THIRD EDITION

Computer Literacy

BASICS

A COMPREHENSIVE GUIDE TO IC³

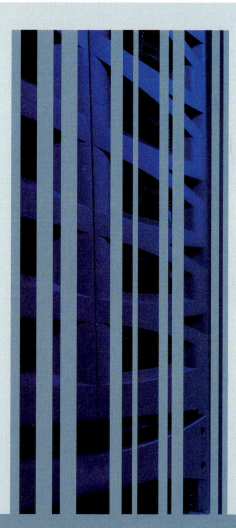

Connie Morrison
Consultant, Encore Training, Inc.

Dr. Dolores Wells
Hillsborough Community College

COURSE TECHNOLOGY
CENGAGE Learning

Australia • Brazil • Japan • Korea • Mexico • Singapore • Spain • United Kingdom • United States

COURSE TECHNOLOGY
CENGAGE Learning™

Computer Literacy BASICS: A Comprehensive Guide to IC³, 3rd Edition
Connie Morrison, Dolores Wells

Executive Editor: Donna Gridley

Product Manager: Allison O'Meara

Development Editors: Karen Porter, Lisa Ruffolo

Associate Product Manager: Amanda Lyons

Editorial Assistant: Kim Klasner

Content Project Manager: Jennifer Feltri

Director of Manufacturing: Denise Powers

Text Designer: Shawn Girsberger

Manuscript Quality Assurance Lead: Jeff Schwartz

Manuscript Quality Assurance Reviewers:
John Freitas, Serge Palladino, Danielle Shaw

Copy Editors: Mark Goodin, Andrew Therriault

Proofreaders: Kim Kosmatka, Vicki Zimmer

Indexer: Liz Cunningham

Art Director: Faith Brosnan

Image credit: Photos.com

Image description: Underneath Gateway Arch, St. Louis, Missouri (#5268043)

Cover Designer: Hanh L. Luu

Compositor: GEX Publishing Services

For product information and technology assistance, contact us at
Cengage Learning Academic Resourse Center, 1-800-354-9706

For permission to use material from this text or product, submit all requests online at **www.cengage.com/permissions**
Further permissions questions can be emailed to
permissionrequest@cengage.com

Hardcover
ISBN-13: 978-1-4390-7853-2
ISBN-10: 1-4390-7853-X

Softcover
ISBN-13: 978-1-4390-7861-7
ISBN-10: 1-4390-7861-0

Course Technology
20 Channel Center Street
Boston, Massachusetts 02210
USA

Cengage Learning is a leading provider of customized learning solutions with office locations around the globe, including Singapore, the United Kingdom, Australia, Mexico, Brazil, and Japan. Locate your local office at:
international.cengage.com/region

Cengage Learning products are represented in Canada by Nelson Education, Ltd.

To learn more about Course Technology, visit **www.cengage.com/coursetechnology**

To learn more about Cengage Learning, visit **www.cengage.com**

Microsoft and the Office logo are either registered trademarks or trademarks of Microsoft Corporation in the United States and/or other countries. Course Technology, a part of Cengage Learning, is an independent entity from the Microsoft Corporation, and not affiliated with Microsoft in any manner.

Any fictional data related to persons or companies or URLs used throughout this book is intended for instructional purposes only. At the time this book was printed, any such data was fictional and not belonging to any real persons or companies.

Printed in the United States of America
3 4 5 6 7 13 12 11 10

Whether you're seeking further education, entering the job market, or advancing your skills through higher ICT certification, IC³ gives you the foundation you need to succeed.

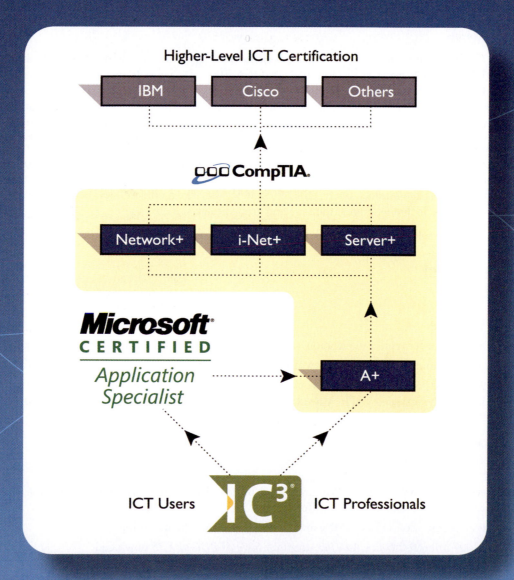

Higher-Level ICT Certification

| IBM | Cisco | Others |

CompTIA

| Network+ | i-Net+ | Server+ |

Microsoft CERTIFIED

Application Specialist

A+

ICT Users · IC³ · ICT Professionals

ABOUT THIS BOOK

Computer Literacy Basics, Third Edition, provides complete coverage on computing basics, including computer hardware and components, operating system software, application software, networks, and the Internet. Lessons are organized in three modules, and within each module, concepts and features are introduced in a logical progression to build on previously learned concepts and features. Illustrations provide visual reinforcement of features and concepts, and sidebars provide notes, tips, and concepts related to the lesson topics. Step-by-Step exercises provide guidance for using the features. End-of-lesson projects include a comprehensive review of the lesson content. Teamwork projects, Critical Thinking activities and Online Discovery challenges provide additional practice and require you to apply your problem-solving skills.

The Computing Fundamentals module focuses on hardware and software and how they work together. The lesson activities include exercises that provide the students with opportunities to explore Windows operating system commands and how to change settings and customize the desktop. Additionally students learn how to manage files and folders. Hands-on exercises, lesson review, and end-of-lesson projects provide the student with additional exploration of these topics. The module review includes additional review questions and projects.

The Key Applications module focuses on four of the Microsoft Office 2007 applications: Microsoft Word, Excel, PowerPoint, and Access. The lesson activities include exercises that introduce how to use the software tools, and the end-of-lesson projects provide additional practice to master using those tools to complete typical day-to-day tasks at home, school, and work. The module review includes an integrated project which entails combining the tools for word processing, spreadsheets, presentations, and databases to process information and then share the information with others.

The Living Online module introduces the student to communication network fundamentals and the relationships between networks and the Internet. Understanding and identifying how to use e-mail and using a Web browser to search the Internet also are discussed. The final section focuses on how computers are used at work, school, and home, and discusses the risks of using hardware and software and using the Internet safely, ethically, and legally. The module review contains a variety of additional projects and hands-on exercises, including critical thinking and group projects.

To complete all lessons and module reviews, this book will require approximately 49 hours.

Start-Up Checklist

Hardware

- PC with Pentium processor
- Hard disk with 400 MB free for typical installation
- CD-ROM drive, or access to network drive for downloading and saving data files and solutions for exercises
- Monitor set at 1024x768 or higher resolution (If your resolution differs, the Ribbon and task panes on your screen may not match the screen shots in the text, and you may need to scroll up or down to view the information on your screen)
- Printer
- Internet connection

Software

- Microsoft Windows Vista running with the Windows Vista Basic color scheme (Windows Aero color scheme not recommended because screen shots and features will differ)
- A typical installation of Microsoft Office 2007 using the Windows Vista theme setting
- Installation of the *2007 Microsoft Office Add-in: Microsoft Save as PDF or XPS* download
- PDF reader software
- Microsoft Internet Explorer 7 browser (or newer version)

INSIDE THE BASICS SERIES

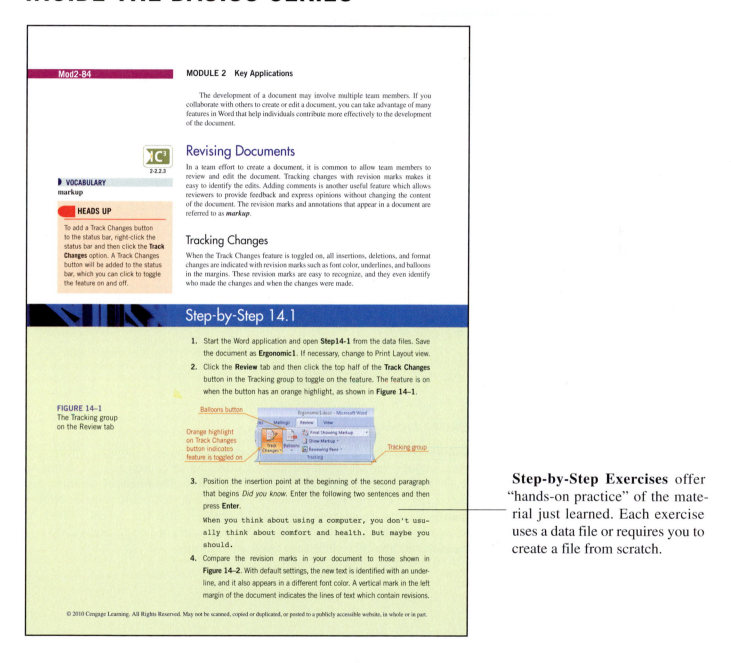

MODULE 2   Key Applications

The development of a document may involve multiple team members. If you collaborate with others to create or edit a document, you can take advantage of many features in Word that help individuals contribute more effectively to the development of the document.

Revising Documents

In a team effort to create a document, it is common to allow team members to review and edit the document. Tracking changes with revision marks makes it easy to identify the edits. Adding comments is another useful feature which allows reviewers to provide feedback and express opinions without changing the content of the document. The revision marks and annotations that appear in a document are referred to as *markup*.

▶ **VOCABULARY**
markup

HEADS UP

To add a Track Changes button to the status bar, right-click the status bar and then click the **Track Changes** option. A Track Changes button will be added to the status bar, which you can click to toggle the feature on and off.

Tracking Changes

When the Track Changes feature is toggled on, all insertions, deletions, and format changes are indicated with revision marks such as font color, underlines, and balloons in the margins. These revision marks are easy to recognize, and they even identify who made the changes and when the changes were made.

Step-by-Step 14.1

1. Start the Word application and open **Step14-1** from the data files. Save the document as **Ergonomic1**. If necessary, change to Print Layout view.

2. Click the **Review** tab and then click the top half of the **Track Changes** button in the Tracking group to toggle on the feature. The feature is on when the button has an orange highlight, as shown in **Figure 14–1**.

FIGURE 14–1
The Tracking group on the Review tab

Balloons button

Orange highlight on Track Changes button indicates feature is toggled on

Tracking group

3. Position the insertion point at the beginning of the second paragraph that begins *Did you know*. Enter the following two sentences and then press **Enter**.

   When you think about using a computer, you don't usually think about comfort and health. But maybe you should.

4. Compare the revision marks in your document to those shown in **Figure 14–2**. With default settings, the new text is identified with an underline, and it also appears in a different font color. A vertical mark in the left margin of the document indicates the lines of text which contain revisions.

Step-by-Step Exercises offer "hands-on practice" of the material just learned. Each exercise uses a data file or requires you to create a file from scratch.

Lesson opener elements include the **Objectives**, **Data Files**, and **Estimated Completion Time**.

End-of-Lesson elements include the **Summary**, **Vocabulary Review**, **Review Questions**, **Lesson Projects**, and **Critical Thinking Activities**.

Instructor Resources Disk

ISBN-13: 978-1-4390-7859-4
ISBN-10: 1-4390-7859-9

The Instructor Resources CD or DVD contains the following teaching resources:

The Data and Solution files for this course

ExamView® tests for each lesson

Instructor's Manual that includes lecture notes for each lesson and references to the end-of-lesson activities and Module Review projects

Answer Keys that include solutions to the lesson and unit review questions

Copies of the figures that appear in the student text

Suggested Syllabus with block, two quarter, and 18-week schedule

PowerPoint presentations for each lesson

IC^3 correlation grid that shows skills required for the Internet and Computing Core Certification (IC^3) exams and references where those skills are discussed within the textbook

Bonus content
Appendix B: Lesson 11 in Windows XP

ExamView

ExamView®. This textbook is accompanied by ExamView, a powerful testing software package that allows instructors to create and administer printed, computer (LAN-based), and Internet exams. ExamView includes hundreds of questions that correspond to the topics covered in this text, enabling students to generate detailed study guides that include page references for further review. The computer-based and Internet testing components allow students to take exams at their computers, and save the instructor time by grading each exam automatically.

IC³

IC³ stands for the Internet and Computing Core Certification program, a global training and certification program. Completing this program and earning IC³ certification shows that you have the necessary computer skills to excel in a digital world, and are capable of using a wide range of computer technology. IC³ provides three exams: Computing Fundamentals, Key Applications, and Living Online. The skills needed for these exams are valuable to any functional user of computer hardware, software, networks, and the Internet. By passing the three IC³ exams, you give yourself a globally accepted and validated credential that provides the proof employees or higher education institutions need.

SAM

SAM 2007 helps bridge the gap between the classroom and the real world by allowing students to train and test on important computer skills in an active, hands-on environment.

SAM 2007's easy-to-use system includes powerful interactive exams, training or projects on critical applications such as Word, Excel, Access, PowerPoint, Outlook, Windows, the Internet, and much more. SAM simulates the application environment, allowing students to demonstrate their knowledge and think through the skills by performing real-world tasks.

SAM 2007 includes built-in page references so students can print helpful study guides that match the textbooks used in class. Powerful administrative options allow instructors to schedule exams and assignments, secure tests, and run reports with almost limitless flexibility.

ACKNOWLEDGMENTS

Connie Morrison: This book represents a true team effort involving several dedicated publishing experts, and it was a pleasure working with everyone. My appreciation goes to that entire team who made this book possible. I owe special thanks to the following individuals:

Donna Gridley, Allison O'Meara, and Amanda Lyons, for their direction and support in the development of this book.

Jeff Schwartz and his team, for the thorough quality assurance reviews.

Karen Porter, for her expertise, experience, and attention to detail, and especially for her cheerful support and humor.

My family, Gene, Al, Amy, and Chris, for their steadfast love and support.

Dolores Wells: Special thanks go to Lisa Ruffolo for all of her help and to Allison O'Meara for her patience, guidance, and assistance.

Bring Your Course Back To the BASICS

Developed with the needs of new learners in mind, the **BASICS** series is ideal for lower-level courses covering basic computer concepts, Microsoft Office, programming, and more. Introductory in nature, these texts are comprehensive enough to cover the most important features of each application.

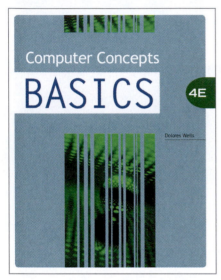

Computer Concepts BASICS, 4th Edition
Hard Spiral
ISBN-10: 1-4239-0461-3
ISBN-13: 978-1-4239-0461-8

Softcover:
ISBN-10: 1-4239-0462-1
ISBN13: 978-1-4239-0462-5

This revised fourth edition puts computer literacy information at your fingertips by learning Microsoft® Office 2007 skills, Web page creation techniques, computer ethics, and more. Whether used for an introductory course or in conjunction with software tutorial instruction, this text proves to be the best solution for computer education.

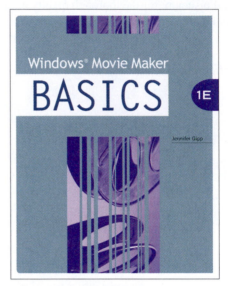

Movie Maker BASICS
ISBN-10: 0-324-78940-8
ISBN-13: 978-0-324-78940-9

This new text in the BASICS series explores Windows® Movie Maker 6.0 using Windows Vista and offers the essential skills for mastering this video-editing program. Topics include importing media, organizing elements, editing movies, adding sounds and texts, and publishing movies. Whether used in an introductory course or in conjunction with software tutorial instruction, this text proves to be the best solution for movie-making education.

CONTENTS

MODULE I | COMPUTING FUNDAMENTALS

LESSON 8
Operating Systems   Mod1-145

LESSON 9
Windows Management   Mod1-163

LESSON 10
Operating System Customization   Mod1-187

MODULE 1 REVIEW
Computing Fundamentals Mod1-215

MODULE 2   KEY APPLICATIONS

LESSON 11
Exploring Microsoft Office 2007   Mod2-3

LESSON 12
Getting Started with Word Essentials   Mod2-27

LESSON 13
Editing and Formatting Documents   Mod2-49

LESSON 14
Sharing Documents   Mod2-83

LESSON 15
Working with Tables   Mod2-109

CONTENTS

MODULE 3   LIVING ONLINE

CONTENTS

*Appendix B: Lesson 11 in Windows XP
is available on the Instructor Resources Disk.*

MODULE I

COMPUTING FUNDAMENTALS

Computer Concepts

LESSON 1   **2 HRS.**
Computers and Computer Systems

LESSON 2   **2 HRS.**
Input, Output, and Processing

LESSON 3   **1 HR.**
Computer Protection

LESSON 4   **1 HR.**
Computer Maintenance

LESSON 5   **1.5 HRS.**
Computer-Related Issues

LESSON 6   **1 HR.**
Software and Hardware Interaction

LESSON 7   **1.5 HRS.**
Software Fundamentals

Introduction to Microsoft Windows

LESSON 8   **1.5 HRS.**
Operating Systems

LESSON 9   **1 HR.**
Windows Management

LESSON 10   **1.5 HRS.**
Operating System Customization

COMPUTING FUNDAMENTALS

Computer Concepts

 LESSON 1
Computers and Computer Systems
| 1-1.1.1 | 1-1.1.3 | 1-1.1.4 |
| 1-1.1.2 | | |

 LESSON 2
Input, Output, and Processing
| 1-1.1.5 | 1-1.1.7 | 1-1.1.9 |
| 1-1.1.6 | 1-1.1.8 | |

 LESSON 3
Computer Protection
| 1-1.2.1 | 1-1.2.2 | 1-1.2.3 |
| 1-1.2.4 | | |

 LESSON 4
Computer Maintenance
| 1-1.2.5 | 1-1.2.6 | 1-1.2.7 |

 LESSON 5
Computer-Related Issues
| 1-1.2.8 | 1-1.2.9 |

 LESSON 6
Software and Hardware Interaction
| 1-2.1.1 | 1-2.1.2 | 1-2.1.3 |

 LESSON 7
Software Fundamentals
1-2.2.1	1-2.2.5	1-2.2.8
1-2.2.2	1-2.2.6	1-2.2.9
1-2.2.3	1-2.2.7	1-2.2.10
1-2.2.4		

Introduction to Microsoft Windows

 LESSON 8
Operating Systems
| 1-3.1.1 | 1-3.1.3 | 1-3.1.5 |
| 1-3.1.2 | 1-3.1.4 | |

 LESSON 9
Windows Management
1-3.2.1	1-3.2.4	1-3.2.7
1-3.2.2	1-3.2.5	1-3.2.8
1-3.2.3	1-3.2.6	

 LESSON 10
Operating System Customization
1-3.3.1	1-3.3.4	1-3.3.6
1-3.3.2	1-3.3.5	1-3.3.7
1-3.3.3		

LESSON 1

Computers and Computer Systems

■ OBJECTIVES

Upon completion of this lesson, you should be able to:

- Understand the importance of computers.
- Define computers and computer systems.
- Classify different types of computer devices.
- Use computer systems.
- Identify system components.
- Describe the role of the central processing unit.
- Define computer memory.
- Describe how data is represented.
- Identify types of storage devices.
- Care for storage media.

■ DATA FILES

You do not need data files to complete this lesson.

■ VOCABULARY

arithmetic/logic unit (ALU)

central processing unit (CPU)

circuit board

computer

control unit

data

hard disks

hardware

information

memory

mobile devices

motherboard

notebook computers

random access memory (RAM)

read-only memory (ROM)

server

software

supercomputer

tablet PC

USB flash drive

This lesson introduces you to computers, starting with a brief history, and ending with a look into the future. You will learn how to classify computers and their components and identify and care for storage devices.

Understanding the Importance of Computers

The computer is one of the most important inventions of the past century. The widespread use of computers affects each of us individually and as a society. You can see computers in use almost everywhere! For instance, consider the following:

- Educational institutions use computers to enhance instruction in all disciplines and to provide online instruction.
- Video game systems transport you to an imaginary world.
- Using ATMs, you can withdraw money from your bank account from almost any location in the world.
- On television and at the movies, you can see instant replays in sports or amazing special effects that take you to outer space.
- Mobile computing, text messaging, e-mail, and online audio/video conferencing allow you to communicate with people at almost any location.

As indicated by these examples, you find computers and computer technology everywhere throughout society—from businesses and financial organizations, to home electronics and appliances, and to personal applications such as clothing embedded with iPod controls.

The importance of the computer is not surprising. Many people consider the computer to be the single most important invention of the 20th century! This technology affects all aspects of everyone's daily lives. Computers are no longer bulky machines that sit on desktops. Computers come in every shape and size and are found everywhere. As more powerful and special-purpose computers become available, society will find more ways to use this technology to enhance everyone's lives. See **Figure 1–1**.

FIGURE 1–1 A group of students playing an online video game

A Brief History of the Computer

Computers have been around for more than 60 years. The first computers were developed in the late 1940s and early 1950s. They were massive, special-purpose machines with names like UNIVAC and ENIAC and were designed initially for use by the military and government. These early computers had less processing power than today's iPhone, occupied small buildings or entire city blocks, and cost millions of dollars. Computers in the mid-1950s through early 1970s were somewhat smaller and more powerful, but still were limited in what they could do. They remained expensive, so only major companies and government organizations could afford these systems. See **Figure 1–2**.

FIGURE 1–2   Early computers

In 1971, Dr. Ted Hoff developed the microprocessor. It took such visionaries as Steve Jobs and Steve Wozniak to see a future for the microprocessor and its application to personal computers. Jobs and Wozniak built the first Apple computer in 1976. Shortly thereafter, a second version, the Apple II, was released. It became an immediate success, especially in schools. In 1980, Bill Gates worked with IBM to develop the disk operating system (DOS) for the IBM PC. This computer, introduced in 1981, quickly became the PC of choice for businesses. See **Figure 1–3**.

EXTRA FOR EXPERTS

In 1969, the Neiman Marcus catalog advertised the first home computer, a Honeywell H316 model called the "Kitchen Computer," for $10,600.

FIGURE 1–3   The Apple II and IBM PC

1-1.1.1

 EXTRA FOR EXPERTS

In 1937, Dr. John Atanasoff and Clifford Berry designed and built the first electronic digital computer.

Defining Computers and Computer Systems

Throughout a normal workday, millions of people interact globally with computers and other digital devices, often without even knowing it. Doctors, lawyers, warehouse workers, store clerks, homemakers, teachers, musicians, and students, to name a few examples, constantly depend on computers to perform part of their daily duties.

So, what exactly is a computer? What does it really do? A *computer* is an electronic device that receives data (input), processes data, stores data, and produces a result (output).

A *computer system* includes hardware, software, data, and people. The actual machine—wires, transistors, and circuits—is called *hardware*. Peripheral devices such as printers and monitors also are hardware. *Software* consists of instructions or programs for controlling the computer. *Data* is text, numbers, sound, images, or video. The computer receives data through an input device, processes the data, stores the data on a storage device, and produces output or *information*. The users, the people who use computers, are also part of the system. See **Figure 1–4**.

FIGURE 1–4   Using a mobile computer to process data into information

Consider the description of a computer system with examples of ways a store clerk might use a computer at a department store:

- *Receives data*: The store clerk enters the customer's name and scans the barcode of an item into the computer through input devices, such as the keyboard or digital scanner.
- *Processes data*: The computer uses stored instructions to process the data into information.
- *Outputs information*: An output device, such as a monitor and/or a printer, displays the information.
- *Stores data*: The data and information are stored in temporary memory and then on a permanent storage device, such as a hard drive.

This series of steps is often referred to as the *information processing cycle*. See **Figure 1–5**.

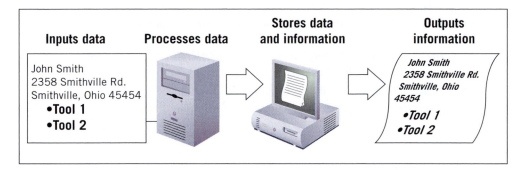

FIGURE 1–5   Information processing cycle

This brief overview of a computer and the listing of some of the tasks you can accomplish with a computer might appear to imply that the computer is a very complicated device. A computer, however, performs only two operations:

- Arithmetic computations such as addition, subtraction, multiplication, and division, and comparisons such as greater than, less than, or equal to
- Logical operations using logical operators, such as AND, OR, and NOT

Classifying Computers

Computers today come in all shapes and sizes, with specific types being especially suited for specific tasks. Computers are classified as either special purpose or general purpose. *Special-purpose computers* are used mostly to control something else. Tiny chips are embedded in devices, such as a dishwasher, bathroom scale, or airport radar system, and these chips control these particular devices.

General-purpose computers are divided into categories, based on their physical size, function, cost, and performance:

- Desktop and notebook computers are today's most widely used personal computers (PCs). A desktop computer is designed so that all components fit on or under a desk. Two popular types of personal computers are the PC (based on the original IBM personal computer design) and the Apple Macintosh. **Notebook computers** (also called laptop computers) are small personal computers that contain the monitor with a built-in keyboard. They are designed to be carried from one location to another.
- A *server* generally is used by small to medium-size companies and can support a few users or hundreds of users. Most servers are referred to as *network servers* or *application servers*. Variations of the server include a file server, a database server, and a Web server. A computer that delivers Web pages to browsers and other files to applications via the HTTP protocol is considered a *Web server*. A *database server* stores databases and database management systems. A *file server* stores remote programs and data files that are shared by a set of designated users.
- **Mobile devices** generally can fit into the palm of your hand. Examples of mobile devices (or handheld devices) are personal digital assistants (PDAs), calculators, smart phones and other cell phones, electronic organizers, handheld games, and other similar tools. Many mobile devices can connect wirelessly to the Internet.

VOCABULARY
notebook computers
server
mobile devices

MODULE 1 Computing Fundamentals

■ A *tablet PC* is a personal computer similar in size and thickness to a notepad. The user can take notes using a stylus or digital pen on a touch screen. This device functions as the user's primary personal computer as well as a note-taking device.

■ The modern *mainframe computer* is a large, expensive computer capable of supporting hundreds or even thousands of users. This type of computer is big compared to personal computers. Large companies use these to perform processing tasks for many users.

■ A *supercomputer* is the fastest type of computer. Government agencies and large corporations use these computers for specialized applications to process enormous amounts of data. The cost of a supercomputer can be as much as several million dollars.

Other types of computer devices include the following:

■ *Embedded computers* perform specific tasks and can be found in a range of devices such as a digital watch, an MP3 player, automobile, household appliance, or as a system controller for a nuclear power plant.

■ *Portable music and media players* are approximately the size of a paperback book. They can store and play back music and video. Examples are MP3 players and portable DVD players.

Today's small personal and handheld computers are more powerful than the mainframes and supercomputers of yesteryear. **Figure 1–6** shows examples of different types of computers.

FIGURE 1–6 (a) Desktop computer (b) Mobile device (c) Notebook computer (d) Contains an embedded computer (e) Mainframe (f) Supercomputer

Other computer devices include the following:

- *Calculators* are used for performing mathematical calculations.

- *Computer game systems* are specialized computers used to play games. Some of the more popular are the Sony PlayStation 3 (PS3), Nintendo Wii, and Microsoft Xbox.

- *Electronic book readers* enable the user to read an electronic version of a traditional print book (see **Figure 1–7**).

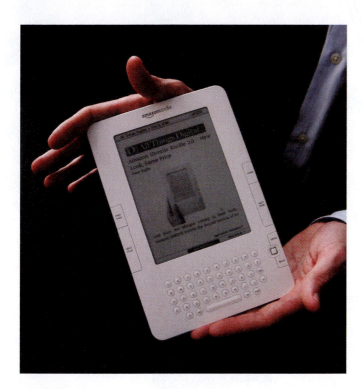

FIGURE 1–7 Electronic book reader

Using Computer Systems

1-1.1.2

Computers are used for all kinds of tasks—to predict weather, to fly airplanes, to control traffic lights, to play games, to access the Internet, to send e-mail, and so on. You might wonder how a machine can do so many things.

To appreciate how a computer operates requires knowledge of calculus, probability, and statistics—all of which are needed to understand physics and circuit analysis. Most of us, however, do not need this level of comprehension. Instead, we need a fundamental understanding. Just about all computers, regardless of size, take raw data and change it into information. The procedure involves input, processing, output, and storage (IPOS). For example:

- You input programs and data with some type of input device.

- The computer uses instructions to process the data and to turn it into information.

- You send the information to some type of output device.

- You store it for later retrieval.

Input, output, and processing devices grouped together represent a computer system. The components that the computer uses to process data are contained within the system case. See **Figure 1–8**.

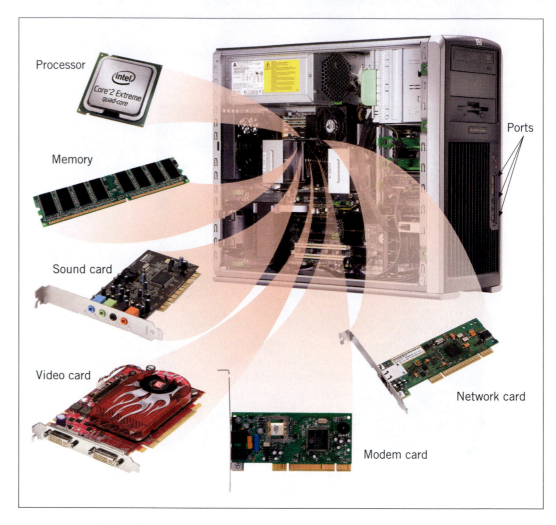

FIGURE 1–8   Computer system components

1-1.1.2
1-1.1.3

▶ **VOCABULARY**

motherboard

circuit board

Identifying System Components

The PC system case is the metal and plastic case that houses the main system components of the computer. Central to all of this is the ***motherboard*** or system board that mounts into the case. The motherboard is a circuit board that contains many integral components. A ***circuit board*** is simply a thin plate or board that contains electronic components. See **Figure 1–9**. The following are some of the most important of these components:

- Central processing unit
- Memory
- Basic controllers
- Expansion ports and expansion slots

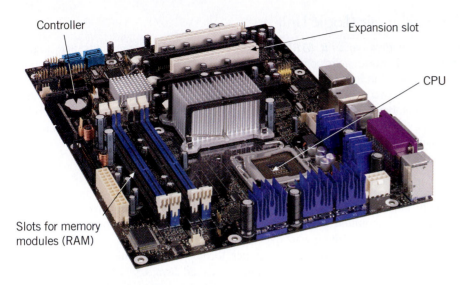

Controller

Expansion slot

CPU

Slots for memory
modules (RAM)

FIGURE 1–9   Motherboard

The Central Processing Unit

The *central processing unit (CPU)*, also called the microprocessor or central processor, is the brains of the computer. The processor is housed on a tiny silicon chip similar to that shown in **Figure 1–10**. This chip contains millions of switches and pathways that help your computer make important decisions. The switches control the flow of the electricity as it travels across the miles of pathways. The processor knows which switches to turn on and which to turn off because it receives its instructions from computer programs. Programs are a set of special instructions, written by programmers, which control the activities of the computer. Programs are also known as software.

FIGURE 1–10   Microprocessor

   Some chip manufacturers now offer dual-core and multicore processors. A *dual-core processor* is a single chip that contains two separate processors, and a *multicore processor* is an expansion that provides for more than two separate processors. These processors do not necessarily double the processing speed of a single-core processor, but do provide increased performance when running multiple programs simultaneously.
   The CPU has two primary sections: the arithmetic/logic unit and the control unit.

▶ **VOCABULARY**

arithmetic/logic unit (ALU)

control unit

binary

bit

byte

The Arithmetic/Logic Unit

The *arithmetic/logic unit (ALU)* performs arithmetic computations and logical operations. The arithmetic computations include addition, subtraction, multiplication, and division. The logical operations involve comparisons—asking the computer to determine if two numbers are equal or if one number is greater than or less than another number. These might seem like simple operations. However, by combining these operations, the ALU can execute complex tasks. For example, a video game uses arithmetic operations and comparisons to determine what appears on your screen.

The Control Unit

The *control unit* is the boss, so to speak, and coordinates all of the processor's activities. Using programming instructions, it controls the flow of information through the processor by controlling what happens inside the processor.

You communicate with the computer through programming languages. You might have heard of programming languages called Java, COBOL, C++, or Visual Basic. These are just a few of the many languages you can use to give instructions to a computer. For example, you might have a programming statement such as *Let X = 2 + 8*. With this statement, you are using a programming language to ask the computer to add the numbers 2 and 8 and assign the calculated value to *X*. However, when you input this instruction, something else has to happen. The computer does not understand human language. It understands only machine language, or *binary*, which is all *1*s and *0*s. This is where the control unit takes over.

Recognizing How a Computer Represents Data

The control unit reads and interprets the program instruction and changes the instruction into machine language. Earlier, this chapter discussed the processor and its pathways and switches. As electricity travels through processor pathways, the turning on and off of switches represents the *1*s and *0*s. When electricity is present, it represents a *1*. The absence of electricity represents a *0*. After changing the instructions into machine language (binary), the control unit then sends out the necessary messages to execute the instructions. A single zero or a single one is called a *bit*. Eight bits are equal to one byte. A *byte* is a single character. See **Table 1–1** for a list of measurement terms. As a comparison, 1 GB of data is equivalent to about 450 digital songs.

TABLE 1–1   Measurement terms

TERM	ABBREVIATION	NUMBER OF BYTES
Kilobyte	K or KB	1,024 (approximately 1,000)
Megabyte	MB	1,048,576 (approximately 1 million)
Gigabyte	GB	1,073,741,824 (approximately 1 billion)
Terabyte	TB	1,099,511,627,776 (approximately 1 trillion)

■ **HEADS UP**

The Step-by-Step exercises in this book are written for a personal or notebook computer with the Windows Vista operating system. The menus and screens for earlier versions of Windows are similar. Please make appropriate adjustments if you are using a different Windows version or working on a network.

To view an example of a binary number, complete Step-by-Step 1.1.

Step-by-Step 1.1

1. Click the **Start** button 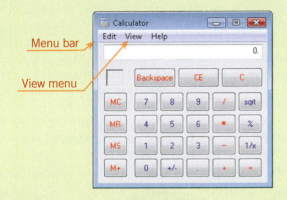 on the taskbar, point to **All Programs**, click **Accessories**, and then click **Calculator**. The Standard calculator is displayed (see **Figure 1–11**).

FIGURE 1–11
Windows Standard calculator

2. Click **View** on the menu bar and then click **Scientific**, if necessary. The Scientific calculator is displayed (see **Figure 1–12**).

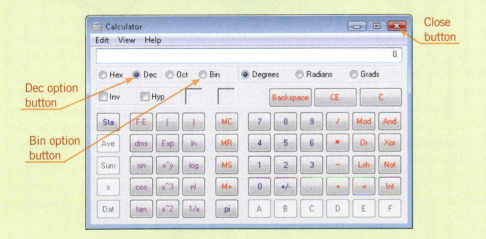

FIGURE 1–12
Windows Scientific calculator

3. If necessary, click the **Dec** (decimal) option button. Enter **30** by clicking the calculator numeric buttons. Click the **Bin** (binary) option button. The number 11110 is displayed.

4. Click the **Dec** option button and convert the following decimal number to binary: **4545**. The number 1000111000001 is displayed. Convert **1112** to binary. The number 10001011000 is displayed.

5. What decimal number is equal to 101101 in the binary system? What decimal number is equal to 1111011? When you are finished, close the calculator by clicking the **Close** [X] button in the upper-right corner.

Memory

Memory is also found on the motherboard. Sometimes understanding memory can be confusing because it can mean different things to different people. The easiest way to understand memory is to think of it as either short term or long term. When you want to store a file or information permanently, you use secondary storage devices such as the computer's hard drive or a USB drive. You might think of this as long term.

Random Access Memory

You can think about the memory on the motherboard as short term. This type of memory is called *random access memory*, or *RAM*. RAM is also referred to as *main memory* and *primary memory*. You might have heard someone ask, "How much memory is in your computer?" Most likely, they are asking how much RAM is in your computer. The computer can read from and write to this type of memory. Data, information, and program instructions are stored temporarily within the CPU on a RAM chip or a set of RAM chips, such as those shown in **Figure 1–13**.

FIGURE 1–13   RAM chips

When the computer is turned off or otherwise loses power, whatever is stored in the RAM memory chips disappears. Therefore, it is considered volatile. To understand how RAM works and how the computer processes data, think about how you would use a word-processing program to create an address list of your family and friends:

1. First, you start your word-processing program. The computer then loads your word-processing program instructions into RAM.

2. You input the names, addresses, and telephone numbers (your data). Your data is also stored in RAM.

3. Next, you give your word-processing program a command to process your data by arranging it in a special format, such as alphabetical order. This command and your processed data, or information, are also now stored in RAM.

4. You then click the Print button. Instructions to print are transmitted to RAM, and your document is sent to your printer.

5. Then, you click the Save button. Instructions to provide you with an opportunity to name and save your file are loaded into RAM. Once you save your file, you exit your word-processing program and turn off the computer.

6. All instructions, data, and information that you used to create your address are erased from RAM.

This process is known as the *instruction cycle* or *I-cycle*, and the *execution cycle* or *E-cycle*. When the CPU receives an instruction to perform a specified task, the instruction cycle is the amount of time it takes to retrieve the instruction and complete the command. The execution cycle refers to the amount of time it takes the CPU to execute the instruction and store the results in RAM. Together, the instruction cycle and one or more execution cycles create a *machine cycle*.

For every instruction, a processor repeats a set of four basic operations, which compose a machine cycle: (1) fetching, (2) decoding, (3) executing, and, if necessary, (4) storing (see **Figure 1–14**). *Fetching* is the process of obtaining a program instruction or data item from RAM. The term *decoding* refers to the process of translating the instruction into signals the computer can execute. *Executing* is the process of carrying out the commands. *Storing*, in this context, means writing the result to memory (not to a storage medium).

▶ **VOCABULARY**

instruction cycle

execution cycle

machine cycle

fetching

decoding

executing

storing

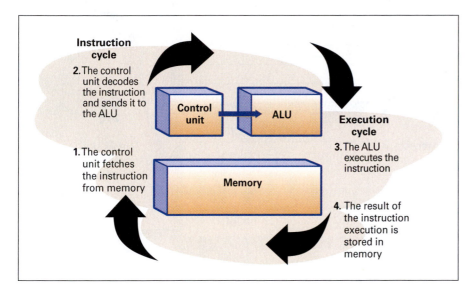

FIGURE 1–14   Processing cycle

Machine cycles are measured in microseconds (millionths of a second), nanoseconds (billionths of a second), and even picoseconds (trillionths of a second) in some of the larger computers. The faster the machine cycle, the faster your computer processes data. The speed of the processor has a lot to do with the speed of the machine cycle. However, the amount of RAM in your computer can also help increase the speed with which the computer processes data. The more RAM you have, the faster the computer processes data. See **Figure 1–15**.

EXTRA FOR EXPERTS

If you have read computer ads lately, you most likely saw the abbreviations MHz (megahertz) and GHz (gigahertz). These speed specifications indicate the speed of the microprocessor clock—a timing device that specifies the speed for executing instructions.

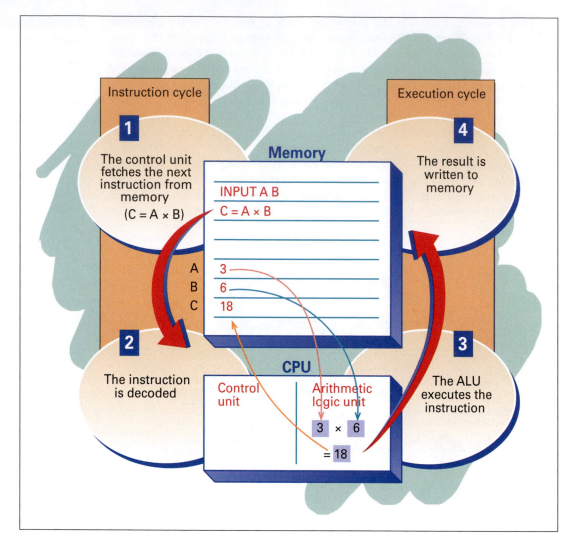

FIGURE 1–15   Machine cycle

Read-Only Memory

Another type of memory you will find on the motherboard is ***read-only memory***, or ***ROM***. ROM chips are found throughout a computer system. The computer manufacturer uses this type of chip to store specific instructions that are needed for computer operations. This type of memory is nonvolatile. These instructions remain on the chip even when the power is turned off. The more common of these is the ***BIOS ROM***. The computer uses instructions contained on this chip to start the system when you turn on your computer. A computer can read from a ROM chip, but cannot write or store data on the chip.

TECHNOLOGY CAREERS

Computers on the Job

In the past few decades, computers have had dramatic effects on how we live, learn, and work. For example, the kinds of jobs available have changed because of computers. Fifty years ago, only a handful of people were computer programmers, and there were no Web designers or "dot.com entrepreneurs." Today, few if any prospective employees will find work that does not require some computer skills.

Time-consuming, labor-intensive communications tasks that used to require face-to-face meetings, telephone calls, overnight deliveries, or paging through printed materials are now performed quickly and efficiently using Internet browsers and e-mail. Students can participate in a distance-learning class to take a course of study not available where they live. Even the electric meter reader and delivery person now carry handheld computers that track a consumer's electric use or the location of a package. Cashiers use computers for retail sales, and computers also update the store's inventory, handle customer calls, and advertise the products. All these advances, now taken for granted by many of us, are very recent innovations.

Identifying Types of Storage Devices

1-1.1.4

As data is entered in the computer and processed, it is stored in RAM (temporary memory). If you want to keep a permanent copy of the data, you must store it on some type of storage medium. Storage devices are categorized by the method they use to store data. The categories include magnetic technology, optical technology, and solid-state storage.

Magnetic Storage Devices

Magnetic storage devices use oxide-coated plastic storage media called Mylar. As the disk rotates in the computer, an electromagnetic read/write head stores or retrieves data in circles called *tracks*. The number of tracks on a disk varies with the type of disk. The tracks are numbered from the outside to the inside. As data is stored on the disk, it is stored on a numbered track. Each track is labeled and the location is kept in a special log on the disk called a *file allocation table (FAT)*. The more common types of magnetic storage media are hard drives, magnetic tape, 3½-inch disks, and Zip disks.

▶ **VOCABULARY**

tracks

file allocation table (FAT)

hard disks

Hard Disk

Most *hard disks* (also called hard drives) are used to store data inside the computer, although removable hard disks are also available. They provide two advantages: speed and capacity. Accessing data is faster, and the amount of data that can be stored is much larger than what can be stored on a 3½-inch disk. The size of the hard disk is measured in megabytes or gigabytes and can contain several platters (**Figure 1–16**).

FIGURE 1–16   Hard disk

Magnetic Tape

Magnetic tape primarily is used for backup purposes and data collection. The tapes come in a variety of shapes and sizes and include reels, cartridges, and cassettes. Companies and other organizations use magnetic tape mostly for making backup copies of large volumes of data. This is a very slow process and therefore is not used for regularly saving data. The backup tape can be used to replace data that might have been lost or deleted from the hard drive or other storage media.

3½-Inch Disks and Zip Disks

A 3½-inch disk, usually just called a *disk*, is a flat circle of iron oxide-coated plastic enclosed in a hard plastic case. Although the 3½-inch is the most common size, you might see other sizes. A 3½-inch disk can hold 1.44 MB or more of data (see **Figure 1–17**). To protect unwanted data from being added to or removed from a disk, write protection is provided. To write-protect a disk, open the write protect window on the disk. Since the introduction of USB drives and solid-state storage media, 3½-inch disks are not as widely used.

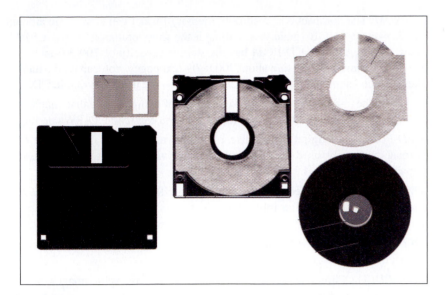

FIGURE 1–17   Parts of a 3½-inch disk

Optical Storage Devices

Optical storage devices use laser technology to read and write data on silver platters (see **Figure 1–18**). The term *disc* is used for optical media. CDs and DVDs are a type of optical storage media. Most computers today come equipped with some type of optical storage—a CD drive or a DVD drive. The technology for CDs and DVDs is similar, but storage capacities are quite different, and several variations exist. These storage devices come in the formats listed below.

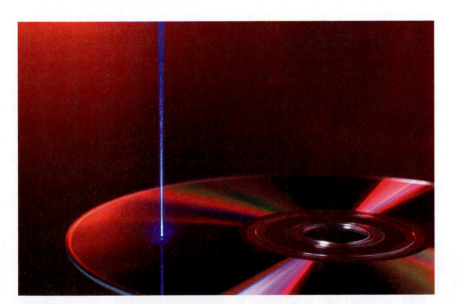

FIGURE 1–18   A laser reads data on a CD or DVD

- *CD-DA*: The compact disc digital audio format is also known as an audio CD; it is the industry-wide standard for music publishing and distribution.
- *CD-R*: The compact disc-recordable format makes it possible for you to create your own compact discs that can be read by any CD-ROM drive. After information is written to this type of disc, it cannot be changed.

- *CD-ROM*: The compact disc read-only memory format can store large amounts of data—up to 1 GB (gigabyte), although the most common size is 650 MB (megabytes). A single CD-ROM has the storage capacity of 700 3½-inch disks with enough memory to store about 300,000+ text pages. You can read data from the CD; you cannot store data on a CD unless you are using a writable CD.

- *CD-RW*: The compact disc-rewritable is a type of compact disc that enables you to write onto it multiple times. Not all CD players can read CD-RWs.

- *DVD-ROM*: The digital video disc read-only memory is a read-only DVD format commonly used for distribution of movies and computer games; its capacity ranges from 4.7 GB to 17 GB.

- *DVD-R*: The digital video disc-recordable is similar to the CD-R except it has a much larger capacity; after information is written to this type of disc, it cannot be changed.

- *DVD-RW*: The digital video disc-rewritable stores data using technology similar to that of a CD-RW, but with a much larger capacity.

- *PhotoCD*: The PhotoCD is used to store digitized photographic images on a CD. The photos stored on these discs can be uploaded to the computer and used in other documents.

- *Blu-ray*: Also known as Blu-ray discs (BD), this is the next-generation optical disc format. The format provides more than five times the storage capacity of traditional DVDs. A single-layer disk can hold up to 25 GB, and a dual-layer disc can hold up to 50 GB. This format was developed for storing large amounts of data and to enable recording and playback of high-definition video.

The color of a CD/DVD indicates its quality. It is best to look for a gold or silver CD/DVD. When viewing the color, look at it from the underside of the disk and not from the top. The shelf-life of a CD/DVD is cited as approximately 2 to 25 years or longer. The quality of the storage media and the storage environment affects the shelf life.

Solid-State Storage Media

Solid-state storage, also referred to as removal media, is a nonvolatile, removable medium that uses integrated circuits. The main advantage of this type of storage medium is that everything is processed electronically, and it contains no mechanical parts. Several types of solid-state storage are available. Miniature mobile storage media, for example, are popular solid-state storage devices for cameras, PDAs, music players, and other such electronics. **Figure 1–19** contains an assortment of miniature mobile storage media, most of which are no larger than a postage stamp.

FIGURE 1–19   Miniature mobile storage media

Another popular solid-state storage medium is the ***USB flash drive***. This small removable data storage device comes in a variety of configurations, such as those shown in **Figure 1–20**. It uses a USB connector to connect to your computer's USB port or other electronic device. Flash drives are also known by other names such as a key drive, thumb drive, jump drive, USB flash memory drive, and USB stick.

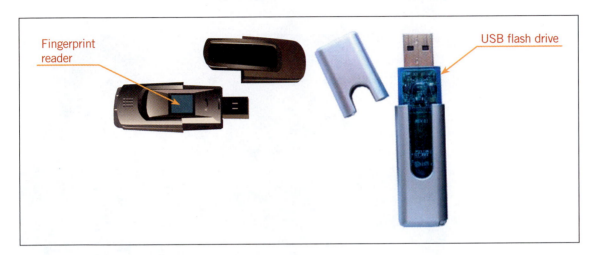

Fingerprint reader

USB flash drive

FIGURE 1–20   Examples of USB flash drives

Network Drives

A ***network drive*** can be a hard drive or a tape drive located on a computer other than the user's local system. It is connected to a network server and is available to and shared by multiple users.

Remote storage is used to extend disk space on a server and to eliminate the addition of more hard disks or other storage devices. When the amount of available space on the server falls below a designated level, the remote storage process frees up disk space by removing excess content to an attached storage device. This frees up additional disk space on the specified server. The storage device could be on the same network, a separate network, or on the Internet.

Caring for Storage Media

Removable storage media require special care if the data stored is to remain undamaged. Here are some safeguards that should be taken:

- Keep away from magnetic fields such as those contained in televisions and computer monitors (magnetic media).
- Avoid extreme temperatures.
- Remove media from drives and store them properly when not in use.
- When handling DVDs and other optical discs, hold them at the edges.
- Never try to remove the media from a drive when the drive indicator light is on.
- Keep discs in a sturdy case when transporting.

Computers in Your Future

It is a fair assumption that computers of the future will be more powerful and less expensive. It is also a fair assumption that almost every type of job will somehow involve a computer. With long-distance connectivity, more people will work full-time or part-time from home. See **Figure 1–21**.

FIGURE 1–21   Working from home

One of the major areas of change in the evolution of computers will be connectivity, or the ability to connect with other computers. Wireless and mobile devices will become the norm. Computer literacy, which is the knowledge and understanding of computers and their uses, will become even more important.

SUMMARY

In this lesson, you learned:

- A computer is an electronic device that receives data, processes data, produces information, and stores the data and information.

- A computer derives its power from its speed, reliability, accuracy, storage, and communications capability.

- Computer classifications include personal computers (desktop and notebook), mobile devices, servers, mainframes, and supercomputers.

- Almost all computers perform the same general functions: input, processing, output, and storage. Input, output, and processing devices grouped together represent a computer system.

- The machine cycle is made up of the instruction cycle and the execution cycle.

- The motherboard is the center of all processing. It contains the central processing unit (CPU), memory, and basic controllers for the system. It also contains ports and expansion slots.

- The motherboard contains different types of memory. Random access memory (RAM) is volatile and is used to store instructions, data, and information temporarily. Read-only memory (ROM) is nonvolatile and is used to store permanent instructions needed for computer operations.

- The CPU is the brains of the computer. The CPU has two main sections—the arithmetic/logic unit (ALU) and the control unit. All calculations and comparisons take place in the ALU. The control unit coordinates the CPU activities.

- To maintain a permanent copy of data, you should store it on some type of storage medium. The three categories of storage media are magnetic storage, optical storage, and solid-state storage.

■ VOCABULARY REVIEW

Define the following terms:

arithmetic/logic unit (ALU)
central processing unit (CPU)
circuit board
computer
control unit
data
hard disks

hardware
information
memory
mobile devices
motherboard
notebook computers
random access memory (RAM)

read-only memory (ROM)
server
software
supercomputer
tablet PC
USB flash drive

■ REVIEW QUESTIONS

TRUE / FALSE

Circle T if the statement is true or F if the statement is false.

T   F   **1.** For every instruction, a processor repeats a set of four basic operations.

T   F   **2.** When data is stored on a disk, it is stored in circles called tracks.

T   F   **3.** Data is stored in temporary memory and on a permanent storage device.

T   F   **4.** A notebook computer can fit in the palm of your hand.

T   F   **5.** The two primary sections of the CPU are the ALU and the control unit.

MULTIPLE CHOICE

Select the best response for the following statements.

1. A _____ consists of hardware, software, data, and users.

   A. client   C. mobile device

   B. node   D. computer system

2. A _____ generally can fit into the palm of your hand.

   A. mainframe computer   C. supercomputer

   B. notebook computer   D. mobile device

3. The _____ is a circuit board that contains many integral components.

   A. supercomputer   C. motherboard

   B. arithmetic/logic unit (ALU)   D. BIOS ROM

4. _____ devices use laser technology to read and write data on silver platters.

   A. Output   C. 3½-inch

   B. Solid state   D. Optical storage

5. Random access memory is _____.

   A. permanent   C. nonvolatile

   B. volatile   D. the same as ROM

FILL IN THE BLANK

1. You can think of RAM as _____-term memory.

2. The instruction cycle and the execution cycle create a(n) _____ cycle.

3. The faster the machine cycle, the _____ your computer processes data.

4. The two primary sections of the CPU are the _____ and the control unit.

5. Read-only memory (ROM) is _____ and is used to store permanent instructions needed for computer operations.

■ PROJECTS

PROJECT 1–1

Access the Dell computer Web site at *www.dell.com*. Select either the Home and Office Laptops or Home and Office Desktops category. Using either a spreadsheet program or paper and pencil, create a comparison table. Include the following elements in your table: processor speed, amount of RAM, number of expansion slots, number of USB ports, other ports, and price. Based on your comparisons, write a short paragraph explaining which computer you would purchase and why.

PROJECT 1–2

Using Google or another search engine, find an image of a computer system with the case removed. Print a copy of the image. Examine the printout and look for the motherboard and the components connected to the motherboard. Locate and count the number of available expansion slots. Locate the RAM chips. See if you can find the CPU. Can you see the chip itself? What other elements are visible? Using your printed copy, label each element you locate.

PROJECT 1–3

Using the Internet or other resources, see what you can find about the history of computers. For the first part of this project, see if you can find the answers to the following questions: (1) What was the name of the first commercially available electronic digital computer? (2) In what year was the IBM PC first introduced? (3) What software sent Bill Gates on his way to becoming one of the richest men in the world? (4) In what year did Apple introduce the Macintosh computer? Use your word-processing program to answer each of these questions and/or provide some additional historical facts.

For the second part of this project, find out who invented the first microprocessor. Launch your Web browser and type the following URL *www.wikipedia.com*. When the Web site is displayed, type *microprocessor* in the Search text box. Scroll down the page and click the History link. Use a presentation program (such as Microsoft PowerPoint) to create a presentation on what you found at this Web site. Find an image of a microprocessor and add it to your presentation. Share your presentation with your class.

 ## TEAMWORK PROJECT

Some people say you should leave your computer on at all times— that turning the computer on and off creates stress on the components. Others argue that computers use a lot of energy, and that computers should be turned off when not in use. Your computer operating system, however, includes power-management settings.

Your instructor has requested that you and your team investigate these options. Use Windows Help and Support and prepare a report describing these power-management options and how you can create a power plan. Describe the steps necessary to modify Sleep mode.

 # CRITICAL THINKING

Think about what you have read in this lesson. Your goal is to purchase a computer. Where would you shop—online, or through a local computer dealer, retail store, or other? What type of processor would you purchase? How much memory would you need? Would

you purchase a desktop, notebook, or other type of computer? Write a one-page report answering the above questions and outlining your thoughts about what other technologies you would include. Explain why you made these selections.

 # ONLINE DISCOVERY

Google has a feature that focuses solely on blog searching. This feature, called Blog Search, is located at *http://www.google.com/blogsearch*. Frequently Asked Questions about Blog Search can be found at *http://www.google.com/help/about_blogsearch.html*.

Access this Web site and then write a one-page report on what you learned. Google also has *https://www.blogger.com/start?hl=en*—a Web site where you can start your own blog. Recruit two or three teammates and start your own blog about your class activities.

LESSON 2

Input, Output, and Processing

■ OBJECTIVES

Upon completion of this lesson, you should be able to:

- Identify and describe standard and specialized input devices.
- Identify and describe standard and specialized output devices.
- Identify and describe how input and output devices are connected to the computer.
- Consider computer performance factors.

■ DATA FILES

You do not need data files to complete this lesson.

■ VOCABULARY

audio input

biometrics

digital camera

expansion slot

FireWire

inkjet printer

input

keyboard

laser printer

modem

monitor

mouse

output

plug-and-play

pointing device

port

printer

scanner

trackball

Universal Serial Bus (USB)

► **VOCABULARY**

input

keyboard

When it comes to processing data, it is the computer that does all of the work. However, it needs help. *Input*, which is data or instructions, must be entered into the computer and then stored temporarily or permanently on a storage media device. To turn the data into information, it must be processed. The central processing unit (CPU), which you learned about in Lesson 1, processes the data. After the data is processed, it is "presented" to the user through an output device.

1-1.1.5

Standard Input Devices

Input devices enable you to enter data and commands into the computer, and output devices enable the computer to give you the results of the processed data. Some devices perform both input and output functions, such as the fax machine and fax modem. You use these devices to send (output) and receive (input) data over communications media.

The type of input device you use is determined by the task you need to complete. An input device can be as simple as the keyboard or as sophisticated as those used for specialized applications such as voice or retinal recognition.

Keyboard

The *keyboard* is the most commonly used input device for entering numeric and alphabetic data into a computer. If you are going to use the computer efficiently, it is important that you learn to type. Most of the keyboards provided with desktop computers are enhanced. An enhanced keyboard has 12 function keys along the top, two Alt keys, two Ctrl keys, and a set of directional/arrow keys between the typing area and the numeric keypad.

Some keyboards, such as the one shown in **Figure 2–1**, have multimedia hot keys that enable you to access e-mail and the Internet, adjust speaker volume, and have other features such as a zoom slider. This device makes it easy to zoom in for a closer look at documents, spreadsheets, pictures, maps, and Web pages.

Zoom slider

 Multimedia hot keys

FIGURE 2–1   Enhanced keyboard

🖭 **EXTRA FOR EXPERTS**

Need more space on your desk? Consider the Nearly Indestructible Keyboard (NIK)—it is flexible, can be rolled up and put into a brief-case, and even washed with soap and water or a spray cleaner *(www. dovecoteglobal.com/nik.html)*.

Not all keyboards, however, are traditional. Some other popular types of keyboards are:

■ *Ergonomic*: This type of keyboard is designed to provide users with more natural, comfortable hand, wrist, and arm positions.

■ *Cordless or wireless*: This is a battery-powered keyboard that transmits data using wireless technology.

■ *Specialized*: This keyboard has specialized keys that represent items such as those used in fast-food restaurants.

■ *Security*: This keyboard provides security features such as a biometric fingerprint reader, magnetic stripe, and smart card readers (see **Figure 2–2**).

Biometric
fingerprint —
reader

FIGURE 2–2   Keyboard with fingerprint reader

■ *Foldable or flexible*: An easily transported keyboard primarily used with PDA and pocket PC-type devices, this type of keyboard has a soft touch and is water resistant (see **Figure 2–3**).

FIGURE 2–3   Foldable keyboard

■ *Laser virtual keyboard*: Packaged in a case smaller than a soda can, a laser beam is used to generate a full-size laser keyboard. This keyboard easily connects to any personal computer, including Macintosh, BlackBerry or other smart phone, and most other handheld devices (see **Figure 2–4**).

FIGURE 2–4   Laser virtual keyboard

Pointing Devices

A *pointing device* is an input device that allows you to position the pointer on the screen. The pointer can have several shapes, but the most common is an arrow. You use a pointing device to move the pointer; select objects, such as text or graphics; and click buttons, icons, menu items, and links. The following sections discuss several pointing devices.

Mouse

The *mouse* is the most commonly used pointing device for personal computers. It moves on a flat surface and controls the pointer on the screen. The mouse fits conveniently in the palm of your hand. You can use any of the following four types of mice:

- *Mechanical*: This type of mouse has a ball located on the bottom that rolls around on a flat surface as the mouse is moved. Sensors inside the mouse determine the direction and distance of the movement. A mouse pad generally is used with a mechanical mouse.

- *Optomechanical*: This mouse is the same as a mechanical mouse, but uses optical sensors to detect motion of the ball.

- *Optical*: An optical mouse (see **Figure 2–5a**) uses a laser to detect the mouse's movement. Optical mice have no mechanical moving parts. They respond more quickly and precisely than mechanical and optomechanical mice.

- *Wireless*: A wireless mouse (see **Figure 2–5b**) is a battery-powered device that relies on infrared or radio waves to communicate with the computer.

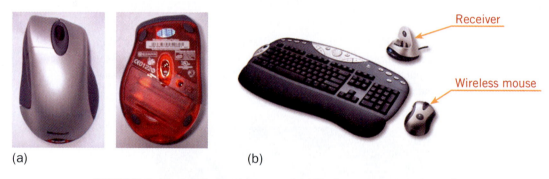

(a)   (b)

FIGURE 2–5   (a) Optical mouse (b) Wireless mouse and receiver

Most mice have two or three buttons; some have a wheel. You use the left button for most mouse operations. Generally, clicking the right button displays a shortcut menu. After you place the on-screen pointer where you want it, press a button on the mouse. This causes some type of action to take place in the computer; the type of action depends on the program. Use the wheel to scroll or zoom a page.

You use the mouse to accomplish the following techniques in most software programs and Web pages:

- *Pointing*: Placing the on-screen pointer at a designated location
- *Clicking*: Pressing and releasing the mouse button to select a specific location within a document
- *Dragging*: Pressing down the mouse button and moving the mouse while continuing to hold down the button to highlight a selected portion of text

- *Double-clicking*: Pressing and releasing the mouse button two times in rapid succession to select a word
- *Triple-clicking*: Pressing and releasing the mouse button three times in rapid succession to select a paragraph
- *Right-clicking*: Pressing the right mouse button to display a menu
- *Rotate wheel*: Rotate wheel forward or backward to scroll vertically
- *Tilt wheel*: Press the wheel right or left to scroll horizontally

Trackball

The *trackball* is a pointing device that works like a mouse turned upside down; the ball is on top of the device. See **Figure 2–6a**. You use your thumb and fingers to operate the ball, thus controlling the pointer on the screen. A trackball is a stationary device and is a good alternative to the mouse when you have limited desktop space. Some trackballs are built into the keyboard. See **Figure 2–6b**.

▶ **VOCABULARY**
trackball

Trackballs

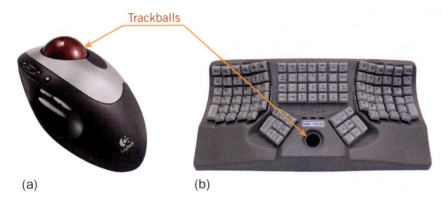

(a)   (b)

FIGURE 2–6   (a) Trackball on a mouse (b) Trackball on a keyboard

Touchpad

A common feature on laptop computers is the touchpad, a pointing device with a specialized surface that can convert the motion and position of your fingers to a relative position on screen. Touchpads are a common feature of laptop computers and can be found on personal digital assistants (PDAs) and portable media players.

Pointing Stick

Many notebook computers contain a pointing stick—a pressure-sensitive device that looks like a pencil eraser. It is located on the keyboard, generally between the G, H, and B keys. See **Figure 2–7**. It is moved with the forefinger, while the thumb is used to press related keys. In a confined space, a lot of people find a pointing stick more convenient than a mouse. IBM popularized this device by introducing the TrackPoint on its ThinkPad notebooks.

FIGURE 2–7   Pointing stick

Audio Input

Audio input is the process of inputting sound into the computer. This could include speech, sound effects, and music. Audio input devices include microphones, CD/DVD players, radios, and other hardware such as electronic keyboards. Voice input is a category of audio input. Voice-recognition devices are used to "speak" commands into the computer and to enter text. These devices usually are microphones. The computer must have some type of voice-recognition software installed before you can use a voice-recognition device. Directory assistance is a type of voice-recognition technology, as are devices that disabled persons use to command wheelchairs and other objects that make them more mobile.

1-1.1.5

Standard Output Devices

Output is data that has been processed into a useful format. Examples of output are printed text, spoken words, music, pictures, video, or graphics. The most common output devices are monitors and printers. Output devices display information.

Monitors

Desktop computers typically use a *monitor* as their display device. The screen is part of the monitor, which also includes the housing for its electrical components. Screen output is called soft copy because it is temporary.

Computer monitors come in many varieties. The cathode ray tube (CRT) was one of the earliest types of monitors. This type of monitor is similar to a standard television and can be either monochrome or color. A monochrome monitor screen has a one-color display, which can be white, green, or amber. Most of today's monitors are color monitors, which display thousands of colors. CRT monitors are available in various sizes, with the more common being 17-, 19-, and 21-inch. See **Figure 2–8a**. Some of the newest monitors are available in sizes up to 30 inches or more.

Flat-panel monitors come in two varieties: liquid crystal display (LCD) and gas plasma. Both types of monitors are more expensive than CRT monitors. They take up less space, however, and are much lighter in weight.

LCD panels produce an image by manipulating light within a layer of liquid crystal cells. See **Figure 2–8b**. Until recently, LCD panels were used primarily on notebook computers and other mobile devices such as cell phones and PDAs. In 1997, several manufacturers started producing full-size LCD panels as alternatives to CRT monitors.

Gas plasma technology consists of a tiny amount of gas that is activated by an electrical charge. See **Figure 2–8c**. The gas illuminates miniature colored fluorescent lights arranged in a panel-like screen. These monitors have a brilliant color display and are available in sizes up to 60 inches or more.

(a)   (b)   (c)

FIGURE 2–8   (a) CRT (b) LCD panel (c) Gas plasma display

Printers

Printers are used to produce a paper or hard copy of the processing results. Printer output is called hard copy because it is permanent. Several types of printers are available, with significant differences in speed, print quality, price, and special features.

When selecting a printer, consider the following features:

- *Speed*: Printer speed is measured in pages per minute (ppm). The number of pages a printer can print per minute varies for text and for graphics. Graphics print more slowly than regular text.

- *Print quality*: Print quality is measured in dots per inch (dpi). The higher the dpi, the higher the resolution or print quality.

- *Price*: The price includes the original cost of the printer as well as what it costs to maintain the printer. A good-quality printer can be purchased very inexpensively; however, a high-output system can cost thousands of dollars. The ink cartridges and toners need to be replaced periodically. Printers are classified as either impact or nonimpact. Impact printers use a mechanism that actually strikes the paper to form letters and images. Dot matrix printers are impact printers. Nonimpact printers form characters without striking the paper. The two most popular types of printers, laser printers and inkjet printers, are examples of nonimpact printers.

Laser Printers

A *laser printer* produces images using the same technology as copier machines. The image is made with a powdery substance called toner. A laser printer produces high-quality output. The cost of laser printers has come down substantially in recent years. Color laser printers, however, are still expensive, some costing thousands of dollars. See **Figure 2–9**.

▶ **VOCABULARY**
printer
laser printer

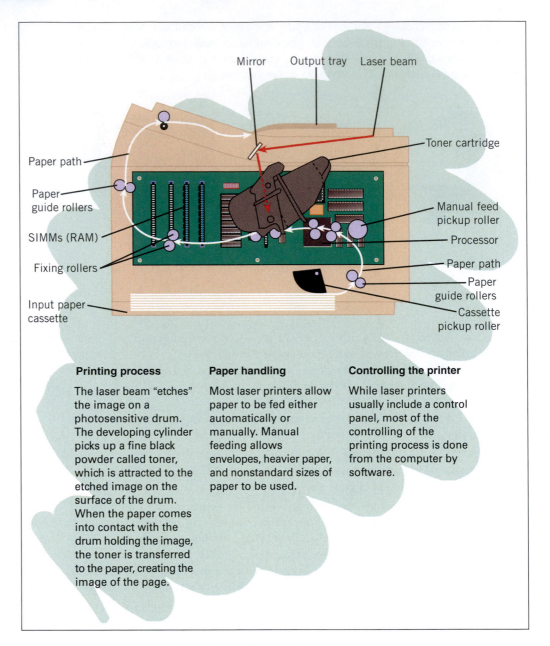

FIGURE 2–9   How a laser printer works

Inkjet Printers

An *inkjet printer* provides good-quality color printing for less expense than a laser printer. See **Figure 2–10**. Inkjet printing, like laser printing, is a nonimpact process. Ink is squirted from nozzles as they pass over the media. Unlike earlier versions of the inkjet printer, newer versions can use regular photocopy paper.

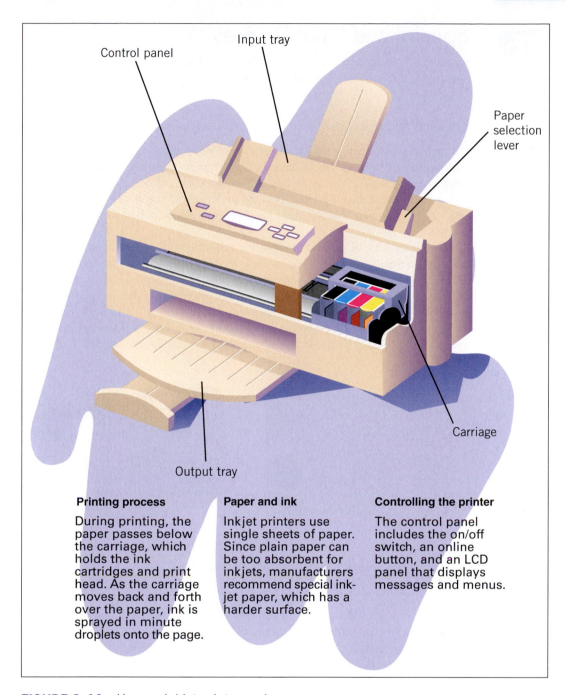

Control panel

Input tray

Paper selection lever

Carriage

Output tray

Printing process

During printing, the paper passes below the carriage, which holds the ink cartridges and print head. As the carriage moves back and forth over the paper, ink is sprayed in minute droplets onto the page.

Paper and ink

Inkjet printers use single sheets of paper. Since plain paper can be too absorbent for inkjets, manufacturers recommend special ink-jet paper, which has a harder surface.

Controlling the printer

The control panel includes the on/off switch, an online button, and an LCD panel that displays messages and menus.

FIGURE 2–10 How an inkjet printer works

Speakers

Speakers are also a type of output device. Speakers and headsets generate sound, such as music or instructions on how to complete a tutorial. Individuals use headsets or earphones to hear the music or other voice output privately.

1-1.1.6

Specialized Input Devices

A variety of other input devices are also available, most of which are used for specialized applications. The following section describes these input devices.

Digital Cameras

The pictures taken with a ***digital camera*** are stored digitally and then transferred to the computer's memory. Digital cameras use a variety of storage media to store the images, including flash memory cards, memory sticks, USB keys, mini-discs, and other solid-state storage devices. After the pictures are transferred to the computer, they can be viewed quickly and any imperfections can be edited with photo-editing software.

Video input is the process of capturing full-motion images with a type of video camera and then saving the video on a storage medium such as a hard drive, CD, or DVD. After the video is saved, you can view and edit it. A digital video (DV) camera records video as digital signals; some cameras also capture still images. Some are just a little larger than a credit card. See **Figure 2–11**. A PC video camera is a type of digital video camera that allows the user to send live images over the Internet, make video telephone calls, and send e-mail messages with video attachments.

FIGURE 2–11   Miniaturized digital video camera

Webcams are video-capturing cameras that are connected to computers or to computer networks and display images through the World Wide Web. Generally, these cameras are used for videoconferencing and or monitoring. Webcams are also used for security purposes, monitoring both movement and sound.

Game Controllers

The joystick and wheel are types of pointing devices. Joysticks and wheels, such as the ones shown in **Figure 2–12**, most often are used for games. The *joystick* consists of a plastic or metal rod mounted on a base. You can move the rod in any direction. Some joysticks have switches or buttons that can input data in an on/off response. A *wheel* is a steering-wheel type of device used to simulate driving a vehicle. Most wheels also include foot pedals used for braking and acceleration actions.

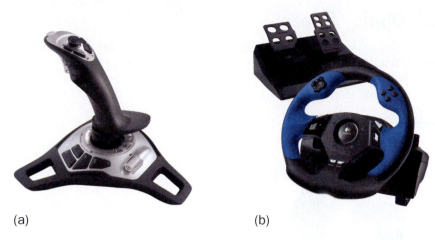

(a)   (b)

FIGURE 2–12   (a) Joystick (b) Wheel

Scanners/Bar Code Readers

Scanners are devices that can change images into codes for input to the computer. Scanners are available in various sizes and types, including the following:

- *Image scanners*: These devices convert images into an electronic form that can be stored in a computer's memory. The image can then be manipulated.

- *Bar code scanners*: This type of scanner reads bar lines that are printed on products (for example, in a grocery store or department store). See **Figure 2–13a**.

- *Magnetic scanners*: These devices read encoded information on the back of credit cards. The magnetic strip on the back of the cards contains the user's encoded account number.

- *Wireless scanners*: A Bluetooth barcode scanner uses Bluetooth wireless technology to scan data, such as from a hospital bracelet, and transmit it to a computer. See **Figure 2–13b**.

- *Optical character recognition (OCR) and optical mark recognition (OMR)*: These devices use a light source to read characters, marks, and codes; the data is then converted into digital data. Banks use OCR technology to scan checks. Commonly known as Scantrons, schools and other organizations use OMR for testing purposes.

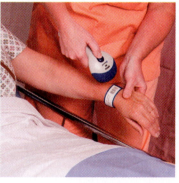

(a)   (b)

FIGURE 2–13   (a) Optical scanner (b) Bluetooth scanner

Touch Display Screen

The touch display screen, shown in **Figure 2–14**, is a special screen with pictures or shapes. You use your fingers to "point" to the desired object to make a selection. You can find these screens in many public places such as airports, hotels, banks, libraries, delivery services, and fast-food restaurants. Many mobile devices have touch screens.

FIGURE 2–14   Touch screen on a handheld device

Stylus

A stylus and digital pen are pen-like writing instruments. See **Figure 2–15**. These devices allow you to input information by writing on a PDA or other mobile device or to use the pen as a pointer.

FIGURE 2–15   Stylus for mobile device

Environmental Probes and Sensors

Environmental monitoring in many industries and companies is a critical component of stabilization in the work area. Workers can use *environmental probes* and *sensors* with a standard Web browser, such as Internet Explorer, to view elements such as the temperature and humidity of a remote environment, smoke detector readings, pollution control readings, and so on. Industries such as farming, tropical fish production, moisture monitoring, and warehouse security use environmental probes and sensors.

Remote Controls

Remote controls, also a type of specialized input device, are used for numerous standard applications, such as television, lights, fans, and so on. Industry and business also use remote controls for various applications. For example, a construction worker can use a remote control to control a crane, or a warehouse worker can have a remote control for a product cart.

Security Devices

Consider the following scenario: You are going on a two-week vacation to Tahiti and Bora Bora—you are packed and ready to go, but you do not need a wallet or credit cards. You use your fingerprint as an input device to pay for all of your expenses.

In information technology, ***biometrics*** is an authentication technique using automated methods of recognizing a person based on a physiological or behavioral characteristic. Biometric devices consist of a reader or scanning device and software that converts the scanned information into a digital format. The scanned information then is compared to a database of stored biometric data.

▶ **VOCABULARY**
biometrics

Several types of biometric identification techniques exist. Some of the more common use a person's fingerprints, face, handwriting, or voice. Other less common techniques are retina (analysis of the capillary vessels located at the back of the eye), iris (analysis of the colored ring surrounding the eye's pupil), hand geometry (analysis of the shape of the hand and length of the fingers), and vein (analysis of pattern of veins on the back of the hand and the wrist).

The process or the way in which biometric technology works, however, is basically the same for all identification techniques:

- *Enrollment*: The user enrolls in the system by establishing a baseline measurement for comparison.

- *Submission*: The user presents biological proof of his or her identity to the capture system.

- *Verification*: The system compares the submitted sample with the stored sample.

Privacy and civil liberties advocates, however, are concerned about the widespread adoption of biometric systems. They argue that by using biometric data, unauthorized parties can access someone's data without their consent and link it to other information, resulting in secondary uses of the information. This erodes the users' personal control over their private information. On the other hand, biometrics can also be applied to private security. For example, several companies now offer biometric computer keyboards and USB flash drives with fingerprint authentication that can be used for personal applications. (Flash drives were discussed in Lesson 1.) See **Figure 2–16**.

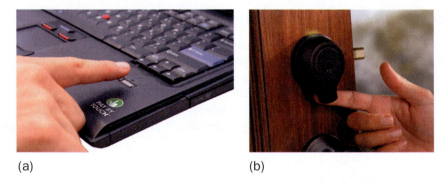

(a)   (b)

FIGURE 2–16   (a) Biometric keyboard scanner (b) Fingerprint scanner

Virtual Devices

Similar to the laser virtual keyboard mentioned earlier, virtual devices use the synchronized positioning of light-emitting and sensing devices to detect user input. **Figure 2–17a** shows a virtual computer keyboard and **Figure 2–17b** shows a virtual piano keyboard.

(a)

(b)

FIGURE 2–17 (a) Virtual computer keyboard (b) Virtual piano keyboard

Touch-Sensitive Pads

The touch-sensitive pad on a portable device, such as an iPod, enables you to scroll through a list, adjust the volume, play music, view videos or pictures, and customize settings.

Input Devices for the Physically Challenged

A variety of special input devices are available for the physically challenged. Following are some examples:

- Some keyboards can be operated with one hand or with the feet.
- A program called Camera Mouse enables users to use a Webcam and control the mouse pointer by moving their heads.
- A human-computer interface uses eye control to move a pointer and make selections.
- A joystick computer mouse can be operated with the lips, chin, or with the tongue for people with little or no head movement.
- Voice input devices allow visually impaired, blind, and physically challenged individuals to more easily interact with computers.
- A computer display screen is sensitive to human touch and allows the user to interact with the computer by touching an active area or a target, or to control data such as pictures or words on the screen.

Specialized Output Devices

1-1.1.7

Similar to specialized input devices, a variety of specialized output devices are also available:

- *Projectors*: A data projector projects the computer image onto a screen; this is mostly used for presentations.
- *Fax machines and fax modems*: A fax machine and fax modem transmit and receive documents over a telephone line or through a computer.
- *Multifunction printer*: A multifunction printer combines various output options such as printing, scanning, copying, and faxing.
- *Control devices/robots*: The field of robotics is defined as the study, design, and use of robot systems for manufacturing. Some of the typical applications of robots include testing, product inspection, painting, assembly, packaging, and painting.

Specialized Printers

Impact printers, such as the dot matrix and line printer, have been around for a long time. Dot matrix printers transfer ink to the paper by striking a ribbon with pins. The higher the number of pins (dpi), the better the resolution or output. The mechanism that actually does the printing is called a printhead. The speed of the dot matrix printer is measured in characters per second (cps). With the reduction in cost of laser and ink jet printers, dot matrix printers are used less often today. A variation of the dot matrix printer is the line printer. This type of high-speed printer is attached primarily to large computers such as mainframes or midrange servers.

Several other types of specialty printers are available. Some examples are:

- *Thermal*: A thermal printer forms characters by heating paper. The printer requires special heat-sensitive paper.
- *Mobile*: A mobile printer is a small, battery-powered printer, primarily used to print from a notebook computer.
- *Label and postage*: A label printer prints labels of various types and sizes on an adhesive-type paper; a postage printer is a special type of label printer. This type of printer contains a built-in digital scale and prints postage stamps.
- *Plotters/large-forma*t: Engineers, architects, and graphic artists use plotters and large-format printers for drawings and drafting output.

Output Devices for the Physically Challenged

Similar to input devices for the physically challenged, output devices are also available. Following are some examples:

- *Screen magnifiers*: These devices contain a range of magnifications and a variety of fonts and are used to enlarge the information displayed on the computer screen.
- *Screen readers*: A screen reader assists people who are blind or otherwise visually impaired. A speech synthesizer generally is used to read the screen content. Some screen readers can also read scanned documents.
- *Voice synthesizers*: Speech synthesis is the computer-generated simulation of human speech. A voice changes written computer text into synthetic speech. This technology is useful especially for people with limited sight.

1-1.1.8

Connecting Input and Output Devices to the Computer

Input and output devices must be connected to the computer. Some devices connect to the computer through a physical connection, such as a port. For instance, you can plug the cable for a physical device into an existing port located on the back or front of the computer. Some monitors also have ports. Wireless devices connect through infrared or radio waves.

Ports and Connectors

A *port*, also called a *jack*, is an interface to which a peripheral device attaches to or communicates with the system unit. Older peripheral devices use serial and parallel ports to connect to the computer. Serial devices transmit data one bit at a time. Parallel devices transfer eight bits at a time. A bit is represented by a 0 or 1. Typically, eight bits make one byte. Most computers traditionally have at least one parallel port and one serial port. In older computers, you will likely find a printer connected to a parallel port and perhaps a mouse connected to a serial port. A *modem* is a device that allows one computer to talk to another.

The *Universal Serial Bus (USB)* port can connect up to 127 different peripherals with a single connector and supports data transfer rates of up to 200 million bits per second (Mbps). USB replaces the standard serial and parallel ports on newer computers. USB 2.0 is a recent and more advanced version of USB technology, with speeds 40 times faster than that of its predecessors. Today's personal computers typically have four to eight USB ports either on the front or back of the system unit. Using a daisy-chain arrangement or a USB hub, you can use a single USB port to connect up to 127 peripheral devices. A USB hub is a device that plugs into a USB port and contains multiple USB ports into which cables from USB devices can be plugged. USB also supports plug-and-play and hot plugging. *Plug-and-play* refers to the ability of a computer system to configure expansion boards and other devices automatically. Hot plugging is the ability to add and remove devices to a computer while the computer is running and have the operating system automatically recognize the change.

Another type of external bus is *FireWire*, also known as IEEE 1394 and IEEE 1394b. The IEEE 1394 bus standard supports data transfer rates of up to 400 Mbps and can connect up to 63 external devices; IEEE 1394b provides speeds up to 3200 Mbps. **Figure 2–18** shows an example of some of the more popular traditional ports and examples of FireWire and USB ports.

▶ **VOCABULARY**

port

modem

Universal Serial Bus (USB)

plug-and-play

FireWire

 EXTRA FOR EXPERTS

USB 3.0 has recently been released, and has ten times the current bandwidth of USB 2.0. Transfer rates are approximately 4.8 Gbits/sec (Gigabits per second) and should be available in commercial products in 2009.

FireWire port

USB ports

Traditional ports

FIGURE 2–18   Traditional, USB, and FireWire ports

MODULE 1   Computing Fundamentals

In addition to the preceding ports, you might find three additional special-purpose ports on various computing devices. These special-purpose ports are:

- *SCSI*: An abbreviation for Small Computer System Interface, SCSI (pronounced skuzzy) is a standard interface for connecting peripherals such as disk drives and printers.

- *IrDA*: A wireless standard that allows data to be transferred between devices using infrared light instead of cables is called IrDA. Both the computer and the device must have an IrDA port, and the IrDA port on the device must align with the IrDA port on the computer.

- *Bluetooth*: Bluetooth uses radio waves and provides wireless short-range communications of data and voice between both mobile and stationary devices. This technology does not require alignment; it is an alternative to IrDA. See **Figure 2–10**.

Bluetooth indicator

FIGURE 2–19   Bluetooth device

▶ VOCABULARY

expansion slot

Expansion slots are openings on the motherboard where an expansion board, also called an adapter card, can be inserted. Expansion boards enhance functions of a component of the system unit and/or provide connections through a port or other connectors to peripheral devices. Expansion boards are also called expansion cards, add-ins, and add-ons. See **Figure 2–20**.

FIGURE 2–20   Expansion slots and card

Traditionally, ports have been located on the back of the system unit. With the introduction of portable devices, such as digital cameras and pocket PCs, many newer computers also include ports on the front of the system unit. This provides for easier access.

Hardware Installation

For most hardware devices to work, they need a set of instructions that communicates with the computer's operating system. This set of instructions is called a driver. In many instances, the operating system includes drivers for the more popular peripheral devices and performs an automatic plug-and-play installation for newly connected devices.

If the operating system does not contain a driver for the hardware, the driver needs to be installed manually. Usually, the software is included with the hardware device. If an installation disk is not available, the manufacturer's Web site generally provides a downloadable file.

Computer Performance Factors

1-1.1.9

A variety of factors can affect a computer's performance. In Lesson 1, you learned about the central processor, computer memory, and input/output devices. These three components, plus video capability and disk organization, affect the speed at which the computer performs.

The following list provides an overview of these various devices and discusses how more than one component can slow down or speed up computer performance.

1. *Microprocessor*: The architecture of the central processor is the most important processing element. CPUs are classified by generations. The higher the generation, the faster and better the processing speed. Some processors support

parallel processing. With this type of processing, while one instruction is being executed, the next instruction is fetched from memory and decoded. Thus, the faster the processor, the more instructions per second it can process.

2. *Random access memory (RAM)*: The amount of RAM also helps to increase the processing cycle and to enhance the computer's performance. When the memory capacity is reached, the CPU stores data on the hard drive. This slows down the processing cycle because it takes longer for the CPU to read from a hard drive compared to reading from RAM.

3. *Hard disk*: The size and speed of the hard drive also affects a computer's performance. The bigger and faster the hard drive, the faster the data is processed. In addition, how the disk is organized affects computer performance. If a hard disk contains many unneeded and outdated files, it takes longer for the computer to find the information it needs.

4. *Video*: The video device that is connected to the computer can enhance or slow down the computer's performance. Having adequate video memory for the video card allows the processor to perform to its full potential.

Windows Vista provides several options to determine what hardware you have in your computer system. In Step-by-Step 2.1, you learn how to view this information. When you view this information, most likely you will see abbreviations such as MB or GB, which are units for measuring bytes. Bits and bytes were discussed in Lesson 1.

Step-by-Step 2.1

1. Click the **Start** button on the taskbar, and then click **Computer**. The Computer window appears, as shown in **Figure 2–21**.

FIGURE 2–21
Computer window

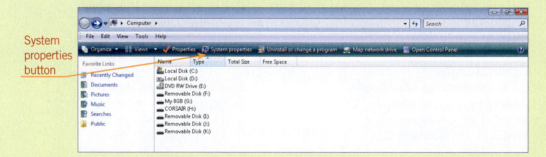

2. Click **System properties** on the menu bar. The System screen is displayed (see **Figure 2–22**). Most likely, your System screen will display different system information than that in **Figure 2–22**.

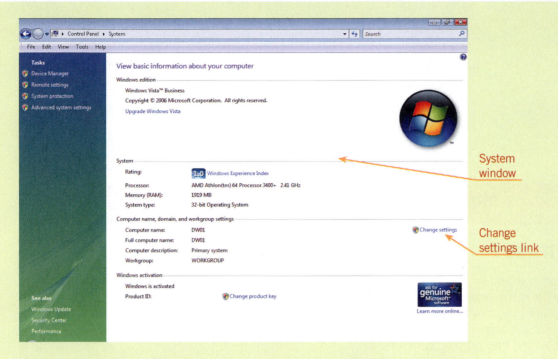

FIGURE 2–22
System window

3. What Microsoft Windows edition is listed for your computer? What processor does your computer contain? How much memory (RAM) is in your computer? What description and name are assigned to your computer?

4. Click the **Change settings** link. If a User Account Control dialog box is displayed, click the **Continue** button. The System Properties dialog box is displayed (see **Figure 2–23**).

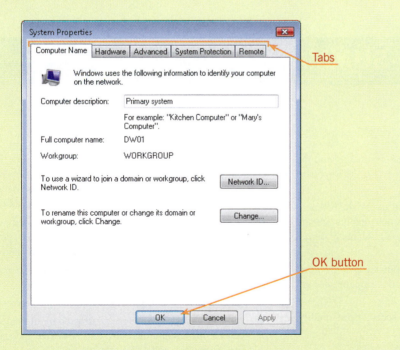

FIGURE 2–23
System Properties
dialog box

5. Click each of the tabs in the dialog box and read the information contained on each tab. If directed by your instructor, use Notepad or your word-processing program and write an overview of the features contained within the System Properties dialog box.

6. Click the **OK** button to close the System Properties dialog box, and then close the System window.

ETHICS IN TECHNOLOGY

Computer Viruses

The word *virus* can put fear into anyone who uses the Internet or exchanges disks. How can such a small word cause such fear? It is because a virus can cause tremendous damage to your computer files!

A virus is a computer program that is written intentionally to attach itself to other programs or disk boot sectors and duplicates itself whenever those programs are executed or the infected disks are accessed. A virus can wipe out all of the files on your computer.

Viruses can sit on your computer for weeks or months and not cause any damage until a predetermined date or time code is activated. Not all viruses cause damage. Some are just pranks; maybe your monitor will display some silly message. Viruses are created by persons who are impressed with the power they possess because of their expertise in the area of computers; sometimes they create them just for fun. To protect your computer from virus damage, install an antivirus software program on your computer and keep it running at all times so that it can continuously scan for viruses.

SUMMARY

In this lesson, you learned:

■ Input devices enable you to input data and commands into the computer. The most common input devices are the keyboard and mouse.

■ Other types of input devices include the trackball, joystick, wheel, pointing stick, graphics tablet, touch display screen, stylus, voice recognition devices, touchpad, scanner, digital camera, video input, and biometric input.

■ Monitors and printers are examples of output devices. Monitors produce soft copy. Printers are used to produce a paper or hard copy of the processed result.

■ Criteria for selecting a printer include speed, print quality, and cost.

■ Input and output devices must be connected to the computer. Some input and output devices communicate with the computer through a physical connection. Wireless devices communicate with the computer through infrared or radio waves.

■ Peripheral devices are connected to the computer through serial, parallel, and Universal Serial Bus (USB) ports. USB is a newer standard expected to replace serial and parallel ports.

■ FireWire is a type of external bus that can connect up to 63 external devices.

■ SCSI, IrDA, and Bluetooth are special-purpose ports.

■ A computer's performance is affected by the speed of the processor, the amount of RAM, hard disk size and speed, capability of monitor, and disk organization.

■ VOCABULARY REVIEW

Define the following terms:

audio input	keyboard	pointing device
biometrics	laser printer	port
digital camera	modem	printer
expansion slot	monitor	scanner
FireWire	mouse	trackball
inkjet printer	output	Universal Serial Bus (USB)
input	plug-and-play	

■ REVIEW QUESTIONS

TRUE / FALSE

Circle T if the statement is true or F if the statement is false.

T   F   **1.** Video input is the process of capturing full-motion images with a video camera.

T   F   **2.** Input and output devices perform the same function.

T   F   **3.** A data projector is a type of specialized output device that projects the computer image onto a screen, usually during a presentation.

T   F   **4.** Input and output devices can stand alone—they do not need to be connected to the computer.

T   F   **5.** An optical mouse uses a laser to detect the mouse's movement.

MULTIPLE CHOICE

Select the best response for the following statements.

1. Which of the following is *not* considered an input device?

   A. keyboard   C. mouse

   B. scanner   D. monitor

2. Which one of the following is a type of scanner that converts graphics into an electronic form?

   A. image scanner   C. bar code scanner

   B. magnetic scanner   D. OCR scanner

3. Plug-and-play refers to a computer's ability to _____.

   A. connect multiple USB devices

   B. configure hardware devices automatically

   C. communicate with the system unit

   D. talk to another computer

4. _____ produce an image by manipulating light within a layer of liquid crystal cells.

   A. Gas plasma monitors   C. CRT monitors

   B. LCD panels   D. Scanners

5. Which of the following is a biometric identification scanning technique?

   A. fingerprint   C. voice

   B. face   D. all of the above

FILL IN THE BLANK

Complete the following sentences by writing the correct word or words in the blanks provided.

1. A(n) _____ is the most widely used device for entering data into the computer.

2. _____ is data or instructions entered into the computer.

3. The _____ port can connect up to 127 different peripherals with a single connector.

4. To improve performance dramatically, increase the amount of _____ on your computer.

5. A(n) _____ is a small, battery-powered printer, primarily used to print from a notebook computer.

■ PROJECTS

PROJECT 2–1

Gmail is a free Web mail service provided through Google. Complete the following steps to create an account.

1. Open your browser and go to *http://mail.google.com/mail/ help/open.html*.

2. When the Welcome to Gmail screen is displayed, read the information provided on the page. Then click the **Create an account** link.

3. Type your first and last name and desired login name. Click the **check availability** button to verify that the name is available.

4. When selecting a password, Google assists with a password strength level—poor, fair, and strong. Your goal is to create a strong password. It must be a minimum of eight characters. Be sure to write down your password or send the password to yourself in an e-mail.

5. If you are using a school computer or a computer other than your own, do not select the "Remember me on this computer" or the "Enable Web History" check boxes.

6. Select a Security Question that you are sure to remember. E-mail the answer to yourself.

7. If you have another e-mail address, you can enter it into the Secondary e-mail text box. However, this is not necessary or required.

8. For Word Verification, type the characters displayed on the form.

9. Read the Terms of Service, and then click the **I accept. Create my account** button.

10. When an Introduction to Gmail page is displayed, read the information on the page and then click **Show me my account**. Sign in to your account using your user name and password.

11. Click the **Compose Mail** link and send a message to your instructor and/or another classmate. List three facts in the message that relate to the topics presented in this lesson. Print a copy of your message and submit it to your instructor.

For additional information, see *http://mail.google.com/support/*.

PROJECT 2–2

Biometric technology is the automated method of recognizing a person based on a physiological or behavioral characteristic. Use the Internet and other sources to research this topic.

1. Use your favorite search engine to search for Web pages discussing biometric technology.

2. Based on your findings, create a document listing the pros and cons of biometric technology. Include your personal opinion about this topic.

3. Submit the document to your instructor as requested.

PROJECT 2–3

Prepare a written report on input devices.

1. Select at least five input devices discussed in this lesson.

2. Create a document for the report. Include a table in your report listing each input device, describing how it could be used, and explaining the device's advantages and disadvantages.

3. Submit the document to your instructor as requested.

TEAMWORK PROJECT

This exercise is a student role-playing activity. Students are given a specific task and a set of rules. They then role-play parts of a computer to accomplish the task. Student roles include a processor, main memory, storage devices, and input/output devices. Following are some of the task examples: (a) inputting pictures from a digital camera, modifying and viewing the pictures, and outputting and printing the pictures; (b) using word-processing software to create a report on a specified school topic, adding pictures to the report, and then printing copies for all students in the class; (c) students use a spreadsheet program to create a worksheet and chart and then print copies for all students in the class; (d) students use a presentation program such as PowerPoint and create a presentation with text, images, and video; they display the presentation to the class.

CRITICAL THINKING

You want to learn more about how the computer processes data and the factors that influence the processing speed. Your instructor thinks this is a great idea and asks you to prepare a report on what factors produce the best overall processing system. Prepare a report listing the devices you would select to produce the best all-around processing system.

ONLINE DISCOVERY

Google has a feature that focuses solely on blog searching. This feature, called Blog Search, is located at *www.google.com/blogsearch*. Access this Web site and then search for *increase computer speed*. Write a one-page report on what you learned.

LESSON 3

Computer Protection

▪ OBJECTIVES

Upon completion of this lesson, you should be able to:

- Identify the importance of protecting computer hardware from theft and damage.
- Explain how to protect data.
- Identify environmental factors that can cause damage to computer hardware and media.
- Identify how to protect computer hardware from power loss and fluctuation.
- Identify common problems associated with computer hardware.

▪ DATA FILES

You do not need data files to complete this lesson.

▪ VOCABULARY

backup

data theft

driver

encryption

humidity

ping

power spikes

surge suppressor

uninterruptible power
  supply (UPS)

MODULE 1   Computing Fundamentals

It is true that computers have made a positive impact in our lives. They have made our daily lives much easier, our work more efficient, our learning more interesting and convenient, and even our game playing more exciting. As the use of computers has grown in volume and importance, protecting computer systems and the information they hold has become increasingly important. Computer users also have certain responsibilities that govern their use of technology, including following guidelines and policies for use as well as protecting their own privacy, exercising ethical conduct online, and maintaining a safe work environment. This lesson explores the many issues of computer maintenance, the risks of computing, and the measures that can be taken to minimize those risks.

1-1.2.1

Protecting Computer Hardware from Theft and Damage

Theft of and damage to computer equipment is a serious problem that many businesses and other organizations face. In addition to the capital loss of equipment and the related down time until it is replaced, the loss of sensitive and confidential information could have long-term consequences to the business or industry. One of the more important safeguards you can implement in the workplace is to physically secure equipment, especially items such as notebook computers, handheld devices, cell phones, and other transportable devices. See **Figure 3–1**.

FIGURE 3–1   Preventing computer theft

EXTRA FOR EXPERTS

Some companies offer security software for notebook computers that can trace the location of a stolen computer when it is connected to the Internet. The location information is forwarded to the company, and they contact law enforcement officials who may be able to recover the computer.

You can apply the following safeguards to help protect computer hardware from theft and loss of data:

- If the equipment is located within an office or open lab, use security locks and/or tabs to secure the equipment to the desk or other furniture.
- Attach an alarm that will sound if the equipment is moved from its designated location.
- Mark all equipment with an identification mark that can be traced easily.

- Insure the equipment. Some insurance policies cover loss due to accidental damage, theft, vandalism, power surges, lightning strike, flood, fire, earthquake, and other natural disasters.
- Use a designated schedule to back up data to a separate system.

Another type of theft that is sometimes overlooked involves employees accessing a company's computer for personal use. Theft of computer time is a crime committed regularly on the job. Some companies use spyware to monitor employee personal use, though this has been challenged in court.

Data Protection

In most instances, hardware can be physically protected or replaced when it is damaged or obsolete. Data, on the other hand, is a critical component of most businesses and is not easily replaced. Many companies protect their data with security devices such as firewalls and intrusion detection devices. Data thieves, however, also steal laptops and servers. They then use the remote software on the stolen system to connect to the organization's network and bypass the company's security measures. In other instances, *data theft* can occur when older systems are discarded and the data is not deleted. The risk and severity of data theft is increasing due to four predominant factors:

- The value of data stored on computers
- Massive amounts of confidential and private data being stored
- Increased use of laptops and other mobile devices outside of a secure network
- Increased proficiency of data hackers and thieves

Many businesses and organizations use data encryption to protect their data. *Encryption* is a secure process for keeping confidential information private. The data is scrambled mathematically with a password or a password key. The encryption process makes the data unreadable unless or until it is decrypted.

Data Backup

Even saved data can be lost or corrupted by equipment failure, software viruses, hackers, fire or water damage, or power irregularities. Because data is so valuable, you must back up important files regularly. To back up files, you save them to removable disks or some other independent storage device that you can use to restore data in case the primary system becomes inaccessible. A hard disk crash (or failure) can result in a catastrophic loss of data if it occurs on a critical system and the files have not been backed up properly.

Backup procedures should place a priority on files that would be difficult or impossible to replace or reconstruct if they were lost, such as a company's financial statements, important projects, and works in progress. Large organizations have secure backup procedures that include a regular schedule for backing up designated files. They store the backup files off site so they will survive intact if the main system is destroyed either by natural disaster or by criminal acts. When flooding is a possibility, it is a good idea to locate computers above the first floor of a building.

> ▶ **VOCABULARY**
> **data theft**
> **encryption**
> **backup**

> **EXTRA FOR EXPERTS**
>
> Data backup systems include disk and tape devices that make archive copies of important files and folders. You should back up data to storage media that can be removed and stored in a separate location from your computer.

1-1.2.2

Environmental Conditions

Computers require the right balance of physical and environmental conditions to properly operate. As indicated previously, computer equipment, as well as data stored on a computer, is subject to various types of hazards. This includes damage caused by improper use by employees and theft of hardware and data. Environmental factors such as temperature, humidity, and electrical fields also can contribute to hardware and software damage. Organizations can prevent many of these conditions through proper planning and by providing employees with appropriate training on how to use and safeguard the equipment.

The following sections describe environmental factors detrimental to computers and how you can control and contain some of these problems.

Temperature

Environmental conditions in a computer room or data center are critical to ensuring a computer system is running properly and reliably, and is accessible to users. A temperature range of 68 to 75 degrees is optimal for system reliability. The general consensus is that you should not operate computer equipment in a room where the temperature exceeds 85 degrees. A separate thermostat can monitor temperature and humidity levels in a computer room (see **Figure 3–2**).

FIGURE 3–2   Temperature control

Humidity

A high level of *humidity* can cause computers to short circuit, resulting in the loss of data and damage to hardware. Excessive humidity also can cause components to rust. For example, taking a cold notebook computer from an air-conditioned office into an automobile on a sunny day could create a thin film of condensation covering the entire interior of the laptop. Also consider the following humidity factors to protect your data and computers:

- For optimal performance, the relative humidity of the computer room should be above 20 percent and below the dew point (which depends on the ambient room temperature).

- Environments that require high reliability should have a humidity alarm that rings when the humidity is out of an acceptable range.

- Some equipment has special humidity restrictions. Generally this information is contained in the equipment manual.

Water Damage

Most computer centers contain some type of sprinkler system. If water sprinklers are activated, newer models of computers most likely will not be damaged, provided that the computer's power is turned off before the water starts to flow. Modern computer systems contain a cut-off device that triggers if the sprinklers turn on. If the computer does suffer water damage, make sure it is completely dried out before you restore the power. Storage devices and printouts out in the open, however, can be damaged or destroyed by water. Other types of water damage may occur from flooding and broken pipes.

Magnetic Fields and Static Electricity

Magnetic fields and static electricity exist wherever electrical current flows. A single spark from static electricity can damage the internal electronics of a computer. Computer technicians should have grounding protection on the floor and use a grounded strap on their wrists. This prevents damaging a computer with a static electrical spark. Data on a hard drive is stored in small magnetic dots on the disk and is therefore sensitive to magnetic fields. Computer rooms should also have tile floors and antistatic carpet.

Maintaining Equipment

One of the best ways to cut down on computer repair is through preventive maintenance. Create a monthly maintenance schedule and follow it regularly to clean equipment and perform tasks to keep computer devices in good working order. For example, if you use a mechanical mouse, you need to remove the ball and clean it periodically. Poorly maintained printers can print pages that are smudged or otherwise difficult to read. Cable connections can be weakened by dust, preventing normal communication with a computer. Damaged cables in general can prevent peripheral devices from communicating with the computer.

Physical Damage

Notebook computers are generally more costly than desktops with similar storage and processing capabilities. They are also more prone to physical wear and tear because they are portable. To help protect the computer and limit the extent of the damage, most portable systems are insulated with shock absorbing material. This reduces damage to internal components if the computer is dropped or subjected to impact with another object. You should take additional steps to prevent damage to portable computers due to physical shock by transporting devices with care, such as in padded cases.

Power Loss and Power Fluctuation Issues

1-1.2.3

One ever-present threat to a computer system is an electrical power failure. Electricity not only provides the power to operate a computer, but it also is the medium by which data is stored. An unexpected power outage, for example, can wipe out any data that has not been properly saved.

To safeguard computer systems against power outages, secure electric cords so that they cannot be accidentally disconnected. You also need to protect electronic devices, including computers, from *power spikes*, which are short, fast transfers of electrical voltage, current, or energy. *Surge suppressors* (see **Figure 3–3**) plug into

▶ **VOCABULARY**
power spikes

surge suppressor

electric outlets, and can protect against power spikes, which can damage computer hardware and software. Some lower end brands of surge suppressors wear out over time, however, and need to be monitored and replaced as necessary.

FIGURE 3–3   Surge suppressor

▶ **VOCABULARY**

uninterruptible power supply (UPS)

One option for preventing data loss due to power outages is to install an **uninterruptible power supply (UPS)**. These devices range from basic kits similar to one shown in **Figure 3–4**, to more sophisticated models designed for desktop computers and networks. A UPS contains a battery that temporarily provides power if the normal current is interrupted, and generally keeps a computer running for several minutes following a power outage. These additional minutes provide an opportunity for you to save data and to properly shut down the computer. Most UPS systems now also provide a software component that automates the backup and shutdown process. The two basic types of UPS systems are standby power systems (SPSs) and online UPS systems. An SPS monitors the electrical power and switches to battery power if it detects a power problem. Depending on the computer system, the switch to battery power can take less than one second. An online UPS constantly provides power, even when the system is functioning properly. In either case, you avoid momentary power lapses.

FIGURE 3–4   Uninterruptible power supply

1-1.2.4

Hardware Issues

Computer equipment and stored data are subject to various types of hardware issues. Some common problems are a failed or "crashed" hard drive, damaged media, printer and monitor problems, loss of network or Internet connectivity, and general failure such as newly installed hardware not working. You can resolve or prevent many of these conditions by proper planning and by receiving appropriate training on how to use and safeguard the equipment. Some of these issues are easily fixed, while others may require the assistance of a professional.

The following sections provide an overview of common hardware problems and suggestions on how to troubleshoot and resolve them.

Crashed Hard Drive

Crashed hard drives generally are caused by software corruption or hardware defects. Hard drives can stop working if they become overheated, are dropped or shaken, become worn out, or are infected with a virus. Some suggestions to evaluate the condition of the drive are as follows:

- Verify that the cable is not damaged and that it is plugged in.
- If a boot disk is available, use the disk to determine if the drive is readable. If so, back up the data and reformat the original disk.
- Several software solutions are available; these diagnostic and data recovery programs can locate and recover bad sectors.
- Use a data recovery service.

Damaged Media

Hard disks and other media eventually fail. Hard disks are mechanical devices with moving parts, and inevitably wear out. CDs and DVDs can be scratched, warped, or physically damaged in another way. Tapes can be harmed by electromagnetic fields. Flash drives can also suffer physical damage, such as from unsafe removal, dust, lint, sun exposure, shock, or force.

Many people assume that information stored on damaged media, such as disks, tapes, or CDs, is unrecoverable. In many instances, however, you can recover the data. The first step is to locate the hardware and damaged media and move it to a secure environment. Secondly, inspect or test the media to determine what type and how much damage has occurred.

The type of damage determines the type of recovery method to use. If the media was damaged by water, do not restart the computer. This could cause a short if even small amounts of water are still in the computer. If the media is wet, do not dry it. Instead, place it in an airtight plastic bag to eliminate any contaminants that remain on the media. If the media was damaged by fire and is still inside a melted computer case, leave it in the case if water or other elements were used to control the fire. The case should be opened by a professional. If the computer was dropped or otherwise physically harmed in some way, do not restart the computer. The read/write heads can be damaged or out of alignment.

Another option is to locate a disaster data recovery company with the knowledge, skills, and equipment necessary to recover data from the computer.

Printer Problems

Printer problems are one of the more frequent issues that occur with the use and operation of a printer. Generally, these problems are easily fixed.

Paper jams are one of the more common printer problems. Using the wrong type of paper can cause a printer jam, as can wrinkled or torn paper. If the rollers that feed the paper are worn or dirty, they might turn slowly or unevenly and cause a jam. When eliminating a paper jam, always pull the paper in the direction of the paper path. Pulling the paper backward can damage the printer (see **Figure 3–5**).

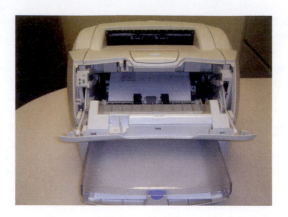

FIGURE 3–5   Paper jam

If ink or toner comes off the paper when touched, look for one of three possible causes. The printer's fuser assembly might be damaged and need to be replaced; the toner cartridge could be defective and need to be replaced; or some toner may have spilled into the printer. If so, the toner needs to be cleaned out of the printer with a dry cloth.

If the printed image is faded, this could indicate one of three conditions: the toner is low, the print density is set too low, or economy mode printing is turned on.

Display Problems

The hardware for your display consists of two elements: the monitor and the video card. It can be more difficult to determine the source of display problems than printer problems, for example, because more hardware is involved (see **Figure 3–6**).

FIGURE 3–6   Video card problem

Consider the following factors as you troubleshoot a display problem:

- Check that the monitor power cord is plugged in and that the monitor cable is connected to the computer.
- Verify that the monitor is turned on and that the settings are correct.
- The majority of display problems are caused by incorrect, corrupted, or missing video drivers. (See the following section for the definition of a driver.) You can usually upgrade the video driver when you update the operating system; otherwise, visit the Web site for the video driver manufacturer and look for instructions on upgrading the video driver.

Inoperable Hardware Devices

When a hardware device such as a printer or monitor does not work, it could be a software problem, an electrical problem, or a mechanical problem. A small program called a *driver* instructs the operating system on how to operate specific hardware. As mentioned in the previous section, most display problems are caused by missing or corrupted drivers. Incorrect installation of the software for the hardware device or hardware failure also can be at fault. Also check the following alternatives:

- Check the power cord and verify that it is plugged in.
- Verify that the circuit breaker has not tripped.
- Check the electrical plug strip, the UPS, and/or the surge protector.

Loss of Network or Internet Connectivity

Local networks and the Internet provide valuable resources for organizations and individuals. As people become dependent on these systems, losing connectivity means they cannot communicate or work effectively. In addition to loss of connectivity, intermittent connectivity and time-out problems can result in poor network performance.

The following are common causes for connectivity problems:

- The network provider's system is not working properly.
- Network adapters and switch ports do not match.
- The network adapter is incompatible with the motherboard or other hardware components.

Some troubleshooting options are:

- Use the DOS *ping* command to test connectivity and isolate hardware problems and any mismatched configurations.
- Verify that other computers on the same network and those plugged into the same switch are also experiencing network connectivity problems.
- If you are using a router, restart the router.
- Check the computer's network board and verify it is using settings as indicated by the manufacturer.
- Try another network cable.

The following Step-by-Step exercise shows you how to use the ping command.

▶ **VOCABULARY**
driver

ping

🖃 **EXTRA FOR EXPERTS**

Connecting computers to a network or the Internet creates opportunities for unauthorized access from outside the network. Software and hardware devices that safeguard a network and provide security from unauthorized entry are called firewalls.

Step-by-Step 3.1

1. Click the **Start** button  on the taskbar, point to **All Programs**, click **Accessories**, and then click **Command Prompt**. The Command Prompt window appears, as shown in **Figure 3–7**.

FIGURE 3–7
Command Prompt window

2. At the command prompt (C:>), type **ping (*Web site address of your school or another Web site address*)** and then press the **Enter** key.

The results will show a series of replies, which indicates the connection is working (see **Figure 3–8**). The time shows the speed of the connection. Your specific results will be different from those in **Figure 3–8**.

FIGURE 3–8
Replies to ping command

If a "timed out" error instead of a reply is displayed, there is a breakdown somewhere between your computer and the site to which you are attempting to connect.

ETHICS IN TECHNOLOGY

The Golden Rule of Computer Ethics

You probably heard the Golden Rule when you were in elementary school: "Do unto others as you would have them do unto you." The Golden Rule applies to computer ethics, too. Would you appreciate it if someone used their computer to cause you financial harm or to ruin your reputation? Of course not, and you should extend the same courtesy to other people. Don't give in to the urge to snoop around in other people's files or interfere with their work by accessing and changing data in files. You wouldn't want someone to mess with your hard work or private files, would you? And if you had spent a few months creating a great computer game, how would you feel if all your friends started passing copies of the game around to all their friends, without even giving you credit for the program, not to mention cheating you out of any potential profit for your work?

If you do write computer programs, think about the social consequences of the programs you write. Don't copy software illegally, and don't take other people's intellectual property and use it as your own. Just because something is posted on the Web does not mean it is "free" for anyone to use. Use your computer in ways that show consideration of and respect for other people, their property, and their resources. In short, think of the Golden Rule and follow it whenever you face an ethical dilemma at your computer.

SUMMARY

In this lesson, you learned:

- Computer equipment needs to be protected from theft and damage.

- Back up data frequently and consistently to avoid losing important information.

- The right balance of physical and environmental conditions are required for computers to operate properly.

- High humidity, water, and electric/magnetic fields can damage computer equipment.

- Preventive maintenance reduces equipment repair needs.

- Electrical power failure can destroy data and equipment.

- Surge suppressors can protect against power spikes.

- Computer centers are vulnerable to problems such as a crashed hard disk, damaged media, printer and display problems, inoperable hardware devices, and loss of network and Internet connectivity.

■ VOCABULARY REVIEW

Define the following terms:

backup	encryption	power spikes
data theft	humidity	surge suppressor
driver	ping	uninterruptible power supply (UPS)

■ REVIEW QUESTIONS

TRUE / FALSE

Circle T if the statement is true or F if the statement is false.

T   F   **1.**   Theft of and damage to computer equipment is a serious problem.

T   F   **2.**   Data theft is decreasing.

T   F   **3.**   Backup procedures are not necessary for most companies.

T   F   **4.**   A temperature range of 68 to 75 degrees is optimal for most data centers.

T   F   **5.**   Magnetic and static electrical fields exist wherever electrical current flows.

MULTIPLE CHOICE

Select the best response for the following statements.

1. A high level of _____ can cause computers to short circuit.

   A.   smoke   C.   dust

   B.   humidity   D.   alarms

2. Generally, a _____ keeps a computer running for several minutes following a power outage.

   A.   driver   C.   backup

   B.   spike   D.   UPS

3. Which of the following safeguards can help protect computer hardware from theft and loss of data?

   A.   security locks   C.   identification mark

   B.   alarm   D.   all of the above

4. _____ can protect against power spikes.

   A.   Surge suppressors   C.   Undamaged media

   B.   Video drivers   D.   Network connections

5. Software corruption or hardware defects can cause a hard drive to _____ .

   A.   become overheated   C.   spin faster

   B.   crash   D.   spin slower

FILL IN THE BLANK

Complete the following sentences by writing the correct word or words in the blanks provided.

1. _____ is a secure process for keeping confidential information private.

2. The hardware for your display consists of two elements: the monitor and the _____ _____ .

3. _____ _____ should be used on a regular basis on files that would be difficult or impossible to replace.

4. The _____ on a mouse should be cleaned periodically.

5. If printer rollers are worn or dirty, they might cause a(n) _____ _____ .

PROJECTS

PROJECT 3-1

Your instructor has requested that you be responsible for maintenance of the school's computer lab. Assume that the lab has thirty networked computers, a server, two color inkjet printers, three laser printers, and a scanner. Hardware and software needs to be updated and maintained on a regular schedule. As part of this job, one of the tasks that you have is to create a maintenance schedule for the equipment. Complete the following:

1. Use a spreadsheet program or word processing software and create a monthly schedule listing required maintenance.

2. Record how often maintenance is scheduled.

3. Submit the document to your instructor as requested.

PROJECT 3-3

Your instructor has assigned you the responsibility of creating an acceptable use policy for the school's computer lab. Complete the following:

1. Write a statement that describes appropriate and inappropriate behavior and acceptable and unacceptable use of equipment.

2. Share your statement with your classmates.

PROJECT 3-2

Computer crimes have been responsible for the loss of millions of dollars. Some crimes result in more loss than others. Complete the following:

1. Use the Internet and other resources to locate information on lost revenue due to the top five computer crimes. Some search terms that may be helpful are "computer crimes," "computer crime costs," "hackers," "viruses," "data loss," and "software piracy." Use various search engines to research each term.

2. Use a spreadsheet program to prepare this information and use formulas that will add the totals and also display the percentage of each crime's portion.

3. Submit the document to your instructor as requested.

 TEAMWORK PROJECT

Working with a partner, research some of the hardware and software issues and problems discussed in this lesson. Select three of the issues and then create a presentation describing these problems. If possible, share your team's presentation with your class.

 CRITICAL THINKING

Use the Internet and other resources to identify early security measures that were used to protect computers and computer data. Describe how these measures counteracted the intrusions made on the computers. Then, visit the Web sites of some companies that now make computer security devices, such as *www.pcguardian.com*. Describe how and why these devices are different. Write a report of your findings.

 ONLINE DISCOVERY

Suppose several computers in the lab at your school have a virus. Use Google or another search engine to determine the best method for eliminating the virus and how to protect the computers from encountering this problem again in the future. Write a report on your findings and include the Web site addresses where you found your information. Submit your report to your instructor.

LESSON 4

Computer Maintenance

■ OBJECTIVES

Upon completion of this lesson, you should be able to:

- Identify problems that can occur if hardware is not properly maintained.
- Identify routine maintenance that can be performed by users.
- Identify maintenance that should be performed by experienced professionals.

■ DATA FILES

You do not need data files to complete this lesson.

■ VOCABULARY

cable management

corona wires

cookie

defragmentation

ergonomic keyboard

fragmentation

maintenance

Recycle Bin

sectors

seek time

touchpad

wireless keyboard

This lesson explores the importance of computer maintenance, the risks of computing if equipment is not properly maintained, and the measures that can be taken to minimize those risks. The type of maintenance determines whether a professional or you as the computer user should perform the maintenance tasks.

1-1.2.5

▶ **VOCABULARY**
maintenance

cable management

Maintenance Issues

Consider the following: To properly maintain a car and have it run smoothly, you change the oil and filter, check the tire pressure, and complete other required maintenance on a regular schedule. The computer is no different. It also requires regular *maintenance*. Sooner or later, you will begin to experience problems with the hardware. For instance, the performance of a hard disk starts to slow and printer problems may start to occur. The keyboard and the mouse can become sluggish, and the monitor may not work properly. This could be the result of loose or incorrect cables, poor power connections, or could be other more severe problems.

Managing computer cables is an overlooked problem when maintaining a computer system. Damaged and poorly maintained cables can prevent peripheral devices from communicating with the computer. Unorganized and unprotected cables can also create safety hazards (see **Figure 4–1**).

FIGURE 4–1   Unprotected cables are a safety hazard

Cable management kits and individual cable management products are available online and through most stores that sell computer equipment (see **Figure 4–2**).

FIGURE 4–2   Managing cables

Hardware Maintenance

One of the best ways to cut down on computer repair is through preventative maintenance performed on a regular schedule. As a general rule, you should clean a computer every 3–6 months. If it is in a dusty environment, however, you should clean it more often. This section provides guidelines that you can easily put into practice.

Keyboard and Mouse

You should check and clean the keyboard periodically. Dirt, dust, hair, and food particles can accumulate, causing the keys to jam or otherwise malfunction. Many people clean the keyboard by turning it upside down and shaking it. A more effective method, however, is to use compressed air. Every 6 months, you can use a can of compressed air to remove the dust from the keyboard (see **Figure 4–3**).

FIGURE 4–3   Cleaning a keyboard

If you spill a liquid onto the keyboard, turn off the computer immediately. Disconnect the keyboard, spray it with water to clean it, turn it upside down and shake to remove the liquid, and then use a cloth to dry it as much as possible. After it is cleaned, leave it upside down for at least 12 hours.

A mouse with a ball (which is a mechanical mouse) can be difficult to move if the rollers are clogged. Cleaning mechanical mice often eliminates jerky or erratic movement of the mouse pointer. To clean the rollers, you need to remove the bottom cover of the mouse (see **Figure 4–4a**). Generally, you will find dirt or hair in the middle of the roller. Remove as much of this debris as much as possible, and then reassemble the mouse (see **Figure 4–4b**).

(A)   (B)

FIGURE 4–4   (A) Removing the bottom cover of a mouse
(B) Cleaning debris

Cleaning a printer helps prolong the printer's life. The first step is to check the printer documentation. If this is unavailable, most likely you can find information online. Clean only the parts recommended. Recall that the two more popular types of printers are inkjet and laser. The following general instructions apply to both types of printers:

- Turn off the printer.
- Use a cleaner recommended by the manufacturer, or a lint-free cloth, and then moisten it with a 50-50 percent solution of water and vinegar. Wring out all excess moisture and thoroughly clean the outside of the printer, making sure that no fluid gets inside the printer.
- Never spray an aerosol directly onto the printer.
- It is not necessary, but consider wearing latex gloves to protect your hands from dirt and other debris.

Inkjet Printer

After so much usage, small deposits of dry ink accumulate on the print head of the printer. Eventually, these deposits begin to clog the printer's ink jets and affect the print quality of the document. This also causes streaks and blotchy printing.

Many inkjet printers have a self-cleaning mode that is accessed through the printer's control panel. If this is not available, an inkjet cleaning cartridge can be used. This flushes dirt and debris out of clogged printer nozzles. Verify that the cleaning cartridge is approved for your printer.

Dust and ink from inexpensive paper can affect the printer's rollers. Before cleaning inside an inkjet printer, turn it off and unplug it. Let it cool down if necessary. Use a small vacuum to remove the debris.

Roller cleaning sheets are available that can be used to clean the print rollers. Check the printer documentation to verify the correct sheets for the printer (see **Figure 4–5**).

FIGURE 4–5   Cleaning an inkjet printer

Laser Printer

Laser printers should be cleaned when print quality deteriorates or when you change the toner cartridge. When you open a laser printer, however, do not touch anything shiny because it might be hot or contain a charge. Perform the following maintenance tasks:

- Turn off the printer and then unplug it. If the printer is warm, let it cool. Remove the paper trays and the toner cartridge. Place the cartridge on a clean surface.

- Use a printer brush or a good paint brush and a lint-free cloth to clean inside the toner opening.

- Remove paper fragments.

- Use a clean cloth to wipe up any spilled toner and dust.

- Clean the rollers, but don't touch the transfer (sponge) roller (see **Figure 4–6**).
- Replace the toner cartridge.

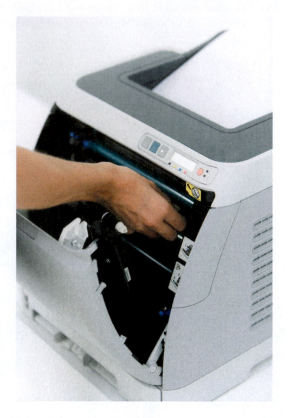

FIGURE 4–6   Maintaining a laser printer

Some laser printers contain exposed *corona wires*. These wires are used to generate a field of positive charges on the surface of the drum and the paper. You should not brush or vacuum these wires.

Upgrades and Consumables

At some point, hardware components may be damaged and need to be changed, or output and production needs to be increased. This can be enhanced by upgrading various elements within the computer system. For instance, adding computer memory is often the best value for increasing overall computer performance. Updating the keyboard and the mouse can also enhance computer performance. The following section describes upgrade options that you can implement and apply.

⚡ WARNING

Exposure to light can damage toner cartridges. Always cover the toner cartridge with an extra lint-free cloth or piece of paper after removing it.

Computer Memory

One way to measure a computer's power is by its capacity to remember. RAM is made up of small memory chips that form a memory module. These modules are installed in the RAM slots on the motherboard of your computer (see **Figure 4–7**).

FIGURE 4–7 RAM chips on the motherboard

The hard drive can be compared to long-term memory and random access memory (RAM) to short-term memory. Data stored in RAM is temporary. When the computer is processing data, it reads and writes to RAM. If RAM fills up, then the processor continually goes to the hard drive to replace old data in RAM with new data. Because hard drive access is considerably slower than RAM, you notice a processing slowdown when a computer's RAM is overloaded. Congested RAM can even affect the speed of the monitor while the disk operates continuously, writing and copying RAM data out to the disk.

Adding RAM to a computer generally helps increase performance, speed, and usability. However, every system has a maximum amount of RAM that it can support. Check the computer's documentation, or verify with a professional technician prior to purchasing additional memory. Complete the following Step-by-Step exercise to explore the amount of RAM contained in your computer.

Step-by-Step 4.1

1. Click the **Start** button 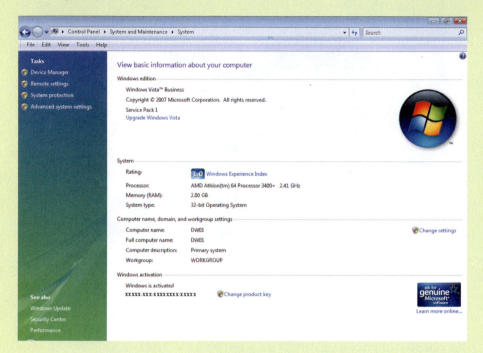 on the taskbar, and then click **Computer**. The Computer window opens.

2. Click **System properties** to display the System window, shown in **Figure 4–8**.

FIGURE 4–8
System window

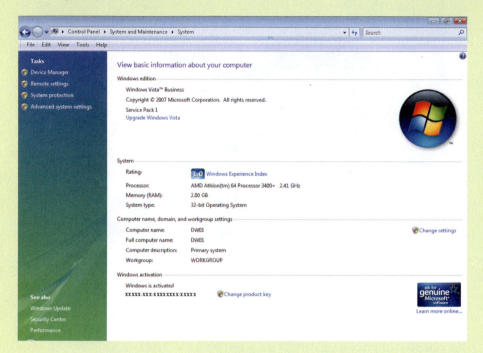

3. Click **Performance** to display the Rate and improve your computer's performance page, shown in **Figure 4–9**. Read the information contained on this page. What is your computer's base score?

FIGURE 4–9
Rate and improve your computer's performance page

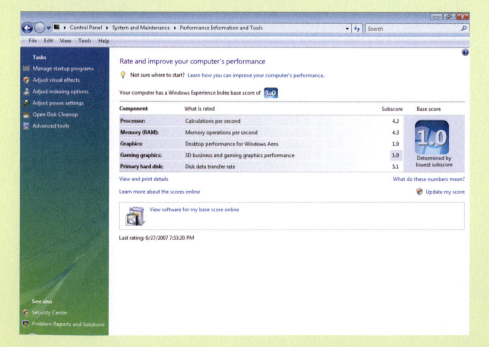

4. Click the **Learn how you can improve your computer's performance** link. Read the information contained in the Windows Help and Support box.

5. List the tasks that you think can help improve your computer's performance.

6. Submit your assignment to your instructor.

Keyboards

Choosing a keyboard is complicated by the vast range of choices. Selecting a keyboard is a choice that should be made by the person who will be using it. The design, performance, and comfort should be considered.

Ergonomic keyboards allow for a more natural positioning of your arms and hands. Many ergonomic keyboards have a smaller width, which keeps the mouse closer to you. This reduces the reach and places the mouse in a more accessible position (see **Figure 4–10**).

▶ **VOCABULARY**

ergonomic keyboard

wireless keyboard

FIGURE 4–10   Ergonomic keyboard

A *wireless keyboard* reduces the clutter of unsightly wires and other cable problems and improves mobility. If necessary, you can move around with a wireless keyboard as necessary and not be bound to the desk.

Mouse

A variety of mouse devices are available, including wireless, optical, and combinations. Some are ergonomic devices such as the one in **Figure 4–11**, which is a wireless ergonomic mouse.

FIGURE 4–11   Wireless ergonomic mouse

> **VOCABULARY**
> **touchpad**

Touchpads are another pointing device you can use instead of a mouse. These devices sense the position of your finger and then move the pointer accordingly. Most notebook computers contain touchpads, but these are also available for desktop computers (see **Figure 4–12**).

FIGURE 4–12   Touchpad

Preventative Maintenance

All computers slow down as you add and delete files, install and uninstall software, and perform normal activities. To eliminate and minimize these problems, Microsoft Windows comes with a set of utilities that perform special functions. You use these tools to defragment hard drives, empty the Recycle Bin, delete temporary files, and remove cookies. You should run these utilities following a routine maintenance schedule so that the computer can run faster and more efficiently.

Disk Defragmentation

As you use a computer, you add and delete files on the computer's hard disk. When the computer is new (or contains a new hard drive), the operating system, such as Windows Vista, writes the file data in a set of side-by-side clusters. As the drive begins to become cluttered and space becomes limited, Windows divides the data for newly created files into sectors. Disk *fragmentation* occurs when a piece of data is broken up into many pieces that are not stored close together. The *sectors* are stored in blocks of nonadjacent clusters, thus creating fragmented files (see **Figure 4–13**). This pattern continues until you begin deleting files and adding new ones.

▶ **VOCABULARY**

fragmentation

sectors

seek time

defragmentation

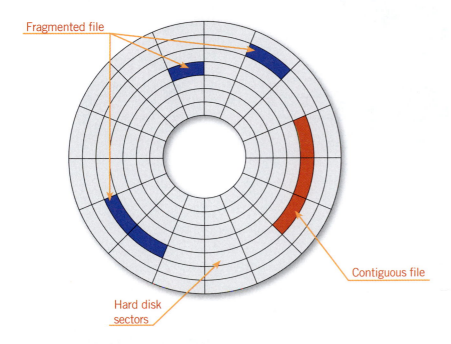

Fragmented file

Contiguous file

Hard disk sectors

FIGURE 4–13   Fragmented file

The computer reads the fragmented file as a single valid file, but to do so, the drive has to scan multiple parts of the drive. Disk *seek time* is one of the more time-consuming elements in a computer's performance and can significantly slow the speed of the processing cycle. Windows contains a *defragmentation* utility that reduces the amount of fragmentation by physically organizing the contents of the disk to store the pieces of each file contiguously. The defragmentation utility, however, does not work with read-only disks, network, or locked drives.

In Step-by-Step 4.2, you run the defragmentation utility. (*Note*: This could be a lengthy process. Verify with your instructor if you should complete this exercise.)

Step-by-Step 4.2

1. Click the **Start** button on the taskbar, and then click **Control Panel** to display the Control Panel window (see **Figure 4–14**).

FIGURE 4–14
Control Panel

System and
Maintenance
category

2. Click **System and Maintenance** to display the System and Maintenance window (see **Figure 4–15**).

FIGURE 4–15
System and
Maintenance window

Defragment
your hard
drive option

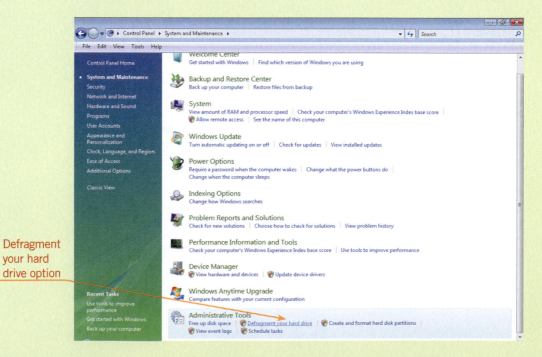

3. Scroll down if necessary, and then click **Defragment your hard drive** to display the Disk Defragmenter dialog box (see **Figure 4–16**). (If a User Account Control dialog box is displayed, click **Continue**.)

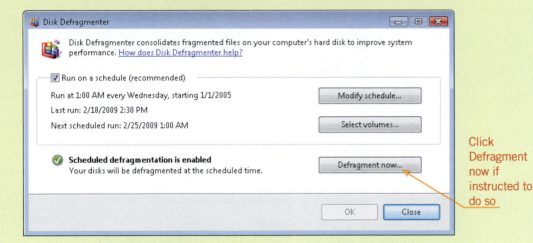

FIGURE 4–16
Disk Defragmenter dialog box

4. If Indicated by your instructor, click the **Defragment now** button. Otherwise, click the **Close** button.

Recycle Bin

The Windows **Recycle Bin** is a holding area for files and folders before their final deletion from a storage device. Generally, you access the Recycle Bin through an icon located on the desktop. The Recycle Bin contains files that have been deleted from the hard disk, whether accidentally or intentionally. You can use special settings to review the contents of the Recycle Bin before permanently deleting the items. Right-click the Recycle Bin and then click Open or Explore on the shortcut menu to view the Recycle Bin contents. Right-click an item to display the shortcut menu, which includes commands to Restore, Cut, Delete, or display the item Properties.

To empty the Recycle Bin, right-click the icon and then click Empty Recycle Bin. A warning box is displayed. Click Yes to continue or No to cancel the command.

To restore a file from the Recycle Bin, right-click the Recycle Bin icon located on the desktop and then click Open or double-click Recycle Bin to display the list of deleted files. Right-click the name of the file to be restored, and then click Restore. Once a file has been deleted from the Recycle Bin, it cannot be restored.

The Recycle Bin settings can be modified by right-clicking the Recycle Bin icon and then clicking Properties to display the Recycle Bin Properties dialog box (see **Figure 4–17**). Select the settings that you want to use and then click the OK button.

▶ **VOCABULARY**
Recycle Bin

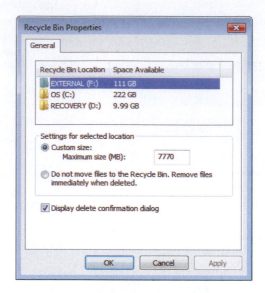

FIGURE 4–17   Recycle Bin Properties dialog box

Temporary Files

Various application programs, such as those in the Microsoft Office suite, create temporary files. This action is used for the following three reasons:

- To free memory for other programs
- To act as a safety net to prevent data loss
- For printing

The software program determines where and when it needs to create temporary files. The temporary files normally exist only during the current session of the software program. When the program is closed through a standard process, the temporary files are closed and then deleted automatically. If, however, there is a power loss or the program is not properly closed, the temporary files remain on the hard drive. The following Step-by-Step exercise provides information on how to use Disk Cleanup to delete the temporary files and other files that are not needed.

Step-by-Step 4.3

1. Click the **Start** button on the taskbar, point to **All Programs**, click **Accessories**, click **System Tools**, and then click **Disk Cleanup** to display the Disk Cleanup Options dialog box (see **Figure 4–18**).

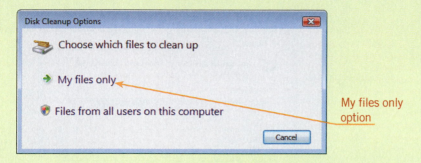

FIGURE 4–18
Disk Cleanup Options dialog box

2. Click **My files only**. The Disk Cleanup: Drive Selection dialog box opens.

3. If your computer contains more than one drive or the drive is partitioned, click the **Drives** box arrow (see **Figure 4–19**), and then select the drive or partition you want to clean. In **Figure 4–19**, the system has two drives (C: and D:), and C: is highlighted.

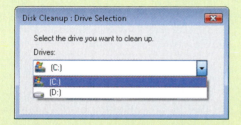

FIGURE 4–19
Disk Cleanup: Drive Selection dialog box

4. Click the **OK** button. Disk Cleanup scans the selected drive and calculates the amount of space that can be freed up through this process (see **Figure 4–20**).

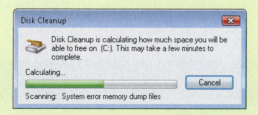

FIGURE 4–20
Scanning a drive

5. The results are displayed, as shown in **Figure 4–21**. Clicking an item in the Files to delete list displays a description of the selection. Click a check box to select the item for deletion. You can use the check boxes to select all of the displayed categories or select specific files to be deleted.

FIGURE 4–21
Results of scanning

Click an item in the Files to delete list to display a description

Description of selected item

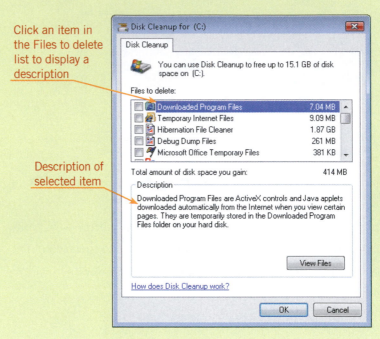

Cookies

A *cookie* is a small text file that a Web site uses to identify a specific computer. The file is created and/or updated on your computer's hard drive each time that the Web site is visited. Cookies are not a threat to your computer's security. The text file contains a code that identifies you to the Web server each time a Web page is accessed. Primarily, cookies are used to gather information about your surfing habits and for targeted advertising. The following Step-by-Step exercise provides information on how to delete cookies from the hard drive.

Step-by-Step 4.4

1. Click the **Start** button 🪟 on the taskbar, and then click **Control Panel**. Click **Network and Internet**. See **Figure 4–22**.

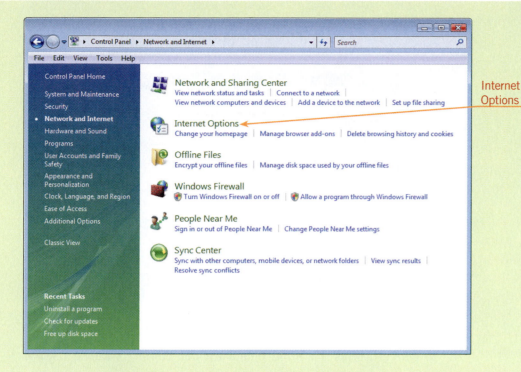

FIGURE 4–22
Network and Internet categories

2. Click **Internet Options** to display the Internet Properties dialog box (see **Figure 4–23**).

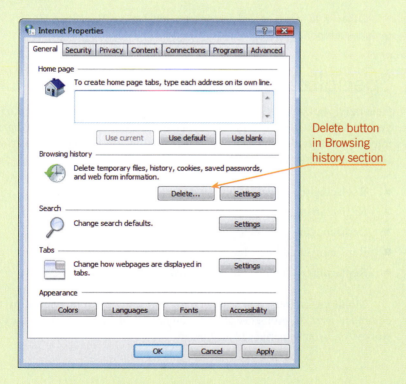

FIGURE 4–23
Internet Properties dialog box

3. In the Browsing history section, click the **Delete** button to display the Delete Browsing History dialog box (see **Figure 4–24**).

FIGURE 4–24
Delete Browsing History dialog box

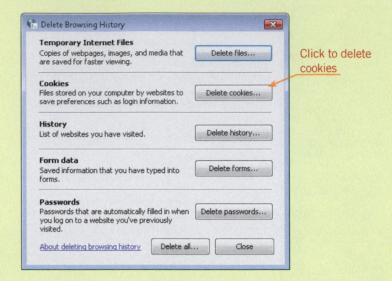

4. To delete cookies, click the **Delete cookies** button. A Delete Cookies confirm dialog box is displayed. Click **Yes** to delete all cookies.

Other data you can delete through the Delete Browsing History dialog box includes temporary Internet files, history, form data, and passwords.

1-1.2.7

Specialized Maintenance

Generally, you can provide routine maintenance as discussed in this lesson. However, you should not attempt some maintenance procedures. The following is a list of internal hardware maintenance or repair that generally should be performed by a computer professional:

- Replacing the power supply or opening the power supply case
- Replacing other electrical components
- Replacing the processor
- Replacing or adding a hard disk
- Replacing or adding additional RAM

Monitors, printers, and scanners are not designed to be opened by the general computer user. If problems are encountered with these devices, they should be worked on by an experienced technician.

ETHICS IN TECHNOLOGY

Risks of Networked Computing

The security of a computer network is challenged every day by equipment malfunctions, system failures, computer hackers, and virus attacks.

Equipment malfunctions and system failures are caused by a number of factors, including natural disasters such as floods or storms, fires, and electrical disturbances, such as a brownout or blackout. Server malfunctions or failures mean users lose temporary access to network resources, such as printers, drives, and information.

Computer hackers and viruses represent a great risk to networked environments. People who break into computer systems are called hackers. They break into systems to steal services and information, such as credit card numbers, test data, and even national security data. Some hackers want to harm a company or organization they do not like or support; sometimes, they do it just for the thrill of being able to get into the system.

People create computer viruses and infect other computers for some of the same reasons. Viruses are very dangerous to networked computers—they usually are designed to sabotage files that are shared.

SUMMARY

In this lesson, you learned:

- A computer requires maintenance on a regular schedule to prevent problems such as the degrading of the hard disk performance and monitor trouble.

- Damaged and poorly maintained cables can prevent peripheral devices from communicating with the computer. Unorganized and unprotected cables can also create safety hazards. Cable management should therefore be part of a regular computer maintenance routine.

- To maintain the computer keyboard, use a can of compressed air to remove the dust from the keyboard every six months.

- Clean a mechanical mouse by removing its bottom cover, removing debris from the roller, and then reassembling the mouse.

- Printer maintenance helps to prevent many common printing problems. Many inkjet printers have a self-cleaning mode. If yours does not, use an inkjet cleaning cartridge to flush dirt and debris out of clogged printer nozzles. Clean a laser printer when you change the toner cartridge.

- Adding computer memory often provides the best value for increasing overall computer performance.

- All computers slow down as you work with them. To improve or maintain computer efficiency, periodically use Windows tools to defragment hard drives, empty the Recycle Bin, delete temporary files, and remove cookies.

- Some maintenance procedures are not suitable for the average computer user, and should be performed by a computer professional, such as replacing the power supply or opening the power supply case, replacing other electrical components, including the processor and RAM, and adding an internal hard disk.

 # VOCABULARY REVIEW

Define the following terms:

cable management	ergonomic keyboard	sectors
corona wires	fragmentation	seek time
cookie	maintenance	touchpad
defragmentation	Recycle Bin	wireless keyboard

■ REVIEW QUESTIONS

TRUE / FALSE

Circle T if the statement is true or F if the statement is false.

T   F   **1.**   Most computers do not require regular maintenance.

T   F   **2.**   A can of compressed air can be used to clean a keyboard.

T   F   **3.**   Small deposits of dry ink can accumulate on the print head of a laser printer.

T   F   **4.**   Disk fragmentation rarely occurs.

T   F   **5.**   Temporary files are always automatically deleted.

MULTIPLE CHOICE

Select the best response for the following statements.

1. A text file that a Web site uses to identify a specific computer is called a _____ .

   A.   cookie   C.   cupcake

   B.   cracker   D.   sandwich

2. Specialized maintenance on a computer should be performed by _____ .

   A.   a carpenter   C.   a professional

   B.   computer owner   D.   a neighbor

3. _____ printers should be cleaned when print quality deteriorates or when toner cartridges are changed.

   A.   Inkjet   C.   Dot matrix

   B.   Laser   D.   Compact

4. The _____ should be checked and cleaned periodically.

   A.   keyboard   C.   monitor

   B.   mouse   D.   all of the above

5. RAM is _____ .

   A.   permanent   C.   permanent or temporary

   B.   temporary   D.   none of the above

FILL IN THE BLANK

Complete the following sentences by writing the correct word or words in the blanks provided.

1. Disk _____ is one of the more time-consuming elements in a computer's performance and can cause considerable slowdown in the processing cycle.

2. A(n) _____ allows for a more natural positioning of your arms and hands.

3. Most notebook computers use a(n) _____ to replace a mouse.

4. Disk _____ occurs when a piece of data is broken up into many pieces that are not stored close together.

5. The _____ is a holding area for files and folders before their final deletion from a storage device.

PROJECTS

PROJECT 4–1

Printers need more frequent maintenance than most types of electronic devices. Complete the following:

1. Using Google or another search engine, find instructions or tips on maintaining the type of printer you have or use regularly.

2. As you research, identify periodic and occasional maintenance tasks.

3. Note any hazards or cautions you should observe when maintaining a printer.

4. Summarize the maintenance routine and cautions in a one-page explanation.

PROJECT 4–3

Consider the computer that you use at home or school. Suppose you want to upgrade the hardware so you can use it productively for another two years or so. Using the Internet and other resources, research what you can upgrade on your computer. Answer the following questions:

1. What type of computer do you have? Is it a notebook or desktop computer?

2. What can you replace or enhance to improve the computer's overall performance?

3. What can you replace or enhance to improve the quality of displayed images?

4. What other types of equipment would you like to replace?

5. Use a presentation program (such as Microsoft Office PowerPoint) to create a presentation on upgrading your computer. Find images of your current computer and the upgraded equipment you want to add, and use them to your presentation. Share your presentation with your class.

PROJECT 4–2

Some people say you should leave your computer on at all times—that turning the computer on and off creates stress on the components. Others argue that computers use a lot of energy, and that computers should be turned off when not in use. Your computer operating system, however, includes power-management settings. Your instructor has requested that you and your team investigate these options.

1. Use Windows Help and Support and prepare a report describing these power-management options.

2. Describe how to create a power plan.

3. Describe how you can change what happens when you press the power button on a mobile PC.

 ## TEAMWORK PROJECT

You work at a video store as a clerk. The computers at the video store are used by many different clerks in the course of a workday. Your supervisor has asked you and another employee to come up with a routine maintenance checklist that any of the clerks can use at the beginning of the day to make sure the terminals are in good working order. Create a checklist that includes daily tasks and weekly tasks to keep the components clean and in good working order.

CRITICAL THINKING

This lesson explains fragmentation and defragmentation, and provides steps for defragmenting a hard drive. Using the Internet and other resources, complete the following:

1. Windows Vista includes a defragmentation tool. Should you supplement that tool with other defragmentation utilities? If so, explain why.

2. How often should you defragment your hard disk? What is a good rule of thumb to follow?

3. Does defragmentation pose any risks to your computer? What can you do to overcome the risks?

4. Write a one-page report answering these questions and summarizing your findings.

ONLINE DISCOVERY

Review the section on keyboards and then consider the elements of design, comfort, and performance. Use your Web browser to research ergonomic keyboards and compare the different options that are available. Use your word-processing program to write a short report describing the keyboard you would select and why you would select that particular keyboard.

LESSON 5

Computer-Related Issues

■ OBJECTIVES

Upon completion of this lesson, you should be able to:

- Define problem solving.
- Identify problem-solving steps.
- Identify criteria for selecting a computer.
- Describe warranties and support agreements.
- Describe the concept of "useful life" as related to a computer.
- Explain the process of discarding equipment.

■ VOCABULARY

Linux PC

problem solving

support agreement

troubleshooting

useful life

warranty

■ DATA FILES

You do not need data files to complete this lesson.

▶ **VOCABULARY**

problem solving

troubleshooting

Sooner or later, you will have a problem relating to your computer hardware or software. To reach a solution and correct the problem involves a process. ***Problem solving*** is a systematic approach leading from an initial situation to a desired situation that is subject to some resource constraints. See **Figure 5–1**.

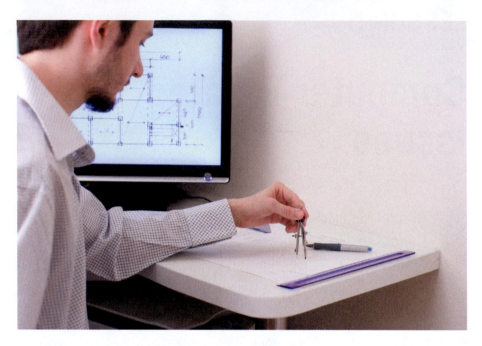

FIGURE 5–1   Solving technology problems

1-1.2.8

The Problem-Solving Process

To solve a problem successfully, you must apply a logical plan to act as a guide or road map. The plan will assist you in defining the problem, gathering information concerning the problem, identifying possible solutions, and selecting and implementing the best solution. The following steps suggests the process that should be taken:

1.   Define the problem.

2.   Investigate and analyze the problem.

3.   Identify possible solutions.

4.   Select and implement a solution.

5.   Evaluate solutions.

Each of the steps is important in the problem-solving process, also called ***troubleshooting***. Each step should be completed fully before going to the next step.

Define the Problem

In the beginning stage, ensure that you actually have a problem and identify what it is. Start with the most obvious or simplest possibilities, and continue troubleshooting from there. For example, if you are having trouble sending e-mail, make sure the computer is turned on and connected to the Internet.

Sometimes the problem may not be as transparent as it appears. Investigation of the situation is necessary to determine the real issue. Ask questions, use what-if statements, eliminate some facts, include others, clarify the current situation, and identify what the situation should be or perhaps what you would like it to be. If necessary, make notes or sketches. For example, if you are having problems with your computer, describe the system behavior and any error messages you receive. If possible, take a screenshot of the behavior or message by pressing the Print Screen key to store an image of the screen on the Clipboard, opening a program such as Paint or Microsoft Office Word, and then pasting the image into the file.

Investigate and Analyze the Problem

After you define the problem, you need all the facts. Collect all available data regarding the situation. Determine why the problem exists and its possible causes. Ask the most basic questions or the ones that are easiest to answer. Continuing with the e-mail example, what do you see on the screen when you try to retrieve your e-mail?

Attempt to reproduce the problem, noting what actions you take to do so. For example, if you are having trouble printing a document from your computer, try printing a different document. Then try printing from a different computer, if possible. Also attempt to print a test page using a button or other feature on the printer itself. Investigating the problem in this way helps to narrow the possible solutions. If you can print a test page from the printer, but cannot print at all from any computer connected to the printer, the problem probably involves the cable connecting the printer to your computer or network.

The investigation and analysis step provides information needed to make an accurate decision. Sometimes during this step, you may decide that a problem really does not exist at all or that what you thought was the problem is being caused by something else. If there is a legitimate problem or need, however, your detective work at this stage should provide you with information you need to solve the problem.

Identify Possible Solutions

After diagnosing the problem, you need to identify possible solutions. What can you do to alleviate the problem? What should you do differently? What needs to be deleted or added? These are the types of questions that need to be answered as you look for a solution. In exploring possible answers, you may identify more than one solution.

In general, start with the most basic possible solutions or those that are the easiest to try. For example, if you are having trouble with hardware, check to make sure the device is properly connected to a power source. If you are having trouble with a software program, close the program and then restart it.

Select and Implement a Solution

If you identify more than one possible solution, critique and test each solution one at a time to determine its likely outcome. Based on this information, choose the solution that provides the best outcome. Avoid combining solutions because you might not know which one solved the problem. If you are not sure about the consequences of your actions, look for help and advice from an expert source, such as hardware or software documentation, information posted on a reputable Web site, technical support personnel, or an experienced colleague or friend. Refer to the notes you took in Step 1 (define the problem) or images you created to accurately describe the problem and any troubleshooting attempts you made.

The next step is to implement the solution. As you did when you defined the problem, take notes about the troubleshooting steps you perform. If the problem recurs, you can refer to the notes to solve the problem again.

Confirm the Solution

After putting the selected solution into place, you need to evaluate its performance. Did it eliminate the problem? Did it accomplish what you needed to have done? If your answer is yes, you now have a solution to a situation that caused you concern. For example, if your computer was running slowly, did performance return to normal after scanning the computer with antivirus software? If not, you need to return to the previous step to select and implement a different solution. If the solution did not work at all, return to the first step and ask better questions before trying new solutions.

Document the Problem and the Solution

Prepare written documentation describing the problem and the solution. Organize the notes you took during the problem-solving process so you can easily refer to the information again. If you discovered a way to avoid or prevent similar problems, begin to follow that practice as soon as possible. For example, if occasional power interruptions cause you to lose work, invest in a UPS (uninterruptible power supply) device and make a habit of backing up your current files at the end of each day.

Keep in mind that solving problems is not a linear process. Instead, you sometimes define the problem, investigate it, and start identifying possible solutions only to determine that you really need to better define the problem. In this case, you take a circular or spiral path, as shown in **Figure 5–2**, rather than a straight path.

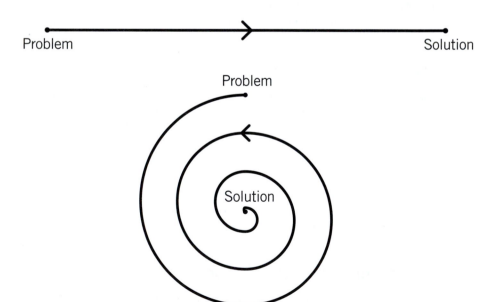

FIGURE 5–2   Following a straight or spiral path to solve problems

Implementing Problem-Solving Solutions

In the following scenario, assume that a printer is not working. The following steps illustrate how to troubleshoot the problem and find a solution. Each step should be completed fully before going to the next step. These same steps can also be applied to other computer-related devices and problems.

1. **Identify the problem**.

   The printer is not working. See **Figure 5–3**.

FIGURE 5–3   Identifying the problem

2. **Investigate and analyze the problem**.

Collect all available data and facts regarding the situation. See **Figure 5–4**.

FIGURE 5–4   Analyzing the problem

This step provides information needed to make an accurate decision. Identify the steps you take to create the problem and then reproduce the steps. Write down the steps. Does the problem always occur when these steps are implemented? Review the manual that came with the printer. Most manuals contain a troubleshooting section. A second resource is the Web site of the manufacturer of the printer.

3. **Identify possible solutions**.

Is the printer plugged in? Is it turned on? Is it online? Is it beeping? Is it out of ink or toner? Are there color printing issues? Does it have paper? Is it jammed? Is the cable connected, and is it connected properly? Is the cable good? Have you cleaned the printer recently?

4. **Select and implement a solution**.

Test all possible solutions until you find one that is likely to work, and then implement the solution.

5. **Confirm the solution**.

Turn off the computer and printer, turn them back on, and then test again.

6. **Document the problem and the solution**.

Describe the symptoms and write down the steps required to resolve the issue. Save the document and print a copy. File the copy or keep it in a notebook.

The following Step-by-Step exercise shows you how to apply the problem-solving process to troubleshoot a problem viewing an e-mail attachment in Windows Mail.

Step-by-Step 5.1

1. Click the **Start** button on the taskbar, and then click **Help and Support**. The Windows Help and Support window opens. See **Figure 5–5**.

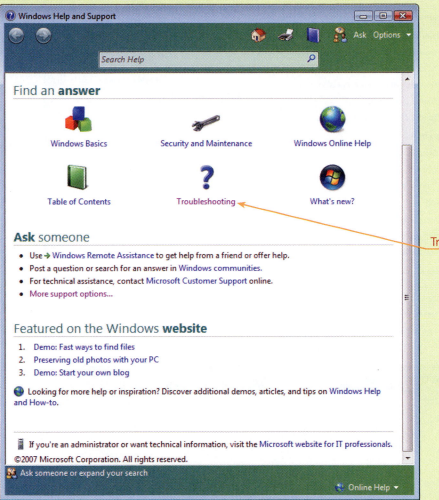

FIGURE 5–5
Windows Help and Support window

Troubleshooting link

2. Click the **Troubleshooting** link. The Troubleshooting in Windows page opens. See **Figure 5–6**.

FIGURE 5–6
Troubleshooting in Windows page

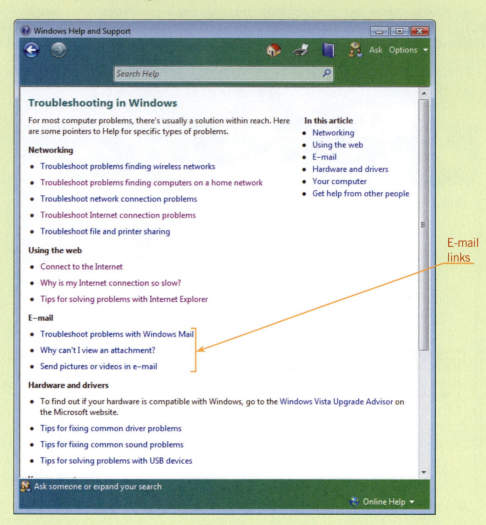

3. In the E-mail section, click the **Why can't I view an attachment?** link to
    display the Why can't I view an attachment in Windows Mail? page. See
    Figure 5-7.

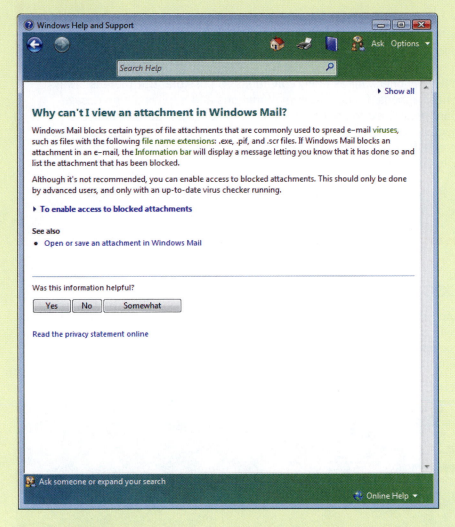

FIGURE 5-7
Why can't I view an attachment in
Windows Mail? page

4. Read the information to find a possible solution. Using your word-
    processing program, create a document that describes the solution and
    explains how you arrived at the solution. Submit the assignment to your
    instructor as requested.

ETHICS IN TECHNOLOGY

Who Is Responsible?

Increasingly, computers participate in decisions that affect human lives. Consider medical safety, for instance, and think about the fact that just about everything in a hospital is tied to a computer. So what happens if these machines don't produce the expected results? What happens if they have been incorrectly programmed?

When programmers write a program, they check for as many conditions as possible. But there is always the chance they might miss one. So what happens if a computer malfunctions and applies a high dosage of radiation? What if two medications are prescribed to an individual and the computer doesn't indicate the medications are incompatible? Imagine the consequences if someone called for an ambulance and the dispatch system didn't work. Then the question becomes who is responsible for these mishaps. Is it the programmer? Is it the company who sold the software or hardware? Is it the person who administered the radiation treatment?

The incidents described here actually happened. These ethical issues are being decided in court to determine who has legal responsibility.

Consumer Issues

Purchasing, maintaining, and repairing a computer requires considerable research and focused decision making. The following section discusses selecting and purchasing a computer for an organization and purchasing a computer for personal use. See **Figure 5–8**.

FIGURE 5–8 Researching personal computers before purchasing one

Purchasing a Computer

Selecting a computer for an organization or business can be critical to the success and efficiency of the business. The first task is to identify the purpose and tasks for which the computer will be used in the present and how it will be used in the future. Some requirements that are common to most businesses are accounting, budgeting, financial record keeping, correspondence, marketing, and presentations. Companies that specialize in unique and unusual types of businesses also most likely require specialized applications.

Purchasing a computer for personal use most often means selecting one that runs the latest version of the Windows or Macintosh operating system. Personal computers, both Windows and Macintosh models, are typically used for writing papers or letters, tracking personal finances, playing games, and connecting to the Internet. There are two primary disadvantages of the Macintosh: (1) most new applications are designed for the Windows operating system first, and (2) you might have difficulty exchanging data between computers with the Windows operating system and the Mac operating system.

A *Linux PC* is a standard personal computer that runs the Linux operating system. All primary applications, such as word processing, spreadsheets, databases, and so on, are available for Linux. There is no comparison, however, to Windows or Macintosh in the number of software titles. Linux desktops primarily are popular with the knowledgeable IT professional and the home user with limited funds.

Most companies and organizations have a list of approved computer models and standard packages of software. If the standards and policies are defined and in place, then the employee would identify the tasks for which he or she would use the computer. Backup procedures and software installations are also standardized within many companies.

▶ **VOCABULARY**
Linux PC
warranty

Maintaining a Computer

Similar to your automobile, computers require maintenance on a regular schedule. Generally, routine maintenance can be performed by the average computer user. However, computers can be difficult to use and can break down easily or even arrive damaged from the manufacturer. For these situations, postsale service and support is critical. Many companies purchase a computer that comes with a 3-year parts-and-labor limited warranty.

Warranties

A *warranty* is a written guarantee that a product or service meets certain specifications. It usually explains that if the product or service doesn't meet the specifications, the manufacturer will repair or replace it. Some warranties also list your responsibilities as a consumer, such as to maintain the product according to the manufacturer's guidelines, or have it serviced only by a licensed technician. Read the warranty to verify that it does not allow the manufacturer to repair the computer with refurbished or used parts. See **Figure 5–9**.

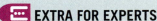 **EXTRA FOR EXPERTS**

The warranty that is provided as a standard part of a computer product is usually sufficient. Some manufacturers and retail services provide extended warranties, which are usually not worth the expense. In some cases, however, they might be worthwhile. If you are purchasing a notebook computer and plan to travel frequently, an extended warranty on the notebook's display can be a good idea.

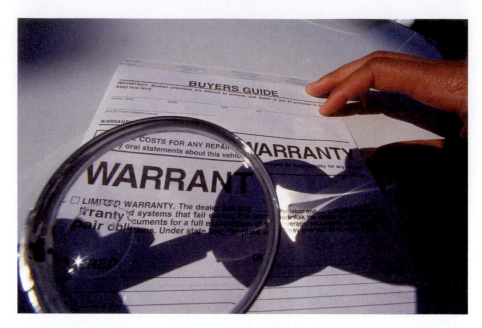

FIGURE 5–9   Reading the computer warranty

In addition, look for the following information in a computer warranty:

- Determine if there is software coverage.
- Check for on-site repair and the length of time it is in force.
- Check the period of free telephone support; look for a minimum of 90 days with no limitations.
- Confirm that technical support is available 24 hours a day, seven days a week.
- Determine if a toll-free number is provided.
- Check if the warranty still applies if the computer is used outside the country.

Support Agreements

A computer manufacturer might provide its customers with a *support agreement*, which is a list of services specifically designed to provide assistance to a company or organization. This allows a company to budget for support just like they would for rent or insurance. The terms of service and the assistance to be provided are specified in the agreement. A support agreement can apply to a variety of services, depending on the type of equipment. Generally, these services are determined by a mutual agreement between the company receiving the service and the company providing the support. An example is a support agreement for a company's network. The company providing the support most likely would first provide a free audit of the network. They would then set forth the terms and conditions of the agreement. Some examples of terms could be a fixed cost per hour, remote telephone assistance, in-house assistance, maximum number of hours over a specified time frame, other additional costs, and so on. Most agreements also include information on services not covered.

▶ **VOCABULARY**
support agreement

📧 **EXTRA FOR EXPERTS**

Most computer manufacturers provide extensive help resources online to guide you in solving problems with your computer. Check their Web site before making an expensive technical support phone call.

Useful Life

Useful life is defined as the estimated time period that an asset, such as computer equipment, will be of use to the owner. Depending on the type of company, the time period can vary from one year to five years. A general rule is that the useful life of a computer for a company in the technology industry is two to three years; for developers, two to four years; and for the general public, three to five years. Some businesses consider the useful life of a computer lasts until it ceases to perform its function.

Depending on the value and condition of the computer, some companies may extend the life of a computer by adding components or upgrading parts of the computer. Other companies may elect to trade in the older equipment.

Discarded Equipment

At some point, you need to dispose of or discard computer equipment. For many companies, this can be a major consideration. The Environmental Protection Agency has a Web site containing basic information on the disposal of electronics (*www.epa.gov/osw/conserve/materials/ecycling/basic.htm*). The suggestions on this Web site address the mounting problem of computer waste and include suggestions for reusing equipment. For example, if the equipment is still usable, donate it to agencies such as schools, nonprofit organizations, and lower-income families. The Web site also contains a list of programs that take donations.

If donating is not an option, consider recycling. Many cities and communities provide recycling centers. See **Figure 5–10**. The EPA Web site provides guidelines and assistance to help locate a recycling center.

> **VOCABULARY**
> **useful life**

> **EXTRA FOR EXPERTS**
>
> If you are replacing one computer system with another, you might not need to discard your monitor if it is working properly. Monitors last longer than CPUs and are often compatible with newer CPUs. Check with your computer provider to determine whether you can use your old monitor with a new system.

FIGURE 5–10   Recycling computer hardware

TECHNOLOGY CAREERS

Science or Science Fiction?

One way to prepare for a career in a technology field is to watch science fiction movies. How so? New technology often can remind us of gadgets from an old science fiction movie. Some people claim that the resemblance is not because the creators of those fictionalized futuristic shows correctly predicted 21st century trends. Instead, some of the inventors and engineers who create today's technology may be science fiction fans who consciously or unconsciously design their devices to imitate what they saw in the movies or read about in books. For example, a cell phone looks a lot like a "communicator" used on spaceships in 1960s television shows, and the Segway scooter provides individual transportation that is a step toward the hovercraft and jetpacks of many tales of the future.

Popular culture has long offered views of a world full of technology, such as those presented in *Twenty Thousand Leagues Under the Sea; I, Robot; and 2001: A Space Odyssey*. Many works of science fiction show a respect for "real science" combined with the imagination to contemplate where it could lead us. Now science imitates science fiction as we flip open our cell phones, swipe our magnetic identification and cash cards, and watch long-deceased actors sell brand-new products on television—or is it a holodeck?

SUMMARY

In this lesson, you learned:

- Problem solving involves defining a problem and finding a solution.

- The sequence of problem solving is as follows: defining the problem, investigating and analyzing the problem, identifying possible solutions, selecting and implementing the best solution, evaluating the chosen solution, and then documenting the problem and solution.

- When purchasing a computer for yourself or for an organization, identify the purpose of the computer and the tasks you or others will perform on it.

- Purchasing a computer for personal use most often means selecting one that runs the latest version of the Windows or Macintosh operating system. Computers running the Linux operating system primarily are popular with knowledgeable IT professionals and home users with limited funds.

- Warranties and support agreements help you maintain computer equipment. If a computer fails to perform according to guidelines the manufacturer specifies, the warranty might provide for the repair or replacement of the computer. A computer manufacturer might provide its customers with a support agreement, which is a list of services specifically designed to provide assistance to a company or organization.

- When you purchase computer equipment, be aware of its useful life, which is the estimated time period the computer equipment will be of use to you.

- To dispose of computer equipment properly, refer to the guidelines on the EPA Web site and consider donating or recycling the equipment.

■ VOCABULARY REVIEW

Define the following terms:

Linux PC	support agreement	useful life
problem solving	troubleshooting	warranty

◼ REVIEW QUESTIONS

TRUE / FALSE

Circle T if the statement is true or F if the statement is false.

T   F   **1.**   Selecting the right computer can be critical to the success of a business.

T   F   **2.**   The first step in the problem-solving process is to select a solution.

T   F   **3.**   To solve a problem, you first must identify the problem.

T   F   **4.**   Once a problem is identified, it is not necessary to create documentation.

T   F   **5.**   When selecting a computer, the last step is to identify the purpose and tasks for which it will be used.

MULTIPLE CHOICE

Select the best response for the following statements.

1. A _____ is defined as the estimated time period that an asset will be of use to the owner.

    A.   useful life   C.   hardware data

    B.   support agreement   D.   presentation program

2. Generally, routine _____ can be performed by the average computer user.

    A.   maintenance   C.   identification

    B.   selection   D.   analysis

3. A possible solution for a nonworking printer is to check if the printer _____.

    A.   is turned on   C.   has a cable connected to the computer

    B.   has paper   D.   all of the above

4. When applying the problem-solving process, the first step is to _____.

    A.   identify possible solutions   C.   analyze the problem

    B.   evaluate solutions   D.   implement a solution

5. A _____ is a list of services designed to provide assistance to a company or an organization.

    A.   warranty   C.   contract

    B.   spreadsheet   D.   support agreement

FILL IN THE BLANK

Complete the following sentences by writing the correct word or words in the blanks provided.

1. The estimated period that computer equipment is useful to the owner is called _____.

2. If electronic equipment is still usable, it is best to _____ it to agencies such as schools or nonprofit organizations.

3. Computers require _____ on a regular schedule.

4. When selecting a computer, the first activity is to identify the _____ and _____ for which the computer will be used.

5. The third step in the problem-solving process is to identify _____.

PROJECTS

PROJECT 5–1

In your new job as project director, you have been asked to present a proposal for the purchase of five new computers for the finance department. Assume that the computers will be used for advanced financial accounting statements that are fairly complex. Complete the following:

1. Use the problem-solving process outlined in this chapter to select the type of computer to be recommended to the purchasing department. Be sure to consider the processor, hard drive, RAM, USB ports, and video ability.

2. Provide detailed information for each step within the process. The completed report should be one to two pages long.

PROJECT 5–3

Arthur C. Clarke, who wrote *2001: A Space Odyssey*, said that advanced technology is indistinguishable from what we call magic. Jules Verne noted that anything one man could imagine, another could invent. If you could invent an advanced technological device that was so wondrous it seemed like magic, what would that device be? How would it work? Write a one-page report describing your technology.

PROJECT 5–2

The question of what to do with used computer equipment is quickly becoming a concern for cities and towns. Complete the following:

1. Using the Internet and other reference materials, research the resources in your city or town for discarding electronic waste.

2. What are the particular problems associated with disposing of computers and other electronic devices? What are the possible solutions? Write an explanation of the problems and solutions. Your explanation should include at least three paragraphs.

TEAMWORK PROJECT

Working with a partner, complete the following steps:

1. Research warranties and support agreements.

2. Prepare a one-page report and a presentation describing these two types of documents and how they differ. Provide examples.

3. If possible, share your team's presentation with your class.

CRITICAL THINKING

Use the problem-solving steps in this lesson to write a strategy for solving a problem that you or a friend have faced, or a problem you have heard about in the news. Complete the following:

1. In a written report, define the problem, then investigate and analyze it, and identify possible solutions that would use a computer program or some other kind of technology.

2. Choose a solution you think will solve the problem. How will you put the solution into action? What could go wrong with the solution you choose? Would the technology need to be updated in a few years, or would the solution remain useful for a long time?

ONLINE DISCOVERY

The E-cycling Central Web site located at *www.eiae.org* contains a map of the United States. Complete the following:

1. Access the E-cycling Central Web site and then click the state in which you live to view a list of events and the number of recycling programs in your state.

2. Create a report listing the number of events and the number of recycling programs.

3. If possible, locate your city, and then create a one-page report describing the programs within your area. If your city does not contain any recycling programs, find a city nearby and create your report on that city's recycling programs.

LESSON 6

Software and Hardware Interaction

■ OBJECTIVES

Upon completion of this lesson, you should be able to:

- Identify how hardware and software interact.
- Explain how a software program works.
- Describe the difference between application software and system software.
- Describe the software distribution process.

■ DATA FILES

You do not need data files to complete this lesson.

■ VOCABULARY

algorithm

application software

beta testing

bundleware

flowchart

inputting

network license

operating systems

patch

service pack

single-user license

software

Software as a Service (SaaS)

software development

software license

software piracy

system software

update

upgrades

Web applications

Over the last 50 years or so, computer technology has changed the world. Not long ago, the typical worker did not use computers on the job. Customers did not order products online or scan ID cards to receive benefits for frequent shopping. Accounting was done using ledgers. When you think about the recent history of computers, you probably think of innovations in hardware—computers have become smaller and faster. Computer usage has changed just as dramatically. Early computers were used as little more than high-speed calculators. Because computers developed the capacity to do many tasks very quickly, they now have a major influence on the culture and economy. Computers have had such an impact due to the vision and desire of software developers, who created thousands of ideas and ways in which to use computers. They created programs that affect you in every aspect of your life.

How Hardware and Software Interact

1-2.1.1

Although software and hardware are clearly distinct parts of a computer system, they often play similar roles and perform similar tasks. Recall that hardware refers to anything you can touch, including objects such as the keyboard, mouse, monitor, printer, chips, disk drives, and CD/DVD recorders. **Inputting** is the process of using an input device to enter data. In Lesson 2, you reviewed input devices. Some of the more popular input devices are the keyboard (used for inputting text and numbers), the mouse (used for selecting items on the screen), scanner (used to input images and documents), microphone (used to input sound), and video camera (used to input video).

Using input devices, you interact with software by typing commands such as providing a name for a word-processing document, selecting an option from a menu, or clicking a button, such as the Save button in most software programs (see **Figure 6–1**).

▶ **VOCABULARY**

inputting

software

EXTRA FOR EXPERTS

An early computer called the Univac I was a sensation in 1952 when it correctly predicted that Dwight D. Eisenhower should win the presidential election in a landslide victory. The election results were remarkably close to the computer's predication, but the computer didn't perform a miracle. The programmers who used statistical vote samples (the data) and shrewd analysis techniques (the program commands) deserve the credit for the accurate prediction.

FIGURE 6–1   Interacting with software

The Role of Software

You cannot touch software because it has no substance. **Software** (or program) is programming code written to provide instructions to the hardware so it can perform tasks, such as printing, displaying a Web page or dialog box, or saving a document on the hard disk. Hardware and software interact as a computer processes data. You use input devices—hardware—to enter data. Then specific programmed instructions tell the computer how to process that data—this is the software component that tells the hardware what to do. Finally, other software instructions format the data correctly so you can understand it when you see it on a monitor, print it on a page, or hear it through the speakers.

For instance, a computer programmer might write a program that lets you use the keyboard to access a Web site and then use the mouse to select a file and download music from the Internet. The software makes it possible to download or retrieve the music file from a server somewhere on the Internet, and other software on your computer allows you to play the music. The CPU, sound card, and speakers in your computer system are hardware devices that function as output devices. Other examples of how data is processed and then sent to an output device are as follows:

■ You use a scanner to scan a document and then print a copy (see **Figure 6–2**).

■ You create video with your digital video camera and then transfer it from your camera to your computer.

■ You use a microphone to create an audio file to accompany a message to your grandmother.

FIGURE 6–2   Scanning a document

The software provides the instructions on what and how to accomplish these tasks and where to save the files.

You may have heard people say they have a problem with how their computer is working. They might say, "It's a software problem." This means there is a problem with the program or data, and not with the computer or hardware itself.

A good analogy is a book. The book, including the pages and the ink, is the hardware. The words and ideas on the pages are the software. One has little value without the other. The same is true of computer software and hardware: the way in which the two interact allows us to use the computer to complete many different tasks.

How a Software Program Works

VOCABULARY
algorithm

A computer processes data by applying rules called algorithms. An *algorithm* is a set of clearly defined, logical steps that solve a problem. For example, if you want to explain to someone who has never done laundry how to do it properly, you would explain the process step by step, as shown in **Figure 6–3**.

HOW TO DO LAUNDRY
Collect the clothes that need to be washed.
Separate the clothes into light and dark piles.
Take the light pile to the washing machine and put clothes in the machine.
Add laundry detergent to the washing machine.
Set the dial on the washing machine for the correct size load.
Set the dial on the washing machine for warm wash and warm rinse water.
Turn on the washing machine.
When the cycle has finished, take wash out and put clothes in dryer.
Add a dryer fabric softener sheet to the dryer.
Set dryer cycle to Permanent Press.
Set dryer timer to 40 minutes.
Turn on dryer.
When the cycle has finished, take clothes out.
Fold clothes.
Put away clothes.
Repeat all previous steps with dark clothes.

FIGURE 6–3   An algorithm lists steps required to perform a task

If these steps seem like they offer very detailed instructions for performing a simple task, remember that the person you are instructing has no idea how to do laundry. You cannot assume he or she knows anything about it. In the same way, when a programmer writes software instructions for a computer, every step must give explicit instructions. A computer cannot do anything without being instructed how to do it through programmed software commands.

The following is a very simple example of how a programmer would begin to write a software program. After writing an algorithm for solving the problem in plain English (or French, Chinese, or Portuguese, depending on the spoken language of the programmer), the next step would be to rewrite the steps in a formal programming language. Even then the computer will not understand the instructions; a specialized computer program translates the programming language to machine language that the computer can understand.

To instruct a computer how to perform a simple task such as output the average of three numbers, the program must break this down into many steps. For example:

1. Let A equal 95.
2. Let B equal 102.
3. Let C equal 88.
4. Add $A + B + C$.
5. Let the sum of $A + B + C$ equal X.
6. Divide X by 3.

7. Let the quotient equal Y.

8. Print the text "The average is" followed by Y.

Software Development

Software development is a multistep process that usually begins when someone recognizes a need to perform a task more effectively and/or efficiently using a computer. As you have seen, the first thing the programmer must do is break down the task into an algorithm or series of steps that will cover all the individual actions needed to perform the task. Often the programmer works out the logic for the steps in the algorithm by using a ***flowchart*** that shows different paths the program will take depending on what data is inputted (see **Figure 6–4**).

▶ **VOCABULARY**
software development
flowchart
beta testing

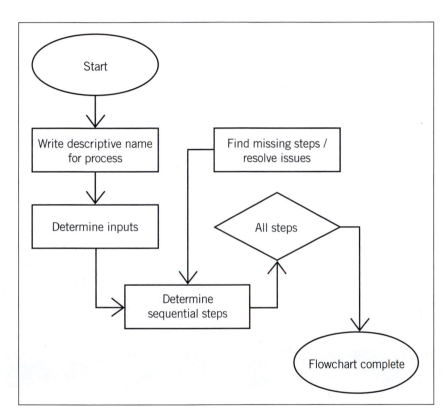

FIGURE 6–4   Flowchart

Next, the programmer writes the steps in a computer programming language or code that uses a formal set of terms and *syntax*, or rules for how the words are used together. The computer then will take that code, translate it into language it can understand, and use the translated commands to execute the program.

This, however, is not the end of the process. Computer programs are written by a person or people who can make mistakes. Someone might enter a line of code with a small error in syntax or spelling, and it can result in very different results than the programmers were expecting. So software development also requires a quality control process that involves running systematic tests, debugging (finding and correcting errors in the code), and ***beta testing***, a process that releases commercial software in development to a cross-section of typical users who evaluate the program and report any problems or "bugs" in the software before it is released to the public.

1-2.1.2

▶ **VOCABULARY**

application software

system software

Application Software and System Software

There are two basic types of computer software: *application software* and *system software*. Application software helps you perform a specific task. System software refers to the operating system and all utility programs that manage computer resources at a low level. Figuratively speaking, application software sits on top of system software. Without the operating system and system utilities, the computer cannot run any applications.

Application Software

Application software generally is referred to as productivity software. This type of software is composed of programs designed for an end user. Some of the more commonly used application programs are word processors, database systems, presentation programs, spreadsheet programs, and graphic design programs. Some other application categories are as follows:

- *Education, home, and personal software*: Includes reference, entertainment, personal finance, calendars, e-mail, and Web browsers
- *Multimedia software*: Includes authoring, animation, music, video and sound capturing and editing, virtual reality, and Web site development
- *Workgroup computing software*: Includes calendars and scheduling, e-mail, Web browsers, electronic conferencing, and project management

Using Application Software

One of the tasks you can perform with application software is to modify and apply rules to data. In Microsoft Office, for instance, you can customize options that determine how you use each program. In Step-by-Step 6.1, you learn how to view this information. Complete Step-by-Step 6.1 to modify the Quick Access Toolbar, which is the toolbar that appears to the right of the Office button on the title bar in Microsoft Office programs.

Step-by-Step 6.1

1. Click the **Start** button on the taskbar, point to **All Programs**, and then click **Microsoft Office**.
2. Click **Microsoft Office Word 2007** to open the program and display a new, blank document.
3. Click the **Office** button and then point to the **Word Options** button (see **Figure 6–5**).

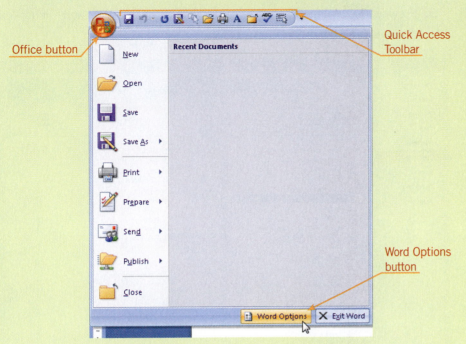

Office button

Quick Access Toolbar

Word Options button

FIGURE 6–5
Office menu and Word Options button

4. Click the **Word Options** button to display the Word Options dialog box. Click **Customize** in the left pane (see **Figure 6–6**). You use the Customize category of options to add and remove buttons on the Quick Access Toolbar. When you add a command to the list on the right, Word adds a corresponding button to the toolbar.

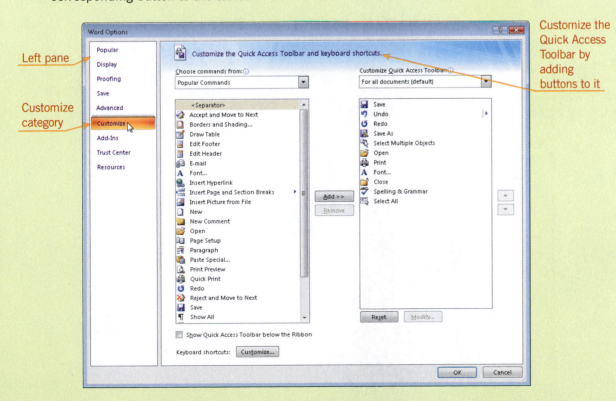

Left pane

Customize category

Customize the Quick Access Toolbar by adding buttons to it

FIGURE 6–6
Word Options dialog box

5. Review the options in the list of commands on the left, and then click **E-mail** (see **Figure 6–7**).

FIGURE 6–7
Selecting the E-mail command

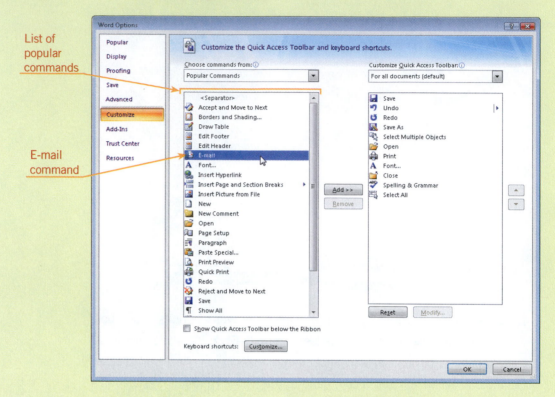

6. Click the **Add** button to add the E-mail command to the Customize Quick Access Toolbar list (see **Figure 6–8**).

FIGURE 6–8
Adding the E-mail command to the Customize Quick Access Toolbar list

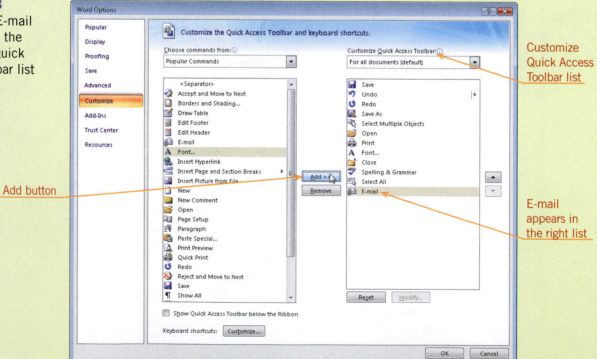

7. Click the **OK** button to add the command to the toolbar. Your Quick Access Toolbar may have fewer or additional icons (see **Figure 6–9**).

E-mail button

FIGURE 6–9
E-mail button on Quick Access Toolbar

System Software

System software is a group of programs that coordinate and control the resources and operations of a computer system. System software enables the many components of the computer system to communicate. There are three categories of system software: operating systems, utilities, and language translators.

Operating Systems

Operating systems provide an interface between the user or application program and the computer hardware. **Figure 6–10** shows how the relationship works.

> ▶ **VOCABULARY**
> **operating systems**

FIGURE 6–10   Operating system: an interface between users and computers

As an interface between you and the hardware, an operating system contains drivers that communicate with the hardware and provides a graphical user interface (GUI) you use to control the computer. An operating system also communicates with application software. A sophisticated operating system such as Microsoft Windows, Mac OS, or Linux includes built-in applications, such as games, basic graphics editors, and e-mail software. Operating systems also communicate with other more complex applications that are not part of the operating system itself, such as word processors, spreadsheets, and multimedia players. The operating system provides a consistent way for applications to interact with the hardware without having to know all the details of the device or driver.

 **EXTRA FOR EXPERTS**

The history of Apple Computer and its founders, Steve Jobs and Steve Wozniak, is a fascinating story. For an overview of the story, check out *http://inventors.about. com/od/cstartinventions/a/Apple_ Computers.htm*.

Utilities and Language Translators

Utilities are programs that help to maintain computer hardware or other software, and usually perform a single task. For example, the disk defragmenting tool used in Lesson 4 is a utility. A language translator, or compiler, is a program that translates computer code written by a programmer into an executable program.

1-2.1.3

Software Distribution

Software and software licensing options are available through a variety of alternatives and distribution methods; these include single copies for installation on a single-user computer, network versions, and Internet options.

Software Licensing

When you purchase a software program, you are not just purchasing the software—you are purchasing a *software license* that gives you permission to use the program. This *single-user license* gives you the right to install the software on a single computer.

Many companies, government organizations, and educational institutions purchase a *network license*. This type of license gives the organization the right to install a program on a server which can be accessed by a specific number of computers. Some of the benefits include the following:

- Lower pricing can decrease a company's per-user cost by purchasing a network license versus purchasing multiple single-user copies, therefore making it more cost effective.

- Most network licenses are offered in five-users increments. Generally the range is from five users to any multiple of five users. Usually, additional licenses can be added at any time.

- Ready-to-use installations can be deployed rapidly.

- Standardization provides the administration more control.

Software as a Service (SaaS), typically pronounced "sass," is a recently developed software delivery method where an application is licensed for use as a service. The software is provided to customers on demand through the Internet, an intranet, or through a network. The demand for SaaS is managed by a company known as Application Service Provider (ASP). This delivery method provides a more cost-effective alternative than traditional packaged applications. In most instances, the product is accessed through a user login. SaaS is one of the fastest growing segments of the information technology (IT) industry. Examples of SaaS include Google Docs and Salesforce.com, which is software for tracking sales and customers.

Updating and Upgrading Software

Software development is a continuous process of updating. Users of the program often discover errors or other problems within the software, or that some hardware devices may not work properly with the software. When this happens, the software is updated. In most instances, users who purchased the original version of the software can download a fix for the problem. These fixes are called a *patch*, an *update*, or a *service pack*. A software patch is applied over software that you already have installed. Revised versions that require patches or updates generally are indicated with numbers such as 1.1 or 1.2 if the modifications are minor.

▶ **VOCABULARY**

software license

single-user license

network license

Software as a Service (SaaS)

patch

update

service pack

EXTRA FOR EXPERTS

A single-user software license is also called an end user license agreement (EULA). The EULA usually appears as you install the software and gives you the option of accepting or rejecting the agreement. If you accept, you can continue to install the software. If you reject the agreement, the installation does not continue.

Some companies also make major improvements to upgrade and modify some of the software's features. This refers to the replacement of a product with a newer version of that same product. In most instances, the modifications generally involve radical changes, so the numbers may be changed to a higher number such as 2.0. *Upgrades* are revised versions of a software program and require the purchase of a newer version of the software.

Generally, you can download updates along with instructions. Once downloaded, follow the instructions to update the software. Upgrades, on the other hand, might be available for downloading after purchasing. Large programs, such as Microsoft Office, generally are installed from CDs or DVDs.

More applications are migrating to the Web. These *Web applications* are without platform constraints or installation requirements and are accessed through a Web browser over a network such as an intranet or the Internet. Some of the more common Web applications include Web-based e-mail, online calendars, personal information managers, photo sharing, as well as many other applications (see **Figure 6–11**). These applications generally are updated online by the company or owner.

▶ **VOCABULARY**
upgrades
Web applications

(A)

(B)

FIGURE 6–11 Web applications: (A) Google Calendar (B) Photoshop.com

In Step-by-Step 6.2, you learn how to access Windows update information. Complete Step-by-Step 6.2 to learn how to apply updates.

Step-by-Step 6.2

1. Click the **Start** button on the taskbar, and then click **Help and Support** to open the Windows Help and Support window.

2. In the Search Help box, type **Windows Updates** (see **Figure 6–12**).

FIGURE 6–12
Windows Help and
Support window

Search
Help box

Search Help
button

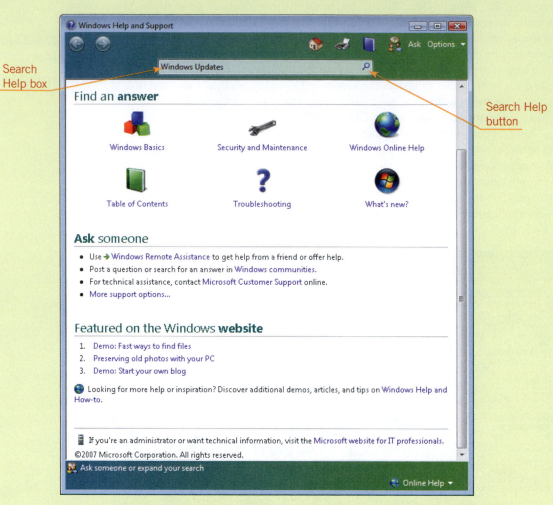

3. Click the **Search Help** button to display the results (see **Figure 6–13**), and then point to the **What are updates?** link.

FIGURE 6–13
Results of searching for
"Windows Updates"

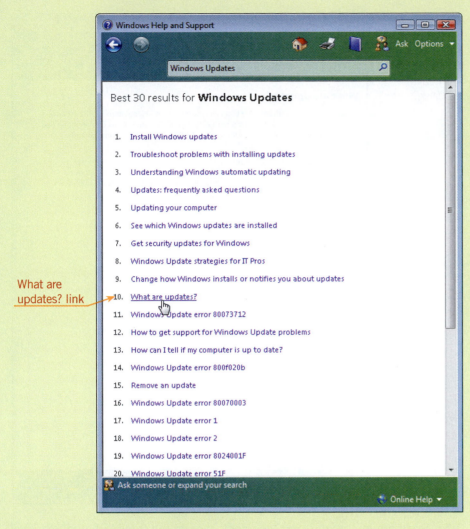

4. Click the **What are updates?** links to display the What are updates? page
   (see **Figure 6–14**).

FIGURE 6–14
What are updates? page

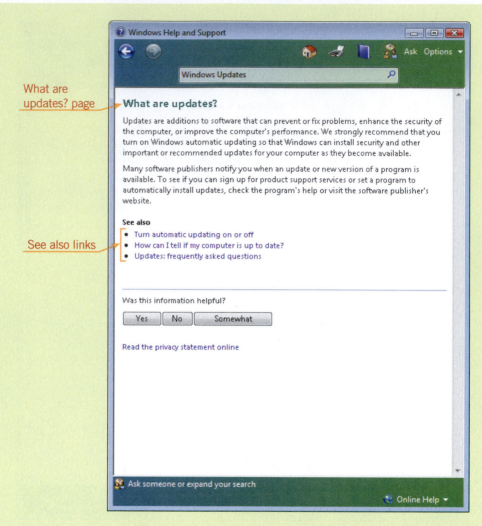

What are
updates? page

See also links

5. Read the information and then click each of the three bulleted See also links (**Turn automatic updating on or off**; **How can I tell if my computer is up to date?**, and **Updates: frequently asked questions**).

6. Using your word-processing program, write a paragraph summarizing the information contained in each of the three bulleted items.

Alternative Methods of Software Distribution

Several other alternative methods of software distribution are available. They include the following:

- *Open source*: A programmer or programmers create a program and make it available to the general public for use without cost; the source code can be modified and redistributed to the software user/developer community.

- *Freeware*: This is copyrighted software given away for free by the author. The author, however, retains the copyright. Code cannot be changed unless it is expressly allowed by the author.

- *Shareware*: This software, usually downloadable from the Internet, is usually made available on a trial basis. Most shareware is free for an evaluation period but requires payment if you continue to use it after that.

- *Software bundled with hardware purchases*: Also called **bundleware**, this software is included with the purchase of a new computer.

▶ **VOCABULARY**
bundleware
software piracy

For individual or personal computers, it is the responsibility of the user to verify and use only legitimately licensed software. A network manager's responsibilities are somewhat more extensive. They must verify that the product is used and distributed within the terms of the license and that licensing and maintenance fees are maintained.

As indicated previously, most commercially marketed software is copyrighted. ***Software piracy*** is the unauthorized copying of software. Originally, many software companies attempted to stop the piracy by copy-protecting their software. They soon discovered, however, that this strategy was not foolproof and that software piracy is almost impossible to stop. Many software companies now require some sort of registration that generally includes a license number. This strategy works somewhat, but is not perfect and does not completely stop software piracy.

TECHNOLOGY CAREERS

Software Developer

A software developer maintains and helps develop new application and system software. When you see a job listing for software developer, it could include many requirements. A company may be looking for someone to develop software using a particular programming language such as Java, Visual Basic, C, or C++, or a company may be looking for someone to develop add-ons to operating systems programs. This could include enhancements to utility programs, updates to language translators, or new additions to the operating system itself. Many companies seek employees with skills in operating systems such as UNIX and Windows Vista.

If you go online to look for software developer jobs, you will find that many of them refer to Oracle, a large information technology software company. Oracle products support database technology, data design and modeling, Web applications, and much more. There is a great variation in salaries and educational requirements for software developers. Educational requirements range from some college to a bachelor's or master's degree, sometimes even a Ph.D. Generally, but not always, the more education you have, the higher your starting salary. Most companies require some experience, but a few have entry-level positions.

SUMMARY

In this lesson, you learned:

- Hardware refers to anything you can touch, including objects such as the keyboard, mouse, monitor, printer, chips, disk drives, and CD/DVD recorders. Inputting refers to using an input device to enter data.

- Software is programming code written to provide instructions to the hardware so that you can perform specific tasks. Using input devices, you interact with the software by typing commands, selecting an option from a menu, or clicking a button, for example.

- Hardware and software interact as a computer processes data.

- A computer processes data by applying rules called algorithms, which are sets of clearly defined, logical steps that solve a problem.

- Software development usually begins when someone recognizes a need to perform a task more effectively using a computer. The programmer breaks down the task into an algorithm that covers all the actions needed to perform the task. The programmer often works out the logic for the steps in the algorithm by using a flowchart that shows different paths the program will take depending on what data is inputted.

- The programmer writes the steps in a computer programming language or code that uses a formal set of terms and syntax, or rules for how the words are used together. The computer translates the code into language it can understand, and uses the translated commands to execute the program.

- Software development also requires quality control, which involves running systematic tests, debugging (finding and correcting errors in the code), and beta testing.

- The two types of software are application software and system software. Application software helps you perform a specific task. System software refers to the operating system and all utility programs that manage computer resources at a low level.

- Operating systems provide an interface between the user or application program and the computer hardware.

- When you purchase a software program, you are purchasing a software license that gives you permission to use the program. A single-user license gives you the right to install the software on a single computer. Organizations using networks can purchase network licenses.

- Software as a Service (SaaS), is a recent software delivery method where an application is licensed for use as a service. The software is provided to customers on demand through the Internet, an intranet, or local network.

- A software update is a fix called a patch, an update, or a service pack. A software patch is applied over software that you already have installed.

- Software upgrades are revised versions of a software program and require the purchase of a newer version of the software.

- Web applications do not have platform constraints or installation requirements and are accessed through a Web browser over a network such as an intranet or the Internet. Common Web applications include Web mail and online calendars.

- Alternative methods of software distribution include open source, freeware, shareware, and bundleware.

■ VOCABULARY REVIEW

Define the following terms:

algorithm	operating systems	software license
application software	patch	software piracy
beta testing	service pack	system software
bundleware	single-user license	update
flowchart	software	upgrades
inputting	Software as a Service (Saas)	Web applications
network license	software development	

◼ REVIEW QUESTIONS

TRUE / FALSE

Circle T if the statement is true or F if the statement is false.

T   F   **1.**   The first step in programming is to develop machine language code.

T   F   **2.**   An operating system is generally referred to as productivity software.

T   F   **3.**   Debugging a program means looking for errors in the instructions to the computer.

T   F   **4.**   Computer hardware is anything you can touch.

T   F   **5.**   There are five categories of system software.

MULTIPLE CHOICE

Select the best response for the following statements.

1. Another word for software is _____.

   A.   hardware   C.   algorithm

   B.   program   D.   interface

2. The two basic types of computer software are _____ and _____.

   A.   program, application   C.   application, system

   B.   productivity, application   D.   system, networking systems

3. A group of programs that coordinate and control the resources of a computer system is called _____.

   A.   system software   C.   shareware

   B.   application software   D.   network

4. When you purchase a software program, you are purchasing _____.

   A.   the programming code   C.   a language translator

   B.   a license   D.   the user interface

5. A software fix is called a(n) _____.

   A.   patch   C.   service pack

   B.   update   D.   any of the above

FILL IN THE BLANK

Complete the following sentences by writing the correct word or words in the blanks provided.

1. The _____ software delivery method provides a more cost-effective alternative than traditional packaged applications.

2. With a(n) _____ program, the source code can be modified and redistributed to the software user and developer community.

3. _____ is the unauthorized copying of software.

4. A(n) _____ is a set of clearly defined, logical steps that solve a problem.

5. A(n) _____ shows different paths the program will take depending on what data is inputted.

■ PROJECTS

PROJECT 6–1

Operating systems have come a long way over the last few years. They are much easier to use and support many more features. Suppose you are designing an operating system for computers for the year 2012. Answer the following questions, and then perform the following task:

1. What features would you include?

2. How would your operating system be different from those that currently are available?

3. Would your operating system be an open source operating system? Why or why not?

4. Use your word-processing program to write a one-page report or give an oral report to your class.

PROJECT 6–2

You are part of a team that is going to write the program for an interactive children's game. The object of the game is similar to the poem Jack and Jill. Your part is to develop the basic flowchart or algorithm for the poem. Complete the following:

1. Identify the steps in the poem.

2. Using the algorithm shown in Figure 6–3 or the flowchart shown in Figure 6–4, write or sketch the steps of the poem.

PROJECT 6–3

Open source, freeware, and shareware are three categories of software described in this lesson. Complete the following:

1. Use the Internet and Web sites such as *download.com*, *directory.fsf.org*, and *freewarefiles. com* and find a minimum of two examples of each of these types of software.

2. Use your word-processing program and create a report listing the name of the software program, the location from where it was downloaded, a short description, and the software category.

TEAMWORK PROJECT

You and two team members have been given the responsibility for purchasing new computers for a small accounting firm. You and your team members are responsible for determining the operating system, the distribution method you will use for software access, and the minimum application software you will need within this company. Research these options online, and then organize your findings into a one-page report and a presentation to present to your class.

■ CRITICAL THINKING

This lesson described three ways in which software can be distributed. Write a short paragraph describing each method. If you were choosing a method for a game, which method would you choose and why? Would you choose a different method for software you use to produce your academic documents? Explain why or why not.

■ ONLINE DISCOVERY

Computer software engineers are one of the occupations projected to grow the fastest and add the most new jobs over the 2006-16 decade. You are considering a career as a software engineer and want to learn more about this profession. Using the Internet and other resources, prepare a report of at least one page describing the level of skill and educational requirements required for this type of career. A minimum of three Web sites should be used.

LESSON 7

Software Fundamentals

■ OBJECTIVES

Upon completion of this lesson, you should be able to:

- Identify the fundamental concepts of word-processing software.
- Identify the fundamental concepts of spreadsheet software.
- Identify the fundamental concepts of presentation software.
- Identify the fundamental concepts of database software.
- Identify the fundamental concepts of graphics and multimedia software.
- Identify the fundamental concepts of education and entertainment software.
- Identify the types and purposes of utility programs.
- Identify other types of miscellaneous software programs.

■ DATA FILES

You do not need data files to complete this lesson.

■ VOCABULARY

bitmapped graphics

cell

database

datasheet

field

multimedia

object

object linking and embedding (OLE)

presentation software

primary key

query

record

spreadsheet

table

text editor

utility program

vector graphics

word-processing software

workbook

worksheet

As you learned in Lesson 6, software is divided into two classes: system software and application software. System software consists of low-level programs that interact with the computer at a basic level and is discussed in detail in Lesson 8. In contrast, application software (also called end-user programs) includes programs such as databases, presentation software, spreadsheets, and word processors. Symbolically speaking, application software sits on top of system software because it cannot run without the operating system and system utilities.

You can purchase application software as individual programs or as a suite. A suite generally contains the following four types of programs: word processing, spreadsheets, presentations, and databases. Some of the more popular suites are Apple iWork, Corel WordPerfect Office, Google Docs, Microsoft Office, Microsoft Works, and StarOffice. Some suites, however, do not include a database program, while others contain add-ons such as Talk and Calendar.

1-2.2.1

▶ VOCABULARY

word-processing software

Word-Processing Programs

Word-processing software is a widely used application program. Primarily, you use this software to create, edit, and print documents and then save the documents electronically. When creating a document, you can easily correct errors and modify data. In most word-processing programs, you can save the document in a variety of formats including a template, earlier versions of the program, Rich Text Format, and plain text format.

Microsoft Office Word (see **Figure 7–1**), one of the more popular word-processing programs, includes basic and sophisticated features for creating, editing, formatting, and producing documents. For example, it includes collaboration features that allow you to track the changes made by multiple users. Reviewers can insert their comments within a document. These features are very useful, particularly when two or more people are working on the same project or when instructors need to comment on a student's work.

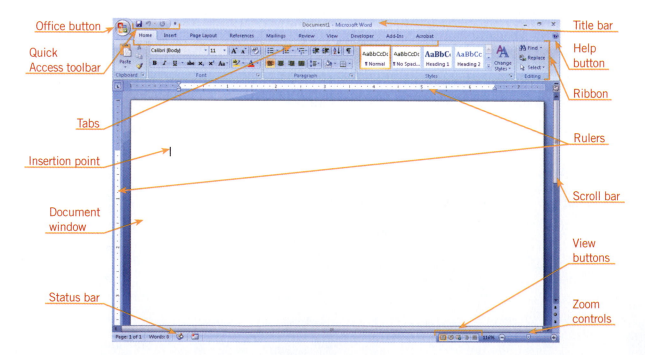

FIGURE 7–1   Opening Word window

Figure 7–1 shows a blank document opened in Microsoft Office Word. The following list describes most of the features displayed in this figure.

- *Document window*: Area where you type and work with a document
- *Help button*: Opens a new window with a Search text box
- *Horizontal scroll bar*: Used to move the page left and right
- *Office button*: Located in the upper-left corner of the Word window, this button replaces the File menu
- *Quick Access Toolbar*: Located in the title bar and contains a repository of the most-used functions; fully customizable
- *Ribbon*: Panels that contain command buttons and icons
- *Rulers*: Show the positioning of text, tabs, margins, insertion point, and any other elements on the page
- *Scroll bars*: Used to scroll vertically and horizontally through a document that is too large to fit in the document window
- *Status bar*: Displays the number of the current page and the total number of pages in the document; also indicates the on/off status of Word features such as spelling and grammar checking
- *Title bar*: Displays the name of the software program and the name of the document on which you are working; the default name of a document is DocumentX, where X is a number
- *View buttons*: Used to switch among the following views: Print Layout, Full Screen Reading, Web Layout Outline, and Draft

The following are basic features in word-processing programs that automate the process of creating and editing professional-quality documents:

- *Accessibility*: Use keyboard shortcuts, size, zoom, color, and sound options
- *Copy and paste*: Select and then duplicate a section of text
- *Cut and paste*: Select and then cut (delete) a segment of text from one place in a document and then insert or paste it somewhere else within the same document or within another document
- *Delete*: Select and then delete characters, words, lines, or pages of text
- *File management*: Access options so you can create, delete, move, save, and search for files
- *Font selection*: Apply font size, font type, italics, underline, and bold properties to the text
- *Graphics*: Insert pictures, clip art, shapes, SmartArt, WordArt, and a variety of other objects
- *Text insertion*: Insert text anywhere in the document; the inserted text can be copied from another word-processing document, an e-mail message, a Web page, or other document type
- *Page size and size margins*: Define various page sizes and margins; text automatically is readjusted to fit the page
- *Print*: Send a document to a printer to produce a hard copy
- *Search and replace*: Search for a particular word or phrase; replace is used to have a word or selection of words replaced with another anywhere within the selection or the entire document
- *Word wrap*: Automatically moves the insertion point to the next line when one line is filled with text; the text is readjusted if the margins are changed

---

EXTRA FOR EXPERTS

If your desktop contains a Word icon or an icon for another Office program, you can double-click the icon to start the program.

WARNING

As you work in a document, it is a good idea to save it regularly.

▶ **VOCABULARY**
text editor

Word processors that support these basic features generally are called *text editors*, whereas word-processing programs that are more robust support additional features. Some of these more advanced features are as follows:

- *Blogs*: Publish blogs directly from the word-processing program.
- *Footnotes*: Automate the numbering and placement of footnotes.
- *Headers and footers*: Specify custom text at the top and bottom of a page.
- *Macros*: Create a series of keystrokes that represent a series of commands.
- *Merge*: Merge text from one file into another; useful for generating such documents as mailing labels and then merging them with a form letter.
- *Page numbering*: Number pages in the format and position you specify.
- *Reference tools*: Access a variety of reference tools such as a spell checker, research, thesaurus, and a language translator.
- *Windows*: Display and edit two or more documents on the same screen.
- *WYSIWYG*: Work with the document on the screen as it will look when printed; stands for "what you see is what you get."

Microsoft Word also provides other options that you can adjust and configure to suit your working style. You can display these options by clicking the Office button and then clicking the Word Options button at the bottom of the menu. **Figure 7–2** shows an example of options you can modify through the Microsoft Word Options dialog box. In this figure, the Proofing category is selected.

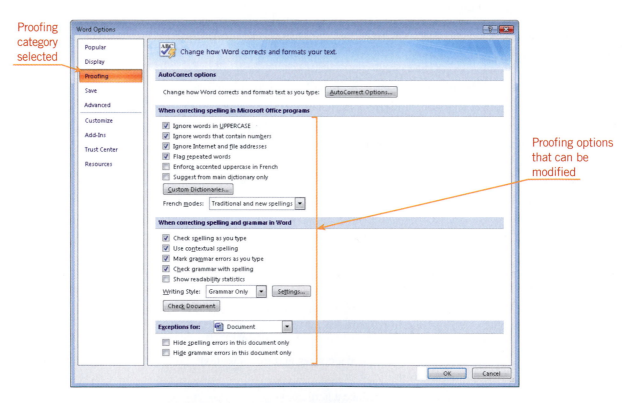

FIGURE 7–2   Word Options dialog box

Spreadsheet Concepts

A *spreadsheet* is a row-and-column arrangement of data. You use electronic spreadsheet software such as Microsoft Office Excel to evaluate, calculate, manipulate, analyze, and present numeric data. Calculations are updated automatically, which makes this type of software very effective for tasks such as preparing budgets, financial statements, payrolls, and sales reports, and for managing orders and inventory. You can also use spreadsheet software to make forecasts and identify trends.

A spreadsheet (see **Figure 7–3**) looks much like a page from a financial journal. It is a grid with columns and rows. The rows and columns can contain text, formulas, and numbers (values). This grid in Excel is referred to as a *worksheet*. The terms *spreadsheet* and *worksheet* are used interchangeably. When you start Excel, you open a file called a *workbook*. Each new workbook comes with three worksheets, like pages in a document.

1-2.2.2

▶ **VOCABULARY**

spreadsheet

worksheet

workbook

cell

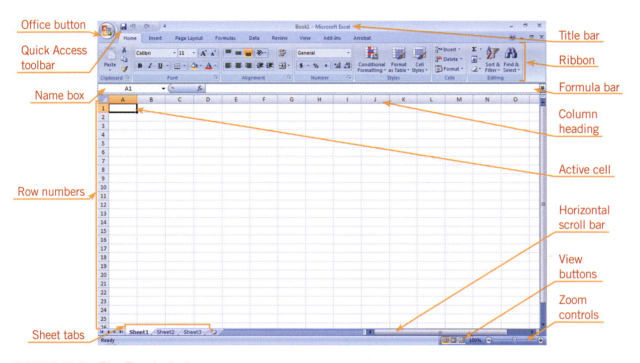

FIGURE 7–3 The Excel window

As shown in **Figure 7–3**, the columns are identified by letters of the alphabet, and the rows are identified by numbers. The point at which a column and a row intersect or meet is called a *cell*. Each cell has a name, called the cell reference (or cell address), which is represented by the column letter and the row number. For example, the first cell in a worksheet is cell A1. It is located in column A and in row 1. The active cell is the cell in which you are working currently and is surrounded by a thick border. Note that cell A1 is the active cell in **Figure 7–3** (as indicated in the Name box) and that 26 rows and the columns A through O are displayed. Some worksheets, however, contain thousands of columns and over a million rows; therefore only a small portion of the worksheet is displayed at one time, as seen in **Figure 7–3**. Individual worksheets are stored within a workbook. By default, a workbook contains three worksheets named Sheet1, Sheet2, and Sheet3, as shown on the sheet tabs at the bottom of the window. (*Sheet* is another word for worksheet.)

The basic features supported by most spreadsheet programs are as follows; many of these features are the same or similar to those contained in word-processing programs:

- *Accessibility*: Use keyboard shortcuts, size, zoom, color, and sound options.

- *Copy and paste*: Select and then duplicate a section of text, a formula, a number, or other data. When a number or formula is copied from one cell and then pasted into a new cell, the spreadsheet program automatically readjusts the formula based on the new location.

- *Cut and paste*: Select and then cut (delete) a segment of text, a number, a formula, or other data and then insert or paste it somewhere else within the same document or within another document. If a formula is part of the selection, it is readjusted automatically to accommodate the new location.

- *Data filtering*: Locate certain records in a spreadsheet based on selected criteria and then display those selected records.

- *Delete*: Select and then delete numbers, text, formulas from cells, charts, and so on.

- *File management*: Create, delete, move, save, and search for files.

- *Font selection*: Apply font size, font type, italics, underline, and bold properties to the data.

- *Formulas*: Use a variety of formula options, including AutoSum, Financial, Logical, Math and Trig, and Statistical.

- *Graphics*: Insert illustrations, images, SmartArt diagrams, symbols, special characters, and a variety of graph types into the spreadsheet.

- *Headers and footers*: Specify custom text at the top and bottom of a page.

- *Insert data*: Insert data anywhere in the spreadsheet; the inserted data can be copied from another spreadsheet, an e-mail message, a Web page, or other document type.

- *Macros*: Create a series of keystrokes that represent a series of commands.

- *Merge*: Merge a selection of cells or split merged cells; this is also used to merge copies of a shared worksheet.

- *Page numbering*: Number pages in the format and position you specify.

- *Print*: Send a document to a printer to produce a hard copy of the worksheet or of the worksheet and chart.

- *Search and replace*: Search for a particular word, phrase, formula, and so on; use replace to have a single selection or multiple selections of text or formulas replaced with another anywhere within the selection or the entire document.

- *Reference and editing tools*: Use a variety of built-in editing tools such as a spell checker, thesaurus, grammar checker, and translate tools.

- *Windows*: Display and edit two or more documents on the same screen.

- *WYSIWYG*: Work with the document on the screen as it will look when printed; this stands for "what you see is what you get."

The appearance of the spreadsheet is almost as important as the accuracy of the data it contains. You can use formatting to emphasize specific entries, enhance the appearance of the spreadsheet, and make the information easier to read and understand. In **Figure 7–4**, you can see how formatting called cell styles and themes can affect the appearance of the data.

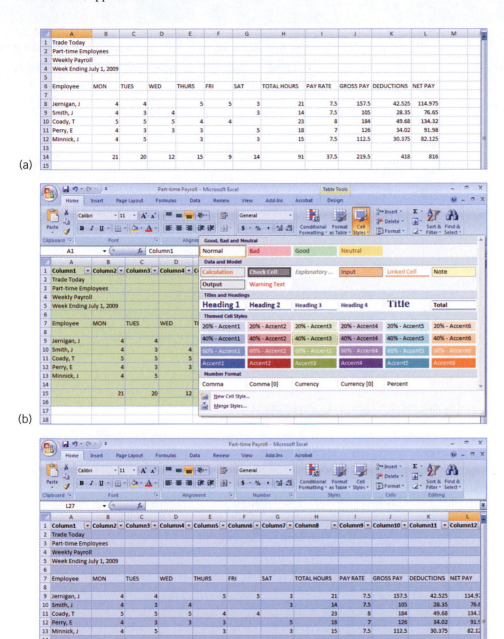

FIGURE 7–4   (a) Unformatted data (b) Cell styles applied (c) Theme applied

In Step-by-Step 7.1, you start Excel and review the commands contained on the Page Layout tab of the Excel Ribbon.

Step-by-Step 7.1

1. Start Excel by clicking the **Start** button on the taskbar, pointing to *All Programs*, clicking **Microsoft Office**, and then clicking **Microsoft Office Excel 2007**.

2. Click the **Page Layout** tab on the Ribbon (see **Figure 7–5**).

FIGURE 7–5
Excel Page Layout tab

Page Layout tab

3. Review the five groups of commands on the Page Layout tab (Themes, Page Setup, Scale to Fit, Sheet Options, and Arrange). Use your word-processing program and summarize the features provided within each of these groups. Submit your summary to your instructor.

1-2.2.3

▶ **VOCABULARY**
presentation software

Presentation Concepts

Presentation software is a computer program you use to organize and present information, normally in the form of a slide show. Through the use of sequential slides enhanced with a variety of special effects such as animation, text, graphics, and other features, a presentation is an effective and professional way to communicate topics and ideas. In addition, presentation software provides options for generating notes for the presenter and handouts for the audience. Equipment requirements for the presentation include a projector and computer (see **Figure 7–6**).

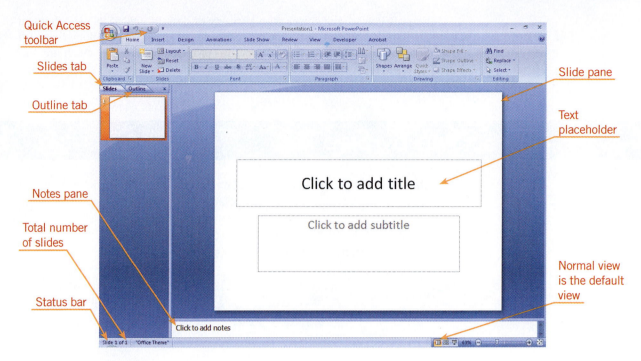

FIGURE 7–6   PowerPoint window

Besides being excellent for creating on-screen shows, presentation software is also useful in the following scenarios:

- *Self-running presentation*: Job fairs, demonstrations, and conventions are a few examples of where you might see a self-running presentation. When the presentation is completed, it automatically restarts.

- *Online meetings*: Using programs such as PowerPoint with Windows Meeting Space makes it easy to set up a meeting and share documents, programs, or your desktop with up to 10 people. The participants can be located in the same city, state, or even another country.

- *Presentation broadcasting*: You can use the Web to broadcast your presentation to locations all over the world.

- *Web presentation*: You can save a presentation as a Web or HTML document and upload it to your organization's Web site or to your own personal Web site.

- *Overhead transparencies*: If you do not have access to a computer and projector for your presentation, you can create and print either black-and-white or color transparencies. This requires using plastic transparency acetate sheets in your printer.

- *35-mm slides*: Each screen can be saved as a separate slide and then converted to 35-mm slides.

- *Audience handouts*: Printed handouts support your presentation. Smaller versions of your slides can be printed two, three, six, or nine to a page.

- *PDF document*: Portable Document Format (PDF) is a common format for sharing documents online and through other channels.

Several software companies produce presentation graphics programs. Some of the more popular of these include Microsoft Office PowerPoint—both Macintosh and Windows versions—Corel Presentations, and Open Office.

MODULE 1   Computing Fundamentals

Microsoft PowerPoint comes with a variety of designs, called themes, that you can apply to a presentation. A theme is a predesigned set of fonts, colors, lines, fill effects, and other formatting. PowerPoint also provides transitions, which are animated effects that play between slides. In Step-by-Step 7.2, you start PowerPoint and then review the themes and transitions.

Step-by-Step 7.2

1. Start PowerPoint by clicking the **Start** button on the taskbar, pointing to *All Programs*, clicking **Microsoft Office**, and then clicking **Microsoft Office PowerPoint 2007**.

2. Click the **Design** tab on the Ribbon (see **Figure 7–7**).

FIGURE 7–7
Design tab on the PowerPoint Ribbon

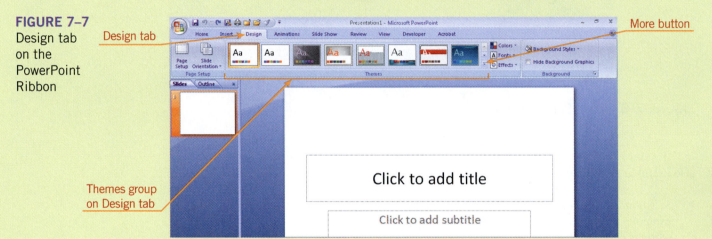

3. Move the mouse pointer over each theme in the Themes group to view a preview and the name of the theme. Click the **More** button to display additional themes in the Themes gallery (see **Figure 7–8**). Click a theme to apply it to the slide.

FIGURE 7–8
Displaying the Themes gallery

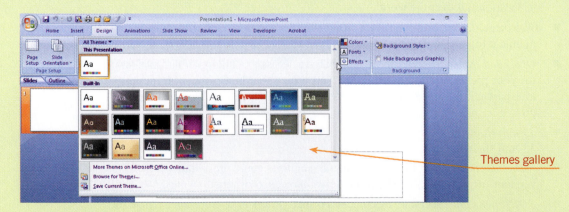

4. Click the **Animations** tab. Move the mouse pointer slowly over each of the five animated transitions in the Transitions to This Slide group. Note that if you rest the pointer on a transition, the name of the transition is displayed.

5. Click the **More** button to display the Transitions gallery.

6. Use your word-processing program to answer the following questions:
   a. Which theme would you select and why?
   b. Which special effect would you use?
   c. Would you use the same design and transition on each slide? Why or why not?
   d. Submit your assignment to your instructor.

Effective Presentation Guidelines

You can use presentation tools to make any presentation more effective and interesting. However, be cautious! Presentation programs contain many features and many options, so it is sometimes difficult to avoid getting carried away. Often, the first-time user is tempted to add distracting sounds, animations, and excessive clip art to each slide. Before you create a presentation, therefore, you need to plan and outline the message that you want to communicate. As you develop the outline for your presentation, consider your audience and determine the presentation's purpose, the location in which it will be given, and the equipment you will need.

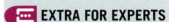 **EXTRA FOR EXPERTS**

Use photos, clip art, and graphics instead of words for a more powerful presentation.

Follow these guidelines to create an effective presentation:

- Keep the text simple—use the "6 by 6 rule," which is six lines of text, six words per line.
- Use no more than 50 words per slide, including titles and subtitles.
- Do not clutter your slide with large paragraphs displayed in a small font size. Use one-sentence comments and fill in the details orally.
- Use bullets, not numbers, unless providing specific step-by-step instructions. Bullets indicate no significant order, while numbers indicate rank or sequence.
- Cover one topic per slide.
- Use readable typefaces and fonts. Use serif fonts for body text and sans serif fonts for titles.
- Choose color carefully.
- Use simple tables to present numbers.
- Add clip art sparingly and only where appropriate.
- Don't try to dazzle your audience with an overabundance of graphics, sound, transitions, and other effects.

TECHNOLOGY CAREERS

Presentation Expert

Presentations are an organization's most direct communication effort. Many times, a presentation can make or break a sale or prevent a company from landing that big contract. As more and more employees are using computers and presentation programs, companies are beginning to realize the importance of this media.

A growing trend in large companies is to hire a presentation expert to oversee the creation and delivery of presentations within the organization. Depending on the size of the company and the number of presentations required, this person might work alone or work as part of a media department. The media department generally functions as a service bureau for the rest of the company. Presentation managers might also be responsible for design. They must stay updated and aware of technological advances in the areas of multimedia. This position will most likely require additional education such as workshops, conferences, and classes.

Many large companies have a standard set of master slides and templates. All employees are expected to use these standards. The presentation manager might be responsible for creating these masters and templates and might even be responsible for teaching physical presentation delivery skills or coaching frequent speakers.

Because there are no certifications or degrees for presentation managers, many people employed in this field have graphics design and/or Web design backgrounds. They may or may not have a 4-year degree. It is not unusual to find someone with a community college 2-year degree in design or someone with design certifications employed in this type of job.

Salaries are varied and can range from as little as $20,000 to as much as $80,000 or more.

1-2.2.4

Database Concepts

Effective information management is the core of a successful business or organization and is important in your personal life. Data is unorganized text, graphics, sound, or video. Information is data that has been organized and processed so that it is meaningful and useful. Every organization and most individuals need a method to store data and convert it into accurate, relevant, and timely information when needed.

Database Software Defined

VOCABULARY

database

A *database* is a collection of related information organized in a manner that allows for rapid search and retrieval. A database management system (DBMS) is a software program that is used to create, maintain, and provide controlled access to data. A database and spreadsheet are somewhat similar. Like spreadsheets, database tables are composed of rows and columns. Both programs enable you to organize, sort, and calculate the data. A database, however, provides additional comprehensive functions for manipulating the data. This lesson introduces you to some basic features of a database for entering, organizing, and reporting data.

Before you begin to design and develop a database, you should do some planning. Consider what data you will include and what information you want to create. After you have made these decisions, you are ready to begin creating your database.

Database Structure

To use a database program effectively, you first need to understand some basic terminology. In Microsoft Office Access, a database can consist of one table or a collection of tables. A **table** is composed of columns and rows, referred to as fields and records in Access. **Figure 7–9** shows a sample database table for customers of the Flower Store. The Flower Store provides wholesale products to florists, so its customers are small flower shops.

▶ VOCABULARY

table

record

field

primary key

object

query

FIGURE 7–9   Records added to Customers table

Following is a description of the three table components identified in **Figure 7–9**:

- The rows in the table are call **records**. Each record is a group of related fields, such as all of the information regarding each member in a membership database or each customer in a customer table.

- The columns in the table are called **fields**. Each field contains a specific piece of information within a record. In the table in **Figure 7–9**, for example, the Phone Number field contains the customer's phone number.

- The **primary key**, which is assigned to a field, uniquely identifies each record in a table. It tells the database program how your records are sorted, and it prevents duplicate entries. In **Figure 7–9**, the primary key is the Contact ID field.

Microsoft Office Access is one of the most widely used database programs. When you start Access, the window you see is similar to other Microsoft Office 2007 applications in several ways—it displays a title bar, the Ribbon, and a status bar. Unlike Word, Excel, and PowerPoint, however, Access does not have a standard document view. The Access window changes based on the **object** you are using as you work with the database. Furthermore, many of the Ribbon buttons are unique to Access.

Using the data stored in the table, you can use Access to create the following objects: queries, forms, and reports. A **query** asks a question about the data stored in the table. The database program searches for and retrieves information from a table or tables to answer the question. You use forms to enter data in a table, and a report to print selected data. All of these objects—tables, forms, queries, and reports—are stored in a single file, which is the database.

After you create and save a new database, the next step is to add fields and then add data to the table. Tables are the primary objects in a database because they contain the data. Most databases contain multiple tables.

Creating a Table

Access provides several ways to create a table, including the following:

- Create a new database.
- Add a table to an existing database using the Tables group on the Create tab.
- Create a table based on a table template using the Tables group on the Create tab, selecting Table Templates, and then selecting an available template.

Creating a table is the first step in a three-step process and adding fields is the second step. The third step is to populate or add records to the table. When editing or adding records to a table, you can create and use a form or use Datasheet view. Views are formats used to display and work with the various objects. Access contains two basic views for working with tables:

- *Design view*: Create a table, form, query, and report.
- *Datasheet view*: Display a row-and-column view of the data in tables, forms, and queries; the table is called a ***datasheet*** and resembles an Excel worksheet.

When you enter data in a cell, it is called an entry. To move from one cell to another, you can use the mouse to click in a cell or you can use the keyboard to navigate in a table.

▶ **VOCABULARY**
datasheet

Forms

In addition to adding and viewing records in Datasheet view, you can also create and use a data-entry form. A form provides a convenient way to enter and view records in a table. When you create a form, you are adding a new object to the database. You can create the form manually or use the Form Wizard. The wizard asks you questions and formats the form according to your preferences.

Queries

A query enables you to locate records that match specified criteria by providing a way for you to ask a question about the information stored in a database table or tables. The database program searches for and retrieves data from the table(s) to answer your question. Microsoft Access provides four query options:

- *Simple Query Wizard*: Creates a select query from the selected fields.
- *Crosstab Query Wizard*: Displays data in a spreadsheet format.
- *Find Duplicates Query Wizard*: Locates records with duplicate field values.
- *Find Unmatched Query Wizard*: Locates records in one table that have no related records in another table.

Suppose, for example, that you want a list of all customers within a specified zip code. When you create a query, you determine what fields you want displayed in the query results. Often, you only need to see certain fields in the query results instead of all the fields in the table. In the preceding example, for instance, you might want only the customer's last name and the zip code displayed. The order in which you select the fields determines the order in which the information is displayed in the query results.

Reports

Another important feature of database management software is the ability to generate sophisticated reports that contain the contents of the database. A report is a database object that allows you to organize, summarize, and print all or a portion of the data in a database. You can create a report based on a table or a query. You can decide what formatting you want to use, such as headings, spacing, and graphics. After the report is generated, you can decide which records you want included in the report, you can sort the report, and you can insert a picture in the report.

Although you can produce a report manually, the Report Wizard, similar to the Query Wizard, provides an easy and fast way to design and create one. The wizard asks questions about which data you want to include in the report and how you want to format the data. An example of a printed report is displayed in **Figure 7–10**.

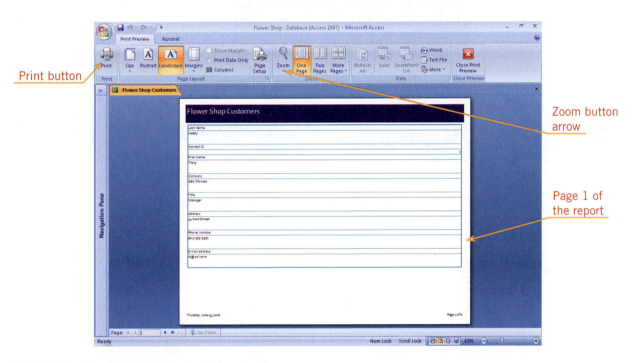

FIGURE 7–10   Access report in Print Preview

Online Databases

Entrepreneurs looking to open an online business often want to find an Internet-based database program. Many Internet-based databases are dynamic and therefore provide the capability for the user to change the content and products frequently.

Using an online database, you can insert new records and modify, delete, and search existing records. You can set up many online databases by uploading a CSV file from Microsoft Excel or Access. A CSV file is a comma-separated value file that can be exported from any spreadsheet or PC database software.

With some online databases, you can create a template for e-mail marketing. Some other features of Web databases are as follows:

- Create and update a contacts list.
- Change photos frequently and update an online catalog.
- Manage and keep your content current.

- Use online documentation.
- Generate formulas and calculated fields to automatically update your data.
- Keep users up to date with the latest information.
- Import and export information easily.

1-2.2.5

Graphics and Multimedia Programs Concepts

You use graphics and multimedia programs to create a variety of illustrations and animation. Most graphics applications fall into one of two main categories: vector or bitmap graphics. A vector image consists of many individual objects with individual properties such as color, fill, and outline. Their resolution can be adjusted to the highest quality. A bitmap image is composed of pixels in a grid. Each pixel contains information about the color to be displayed. These images have fixed resolution and cannot be resized without losing image quality. Other types of images are identified in **Table 7–1**.

TABLE 7–1 Computer images

IMAGE TYPE	DESCRIPTION
FLV	Adobe format for streaming Web video content
GIF	Image format for pictures with up to 256 distinct colors
JPG	File method for compressing graphics
MOV	File extension for digital video files in QuickTime format
MP3	Compressed audio format
PNG	Bitmapped image format that uses lossless data compression
QuickTime	Video and audio format that allows for the production of video and multimedia
SWF	Shockwave file format; supports exact positioning of graphical objects
WAV	Standard audio format

EXTRA FOR EXPERTS

Some Web sites offer free clip art that you can download.

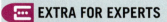 **VOCABULARY**
vector graphics

Most graphics programs use a variety of tools to create and modify images. The following sections briefly describe types of graphic programs.

Drawing Programs

A drawing program is a graphics program that is used for creating illustrations. The image is saved in a *vector graphics* format. This allows all individual parts of the picture to be moved, isolated, and scaled independently of the other parts. Examples of popular drawing programs are Adobe Illustrator and Corel Draw.

Paint Programs

A paint program allows the user to simulate painting on the computer through the use of a graphics tablet or a mouse. The images are created with a matrix of picture elements (pixels) and are generated as *bitmapped graphics*. A program titled Paint is part of Microsoft Windows. Another popular paint program is Corel Painter. These programs use a variety of tools, such as a line tool, fill tool, shape, and curve tools (see **Figure 7–11**).

▶ VOCABULARY
bitmapped graphics
multimedia

FIGURE 7–11 Image in Paint

Photo/Image Manipulation Programs

You use digital editing software to edit images, photos, and logos. Adobe Photoshop is one of the more popular photo/image-editing programs.

Animation Programs

You use animation software to create moving images and 3D graphics. Some of the more popular uses for these programs are online animations and game development. Adobe Flash, 3D Studio Max, and LightWave 3D are examples of this type of software.

Multimedia Programs

Multimedia is defined as the use of text, graphics, audio, and video in some combination to create an effective means of communication and interaction. Some examples of how this software is used are games, interactive presentations, advertisements, screen savers, and interactive books.

Education and Entertainment Programs

A wide variety of educational programs are available for children as young as 1 year old, as well as software programs for ages up to adult. Many of these programs apply an entertainment motif to the software. The following describes this type of software:

- *Computer-based training (CBT)*: Web based and/or computer-based training programs
- *Computer games*: Single-user and multiuser games; combines an educational component with a game format
- *Audio and video*: Software applications used to play audio and video; Media Player is bundled with Windows
- *Virtual reality*: A technology that lets users interact with a computer-simulated environment

Utility Programs

VOCABULARY
utility program

Utility programs help you perform computer housekeeping chores. You use these programs to complete specialized tasks related to managing the computer's resources, files, and so on. Some utility programs are part of the operating system, and others are self-contained programs. Some examples of utility program functions are the following:

- *File compression programs*: Compress a file or files to reduce the amount of disk space it requires. WinZip is one of the more popular programs. Microsoft Windows also contains a compression utility.
- *Antivirus, antiadware, and antispyware programs*: Use these types of software programs to protect against viruses, remove spyware, and prevent adware from playing or downloading advertisements.
- *Defragmentation*: Reduce the amount of fragmentation by organizing the contents of the disk to store the pieces of each file contiguously.
- *Backup program*: Create a copy of data on a drive; you should back up your data files on a regular schedule.
- *Single-purpose tools and accessories*: Use *widgets* or *gadgets*, mini-applications that can access online services or information such as the weather, or to provide a desktop calculator or clock.

Miscellaneous Software

In addition to the software programs described, the following are other types of software:

- *Financial and accounting programs*: Prepare financial statements for stockholders, employees, banks, and owners.
- *Electronic mail*: Send and receive messages on the Internet or through company or individual networks.
- *Chat, messaging, and instant messaging software*: Communicate in real time over the Internet by exchanging text messages.
- *Web browser*: Visit Web sites using programs such as Internet Explorer or Firefox to browse the World Wide Web.

- *Computer-aided design (CAD)*: Design houses, buildings, airplanes, and so on; includes ability to view a design from any angle and to zoom in and out.

- *Project management*: Plan, organize, and manage resources of the goals and objectives of a specific project.

- *Groupware*: Participate as a member of a workgroup attached to a local area network to organize your activities; also called *workgroup productivity software*.

- *Web conferencing*: Attend online meetings, share desktop presentations, and use VoIP, whiteboard, and chat, among other features. Some of the more popular programs are Adobe Connect Pro, Microsoft Office Live Meeting, and GoToMeeting.

- *Integrated programs*: Use programs such as Microsoft Office or Adobe Design, which contain a collection of programs within a single suite.

- *Specialized software*: Programs such as airline reservation systems, manufacturing-plant automatic/process control, sales force/customer service automation, and school information management are used for specific activities.

Selecting Software

When selecting a software product, it is important to select a product that is appropriate for the task. You can use Microsoft Word, for example, to integrate a variety of extra features in addition to creating general text documents. For example, you can create tables using Microsoft Word; however, you can also create tables through a spreadsheet program such as Microsoft Excel or through a database program such as Microsoft Access. The end result needs to be examined to determine which of the three programs would be more appropriate for creating a table.

A second example of incorrectly selecting software is using word-processing software to keep copies of financial records when a spreadsheet or an accounting program would be a better choice.

1-2.2.9

Software Integration

As indicated previously, you can use individual application programs, such as those in Microsoft Office, to perform common tasks in the workplace, in education, and for personal use. In addition to producing individual documents with these applications, you can also integrate data from one program into the other programs. In this context, an object is the data or information that you want to share between the programs. Microsoft Office, for example, provides three methods for inserting objects from one Office document into another Office document: copying and pasting, embedding, and linking. Each method has advantages and disadvantages.

The copy-and-paste process between documents is similar to copying and pasting text or other objects within a single document. Assume that you have a chart or worksheet in Excel and you would like to add a copy of it to a Word document. In the Excel document you select and copy the content. Next, you open a Word document, click the location where you want to paste the copied data and then click the Paste button.

Object linking and embedding (OLE) is a technology developed by Microsoft that lets you create a document or object in one program and then link and/or embed that data into another program. You can embed or link all or part of an existing file. For example, you can create a form letter using Microsoft Word, link it to an Access database file that contains a list of names and addresses, and then merge the form letter with the names and addresses.

1-2.2.10

📧 EXTRA FOR EXPERTS

In addition to embedding and linking Microsoft Office files, you can also link a variety of other files, including Adobe and Paint Shop Pro files, video clips, wave sounds, media clips, and others.

▶ **VOCABULARY**
object linking and embedding (OLE)

Keeping data current, however, can be an issue if the information changes often. A linked object, on the other hand, retains a connection to the original file, and the source document displays a representation of the linked data. Any changes made to the source file are reflected in the linked object. Assume that you have inserted a linked spreadsheet object into a PowerPoint document. If the spreadsheet data in the Excel program is modified, then the linked spreadsheet object in the PowerPoint document is also modified.

Linking is useful when information is maintained independently. You can also link an entire file to another program. For example, employee records are maintained by the personnel department. Other departments within the company use this data for sending mailings, creating interoffice documents, and so on. A link to the employee records would verify that the information was current.

Internet applications can also interact with a user's desktop or network. Adobe Air applications, for example, can update themselves, interact with the system clipboard, use the file system, use native windows and menus, use a local SQL database, and store encrypted data.

SUMMARY

In this lesson, you learned:

- How to use word-processing software to create, edit, and print documents and then save the documents electronically. When creating a document, you can easily correct errors and modify data.

- A spreadsheet is a row-and-column arrangement of data. You use electronic spreadsheet software to evaluate, calculate, manipulate, analyze, and present numeric data. Calculations are updated automatically.

- A database is a collection of related information organized in a manner that provides for rapid search and retrieval. You use database software to create, maintain, and provide controlled access to data.

- A database can consist of one table or a collection of tables, which are composed of columns and rows, referred to as fields and records. The primary key, which is assigned to a field, uniquely identifies each record in a table. You can also create queries, forms, and reports using database software.

- How to use graphics and multimedia programs to create a variety of illustrations and animation. Most graphics applications fall into one of two main categories: vector or bitmap graphics.

- Educational programs include computer-based training, computer games, audio and video software, and virtual reality programs.

- Utility programs help you perform computer housekeeping chores such as managing the computer's resources and managing files.

- Miscellaneous software includes programs such as e-mail applications, Web browsers, and project management software.

 **VOCABULARY REVIEW**

Define the following terms:

bitmapped graphics	object linking and embedding (OLE)	text editor
cell	presentation software	utility program
database	primary key	vector graphics
datasheet	query	word-processing software
field	record	workbook
multimedia	spreadsheet	worksheet
object	table	

REVIEW QUESTIONS

TRUE / FALSE

Circle T if the statement is true or F if the statement is false.

T   F   **1.**   Word-processing software is one of the more widely used application programs.

T   F   **2.**   Macros are used to create a series of keystrokes that represent a series of commands.

T   F   **3.**   In Excel, individual worksheets are stored within a workbook.

T   F   **4.**   In PowerPoint, a theme is a predesigned set of fonts, colors, lines, fill effects, and other formatting.

T   F   **5.**   A database and a word-processing program have the same purpose.

MULTIPLE CHOICE

Select the best response for each of the following statements.

1. The _____ in a database table are called records.

   A.   rows   C.   menus

   B.   columns   D.   add-ons

2. In a database program, a _____ enables you to locate records that match specified criteria.

   A.   request   C.   formula

   B.   query   D.   all of the above

3. A _____ is an animated effect that plays between slides.

   A.   vector graphic   C.   theme

   B.   worksheet   D.   transition

4. A(n) _____ image is composed of pixels in a grid.

   A.   access   C.   pixel

   B.   vector   D.   bitmap

5. In a worksheet, the point at which a column and a row intersect or meet is called a(n) _____.

   A.   field   C.   view

   B.   cell   D.   object

FILL IN THE BLANK

Complete the following sentences by writing the correct word or words in the blanks provided.

1. _____ programs help you perform computer housekeeping chores.

2. _____ software is used to design houses, buildings, and airplanes, and so on.

3. A(n) _____ is the data or information that you want to share between the programs.

4. In OLE, _____ is useful when information is maintained independently.

5. A(n) _____ provides a convenient way to enter and view records in a database table.

PROJECTS

PROJECT 7–1

This lesson discussed the differences between types of application software. Complete the following:

1. Use your word-processing program and create a table with four columns and five rows.

2. Name the columns *word processing*, *spreadsheet*, *database*, and *presentation*. Bold the headings.

3. In column 1, list four activities for which you would use a word-processing program; in column 2, list four activities for which you would use a spreadsheet program; in column 3, list four activities for which you would use a database program; and in column 4, list four activities for which you would use a presentation program.

PROJECT 7–3

This lesson discussed widgets and gadgets. Complete the following:

1. Use the Internet to research the terms *widget* and *gadget*.

2. Locate a minimum of 10 widgets and gadgets. Note the Web addresses of the most useful Web pages.

3. Use your word-processing program to write a short overview of each one.

PROJECT 7–2

You can find many graphics programs to suit your needs. Complete the following:

1. Use your favorite search engine to research the topic of *graphics programs*. Note the Web addresses of the most useful Web pages.

2. Use your word-processing program to list the various programs and their cost or approximate cost.

3. If you were going to select one of these programs to purchase, explain which program you would choose and why. Price is no object.

TEAMWORK PROJECT

This lesson discussed specialized software. Interview the technology specialist at your school or at the school district level. Ask such questions as what types of programs are used, how textbooks are ordered, what is used for class scheduling, how is the payroll handled, what other financial programs are used, and other pertinent topics. As a group, use the information you obtain to create a presentation to share with your classmates.

CRITICAL THINKING

You have been selected as the lucky recipient of a $500 gift certificate that can be used to purchase integrated software. Review the various programs online and then select the one you would purchase. Use your word-processing program to describe the software and why you selected this particular program.

ONLINE DISCOVERY

Defragmentation was discussed briefly in this lesson. Research defragmentation and expand the definition. Explain the advantages of defragmentation and describe how this process increases and improves startup times.

LESSON 8

Operating Systems

■ OBJECTIVES

Upon completion of this lesson, you should be able to:

■ Identify the purpose of an operating system.

■ Identify different operating systems.

■ Describe computer user interaction with multiple operating systems.

■ Identify system limitations.

■ Describe common problems related to operating systems.

■ DATA FILES

You do not need data files to complete this lesson.

■ VOCABULARY

administrative rights

administrator account

driver

embedded operating system

emulation card

file system

handheld operating system

Linux

Mac OS X

operating system (OS)

Palm OS

system administrator

UNIX

Windows Embedded CE

Windows Mobile

As indicated in Lesson 7, there are two basic types of software: application software and system software. Fundamental concepts of applications were discussed in detail in Lesson 7. This lesson focuses on system software and how it relates to the operating system and the utility programs that manage computer resources at a low level.

1-3.1.1

▶ **VOCABULARY**

operating system (OS)

driver

file system

Understanding the Purpose of an Operating System

Recall that system software facilitates the use of a computer system. An *operating system (OS)* is system software that enables the computer hardware to communicate and operate with the application software. Without an operating system, a computer would not function because the operating system manages and coordinates the activities and resources of the computer. For example, operating systems perform jobs such as recognizing input from the keyboard, sending output to the monitor and printer, keeping track of files and directories, and controlling peripheral devices such as printers, monitors, and the keyboard. Manufacturers of peripheral devices, such as printers or monitors, provide programs called *drivers* that the operating system uses to communicate with various hardware devices.

An operating system also manages resources for applications. It provides a consistent way for applications to communicate with hardware without duplicating settings or learning details about the hardware. This is why your computer system can use different hardware and settings from another computer, but still reliably run the same applications—the operating system takes care of that task for the applications.

Another way an operating system helps applications is by performing system and file maintenance tasks. For example, the operating system is responsible for such system tasks as preparing the desktop, managing visual and audio effects, handling memory, and maintaining power settings. Its file maintenance responsibilities are just as important. The operating system controls access to files stored on disks and manages the amount of space those files can use. The way an operating system stores files on disk is called a *file system*. The file system regulates the types of names and other attributes a file can have and organizes the files into folders arranged in a hierarchy, where a main folder can contain subfolders that contain files. The file system allows you to find and retrieve files you store on a computer by keeping track of the files you save and where you save them. The file system also identifies sections of a disk that are not being used.

EXTRA FOR EXPERTS

The Windows and Macintosh operating systems call file containers *folders*, while UNIX calls them *directories*.

1-3.1.2

Personal Computer Operating Systems

An operating system provides an interface between the user or application program and the computer hardware. See **Figure 8–1**.

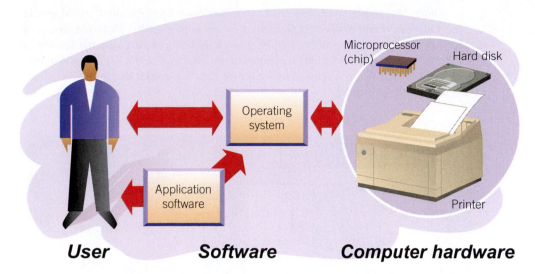

Microprocessor (chip)

Hard disk

Operating system

Application software

Printer

User **Software** **Computer hardware**

FIGURE 8–1 Operating system: an interface between users and computers

Several brands and versions of operating system software are available for personal computers. Each is designed to work with one or more particular processors. For example, the Windows operating system is designed to work with an Intel processor or clone. Currently, Microsoft Windows runs on more personal computers worldwide than other operating systems. The most widely used version of Windows is Windows XP, released in 2001. Windows Vista was released in 2006, and Windows 7 is scheduled for release in 2009. **Figure 8–2** shows the Windows Vista desktop.

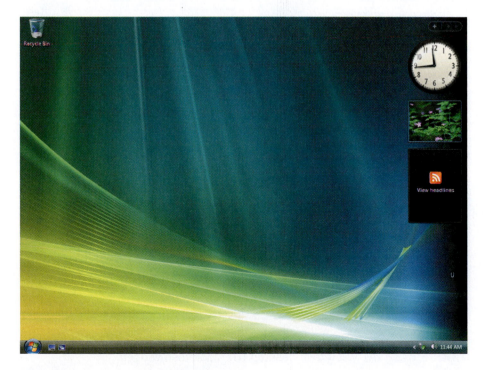

FIGURE 8–2 Windows Vista desktop

MODULE 1 Computing Fundamentals

Older Macintosh computers contain a processor manufactured by Motorola. Generally, the Windows operating system does not work with this Motorola processor. Recently, however, Microsoft and Apple have released operating systems for use on both platforms. Current Macintosh computers use Intel processors similar to Windows computers. The Macintosh operating system is called *Mac OS X*. **Figure 8–3** shows the Mac OS X version 10.5.

▶ **VOCABULARY**

Mac OS X

(A)

(B)

FIGURE 8–3 (A) Macintosh desktop (B) Macintosh widgets

EXTRA FOR EXPERTS

Macintosh popularized the first graphical user interface; however, Apple did not invent the interface. Xerox Corporation developed the idea of using pictorial icons for a computer interface.

Still another operating system is **UNIX**. This operating system is frequently used by scientists and programmers. UNIX was developed by a group of programmers for AT&T and is considered a multitasking, portable operating system. This means it can run on just about any hardware platform. Some versions of UNIX have a command-line interface, where you enter text commands instead of manipulating objects with a mouse, but most versions provide a graphical user interface such as that shown in **Figure 8–4**. There are several variants of the operating system, such as **Linux** and IBM's AIX.

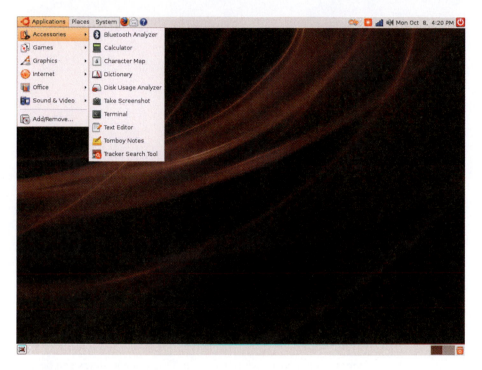

FIGURE 8–4   Linux desktop

Both the IBM AIX system and Linux are based on UNIX. Linux is an open source program that is free, and programmers and developers can use or modify it as they wish. Linux has a reputation of being stable and rarely crashing. One Linux user interface is called GNOME (pronounced *gah-NOHM*) and allows the user to select a desktop similar to Windows or Macintosh. GNOME also includes software applications such as word processing, spreadsheet, database, presentation, e-mail, and a Web browser. Even with these included applications, however, the number of available application programs is far fewer than those for Windows or the Mac OS.

Handheld and Embedded Operating Systems

As the interface between hardware and the user, the operating system is responsible for coordinating and managing the activities the device performs. **Handheld operating systems** and **embedded operating systems**, also known as mobile operating systems, are similar in principle to operating systems such as Windows or Linux. These systems, however, are smaller and generally less capable than desktop operating systems.

The diminutive operating systems can fit into the limited memory of mobile and handheld devices, such as cell phones, PDAs, handheld computers, mobile game players, and cameras. Mobile and handheld computers and other devices are used in a variety of application areas, including education, health care, automobile navigation, and for people with disabilities. The more popular handheld computers are those that are specifically designed to provide personal information manager (PIM) functions, such as a calendar and address book. These diminutive devices have plenty of memory to hold software applications, electronic texts, audio, and video (see **Figure 8–5**).

FIGURE 8–5   Handheld computer

All of these devices contain an operating system. Operating systems can be categorized by a number of characteristics, including technology, usage, and licensing. In some instances, these groupings may overlap. The operating system on most small devices and smart phones resides on a ROM chip. Some of the more popular of these handheld and embedded operating systems are listed below:

- *BlackBerry*: The BlackBerry operating system runs on handheld devices supplied by Research in Motion (RIM). In addition to phone capabilities, this system also provides services such as multitasking, instant messaging, PIM capabilities, and access to Bluetooth devices.

- *Embedded Linux*: This is a scaled-down Linux operating system used in devices such as mobile phones, media players, PDAs, smart watches, and many other types of devices that require an embedded operating system.

- *Palm OS*: A competing operating system to Windows Mobile, **Palm OS** runs on Palm handhelds and other third-party devices. Some of the more common built-in applications include an address book and calculator, schedule management, contacts, and phone book tools. This OS also includes handwriting-recognition software.

- *Symbian OS*: This is an open source multitasking operating system designed for smart phones. Some of the more popular features include the capability to send and receive e-mail messages and faxes, maintain contact lists, and browse the Web.

▶ **VOCABULARY**
Palm OS

- *Windows Embedded CE*: A scaled-down version of the Windows operating system, **Windows Embedded CE** is designed for devices such as digital cameras, security robots, intelligent appliances, gaming devices, GPSs, and set-top boxes.

- *Windows Mobile*: Based on Windows Embedded CE, **Windows Mobile** runs on smart phones and other types of handheld computers. It allows you to perform tasks such as accessing e-mail, recording and watching video, exchanging instant messages, reading an e-book, playing games, and managing finances. See **Figure 8–6**.

FIGURE 8–6   Smartphone with Windows Mobile

Sharing Files on Different Operating Systems

1-3.1.3

In many business, personal, and educational settings, it is necessary to share files across operating system platforms. A business might have workers using both Macintosh and Windows computers. Depending on the task, artists and designers might use Macintosh computers, while accountants and writers might have PCs. In the classroom, all of the computers might be the same type, but students might have different types of computers at home. These situations require that multiple systems be able to read disks and share files. Hardware and software solutions are available for these problems.

One type of hardware solution is an *emulation card* that is added to the motherboard of a computer. These cards provide the ability for the computer to run a program that was designed for a different operating system. For example, a card can be added to a Macintosh that allows it to run Windows programs. Software emulation programs are also available to provide this capability for some programs. Or, a Macintosh computer could have software installed that allows it to read disks that were formatted on PCs.

Some file types are readable on different operating systems. One example for word-processing documents is the basic text format (.txt). This format usually is readable by most word-processing programs on different systems. However, documents saved as .txt do not retain complicated formatting. Another text format, Rich Text Format (.rtf), does retain more formatting commands, such as paragraph breaks, fonts, and styles such as bold and italic. To save a file in text format or Rich Text Format, you use the Save As command in your word-processing program and specifically select Text or Rich Text Format as the file type. This type of document file type can generally be transferred to other operating systems across a network, to a Linux server, or to a handheld or mobile device (see **Figure 8–7**).

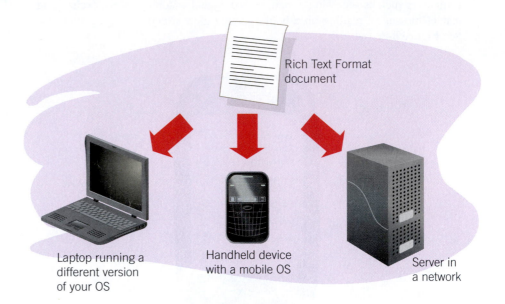

FIGURE 8–7   Transferring files from one operating system to another

If you use the Internet, you also share files across different operating systems regularly. Your desktop or laptop computer uses an operating system such as Windows or Mac OS. If you use an Internet service provider to connect to the Internet, you are probably connecting to a UNIX system. If you connect to the Internet using a direct network connection, such as through a school or other organization, you are connecting to computers that use a network operating system. Each operating system provides ways to communicate and exchange information with other operating systems so that you can use more than one operating system simultaneously.

1-3.1.4

User Rights

An operating system allows you to interact with a computer and take advantage of the computer's technology, but it also sets limitations to protect itself and the data on the computer. The operating system grants permission to you to perform some tasks but prevents you from performing others. The tasks you are allowed to perform are defined by your user rights. The system administrator sets the user rights to protect the computer's security. The ***system administrator*** is a user who has an ***administrator account***, which is a local account or a local security group. (An account is a collection of information that determines which files you can access and which settings you use; you access your user account by providing your user name and password.) The administrator account provides unrestricted access to make systemwide changes to the computer, including those that affect other users. Without administrative rights, you cannot make changes such as system modifications, installing software, or changing network settings.

▶ **VOCABULARY**
system administrator

administrator account

A typical system administrator has a variety of duties including the following:

- Creating account passwords and assigning user accounts and passwords
- Creating or deleting user accounts on the computer
- Changing account names, pictures, passwords, and other data
- Establishing security access levels
- Allocating storage space
- Monitoring systems to prevent unauthorized access and attacks by malicious software

The administrator can grant *administrative rights* to other users, allowing them to make changes based on the specified right. Without administrative rights, the typical user cannot perform many system modifications, such as installing or deleting software or changing network settings. To have administrative rights, you must know the administrative password. For example, if you want to install software on a computer, the operating system usually asks for the administrative password before it starts the setup process. If you provide the correct password, the operating system continues the installation. If you don't provide the correct password, it stops the setup process.

▶ **VOCABULARY**
administrative rights

ETHICS IN TECHNOLOGY

What Is Computer Ethics?

Ethics is the branch of philosophy concerned with evaluating human action, and a system or code of morals of a particular religion, group, or profession.

Ethical judgments are no different in the area of computing than they are in any other area. The use of computers can raise many issues of privacy, copyright, theft, and power, to name just a few. For example, many computer professionals condemn hacking into other computers as unethical, while some defend so-called white-hat hackers who breech computer security because they want to gain a deeper understanding of computers and networks.

In 1990, the Institute of Electrical and Electronics Engineers created a code of ethics. The organization reapproved it in 2006. This code is available at *www.ieee.org/portal/pages/iportals/aboutus/ethics/code. html*. The Association for Computing Machinery (ACM) also has a code of ethics and professional conduct provided at *www.acm.org/about/code-of-ethics*. This code is considered one of the most definitive sets of ethical standards for computer professionals, and contains 24 statements of personal responsibility. Many businesses and organizations have adopted one of these codes as their ethical code. Remember that they are only codes—not laws. People choose to follow them voluntarily.

1-3.1.5

Common Operating System Problems

Sooner or later, you will have trouble on your computer that affects the operating system. Examples of these issues are as follows:

- *Incompatibility*: A copy of Quicken for Windows does not run on a computer with a Macintosh operating system. Application software and files need to be compatible with the computer's operating system. Usually, the operating system will not let you install or run an incompatible program. Similarly, an operating system will not let you open a file or use a media device (such as a DVD) if it doesn't recognize the file or media type.

- *File corruption*: Files can become corrupt as the result of a power failure, turning off the computer without properly shutting it down, a virus, resource conflicts, outdated drivers, bad sectors or lost clusters on the hard drive, bad software installation, and so on. If your operating system is unpredictable, its files might be damaged or corrupted. You can use a system utility that identifies and repairs corrupted files.

- *Disk crashes*: If your system is unstable, programs and even the operating system shut down unexpectedly and you receive error messages when you try to use the operating system and applications. In some instances, restarting, or rebooting, the system can solve the problem. If the problem is more severe, you might need to upgrade or reinstall the operating system.

Other common types of problems include having trouble completing tasks you normally perform on your computer, such as connecting to the Internet, retrieving e-mail, opening and saving files, or playing music through your speakers. If you are using a Windows Vista computer, Windows Help and Support might provide solutions to your problem. Complete the following exercise to access Windows Help and Support for troubleshooting Windows. The following steps assume you are connected to the Internet and using Online Help.

EXTRA FOR EXPERTS

Sometimes Windows does not boot properly. Instead, a dialog box indicating that you are in safe mode is displayed on the screen. This means that something did not function properly during the boot process. Safe mode provides functionality so you or an expert user can do diagnostic testing.

Step-by-Step 8.1

1. Click the **Start** button 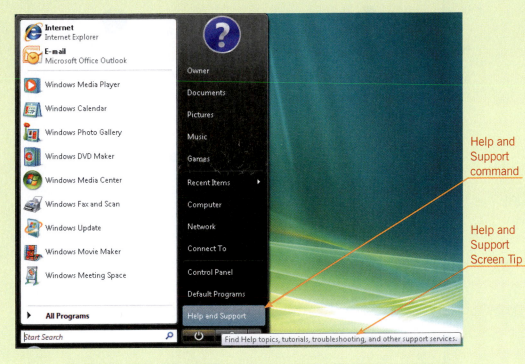 on the taskbar, and then point to *Help and Support*. See **Figure 8–8**.

FIGURE 8–8
Help and Support on the Start menu

Help and Support command

Help and Support Screen Tip

2. Click **Help and Support** to open the Windows Help and Support window. In the Find an Answer section, point to *Troubleshooting*, as shown in **Figure 8–9**.

Troubleshooting in
Windows Help and
Support

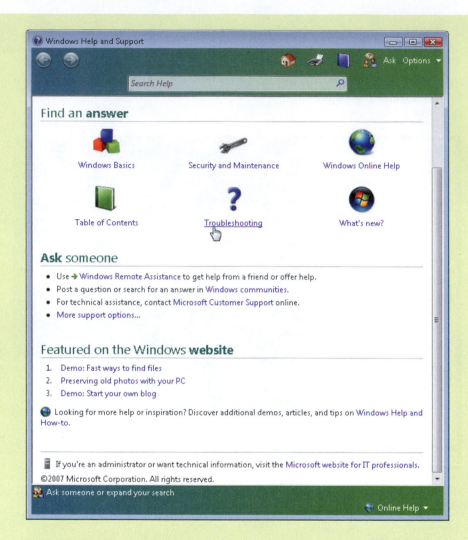

3. Click **Troubleshooting** to display the Troubleshooting in Windows page. In the Hardware and drivers section, point to *Tips for fixing common sound problems*, as shown in **Figure 8–10**.

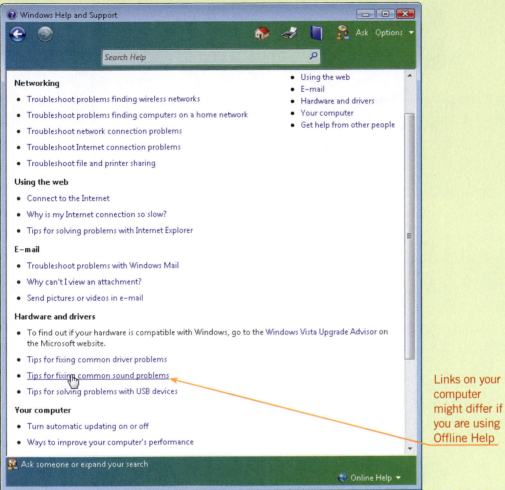

FIGURE 8–10
Troubleshooting in
Windows page

4. Click the **Tips for fixing common sound problems** link to display the Tips
   for fixing common sound problems page, shown in **Figure 8–11**.

FIGURE 8–11
Tips for fixing common sound problems page

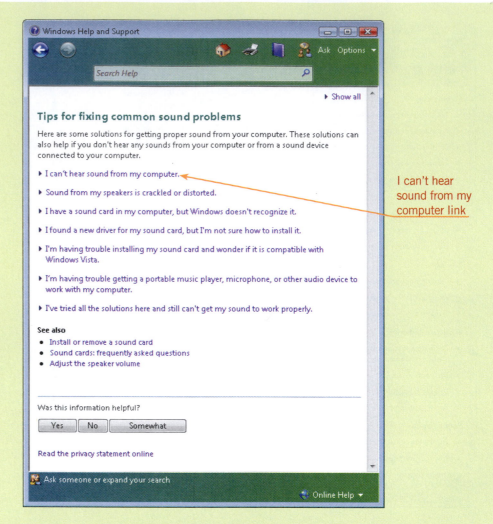

I can't hear sound from my computer link

5. Click the **I can't hear sound from my computer** link to display tips for solving this problem. See **Figure 8–12**.

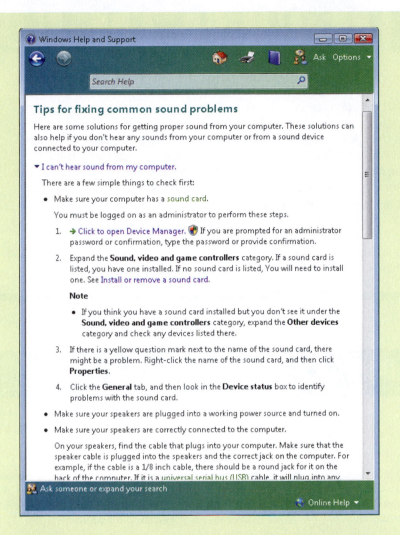

FIGURE 8–12
Suggestions for
fixing sound
problems

6. Read this information and then use your word-processing program to type a summary of options that could help correct this problem.

7. If necessary, scroll down and then click the **Sound from my speakers is crackled or distorted**. Read this information and then use your word-processing program to type a summary of options that could help correct this problem.

8. Submit your word-processing documents to your instructor.

TECHNOLOGY CAREERS

PC Support Specialist

The PC support specialist provides support for application software and related hardware via telephone or site visits to computer users.

As a PC support specialist, you need to be knowledgeable about current software and have good oral communication and organizational skills. You are required to interact with all departments within the company and with users who have varying skill levels ranging from novice to expert. You might be required to configure and maintain computer systems running Microsoft Windows, Macintosh OS X, or Linux. You might also test new technologies and techniques, develop and follow computer maintenance and backup procedures, manage upgrades and patches to the operating system and other software, and track computer problems and solutions.

A bachelor's degree is preferred for most of these jobs; however, impressive experience is also accepted. Experience performing actual hands-on hardware and software upgrades is important.

SUMMARY

In this lesson, you learned:

- An operating system is system software that enables computer hardware to communicate and operate with the application software. Without an operating system, a computer would not function because the operating system manages and coordinates the activities and resources of the computer.

- Operating systems provide a consistent way for applications to communicate with hardware without duplicating settings or learning details about the hardware. They also perform system and file maintenance tasks.

- Windows, Mac OS X, and Linux are common operating systems for personal computers.

- Handheld and embedded operating systems, also known as mobile operating systems, are similar in principle to operating systems such as Windows or Linux. These systems, however, are smaller and generally less capable than desktop operating systems.

- To share files across operating system platforms, you can use solutions involving hardware, software, and data. For example, saving data or work files in the Rich Text Format means that most other operating systems can read the file.

- An operating system sets limitations to protect itself and the data on the computer. The operating system grants permission to you to perform some tasks but prevents you from performing others according to your user rights.

- The system administrator has unrestricted access to make systemwide changes to the computer, including those that affect other users. Without administrative rights, you cannot make changes such as system modifications, installing software, or changing network settings.

- Typical operating system problems include file incompatibility, file corruption, and disk crashes.

VOCABULARY REVIEW

Define the following terms:

administrative rights	file system	Palm OS
administrator account	handheld operating system	system administrator
driver	Linux	UNIX
embedded operating system	Mac OS X	Windows Embedded CE
emulation card	operating system (OS)	Windows Mobile

■ REVIEW QUESTIONS

TRUE / FALSE

Circle T if the statement is true or F if the statement is false.

T   F   **1.**   Handheld operating systems are smaller and less capable than desktop operating systems.

T   F   **2.**   The computer cannot run any applications without an operating system.

T   F   **3.**   Embedded operating systems reside on a ROM chip.

T   F   **4.**   Computer software is anything you can touch.

T   F   **5.**   An administrator is a local account or a local security group.

MULTIPLE CHOICE

Select the best response for the following statements.

1. _____ are programs used by the operating system to communicate with various hardware devices.

   A.   Drivers   C.   Borders

   B.   Mice   D.   Interfaces

2. Which document file type can be transferred from one operating system to another?

   A.   emulation files   C.   Rich Text Format (RTF)

   B.   Portable Transfer Documents   D.   networking files
       (PTD)

3. Files can become corrupt as the result of a _____.

   A.   power failure   C.   bad software installation

   B.   virus   D.   any of the above

4. The tasks an operating system allows you to perform are defined by your _____.

   A.   password   C.   user rights

   B.   system administrator   D.   user interface

5. The _____ operating system is considered a multitasking, portable operating system.

   A.   Apple Macintosh   C.   UNIX

   B.   IBM PC   D.   Windows

FILL IN THE BLANK

Complete the following sentences by writing the correct word or words in the blanks provided.

1. A handheld or _____ operating system can fit into the limited memory of mobile and handheld devices.

2. Software _____ programs allow a Macintosh to run Windows programs.

3. The _____ operating system is an open source program.

4. The _____ can grant administrative rights to other users.

5. Application software and files need to be _____ with the computer's operating system.

PROJECTS

PROJECT 8–1

Windows Disk Cleanup utility helps you free up space on your computer by deleting temporary and other unnecessary files from a drive. Complete the following:

1. Use Windows Help and Support and research this utility program.

2. In a word-processing document, explain the purpose of this utility and provide an example of how you would access the program and then use it.

PROJECT 8–2

Besides Windows, Mac OS X, and UNIX/Linux, other operating systems have been developed for personal computers. Complete the following:

1. Use your favorite search engine to research personal computer operating systems. (*Desktop operating systems* and *PC operating systems* are also good search terms.)

2. Select one that interests you and research its history, notable features, and innovations for its time.

3. Use your word-processing program to write a one-page report or give an oral report to the class.

PROJECT 8–3

IBM introduced its first IBM PC in 1981. With the introduction of this new microcomputer came a new operating system. This system was called DOS (Disk Operating System). IBM referred to this operating system as PC-DOS. Complete the following:

1. Use your favorite search engine to research DOS.

2. In a word-processing document, provide a brief overview of this operating system.

TEAMWORK PROJECT

You and two team members have been given the responsibility for purchasing new computers for your company's front office. One team member wants to purchase an Apple Macintosh with the latest version of the Mac operating system and the latest software suite; another wants to purchase a PC with the latest version of the Windows OS; and the third wants to purchase a PC with the UNIX operating system. The manager has requested that your team do some research and present her with a report so that she can make the best choice. Your report should include the positives and negatives for each of these operating systems. Also include information on how these computers could interact if more than one type of computer was selected.

CRITICAL THINKING

Assume you are a member of a team and your objective is to come up with three ideas on how the Windows Vista operating system can be improved. Provide a thorough explanation of why you think your ideas would make the operating system better and easier to use.

ONLINE DISCOVERY

Google Phone's operating system is called Android and is an open source mobile operating system. Use the Internet to research this topic. Use your word-processing program and write a one-page report that includes the following:

1. On which operating system is Android based?

2. What is the Apache license?

3. How long has Android been available as open source?

4. In what programming language is Android written?

5. What media formats are supported by Android?

Estimated Time:
1 hour

LESSON 9

Windows Management

■ OBJECTIVES

Upon completion of this lesson, you should be able to:

- Log on and off, shut down, and restart the computer.
- Identify elements of the operating system desktop.
- Identify the icons used to represent drives, disks, files, and folders.
- Manipulate windows.
- Start and run programs.
- Manage files.
- Identify precautions when manipulating files.
- Solve common file problems.

■ DATA FILES

You do not need data files to complete this lesson.

■ VOCABULARY

active window

application file

Computer

data file

directory

file properties

gadgets

hidden file

icons

Quick Launch toolbar

Recycle Bin

shortcut

Sidebar

system file

▶ VOCABULARY
Computer

The utility program *Computer* (called My Computer in Windows XP) is designed to help you find, view, and manage files easily and effectively. In earlier versions of Windows, My Computer and Windows Explorer were separate programs. In Windows XP, My Computer and Windows Explorer were the same program. Windows Vista also merges these tools into one window. All the disk and folder maintenance operations you use with Windows Explorer now are available through the Computer window. In this lesson, you will learn how to use options in the Computer window to control the display of files and folders.

1-3.2.1

Logging On and Off the Computer

To start Windows, you only need to turn on your computer. Windows automatically starts, and a Welcome screen is displayed. After a short time, the Windows Vista logo is displayed. If the computer is set to automatic logon, you are not required to type a user name or password. Otherwise, you log on to Windows by selecting your user name or picture, and then entering a password. The next screen that appears is the Welcome screen.

After completing your work, you log off the system to let another user work with Windows by clicking the Start button, pointing to the Lock Button menu, and then clicking Log Off. You can also end your session by selecting any of the other available options described in **Table 9–1**.

TABLE 9–1   Ending a Windows session

OPTION	METHOD
Switch User	Click the Switch User command to allow another user to log on; your programs continue to run in the background
Log Off	Click the Log Off command to close all open programs and the user account; the computer does not close down but instead continues running so that another user can log on
Lock	Click the Lock command to prevent any unauthorized users from logging on to the computer
Restart	Click the Restart command to shut down the system and then restart the computer
Sleep	Click the Sleep command to have Windows automatically save your documents and then power down to a low-power state; this option is useful for short intermissions away from the computer
Hibernate	Click the Hibernate command to have Windows automatically save your documents and then power down the computer; this option is useful for longer intermissions of a few hours or so
Shut Down	Click the Shut Down command to close all open programs and turn off the computer

Shutting Down an Application

Sometimes a Windows application stops functioning or does not respond, and you cannot close the program or perform any other tasks in Windows, such as turning off the computer. The following Step-by-Step exercise shows how to use the Task Manager to close an unresponsive application or process.

Step-by-Step 9.1

1. Right-click the **taskbar** and then click **Task Manager** or press **Ctrl+Shift+Esc** (press all three keys at the same time) to display Windows Task Manager shown in **Figure 9–1**. If necessary, click the **Applications** tab, which displays the applications that are currently running.

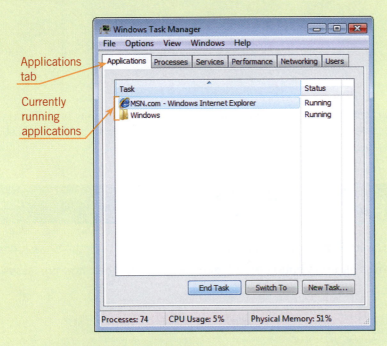

FIGURE 9–1
Windows Task Manager

Applications tab

Currently running applications

2. Click the **Processes** tab and then click the application you want to close; it will be highlighted in the Processes list (see **Figure 9–2** on the next page.) Click the **End Process** button. If a message appears requesting confirmation, click the **Continue** button. Leave Windows Task Manager open for the next Step-by-Step exercise.

FIGURE 9–2
Processes tab in Windows
Task Manager

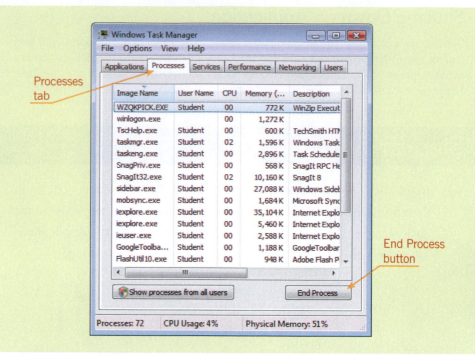

In other instances, an application or process may be running in the background. The following Step-by-Step exercise shows you how to force the application or process to close.

Step-by-Step 9.2

1. On the Processes tab of Windows Task Manager, click the **Show processes from all users** button as in **Figure 9–2** or click the **Show processes from all users** check box (see **Figure 9–3**).

FIGURE 9–3
Showing processes
from all users

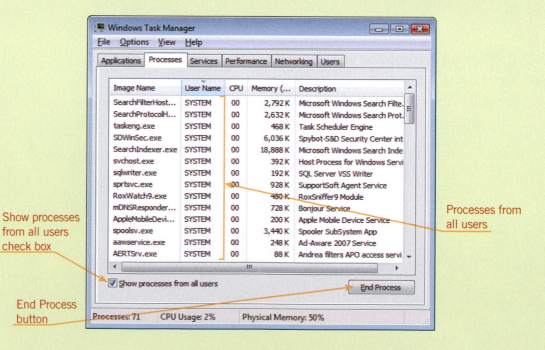

2. Click the application or process that you want to stop and then click the **End Process** button to close the selected application or process.

3. Close Windows Task Manager.

Desktop Elements

The Windows Vista desktop is the main screen area that you see after you turn on your computer. The objects on the desktop simulate a work area in an office. You can place objects on the desktop, delete the objects, move the objects, rename the objects, and so on. You can use these objects, called *icons*, as shortcuts to start a program, open a window, access a Web site, and perform various other applications. The *Recycle Bin* is a standard element and generally is installed and displayed when you start your computer for the first time. You use this icon to discard unnecessary items. The Recycle Bin stores the discarded items until you empty it. Depending on your computer, you may have additional icons displayed.

The desktop contains five main sections:

1. The taskbar, which is located at the bottom of the screen

2. The Start button, which opens the Start menu

3. The *Quick Launch toolbar*, which starts a program with one mouse click

4. The *Sidebar*, which displays small programs called *gadgets*

5. The middle section, which contains program and document icons

Customizing the Icons on the Desktop

If the default icons that are displayed on your desktop are not the icons that you prefer, you can easily modify these icons. Step-by-Step 9.3 shows how to modify the desktop icons.

1-3.2.2

▶ **VOCABULARY**

icon

Recycle Bin

Quick Launch toolbar

Sidebar

gadgets

Step-by-Step 9.3

1. Right-click an empty space on the desktop to display a shortcut menu. Click **Personalize** to display the Personalization window (see **Figure 9–4**).

FIGURE 9–4
Personalization window

Change desktop
icons link

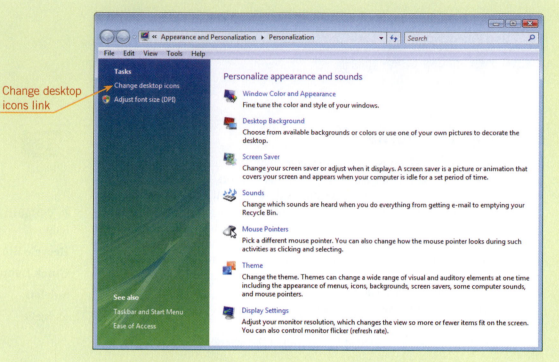

2. Click the **Change desktop icons** link in the Tasks column to display the Desktop Icon Settings dialog box (see **Figure 9–5**).

FIGURE 9–5
Desktop Icon Settings dialog box

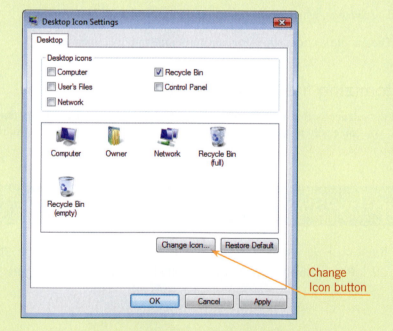

Change
Icon button

3. If necessary, click the **Computer** check box to display the Computer icon on the desktop.

4. Click the **Computer** icon in the Desktop Icon Settings dialog box, and then click the **Change Icon** button to display the Change Icon dialog box. Select an icon that you prefer (see **Figure 9–6**).

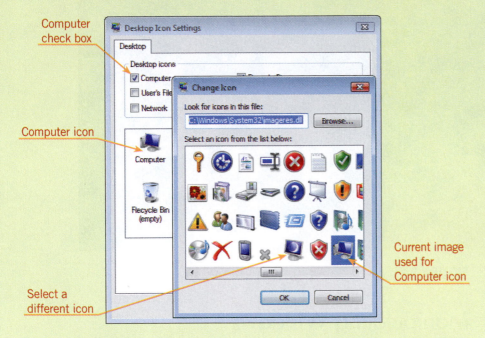

FIGURE 9–6
Change Icon dialog box

5. Click the **OK** button to close the Change Icon dialog box and then click the **Apply** button in the Desktop Icon Settings dialog box. Click the **OK** button to close the Desktop Icon Settings dialog box. Close the Personalization window.

Most users generally have a variety of icons located on the desktop that start a program, open a file, and so on. Some example icons for window types include program, document, help, games, instructional, folders, mail, and utilities. Each of these types of windows has its own special icon. For instance, folder icons contain additional folders and/or files. Microsoft Office Word has its own designated icon, as does Windows Mail. This standardization of icons helps you easily recognize various programs.

Other Graphical Elements

You can also add other items to the desktop. Windows Vista provides the Gadget Gallery, with a link to additional online gadgets. You can drag and drop these gadgets from the Gadgets window to the Windows Sidebar or elsewhere on the desktop. In **Figure 9–7**, the Sidebar contains three gadgets—a clock, a CPU meter, and the temperature. The currency gadget is located on the desktop.

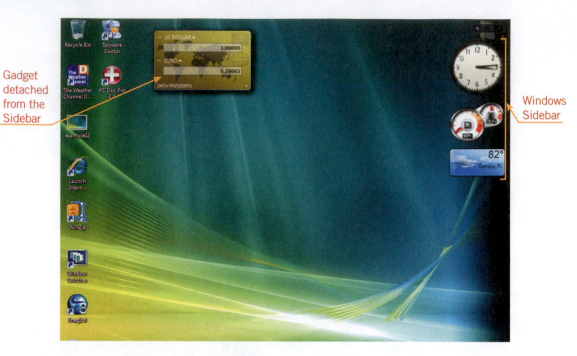

Gadget detached from the Sidebar

Windows Sidebar

FIGURE 9–7   Windows Sidebar and gadgets

1-3.2.3

Manipulating Windows

Similar to icons, Windows also contain standardized tools. You use three buttons on the Window title bar—the Minimize button, the Maximize/Restore button, and the Close button—to control the way in which a window is or is not displayed. **Figure 9–8** shows these buttons.

Close button

Minimize button   Restore Down button

FIGURE 9–8   Window manipulation buttons

- Click the Minimize button to minimize the window, but still keep it in memory; you can restore the window by clicking its button on the taskbar.
- Click the Restore Down button to display the window in less than a full screen. The button in this position becomes the Maximize button after you click the Restore Down button.
- Click the Maximize button to have the window fill the full screen.
- Click the Close button to close the window.

To minimize all open windows at one time using the mouse, click the Show desktop icon on the Quick Launch toolbar. Click it again to reopen all of the windows. To minimize all open windows using the keyboard, press the Windows logo key plus the letter "M".

Starting Programs and Switching Between Windows

1-3.2.4

To start a program in Windows Vista is a simple task. Click the Start button and then click the program name. You can also double-click the program icon located on the desktop. More than one program can be in memory at the same time. When multiple windows are open on your desktop, the one you are working with is called the *active window*. The active window is easy to recognize because its title bar is a different color or intensity. You can make any open window the active window in the following ways:

- If any portion of the window you want to work with is visible, click it. It moves to the front and becomes the active window.

- Press and hold down the Alt key; then press Tab. A small window appears in the center of the screen. The window contains icons for all items currently open, including items minimized on the taskbar. Hold down the Alt key and then press and release Tab to cycle through all the icons. A box surrounds the item's icon and a description appears at the bottom of the window as it is selected. When the one you want is selected, release the Alt key. That item comes to the front and becomes the active window. This is called the fast Alt+Tab method for switching to a different window.

Accessing Online Support

The Help and Support Center provides three options for online help:

- *Windows Remote Assistance*: Remote Assistance is a convenient way for someone you know to connect to your computer from another computer running Windows Vista, chat with you, and observe your computer screen as you work. With your permission, you can receive the remote user's keystrokes as if he or she were keying on your keyboard. In this way, you can watch the remote user demonstrate the solution to your problem. In this same category, you can also offer Remote Assistance or open a Remote Assistance invitation.

- *Windows communities*: Post a question or search for an answer in Windows communities.

- *Microsoft customer support*: Use this service to get support online from a technician who can answer your questions in e-mail, an online chat session, or by phone. This option also gives you access to newsgroups that can offer tips and guidelines about working with Windows Vista.

To access Help and Support, click the Start button and then click Help and Support.

Operating System Version

Windows Vista is available for purchase in four different versions: Home Basic, Home Premium, Business, and Ultimate. Microsoft regularly releases updates for the Windows Vista operating system. It is important to know the version of your software so that you use the correct update. To determine the version of the operating system you are using, complete the following Step-by-Step exercise:

▶ **VOCABULARY**
active window

▣ **EXTRA FOR EXPERTS**

Another way to switch between open windows is to click the Switch between windows button on the Quick Launch toolbar. If you are using Windows Vista with the Aero color scheme, you can also use Flip 3D, which previews all the open windows, without clicking the taskbar. To switch windows using Flip 3D, click the Windows Logo key and the Tab key, and then cycle through the windows as you do when you press Alt+Tab.

Step-by-Step 9.4

1. Click the **Start** button on the taskbar, and then click **Help and Support** to display the Windows Help and Support window.

2. In the Search Help text box, type **operating system version** and then press the **Enter** key.

3. When the results are displayed, click item number six or the item number with the question *Find which edition of Windows Vista you are using* to open another Help window.

4. The first option in the new window is **Click to open Welcome Center**. Click this option to display the Welcome Center. Information about your computer is displayed on the left in the top pane. You can view additional information about your computer by clicking the **Show more details** link.

1-3.2.5

Desktop Folders and Icons

The first task many people want to complete when they start using Windows is to customize the desktop to better suit how they work. Adding desktop folders and icons or shortcuts to the desktop helps you to create a personal environment best suited for your particular style and purpose. A *shortcut* is an icon that represents a link to an item, rather than the item itself. Shortcuts contain arrows on their icon. **Table 9–2** provides an overview of desktop customization methods.

▶ **VOCABULARY**

shortcut

TABLE 9–2   Desktop folders and icons

TASK	DESCRIPTION
Create desktop folders	Right-click a blank space on the desktop, point to New, and then click Folder to display a new folder. Type a name for the folder.
Create desktop icon/shortcut	Right-click a blank space on the desktop, point to New, and then click Shortcut to display the Create Shortcut dialog box. Click the Browse button to locate the location of the item, click OK, and then click the Next button in the Create Shortcut dialog box. Type a name for the shortcut and then click the Finish button to add the shortcut to the desktop.
Delete desktop folders and icons/shortcuts	To delete desktop folders and icons/shortcuts, right-click the item you want to delete, and then click Delete. The Delete File/Folder dialog box is displayed. Click Yes to move the file to the Recycle Bin or No to cancel the command.
Move and copy desktop folders and icons/shortcuts	Right-click the item you want to move and or copy to display the shortcut menu. To copy the item, click the Copy command and then right-click the desktop to display the shortcut menu. Click the Paste or Paste Shortcut command.
Rename desktop folders and icons/shortcuts	Right-click the item you want to rename to display the shortcut menu. Click the Rename command to edit the text.
Display properties of desktop folders and icons/shortcuts	Right-click the item for which you want to display the properties, and then click Properties on the shortcut menu. The type, location, size, and date of creation is displayed in the Properties dialog box.

Managing Files

1-3.2.6

As you have learned, you use folders to organize files on a disk, and folders are represented by icons that actually look like file folders. As you create and use folders and files, they often multiply over time. The utility program, Windows Computer, is designed to help you find, view, and manage files easily and effectively. The Computer window gives you control over the organization and management of your files and folders.

Displaying Files

Windows Computer provides tools you use to search for files and folders and to view details about the contents of the files and folders. Using Windows Computer, you can delete, copy, and move files and folders as necessary. To open the window, click the Start button and then click Computer, or double-click the Computer icon on your desktop to display the Computer window (see **Figure 9–9**).

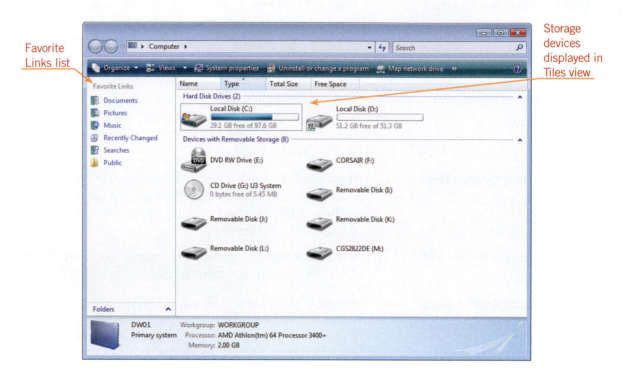

FIGURE 9–9 Computer window

In **Figure 9–9**, the Favorite Links list is displayed in the left pane and a list of storage devices is displayed in Tiles view in the right pane. The devices displayed in this figure include two local hard drives (C and D), a CD drive, a DVD drive, and several portable storage devices such as USB drives. Other storage devices could include remote devices such as those on a network or the Internet. In **Figure 9–10**, the selected view is Medium Icons. Clicking the Views menu, however, provides several other view options.

Click to display Views menu

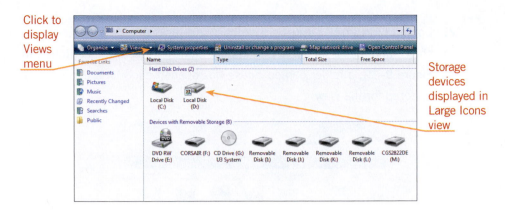

FIGURE 9–10   Computer window in Large Icons view

Windows uses a directory/folder structure to organize and store files. When the right pane of the Computer window contains a folder, you can double-click the folder to display the folder content. In the following Step-by-Step exercise, you view the contents of a folder.

Step-by-Step 9.5

1. Double-click the **Computer** icon on the desktop to display the Computer window, shown in **Figure 9–11**, which displays the window contents in Details view. The view displayed on your computer may be different than the one displayed in **Figure 9–11**.

Local Disk (C:)

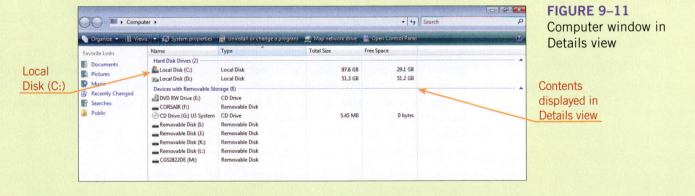

FIGURE 9–11
Computer window in Details view

Contents displayed in Details view

2. Double-click **Local Disk (C:)** or other hard disk. Select a folder of your choice and then double-click the folder name to display the contents. In **Figure 9–12**, a folder named *house* was opened and Medium Icons was selected for the view.

FIGURE 9–12
Contents of a folder in
Medium Icons view

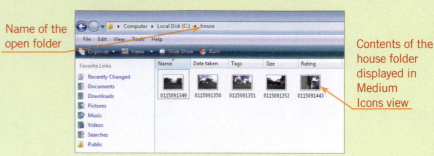

Name of the open folder

Contents of the house folder displayed in Medium Icons view

3. Click the **Views** button arrow and then drag the slider from one menu option to another to experiment with the other views.

File Types

A computer can contain three types of files: system files, application files, and data files. *System files* usually are found in the Windows or Program Files folder and are essential files necessary for running Windows. An *application file* is part of an application program, such as a word-processing program, a graphics program, and so on. A *data file* is one you create when working with an application program such as Microsoft Word.

Directory and File Views

A *directory*, or folder, is a container for files and other directories. Windows Vista generally uses the term *folder*, while operating systems such as Linux use the term *directory*. To view the contents of the folder, double-click the folder name. Using the Computer window, you can view files using these options: Extra Large Icons, Large Icons, Medium Icons, Small Icons, List, Details, and Tiles.

▶ **VOCABULARY**
system file
application file
data file
directory

Sorting Files

You can use the Computer window to sort files by name, size, type, date, or other characteristics. Sorting creates a list of files organized by that characteristic. You can sort the entire drive by selecting the hard drive letter, or sort the contents of a folder by name, date modified, and type. You can also sort the desktop by right-clicking an empty spot on the desktop, pointing to Sort By, and selecting Name, Size, Type, or Date modified.

Managing Folders

You use folders to store, manage, and organize files. To create a folder, go to the location (desktop or another folder) and right-click a blank spot on the desktop or folder window. Point to New on the shortcut menu, and then click Folder. Type a name for the new folder, and then press Enter.

Selecting Files

To select a single file, click the filename. To select a consecutive group of files, click the first item, hold down the Shift key, and then click the last item. Using the mouse pointer, you can also select a consecutive group of files by dragging the pointer around the outside of all of the items to be included. To select nonconsecutive files, click the first file, hold down the Ctrl key, and then click the next file.

Move, Copy, Delete, and Rename Files

To move a file, select the file and drag it to the new location. Or, select the file, right-click to display the shortcut menu, and then click Cut. Access the location where you want to move the file, right-click a blank spot in the folder window to display the shortcut menu, and then click Paste. You can use the same steps to *copy* a file by clicking Copy instead of Cut. To delete a file, click the filename, right-click it to display the shortcut menu, and then click Delete. To rename a file, click the filename, right-click it to display the shortcut menu, and then click Rename. Type the new name for the file.

 **EXTRA FOR EXPERTS**

Windows Vista hides filename extensions by default to make the names easier to read. You can still distinguish between a Word document named Budget and an Excel workbook named Budget because the file icons are different.

Retrieve Deleted Files

At some point, you may find that you have unintentionally deleted a file, folder, or other element. If the Recycle Bin has not been emptied and still contains the file, it can be restored. To restore a file, double-click the Recycle Bin to open it. Look through the files and then right-click the filename that you want to restore. When the shortcut menu is displayed, click Restore to restore the file to its original location.

Empty the Recycle Bin

Similar to the trash in your home or office, Windows Recycle Bin also needs to be emptied. To empty the Recycle Bin, right-click the Recycle Bin icon on the desktop and then select Empty Recycle Bin. A Delete File or Multiple Items warning box is displayed. Click the Yes button to permanently delete the files contained in the Recycle Bin or click the No button to cancel the command.

WARNING

If you choose to Empty the Recycle Bin, keep in mind that the files are deleted permanently and cannot be restored.

Display File Properties

File properties are characteristics that help you locate and organize files. The properties provide information about the selected file. You can view file properties for folders, documents, icons, images, and so on. To view the properties of a file, right-click the file, and then select Properties on the shortcut menu to display the Properties dialog box (see **Figure 9–13**). The Properties dialog box can contain a number of tabs: General, Sharing, Security, Previous Versions, Customize, and Compatibility. Most of these tabs contain information about the file. You use the Customize tab to add properties and other information to the file. The Compatibility tab relates to working with Windows.

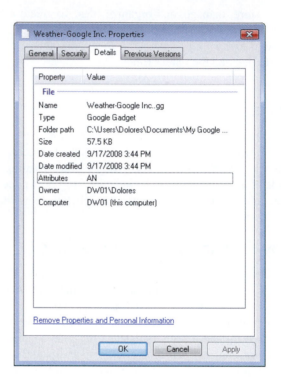

FIGURE 9–13   Properties dialog box for a file

Find Files

Windows Computer provides tools to help you search for files and folders, to find details about the contents of the files and folders, and to manage them—deleting, copying, and moving files and folders as necessary. **Figure 9–14** shows the Search text box, which is displayed in every Windows Vista folder window. In **Figure 9–14**, the Search pane is also open in the Computer window.

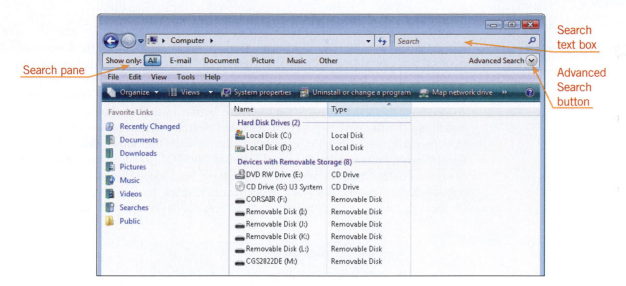

FIGURE 9–14 Search tools in the Computer window

To find a file or folder using the Search text box, click in the Search text box, and then type a word or part of a word. As you type, the contents of the folder are filtered to include each character you type. When you see the file you want, stop typing. After you search for a file or folder, the toolbar in the Computer window changes to include a Search Tools button. Click the Search Tools button and then click Search Pane to display the Search pane shown in **Figure 9–14**. You can use the Search pane to narrow your search as necessary. For example, you can search for only picture files that contain the search text you typed. Click the Advanced Search button on the Search pane to search for files by date, size, author, and other properties. To close the Search pane, click the Organize button on the toolbar, point to Layout, and then click Search Pane.

TECHNOLOGY TIMELINE

Logical Search Tools

In the 1840s, George Boole, a self-educated mathematician from England, developed ways of expressing logical processes using algebraic symbols. The Boolean logic uses words called "operators" to determine whether a statement is true or false. This Boolean logic has become the basis for computer database searches. The most common operators used are AND, OR, and NOT. These three simple words can be extremely helpful when searching for data. For example, if you search for "railroad AND models," the results include documents with both words. If you search for "railroad OR models," the results include the greatest amount of matches listing documents with either word. A good way to limit the search is to search for "railroad NOT models." The results then include all documents about railroads but not documents about models.

Display and Identify Hidden Files

A *hidden file* is a file like any other except it is not displayed in the Computer window. You can hide a file using the General tab in the Properties dialog box for the file. To hide a file, right-click the filename, and then click Properties to display the Properties dialog box. On the tab, click the Hidden check box (see **Figure 9–15**). To display a hidden file, click the Organize button in the window of the folder containing the file, and then click Folder and Search Options to open the Folder Options dialog box. Click the View tab, and then click the Show hidden files and folders option button under Advanced settings. Click OK to apply the settings and close the Folder Options dialog box. To remove the hidden attribute from a file, right-click the filename and select Properties to display the Properties dialog box. On the General tab, in the Attributes section, deselect the Hidden option.

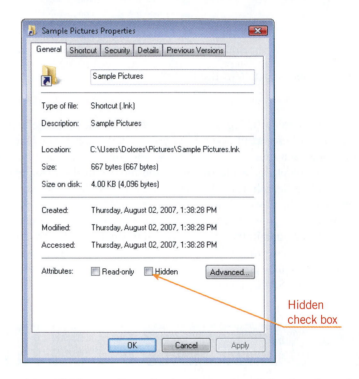

FIGURE 9–15   Hidden attribute in the Properties dialog box for selected file

1-3.2.7

Strategies for Working with Files

If you have worked with older versions of Windows, you might be familiar with the file-naming convention called "8.3" (pronounced "eight dot three"). The "eight" part means that a file's name may be up to eight characters long. The "three" part is an extension (no longer than three characters) to the name. And the "dot" is the period that separates the eight characters from the three characters. Neither spaces nor special characters can be used in this naming system. For example, in the filename *letter.doc*, the name is *letter*, the separator is the standard period, and the extension is *doc*.

Naming and Organizing Files and Folders

Newer versions of Windows, including Windows Vista, allow longer names (up to 255 characters) for folders and files, and allows spaces, punctuation marks, and some characters in the names. For example, you can name a folder *Myrtles Cookies and Cream* instead of a code name such as *myrtlecc*. In some instances, extensions also are longer. Examples include the "jpeg" extension, which is used for some graphics files, and the "html" extension, short for hypertext markup language, which is used to designate files in a format used for Web pages.

Similar naming conventions also apply to folder names. When you create a new folder (before you click anywhere else or press Enter), simply type the folder name. As you type, your folder name replaces the words *New Folder* below the folder's icon. Press Enter to display the new folder name. The folder name should indicate the content of the folder.

You may find that after you have used a folder for a time, you need to rename it. You can rename a folder in four ways:

- Click the folder in the contents pane to select it, press the F2 key, and then type the new name in the text box.
- Click the folder to select it, choose Rename from the File menu, and then type the new name in the text box.
- Right-click the folder name, choose Rename on the shortcut menu, and then type the new name in the text box.
- Click the folder you want to rename, click the Organize button on the toolbar, click Rename, and then type the new name in the text box.

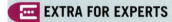

EXTRA FOR EXPERTS

Rename folders with care. Application programs will not work if they cannot locate the folder names they are searching for.

Deleting Unneeded Files and Folders

Deleting unused files and folders saves disk space, helps avoid clutter, and enables better access to the hard drive. You can delete a file or a folder in several ways:

- Click the file or folder to select it and then click Delete on the File menu.
- Click the file or folder to select it and then press the Delete key.
- Right-click the file or folder and then click Delete on the shortcut menu.

When you delete a folder or subfolder, you also delete all the files in it. Use extreme caution, therefore, before you delete a folder. To verify that is what you really want to do, Windows displays a Delete Folder message box. Windows also provides one additional safety net when you are deleting a folder from a hard disk. Folders deleted from a hard disk are transferred by default to the Recycle Bin, from which they can be recovered. A folder or a file deleted from a floppy disk, however, cannot be recovered. No Recycle Bin is available.

Backing up Files and Folders

Occasionally a hard drive fails or a particular file cannot be located. To protect these important documents, files and folders should be backed up to an external device on a regular basis. Depending on the size of the file or folder, the external device could be a USB drive, a CD, or an external hard drive. Another option is online storage.

1-3.2.8

Solving Common File Problems

Several problems can occur with files. For instance, you may "lose" a file, or a file could be hidden. A file could be protected with a password, or it could be a read-only file. Following are common problems associated with file management.

- You cannot find a file because it is hidden. As mentioned earlier, you can view hidden files by clicking the Organize button in the window of the folder containing the file, and then clicking Folder and Search Options to open the Folder Options dialog box. Click the View tab, and then click the Show hidden files and folders option button under Advanced settings. Click OK to apply the settings and close the Folder Options dialog box.

- Another file issue may be the result of a file being password protected. To view a password-protected file, you must know the password. Generally, password-protected files are located on a server or on a computer that is used by more than one person.

- Read-only files can be read or copied, but they cannot be modified. To make a change in a read-only file, you need to save it with a new filename.

- Occasionally, when attempting to open a file, you may receive a "file access denied" message. Generally, this type of file is on a network. In some instances, you might have access to the document but only be able to read it and not change it.

- When a file is not saved properly, it may become corrupted. This could happen with an intermittent power outage, a hard drive issue, and so on. When attempting to open this type of file, the Document Recovery task pane may be displayed. When this happens, there are two possibilities: (a) The program opens the file so you can continue your work, or (b) the Document Recovery task pane appears, with up to three recovered versions of your document. You can identify a version to keep. In some instances, the file may be damaged and not be recoverable.

- Different file types often are identified by the file extension—the three or four characters separated by a period from the file name. If the file extension is changed or deleted through an error, then the parent software program will not be able to open the file. To correct this situation, the file extension must be manually changed to the default program extension.

SUMMARY

In this lesson, you learned:

- To start Windows, you turn on your computer, and then, if necessary, log on by selecting your user name or picture and entering a password. To end your Windows session, you can log off and let another user work with Windows by clicking the Start button, pointing to the Lock Button menu, and then clicking Log Off.

- If you are working with an application that does not respond to your actions, you can use the Task Manager to close the nonresponsive application or process.

- The Windows Vista desktop is the main screen area that appears after you turn on your computer. You can place icons on the desktop that are shortcuts to start a program, open a window, or access a Web site, for example. You can also delete, move, and rename the icons on the desktop.

- The Recycle Bin appears on your desktop by default. You use the Recycle Bin to discard unnecessary items, such as folders. The Recycle Bin stores the discarded items until you empty it.

- The desktop contains five main sections: the taskbar, which is located at the bottom of the screen; the Start button, which opens the Start menu; the Quick Launch toolbar, which starts a program with one click; the Sidebar, which displays gadgets; and the middle section, which contains program and document icons.

- You use three buttons on the window title bar—the Minimize button, the Maximize/Restore button, and the Close button—to control the way in which a window is or is not displayed.

- To start a program in Windows Vista, you click the Start button and then click the program name. You can also double-click the program icon located on the desktop. More than one program can be in memory at the same time. When multiple windows are open on your desktop, the one you are working with is called the active window.

- To customize the desktop, you can create desktop folders, add desktop icons or shortcuts, and delete, move, and rename these objects.

- Windows Computer is designed to help you find, view, and manage files easily and effectively. Besides displaying files and folders, you use the Computer window to examine file types; change the view of the folder and its files; sort files; manage folders; select, move, copy, delete, and rename files; display file properties; and find files.

- You should take caution when manipulating files by using a standard naming convention when naming folders, by organizing files and folders logically, by deleting unnecessary files, and by regularly backing up important files.

- Be aware of common file management problems, including locating files that are difficult to find; learning how to work with attributes to open files that are read-only, hidden, or shared; and naming files to preserve their file extension so they are associated with the appropriate application.

VOCABULARY REVIEW

Define the following terms:

active window	file properties	Recycle Bin
application file	gadgets	shortcut
Computer	hidden file	Sidebar
data file	icon	system file
directory	Quick Launch toolbar	

REVIEW QUESTIONS

TRUE / FALSE

Circle T if the statement is true or F if the statement is false.

T   F   1.   To open the Computer window, you select Computer on the Start menu.

T   F   2.   When you turn on your computer, you have to click the Office button to start the computer.

T   F   3.   Click the Restore Down button to minimize a window, but still keep it in memory.

T   F   4.   When you select hibernate, Windows automatically saves your documents and then powers down the computer.

T   F   5.   If you delete a file by accident, you can restore the file even if you have emptied the Recycle Bin.

MULTIPLE CHOICE

Select the best response for the following statements.

1. The _____ is the main screen area that you see after you turn on your computer.

   A.   desktop   C.   Process tab

   B.   Task Manager   D.   Recycle Bin

2. _____ creates a list of files organized on a specific criterion.

   A. Searching   C. Exploring

   B. Sorting   D. Tiling

3. You can drag gadgets from the Gadgets window to the _____.

   A. Windows Sidebar   C. a word-processing document

   B. desktop   D. A and B

4. The Windows Sidebar can contain which of the following gadgets?

   A. clock   C. temperature

   B. CPU meter   D. all of the above

5. _____ files are essential files necessary for running Windows.

   A. Database   C. Application

   B. System   D. Data

FILL IN THE BLANK

1. The _____ is used to discard unnecessary files.

2. The window on which you are working is called the _____.

3. Windows Vista is available in _____ different versions.

4. A word-processing program is an example of a(n) _____ program.

5. A(n) _____ is an item that represents a link to the item, rather than the item itself.

■ PROJECTS

PROJECT 9–1

Details view in the Computer window provides information regarding the storage media devices on your computer. Complete the following:

1. Using Details view, select the various media devices on your computer.

2. Create a list indicating the total size, free space, and number of items on each device. To display the number of items, double-click the storage device icon. The number of items is indicated in the Details pane.

PROJECT 9–2

Windows System Restore can help fix problems that are causing your computer to run slowly or not respond. Complete the following:

1. Use Windows Help and Support to review the Windows System Restore feature.

2. Use your word-processing program and write a short overview of what you learned.

PROJECT 9–3

When you are online, Windows can check for updates and install them automatically. On the other hand, you can also select to manually install updates. Complete the following:

1. Do you think it is better to have the updates installed automatically, or would you prefer to do it yourself?

2. Use your word-processing program and compose a paragraph explaining your views.

■ WEB PROJECT

Windows Vista includes the Backup and Restore tool, but many other backup programs are available that work with Windows Vista. Complete the following:

1. Using your favorite search engine, research backup and restore programs for Windows Vista online.

2. Select three programs and create a table that compares at least five features in each program.

TEAMWORK PROJECT

Windows Vista includes many tools and techniques for finding files. Complete the following:

1. Team up with one or two of your classmates and research the four following ways to find files: using file list headings, using the Search folder and saving a search, using tags, by

creating advanced searches in the Search text box, and using the Start menu.

2. Create an outline that lists the major steps for the four ways that you selected to find files.

CRITICAL THINKING

Windows Vista includes 11 accessibility options. Complete the following:

1. Visit the Microsoft Web site at *www.microsoft.com/enable/ products/windowsvista*.

2. Select three of the accessibility options, and read all the information provided about each one.

3. In a word-processing document, describe each option and give examples of how someone could use the option.

ONLINE DISCOVERY

Office Live is a free online workspace where you can store all types of documents, even those not created with Microsoft Office. Complete the following:

1. Visit the Office Live Web site at *www.officelive.com*, read about the Office Live service, and then create and save a document with a bulleted list of the top five features of Office Live.

2. On the Office Live home page, click the Get a Free Workspace button (or similar option) to set up a free Office Live account.

3. In the Office Live Workspace, click Add Documents, and then copy to your workspace the document with the bulleted list of Office Live features.

4. Click the check box for the document, and then click Share and Share Document.

5. In the Editors and Viewers text box, enter your instructor's e-mail address, and then send the e-mail to your instructor.

Estimated Time:
1.5 hours

LESSON 10

Operating System Customization

■ OBJECTIVES

Upon completion of this lesson, you should be able to:

■ Understand the settings on the Control Panel.

■ Identify different Control Panel and system preference settings.

■ Change settings.

■ Display a list of installed printers.

■ Describe system settings and modifications to system settings.

■ Describe how to install and uninstall software.

■ Identify common problems related to installing and uninstalling application programs.

■ DATA FILES

You do not need data files to complete this lesson.

■ VOCABULARY

Appearance and Personalization category

Clock, Language, and Region category

Control Panel

Ease of Access category

Hardware and Sound category

Mail Setup

Network and Internet category

notification area

Program Compatibility Wizard

Programs category

Security category

Startup program

System and Maintenance category

System Restore

system settings

User Accounts category

Windows CardSpace

Windows Vista provides a number of ways to change system preferences and settings and to install and uninstall hardware and software. You can access most operations through the Windows Control Panel. This lesson focuses on how to use the Control Panel to view and modify preferences.

1-3.3.1

▶ **VOCABULARY**
Control Panel

Using the Control Panel

You use the *Control Panel* to change and customize settings on your computer, such as the desktop, time zone, and account picture. Recall that the left pane of the Start menu includes a list of programs. The right pane has links to some of the more commonly used programs and commands. One of these commands is the Control Panel. To open the Control Panel, click the Start button and then click the Control Panel link on the Start menu (see **Figure 10–1**).

FIGURE 10–1   Selecting Control Panel on the Start menu

Clicking the Control Panel command displays the window shown in **Figure 10–2**.

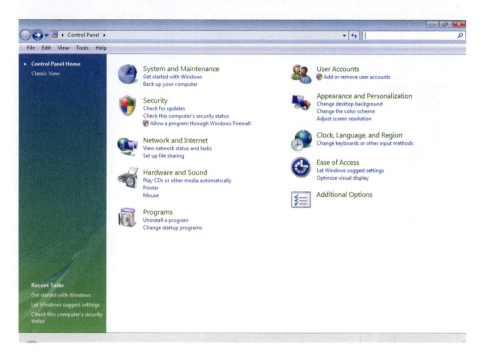

FIGURE 10–2   Control Panel

This section provides an overview of the Control Panel categories, including a brief explanation of how to apply these features. In each case, the settings and options on your computer might be different depending on the hardware and software installed.

▶ **VOCABULARY**

System and Maintenance category

Security category

The *System and Maintenance category* includes settings for a variety of system tasks, such as backup and restore, systems options, power options, Windows Update, and so on. **Figure 10–3** provides an overview of the options within this window.

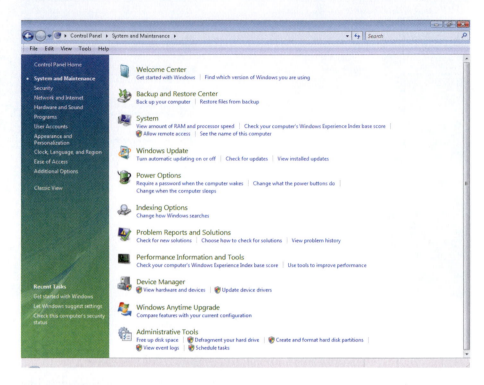

FIGURE 10–3   System and Maintenance window

Use the options in the *Security category* to check for Windows updates and for Windows security features. **Figure 10–4** shows a list of the security choices.

FIGURE 10–4   Security window

The options in the ***Network and Internet category*** help you connect to and view a network and network computers and devices, sync with other computers, and perform other networking tasks. **Figure 10–5** provides an overview of the other options accessed through this feature.

▶ **VOCABULARY**
Network and Internet category
Hardware and Sound category

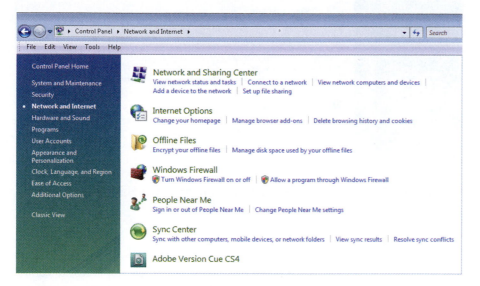

FIGURE 10–5 Network and Internet window

The settings in the ***Hardware and Sound category*** let you manage hardware devices such as printers, the mouse, and the keyboard, for example. You can also set power options and personalize the display. See **Figures 10–6a** and **10–6b** for other features available through this option.

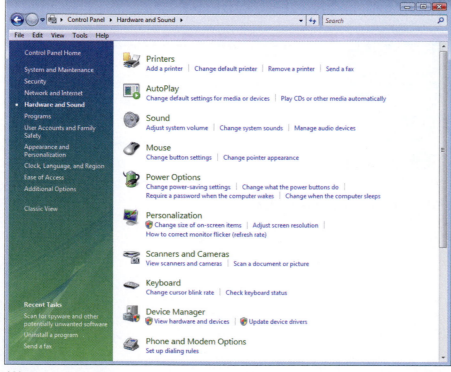

(A)

FIGURE 10–6 (A) First 10 options in the Hardware and Sound window (*continued*)

(B)

FIGURE 10–6   (*continued*) (B) Last five options in the Hardware and Sound window

The ***Programs category*** provides options to install, change, or remove software and Windows components; see a list of installed software; control access to certain programs; and add gadgets to the Sidebar. **Figure 10–7** shows a list of these options.

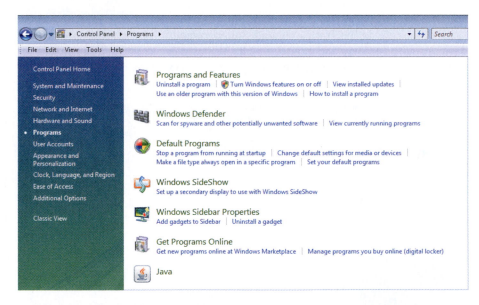

FIGURE 10–7   Programs window

Using the *User Accounts category*, you can change user accounts and passwords; change a user's mail profile, and change your Windows password (see **Figure 10–8**). Your window might contain the User Accounts and Family Safety category.

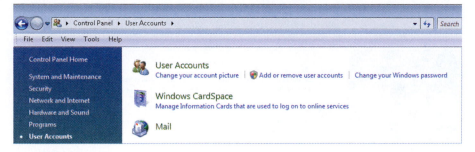

FIGURE 10–8   User Accounts window

The *Appearance and Personalization category* provides options to personalize the desktop by selecting a new color scheme, changing the background, adjusting the screen resolution, and so on. **Figure 10–9** shows the other options that can be modified.

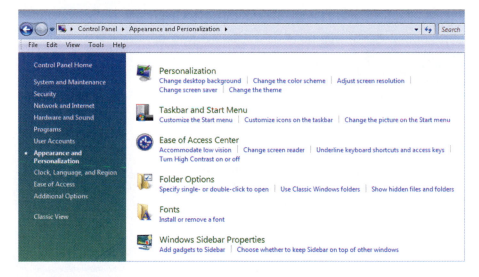

FIGURE 10–9   Appearance and Personalization window

MODULE 1   Computing Fundamentals

Clock, Language, and Region category

Ease of Access category

Use the options in the ***Clock, Language, and Region category*** to change the language your system uses or the date, time, or time zone; and change the way numbers, currency, dates, and times are formatted and displayed (see **Figure 10–10**).

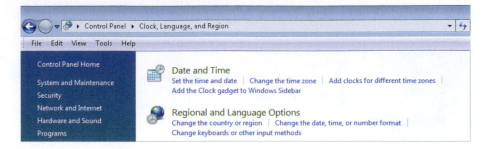

FIGURE 10–10   Clock, Language, and Region category

In the ***Ease of Access category***, you can adjust hardware and operating system settings for users with vision, hearing, and mobility disabilities (see **Figure 10–11**).

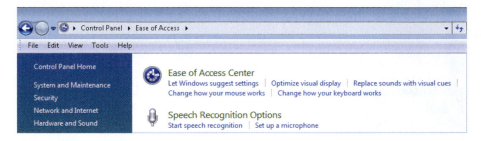

FIGURE 10–11   Ease of Access window

The Additional Options category includes specialized programs such as QuickTime or Weather Services (see **Figure 10–12**). The specialized programs on your computer most likely are different.

FIGURE 10–12   Additional Options window

If the computer on which you are working is a networked computer, you may not have permission to change all the Control Panel settings. The network administrator can restrict access to settings to prevent unauthorized users from making changes that can affect other users in a network. Examples include creating a new user account or altering regional or language settings. Some hardware settings that control peripherals (such as printers and modems) are allocated through the network and can be protected so that changes made by one user will not affect the entire network.

In Step-by-Step 10.1, you open the Control Panel and then change the screen saver.

Step-by-Step 10.1

1. Click the **Start** button ⊞ on the taskbar, and then click **Control Panel** to display the Control Panel window. (If the Classic view is selected, click the **Control Panel Home** link in the left pane to switch to Category view.)

2. Click the **Appearance and Personalization** category in the right pane.

3. In the Appearance and Personalization window, click **Change screen saver** in the Personalization category to open the Screen Saver Settings dialog box (see **Figure 10–13**). The screen saver on your computer might be different.

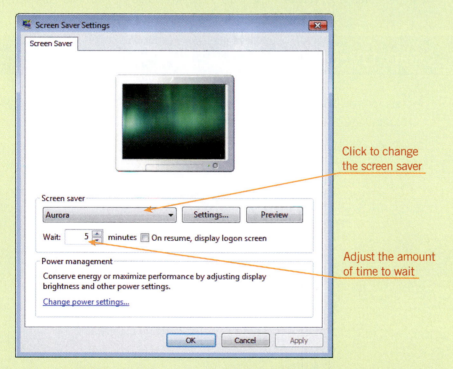

Click to change the screen saver

Adjust the amount of time to wait

FIGURE 10–13
Screen Saver Settings dialog box

4. Click the **Screen saver** button, and then click a different screen saver.

5. Click in the **Wait** text box, and then enter the number of minutes you want the computer to wait before the screen saver starts. Use your word-processing program to open a new document, and then type **Step-by-Step 10.1** at the top of the page. Describe the two changes you made in the Screen Saver Settings dialog box. Save your document using the filename **ic3_ch10**. Keep the document open for Step-by-Step 10.2.

6. Click **OK** to accept the settings. Then click the **Back** button ⊙ until you return to the Control Panel window.

7. Leave the Control Panel window open for the next Step-by-Step exercise.

Selecting Control Panel Settings

1-3.3.2

As noted earlier in this lesson, the Control Panel lets you view and manipulate basic operating system settings and controls. You use some options to change the appearance of the screen or to modify the behavior of input devices. Other options affect various functions such as security or disability settings. The Control Panel has two views: Control Panel Home (Category view) and Classic view. This lesson uses the Control Panel Home view.

Common Control Panel System Settings

1-3.3.3

The following step-by-step exercises illustrate how to change typical settings such as date and time, display settings, audio volume, mouse and keyboard, disability settings, and security settings.

Date and Time Settings

In Step-by-Step 10.2, you use the Control Panel to change the Date and Time settings.

Step-by-Step 10.2

1. If necessary, display the Control Panel window. Click the **Clock, Language, and Region** link (refer back to **Figure 10–10**).

2. Click the **Date and Time** link to display the Date and Time dialog box (see **Figure 10–14**).

FIGURE 10–14
Date and Time dialog box

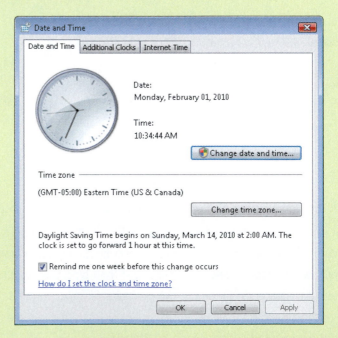

3. The Date and Time tab displays the current date and time. Click the **Change date and time** button to display the Date and Time Settings dialog box. (If a User Account Control dialog box opens, click the **Continue** button and enter a password, if requested.) Review the settings and then click the **OK** button to return to the Date and Time dialog box.

4. Click the **Change time zone** button to display the Time Zone Settings dialog box. The Automatically adjust clock for Daylight Saving Time box should be checked. Click the **OK** button to return to the Date and Time dialog box.

5. Click the **Additional Clocks** tab. Note that through this dialog box, you can select additional clocks to display the time in other time zones.

6. Click the **Internet Time** tab (see **Figure 10–15**). Note that the computer in **Figure 10–15** is set to synchronize with *time.windows.com*. (Your computer might be set to synchronize with a different Web site.) Close the Date and Time dialog box.

FIGURE 10–15
Internet Time tab in the Date and Time dialog box

7. Click the **Back** button ◀ to return to the Control Panel window. Click the **Hardware and Sound** link and then click the **Sound** link to display the Sound dialog box (see **Figure 10–16**). This same dialog box also is displayed when you click the Manage audio devices link.

FIGURE 10–16
Sound dialog box

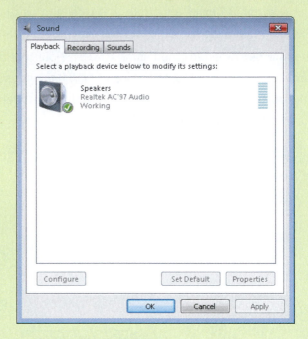

8. If necessary, click the **Playback** tab, and then review the information and settings on the tab. Do the same for the **Recording** and **Sounds** tabs. Click the **Cancel** button to close the dialog box.

9. Click the **Adjust system volume** link to display the Volume Mixer dialog box. In the Volume Mixer dialog box, drag the **slide control** for the speakers to make the volume slightly louder. You might hear a sound when you adjust the setting.

10. Click the **Close** button to close the dialog box and save the change you made to the volume setting.

11. If necessary, open your **ic3_ch10** word-processing document. Enter **Step-by-Step 10.2** as a new heading. Then write a paragraph describing what you learned in this exercise.

In addition to using the Control Panel, you also can change some settings by double-clicking the appropriate icon on the right side of the taskbar, which is called the *notification area*. See **Figure 10–17**.

▶ **VOCABULARY**
notification area

FIGURE 10–17   Notification area of the Windows Vista taskbar

Different icons may appear in the notification area depending on the way your taskbar is customized. For example, clicking the time display opens the Date and Time Properties dialog box, If you have an icon that looks like a horn or speaker, you can click it to open the Volume Control dialog box and then adjust the speaker volume.

Mouse and Keyboard Settings

Mouse and keyboard settings also can be changed to meet your particular needs and requirements. In Step-by-Step 10.3, you explore how to change mouse and keyboard options.

Step-by-Step 10.3

1. If necessary, open the Control Panel, and then click the **Hardware and Sound** link.

2. In the Mouse category, click **Change button settings** to display the Mouse Properties dialog box (see **Figure 10–18**).

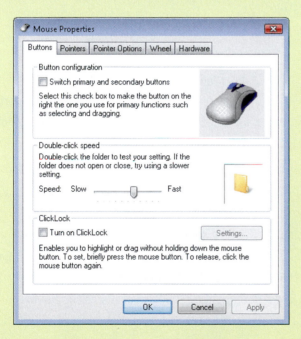

FIGURE 10–18
Mouse Properties dialog box

3. Review each of the five tabs in the Mouse Properties dialog box: Buttons, Pointers, Pointer Options, Wheel, and Hardware. Then click the **Cancel** button to close the dialog box without changing any settings and return to the Hardware and Sound page.

4. Click the **Keyboard** link to display the Keyboard Properties dialog box and to review the Keyboard settings (see **Figure 10–19**). Then click **OK** to close the Keyboard Properties dialog box.

FIGURE 10–19
Keyboard Properties dialog box

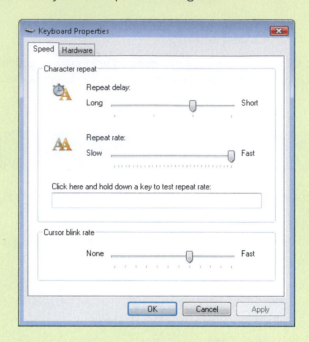

5. If necessary, open your **ic3_ch10** word-processing document. Enter **Step-by-Step 10.3** as a new heading. Enter **Mouse Properties** as a sub-heading. Write a short description of each of the five options contained in the Mouse Properties dialog box.

6. Click the **Back** button ⬅ until you return to the Control Panel window.

7. Click the **Ease of Access** link (refer back to **Figure 10–11**). Review the five options in this window: Let Windows suggest settings, Optimize visual display, Replace sounds with visual cues, Change how your mouse works, and Change how your keyboard works. Then click **Ease of Access Center** to display disability options. On the Step-by-Step 10.3 page of the ic3_ch10 document, enter **Ease of Access** as a subheading, and then describe the Ease of Access options. Save the ic3_ch10 document.

8. Click the **Back** button ⬅ to return to the **Ease of Access** page. Click the **Speech Recognition Options** and review the various options (see **Figure 10–20**). When you're finished, close the Speech Recognition Options window.

FIGURE 10–20
Speech Recognition Options window

Security Settings

Windows contains a number of security options. All of the options are in one central location that is accessed easily: the Security Center. On the Control Panel Home page, click the Security link to display the Security options (refer back to **Figure 10–4**). The following provides an overview of the Windows Vista Security Center options.

- *Security Center*: Provides options to check for updates, check the computer's security status, turn automatic updating on or off, check firewall status, and require a password when the computer wakes

- *Windows Firewall*: Monitors the system to verify that a firewall is installed, determines if the firewall should be on or off, and determines if a program should be allowed through the firewall

- *Windows Update*: Turns automatic updating on or off, checks for updates, and views installed updates

- *Windows Defender*: Scans for spyware and other unwanted software

- *Internet Options*: Includes changing security settings, deleting browsing history and cookies, and managing browser add-ons

ETHICS IN TECHNOLOGY

Spyware and Phishing

As you know, harmful software such as viruses are programs that are attached to a file and run when you open the file. Another type of harmful software is spyware, which is software that secretly monitors your computer activity and collects personal or private information such as credit card numbers and passwords. Windows Vista includes a tool called Windows Defender to protect against spyware. You can access Windows Defender from the Control Panel.

When spyware installs itself on your computer, it can change system settings, interrupt programs, and generally slow down your computer. Spyware often infects your computer when you visit certain Web sites or download a free program, such as a screen saver or search toolbar.

Occasionally, a type of spyware called adware changes your browser settings to open pop-up ads or divert your browser to Web sites that advertise a product or service. These Web sites might be phishing sites, which attempt to deceive you into revealing personal or financial information. Phishing sites often look like official sites by including logos from reputable businesses, and provide text boxes for entering sensitive information such as account numbers and passwords. Beware of any upsetting or exciting but false statements in an e-mail message or Web site that want you to react immediately by providing sensitive information. Always make sure you're using a secure Web site when submitting credit card or other confidential information by verifying the address in the Address bar, looking for a Web address that starts with "*https*" and verifying a security lock icon appears in the browser's status bar. Some phishing sites can display fake versions of these security devices, so the best advice is to avoid providing any information unless you know or can verify the recipient.

1-3.3.4

Printers

You may have access to one or more printers or have several printers installed on your computer. Using the Printers option, located on the Hardware and Sound page, makes it easy to add or remove printers. The following Step-by-Step exercise shows how to display and update printers.

Step-by-Step 10.4

1. If necessary, open the Control Panel. Click **Hardware and Sound**, and then click Printers. The available printers and fax devices appear in the right pane, and the toolbar includes buttons for performing common tasks (see **Figure 10–21**). Click a printer to select it. Most likely your list will be different from that in **Figure 10–21**.

FIGURE 10–21
Printers window

2. To add a printer, click the **Add a printer** button on the toolbar to start the Add Printer Wizard. Click **Add a local printer**, and then click **Next** on the next three dialog boxes to review printer information. Click the **Cancel** button to return to the Printers window.

3. To change the default printer, select the printer you want to use as the default, and then click the **Set as default** button on the toolbar. Click the **Select printing preferences** button to display the Printing Preferences dialog box.

4. Review each tab in the Printing Preferences dialog box. If necessary, open your **ic3_ch10** word-processing document. Enter **Step-by-Step 10.4** as a new heading, and then write a short description of each of the three options contained in the Printing Preferences dialog box. Close the Printing Preferences dialog box.

5. To remove a printer, select the printer, and then click the **Delete this printer** button.

6. In the Address bar of the Printers window, click **Hardware and Sound** to return to the Hardware and Sound window.

7. In the Printers category, click **Send a fax**. The Windows Fax and Scan window opens (see **Figure 10–22**). Note the options in this window: New Fax, New Scan, Reply, Forward as E-mail, and Receive a Fax Now.

FIGURE 10–22
Windows Fax and Scan window

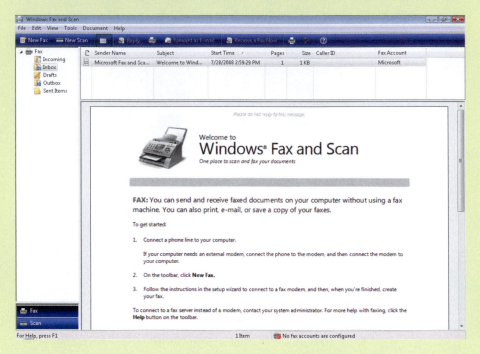

8. Close the Windows Fax and Scan window, and then close the Hardware and Sound window.

1-3.3.5

Changing System Settings

As you have learned, if you have permission within your particular environment, you can use the Control Panel to change your computer's *system settings*. When making changes to the settings, however, it is important to understand the effect the change will have on the computer. For example, suppose you incorrectly change the system date and/or time. This will prevent your documents, e-mails, and other files from displaying the correct date/time. Or, you select a printer not connected to your network or make a change to your Internet connection. This type of change could result in endless hours of trying to resolve the problem. In some instances, you may not be able to make changes. If you are connected to a network, for example, you might not have permission to change specific settings.

When you do make changes, it is a good idea to record the original settings. If the new settings are not correct or need to be returned to the original settings, you have access to these settings.

If you do change a system setting that makes your system unstable, you can use Windows System Restore. *System Restore* creates and saves restore points on a regular basis. If an issue occurs and the system is not working correctly, you can use this feature to return the system files to an earlier point in time. To access System Restore, select the Control Panel and then type System Restore in the search box.

Installing and Uninstalling Software

1-3.3.6

Your computer most likely has many software programs already installed. Based on the installation media, it may be necessary to make a backup of the program. If the media is on a CD or DVD, most likely a backup is not necessary. The CD or DVD should be stored in a safe place. It also is a good idea to record the product key provided with the installation package. You can write the number on a label and attach it to the CD or DVD. If the software is downloaded from the Internet, then you can make a backup by copying the program to other media such as a CD, a USB drive, or an external hard drive. You also might consider e-mailing to yourself the product key for your software programs.

At some point, however, you will want to install a new program, or an updated version (upgrade) of a program you already have. An upgrade generally is not free, but usually costs less than purchasing the software for the first time. If an upgrade is made available, most likely it is to fix a problem or problems or to enhance an existing feature. In some instances, an upgrade may cause compatibility problems if you attempt to install the software on older hardware.

If you register with the software manufacturer, you may be notified of upgrades to the program by e-mail. You also can check the manufacturer's Web site for information about the most recent version of the software. Sometimes minor patches and updated material are offered to registered users at no cost.

Installing new or updated software is a simple procedure that starts by inserting a CD or DVD, or by downloading a program from the Internet. Step-by-Step 10.5 provides instructions on software installation from a CD or DVD. Depending on the software, however, the steps may be somewhat different.

Step-by-Step 10.5

1. Insert the installation disc into the appropriate drive, such as a CD or DVD drive.

2. Most likely an AutoPlay dialog box similar to the one in **Figure 10–23** will be displayed. Click **Run setup.exe**.

FIGURE 10–23
AutoPlay dialog box

If a dialog box or prompt is not displayed, then complete the following:

a.   If necessary, use the Computer window to change to the drive that contains the disc.

b.   If necessary, change the View to **Details**.

c.   Locate the file named Setup or Install and then double-click the filename.

d.   Generally, an installation wizard is displayed, and you might have to click a button to indicate that you agree to the software terms of use. After reading the terms, click the Yes or Continue button.

3.   When the installation is complete, the installation wizard might indicate that the computer needs to reboot before the program will be available. If you see this message, verify that all other programs are closed before clicking **OK** or **Finish** to reboot the system.

4.   After the computer restarts, double-click the **shortcut icon** on the desktop (or locate the name of the program in the All Programs list of the Start menu, and then click the program name).

5.   You might be requested to register the program. It is a good idea to register a new software program so that you can take advantage of technical support and upgrades offered by the software company. If you have an Internet connection, you can register the program online. If not, click the **Register Later** option to begin using the program.

The same basic instructions apply for installing downloaded software. To install software downloaded from the Internet, complete Step-by-Step 10.6.

Step-by-Step 10.6

1.   Download a file from a Web site, and then locate the file you downloaded. In many instances, you may need to unzip the file. If you do, right-click the filename, select **Open with WinZip** or select **Open With**, and then select the appropriate program to unzip the file. Make a note of the location of the unzipped files. If you don't have WinZip, you can double-click the file to open it and extract its contents using Windows Vista.

2.   Locate the unzipped files, and then look for the filename Setup or Install. Double-click the file and follow the prompts to install the software.

Uninstall Software Programs

When software programs become outdated or are no longer used, you should uninstall them from the computer's hard drive. Step-by-Step 10.7 provides instructions on how to remove (uninstall) software programs.

Step-by-Step 10.7

1. Open the Control Panel, and then click **Uninstall a program** in the Programs category. Wait a moment while Windows Vista compiles a list of installed programs.

2. If necessary, scroll the list to locate the name of the program you want to uninstall. Click the program name to select it (see **Figure 10–24**).

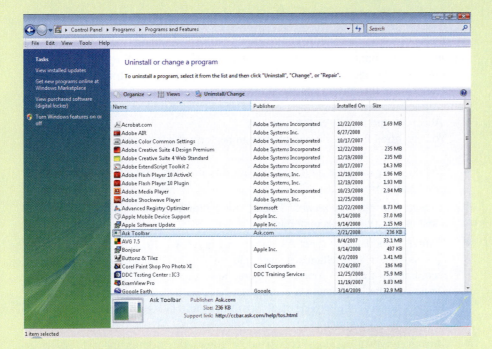

FIGURE 10–24
Programs and Features window

3. Click the **Uninstall/Change** button on the toolbar. A dialog box is displayed verifying that you want to remove the program. A User Account Control dialog box might also appear, asking you to verify that you want to continue and to enter a password. Click **Continue**.

4. To remove the program, click the **Yes** button. Click the **No** button or the Cancel button to leave the program installed on your computer. (These instructions might vary depending on the program you are removing.)

You use similar steps to install updates and upgrades to existing programs. An update is a fix for a specific problem in the software. If automatic updating is turned on, updates are installed automatically. Otherwise, to install an update, you need to review and then select the updates from the list that Windows finds for your computer. Optional updates are not installed automatically.

Software as a Service (SaaS)

Recall from Chapter 6 that Software as a Service (SaaS) is a type of software delivery method. The software is provided to customers through the Internet, an intranet, or another network. Bill Gates described the software "services wave" as the "next sea change that is upon us." To subscribe to a SaaS application, you must pay a monthly or annual subscription fee, and then access the software online. This eliminates factors such as hardware, installation fees, and upkeep. Some concerns with this model are the security of the data, the availability of the software program, and the control of the data.

User Accounts and Software Installation

Windows Vista has two types of user accounts: standard user accounts and administrator accounts. Standard users cannot install or uninstall applications in the root directory, change system settings, or perform other administrative tasks unless they can provide the correct password for the Administrator account. User Accounts options are accessed through the Control Panel. Clicking User Accounts opens the User Accounts and Family Safety window.

You can click the User Accounts link to perform the following tasks:

- *Change your account picture*: Clicking this link lets you select a new picture (see **Figure 10–25**).

- *Change your account name*: Clicking this option opens a window and provides a text box for a new account name.

- *Change your account type*: As shown in **Figure 10–26**, this window provides options to create a Standard user and an Administrator account. Microsoft recommends that everyone using a computer should have a Standard account. Doing so helps to protect your computer because it prevents users from making changes that affect everyone else. Recall that only the Administrator can install software on a computer.

- *Manage another account*: This window allows the Administrator to select an account and turn it on or off and to make other changes, including changing the account name, picture, and account type, creating a password, and deleting the account.

FIGURE 10–25   Change Your Picture window

FIGURE 10–26   Change Your Account Type window

Also available in the User Accounts window is ***Windows CardSpace***. This feature provides a system for creating relationships with Web sites and online services that use credit cards and membership cards for payment or credentials. Using Windows CardSpace, you can send information across the Internet or other networks to review the identity of a site, manage your information by using Information Cards, and review card information before you send it. Personal cards are cards that you create and managed cards are provided by businesses and organizations. The managed card generally contains credit card and membership card information. This information is encrypted before it is sent.

Mail is another option available in the User Accounts window. Using ***Mail Setup***, you can create e-mail accounts and directories, change settings for Outlook files, and set up multiple profiles of e-mail accounts and data files (see **Figure 10–27**).

FIGURE 10–27   Mail Setup dialog box

1-3.3.7

Troubleshooting Common Software Problems

Generally, software installation is a fairly smooth process. You insert the installation media, double-click the setup or install file, and follow the prompts. Occasionally, however, issues occur that prevent the installation for one reason or another. The following list describes some common installation problems.

- *Install/uninstall software on a network*: Software installation on a network generally is reserved for the administrator or other designated employees. If software is being installed or uninstalled on a computer connected to a network or another computer that does not contain your username or if you are not an administrator, a network policy may prohibit installation rights except for those individuals who have been approved. Contact the administrator or supervisor to resolve the issue.

- *Defective or lost installation media*: When installing software, you might not always want to install the entire program—you might not need all the features, for example, or have enough disk space. Later on, you might decide to add features and discover that the disk is damaged or missing. If you have registered your software or have proof of purchase, then in most instances you can contact the manufacturer and ask for a replacement disc. Depending on the company, a fee may be charged, or the company may provide the software free of charge.

- *Installation program will not start*: When you insert the CD or other disk, generally the **Startup program** runs automatically. When this does not occur, use the Computer program to view the CD and search for a file named setup.exe, startup.exe or install.exe. Double-click this program name to start the program. If this does not work, check the information that came with your file or go to the manufacturer's Web site.

- *Installation stops before completion*: If the program stops responding during installation, most likely there is a problem with the program. If this does not work, close the program and then restart it. If the program still will not work, there could be issues with your computer or the media could be damaged. Sometimes if you wait, some programs will start responding again. Your next step would be to view the manufacturer's Web site and see if there is a solution. If not, then contact the manufacturer. If a program is not working, most likely it means that a problem has occurred in the program itself. If a program freezes, you can press the Ctrl+Alt+Del keys or right-click the taskbar to display a shortcut menu, and then select Task Manager. In the Windows Task Manager dialog box, select the End Process button (see **Figure 10–28**).

- *Installed program is not displayed*: The program could be an older version that is not compatible with Windows Vista or a driver could be damaged or needs to be updated. Another possibility is that the executable file that starts the program could have been deleted or damaged. Reviewing the folder that contained the program files would verify if this was or was not the issue. Using Windows **Program Compatibility Wizard**, you can change the compatibility settings for the program. To access the Program Compatibility Wizard, click Programs in the Control Panel and then click Use an older program with this version of Windows.

- *Installed program fails to work*: Similar issues to those of programs that are not displayed. It could be an operating system compatibility problem, program files could be damaged and/or deleted, or it could be an incompatibility issue with other programs. Running Windows Program Compatibility Wizard would eliminate any compatibility issues. If this does not work, the program may have to be uninstalled and then reinstalled.

■ *Other programs fail to work after new product is installed*: This could be due to a conflict with another program. Virtualization tools, such as Virtual PC and VMware, are free downloads on the Internet. You can use these programs for compatibility testing. Some Vista background processes also can cause issues. Using the System Configuration Utility (MSCONFIG) can help resolve the background conflicts.

■ *Files cannot be read by new application*: Several reasons could account for this issue: a) you might not have permission to access the file; b) the file may be damaged; c) the file could have been created in an older version of the software and the newer version does not read older versions; d) the file does not have the correct extension; or e) the file may be encrypted. To check the file, right-click the filename and then click Properties. Click the General tab and then click Advanced. If the Encrypt contents to secure data check box is selected, open the file by using the certificate that was used to encrypt the file.

■ *Access to online application denied*: Several reasons could account for the denial. The logon could be incorrect or not activated; the site fee could be past due; or the site could be going through an update process. Wait for 10 minutes or so and then try to access the Web site again. Otherwise, contact the Web site through e-mail or telephone to determine the problem.

■ *Online application not available*: Several reasons could account for an online application not being available: the Web site could be down or the site could be busy with the maximum number of users. Wait for 10 minutes or so and then try to access the Web site again. Otherwise, contact the Web site through e-mail or telephone to determine the problem.

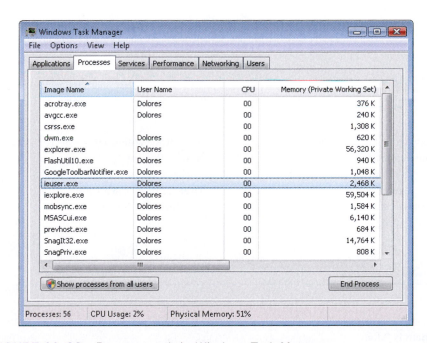

FIGURE 10–28   Processes tab in Windows Task Manager

SUMMARY

In this lesson, you learned:

- You use the Control Panel to change and customize settings on your computer. One popular category is System and Maintenance, which provides settings for a variety of system tasks, such as backup and restore, power options, and Windows Update. Another frequently used category is Appearance and Personalization, which provides options to personalize the desktop by selecting a new color scheme, changing the background, and adjusting the screen resolution.

- You also can change some system and program settings by double-clicking the appropriate icon in the notification area of the taskbar.

- The Windows Security Center provides options to check the computer's security status, turn Windows Firewall on or off, set up Windows Update for automatic updating, use Windows Defender to scan for harmful software, and set Internet security options.

- When you use the Control Panel to change your computer's system settings, make sure you understand the effect the change will have on the computer. It is also a good idea to record the original settings. If you do make a system change that makes your system unstable, you can use Windows System Restore, a built-in tool that creates and saves restore points on a regular basis.

- You can install software from installation media such as a CD or DVD, or from a file downloaded from a Web site. In either case, you follow similar steps: double-click the setup or install file, and then follow the prompts to install the software.

- To uninstall software, open the Control Panel, and then use the Uninstall a program link in the Programs category to remove the software from your computer.

- Windows Vista has two types of user accounts: standard user accounts and administrator accounts. Standard users cannot install or uninstall applications in the root directory, change system settings, or perform other administrative tasks unless they can provide the correct password for the Administrator account.

- Typical software problems include defective or lost installation media, an installation program that does not start or starts and then stops, an installed program that does not open, and other programs failing to work after a new product is installed.

 ## VOCABULARY REVIEW

Define the following terms:

Appearance and Personalization category
Clock, Language, and Region category
Control Panel
Ease of Access category
Hardware and Sound category
Mail Setup

Network and Internet category
notification area
Program Compatibility Wizard
Programs category
Security category
Startup program

System and Maintenance category
System Restore
system settings
User Accounts category
Windows CardSpace

REVIEW QUESTIONS

TRUE / FALSE

Circle T if the statement is true or F if the statement is false.

T   F   **1.**   The Control Panel is a part of the Microsoft Windows graphical user interface.

T   F   **2.**   If you change a system setting that makes your system unstable, your only option is to reinstall Windows.

T   F   **3.**   Installing new or updated software is difficult, and is best handled by a certified technician.

T   F   **4.**   Windows Defender can scan for spyware.

T   F   **5.**   If an installed program does not open, the program might be an older version that is not compatible with Windows Vista.

MULTIPLE CHOICE

Select the best response for the following statements.

1. You use the _____ in the Control Panel to adjust screen resolution.

    A.   System and Maintenance category

    B.   AutoPlay option

    C.   Sound category

    D.   Appearance and Personalization category

2. You can use the Windows _____ to accommodate low vision, change screen readers, and turn high contrast on or off.

    A.   Ease of Access Center   C.   Screen reader

    B.   Sidebar properties   D.   all of the above

3. In the Windows Mouse Properties dialog box, you can change _____.

    A.   button configurations   C.   vertical and horizontal scrolling

    B.   pointer options   D.   any of the above

4. To change the date and time, you would use the _____ option.

    A.   New Clock   C.   Time and Access

    B.   Clock, Language, and Region   D.   Current Time

5. When you insert an installation CD or DVD into the appropriate drive, generally the _____ runs automatically.

    A.   Programs window   C.   Startup program

    B.   screen saver   D.   Administrator account

FILL IN THE BLANK

Complete the following sentences by writing the correct word or words in the blanks provided.

1. You can change the desktop background through the Appearance Settings options of the _____ window.

2. If your computer system is not working correctly, you can use _____ _____ to return the system files to an earlier point in time.

3. In Windows Vista, only someone with a(n) _____ account can install software on a computer.

4. When software programs become outdated or are no longer used, you should _____ them from the computer.

5. If a program freezes, you can press the Ctrl+Alt+Del keys or right-click the taskbar to display a shortcut menu, and then select _____.

■ PROJECTS

PROJECT 10–1

The Control Panel provides access to information about what's new in Windows Vista. Complete the following:

1. Open the Control Panel and then click System and Maintenance.

2. Click Welcome Center and then click Get started with Windows. Review the information contained in the window.

3. Click the What's new in Windows Vista link. Read the information and then use your word-processing program to write a paragraph describing three new features. Explain why you think these features are valuable and how you could apply these features.

4. In the Get started with Windows window, click the Personalize Windows link. Find two ways to personalize Windows that have not been covered in this lesson or in Project 10-2. Add a paragraph to your document describing these features.

PROJECT 10–2

Windows Vista lets you select a set of colors, called a color scheme, to display on your desktop according to your preferences. Complete the following:

1. Open the Control Panel and then click Hardware and Sound.

2. Click Personalization and then click Window Color and Appearance to display the Appearance Settings dialog box. If you are using Windows Aero, a different window opens that also displays color schemes.

3. Review the various color schemes. Which color scheme do you prefer?

4. If you are not using Windows Aero, click the Effects button, and then click OK. What is the purpose of this button?

5. Click the Advanced button and describe the options that are available through the Advanced Appearance dialog box.

6. In a word-processing document, provide your written responses to Steps 3–5.

TEAMWORK PROJECT

One of your coworkers is collecting informal inventories of all employees' installed programs. She has requested a list of the software on your computer in the following categories: security, multimedia, and communications. Complete the following:

1. Working with another student, create a table that includes your name and the three categories of software your coworker requested: security, multimedia, and communications.

2. Add a column called "Location" that identifies where you found information about the program.

3. Complete the table using the Control Panel and other resources on your computer.

PROJECT 10–3

Many organizations and schools deny access to the Control Panel or to some system settings. Complete the following:

1. In a word-processing document, create a table that lists other advantages and disadvantages of providing access to Control Panel settings.

2. In a word-processing document, explain why you agree or disagree with the policy to prevent computer users from changing system settings.

■ CRITICAL THINKING

One popular use of the Control Panel is to change the desktop on your computer. Complete the following:

1. In one or two paragraphs, answer the following question: Beyond aesthetics, is there a practical use for applying a desktop background?

2. Include a brief explanation in your answer. If your answer is yes, include an example of a practical application. If your answer is no, cite an example of how a desktop background might impair productivity.

■ ONLINE DISCOVERY

Access Microsoft's Windows Vista Web page at *www.microsoft.com/windows/windows-vista* and then click the Compare Editions link.

A. How many versions are there of Windows Vista?

B. Which is the most expensive version?

Review the table containing the comparisons and then answer the following questions:

C. Which is the least expensive version?

D. Which version would you prefer and why?

MODULE 1 REVIEW

Computing Fundamentals

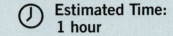

■ REVIEW QUESTIONS

TRUE / FALSE

Circle T if the statement is true or F if the statement is false.

T　F　**1.** A local area network connects one computer to other computers and peripheral devices within an office or building.

T　F　**2.** Output devices enable you to input data and commands into the computer, and input devices enable the computer to give you the results of the processed data.

T　F　**3.** An uninterruptible power supply (UPS) usually contains a battery that provides power if the normal current is interrupted.

T　F　**4.** Disk fragmentation occurs when a piece of data is broken up into many pieces that are not stored close together.

T　F　**5.** Each zero or one used in computer binary code is referred to as a byte of information.

T　F　**6.** Hardware is programming code written to provide instructions to the hardware so that specific tasks may be performed.

T　F　**7.** You use electronic spreadsheet software such as Microsoft Office Excel to evaluate, calculate, manipulate, analyze, and present numeric data.

T　F　**8.** An algorithm is a set of clearly defined, logical steps that solve a problem.

T　F　**9.** Windows Vista can be purchased in four different versions.

T　F　**10.** The Control Panel is used to change settings on your computer and to customize the display.

MULTIPLE CHOICE

Select the best response for each of the following statements.

1. The _____ is a circuit board that contains many integral components.

   A.　supercomputer　　　　　　　C.　motherboard

   B.　arithmetic/logic unit (ALU)　　D.　BIOS ROM

2. _____ produce an image by manipulating light within a layer of liquid crystal cells.

   A. Gas plasma monitors   C. CRT monitors

   B. LCD panels   D. Scanners

3. Damaged _____ can prevent peripheral devices from communicating with the computer.

   A. cables   C. humidity

   B. antivirus program   D. static electricity

4. _____ printers should be cleaned when print quality deteriorates or when toner cartridges are changed.

   A. Inkjet   C. Dot matrix

   B. Laser   D. Compact

5. A _____ is a list of services designed to provide assistance to a company or an organization.

   A. warranty   C. contract

   B. spreadsheet   D. support agreement

6. The two basic types of computer software are _____ and _____.

   A. program, application   C. application, system

   B. productivity, application   D. system, networking systems

7. A(n) _____ image is composed of pixels in a grid.

   A. access   C. pixel

   B. vector   D. bitmap

8. _____ are programs used by the operating system to communicate with various hardware devices.

   A. Drivers   C. Spreadsheets

   B. Mice   D. Interfaces

9. _____ files are essential files necessary for running Windows.

   A. Database   C. Application

   B. System   D. Data

10. When you insert an installation CD or DVD into the appropriate drive, generally the _____ runs automatically.

    A. Programs window   C. Startup program

    B. screen saver   D. Administrator account

FILL IN THE BLANK

Complete the following sentences by writing the correct word or words in the blanks provided.

1. You can think of RAM as _____-term memory.

2. The _____ port can connect up to 127 different peripherals with a single connector.

3. _____ _____ should be used on a regular basis on files that would be difficult or impossible to replace.

4. _____ scans for spyware and other unwanted software.

5. Computers require _____ on a regular schedule.

6. A(n) _____ shows different paths the program will take depending on what data is inputted.

7. In OLE, _____ is useful when information is maintained independently.

8. Application software and files need to be _____ with the computer's operating system.

9. The _____ is used to discard unnecessary files.

10. In Windows Vista, only someone with a(n) _____ account can install software on a computer.

PROJECTS

PROJECT 1–1

You can find many styles of keyboards for computers. Some designs were developed to address various health issues related to keyboard use. Use appropriate research sources to locate information on various keyboard designs and report on the theory on which they are designed. You also may visit retail stores that sell computers to obtain additional information. Prepare a written report outlining the information you located.

PROJECT 1–2

Use the Internet and other resources to locate information on how computers transmit data—broadband and baseband. Prepare a one-page report listing the difference between these two bandwidths. Provide examples of each.

PROJECT 1–3

You are ready to purchase a new computer, but are not sure what operating system you would like to have. Review the three operating systems discussed in Lesson 8 and then select the operating system you would prefer to use. Explain why you selected this particular system and describe at least three features that helped you make this decision.

PROJECT 1–4

You and your family have four computers in your house and have decided it is time for a wireless home network. You would like to share files and a printer. In a report of two or three pages, describe the type of equipment you need to set up the network. Also describe the type of software and security you need.

SIMULATION

You and a friend started a small computer consulting business. You offer technical support to computer users at home and at work, providing assistance with setting up hardware, troubleshooting problems, and using software effectively.

JOB 1–1

Your first client is a medical clinic. The clinic manager asks you to research and make suggestions on why the clinic's current computer system needs to be updated. Use the information you have learned in this module for your research, and supplement the information with research on the Internet or from print sources in the library. Prepare two reports. One report should list the pros of upgrading the system, and the second report should summarize the cons of not upgrading the system.

JOB 1–2

A new client wants to purchase new computers for himself, his spouse, and his two high-school age children. They will use the computers to work on job and school projects, manage family information, such as finances and college searches, and enjoy entertainment such as games and video. He has a budget of $5000. Use store ads, the Internet, catalogs, and other resources to identify the hardware and software he should purchase that would best meet the needs of the family. Prepare a written recommendation on the configuration you think will work best for your client.

ONLINE DISCOVERY

If you are looking for the meaning of a particular word, then you might want to use Google's definition feature. Google has two options you can use to find the definition of a word. First, you can type a word in the Google search box. If Google has the definition, then the word will appear in the right side of the blue bar that stretches across the top of your search results. If it is a one-word term, "[definition]" appears to the right of the word. Clicking that link will display the word's dictionary definition. If your search contains more than one word, each word will appear underlined. Simply click a word to view its dictionary definition. A second option is to type [*define:*] into the Google search box followed by the word or phrase for which you are searching. An example: *define: dictionary*.

Now, use Google's definition feature to find the definition of the following terms. Define each term in your own words: **VPN network**, **gateway** (in computer networking), **wireless network**, **extranet**, **CAT 6**, and **Satellite Internet**.

MODULE 2

KEY APPLICATIONS

KEY APPLICATIONS

LESSON 11
Exploring Microsoft Office 2007

2-1.1.1	2-1.1.7	2-1.2.3
2-1.1.2	2-1.1.8	2-1.2.4
2-1.1.3	2-1.1.9	2-1.2.5
2-1.1.4	2-1.2.2	2-1.2.6

Word Processing

LESSON 12
Getting Started with Word Essentials

2-1.1.3	2-1.1.7	2-1.3.1
2-1.1.5	2-1.2.1	2-2.1.6
2-1.1.6	2-1.2.4	

LESSON 13
Editing and Formatting Documents

2-1.1.7	2-1.4.1	2-2.1.4
2-1.3.2	2-1.4.2	2-2.1.5
2-1.3.3	2-2.1.1	2-2.1.7
2-1.3.4	2-2.1.2	2-2.1.16
2-1.3.5	2-2.1.3	2-2.2.1
2-1.3.6		

LESSON 14
Sharing Document

2-1.4.1	2-1.4.5	2-2.2.3
2-1.4.3	2-1.4.6	2-2.2.4
2-1.4.4	2-1.4.7	

LESSON 15
Working with Tables

2-2.1.3	2-2.1.13	2-2.1.14
2-2.1.15		

LESSON 16
Enhancing Documents

2-1.2.1	2-2.1.9	2-2.1.12
2-1.3.7	2-2.1.10	2-2.1.16
2-2.1.5	2-2.1.11	2-2.2.2
2-2.1.8		

Spreadsheets

LESSON 17
Getting Started with Excel Essentials

2-1.1.1	2-1.1.6	2-1.3.3
2-1.1.2	2-1.2.4	2-3.1.1
2-1.1.3	2-1.2.5	2-3.1.3
2-1.1.4	2-1.3.1	2-3.1.4
2-1.1.5	2-1.3.2	

LESSON 18
Organizing and Enhancing Worksheets

2-3.1.1	2-3.1.5	2-3.1.9
2-3.1.2	2-3.1.6	2-3.1.10
2-3.1.3	2-3.1.7	2-3.2.1
2-3.1.4	2-3.1.8	2-3.2.2

LESSON 19
Creating Formulas and Charting Data

2-1.3.2	2-3.2.3	2-3.2.7
2-1.3.7	2-3.2.4	2-3.2.8
2-3.1.1	2-3.2.5	2-3.2.9
2-3.1.2	2-3.2.6	2-3.2.10

Presentations

LESSON 20
Getting Started with PowerPoint Essentials

2-1.1.2	2-1.3.2	2-4.1.5
2-1.1.3	2-1.3.3	2-4.1.7
2-1.1.5	2-1.3.5	2-4.1.9
2-1.2.1	2-4.1.1	2-4.1.10
2-1.2.2	2-4.1.2	2-4.1.11
2-1.2.4	2-4.1.3	2-4.1.12
2-1.2.5	2-4.1.4	

LESSON 21
Enhancing Presentations with Multimedia Effects

2-1.3.7	2-4.1.6	2-4.1.9
2-4.1.2	2-4.1.8	2-4.1.11
		2-4.1.12

LESSON 11

Exploring Microsoft Office 2007

■ OBJECTIVES

Upon completion of this lesson, you should be able to:

- Start Microsoft Office 2007 applications.
- Switch between application windows.
- Navigate and identify the common elements in application windows.
- Identify the elements in the new Office 2007 user interface.
- Customize the Quick Access Toolbar.
- Close documents and applications.
- Open, save, and print documents.
- Use onscreen and online Help features.

■ DATA FILES

To complete this lesson, you will need these data files:

Lesson 11A (a folder containing First Draft Report.docx and
       Lesson 11 Worksheet.xlsx)

Step11–7a.docx

Step11–7b.xlsx

Project11–1.docx

Project11–3.pptx

■ VOCABULARY

application window

Dialog Box Launcher

document window

file

file compatibility

file extension

folders

I-beam

insertion point

open a document

path

Ribbon

save a document

ScreenTip

scroll

Microsoft Office 2007 is an integrated software package that enables you to share information between several applications. The applications available in Office 2007 are Word, PowerPoint, Excel, Access, Outlook, OneNote, Publisher, and Accounting Express. The applications available on your computer depend on which Office 2007 suite is installed and the selections made during the installation. Microsoft offers several different Office 2007 suites, such as Office Professional 2007 and Office Home and Student 2007. Each suite offers a different combination of applications.

Each application performs specific tasks. **Table 11–1** provides a brief description of the applications covered in depth in this module: Word, Excel, PowerPoint, and Access. You will find an introduction to Outlook in the Living Online module of this text.

TABLE 11–1   Microsoft Office 2007 applications

APPLICATION	DESCRIPTION
Access	A database application that enables you to organize, manipulate, and analyze information such as addresses and inventory data
Excel	A spreadsheet application that enables you to work with text, numbers, and formulas to create tables, worksheets, and financial documents
Outlook	An e-mail and scheduling application that enables you to manage e-mail, appointments, tasks, contacts, and events efficiently
PowerPoint	A presentation application that enables you to create multimedia slide shows, transparencies, outlines, and organizational charts
Word	A word-processing application that enables you to create and share documents such as letters, memos, and reports

2-1.1.1
2-1.2.3

Starting Office 2007 Applications

Depending on your computer setup and operating system, you can start Office 2007 applications by double-clicking the application icon on the desktop, clicking the application button on the taskbar, or by using the Start button in the bottom-left corner of the screen.

You can have multiple applications open at the same time. Each open application appears on the taskbar at the bottom of the screen. To switch from one open application to another, click the application button on the taskbar or click the Switch between windows button on the Quick Launch toolbar to the right of the Start button.

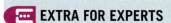

EXTRA FOR EXPERTS

To create a desktop shortcut, right-click the application name on the Start menu, click **Send To**, and then click **Desktop (create shortcut)**.

Step-by-Step 11.1

1. Click the **Start** button 🪟 on the taskbar. The Word application name may appear in the most frequently used programs list, as shown in **Figure 11–1**.

FIGURE 11–1
The Start menu

Programs used most frequently

Start button

2. Click **All Programs**. A complete list of your programs will appear.

3. When the submenu appears, click the **Microsoft Office** folder. You may need to move down through the list to see the folder name.

4. When the next submenu appears, click **Microsoft Office Word 2007**.

5. Click the **Start** button, click **All Programs**, click **Microsoft Office**, and then click **Microsoft Office Excel 2007**. Excel is now the active application, although Word is still open and running.

6. Click the **Start** button, click **All Programs**, click **Microsoft Office**, and then click **Microsoft Office PowerPoint 2007**.

7. Microsoft PowerPoint is now the active application, although Word and Excel are both still open and running. The taskbar, with three open applications, is shown in **Figure 11–2**.

> **EXTRA FOR EXPERTS**
>
> If the application icon appears on the desktop, click the **Show desktop** button on the Quick Launch toolbar, or right-click in a blank area on the taskbar and click **Show the Desktop**. Then to start the application, you can double-click the application icon on the desktop.

Show desktop button

Quick Launch toolbar

Switch between windows button

Applications that are open

FIGURE 11–2
The taskbar with multiple open application buttons

8. Click the Excel spreadsheet document button on the taskbar to switch to that application.

9. Click the **Switch between windows** button on the Quick Launch toolbar. Icons for all of the open documents will show on your desktop, and when you move the mouse pointer over the icon, the document title will show.

10. Select the icon for the Word document to switch to that application.

11. Leave the Word, Excel, and PowerPoint applications open.

Navigating Application Windows

2-1.1.2
2-1.1.3

When an application is launched, an application window similar to the one shown in **Figure 11–3** appears. The *application window* serves as the primary interface between the user and the application. The application window includes many of the elements of all Windows screens, including the title bar, scroll bars, and the status bar. Most Office 2007 applications will automatically open a new blank document when the application is launched. The *document window* is the area where you enter new text and data or change existing text and data.

▶ **VOCABULARY**
application window
document window

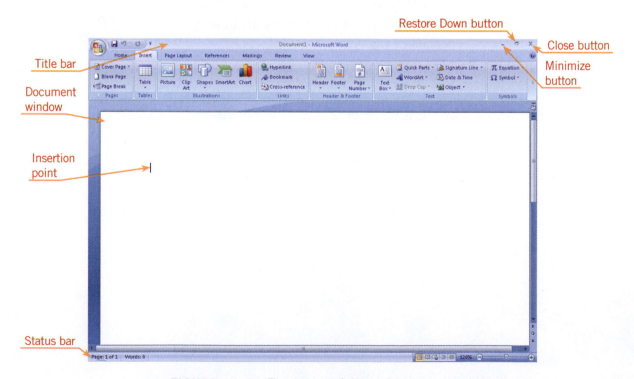

FIGURE 11–3   The Microsoft Word 2007 application window

The Microsoft Word window can be resized and moved just like other windows on your screen by using the Minimize, Maximize, and Restore Down buttons. The Minimize and Restore Down buttons are shown in **Figure 11–3**.

The *insertion point* is a blinking vertical line that indicates the location in the document where the new text and data will be entered. The arrow keys on the keyboard move the insertion point up, down, left, and right in the document. The Page Up and Page Down keys move the insertion point in bigger increments. To use the mouse to reposition the insertion point, simply move the mouse pointer to the desired location within the document. When positioned within the document window, the pointer changes from an arrow to an *I-beam*, which looks like a capital letter I. Position the I-beam over the text in the document where you would like the insertion point, and then click.

When you *scroll* through a document, you move through the document on the screen without changing the location of the insertion point. To scroll, use the horizontal or vertical scroll bars. Another convenient way to scroll, if available, is to use the wheel on the mouse. The display on the screen adjusts as you scroll. **Figure 11–4** identifies the scroll bar tools.

▶ **VOCABULARY**
insertion point
I-beam
scroll

◗ **HEADS UP**

The arrow keys and Page Up and Page Down keys will not move the insertion point in a blank document. As soon as text and data are added to the document, the keys will perform as described.

Scroll up arrow

Vertical scroll bar

Drag scroll box left or right

Drag scroll box up or down

Horizontal scroll bar

Scroll down arrow

Scroll left arrow

Scroll right arrow

Page 1 of 1   Words: 0   200%

FIGURE 11–4   Using the mouse to scroll

Step-by-Step 11.2

1. If necessary, click the Word document button in the taskbar to show the blank Word document.

2. Enter your first and last names. Notice that the insertion point moves as you enter text.

3. Press **Enter** about 10 times. Notice that the insertion point moves each time you press Enter.

4. Use the arrow keys and the **Page Up** and **Page Down** keys to navigate in the document window. Each time you press Page Up or Page Down, the

insertion point will move up or down in the document about the depth of your screen.

5. Drag the scroll box and click the arrows on the vertical scroll bar to move through the document window without moving the insertion point.

6. Position the mouse pointer between your first and last names and then click. The insertion point will appear now in the new position. Enter your middle name or middle initial.

7. If necessary, click the **Maximize** button 🔲 to change the size of the window to fill the screen. If the Maximize button does not show in the top-right corner of the screen, the document is already maximized.

8. To adjust the size of the window, click the **Restore Down** button 🔲. The window will appear smaller, and you can drag the borders to adjust its size, and you can reposition the window by dragging the title bar. When the window is restored down, the Maximize button will appear in place of the Restore Down button.

9. Click the **Minimize** button ▬ to reduce the document to a button on the taskbar. You should see the Excel document. Notice that the Word document still appears in the taskbar.

10. Click the Word document button in the taskbar to make it active again, and if necessary, click the **Maximize** button to change the size of the window to fill the screen.

11. To return to the previous customized window size, click the **Restore Down** button. Then, click the **Maximize** button once more.

12. Leave the application open.

2-1.1.2
2-1.1.3
2-1.1.4

Using the New Office User Interface

Several of the Office 2007 applications use a new visual design which is referred to as the Microsoft Office Fluent user interface. There are many new features in this new design which make the software more intuitive and easier to use.

Using the Office Ribbon

The **Ribbon** is the blue banner that stretches across the top of the screen, just below the title bar. As shown in **Figure 11–5**, the Ribbon shows several tabs, beginning with the Home tab at the left. The Ribbon makes it easy to find commands because related commands and options are organized in groups on each tab. For example,

▶ **VOCABULARY**
Ribbon

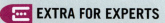 **EXTRA FOR EXPERTS**

For users who are familiar with earlier versions of Microsoft Office, the Ribbon has replaced the menu bar.

all of the commands for formatting characters appear in the Font group. A *Dialog Box Launcher* (a small arrow) appears in the lower-right corner of some groups, and when clicked, a dialog box will open with even more options.

Paste button

Dialog Box Launcher for the Font group

FIGURE 11–5 The Home tab on the Ribbon

What makes the Ribbon so unique is that it changes to meet your needs. As you work in a document, the Ribbon adapts by providing appropriate commands and options. For example, if you insert a picture in your document, the Ribbon will change to show options for formatting the picture—hence, the word "fluent" in Office Fluent user interface.

If you do not know the function of a button in any of the groups, position the mouse pointer over the button, but do not click. After a second or two, the name of the command and a description of the command shows in a small window called a *ScreenTip*.

If you prefer to use the keyboard instead of the mouse, you can access the tabs on the Ribbon by using keyboard shortcuts that you can show on the Ribbon. Commands can also be accessed with legacy keyboard shortcuts, which have been around for many versions of the application. When a keyboard shortcut is available for the command, the shortcut is included in the ScreenTip.

Step-by-Step 11.3

1. If necessary, click the Word button in the taskbar to show the Word document.

2. On the Home tab, in the Clipboard group, position the mouse pointer over the **Paste** button, shown in **Figure 11–5**. Wait a second or two for the ScreenTip to appear. The ScreenTip provides the button name, a keyboard shortcut, and a description of its function.

3. Click the **Insert** tab on the Ribbon. The groups and options will change.

4. Position the mouse pointer over several of the commands on the Insert tab to show the ScreenTips.

5. Click each of the remaining tabs to view the groups and commands. You will see that the groups and commands are very different on each tab.

6. Press the **Alt** key. Letters for keyboard shortcuts will appear under each tab name on the Ribbon. Notice that the letter P appears under the Page Layout tab name.

7.   Press **P** to show the Page Layout tab. More shortcut keys appear. Press **M** to show the margin options. When a command or option is executed, the shortcut keys will disappear. To hide the keyboard shortcuts without executing a command, press the Alt key once again, or click a different tab name.

8.   Click anywhere in the white area of the document window to close the margin options without making any changes. Even though you didn't execute a command or option, the shortcut keys will disappear.

9.   Click the **Home** tab to make it active.

10. Click the **Dialog Box Launcher** in the Font group. The Font dialog box shown in **Figure 11–6** will open.

FIGURE 11–6
The Font dialog box

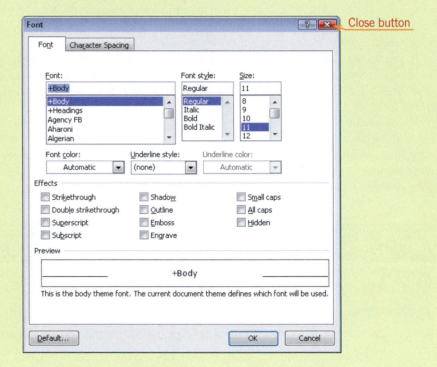

11. Click the **Close** button to close the dialog box.

12. Leave the applications open.

Minimizing the Ribbon

If you want to maximize the screen space for your document window, you can minimize the Ribbon.

Step-by-Step 11.4

1. If necessary, click the Word button in the taskbar to show the Word document.

2. If necessary, click the **Home** tab to make it active. Double-click the **Home** tab. The groups and command buttons will be hidden, and only the tab names will appear, as shown in **Figure 11–7**.

3. Click the **Insert** tab. All the groups on that tab will show.

4. Click anywhere within the document window. The Ribbon will automatically minimize again. The Ribbon will also minimize again if you choose a command or option.

5. Double-click any one of the tabs to maximize the Ribbon and restore its original appearance.

6. Leave the applications open.

Using and Customizing the Quick Access Toolbar

By default, the Quick Access Toolbar is positioned above the Ribbon in the upper-left corner of the application window. This toolbar offers quick access to commands you use frequently. The default settings, as shown in **Figure 11–8**, include only three options, the Save, Undo, and Redo or Repeat commands; but you can customize the toolbar to include the commands you use most often. Keep in mind that the intent of the toolbar is for quick access. If you add too many commands and the toolbar becomes cluttered, it may slow you down.

> **EXTRA FOR EXPERTS**
>
> You can move the Quick Access Toolbar so that it appears below the Ribbon. Click the **Customize Quick Access Toolbar** button and then click the option **Show Below the Ribbon**.

Customize Quick Access Toolbar button

FIGURE 11–8   The Quick Access Toolbar

Step-by-Step 11.5

1. If necessary, click the Word button in the taskbar to show the Word document.

2. Click the **Customize Quick Access Toolbar** button 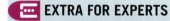. The current commands on the toolbar are identified with a check mark.

3. Click **More Commands** to open the Word Options dialog box. The Customize option is already selected.

4. Double-click a command that is not currently on the Quick Access Toolbar. Be sure to remember which command you clicked. Click **OK**. The width of the toolbar will expand and a new button for the command will show on the toolbar.

5. Click the **Customize Quick Access Toolbar** button, and then click the same command that you clicked in Step 4. This will remove the command from the toolbar.

6. Leave the applications open.

2-1.1.1
2-1.2.5

HEADS UP

Press **Ctrl+F4** as an alternative to using the Close button to close the active document window. Press **Alt+F4** to close the application window.

Closing Documents and Applications

You use the same procedures to close documents and applications in all Office applications. To close a document, you can click the Close button in the application window, or you can click the Office Button and choose the Close command. The Office Button, positioned at the upper-left corner of application window, is available in many Office 2007 applications to access basic commands such as Open, Save, Print, and Close.

If you have multiple documents open in the application, clicking the Close button or using the Close command will close only the active document. To close an application and all documents at the same time, you can click the Office Button and click the Exit command. If you attempt to close a document without saving changes, you will be prompted to save the changes before closing.

Step-by-Step 11.6

1. If necessary, click the Word button in the taskbar to show the Word document.

2. Click the **Office Button** to show the commands and options shown in **Figure 11–9**.

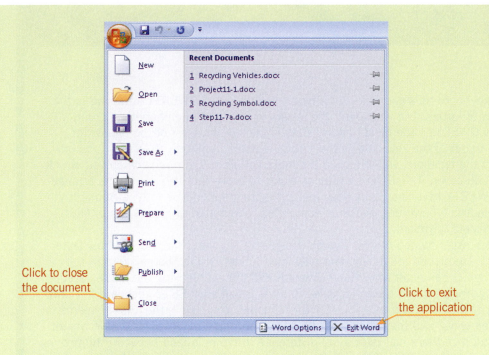

FIGURE 11–9
The Close and Exit commands

Click to close
the document

Click to exit
the application

3. Click **Close**. You will be prompted to save the changes to the document. Click **No**. The document window will close, but the application will still be active.

4. Click the **Office Button**, and then click **Exit Word**. The application window will close. You should see the Excel application window, but if not, click the button on the taskbar to switch to the Excel document.

5. Click the **Office Button**, and then click **Exit Excel**. If prompted to save the changes, click **No**. The document window and the application window will both close. The PowerPoint application and document are still open.

6. Click the **Close** button in the upper-right corner of the application window. If prompted to save changes to the document, click **No**. No application or document buttons should appear in the taskbar, and you should see the desktop.

Opening, Saving, and Printing Documents

You use similar procedures to open and save documents in all Office applications. To ***open a document*** means to load a file into an application. A ***file*** is a collection of information saved as a unit. Each file is identified by a filename. Remember that the terms document and file are used interchangeably.

2-1.1.4
2-1.1.7
2-1.2.2
2-1.2.3
2-1.2.4
2-1.2.6

▶ **VOCABULARY**
open a document
file

TECHNOLOGY TIMELINE

Why QWERTY?

The arrangement of a standard keyboard on a computer (or a typewriter) is called QWERTY, referring to the first six characters in the top row of letters. But why aren't the letters in arranged in alphabetical order, or some other logical order? Why QWERTY? The most popular story is that the inventor of the typewriter, Christopher Sholes, created the layout of the keyboard in the 1860s to keep commonly used key combinations separated. This was so that the typebars, which moved the metal letters to the ribbon when you struck the keys, would not crash into each other. Although no evidence exists to prove that this is why the arrangement of keys was chosen, the QWERTY keyboard really does make it more cumbersome to type frequently used letters. And even though electric typewriters, and then computers, eliminated all possibility of keys crashing together, we still use this old keyboard.

In the 1930s, a university professor named August Dvorak designed a keyboard that would allow faster typing with less finger movement. He placed the most commonly used letters on the "home" keys in the middle row of letter keys, and a typist can enter many English words without ever leaving the home keys. It's been estimated that a typist's fingers might travel 16 miles in a day using a QWERTY keyboard but only 1 mile using the Dvorak keyboard. Yet we're still using the QWERTY model. Why? Well, the answer seems to be that people are just set in their ways, and they don't want to learn a new system. Also, U.S. government tests in the 1950s actually found that there just isn't a big difference in typing speed between the two keyboards to make it worth changing the standard layout. Good typists type faster than bad typists, no matter what keyboard they use.

EXTRA FOR EXPERTS

To preview a file before opening it, click the **Start** button and then click **Documents** in the list at the right. When the dialog box opens, click **Organize** and then click **Layout**. If necessary, click **Preview Pane** to enable the option. The icon at the left of the option will be surrounded by a blue box when enabled. Navigate to the file and click the filename to show the document in the Preview pane. Click anywhere in the Preview pane, and then you can scroll through the document.

▶ VOCABULARY

file extension

folders

path

Opening a Document

The Open command, which is accessed using the Office Button in most Office 2007 applications, enables you to open a file from any available disk and folder. You can also open a document by navigating to the document on the desktop or by using the file management system on the computer. Once you locate the file, double-click the filename. If necessary, your computer will launch the associated application (such as Word or Excel), and then the document will open.

A *file extension* typically identifies the type of file. A period separates the filename and the extension. The extension is usually three or four characters and varies depending on the application used to create the document. For example, Word 2007 automatically assigns the extension docx, PowerPoint 2007 assigns the extension pptx, and Excel 2007 assigns the extension xlsx. The "x" in the extension indicates the XML format. You can quickly identify documents created in earlier versions of these applications because the file extensions are doc, ppt, and xls.

Folders are containers used to organize the documents into manageable groups on a designated storage device. All computer files are saved in folders, and folders can also be created within folders. The *path* is the route the operating system uses to locate a document. The path identifies the disk and any folders relative to the location of the document. **Figure 11–10** shows two typical paths and identifies the items in the paths. The first example shows a document named Volunteer.docx saved in a folder called Assignments. The Assignments folder is, in turn, stored in a folder called CLB Key Applications, which can be found on the local (this computer's) hard drive—drive C. In the second example, the Word document named Volunteer.docx is saved in a folder called Assignments, which can be found on a Flash/USB removable memory drive, which in this example is identified as Removable Disk (E:).

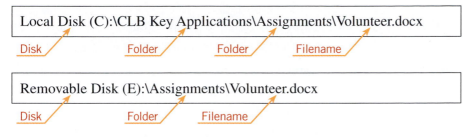

FIGURE 11–10   Typical paths to file locations

Just as you can open multiple applications, you can also open multiple documents within each application. Each open document appears on the taskbar. When several documents are open for one application, the taskbar shows only the name of the application on the taskbar. Click the application button on the taskbar to open a list of all open documents for that application. To make a document active, click the filename from the list.

Step-by-Step 11.7

1. Start the Word application.

2. Click the **Office Button**. To the right of the commands, you will see a list of documents that have been accessed recently in this application, as shown in **Figure 11–9**. If the document you want to open is in that list, you can click the document filename and it will open.

3. Click **Open**. An Open dialog box appears. Word automatically takes you to the drive and folder of the last folder you opened, so your dialog box will be similar to the one shown in **Figure 11–11**, but it may not be identical.

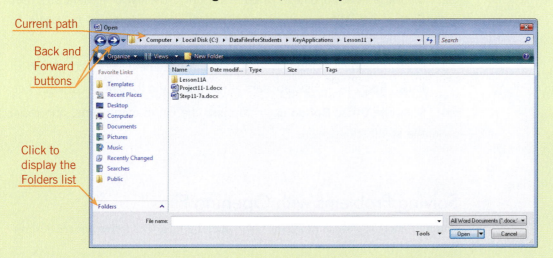

FIGURE 11–11
The Open dialog box

4. Navigate to the location where the data files are stored. (Your instructor can provide this information.) To locate the **DataFilesforStudents** folder, select the folder from the Favorite Links list or use the Folders list. Clicking the Back button will return you to the previous drive or folder.

After you click the Back button, the Forward button will appear and then you can navigate through the folders in both directions.

5. Double-click the **DataFilesforStudents** folder, then double-click the **KeyApplications** folder, and then double-click the **Lesson11** folder. There is one folder, Lesson 11A, and two Word files, Step11–7a.docx and Project11–1.docx, in the Lesson11 folder.

6. Click the **All Word Documents (*.docx;...)** list arrow at the lower-right corner of the dialog box, and then click **All Files (*.*)**. The names of all files in the Lesson11 folder are listed, including those created in applications other than Word.

7. Click the filename **Step11–7a.docx** once to select it, and then click **Open**, or double-click the filename.

8. Start Excel.

9. Click the **Office Button**, and then click **Open**.

10. Navigate to the **DataFilesforStudents** folder again and open the **KeyApplications** folder. Double-click the **Lesson11** folder to open it. Then double-click the **Lesson 11A** folder to show the Excel file in that folder. Notice that the current path for the location of the document shows at the top of the Open dialog box.

11. Click the **Back** button at the upper-left corner of the dialog box to return to the list of folders and files in the Lesson11 folder. Click the **Back** button again to return to the list of folders and files in the KeyApplications folder.

12. Click the **Forward** button twice to return to the list of folders and files in the Lesson11 folder. Double-click the filename **Step11–7b.xlsx** to open it.

13. Click the **Office Button**. Notice that the document you just opened in Excel, Step11–7b.xlsx, appears at the top of the Recent Documents list.

14. Click the **Office Button** again to close the list of commands, and leave the applications open.

> ▶ **HEADS UP**
>
> To open multiple documents at the same time, click the first filename in the Open dialog box, hold down the **Ctrl** key, and click one or more additional filenames, then click **Open**.

Solving Problems with Opening Files

You may encounter some problems when opening files. The following are descriptions of common problems.

- There is a problem with file compatibility. *File compatibility* refers to the ability to open and work with files without a format conflict. In most cases, files that were created with an older version of application software can be opened in

> ▶ **VOCABULARY**
> **file compatibility**

the newer version of the software. But sometimes, files created in newer applications are not backwards compatible, meaning that they cannot be opened in older versions of the software. Office 2007 files are saved in a new format, and they will not normally open in earlier versions of Office applications. Microsoft does, however, provide a free download of compatibility software to enable users with older versions of Office to open, edit, and save files created and saved in the new Office 2007 format.

■ You may also encounter compatibility problems if you are working in a different operating system than the one in which the file was created. For example, if a file was created in PowerPoint on a Macintosh, it may not open in PowerPoint on a PC. This problem generally occurs if you are working with different versions of the software across the different platforms. With a little effort, however, you can usually find a way to open and use almost any Office file.

■ When you use the Open command from the Office Button, you do not see the file for which you are looking. This could be caused by a number of things. First, you need to verify that the document was saved before it was closed. Second, you need to verify that you are looking in the right drive and the right folder, as the file for which you are looking may be stored in a different location. If the file is stored in a remote storage area or on a network, you must make sure you have access to the storage area or the network. If you are unsure of the location of the file, you can use the Search command, available in the upper-right corner of the Open dialog box, to locate the file. To use the Search feature, you must identify the drive and/or folders in the box to the left of the Search box. Or, you can click the Start button and enter the filename in the Search box.

■ The file is in a format that cannot be read by the application you are using. For example, if you attempt to open an Access file using the Open command in the Word application, you will not see the file listed. You can switch the file type within the Open dialog box to show All Files, but that does not necessarily mean that the application you are using will be able to open the file. In general, it is better to open a file in its associated application and then export to the appropriate file format for the application in which you want to open the file.

■ You encounter a corrupted file or a file that will not open. The application may give you an error message when you try to open the file, it may cause the application to shut down, or it may just not open. In these cases you can try to open the file on a different computer to verify that the file is indeed corrupt and that there isn't something wrong with your computer.

Saving a Document

To *save a document* means to store it on a disk or other storage medium. You can save a document to the hard drive on your computer, to the computer desktop, to an auxiliary drive or a network location, or to portable media such as Flash/USB removable memory, or a writable CD/DVD disk. A file extension is automatically added to the filename when the document is saved.

To make it easier to find documents, choose filenames with words that help describe the document. The complete path to the file can include up to 255 characters. Filenames cannot include any of the following characters: \, /, :, *, ?, ", <, >, |.

You should make a habit of saving frequently and after making any major changes to your document. The quickest and easiest way to save a document is to click the Save button on the Quick Access Toolbar. When you click the Save button on the toolbar, the document is saved with the same filename and in the same location. If the file does not already have a name, the Save As dialog box will open and you can enter a name for the file. Unless you specify a different location, the file will be saved to the default location.

HEADS UP

The new file format for Word 2007, PowerPoint 2007, and Excel 2007 is based on an XML (Extensible Markup Language) format, which affects how files are stored. The benefits of the XML format include a smaller file size and improved recovery of damaged or corrupted files.

VOCABULARY
save a document

EXTRA FOR EXPERTS

You can show file extensions in Windows Vista by changing an option in your system settings. Open the **Start** menu, click **Control Panel**, click **Appearance and Personalization**, and then choose **Folder Options**. Click the **View** tab. Under Advanced settings, you will see the option **Hide extensions for known file types**. The option is turned off when the check mark is removed.

When you change the filename or the location in which the file is stored, the original document, with the original name, remains unchanged. When you use the Save As command, you also have the opportunity to change the document format. Each application offers a number of choices for formats in which to save files.

Step-by-Step 11.8

1. Click the Word button on the taskbar to switch to the Step 11–7a.docx document.

2. Click the **Office Button** and then click **Save As**. The Save As dialog box shown in **Figure 11–12** will open. The current path appears at the top of the dialog box.

FIGURE 11–12
The Save As dialog box

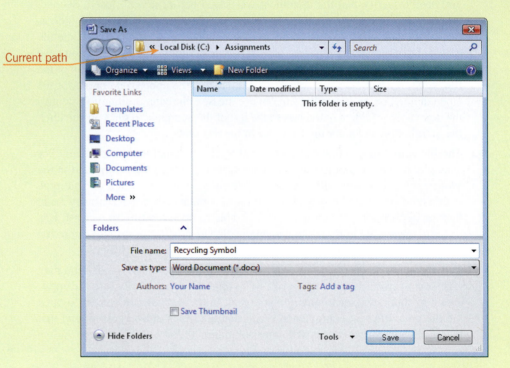

3. If you have an Assignments folder, use the Favorite Links list or the Folders list to locate it. You can specify the folder, directory, network drive, or other remote drive in the Folders list. If you do not have an Assignments folder, follow your instructor's directions about where to save the document.

4. In the File name box, the filename Step11–7a.docx is already selected. (If the text in the File name box is not highlighted, click in the box and select or delete that text.) Then enter **Recycling Symbol**.

5. Click the **Save** button in the dialog box. The document is saved in a new location and with a different filename.

⊞ EXTRA FOR EXPERTS

You can create a new folder by clicking the **New Folder** button 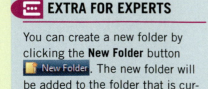. The new folder will be added to the folder that is currently open in the dialog box.

6. Click the Excel button on the taskbar to switch to the Step11–7b document.

7. Click the **Office Button** and click **Save As**. Save the file in your Assignments folder (or as directed by your instructor). Change the file-name to **Expense Report**.

8. In the Save as type box, the default setting for the Excel file format is Excel Workbook (*.xslx). Click the **Save as type** list arrow and change the file type to **Text (Tab delimited) (*.txt)**. You may need to scroll down in the list to find this option.

9. Click **Save**. If you see a message box warning you that the selected file format does not support multiple worksheets, click **OK** and **Yes** to continue.

10. Leave the applications open.

Printing a Document

Some of the commands in the Office Button include submenus, which provide more options without first opening a dialog box. When you point to the arrow next to the Print command, three print options appear in a submenu, as shown in **Figure 11–13**.

FIGURE 11–13   The Print submenu

- The Print option opens the Print dialog box, and you can select a printer, the number of copies to print, and the range of pages to print. You can also change the printer settings (such as print quality or the color settings using the Properties button). The options within the Print dialog box will vary, but most of the print options are similar for all applications. If your computer accesses more than one printer, you will want to choose the Print command so you can select the printer you want to use.

- The Quick Print option sends the content in the active window or document directly to the printer, and you will not have the opportunity to change the printing options or printer settings. The default printer options will be applied.

- The Print Preview option enables you to see exactly how the document will look when it is printed. The printed copy produced by the printer may not look exactly the same as what you see on your screen, so it is good practice to use the Print Preview option.

⟶● WARNING

Check with your instructor about the policy for printing documents in this course.

Step-by-Step 11.9

1. Click the Word button on the taskbar to switch to the **Recycling Symbol.docx** document.

2. Click the **Office Button** and click **Print**. A Print dialog box similar to the one shown in **Figure 11–14** will open.

FIGURE 11–14
The Print dialog box

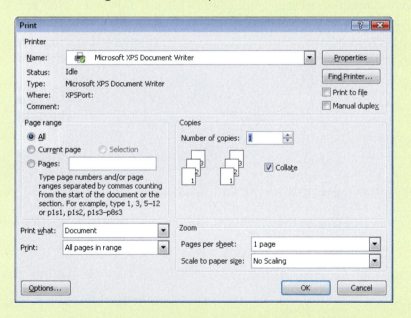

3. In the Printer section, click the list arrow in the **Name** box. If your computer is connected to more than one printer, the other printers will appear in this list. Click on the title bar of the dialog box to close the list without making any changes.

4. In the Page range section, click to select **Current page**. When this option is selected, only the page where you last positioned the insertion point will print.

5. Click the option for **Pages**. When this option is selected, you can enter a specific page number in the text box (for example, 2). Use hyphens for a page range (for example, 1-3), and use commas to separate pages or page ranges (for example, 1, 3-5).

6. Click **Cancel** to close the dialog box without printing. (To print, you would click OK, but there is no reason to print this document.)

7. Click the **Office Button**, position the mouse pointer over the Print command, and then click **Print Preview** in the submenu. The document will appear in the Print Preview window, and the Ribbon will adapt to provide commands and options for printing, changing the page layout, and viewing the document.

8. On the far right of the Print Preview tab, click the **Close Print Preview** button.

9. Close the Word and Excel applications. If you are prompted to save changes to the documents, click **No**.

Getting Help

2-1.1.8
2-1.1.9

The Office 2007 applications have some very powerful Help features to assist you as you work. You have access to documentation including books and manuals and online help as well. Do not overlook another vital source of help: assistance from others. There may be classmates, instructors, or coworkers who are familiar with the application you are using. Or perhaps your workplace has a help desk. You can communicate with support personnel via phone, e-mail, user groups, and blogs.

The key to using these various sources of help is determining what sort of help you need and the quickest or most efficient way to access that help. The idea is to find the assistance you need without interrupting or delaying your work. Whenever you encounter a problem, your first source of help should be the Help features in each Office application. Help is always readily available and is just a few mouse clicks away. For example, you can find out more about most dialog box options by clicking the Help button, which looks like a question mark, on the title bar of the dialog box. This button opens a Help window that provides information about the options available in that dialog box.

Navigating the Help screens is much like navigating a Web page. You can browse the categories presented and click on links to get information about a topic. You can also enter keywords (specific words or phrases) in the Search box. The results for your search will be listed, with links for the most relevant results at the top of the list. Your success in getting useful search results depends on your ability to identify the keywords that relate to your query. The more you search, the better you get at recognizing keywords for your searches. To access previous searches, click the Search list arrow.

If your computer is connected to the Internet, you will also have access to all the current Help information available at the Microsoft Web site or other support specialists. At the Microsoft Office Online Web site you will find a variety of resources, including tours, slide shows, tutorials, training videos, articles, product user groups, blogs, and the opportunity to chat with Microsoft support personnel. If the word Offline appears at the bottom of the Help dialog box, your computer is not currently

HEADS UP

The keyboard shortcut to access the Help feature is **F1**.

HEADS UP

To reposition the Help dialog box, drag the title bar. You can also resize the dialog box by dragging one of the borders.

connected to the Internet, but you can still access Help information from files stored on your computer. You may need to check with your instructor about how to connect to the Internet from your computer.

Step-by-Step 11.10

1. Start Microsoft Office Word 2007.

2. Click the **Help** button on the upper-right corner of the application window. The Word Help dialog box shown in **Figure 11–15** will open. The dialog box includes a search box and several links for browsing Word Help topics.

FIGURE 11–15
The Word Help dialog box

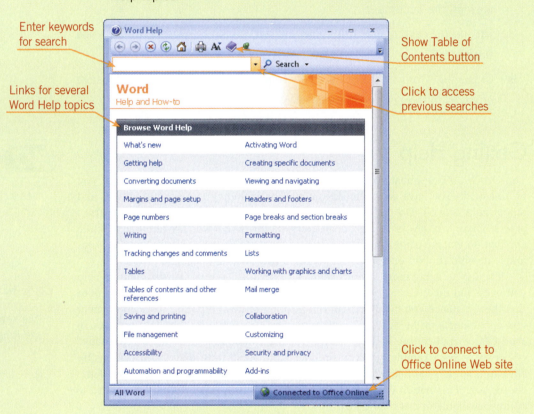

Enter keywords for search

Links for several Word Help topics

Show Table of Contents button

Click to access previous searches

Click to connect to Office Online Web site

3. Click the **Show Table of Contents** button in the dialog box to show the Table of Contents, which will appear on the left side of the dialog box.

4. Click **Getting help** in the Table of Contents. More links related to the topic will appear. Click **Getting help** again to hide the links.

5. Position the insertion point in the Search box. Enter the keywords **display recent documents**.

6. Click **Search**. Topics that may provide an answer are listed in the dialog box.

7. Click the link **Customize the list of recently used files**. If your computer is connected to the Internet, you may need to scroll down to see the option in the list. A new Help screen will open.

8. Scroll down and click the link **Word** to choose the program you are using.

9. Read and follow the three steps. You can keep the Word Help dialog box open as you complete the task. If the dialog box is in the way, reposition it or resize it.

10. After you complete the third step, instead of clicking OK, click **Cancel** in the Word Options dialog box.

11. Close the Word Help dialog box.

12. Close Word.

SUMMARY

In this lesson, you learned:

- You can start Office applications by clicking the Start button on the taskbar and selecting the application from the All Programs menu, or you can double-click the application icon on the desktop.

- Common elements found in Office application windows include the title bar, scroll bars, and status bar.

- You can maximize the space for the document window by minimizing the Ribbon.

- You can customize the Quick Access Toolbar by adding or removing command buttons.

- To close document windows and application windows, you click the Close button in the application window or click the Office Button and then click the Close command or Exit.

- The Open dialog box enables you to open a file from any available disk and folder.

- Problems opening files can involve corrupted data or file compatibility issues, such as trying to open a file in a different application, in an earlier version of an application, or in an operating system other than that used to create it.

- To save a document using a new filename, you click the Office Button and then click the Save As command.

- To print a document, you click the Office Button, point to Print, and then choose a print option.

- ScreenTips provide immediate help without interrupting your work. The Help window and the Office Online Web site are also sources of assistance.

■ VOCABULARY REVIEW

Define the following terms:

application window	file extension	path
Dialog Box Launcher	folders	Ribbon
document window	I-beam	save a document
file	insertion point	ScreenTip
file compatibility	open a document	scroll

REVIEW QUESTIONS

TRUE / FALSE

Circle T if the statement is true or F if the statement is false.

T   F   **1.**   The Ribbon is one of the new features in the Microsoft Office Fluent user interface.

T   F   **2.**   A disk is a collection of information saved as a unit.

T   F   **3.**   Using the scroll bar to navigate through a document also repositions the insertion point.

T   F   **4.**   The insertion point is a blinking vertical line that indicates the location in the document where the new text and data will be entered.

T   F   **5.**   Even though Office 2007 files are saved in a new format, they are backwards compatible, meaning they will normally open in earlier versions of Office applications.

MULTIPLE CHOICE

Select the best response for the following statements.

1. The Office application you would use to organize and manipulate information such as addresses and inventory data is _____.

   A.   Outlook   C.   Access

   B.   Word   D.   Excel

2. To save a file with a new filename or to a new location, _____.

   A.   click the Save button on the Quick Access Toolbar

   B.   click the Save As New button on the Quick Access Toolbar

   C.   click the Office Button and then click New

   D.   click the Office Button and then click Save As

3. The _____ serves as the primary interface between the user and the application.

   A.   document window   C.   Switch between windows button

   B.   application window   D.   Start button

4. To view more options in a group on the Ribbon, _____.

   A.   maximize the Ribbon   C.   double-click a Ribbon tab

   B.   click the Dialog Box Launcher   D.   customize the Quick Access Toolbar

5. The _____ is the route the operating system uses to locate a document.

   A.   file extension   C.   path

   B.   folder   D.   navigation trail

FILL IN THE BLANK

Complete the following sentences by writing the correct word or words in the blanks provided.

1. _____ are used to organize the documents within a disk.

2. When positioned within the document window, the mouse pointer changes from an arrow to a(n) _____, which looks like a capital letter I.

3. A(n) _____ is usually three or four characters in length and defines the type of file.

4. _____ refers to the ability to open and work with files without a format conflict.

5. A(n) _____ is a small window with descriptive text that appears when you position the mouse pointer over a command or control in the application window.

 PROJECTS

PROJECT 11–1

1. Start the Word 2007 application.

2. Start the PowerPoint 2007 application.

3. Switch to the Word application.

4. Navigate to the data files and open the file **Project11–1.docx**. The path for the data file is DataFilesforStudents\KeyApplications\Lesson11.

5. Save the document in your Assignments folder with the new filename **Recycling Vehicles**.

6. Click the **Page Layout** tab on the Ribbon.

7. In the Page Setup group, show the ScreenTip for the Margins button.

8. Minimize the Ribbon, and then restore it.

9. Use the keyboard to move the insertion point to the end of the document, and enter your first and last name.

10. Click the **Office Button** and click **Save** to save the changes to the document.

11. Scroll back to the top of the document.

12. Leave the document and applications open.

PROJECT 11–3

1. Switch to the PowerPoint application.

2. Open **Project11–3.pptx** from the data files. The path for the data file is DataFilesforStudents\KeyApplications\Lesson11. The PowerPoint window shows a slide, an outline of the current presentation, and an area where you can add notes.

3. Save the PowerPoint presentation in your Assignments folder using the new filename **Three Rs**.

4. Click the **View** tab. Notice that there are seven buttons in the Presentation Views group.

5. To learn more about the different views you can use in PowerPoint, open the PowerPoint Help dialog box, enter **change views** in the Search box, and click **Search**. In the list of results for the search, click **When and how to use views in PowerPoint 2007**.

6. Read about the Normal view and the Slide Sorter view, and then close the PowerPoint Help dialog box.

7. Close the PowerPoint application.

8. Close the Word application.

PROJECT 11–2

1. If necessary, open the file **Recycling Vehicles** from your solution files.

2. Add the Open command button to the Quick Access Toolbar.

3. Remove the Open command button from the Quick Access Toolbar.

4. View the document in Print Preview, and then close the Print Preview window.

5. Close the Recycling Vehicles document. If prompted to save any changes, click **No**, and leave the applications open.

 TEAMWORK PROJECT

Your supervisor has decided to assign some projects to teams of employees, and he has asked you and a coworker to investigate what tools Office 2007 offers for collaborative work. Working as a team, use the Office Help features, the Internet, and other resources such as people you know who use Office applications to find out how Office application features enable more than one person to work on a document in Word, PowerPoint, and Excel. Make a list of the reviewing, tracking, and other applicable features in each of the three applications and indicate how you access the features from the applications.

CRITICAL THINKING

ACTIVITY 11–1

In exchange for riding privileges, you have agreed to help the owner of a local riding stable with a number of computer-related tasks. The owner has created the following list of jobs she needs to have done:

A. Write letters to people who board their horses at the stable to tell them feed bills will go up at the beginning of the year.

B. Store information on owners, frequent riders, equipment, and employees.

C. Schedule regular visits by the vet, keep track of regular chores, and plan activities in coming months.

D. Calculate expenses for running the stable as well as income from riders and boarders.

E. Prepare a presentation that can be used to train new employees and new riders.

Which Office applications would you use to complete each of these jobs? Make a table that lists each job and the Office application you would use to complete the task. Are there other jobs you could do for the stable owner using Office applications?

 # ONLINE DISCOVERY

At the beginning of this lesson, **Table 11–1** provides a brief overview of the Microsoft Office applications covered in this textbook: Word, Excel, PowerPoint, Access, and Outlook. Microsoft offers several more Office applications. Browse *www.microsoft.com* to learn about other Office applications that are available. Create a list of these other Office applications, and include a brief description about the purpose of each of application.

LESSON 12

Getting Started with Word Essentials

■ OBJECTIVES

Upon completion of this lesson, you should be able to:

- Create a new document.
- Change Word settings.
- Enter text in a document.
- Change views and magnification in the document window.
- Show nonprinting characters in a document.
- Use the click and type feature.
- Navigate through a document.

■ VOCABULARY

default settings

Normal.dotm template

toggle

word wrap

■ DATA FILES

To complete this lesson, you will need these data files:

Step12-4.docx

Project12-2.docx

Project12-3.docx

Word is a powerful, full-featured word-processing application. You can use Word to create reports, tables, letters, memos, Web pages, and much more. The Word lessons in this course will introduce you to features that enable you to prepare documents efficiently. You will also learn how to change the way the document looks on the screen and how to navigate through a document.

2-1.2.1

▶ **VOCABULARY**

default settings

Normal.dotm template

Creating a New Document

When you first start the Word application, a new blank document appears and is automatically titled Document1. The blank document is formatted with *default settings*, which are the preset options or variables automatically in effect when the document is created. The default settings for Word are stored in the *Normal.dotm template*, a file containing default styles and customizations that determine the structure and page layout of a document. Using the Normal.dotm template greatly increases the speed and efficiency of your work since you do not need to spend time setting up the details of the page. Information about overriding the default settings and changing document formats is provided in Lesson 13.

As you already know, you can open additional documents on top of Document1. All new blank document filenames will be numbered sequentially during the session that Word is open. The filenames for each open document stay the same until you assign a new filename. When the Word application is closed and then reopened, the new blank document filenames begin again with Document1.

Step-by-Step 12.1

1. Start the Word application.

2. Click the **Office Button** and then click **New** to display the New Document dialog box shown in **Figure 12–1**. The options in the dialog box will vary, but you should see the Blank document icon, and it should be highlighted. Because it's a blank document, there's nothing to show in the preview pane.

FIGURE 12–1
The New Document dialog box

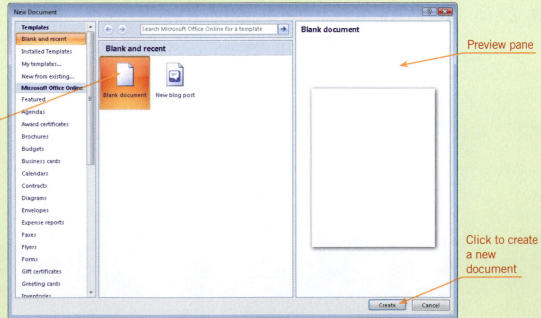

Blank document icon

Preview pane

Click to create a new document

3. Double-click the **Blank document** icon, or click **Create**. A new document based on the Normal.dotm template opens. Notice that the document title bar shows Document2. (If Word was already started when you began this exercise, the document number might be higher than the number 2.)

4. Leave the document open.

Changing Word Settings

2-1.1.7
2-1.2.4

As you work with Word, you will begin to recognize "behind the scenes" application settings that are designed to protect your work and improve your efficiency. If you've ever experienced your computer locking up or shutting down while you are working with a document, you know that when you restart an application, one or more of your documents may be recovered. This is because there is a setting to schedule an automatic save of the document information as you work with the document. You can easily customize a setting like this to fit your preferences and meet your needs.

Step-by-Step 12.2

1. Click the **Office Button**.

2. Click **Word Options**. The Word Options dialog box shown in **Figure 12–2** will open.

Click to show the Save settings

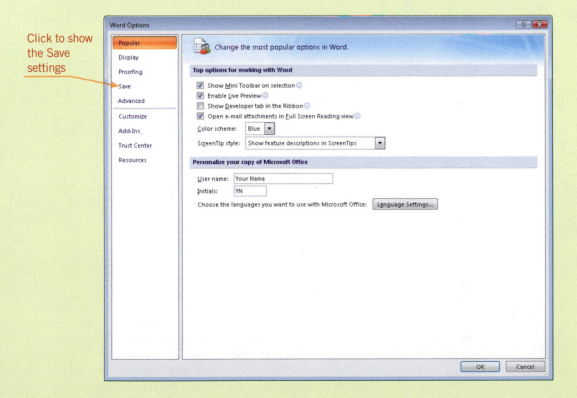

FIGURE 12–2
The Word Options dialog box

3. Click the **Save** option in the list on the left side of the dialog box to review the Save settings, as shown in **Figure 12–3**.

FIGURE 12–3
Save settings in the Word Options dialog box

File format

AutoRecover schedule

Default file location

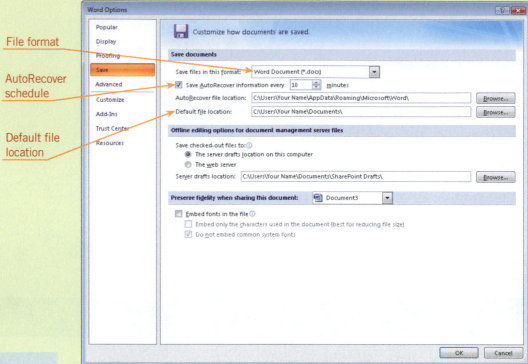

4. Make a note of the file format that is currently selected under Save documents. The default settings in Word 2007 provide that the document is saved in the new XML format (.docx). Click the **Save files in this format** list arrow to view the available settings, but do not make any changes.

5. Notice that there is a setting for saving AutoRecover information. The default setting is every ten minutes, but your setting may be different. Do not make any changes to this setting.

6. Make note of the Default file location box. To change this setting, you would click Browse and identify a new path. Do not make any changes to this setting.

7. Click **Cancel** so that no changes are made to any of the settings.

8. Leave the document open.

2-1.3.1

Entering Text in a Document

As you enter text in a Word document, the insertion point moves to the right and the page number in the status bar at the bottom of the document window changes to reflect the current position of the insertion point. The information in the status bar also continually changes to show the current total number of words in the document. As you add text to the document, you may see a red or green wavy line under some of the words. Word automatically checks the spelling and grammar in a document as you are entering the text, and the wavy lines suggest there may be spelling or grammar errors. If you see any wavy lines while entering text in this lesson, just ignore them. You will learn more about the spelling and grammar features in Lesson 13.

If the text you are entering extends beyond the right margin, Word will automatically wrap the text to the next line. This feature is called *word wrap*. When you press Enter to start a new line in the document, you create a new paragraph. In a document based on the Normal.dotm template, Word automatically adds extra space after each paragraph, so you need to press the Enter key only once.

▶ **VOCABULARY**
word wrap

Step-by-Step 12.3

1. If necessary, click the Word button on the taskbar to make Document2 the active document.

2. Press **Tab**, and then enter the sentence below. Notice as you enter the text that the insertion point moves and the status bar reflects the number of words in the document. Remember: Do not press Enter when the text expands to the right side of the screen.

   ```
   Today, the majority of the American population
   lives in cities and suburbs. The people who live in
   metropolitan areas depend on parks and recreational
   paths close to their homes for both recreation and
   contact with nature.
   ```

3. Press **Enter** to start a new paragraph.

4. Press **Tab** and then enter the sentence below.

   ```
   To preserve acres of green open space, parks
   surrounding and running through metropolitan areas
   are interconnected to create greenways. Sometimes
   these greenways even link cities together.
   ```

5. Click the **Office Button** and then click **Save As**. The Save As dialog box will open. Compare the folder structure at the top of the dialog box to the default file location setting. They may not be the same because the path will show the last folder into which a Word file was saved.

6. Locate the folder where you are to save your documents. (Your instructor will provide this information.)

7. In the File name box, enter **Greenways1**, and then click **Save**.

8. Check the word count in the status bar at the bottom-left corner of the window. The word count should be 62.

9. Leave the document open.

2-1.1.5
2-1.1.6

Changing Views and Magnification

Changing the way the document looks on your screen can make working with the document much easier. You can change the way you view your document, and you can also control how much of the document shows on the screen. The appearance of the document on the screen should be appropriate for the current task.

Viewing a Document

Word offers different options for viewing a document, and you can change the view by selecting options from the Document Views group on the View tab, shown in **Figure 12–4**. You can also change the view by clicking one of the view buttons in the status bar at the lower-right corner of the document window, shown in **Figure 12–5**.

Active view is highlighted

Options for viewing a document

FIGURE 12–4   The Document Views group on the View tab

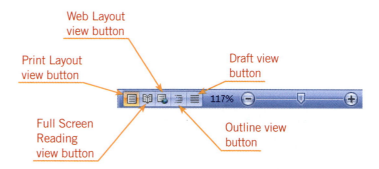

Web Layout view button

Print Layout view button

Draft view button

Full Screen Reading view button

Outline view button

FIGURE 12–5   View buttons in the status bar

Each view provides a different way to look at and work with a document. **Table 12–1** describes each of the views. As you work with documents in the different views, you may find that you prefer one view for certain tasks and another view for other tasks.

TABLE 12–1   View options for Word

VIEW	DESCRIPTION
Print Layout	The document shows on the screen as it will appear when printed; this is the default view in Word
Full Screen Reading	The screen space is maximized for reading the document; when two pages are shown side by side in Full Screen Reading view, it appears as though you are reading a book
Web Layout	The document shows on the screen as it will appear in a Web browser
Outline	The document content shows on the screen in an outline format, which makes it easy to see the structure of the document and to quickly and easily reorganize the content
Draft	Only the basic document, without elements such as headers and footers, shows on the screen; the purpose of Draft view is to make the editing process quicker

Step-by-Step 12.4

1. Open **Step12-4.docx** from the data files, and save the document as **Ruts**.

2. Click the **View** tab on the Ribbon. Notice that the document opened in Print Layout view.

3. Click the **Full Screen Reading** button in the Document Views group on the View tab. Your screen should look similar to **Figure 12–6**. Notice that the Ribbon, the scroll bars, and the status bar are hidden.

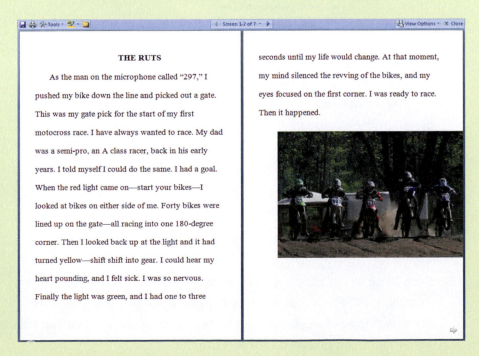

FIGURE 12–6
The document in Full Screen Reading view

4. If your screen does not show two pages side by side, click **View Options** in the upper-right corner of the screen and then click **Show Two Pages**.  Your screen should now show two pages side by side.

5. Click **View Options**. If the Allow Typing button is already highlighted, as shown in **Figure 12–7**, the option is already selected, and you can click **View Options** again to close the menu. If the **Allow Typing** button is not highlighted, click the button to select it. Selecting this option will enable you to edit the document in Full Screen Reading view.

FIGURE 12–7
The View Options menu in Full Screen Reading view

Orange highlight indicates the option is selected

6. To scroll through the pages in the document, do one of the following:
   a. Press the **up** and **down arrow** keys ↑ ↓ or the **PageUp** and **PageDown** keys.
   b. Click the arrows that appear at the lower corners of the pages.
   c. Move the wheel on the mouse.

7. Show the first page of the document, and position the insertion point in front of the letter T in the document title. Enter the words **GETTING THROUGH** so the revised title reads *GETTING THROUGH THE RUTS*.

8. Click the **Save** button in the upper-left corner to quickly save the changes.

9. Click **Close** in the upper-right corner of the screen to close Full Screen Reading view. Your document now appears again in Print Layout view, the view that was used before Full Screen Reading view. Notice that the words you added to the title are still there.

HEADS UP

If the Research task pane appears when you change views, close the task pane.

10. Click the **Web Layout** button. You will most likely notice a difference in the width of the document and changes to the text wrapping.

11. Click the **Outline** button. Notice the Ribbon changes and provides many new tools for navigating and editing the outline. You will have an opportunity to work in Outline view in Lesson 16.

12. In the Close group, click the **Close Outline View** button. The document returns to Print Layout view, with the Home tab active.

13. Click the **View** tab and then click the **Draft** button in the Document Views group. You will probably notice a change in the magnification. Change back to Print Layout view.

14. Leave the document open.

Changing the Zoom and Magnification Settings

Word also provides zoom options to increase and decrease the size of text and graphics on the screen, and you can also show an entire page or multiple pages at the same time. The zoom options are in the Zoom group on the View tab shown in **Figure 12–8**. You will also find zoom controls in the status bar at the lower-right corner of the screen, as shown in **Figure 12–9**.

EXTRA FOR EXPERTS

If your mouse has a wheel, you can press and hold **Ctrl** and move the wheel away from you to increase the magnification and move the wheel toward you to decrease the magnification.

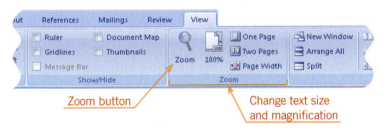

Zoom button

Change text size and magnification

FIGURE 12–8   The Zoom group on the View tab

FIGURE 12–9   Zoom controls in the status bar

Step-by-Step 12.5

1. If necessary, open the **Ruts** document from your solution files.

2. On the View tab, in the Zoom group, click the **Zoom** button to open the Zoom dialog box shown in **Figure 12–10**. The Zoom dialog box provides a Preview screen and a text preview panel in the Zoom dialog box so you can preview how the changes you select will show on the screen.

FIGURE 12–10
The Zoom dialog box

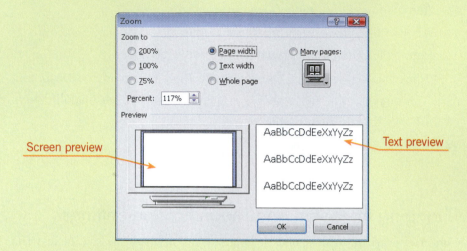

Screen preview   Text preview

3. Notice that the current setting is Page width. Make a note of the percent. Click to select the **75%** option and preview that setting.

4. Click to select the **Whole page** option. Notice that the percentage changes again.

5. Click to select the **Many pages** option. The percentage will change to 10% and you will be able to view all the pages in the document at the same time.

6. Click **OK** to accept the change. All four pages of the document will appear on your screen.

7. Click the **Page Width** button 🖼 Page Width in the Zoom group on the View tab. The first page of the document should appear on your screen.

8. Leave the document open.

2-2.1.6

Showing Characters

As you have learned, changing the way a document looks on the screen can make tasks easier. To make editing a document easier, you can also show some special characters. These characters are known as nonprinting characters because, although you can show these symbols on the screen, they do not print.

The Show/Hide ¶ button, in the Paragraph group on the Home tab, enables you to toggle the option to show these nonprinting characters. When you *toggle* an option, you alternate between the off and on states by repeating a procedure, such as clicking a button. Nonprinting characters include paragraph markers, blank spaces, page or section breaks, and tab markers, as shown in **Figure 12–11**. Initially, you may not like showing nonprinting characters while you work with a document, but give it a try. Once you get used to seeing the nonprinting characters on the screen, you will find them very useful as you create and edit the document.

▶ **VOCABULARY**
toggle

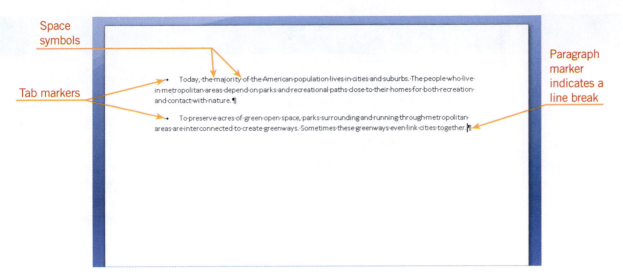

FIGURE 12–11   A document with nonprinting characters showing

Step-by-Step 12.6

1. If necessary, open the **Greenways1** document from your solution files. Save the document Greenways1 as **Greenways2**.

2. Click the **Home** tab. In the Paragraph group, click the **Show/Hide¶** button ¶ to toggle the feature on. The button will have an orange background when it is activated.

3. Compare your document to **Figure 12–11**. The nonprinting symbols are identified in the figure. If necessary, scroll up in the document to see the symbols. If you do not see the nonprinting characters on your screen, click the Home tab and then click the Show/Hide ¶ button again.

4. Leave the document open.

Using Click and Type

2-1.3.1
2-2.1.6

Click and type is a Word setting that enables you to quickly position the insertion point within a blank area of a document. When you double-click in a blank space in the document, Word automatically adds blank paragraphs or tabs to position the insertion point where you click. Showing the nonprinting characters can be very helpful when using click and type. If the nonprinting characters are visible when you reposition the insertion point in a blank area of the document, new nonprinting paragraph markers and tab markers will appear so you will know how many blank paragraphs or tabs were created to move the insertion point to the new location.

Step-by-Step 12.7

1. If necessary, open the **Greenways2** document from your solution files.

2. Make sure that the click and type setting is enabled. Click the **Office Button**, click **Word Options**, and then click **Advanced**. At the bottom of the list below Editing options, make sure there is a check mark in the box for **Enable click and type**. The option is turned on when there is a check mark in the check box, as shown in **Figure 12–12**.

FIGURE 12–12
Advanced settings in the Word Options dialog box

Enable click and type

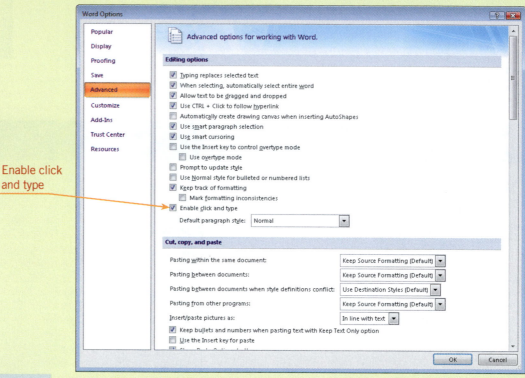

EXTRA FOR EXPERTS

If a graphic is visible next to the I-beam, it indicates the format for the text. For example, the I-beam shown in **Figure 12–13** indicates that the text will be aligned at the left, beginning where you position the insertion point.

3. Click **OK** to apply the option and close the dialog box.

4. If necessary, click the **Print Layout** button 📄 in the status bar to switch to Print Layout view.

5. Use the scroll bar to move to the bottom of the document. All or most of the document window will be white. Point to the middle of the document window. The mouse pointer will change to an I-beam, indicating text can be entered in that area of the document. The I-beam is shown in **Figure 12–13**.

FIGURE 12–13
The I-beam in a blank area of the document

Insertion point

I-beam pointer

6. With the mouse pointer positioned in the white area, double-click. The insertion point is now positioned where you clicked. Several new paragraph markers and a tab marker will appear above and before the new location of the insertion point.

7. Enter your first and last names.

8. Click the **Save** button on the Quick Access Toolbar and close the document.

Navigating Through the Document

2-1.1.3

It's easy to move around in a one-page document, but if the document is several pages in length, it takes much longer to navigate. There are several ways to move around in Word, including changing the view, using the mouse, and using the keyboard. For both short and long documents, there are many ways to save time moving through a document.

Using Thumbnails

You've already learned about several ways to view a document, but there's another option on the View tab that you have not yet explored. When the Thumbnails check box in the Show/Hide group on the View tab is checked as shown in **Figure 12–14**, thumbnails for each page in the document will show in a pane on the left side of the document. **Figure 12–14** shows thumbnails for the first three pages of a four-page document. Each thumbnail is identified with a page number, and the current page is also identified in the status bar. Although most words may be too small to read on a thumbnail, usually graphics or headings will help you identify the page. To go directly to a specific page, click on the thumbnail for that page.

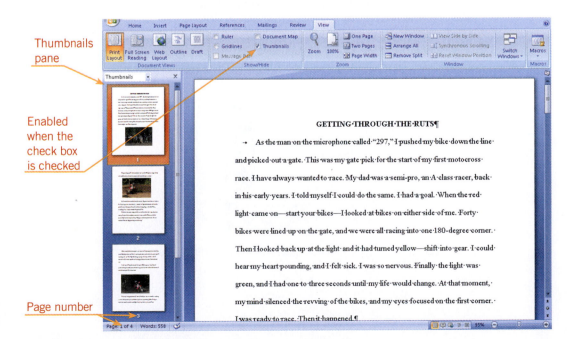

FIGURE 12–14   The Thumbnails pane

Step-by-Step 12.8

1. If necessary, open the **Ruts** document from your solution files.
2. On the View tab, click to select the **Thumbnails** check box 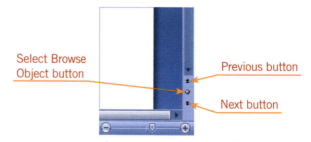 in the Show/Hide group. Four thumbnails will appear in a task pane at the left side of the document.
3. Click the thumbnail for page 3 in the task pane.
4. Click the **Thumbnails** check box on the View tab to deselect the option and hide the Thumbnails task pane.
5. Leave the document open.

Using the Mouse

If the location you want to navigate to is currently on the screen, you can simply position the mouse pointer and click. If the part of the document you want to view is currently not visible, you can use the scroll bars to navigate to that part of the document. The scroll bars enable you to quickly move to other areas of the document. If the zoom settings are set for page width (the default setting) or an even smaller percentage, the horizontal scroll bar will not appear because the entire width of the document is already visible.

If your mouse has a scroll wheel, you can use it to scroll vertically through a Word document. To scroll down, roll the wheel toward you, and to scroll up, roll the wheel away from you.

The position of the scroll box on the scroll bar helps you identify what part of the document you are viewing. As you drag the scroll box, a ScreenTip tells you what page you are viewing. As you learned in Lesson 11, when you scroll through a document, the insertion point does not move. If you scroll to a new part of the document and then want to reposition the insertion point on that page, simply click where you want to position the insertion point.

Browsing is another option for navigating through the document. When you browse, you focus on an object such as a page or a footnote. To browse, you use the three Browse buttons at the bottom of the vertical scroll bar shown in **Figure 12–15**.

Select Browse
Object button

Previous button

Next button

FIGURE 12–15   The Browse buttons on the vertical scroll bar

Step-by-Step 12.9

1. If necessary, open the **Ruts** document from your solution files.

2. Click the **Zoom** button on the View tab to open the Zoom dialog box, and click to change the percentage setting to **200%**. Click **OK**. The horizontal scroll bar will appear. Drag the scroll box in the horizontal scroll bar at the bottom of the screen to the right side of the scroll bar.

3. Click the **Page Width** button in the Zoom group to reduce the magnification of the document.

4. Use the vertical scroll bar to move to the top of the document. Position the insertion point in front of the document title.

5. Click the **Select Browse Object** button at the bottom of the vertical scroll bar. The options shown in **Figure 12–16** will appear.

FIGURE 12–16
Browse options

6. Move the mouse pointer over the options, and the name of the object will appear in the box. Notice that you can also access the Go To command in these options.

7. Click the **Browse by Page** option. The insertion point will move to the top of the second page.

8. Click the **Previous Page** button on the vertical scroll bar to move the insertion point back to page 1.

9. Click the **Next Page** button on the vertical scroll bar twice to move the insertion point to page 3.

10. Leave the document open.

Using the Keyboard

If you have good keyboarding skills, learning keyboard shortcuts to move the insertion point can speed up your work. Using the keyboard shortcuts eliminates the need to move your hands away from the keyboard. You can use the arrow keys on the keyboard to move the insertion point one character at a time or one line at a time. If you need to move across several characters or lines, however, the keyboard shortcuts shown in **Table 12–2** will make the task easier and quicker.

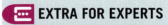 **EXTRA FOR EXPERTS**

You can find a comprehensive list of keyboard shortcuts by searching for the keywords *keyboard shortcuts* in the Word Help dialog box.

TABLE 12–2   Keyboard shortcuts for moving the insertion point

TO MOVE THE INSERTION POINT	PRESS
Right one character	right arrow
Left one character	left arrow
Down one line	down arrow
Up one line	up arrow
To the end of a line	End
To the beginning of a line	Home
To the next screen	Page Down
To the previous screen	Page Up
To the next word	Ctrl+right arrow
To the previous word	Ctrl+left arrow
To the end of the document	Ctrl+End
To the beginning of the document	Ctrl+Home
Up one paragraph	Ctrl+up arrow
Down one paragraph	Ctrl+down arrow

When navigating a multi-page document, the Go To command can also be very useful, because you can go directly to a specific page, line, or footnote in the document.

Step-by-Step 12.10

1. If necessary, open the **Ruts** document from your solution files.
2. Press **Ctrl+Home** to move the insertion point to the beginning of the document.
3. Press the **down arrow** twice to move the insertion point down two lines. Press the **right arrow** three times to move the insertion point three characters to the right.
4. Press **End** to move the insertion point to the end of the line.
5. Press and hold **Ctrl** and then press the **left arrow** to move the insertion point to the previous word.
6. Press **Home** to move the insertion point to the beginning of the line.
7. Press and hold **Ctrl** and then press the **down arrow** to move down one paragraph. Press and hold **Ctrl** and then press **End** to move the insertion point to the end of the document.

8. Press **Page Down** once to move down one screen.

9. Click the **Find** button arrow in the Editing group on the Home tab, as shown in **Figure 12–17**.

Find button arrow

FIGURE 12–17
The Find button in the Editing group

10. Click **Go To**. The Go To tab in the Find and Replace dialog box shown in **Figure 12–18** will appear. Under Go to what, select **Page**. In the Enter page number box, enter **2** and then click **Go To**. The insertion point is repositioned at the top of page 2. The information in the dialog box will adapt to the option you select.

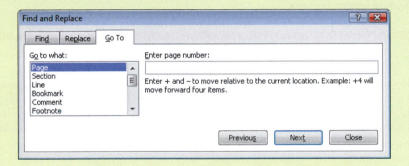

FIGURE 12–18
The Go To tab in the Find and Replace dialog box

11. Enter **1** in the Enter page number box and click **Go To** to go to the first page. The dialog box will remain open, and you can drag the title bar to reposition it if you want to keep it open for future searches.

12. Close the Find and Replace dialog box. The last option you chose in the Go to what box will appear when you open the dialog box again.

13. Press and hold **Ctrl** and then press **Page Down**. The insertion point moves to the top of page 2.

14. Close the document and the application. If prompted to save changes, click **No**.

ETHICS IN TECHNOLOGY

Watermarks

A watermark was originally an image embedded in a sheet of paper when the paper was produced to show the name or logo of the paper company. The term is also used to describe a very light image or text printed in the background of a document. Watermarks are no longer limited to paper; they are also added to digital files. The digital watermark identifies the owner of files and provides copyright protection. For example, corporations add their logo to the bottom corner of a video or slide show presentation. When used for photos, the watermark is often translucent and superimposed on the image. Although these types of watermarks don't prevent unlawful copying of images, video, and audio files, they show ownership and discourage illegal copying. Also, not all digital watermarks are visible to the human eye or audible to the human ear. Invisible watermarks are often embedded in the file and can be used to provide legal evidence of copyright infringement if digital media is copied illegally.

Another new technology, digital fingerprinting, provides information in the file about the originator or the purchaser. The fingerprint can be either visible or invisible. If the media is copied, the fingerprint is copied in the file, and the fingerprint can be traced back to the originator or purchaser. Software programs are designed to read digital watermarks and fingerprints. More new tools are on the horizon to protect the ownership of files and prevent people from stealing content.

SUMMARY

In this lesson, you learned:

- New blank documents are created based on a template with default settings.

- There are many "behind the scenes" settings in Word which can be changed to meet your preferences.

- Word automatically wraps text to the next line when the line of text extends beyond the right margin.

- Word provides several options for viewing a document.

- You can use zoom options to increase or decrease the size of the text and graphics on the screen.

- To make editing easier, you can show the nonprinting characters, such as tab markers, blank spaces, page breaks, and paragraph markers.

- The click and type setting lets you position the insertion point in a blank area of a document.

- You can view thumbnails of the document pages to make it easier and faster to move through the document.

- You can also use the mouse, keyboard shortcuts, or the Go To command to move through a document quickly.

 VOCABULARY REVIEW

Define the following terms:

default settings   toggle
Normal.dotm template   word wrap

■ REVIEW QUESTIONS

TRUE / FALSE

Circle T if the statement is true or F if the statement is false.

T   F   **1.**   All Word settings appear on the Ribbon or in dialog boxes.

T   F   **2.**   As you enter a paragraph of text, you should press Enter to end each line at the right margin.

T   F   **3.**   Word offers five different views for the document window.

T   F   **4.**   The scroll bar includes buttons for browsing objects in the document.

T   F   **5.**   The vertical and horizontal scroll bars are always visible for open documents.

MULTIPLE CHOICE

Select the best response for the following statements.

1. The _____ view allows you to quickly and easily reorganize the content.

   A.   Outline   C.   Full Screen Reading

   B.   Draft   D.   Print Layout

2. Nonprinting characters include _____.

   A.   paragraph markers, blank spaces, and page markers

   B.   paragraph markers, tab markers, and page markers

   C.   paragraph markers, blank spaces, tab markers, and page or section breaks

   D.   paragraph markers and page markers

3. When you _____ a document, you focus on an object such as a page or a footnote.

   A.   browse   C.   magnify

   B.   navigate   D.   scroll

4. You use the _____ options to increase and decrease the size of text and graphics on the screen.

   A.   document view   C.   zoom

   B.   scroll bar   D.   Go To

5. To move the insertion point to the top of the document, press _____.

   A.   Ctrl+up arrow   C.   Ctrl+Home

   B.   Shift+up arrow   D.   Ctrl+up arrow

FILL IN THE BLANK

Complete the following sentences by writing the correct word or words in the blanks provided.

1. Preset options already in place in a new document are called _____.

2. The _____ feature automatically moves text to the next line when you reach the right margin.

3. The _____ feature enables you to position the insertion point in a blank area of the document.

4. The _____ is a file containing default styles and customizations that determine the structure and page layout of a document.

5. When you _____ a setting, you are alternating between the off and on states by repeating a procedure, such as clicking a button.

■ PROJECTS

PROJECT 12–1

1. If necessary, start Word. If Word is already open, create a new blank document.

2. Enter the following two paragraphs.

   Almost everyone knows about the San Andreas Fault in California. Shifting along this fault line resulted in numerous damaging earthquakes throughout the twentieth century.

   Relatively unknown by comparison, the New Madrid Fault in the central United States caused three of the most powerful earthquakes in U.S. history in the nineteenth century. One earthquake along this fault line was so powerful that it caused the Mississippi River to change course. Damage from the earthquake was reported as far away as Charleston, South Carolina, and Washington, DC.

3. Save the document as **Fault**.

4. Switch to Full Screen Reading view.

5. Position the insertion point at the beginning of the document and enter **Someone Else's Fault**.

6. Press **Enter** twice to create extra space after the new line of text.

7. Save the changes and close Full Screen Reading view.

8. Change the zoom to **150%** by changing the setting in the Percent box.

9. Close the document.

PROJECT 12–2

1. Open **Project12–2** from the data files.

2. Save the document as **Interview Preparation**.

3. Show the nonprinting characters in the document.

4. Scroll down to the middle of the document. Position the insertion point in the white space about two inches below the last question.

5. Choose one of the questions and enter your response to that question.

6. There should be at least four blank paragraphs between the last question and the response that you entered. If necessary, position the insertion point between the last question and your response and press **Enter** to add more blank lines.

7. Save your changes and close the document.

PROJECT 12–3

1. Open **Project12–3** from the data files.

2. Scroll to the middle of the document until you see the heading *Similarities*.

3. Use keyboard shortcuts to do the following:
   a. move the insertion point to the end of the document
   b. move the insertion point up one paragraph
   c. move the insertion point to the beginning of the document

4. Use the Go To command to locate line 64, and then go to line 51. The insertion point should first be positioned near the heading *Differences* and then near the heading *Similarities*.

5. Show the Thumbnails pane and use the thumbnails to go to page 1. The first page in the document is a cover page, so it is numbered 0.

6. Browse the document by page until page 4 is the active page.

7. Close the document. If prompted to save changes, click **No**.

TEAMWORK PROJECT

Microsoft released the first version of Word for an IBM PC in 1983. The early versions of the Word software were created for MS-DOS, not Windows. Word made full use of the mouse, but few people used the mouse at this time. They usually accessed the commands by keystrokes, and users often memorized the necessary keystrokes. So, keyboard shortcuts have been around for a long time. You learned several keyboard shortcuts in this lesson, but there are many more.

1. Choose a partner to find keyboard shortcuts for commands related to one of the following Word topics:
   - Display and use windows
   - Switch to another view/Full Screen Reading view
   - Use dialog boxes
   - Use the Open and Save As dialog boxes
   - Create, view, and save documents

2. Explore the ScreenTips in Word and use the Word Help system to create a list of the commands and keyboard shortcuts for commands related to the topic.

3. Try each of the shortcuts described in your list to see if the shortcuts work on your computer.

4. Share your list with the class.

CRITICAL THINKING

ACTIVITY 12–1

In this lesson you viewed documents in several different views. Which of these views do you prefer? Describe your preference and explain why.

ACTIVITY 12–2

When you open a Word document attached to an e-mail, the document will most likely open in Full Screen Reading view as a result of default settings. Explore the Word Options and describe how you can change this setting so Word documents will open in Print Layout View when launched from an e-mail attachment.

ONLINE DISCOVERY

Open your Web browser and experiment changing the text size and zoom settings when you view Web pages. Compare changing the view of a Web page to changing the view of a Word document. Write a brief summary of the similarities you find.

LESSON 13

Editing and Formatting Documents

■ OBJECTIVES

Upon completion of this lesson, you should be able to:

■ Delete and insert text using the Backspace and Delete keys and Insert and Overtype modes.

■ Undo, redo, and repeat actions.

■ Edit text using drag-and-drop editing and the Cut, Copy, and Paste commands.

■ Use proofing tools to check and correct spelling and grammar and use research services.

■ Format characters with fonts and attributes.

■ Format paragraphs with fonts, line spacing, alignment, tabs and indents, and bulleted and numbered lists.

■ Format documents with margin settings, page orientation settings, and page breaks.

■ Find and replace text.

■ DATA FILES

To complete this lesson, you will need these data files:

Step13-1.docx   Step13-12.docx

Step13-4.docx   Step13-13.docx

Step13-7.docx   Project13-1.docx

Step13-9.docx   Project13-2.docx

Step13-10.docx

■ VOCABULARY

alignment

Clipboard

drag-and-drop editing

edit

first line indent

font

format

Format Painter

hanging indent

indent

Insert mode

landscape orientation

manual line break

manual page break

margin

Overtype mode

points

portrait orientation

select

soft page break

2-1.1.7
2-1.3.2
2-1.3.3
2-1.3.5
2-2.2.1

Word provides many features that give you the ability to improve and enhance your documents. Editing and formatting features give you the ability to refine your documents and determine how they will look on the screen, on the Web, or as printed pages.

Editing Documents

When you *edit* a document, you modify or adapt the document and make revisions or corrections. Editing a document involves adding, deleting, changing, or moving text, and Word provides many features that enable you to make changes, correct errors, and check the spelling and the grammar in your document.

Selecting Text

When you *select* text, you identify a block of text you want to edit. The text can be a single character, several characters, a word, a sentence, one or more paragraphs, or even the entire document. Once you select text, you can delete it, replace it, change its appearance, move it, copy it, and so on. You can use the mouse or the keyboard to select text. The quickest way to select text using the mouse is to click and hold the mouse button, drag the mouse pointer over the desired text, and then release the mouse button.

Sometimes it is difficult to select precisely when you are dragging the mouse. **Table 13–1** lists several options for selecting text using the mouse and the keyboard. To deselect the text (remove the selection), click anywhere in the document window or press an arrow key. If you accidentally delete or replace selected text, or if you just change your mind, click the Undo button.

TABLE 13–1   Ways to select text

TO SELECT	DO THIS:
Any amount of text	Click and hold the mouse button, drag the pointer over the text, then release the mouse button
A word	Double-click the word
A sentence	With no other text or objects selected, press and hold Ctrl, then click anywhere in the sentence
A paragraph	Triple-click anywhere in the paragraph, or double-click in the left margin
An entire document	Press Ctrl+A; or move the pointer to the left of any text, and when the pointer changes to a right-pointing arrow, triple-click
A line	Click in the left margin
Multiple lines	Click and hold the mouse button, and drag the pointer in the left margin
One or more characters to the right	Press and hold Shift and press the right arrow
One or more characters to the left	Press and hold Shift and press the left arrow
To the beginning of a word	Press and hold Ctrl+Shift and press the left arrow
To the end of a word	Press and hold Ctrl+Shift and press the right arrow
Any amount of text	Click where you want the selection to begin, press and hold Shift, and then click where you want the selection to end; everything between the two clicks is selected or Position the insertion point where you want the selection to begin, press F8 to toggle on the select mode, then use the arrow keys or the mouse to indicate where you want the selection to end (If you don't execute a command such as Delete or applying a format, press the Escape key to toggle the selected mode off)

Step-by-Step 13.1

1. Start the Word application.
2. Open **Step13-1** from the data files and save the document as **Carbohydrates1**.
3. If necessary, click the **Show/Hide ¶** button to show the nonprinting characters.

4. Move the I-beam mouse pointer until it is at the beginning of the first line of text. Click and hold the mouse button and drag the pointer through the first sentence of text. When the whole first sentence is selected, release the mouse button. The sentence is now selected, as shown in **Figure 13–1**.

FIGURE 13–1
Selected text

Selected text

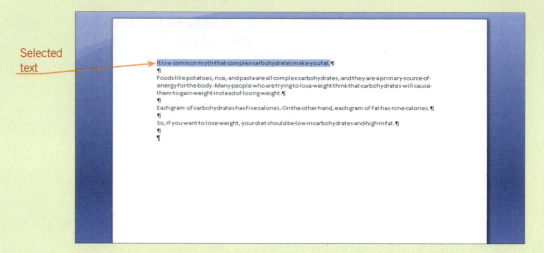

5. Double-click the word *diet* in the last paragraph to select it.

6. Press **Ctrl+A** to select the entire document. Click anywhere in the document window to deselect the text.

7. Click to position the insertion point at the beginning of the second paragraph. Press and hold the **Shift** key, and then click after the word *rice*. Everything between the two clicks is selected.

8. Continue to hold the **Shift** key and press the **right arrow** key to extend the selection. Press the **left arrow** key to reverse direction of the selection. Continue to press the **left arrow** key until text in the previous paragraph is selected. Press the **down** and **up arrow** keys to reverse and extend the direction of the selection. Release the **Shift** key.

9. Position the insertion point at the end of the first paragraph. The insertion point will appear between the period and the paragraph marker. Press and hold the **Ctrl** and **Shift** keys and then press the **Home** key. All of the text from the insertion point to the beginning of the document is selected.

10. Click anywhere in the document window to deselect the text. Practice other methods of selecting text following the instructions in **Table 13–1**.

11. Leave the document open.

Deleting and Inserting Characters

Editing often involves deleting and replacing existing text. You can quickly delete characters one at a time by using either the Backspace or Delete key. The Backspace key deletes the character to the left of the insertion point. The Delete key removes the character to the right of the insertion point. When you hold down either of these keys, the characters will continue to be deleted until you release the key. You can also select characters, words, sentences, or paragraphs and then press the Delete or Backspace key to delete the selected text.

By default, Word enters text in a document using the Insert mode. In *Insert mode*, when you enter new text in front of existing text, the existing text shifts to the right to make room for the new text. When the Insert mode is turned off, the Overtype mode is activated. In *Overtype mode*, new text replaces the existing text. You can change the settings for Insert mode and Overtype mode in the Word Options dialog box.

▶ **VOCABULARY**

Insert mode

Overtype mode

TECHNOLOGY TIMELINE

Typewriter Fonts

Before computers and word-processing programs, typewriters were used to create formal documents. The first machines typed only in capital letters. The Remington Company was the first to offer a typewriter that could print both upper- and lowercase letters with the addition of the Shift key. The action was called a *shift* because the carriage on a typewriter would actually shift the position of the typebar to print either of two letter cases. Modern electronic machines such as computers no longer use a mechanical shift to print upper- and lowercase letters, but the Shift key remains on keyboards for this process.

When using typewriters, it was also common practice to include two blank spaces between sentences. The typewriters used a monospace typeface, which means all characters were the exact same width. For example, the amount of horizontal space provided for the letter i was the same as the amount of horizontal space for the letter m. The extra blank space created more blank space and made it easier to see the break between sentences. Today's word-processing applications are more sophisticated, and the extra spaces are not necessary because the fonts generally allow for proportional spacing, which eliminates excess blank space between characters. The blank space between sentences is more obvious so you need only enter one blank space between sentences. In spite of this, monospace fonts have not vanished. They are especially useful when aligning text in columns.

Step-by-Step 13.2

1. If necessary, open **Carbohydrates1** from your solution files.

2. Position the insertion point right before the period at the end of the last sentence in the second paragraph. Press the **Backspace** key several times to erase the last four words in the sentence (*instead of losing weight*).

3. Move the insertion point to the beginning of the word *complex* in the second paragraph. Press **Delete** to remove the first letter of the word. Double-click the remaining part of the word to select it, and then press **Delete**.

4. Double-click the word **carbohydrates** in the last paragraph to select it, and enter **fat**. The selected text is replaced with the new text.

5. Double-click the second occurrence of the word **fat** in the last paragraph and enter **complex carbohydrates**.

6. Make sure the Insert mode is activated. Click the **Office Button**, click **Word Options**, and then click **Advanced**. Under Editing options, make sure there is no check mark for the option Use Overtype mode. Also, if necessary, enable the option **Use the Insert key to control Overtype mode**. Compare your screen to **Figure 13–2**.

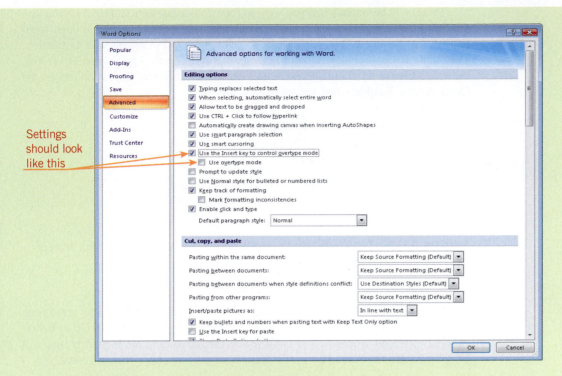

Settings should look like this

FIGURE 13–2
The Insert/Overtype mode options

7. Click **OK** to accept any changes and close the Word Options dialog box.

8. Position the insertion point right before the first occurrence of the word *and* in the first sentence of the second paragraph. Enter **bread**, and then a space. Because you are in Insert mode, Word inserts the text between the existing characters.

9. Press **Insert** to toggle on Overtype mode.

10. Position the insertion point in front of the word *five* in the first sentence of the third paragraph. Enter **four**. The new text replaces the word *five*.

11. Press **Insert** to toggle to Insert mode.

12. Save the changes and leave the document open. You must complete Step-by-Step 13.3 before closing the document.

Undoing, Redoing, and Repeating

Sometimes you may delete or replace text unintentionally. Whenever you perform an action that you want to reverse, you can use the Undo command. If you undo an action and then change your mind, you can reverse the undo action by using the Redo command. You can even undo and redo multiple actions at one time.

There may be times when you want to repeat your last action. For example, you may enter new text in a document and then want to add the same text in other locations in the document. You can use the Repeat command to repeat your last action. The Undo, Redo, and Repeat buttons can be accessed on the Quick Access Toolbar, shown in **Figure 13–3**. The Redo button exchanges with the Repeat button on the Quick Access Toolbar when you undo an action.

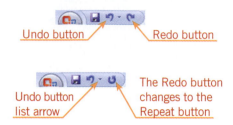

FIGURE 13–3   The Undo, Redo, and Repeat buttons on the Quick Access Toolbar

ScreenTips for these buttons are conditional and will reflect your recent action. Sometimes an action cannot be reversed, and the ScreenTip for the Undo button changes to "Can't Undo." If you can't repeat the last action, the Repeat button will be dimmed and the ScreenTip for the Repeat button will show "Can't Repeat."

Step-by-Step 13.3

1. The document **Carbohydrates1** should already be open from the previous Step-by-Step. Save the document Carbohydrates1 as **Carbohydrates2**.

2. Position the insertion point at the end of the document. Enter your name, and then press **Enter** twice.

3. Move the insertion point to the beginning of the document.

4. Position the mouse pointer over the Repeat button 🔄 on the Quick Access Toolbar to show the ScreenTip *Repeat Typing (Ctrl + Y)*. Then, click the **Repeat** button. Your name and a blank line are inserted at the position of the insertion point.

5. You change your mind. Position the mouse pointer over the Undo button 🔙 on the Quick Access Toolbar to show the ScreenTip *Undo Typing (Ctrl + Z)*. Then, click the **Undo** button. Your name and the blank line are removed from the top of the document.

6. Click the **Undo** button arrow and position the mouse pointer over *Typing "bread,"*. All the previous actions above that action in the list will also be highlighted, as shown in **Figure 13–4**. Click **Typing "bread,"**. The last six actions are reversed.

FIGURE 13–4
Select multiple actions in the Undo list box

7. Click the **Redo** button 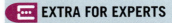 on the Quick Access Toolbar to reverse only the last undo. The word *bread* is reinserted in the second paragraph.

8. Click the **Redo** button four more times to replace the word *five* with *four*.

9. Click the **Undo** button arrow. The list includes *Typing "bread,"* and *Typing the letters f, o, u, and r.*

10. Click anywhere in the document window to close the Undo list. Save the changes and leave the document open.

Copying and Moving Text

Selected text can be copied or moved within a document and between documents. For example, you can copy text from an e-mail message to a Word document. There are several ways to copy and move text.

Using Drag-and-Drop Editing

When you use the mouse to drag selected text from the existing location and then drop the selected text in a new location, it is called ***drag-and-drop editing***. Drag-and-drop editing makes moving text quick and easy, especially when you are moving the text short distances. You simply drag selected text to the new location and then release the mouse button. You can also copy text using drag-and-drop editing. Hold down Ctrl as you drag, and the selected text will be copied instead of moved.

Using the Cut, Copy, and Paste Commands

You can also use the Cut, Copy, and Paste commands to move and copy selected text. When you use the Cut, Copy, and Paste commands, Word stores the selected text on the Clipboard. The ***Clipboard*** is a temporary storage place in your computer's memory, and it is shared among all the Office applications. You send selected contents of your document to the Clipboard by using the Cut or Copy commands. The Clipboard stores up to 24 items, which you can view by showing the Clipboard task pane. If you prefer, you can work with the Clipboard task pane open.

▶ **VOCABULARY**

drag-and-drop editing

Clipboard

⌨ **EXTRA FOR EXPERTS**

Word offers many options for using the Clipboard. Use the Help feature to find out more about the Clipboard and to determine which options best meet your needs.

The Clipboard can store data of all Office types, and that data can be inserted into the same document, into other documents in the same application, or into files in other Office programs. You can retrieve the contents of the Clipboard by using the Paste command. You can select any one of the items on the Clipboard and paste it, or you can paste all of the items at once. Pasting the contents of the Clipboard does not delete the contents from the Clipboard. Therefore, you can paste Clipboard items as many times as you want. However, when you turn off the computer, the Clipboard contents are erased.

Step-by-Step 13.4

1. If necessary, open **Carbohydrates2** from your solution files. Save the document Carbohydrates2 as **Carbohydrates3**. Also, if necessary, click the **Show/Hide ¶** button to show the nonprinting characters.

2. Select all of the text in the third paragraph, but do not include the paragraph marker in the selection.

3. Point to the selection and hold down the left mouse button. Drag the insertion point to the end of the first paragraph, and then release. If you look closely as you drag the selected text, you will see that the insertion point changes to a dotted vertical line. Word automatically adjusts the spacing by adding a blank space between the two sentences.

4. With the sentence still selected, press and hold **Ctrl** and use the left mouse button to drag the text to the end of the document. Notice as you drag the text that the mouse pointer has changed and includes a plus sign. Release the mouse button. The text is copied to the new location.

5. Click the **Undo** button and then click anywhere in the document window to deselect the text.

6. Click the **Dialog Box Launcher** button in the Clipboard group on the Home tab to open the Clipboard task pane, as shown in **Figure 13–5**. Your Clipboard may show different items or no items at all. If items appear on the Clipboard, click the **Clear All** button to remove any items from the Clipboard.

⬛ EXTRA FOR EXPERTS

To drag text beyond the current screen of text, drag the pointer toward the top or bottom of the screen. As you hold the pointer at the edge, the document will automatically scroll in that direction.

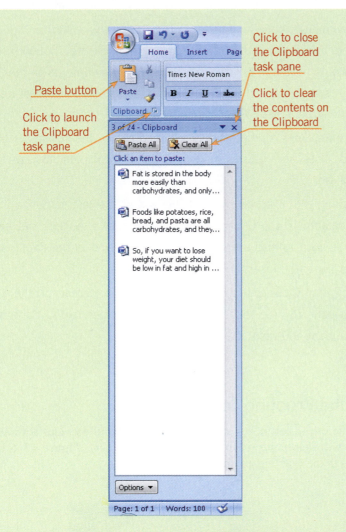

FIGURE 13–5
The Clipboard task pane with data items

Paste button

Click to launch the Clipboard task pane

Click to close the Clipboard task pane

Click to clear the contents on the Clipboard

7. Press and hold **Ctrl** and click anywhere within the last sentence in the document to select the whole sentence. In the Clipboard group, click the **Cut** button . The selected text appears on the Clipboard. Cutting removes text from the document and stores it on the Clipboard.

8. Triple-click anywhere in the second paragraph in the document to select the whole paragraph. In the Clipboard group, click the **Copy** button . The selected text appears on the Clipboard. Copying stores the text or data on the Clipboard, but it leaves the text in the document.

9. Open **Step13-4** from the data files. Press and hold **Ctrl** and press **A** to select the entire document, and click the **Copy** button. The text is stored on the Clipboard.

10. Switch to the **Carbohydrates3** document and position the insertion point at the beginning of the second paragraph. In the Clipboard group, click the **Paste** button. Word inserts the most recent item added to the Clipboard at the location of the insertion point. Notice that the copied text still appears on the Clipboard.

HEADS UP

You can also access the Cut, Copy, and Paste commands by right-clicking the selected text and choosing the desired command from the shortcut menu that appears. The keyboard shortcuts for Cut are **Ctrl+X**; for Copy, **Ctrl+C**; and for Paste, **Ctrl+V**.

11. Open a new blank document, and, if necessary, open the Clipboard task pane. There should be at least three items on the Clipboard. Click the **Paste All** button in the Clipboard pane. All the contents on the Clipboard are inserted at the location of the insertion point. The oldest item on the Clipboard is pasted first.

12. Save the new document as **Carbohydrates4** and then close the document. Also close the Step13-4 document. If prompted to save changes, click **No**.

13. Position the insertion point at the end of the last sentence in the last paragraph. In the Clipboard task pane, click the item that begins *So, if you want to lose weight*. The text is inserted in the document at the location of the insertion point.

14. Click the **Close** button in the upper-right corner of the Clipboard task pane to hide the pane. Save the changes to the Carbohydrates3 document and then close the document.

Using the Proofing Tools

An accurate document makes a good impression. Word provides several proofing tools that will help you prepare an error-free document. **Figure 13–6** shows the commands in the Proofing group on the Review tab.

FIGURE 13–6   The Proofing group on the Review tab

Checking Spelling and Grammar

Checking the spelling in a document can significantly reduce the amount of time you spend proofreading. As you enter text, Word automatically checks the spelling of each word against its standard dictionary. If Word cannot find the word in its dictionary, it will underline the word with a wavy red line. This does not necessarily mean the word is misspelled. It simply means the word is not listed in Word's dictionary. You can access a shortcut menu to view suggestions for changes.

Good proofreading skills also include checking grammar. When you check for the grammar in a document, you read for content and make sure each sentence makes sense. Word also automatically checks for grammar errors such as incomplete sentences, the wrong use of words, and capitalization and punctuation errors. Possible errors are identified with a wavy green line below a word, phrase, or sentence. You can access a shortcut menu to view suggestions for changes.

The red or green underlines are only visible on your screen. They will not appear when you print the document.

Using AutoCorrect and AutoComplete

It is common for us to make the same spelling error over and over. For example, you may often enter *hte* instead of *the*. The AutoCorrect feature automatically corrects errors as you enter text, which saves editing time. The AutoComplete feature suggests the spelling for frequently used words and phrases. For example, as you begin to enter the day of the week or the month, AutoComplete will provide an option for completing the word for you.

Step-by-Step 13.5

1. Open a new blank document and enter the following text exactly as shown here: **It is beleived**. Watch the screen as you press **Spacebar**. Word will automatically correct the spelling and change the word to *believed*.

2. Complete the sentence by entering **the potawatomi indians were originally part of the ancient tribe Anishinabe**. and then press **Enter**. Notice that there are red wavy lines under the words *potawatomi* and *Anishinabe*. Word automatically corrected the capitalization of the word *indians*.

3. Save the document as **Neighbors1**.

4. Point to the word *potawatomi* and right-click. A shortcut menu appears and shows two alternative spellings at the top of the menu. Click the first option **Potawatomi** in the shortcut menu, and the word in the document is corrected.

5. Right-click the word **Anishinabe**. The spelling you entered is correct, but this word is not included in the Word standard dictionary, so that is why the word is flagged. Click **Ignore All** in the shortcut menu. The red wavy line is removed, and the word *Anishinabe* will not be flagged as misspelled if entered again in this document.

6. Position the insertion point at the end of the document and enter **In the early 1700s, lived near Green Bay, Wisconsin**. and then press **Enter**. The entire sentence is underlined with a green wavy line.

7. Point to any part of the green underlined sentence and right-click. A shortcut menu appears, and the words *Fragment (consider revising)* appear at the top of the menu. Click outside the shortcut menu to close it. Position the insertion point in front of the word *lived* and enter **they**. The green wavy line disappears.

8. Save the changes and leave the document open.

Using the Research Tools

Creating a report often requires research. As you write a report, you may struggle to think of the appropriate word or phrase to make the content easier for the reader to understand. Or, you may want to use a synonym to avoid overusing a word. The commands in the Proofing group on the Review tab provide you quick access to several resources including dictionaries, a thesaurus, encyclopedia articles, translation services, and research Web sites.

Counting the Words

How many times have you counted the words in an essay to confirm it meets the minimum or maximum requirement for total words? The Word Count command provides statistics about your document that include the number of pages, sentences, lines, and characters as well as how many words are in your document. You can see the current number of words in the document in the status bar at the bottom of the window.

Step-by-Step 13.6

1. If necessary, open **Neighbors1** from your solution files. Save the document Neighbors1 as **Neighbors2**.

2. Position the insertion point anywhere within the word *near* in the last sentence. Click the **Review** tab, and, in the Proofing group, click the **Thesaurus** button. The Research task pane, shown in **Figure 13–7**, appears, showing a list of synonyms for the word *near*.

FIGURE 13–7
The Research task pane with results for a Thesaurus search

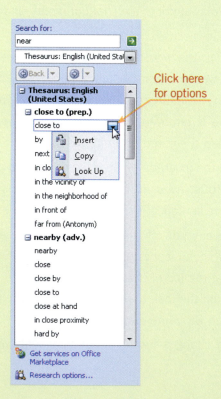

3. In the Thesaurus list, point to *close to*, as shown in **Figure 13–7**, and then click the list arrow. Click **Insert**. The word *near* in the document is replaced with *close to*.

4. In the Proofing group, click the **Translate** button . The Research task pane will change and show the translation options. The Search for box will most likely show *Green* because the insertion point is closest to the word *Green*. The From box should show *English (United States)*.

5. Click the list arrow in the To box and then click **French (France)**.

6. Click the green arrow below *Translate the whole document*. When prompted to translate the whole document, click **Yes**.

7. A window will open in your browser. If necessary, launch your browser from the taskbar to show the translation text.

8. Select all of the translation text, right-click anywhere within the selection, and click **Copy** in the shortcut menu. The selected text is saved on the Clipboard.

9. Switch to the **Neighbors2** document, position the insertion point at the end of the document, right-click, and click **Paste** in the shortcut menu. The translation text is inserted in the document.

10. In the Search for box at the top of the Research pane, enter **Potawatomi**. Click the list arrow in the box directly below, and then click **Encarta Encyclopedia: English (North America)**. Links for online Encarta Encyclopedia articles about Potawatomi Indians appear.

11. In the Proofing group, click the **Word Count** button . The Word Count dialog box opens, revealing the statistics for the document. Close the Word Count dialog box.

12. Save the changes, close the Research task pane, and then close the document. Also, close the browser.

Formatting Documents

When you *format* a document, you change the appearance of the text or of the whole document. The formats and design elements used in a document should be based on the purpose of the document and the needs of reader. Formats can be applied either before or after you enter text in your document.

Word offers a number of formats, including character formats, paragraph formats, and document formats.

- Text color and underline are examples of character formats. You can apply more than one character format at a time. For example, you can apply both color and underline formats to characters.

▶ **VOCABULARY**
format

IC³

2-1.3.4
2-1.3.6
2-1.4.1
2-1.4.2
2-2.1.1
2-2.1.2
2-2.1.3
2-2.1.4
2-2.1.5
2-2.1.7
2-2.1.16

- A paragraph format is applied to an entire paragraph and cannot be applied to only a portion of a paragraph. For example, you cannot single space part of a paragraph and double space the rest. Word defines a paragraph as any amount of text that ends with a paragraph marker. A paragraph marker is inserted by pressing the Enter key, which creates a *manual line break*.

- Document formats apply to an entire document. For example, margins and paper size are document formats. You can position the insertion point anywhere in a document to change the entire document format.

▶ **VOCABULARY**

manual line break

font

points

Applying Character Formats

Changing the character format can actually make a document easier to read. A *font* is the design of the typeface in your document. Fonts are available in a variety of styles and sizes, and you can use multiple fonts in one document. The size of the font is measured in *points*. The larger the point number, the larger the font size will be. You can quickly change the appearance of the font by using the command buttons in the Font group on the Home tab, as shown in **Figure 13–8**. When you open the Font dialog box, more font options are available, and you can make several font changes at one time.

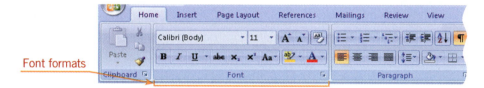

Font formats

FIGURE 13–8   The Font group on the Home tab

Changing the character format can also set the tone for a document. Consider the purpose of the document when you apply these design elements. While formatting text in all caps can draw the reader's attention, it can also send the wrong message. Some readers may feel you are yelling at them. Changing font styles and font colors may make the text look pretty or cool, but some formats may make it harder to read the text.

Step-by-Step 13.7

1. Open **Step13-7** from the data files and save the document as **H2O1**.

2. Click the **Page Layout** tab. Click the **Line Numbers** button [Line Numbers ▾] and click **Continuous** from the list of options. Line numbers will appear to the left of each line, which will make it easier to identify the lines of text in the document.

3. Select all of the text in line 1. Word is intuitive, and because you selected text, a semitransparent image of the Mini toolbar with common formatting commands appears above the selection. Your screen should look similar to **Figure 13–9** . If you do not see the Mini toolbar, select the text again, and do not move the mouse pointer away from the selection.

FIGURE 13–9
The semitransparent image of the Mini toolbar

Mini toolbar

4. Position the mouse pointer over the Mini toolbar, and the image will brighten. Click the **Bold** button **B** to apply the bold format. Move the mouse pointer away from the Mini toolbar, and it disappears.

5. Click the **Home** tab. Notice the Bold button is highlighted to indicate that the selected text is formatted bold. With the text still selected, click the **Change Case** button **Aa** in the Font group. Click **UPPERCASE**.

6. Select all of the text in line 2. Click the **Bold** button and the **Italic** button **I** on the Mini toolbar. Then click the **Font Color** button arrow **A** on the Mini toolbar and click a color.

7. Select all of the text in line 4. In the Font group on the Home tab, click the **Underline** button arrow **U** and then click the last option in the list (the wavy line). Click the **Underline** button to remove the format. Click the **Underline** button again. The wavy line underline option is applied because it is the last underline option used.

8. Select all of the text in lines 8 and 9. Click the **Font** button arrow **Calibri (Body)** in the Font group to show the font options. Position the mouse pointer over one of the font options in the list to show a live preview of the new font in the document window, as shown in **Figure 13–10**. Position the mouse pointer over a different font option, and the live preview reflects the change in fonts. The text does not change, however, until you choose a new font style.

FIGURE 13–10
Live preview for a font style

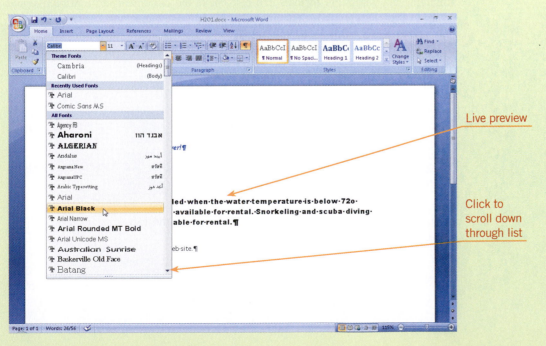

Live preview

Click to scroll down through list

9. Scroll down the list of fonts and select **Comic Sans MS**. The text in the document changes, and the name of the new font appears in the Font box.

10. With the text still selected, click the **Font Size** list arrow. The point sizes are listed in increments. Click **14**. With the text still selected, click the **Shrink Font** button $\overset{\vee}{\text{A}}$ in the Font group three times to decrease the size by three increments. Click the **Grow Font** button $\overset{\wedge}{\text{A}}$ in the Font group once. The point size increases by one increment and *11* appears in the Font Size box.

11. Select the *o* after *72* in the same paragraph. Click the **Superscript** button x^2 in the Font group. Select the number *2* in *H2O* in line 1. Click the **Subscript** button x_2 in the Font group.

12. Position the insertion point at the end of the document on line 14. Change the font size to **14** and enter **www.H2OCove.net**. Press **Enter**. A hyperlink format is automatically applied to the URL. Because this document will not be published on the Web, you do not need a hyperlink format. Right-click the hyperlink and click **Remove Hyperlink** in the shortcut menu.

13. Select the text in line 12 and click the **Text Highlight Color** button arrow $\boxed{\text{ab}}$ in the Font Group. Click a color, and the highlight is applied to the selected text.

14. Save the changes and leave the document open.

HEADS UP

To highlight multiple sections of text throughout the document, select the highlight color first. The pointer will change to show a highlighter pen, and then you can drag the pointer over text to apply the highlight. To toggle the highlight option off, click the **Text Highlight Color** button or press the **Escape** key.

Applying Paragraph Formats

Changing the paragraph formats can also make the document more attractive and easier to read. Paragraph formats include adjusting the blank space between lines of text, aligning text, setting tabs and indents, and adding bullets and numbering. Most of the paragraph formats can be applied using the commands in the Paragraph group on the Home tab, shown in **Figure 13–11**.

FIGURE 13–11   The Paragraph group on the Home tab

Changing the Line Spacing and Alignment

The default line spacing in Word is single spacing. When text is double-spaced, there is a blank line between each line of text, which makes it easier to read. Many reports are formatted with double line spacing. You can also adjust the spacing both before and after the paragraph, which is common in newsletters to help to save space on a page and/or to make a headline stand out.

Alignment refers to how text is positioned between the left and right margins. Text can be aligned in four different ways: left, center, right, or justified. The default setting is left alignment. Center alignment is often used for titles, headings, and invitations. Right alignment is often used in tables for dollar amounts and dates. You can quickly apply any of these alignments using the buttons in the Paragraph group on the Home tab.

> **HEADS UP**
>
> The keyboard shortcuts for single spacing is **Ctrl+1**. For 1.5 spacing, the shortcut key combination is **Ctrl+5**; and for double spacing it is **Ctrl+2**.

▶ **VOCABULARY**
alignment

Step-by-Step 13.8

1. If necessary, open **H2O1** from your solution files. Save the document H2O1 as **H2O2**.

2. Select all of the text in the document, and then click the **Line spacing** button. Click the **2.0** line spacing option. All of the lines are now double-spaced. There are still 15 lines in the document, but there is more blank space between the lines.

3. With all of the text still selected, click the **Line spacing** button and then click **1.5**. The spacing between lines is reduced to 1½ line spacing, and there is less blank space between each line of text.

4. Position the insertion point in line 14. Click the **Line spacing** button, and then click **Add Space Before Paragraph**. Extra blank space is added between lines 13 and 14.

5. With the insertion point positioned in line 14, click the **Line spacing** button again. The next to last option has changed. Click **Remove Space Before Paragraph**.

6. Position the insertion point in line 1. Click the **Line spacing** button, and then click **Add Space After Paragraph** at the bottom of the list of options. Extra blank space is added between lines 1 and 2.

7. Click the **Dialog Box Launcher** in the Paragraph group to open the Paragraph dialog box. Notice that under Spacing, the After box shows 12 pt. Click the down arrow once to reduce the setting to 6 pt. Click **OK** to apply the change and close the dialog box. The space between lines 1 and 2 is adjusted.

8. With the insertion point positioned in line 1, click the **Center** button ≣ in the Paragraph group. Select all the remaining lines in the document and then click the **Center** button. All the lines are centered horizontally on the page.

9. Position the insertion point in line 8, 9, or 10. Click the **Justify** button ≣ in the Paragraph group. The text is aligned at both the left and right margins. Because all three lines are in the same paragraph, the format is applied to all three lines of text.

10. Select all of the text in lines 12, 13, and 14. Click the **Align Text Left** button ≣ to move the text back to the left margin. Click the **Align Text Right** button ≣ to align the text at the right margin.

11. Select all of the text in lines 1 and 2 and increase the font size to **18**. Select all of the text in lines 4 through 14 and increase the font size to **14**.

12. Deselect the text. Save the changes and close the document.

▓ EXTRA FOR EXPERTS

If you want to set precise measurements for tabs, click the Paragraph group **Dialog Box Launcher**, and then click **Tabs** to open the Tabs dialog box.

Setting Tabs and Indents

Tabs are useful for indenting paragraphs and lining up columns of text. Word's default tabs are set at every half inch. You can, however, set custom tabs at other locations. There are four alignment options and a vertical bar for tabs. **Table 13–2** describes each of the options.

TABLE 13–2   Options for tabs

TAB SETTING	DESCRIPTION
∟ Left tab	This is the default tab style; when you begin to enter text at the tab, the text is aligned on the left and extends to the right
⊥ Center tab	Text is aligned evenly on either side of the tab position
⌐ Right tab	Text is aligned on the right and extends to the left
⊥ Decimal tab	Numbers with decimals are all aligned at the decimal point, and text aligns on either side of the tab; a decimal tab can be used to align numbers or text
▯ Bar tab	This setting does not position the text, but a vertical bar appears in the paragraph at the tab position; if the tab is formatted for multiple paragraphs, the vertical bar appears in all the paragraphs to create a vertical line along the column of text or numbers

The ruler, which is available from the Show/Hide group on the View tab, can be used to quickly set tabs, indents, and margins in your document. The ruler is also a handy reference to see the "true" size of your text and document.

An *indent* is a space inserted between the margin and where the line of text appears. You can indent text from the left margin, from the right margin, or from both the left and right margins. For example, to draw attention to specific paragraphs in a document, you can indent all the lines of the paragraph from the left and right margins. If you want the first line of paragraphs to be indented, you can format a *first line indent*. A first line indent makes a long document with several paragraphs easier to read because the reader can easily tell where a new paragraph begins. When creating a bibliography for a report, you need to format a *hanging indent*, where the first line of text begins at the left margin, and all other lines of the paragraph hang, or are indented, to the right of the first line.

HEADS UP

When you press **Enter** to create a new paragraph, the new paragraph will include the same paragraph formats, such as alignment, tabs, and line spacing.

▶ **VOCABULARY**

indent

first line indent

hanging indent

Step-by-Step 13.9

1. Open **Step13-9** from the data files and save the document as **Parks**. Show nonprinting characters and continuous line numbers.

2. Click the **View** tab and, if necessary, click the **View Ruler** check box ☐ Ruler in the Show/Hide group. The ruler is visible when there is a check mark in the box.

3. Position the insertion point at the beginning of line 3. Press **Tab** three times. Although they do not appear on the ruler, default tabs are already set for every ½ inch. The three tab symbols are spaced every ½ inch.

4. Position the insertion point anywhere in line 4. Click the **tab selector** at the left end of the ruler until the Right Tab symbol ⌐ appears, as shown in **Figure 13–12**.

HEADS UP

You can also show the Ruler by clicking the **View Ruler** button at the top of the vertical scroll bar.

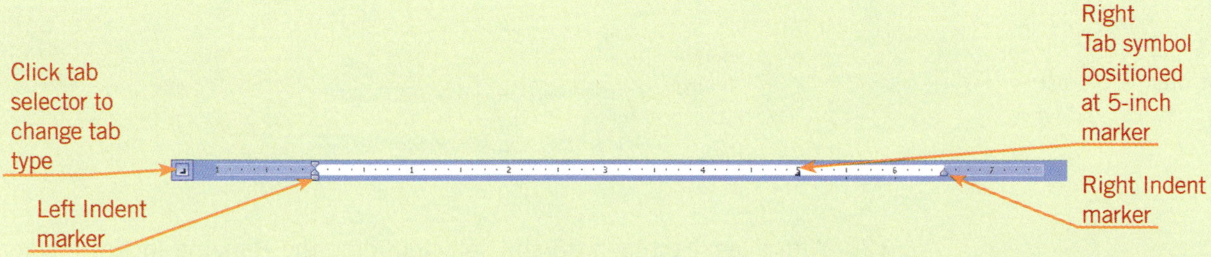

Click tab selector to change tab type

Left Indent marker

Right Tab symbol positioned at 5-inch marker

Right Indent marker

FIGURE 13–12 Tab symbols and indent markers on the ruler

5. Click the **5-inch** mark on the ruler (just to the left of the Right Indent marker). See **Figure 13–12**. Then drag the Right Indent marker on the ruler and position it exactly on top of the Right Tab symbol. The tab symbol will appear on top of the Right Indent marker.

6. Position the insertion point in front of *April 11* and press **Tab**. The date is now aligned at the right indent, which was moved to the 5-inch mark on the ruler.

7. Position the insertion point anywhere in line 6. Notice that no tab markers show on the ruler, and the Right Indent marker is positioned at the 6.5-inch mark on the ruler. The tab and right indent you set in line 5 was applied to that paragraph only, and that paragraph has only one line of text.

8. Select all of the text in lines 5 through 24. Be sure to include the paragraph symbol at the end of line 24.

9. Click the **tab selector** until the Decimal Tab symbol shows ⬒, and then click the **3-inch** mark on the ruler. Then, remove the symbol from the ruler by dragging it off.

10. With lines 5 through 24 still selected, click the **tab selector** until the Right Tab symbol shows, and then click the **5-inch** mark on the ruler. Click and drag the **Right Indent** marker to the 5-inch mark on the ruler. Insert a tab character in front of the dates in line 9 and 16.

11. Select all of the text in lines 4 through 28. Click and drag the **Left Indent** marker to the 1/2-inch mark on the ruler. Notice that the First Line Indent and Hanging Indent markers also move. See **Figure 13–13**.

FIGURE 13–13
Left Indent Markers on the ruler

Margin marker   First Line Indent marker

Left Indent marker   Hanging Indent marker

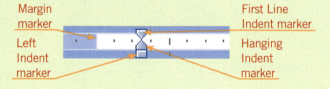

12. With lines 4 through 28 still selected, drag the **Hanging Indent** marker to the ¾-inch mark on the ruler. All lines except the first line of each paragraph are indented from the left three-quarters of an inch.

13. Deselect the text. Save the changes and close the document.

Adding Bullets and Numbers

Bullets are used to list items when order does not matter—an unordered list. Numbered lists are used to identify steps that should be completed in a specific order, which are often referred to as an ordered list. Bulleted and numbered lists are automatically formatted with a hanging indent. Word automatically calculates the best distance for the hanging indent. You can change the bullet symbol, the number style, or the distance for the hanging indent in the Bullets and Numbering dialog box.

Step-by-Step 13.10

1. Open **Step13-10** from the data files, and save the document as **Exhibition1**.

2. Select the list of eight items under the heading that begins *Displays and Demonstrations.* Click the **Bullets** button ⠿ in the Paragraph group on the Home tab. Each paragraph in the selection is formatted with a bullet symbol. The symbol will vary depending on the symbol last used. If necessary, click the Bullet button arrow to show the bullet options and select one of the bullet symbols.

3. Select the list of four items below the next heading that begins *A Look at...* and click the **Repeat** button on the Quick Access Toolbar. The last action (formatting bullets) is repeated, and bullets are applied to the selected text.

4. Select the list of seven items below the next heading *Seminars and Films.* Click the **Numbering** button ⠿ in the Paragraph group. The number format varies depending on the format last used. If necessary, click the Numbering button arrow to show the number format options and select the number format 1., 2., 3.

5. Deselect the text and position the insertion point at the end of the last line in the numbered list, 7. *Transportation.* Press **Enter.** Word automatically formats the next paragraph with the number 8 and a hanging indent. Enter **Water conservation.**

6. Press **Enter,** and the next paragraph is formatted for item number 9. Click the **Numbering** button to toggle the option off.

7. Select the numbered list and click the **Bullets** button. The numbers are converted to bullets.

8. Save the changes and close the document.

Applying Document Formats

Document formats are applied to an entire document. These formats include layout settings such as margins, page orientation, paper size, and page breaks, and you will look at adjusting these settings in this lesson. More document formats will be covered in Lesson 16. Most of the document formats can be accessed in the Page Setup group on the Page Layout tab, shown in **Figure 13–14**.

Document
formats

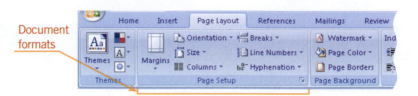

FIGURE 13–14   The Page Setup group on the Page Layout tab

Changing the Margins and the Page Orientation

The margin and page orientation formats you choose should be based on the purpose and content of the document and also on the paper size. If you want more or less content to fit on a page, you can modify the margin settings. The *margin* is the blank space around the edges of the page. The default margin settings are 1 inch for top, bottom, left, and right margins, but you can easily change those settings.

Portrait orientation formats the content of the document with the short edge of the page at the top. This is the default setting. You can change to *landscape orientation*, which formats the content of the document with the long edge of the page at the top. Your on-screen document accurately reflects the page orientation you choose.

Inserting Page Breaks

When you fill a page with text or graphics, Word begins a new page by automatically inserting a *soft page break*. You can also break pages manually by inserting a *manual page break*, which forces a page break at a specific location, regardless of how much text or graphics are on the page. The location of a soft page break will change when you add or delete text so that each page remains completely filled with text. A manual page break will remain where you insert it until it is deleted.

In Print Layout, Outline, and Draft views, the page break is indicated with a dotted line across the page. In Full Screen Reading view the dotted line does not appear, but the pages actually look like separate sheets of paper, so you will clearly see where page breaks are located. You may not see any indication of page breaks at all in Web Layout view.

▶ **VOCABULARY**

margin

portrait orientation

landscape orientation

soft page break

manual page break

Step-by-Step 13.11

1. Open the **Exhibition1** document from your solution files and save the document Exhibition1 as **Exhibition2**.

2. Press **Ctrl+A** to select all the text in the document. In the Font group, click the **Grow Font** button three times. All the selected text increases by three increments.

3. Position the insertion point at the beginning of the third heading, *Seminars and Films*. Click the **Page Layout** tab, and click the **Insert Page and Section Breaks** button [Breaks ▾] to show a list of options. Under Page Breaks, click **Page** to add a manual page break.

4. The paragraph and all of the text below the paragraph now appear on page 2 of the document. The nonprinting characters reveal a page break, as shown in **Figure 13–15**. Click the **View** tab and then, in the Zoom group, click the **Two Pages** button [Two Pages].

Page break

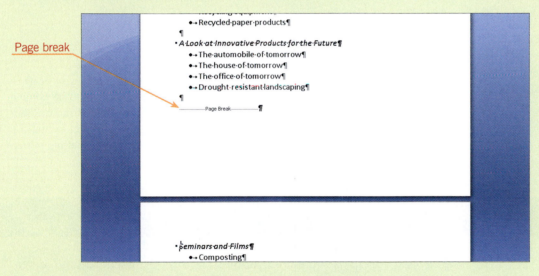

FIGURE 13–15
A manual page break in a document

5. Click the **Page Layout** tab and then, in the Page Setup group, click the **Page Size** button [Size ▾] to show the page size options. Click an option for a paper size smaller than 8.5"×11" and the layout will likely change in the document window. Click the **Page Size** button again, and then click **Letter 8.5"×11"** to return to the default setting.

6. Click the **Margins** button in the Page Setup group to show the options. Click **Wide**.

7. Click the **Page Orientation** button in the Page Setup group. Click **Landscape**. The content is now spread out over three pages. Click the **Undo** button.

8. Select the paragraph containing the page break and press **Delete**.

9. Click the **Office Button**, point to **Print**, and then click **Print Preview**.

10. Uncheck the **Magnifier** option in the Preview group. When this option is unchecked, you can position the insertion point in the document in the Print Preview window. Scroll up if necessary and edit the date in the heading so it reads **September 8-10**.

11. Click the **Margins** button and change the setting to **Normal**.

12. Click the **Shrink One Page** button ⊞ Shrink One Page in the Preview group. The document will be resized so all the content fits on one page.

13. Click the **Close Print Preview** button on the Print Preview tab.

14. Save the changes and close the document.

◗ HEADS UP

You can also change margins by dragging the margin markers on the ruler.

◗ HEADS UP

You can use Format Painter to copy formats from one Word document to another Word document.

▶ VOCABULARY
Format Painter

Using Format Painter

When you apply multiple character or paragraph formats to text, and you need to repeat those formats throughout the document, you want the formats to be consistent. You can use the Format Painter button to quickly copy the formatting to other text and objects. *Format Painter* will copy and apply font and paragraph formatting as well as some basic graphic formatting, such as borders, fills, and shading, which you will learn more about in Lesson 16.

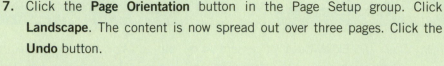

Step-by-Step 13.12

1. Open **Step13-12** from the data files and save the document as **Garden**. If necessary, show the nonprinting characters.

2. Format the first subheading *Creating an "Attractive" Garden* as follows: Arial font, 11 point, bold, and underlined with a single line.

3. With the first subheading text selected, including the paragraph marker, click the **Format Painter** button 🖌 in the Clipboard group. The mouse pointer changes to show a paintbrush when positioned over text.

4. Click the first word in the second subheading *Tips for Attracting Butterflies and Hummingbirds.* The formats are applied only to the one word. Also, the mouse pointer no longer displays a paintbrush, so you cannot continue copying the formats.

5. Select the first subheading text again, and this time double-click the **Format Painter** button. The mouse pointer changes to show a paintbrush, and because you double-clicked the Format Painter button, you now have unlimited opportunities to copy the formats.

6. Click and drag the mouse pointer to select all of the text of the second subheading. The copied formats will be applied to all of the selected text. Click and drag the mouse pointer to select all of the text of the third subheading, *Modifying an Existing Garden.* Click the **Format Painter** button to turn off Format Painter.

7. Select the first two paragraphs under the title. Justify the alignment of text. Change the line spacing to 1.5 lines, and format the font as Arial, 10 point. Add space before the paragraphs. With the paragraphs still selected, double-click the **Format Painter** button.

8. Click and drag the mouse pointer over all of the paragraphs below each of the three subheadings, but do not drag across the bulleted and numbered lists. The paragraphs should now be justified with 1.5 line spacing and extra spacing before the paragraphs, and the characters should be Arial font, 10 point. Press **Escape** to turn off the Format Painter.

9. Notice that the formatting changes have made the document more than one page, and Word automatically added a soft page break.

10. Save the changes and close the document.

> **HEADS UP**
>
> To turn off the Format Painter without applying the format to other text, click the **Format Painter** button again or press **Escape**.

Finding and Replacing Text

Scrolling through a long document to locate a specific section of text is time consuming. The Find command makes locating text and/or formats easier and more efficient. You can use the Find command to search a document for every occurrence of a word or phrase or for character and paragraph formats.

When you need to replace or reformat multiple occurrences of the same text, you can use the Replace command. The replacements can be made individually, or all occurrences can be replaced at once.

Step-by-Step 13.13

1. Open **Step13-13** from the data files and save the document as **Workout**. If necessary, position the insertion point at the beginning of the document.

2. In the Editing group, click the **Find** button 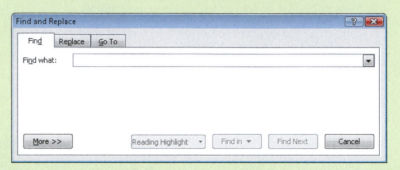. The Find tab in the Find and Replace dialog box, shown in **Figure 13–16**, opens.

3. In the Find what text box, enter **training**, and then click **Find Next** in the dialog box. The search begins at the location of the insertion point. Word locates and selects the first occurrence of the search text *training*. The dialog box remains open.

4. Click **Find Next** again. Word finds the next occurrence of the search text in the open document. Click **Cancel** to close the dialog box.

5. Press and hold **Shift** and press **F4**. The next occurrence of *training* is selected. When you use the Shift+F4 key combination, Word repeats the last search. This shortcut is convenient because you can continue searching the same word without leaving the Find and Replace dialog box open.

6. Position the insertion point at the beginning of the document. Click the **Replace** button on the Home tab. The Replace tab in the Find and Replace dialog box appears. Click the **More** button for more options, as shown in **Figure 13–17**. Notice the word *training* from your last search still appears in the Find what text box.

HEADS UP

If you want to search only a specific portion of a document, you can select the desired text before beginning the search.

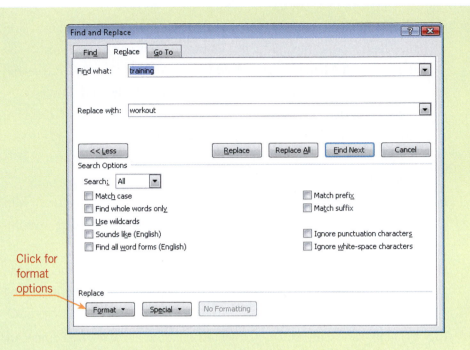

FIGURE 13-17
The Replace tab in the Find and Replace dialog box with more options

7. In the Find what text box, enter **work out** to replace *training*. With the insertion point still in the Find what box, click the **Format** button in the dialog box, and then click **Font** to show the Find Font dialog box, shown in **Figure 13-18**.

HEADS UP

The keyboard shortcuts to execute the Find command are **Ctrl+F**. Use **Ctrl+H** to execute the Replace command.

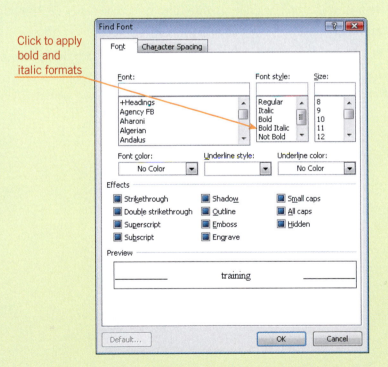

FIGURE 13-18
The Find Font dialog box

8. Under Font style, click **Bold**, and then click **OK**. Notice that *Font: Bold* appears under the Find what box on the Replace tab. Word will now search for all occurrences of *work out* with the bold format.

9. In the Replace with box, enter **workout**. With the insertion point still in the Replace with box, click the **Format** button and click **Font**. In the Replace Font dialog box, click **Bold Italic**, and then click **OK**. The search text will be replaced with the new text formatted bold and italic.

10. Click **Find Next** in the dialog box. The first occurrence of the bold text *work out* is selected. Click **Find Next** again. No replacements are made in the document, and the next occurrence of the search text is selected.

11. Click **Replace** in the dialog box. The selected text is replaced with *workout*, formatted bold and italic, and the next occurrence of *work out* is selected.

12. Click **Replace All** in the dialog box. Word replaces all occurrences of the search text with the replacement text. A message box opens indicating that three replacements were made. Click **OK** to close the message box.

13. Position the insertion point in the Find what box and click **No Formatting** at the bottom of the Find and Replace dialog box. Position the insertion point in the Replace with box and click **No Formatting** to remove the formats. Click **Find Next** once to complete a search without formats. This clears the format settings from the Find what and Replace with boxes so your next search does not include formats. Click **Yes** in the message box and then close the dialog box.

14. Click **Less** to hide the options in the dialog box, and then close the dialog box. Save the changes and then close the document.

SUMMARY

In this lesson, you learned:

- When you add new text in Insert mode, the new characters are inserted between existing text. When text is entered in Overtype mode, the new text replaces existing text.

- The Undo, Redo, and Repeat commands make editing easy when you make mistakes, change your mind, or repeat actions.

- Selected text can be copied or moved from one location in a Word document to a new location in the same document, to a different Word document, or to another application. Drag-and-drop editing is especially helpful when you are moving or copying text short distances.

- When you use the Cut, Copy, and Paste commands, Word stores the selected text on the Clipboard, which stores up to 24 items.

- Word checks spelling and grammar as you enter text.

- Formatting a paragraph for left, center, right, or justified alignment positions the text appropriately between the left and right margins.

- You can use the ruler to format tabs and indents.

- The Bullets and Numbering feature automatically adds and formats bullets and numbers in lists.

- The page orientation determines how the document is printed on the page. Adjusting the margins affects the blank space around the edges of the page.

- The Find command makes searching for text easy and efficient. The Replace command replaces multiple occurrences of search text automatically.

VOCABULARY REVIEW

Define the following terms:

alignment	Format Painter	margin
Clipboard	hanging indent	Overtype mode
drag-and-drop editing	indent	points
edit	Insert mode	portrait orientation
first line indent	landscape orientation	select
font	manual line break	soft page break
format	manual page break	

REVIEW QUESTIONS

TRUE / FALSE

Circle T if the statement is true or F if the statement is false.

T F **1.** You can make several font changes at the same time by using the Font dialog box.

T F **2.** You cannot edit a document while viewing the document in Print Preview.

T F **3.** Word defines a paragraph as any amount of text that ends with a paragraph marker.

T F **4.** If you hold down Ctrl as you drag and drop text, the selected text will be copied instead of moved.

T F **5.** Portrait orientation is the default setting for Word documents.

MULTIPLE CHOICE

Select the best response for the following statements.

1. A _____ makes a long document with several paragraphs easier to read, because the reader can easily tell where a new paragraph begins.

   A. first line indent   C. paragraph marker

   B. hanging indent   D. line number

2. _____ orientation formats the content of the document with the long edge of the page at the top.

   A. Horizontal   C. Portrait

   B. Landscape   D. Layout

3. _____ refers to how text is positioned between the left and right margins.

   A. Line format   C. Line adjustment

   B. Alignment   D. Line spacing

4. A(n) _____ is the space inserted between the margin and the line of text.

   A. first line indent   C. hanging indent

   B. indent   D. manual line break

5. Bulleted and numbered lists are automatically formatted using a _____ indent.

   A. left   C. first line

   B. right   D. hanging

FILL IN THE BLANK

Complete the following sentences by writing the correct word or words in the blanks provided.

1. When you use the Copy or Cut commands, the selected text is stored on the _____.

2. In _____ mode, new text is inserted between existing text.

3. The size of the font is measured in _____.

4. Word automatically inserts a(n) _____ when a page is full.

5. The _____ is the blank space around the edges of a page.

■ PROJECTS

PROJECT 13–1

1. Open **Project13-1** from the data files. Save the document as **Languages**. If necessary, show nonprinting characters.

2. Scroll down the page and notice that there is a course title separated from its description. Cut the *Japanese for Beginners* title from its current location and paste it above the course description that begins *Build a solid foundation for communicating in Japanese.*

3. Remove the extra blank line that remains above the *English as a Second Language* heading after you moved the *Japanese for Beginners* heading.

4. According to the director's notes, Spanish for Beginners and Japanese for Beginners are offered on the same day and time and for the same number of weeks. You need to add information to both class descriptions.

   a. Copy the class dates, *September 25–November 13*, that appear below the Japanese instructor's name. Do not include the paragraph marker at the end of the dates in the selection.

   b. Position the insertion point below the Spanish instructor's name and paste the dates. Press **Enter** to insert a blank line below the dates.

c. Position the insertion point after the Spanish instructor's name, *Ken Grazzi*, and press **Enter** to insert a new line. Enter **Tuesday, 6-8 p.m.**.

d. Position the insertion point after the Japanese instructor's name, *Hiroki Sasaki*, and use the Repeat command. Word should move to a new line and insert the same day and time you entered for the Spanish class.

5. Show the Clipboard task pane, and clear all the items from the Clipboard. Copy to the clipboard the name of the German for Beginners instructor and the fee for the German for Beginners class.

6. Paste the German instructor's name after the course number for Continuing German for Beginners.

7. All classes have the same fee, so you can paste the class fee after the dates for each class.

8. The director's notes indicate that Ken Grazzi may not be able to teach the Spanish class. Delete his name.

9. You just received an e-mail from the director, and you learn that Mr. Grazzi will be able to teach the class after all. Use Undo to restore his name.

10. Using cut and paste and/or drag-and-drop editing, reorganize the information so that the classes are listed alphabetically by class title.

11. Hide the Clipboard task pane, save the changes, and close the document.

PROJECT 13–2

1. Open **Project13-2** from the data files. Save the document as **Oak Creek**.

2. Change the page orientation to landscape. Change the top and bottom margins to 1 inch, and the left and right margins to 2 inches.

3. Center the first eight lines of text, beginning with *Oak Creek Recreation Commission* and ending with *Mt. Washington Recreation Center*.

4. Format the centered text as follows:
   a. Change the font style of the first line (*Oak Creek Recreation Center*) to bold and the font size to 28 points.
   b. Change the size of the next two lines (*Community Center and Program Guide*) to 20 points.
   c. Change the size of the next line (*Fall*) to 20 points and apply bold style.
   d. Change the size of the last four centered lines to 20 points.

5. Position the insertion point in front of the word *Contents* and insert a page break. On the new page, format the word *Contents* as 20 point bold.

6. Select all of the text below the *Contents* heading and then set a right tab at the 6.5-inch mark on the ruler. Format the program listings as follows:
   a. Apply bold and italic formatting to the first three lines of text below the *Contents* heading (*Registration, Memberships, and Hours*) and the last two lines of text (*Special Events* and *Community Meetings*). Change the size of these lines to 12 points and the font to Arial. Include the page numbers in all formatting changes.
   b. Apply bold and underline formatting to the headings (including the page number) for each age group (*ELEMENTARY PROGRAMS, TEEN PROGRAMS*, and *ADULT PROGRAMS*). Change the size of these headings to 12 points and the font to Arial.
   c. Apply a 0.25-inch left indent to the lists of programs under each age group heading and change their size to 12 points.

7. View the document in Print Preview. You decide that the first page could be spread out a little to fill up more of the page. Add blank lines as desired to improve the look of the first page. Close Print Preview.

8. If necessary, delete blank paragraphs at the end of the document, or adjust the document margins, to fit all the content on two pages.

9. Save your changes and close the document.

TEAMWORK PROJECT

The fonts you use to format a document can be divided into two types: serif and sans serif. Serif faces are often used for the main body of a document, and sans serif faces are used for headings and other display items. Learn more about the differences between these two types of typefaces with a partner.

1. With your partner, decide who will research serif typefaces and who will research sans serif typefaces.

2. Use the Web, an online encyclopedia, or other references to read about typography, the art of designing typefaces. Concentrate on your chosen typeface, either serif or sans serif.

3. You and your partner should be able to answer these questions after your research:

   a. What is a serif?

   b. What is the main difference between a serif typeface and a sans serif typeface?

4. Select a paragraph of text and a heading from any source and enter the material using the type of typeface you have been studying (you use serif, for example, and your partner uses sans serif). Copy the text several times and apply different fonts of either serif or sans serif to each copy.

5. With your partner, decide which of the fonts is most readable and appropriate for each type of text.

CRITICAL THINKING

ACTIVITY 13–1

You have been copying multiple items to the Clipboard. You learned in this lesson that the Clipboard holds up to 24 items. What do you think happens when you copy a 25th item? Use the Help feature to see if your answer was correct.

ACTIVITY 13–2

If you completed Project 13-2, you had to add blank lines to center the text vertically on the first page of the document. There is another way to center text vertically. Use Word's Help feature to find out how to do this. Using Word, write a brief explanation of the steps you need to take. What would happen to the second page of the Oak Creek document if you follow these steps? Describe at least two other types of documents in which you could use this feature.

ONLINE DISCOVERY

Selecting and copying text on a Web page is very similar to selecting and copying text in a Word document. Open a Web page that shows an article with several paragraphs of text. Refer to **Table 13–1**, and test all the select text options listed in the table, noting whether each option works or doesn't work in a Web page. Then, open a new blank Word document and test copying text from the Web page and pasting the selected test into the Word document. Write a brief summary describing what is similar when selecting and copying text in Word and in Web pages.

LESSON 14

Sharing Documents

■ OBJECTIVES

Upon completion of this lesson, you should be able to:

- Track changes and add comments.
- Protect documents by restricting access and by restricting revisions and comments.
- Modify printer settings.
- Pause and cancel print jobs.
- Troubleshoot printing problems.
- Prepare documents for electronic distribution.
- Send documents via e-mail or fax.

■ DATA FILES

To complete this lesson, you will need these data files:

Step14-1.docx

Project14-1.docx

Project14-2.docx

Project14-3.docx

Project14-4.docx

■ VOCABULARY

comment

document management server

document workspace

duplex printing

encryption

hard copy

markup

metadata

Portable Document Format (PDF)

read-only document

print queue

soft copy

XML Paper Specification (XPS)

The development of a document may involve multiple team members. If you collaborate with others to create or edit a document, you can take advantage of many features in Word that help individuals contribute more effectively to the development of the document.

2-2.2.3

▶ **VOCABULARY**
markup

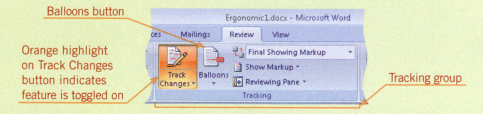

● **HEADS UP**

To add a Track Changes button to the status bar, right-click the status bar and then click the **Track Changes** option. A Track Changes button will be added to the status bar, which you can click to toggle the feature on and off.

Revising Documents

In a team effort to create a document, it is common to allow team members to review and edit the document. Tracking changes with revision marks makes it easy to identify the edits. Adding comments is another useful feature which allows reviewers to provide feedback and express opinions without changing the content of the document. The revision marks and annotations that appear in a document are referred to as *markup*.

Tracking Changes

When the Track Changes feature is toggled on, all insertions, deletions, and format changes are indicated with revision marks such as font color, underlines, and balloons in the margins. These revision marks are easy to recognize, and they even identify who made the changes and when the changes were made.

Step-by-Step 14.1

1. Start the Word application and open **Step14-1** from the data files. Save the document as **Ergonomic1**. If necessary, change to Print Layout view.

2. Click the **Review** tab and then click the top half of the **Track Changes** button in the Tracking group to toggle on the feature. The feature is on when the button has an orange highlight, as shown in **Figure 14–1**.

FIGURE 14–1
The Tracking group on the Review tab

3. Position the insertion point at the beginning of the second paragraph that begins *Did you know*. Enter the following two sentences and then press **Enter**.

   When you think about using a computer, you don't usually think about comfort and health. But maybe you should.

4. Compare the revision marks in your document to those shown in **Figure 14–2**. With default settings, the new text is identified with an underline, and it also appears in a different font color. A vertical mark in the left margin of the document indicates the lines of text which contain revisions.

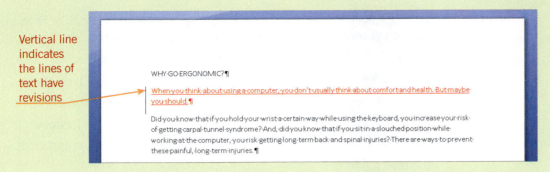

FIGURE 14–2
Markup for inserted text

5. Click the **Track Changes** button arrow and then click **Change Tracking Options**. The Track Changes Options dialog box shown in **Figure 14–3** will open. Compare your settings, and make changes if necessary, so your settings match those shown in **Figure 14–3**. Click **OK** to close the dialog box.

FIGURE 14–3
The Track Changes Options dialog box

6. In the second sentence in the last paragraph, delete the word *office* and the space that follows so that the sentence reads *Using ergonomic elements will....* The deleted text will remain in the document with a strikethrough format.

7. Position the mouse pointer over the deleted text. A ScreenTip will appear showing a user name, a date, and a time. This helps you identify the reviewer who made the change and when the change was made.

8. Click the **Track Changes** button arrow, and then click **Change User Name**. The Word Options dialog shown in **Figure 14–4** will open. Make note of the user name and the initials. Change the User name to **Reviewer 1** and change the Initials to **R1**. Click **OK** to accept the changes and close the dialog box.

FIGURE 14–4
The Word Options dialog box

Change user information here

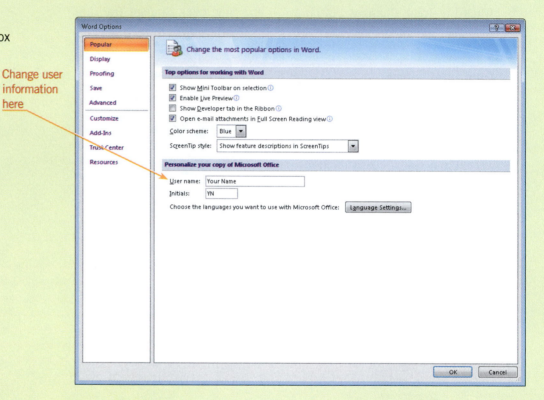

9. In the first sentence in the fourth paragraph, double-click the word *growing* to select the word and then enter **increase in**. The word *growing* is deleted and the new text is inserted. The markup appears in a different font color to distinguish that this is from a different reviewer, and when you show the ScreenTip you will see that the new reviewer name appears.

10. Click the **Balloons** button in the Tracking group. A list with three options will appear. If necessary, click **Show Only Comments and Formatting in Balloons** to select the option. A check mark will indicate the option is selected. If the option already has a check mark, click in the document window to close the list.

11. Select the entire first line. Click the **Home** tab, apply the bold format, and center the text alignment. Notice that the changes for the character and paragraph formats are identified in balloons in the right margin. The border color for the balloons matches the color for the markup related to this reviewer.

12. Click the **Review** tab, click the **Balloons** button and then click **Show Revisions in Balloons**. The deleted text now appears in a balloon in the right margin. Click the **Balloons** button again, and then click **Show All Revisions Inline**. The insertions and deletions appear in the document window, but the format changes do not show. Click the **Balloons** button and then click **Show Only Comments and Formatting in Balloons** to return to the default setting.

13. Click the **Track Changes** button arrow, and then click **Change User Name**. Change the user name and the initials back to the original setting and click **OK**. This setting change now applies to all Office applications.

14. Deselect the text, save the changes, and leave the document open.

Adding Comments

A *comment* is a note that the author or a reviewer adds to the document. A comment can be inserted anywhere in a Word document. You can choose how the comments will appear in the document and whether or not the comments will be included when you print the document.

▶ **VOCABULARY**
comment

HEADS UP

If your computer has a micro-phone, you can record a voice comment. An icon will appear as a sound object inside the comment balloon or in the reviewing pane. To listen to the voice comment, double-click the sound object.

Step-by-Step 14.2

1. If necessary, open **Ergonomic1** from your solution files. Save the document Ergonomic1 as **Ergonomic2**.

2. If necessary, set the document to Print Layout view, click the **Review** tab, and toggle on the Track Changes feature.

3. Select the first two sentences you inserted at the beginning of the document, beginning *When you think*. Click the **Insert Comment** button, shown in **Figure 14–5**.

FIGURE 14–5
The Comments group
on the Review tab

4. You will see shading that highlights the text you selected, and you will also see a dashed line leading to the comment balloon in the margin, as shown in **Figure 14–6**. If you do not select text, the comment will be connected to the word closest to the location of the insertion point.

FIGURE 14–6
Markup showing a
comment and
format changes

5. The initials at the beginning of the comment text indicate the author of the comment, based on the user information provided in the Word Options dialog box. The number *1* indicates that this is the first comment in the document. With the insertion point positioned in the comment balloon, enter **I thought this would be a better intro.**.

6. In the fourth paragraph, double-click the first instance of the word *posture*. Click the **Insert Comment** button, and then enter **My keyboarding instructor made us keep our feet flat on the floor!** in the comment balloon. Notice that the comments are automatically numbered sequentially.

7. Position the mouse pointer over either one of the comments, and a ScreenTip will appear with the reviewer name, and the date and time the comment was added to the document.

8. To show comments and revisions in the Reviewing Pane, click the **Reviewing Pane** button arrow in the Tracking group, and then click **Reviewing Pane Vertical**. The changes and comments appear at the left side of the document as shown in **Figure 14–7**. You can scroll through the list to view the changes, and you can also edit the comments in the Reviewing Pane.

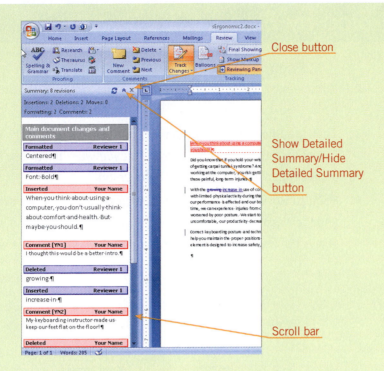

FIGURE 14–7
The Vertical Reviewing Pane

9. At the top of the pane is a summary that shows the number of revisions. If you do not see the details about the summary as shown in **Figure 14–7**, click the **Show Detailed Summary** button.

10. Click the **Hide Detailed Summary** button to hide the summary details.

11. Click the **Reviewing Pane** button arrow in the Tracking group and select **Reviewing Pane Horizontal**. The changes and comments appear at the bottom of the document.

12. Click the **Close** button next to the Show Detailed Summary button to close the Reviewing Pane.

13. Deselect the text, save the changes, and leave the document open.

Showing Markup

Multiple comments and revisions often clutter the document and make it difficult to read. Moreover, if there are multiple users, the revisions may be even more complex to review. You can choose from several options to show the markup. For example, you can choose to show only the edits from a specific reviewer, or you can choose to view only the comments added to the document. To see what the final document will look like, you can hide all of the markup.

There is no limit on the number of reviewers for a document. Word will assign a different color for each of the first eight reviewers. The colors will be reused for additional reviewers beyond the first eight. You can still easily identify reviewers by their initials in the ScreenTips.

HEADS UP

When you move or copy text with a comment, the comment markup is pasted with the text.

Step-by-Step 14.3

1. If necessary, open **Ergonomic2** from your solution files.

2. If necessary, click the **Review** tab and set the document to Print Layout view.

3. Click the **Show Markup** button [Show Markup ▾] in the Tracking group. You can choose the type of revisions that you want to review. All types with a check mark will appear in the document.

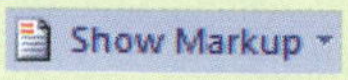

4. Point to **Reviewers**, the last option, to show the names of the reviewers and their associated colors, as shown in **Figure 14–8**. The default setting shows the comments and changes for all who reviewed the document.

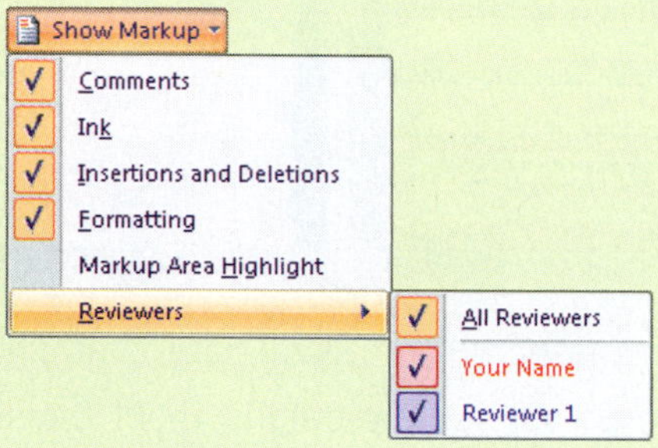

FIGURE 14–8
The Show Markup options with the names of the reviewers

5. Click **Reviewer 1** to uncheck that reviewer name. Now only the changes and comments from the first reviewer will appear in the document.

6. Click the **Show Markup** button, point to **Reviewers**, and then click **All Reviewers** to show all comments and changes.

7. Click the **Display for Review** list arrow [Final Showing Markup ▾] in the Tracking group on the Review tab. Click **Final**. The document appears on the screen exactly as it will print, with all the revisions accepted and the comments hidden. The markup has not been accepted or removed from the document; it just doesn't appear on the screen.

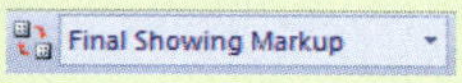

8. Click the **Display for Review** list arrow again, and then click **Final Showing Markup**.

9. Click the **Office Button**, point to **Print**, and then click **Print Preview**. Print Preview reveals that the revision marks and comments will also print. The document is reduced in size so the comments will also print on the same page. Click the **Close Print Preview** button in the Preview group on the Print Preview tab.

10. Click the **Office Button** and then click **Print** to open the Print dialog box, similar to the one shown in **Figure 14–9**. Notice that the option in the Print what box shows Document showing markup. With this option selected, the revision marks and comments will print, and that's why you saw the markup in Print Preview.

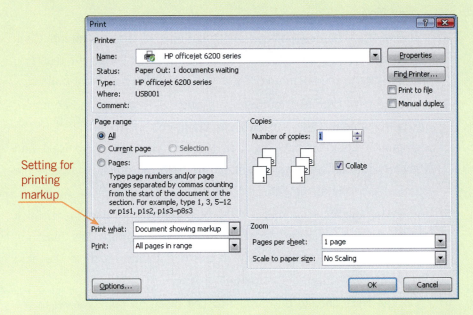

FIGURE 14–9
The Print dialog box

Setting for printing markup

11. In the Print what box, click the list arrow and then click **List of markup**. This option prints a list of all changes, but the document does not print. The list is very similar to the format shown in the Reviewing Pane.

12. Click the **Cancel** button in the Print dialog box to close the dialog box without printing.

13. Click the **Display for Review** list arrow again, and then click **Final**. Return to Print Preview, and you will see that the markup will not appear in the printed copy if the document is sent to the printer when the document is shown on the screen in Final view. Close Print Preview.

14. Click the **Display for Review** list arrow and click **Final Showing Markup**. Leave the document open.

Accepting/Rejecting Changes

After changes and comments are added to a document, the edited document is usually passed on to another person, either the original author or another reviewer, to make a decision about the revisions and comments. That person can decide whether to accept or reject the changes, and they can also remove the comments from the document.

Step-by-Step 14.4

1. If necessary, open **Ergonomic2** from your solution files. Save the document Ergonomic2 as **Ergonomic3**.

2. If necessary, click the **Review** tab and set the document to Print Layout view.

3. Position the insertion point at the beginning of the document. Click the **Next Comment** button ⬛Next in the Comments group. The insertion point moves to the beginning of the text in the first comment balloon.

4. Click the **Next Comment** button again to move to the second comment in the document. Click the **Previous Comment** button ⬛Previous in the Comments group to move back to the first comment. The Next and Previous buttons in the Comments group help you quickly navigate the comments in the document.

5. Reposition the insertion point at the beginning of the document. Click the **Next Change** button ⬛Next in the Changes group. The insertion point moves to the first revision in the document, which is the bold format applied to the first paragraph of text.

6. Click the **Next Change** button again. The insertion point moves to the second change in the document, which is the center alignment format for the same paragraph.

7. Click the **Next Change** button again. The insertion point moves to the beginning of the text in the first comment in the document. The Next Change button locates the next revision or comment.

8. Click the **Next Change** button until the word *growing* is selected. Click the top half of the **Accept and Move to Next** button ⬛ in the Changes group on the Review tab. The word is deleted and the next revision is selected.

9. Click the **Next Change** button, until the word *office* is selected. Click the **Reject and Move to Next** button ⬛Reject in the Changes group. The text is changed back to its original form, and a prompt appears asking if you want to continue searching from the beginning of the document. Click **OK**.

10. In the Comments group, click the **Next Comment** button, and then click the **Delete Comment** button arrow ⬛Delete ▾. Click **Delete All Comments in Document** to remove all the comments from the document.

🔴 HEADS UP

If you don't want to review all of the changes and comments in sequence, show the Reviewing Pane, so you can scroll through the list and quickly locate the change or comment. When you click a comment in the Reviewing Pane, the insertion point is moved to that location in the document window.

11. In the Changes group, click the **Accept and Move to Next** button arrow and then click **Accept All Changes in Document**. All revisions are accepted.

12. Save the changes and leave the document open.

Protecting Documents

2-2.2.4

If a document contains important or even confidential information, you need secure ways to share the information. Word offers features that enable you to control sensitive information and collaborate in confidence.

Restricting Access

Before you share a document, you can save it as a *read-only document*, which will permit others to open and view the document, but they won't be able to make any changes to the document. If you want to permit some users to modify the document, you can create a password which will allow them to save changes to the document. This option doesn't secure the document, but it does limit those who can edit the document. The most secure option is to encrypt the document so it is unreadable without a password. *Encryption* is a standard method for encoding data. When Word encrypts a file, a password is assigned, and then all users must enter the password to open the document.

▶ **VOCABULARY**
read-only document

encryption

> **WARNING**
>
> If you forget the password, the file cannot be reopened. When you assign a password to a document, write it down and keep the note in a secure place.

Step-by-Step 14.5

1. If necessary, open **Ergonomic3** from your solution files.

2. Click the **Office Button** and then click the **Save As** command to open the Save As dialog box.

3. Click the **Tools** button at the bottom of the dialog box, and then click **General Options** to open the General Options dialog box. You can choose to assign one or both passwords. If you choose to use two passwords, make sure the passwords are not the same.

FIGURE 14–10
The General Options dialog box

Enter passwords here

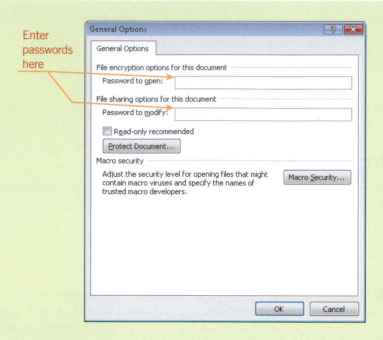

4. In the first Password box shown in **Figure 14–10**, enter **jck0429OH!**. The document will be encrypted and this password will be required to open the document.

5. In the second password box, enter **AEM#1mx50+**. This password will be required for the user to save changes to the document, but is not related to the encryption process.

6. Click **OK**. When prompted, enter the first password and click **OK**. Enter the second password and click **OK**.

7. In the File name box, change the name to **Ergonomic4** and then click **Save** in the dialog box. Because you created a password in the encryption box, the encryption process will be completed.

8. Close the document, and then reopen the **Ergonomic4** document, using the first password you created in Step 4 above. Users who do not know this password will not be able to access the document.

9. When prompted to enter the password to modify, enter the second password you created in Step 5 above. Users who do not know this password can click the Read Only button to view the document.

10. To remove the encryption, click the **Office Button**, click **Save As**, click **Tools**, and then click **General Options**. Delete all the characters in the two password boxes and then click **OK**.

11. In the File name box, change the filename to **Ergonomic5** and click **Save**. There is no restricted access for the Ergonomic5 document.

12. Leave the document open.

▭ EXTRA FOR EXPERTS

It is recommended that passwords include a combination of text, numbers, and symbols and be at least eight characters in length— the more characters the better. In this dialog box, you can enter up to 15 characters.

Restricting Formatting and Edits

Even when you choose to allow others to make revisions and add comments, you can still be selective about who is allowed to make edits as well as the types of edits they can make.

Step-by-Step 14.6

1. If necessary, open **Ergonomic5** from your solution files.

2. Click the **Review** tab and then click the **Protect Document** button in the Protect group at the far right side of the Review tab. The task pane shown in **Figure 14–11** will open.

FIGURE 14–11
The Restrict Formatting and Editing task pane

3. Under 2. Editing restrictions, click to enable the option **Allow only this type of editing in the document:**. The option will show a check mark when enabled. New Exceptions options appear in the task pane, and the current Editing restrictions setting is No changes (Read only).

4. Under Editing restrictions, click the list arrow next to No changes (Read only) and then click **Tracked changes**. Notice that the options in the task pane change again. When the Tracked changes option is enabled, reviewers can make revisions and also add comments to the document.

5. Click the **Editing restrictions** list arrow again and click **Comments**. New Exceptions options appear again in the task pane. With the Comments option enabled, you can make exceptions and allow specified reviewers to edit all or part of the document.

6. Click the **Editing restrictions** list arrow and click **Filling in forms**. When this option is enabled, the exceptions are not available, and users cannot track changes or add comments.

7. Click the **Editing restrictions** list arrow and click **No changes (Read only)**.

8. Select the first four paragraphs in the document, including the title. Then click **Everyone** under Exceptions (optional). The option will show a check mark when enabled. Anyone with access to the document can edit the selected paragraphs.

9. Click anywhere in the last paragraph of text. Notice that the check mark no longer appears next to the Everyone option. With this setting, no users would be permitted to edit this part of the document.

10. Select the last paragraph in the document and then click to enable the **Everyone** option.

11. Point to the **Everyone** option. A list arrow will appear. Click the list arrow and then click **Remove all editing permissions for this user**. With this setting, no one can edit any part of this document.

12. Under 3. Start enforcement, click **Yes, Start Enforcing Protection**. Enter the password **88*A*03*13/** in the first box. Click in the second password box, reenter the password, and click **OK**.

13. Click the **Close** button in the top right corner of the Restrict Formatting and Editing task pane.

14. Save the changes and leave the document open.

HEADS UP

To remove the restrictions from a document, click the Stop Protection button at the bottom of the Restrict Formatting and Editing task pane. You will be prompted to enter the password, and then the restrictions will be disabled.

2-1.4.1
2-1.4.3
2-1.4.4
2-1.4.5

▶ **VOCABULARY**
hard copy

Preparing a Document for Printing

After the document is finalized, you can prepare a *hard copy*—a printed copy—of the document to share the information. Often, multiple copies are prepared and distributed. Your system may have two or more printers available, including inkjet printers, laser printers, fax programs that also serve as a type of printer, and others. The benefit of having more than one printer to choose from is that different printers offer different features.

Selecting Print Options

Many people use their printer default settings, and they're not aware of all the additional features and options that are available. Most printers have settings for adjusting the printing speed and the print quality. Some printers provide special features like *duplex printing*, which is printing on both sides of the page. Of course, you can manually feed the paper back into the printer to print the back side of the page, but it's very convenient when the printer will do that automatically. Another time-saving print option is to collate, which automatically arranges the pages in the proper order when you print several copies of a multi-page document. Deciding which printer to use is usually not the challenge; finding the printer options is.

Showing the Print Queue

The *print queue* shows information about documents that are waiting to print. When you open the print queue, you can see the sequence of the active print jobs, the document owner, and the number of pages to print. In addition to viewing the status and information about the waiting print jobs, you can also use the print queue to pause, resume, restart, or cancel print jobs.

HEADS UP

To access the printer properties, you might need to click a button in the Print dialog box labeled Properties.

▶ **VOCABULARY**

duplex printing

print queue

Step-by-Step 14.7

1. If necessary, open **Ergonomic5** from your solution files.

2. Click the **Office Button** and then click the **Print** command to open the Print dialog box. Notice the printer name shown in the Name text box in the Printer section of the dialog box. This is your system's default printer.

3. Click the list arrow in the Name text box to access a list of other printers available on your system. Click any of the printer names to change from the default printer to a different printer for this job.

4. Under Page range, click to select **Pages** and enter **2** in the text box to the right. Under Copies, change the Number of copies to **3**. This setting indicates that three copies of the second page will print.

5. Click the **Properties** button. Options will vary depending on the printer selected, but they will most likely include paper size, print quality, and color management.

6. Click **Cancel** to close the Properties dialog box, and then click **Close** to close the Print dialog box without printing. Do not print the document.

HEADS UP

To quickly open the print queue during the print process, double-click the printer icon in the tray on the right side of the task bar.

FIGURE 14–12
The print queue with documents waiting to print

7. Click the **Start** button, click **Control Panel**, click **Hardware and Sound**, and then click **Printers**. A check mark next to the printer name identifies the default printer. Double-click the name of the printer you are using. A printer dialog box showing the print queue, similar to the one shown in **Figure 14–12**, will open.

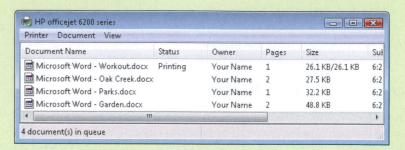

8. If you are the only one accessing the printer, the print queue may already be empty by the time you open it. However, if multiple documents are waiting to print on the printer you selected, the print queue will look similar to the one shown in **Figure 14–12**, which shows multiple documents waiting to be printed.

9. To cancel a print job, you would select the job(s) in the list. You don't have a document to select, but you can look at the commands. Click **Document** in the menu bar.

    a. Cancel removes the document from the print queue. The current printer job may take a while to cancel, and it may finish printing without canceling, but the remaining jobs in the list will be cancelled.

    b. Pause stops the document from being printed, but the document is not removed from the queue.

    c. Resume restarts the printing process for the selected document.

10. Close the print queue dialog box and any Control Panel windows, and close the document.

Troubleshooting Common Printing Problems

Even when using Print Preview, there are times when the print results do not meet expectations. This could be due to a variety of different things, as shown in **Table 14–1**.

TABLE 14–1   Troubleshooting printer problems

PROBLEM	CAUSE/SOLUTION
The entire document does not print, or some of the document looks blurry and faded	If the colors don't print correctly, the printer may be low on or out of ink or toner
The document doesn't look the same	Sometimes the font in your document might not be available on the printer you are using; change the font in your document to a TrueType font, which looks the same on the printed page as it does on the screen, or change the font to one that is available on your printer
The layout looks wrong	• You may be printing a document that was created with a different version of Microsoft Word or was formatted for different printer settings, such as margins and paper size • Some printers will not print documents with margins less than 0.5" • To have Word format the document to your printer's paper size for this printing session only, open the Print dialog box and then show the printer properties; choose the appropriate paper size and scale the document to fit the paper size
Nothing happens	• Check the print queue; your document may be blocked by one or more documents waiting to be printed • Make sure the printer is not out of paper • Make sure the printer is connected to the computer, the printer power is turned on, and the printer is online • Make sure the printer cable is connected to the right port • Check for paper jams • Open the Print dialog box and confirm that the correct printer shows in the Printer Name text box • Run the Windows Printing Troubleshooter; click the Start button, click Help and Support, enter printing troubleshooter in the Search box, and then select the problem or problems you are having and follow the instructions
You don't get a printed document, and Microsoft Word itself stops responding	It is likely that printer is not installed or you do not have the correct printer driver; you can try installing an updated printer driver from the printer's manufacturer to resolve this problem

Sharing Electronic Files

The use of computers and telecommunications in the workplace has changed how we work. The majority of the information we work with is now generated by email and electronic files. Instead of producing a hard copy of a document, it is now common practice to share a soft copy. A *soft copy* is a digital copy of data, such as a file viewed on a computer's display or shared via an e-mail attachment.

IC³
2-1.4.6
2-1.4.7

▶ **VOCABULARY**
soft copy

Preparing Documents for Electronic Distribution

You may want to control what others can see in the document. For example, you may not want them to see the author of the document or the date the document was created. Information like this is referred to as *metadata*—data that describes other data—and although it is invisible, it is still easy to find.

If you know the reviewers of the document are working with an older version of Word, you can choose to save the document in a previous Word version format. Be aware, though, that when you save the document in the older format, some information and/or formatting may be lost.

▶ **VOCABULARY**

metadata

HEADS UP

Be sure to check if a document is linked with other information sources, such as databases or spreadsheets, to avoid unintentionally sending or publishing information about the linked data.

Step-by-Step 14.8

1. Open **Ergonomic2** from your solution files and save the document Ergonomic2 as **Ergonomic6**.

2. Click the **Office Button**, point to **Prepare**, and then click **Properties**. The Document Information Panel shown in **Figure 14–13** will appear at the top of the document window, showing information about the author, title, subject matter, keywords, and so on. This information can be updated and is useful when searching for documents.

FIGURE 14–13
The Document Information Panel

Click here to show Advanced Properties

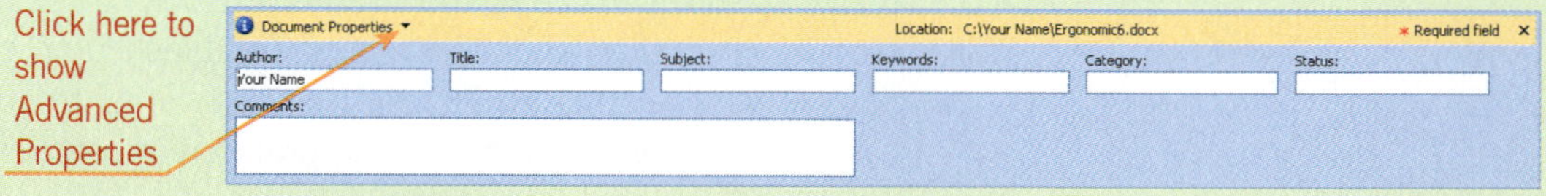

3. To update the information, click in the **Title** box and enter **Why Go Ergonomic?** Click in the **Subject** box and enter **increase safety, comfort, and productivity**.

4. Click the **Document Properties** list arrow and then click **Advanced Properties**. Click the **Statistics** tab in the document Properties dialog box, as shown in **Figure 14–14**. Notice that this information includes the number of times the document has been revised and the total editing time.

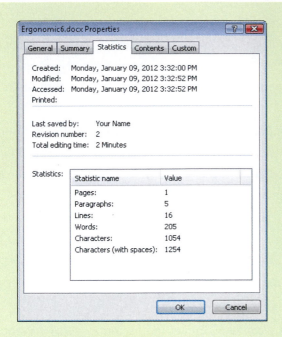

FIGURE 14–14
The Statistics tab in the document
Properties dialog box

5. Click **OK** or **Cancel** to close the dialog box. Then, close the Document
    Information Panel by clicking the **Close** button in the top right corner.

6. Click the **Office Button**, point to **Prepare**, and then click **Inspect**
    Document. When prompted to save the changes, click **Yes**.

7. The Document Inspector dialog box shown in **Figure 14–15** opens. Word
    proposes some features to check.

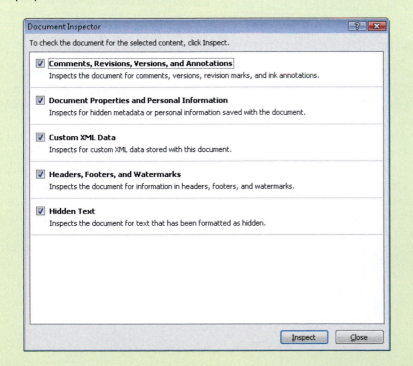

FIGURE 14–15
The Document Inspector dialog box

8. Click **Inspect** at the bottom of the dialog box. The inspection results appear. You want to leave the revision marks in the document, so don't make any changes regarding the markup. However, you do want to remove the personal information, so click **Remove All** in the Document Properties and Personal Information section.

9. Close the Document Inspector dialog box and save the changes to the document. Notice when you save the changes that the initials in the comment balloons change to *A1* and *A2*. Position the mouse pointer over a markup for a revision in the document. The name of the reviewer has been changed to *Author*, and all the markup is the same color. Removing the personal information made the comments anonymous.

10. Click the **Office Button**, point to **Prepare**, and then click **Properties**. Notice that all the personal and property information has been removed.

11. Click the **Document Properties** list arrow, click **Advanced Properties**, and if necessary, click the **Statistics** tab. Much of the data is still visible, but the name of the user who last saved the document has been removed, as well as the total editing time.

12. Click **OK** or **Cancel** to close the Properties dialog box.

13. Save the changes and close the document.

Saving the Document in a PDF or XPS Format

When sharing documents with others, you need to consider that not all users will be using Word 2007. They may be working with different applications, platforms, and operating systems, so before distributing the soft copy, you need to choose an appropriate format so they will be able to access the file.

The ***Portable Document Format (PDF)***, created by Adobe Systems in 1993, is commonly used. Microsoft included the ***XML Paper Specification (XPS)*** format in the Office 2007 applications. Both document formats are designed to preserve the visual appearance and layout of each page, and they enable fast viewing and printing. These document formats are especially useful for resumes and newsletters because the appearance of each page is unchanged and the document will print exactly as intended.

▶ **VOCABULARY**

Portable Document Format (PDF)

XML Paper Specification (XPS)

◀ **HEADS UP**

A computer must be properly configured to output or receive and open documents as a PDF, XPS, fax, e-mail attachment or Web page. Microsoft provides a free add-in that you can download so you can use the XPS and PDF format.

Step-by-Step 14.9

1. Open **Ergonomic3** from your solution files.

2. Click the **Office Button**, point to **Save As**, and then click **PDF or XPS**. The Publish as PDF or XPS dialog box will open.

3. In the File name box enter **Ergonomic7**.

4. In the Save as type box, click the list arrow and then click **XPS Document (*.xps)**.

5. Click **Publish**. The document will open in XPS format in Internet Explorer, if you use that as your default browser.

6. Drag across some text to select it. Press **Delete**. The read-only format will not allow any changes.

7. Close the browser and leave the Ergonomic3 document open.

Sending and Publishing Documents

When distributing electronic copies of the document, you can choose to send the content in an e-mail message or in a fax message, or you can send the file as an attachment to an e-mail message. Of course, you must be connected to a network or the Internet, and you must have sufficient bandwidth (the speed of data transfer) for transferring the electronic files.

Another way to distribute a document is to publish the document to a ***document management server***, which is a central location for storing, managing, and tracking files. Some document management servers, like Windows SharePoint Services, also provide features to help organizations manage business processes. Documents are stored in a library, and access to those documents and the rights of users can be controlled. For example, the files can be encrypted and users must know the password to open folders or files.

Word makes it easy for you to create a document workspace where you can make the document available. A ***document workspace*** is a Windows SharePoint Services Web site that provides tools for sharing and updating files and keeping colleagues informed about document status. You can publish the document at the Web site and keep the local document on your computer synchronized with the changes and updates.

You must have authorization to publish or access files at a Microsoft Windows SharePoint Services Web site. Therefore, using document management server and new document workspace features is beyond the scope of this lesson.

Publishing to a blog is another alternative. You will learn more about creating blog posts in Lesson 16.

▶ **VOCABULARY**
document management server

document workspace

Step-by-Step 14.10

1. If necessary, open **Ergonomic3** from your solution files.

2. Click the **Office Button**, point to **Send**, and then click **E-mail**. If Microsoft Outlook is your default e-mail application, a new message window will open. If Outlook is not your default e-mail application, most likely your e-mail application will open with a new message form.

3. The document is already attached to the e-mail message. Close the message document window without saving any changes.

4. Click the **Office Button**, point to **Publish**, and then click **Document Management Server**. The Save As dialog box will open with My Network Places already selected. At this point you would navigate to the server space and click Save, and the document would be uploaded to document management server.

5. Click **Cancel** to exit the dialog box.

6. Click the **Office Button**, point to **Publish**, and then click **Create Document Workspace**. The Document Management task pane will appear on the right side of the screen. Here you would enter a name for the workspace and the URL for the location.

7. Close the Document Management task pane.

8. Close the document and the application. If prompted to save changes to the document, click **No**.

HEADS UP

When you choose the E-mail as PDF Attachment or the E-mail as XPS Attachment option, the document will be sent in that format.

ETHICS IN TECHNOLOGY

Computer use is a privilege, and it imposes certain obligations and responsibilities. The behavior, courtesy, and etiquette expected in verbal and written communications is extended to electronic communications. When sharing documents, users must maintain integrity and discipline themselves to do what is right. It is important that shared documents are maintained in a manner that is accurate and honest.

Only view and edit the files which you are authorized to access. Do not move, alter, or delete documents without permission. Respect the property of others. The use of the documents should be limited to the intended objectives, and release of information without permission is unethical. Passwords are used to restrict access, so do not share passwords with those who are not authorized to access the files. To protect confidential information, remove metadata and follow the correct procedures to keep the information secure.

SUMMARY

In this lesson, you learned:

- Tracking changes with revision marks makes it easy to identify who made the changes and when the changes were made.

- Reviewers can provide feedback without changing the content by adding comments to the document.

- You can choose the markup that you want to appear on the screen and when the document is printed.

- Revisions can be accepted or rejected, and comments can easily be removed from the document.

- You can protect documents by restricting access and by restricting revisions and comments.

- You can change your default printer and printer settings using the Print command.

- You can view, pause, and cancel print jobs waiting in the print queue.

- When sharing documents with others, you need to choose the appropriate document format.

- Before distributing a soft copy of a document, you may want to remove metadata.

■ VOCABULARY REVIEW

Define the following terms:

comment
document management server
document workspace
duplex printing
encryption

hard copy
markup
metadata
Portable Document Format (PDF)
read-only document

print queue
soft copy
XML Paper Specification (XPS)

■ REVIEW QUESTIONS

TRUE / FALSE

Circle T if the statement is true or F if the statement is false.

T   F   **1.**   When tracking changes, insertions are always blue and deletions are always strikethrough.

T   F   **2.**   When showing markup for multiple reviewers, you can choose to show revisions for only one of the reviewers.

T   F   **3.**   You can restrict formatting changes for a portion of a document.

T   F   **4.**   Adding comments to a document allows reviewers to provide feedback and express opinions without changing the content of the document.

T   F   **5.**   An easy way to restrict access to a file is to assign a password.

MULTIPLE CHOICE

Select the best response for the following statements.

1. Duplex printing is _____.

    A.   when your computer has access to two printers on the system

    B.   a special printer feature for automatically printing two copies of each page in the document

    C.   a special printer feature for automatically printing content on both sides of the page

    D.   when you manually reload paper in the printer to print on the back side of the page

2. _____ is invisible data in a document that describes other data.

   A.   Hidden text   C.   Transparent text

   B.   Metadata   D.   Soft copy

3. When a document is encrypted, _____.

   A.   the user can view the document but cannot make any changes to the document

   B.   the user must enter a password to open the document

   C.   all personal information is removed from the document

   D.   the document will open in most applications, operating systems, and platforms

4. If you don't want others to make changes in your document, you should save the document as _____.

   A.   a read-only document   C. a PDF document

   B.   an XPS document   D. any of the above

5. _____ can be viewed in a balloon in the margin or in the Reviewing Pane.

   A.   Insertions   C. Deletions

   B.   Comments   D. any of the above

FILL IN THE BLANK

Complete the following sentences by writing the correct word or words in the blanks provided.

1. The _____ shows information about documents that are waiting to print.

2. A(n) _____ provides tools for sharing and updating files and keeping colleagues informed about document status.

3. The revision marks and annotations that appear in a document are referred to as _____.

4. _____ is a standard method for encoding data.

5. A digital copy of data, such as a file viewed on a computer's display or shared via an e-mail attachment, is referred to as a _____.

■ PROJECTS

PROJECT 14–1

1. Start the Word application and open the data file **Project14-1**. Save the document as **Facilities1**.

2. Toggle on the Track Changes feature.

3. Make note of the current user name and initials, and then change the user name to **Top Chief** and change the user initials to **TC**.

4. Add the following three items in the bulleted list, in the correct alphabetical order: **pilates classes, strength and conditioning**, and **yoga classes**.

5. Select *pilates* and insert the comment **Should this be initial caps?**.

6. In the first paragraph, find the text *help people* and following that text, insert **of all ages**.

7. In the last sentence of the first paragraph, find the text *assist patients* and add **both young and old**.

8. Find and replace all occurrences of *rehab* with **rehabilitation**.

9. Find all occurrences of *clinics* and replace them with **facilities**.

10. Save the changes to the document, and then toggle off the Track Changes feature.

11. Save the document as **Facilities2**.

12. Inspect the document and remove the personal information. Do not remove the revision marks and comments. Check the document properties to make sure all the personal information was removed.

13. Restore the user name and initials to what they were before you changed them in Step 3.

14. Save the changes to the document and then close the document.

PROJECT 14–2

1. Open the data file **Project14-2** and save the document as **Furniture1**.

2. Show only the insertions and deletions in the document.

3. Move to the first revision and reject the change.

4. Move to the second revision and accept the change.

5. Show the markup for comments and formatting.

6. Delete all the comments in the document.

7. Accept all changes in the document.

8. Save the changes, and then save the document as **Furniture2** in the PDF format. The document will open in Adobe Reader if the application is installed on your computer.

9. Close the Adobe Reader window and the Furniture1 document.

PROJECT 14–4

1. Open the data file **Project14-4** and save the document as **Safety**.

2. Show the Document Information Panel. Enter the title **Work Place Safety** and then enter the subject **industrial ergonomic assessment**.

3. To secure the document and limit access, encrypt the document by assigning the password **BLP9VJ5TMP**.

4. Save the changes and close the document.

5. Attempt to open the document to make sure a password is required. When the Password dialog box appears, click **Cancel**, and then close the application.

PROJECT 14–3

1. Open the data file **Project14-3** and save the document as **Walking**.

2. Protect the document by setting editing restrictions for **No changes (Read only)**. Make exceptions for **Everyone** to edit the last two paragraphs in the document.

3. Start enforcing the protection by assigning the password **Mac@57MCV7**.

4. Close the Restrict Formatting and Editing pane.

5. Save the changes to the document and then close the document.

6. Open the document and make sure the restrictions are applied as intended. Delete the last paragraph.

7. Save the changes and close the document.

TEAMWORK PROJECT

The document you worked with in Project 14-3 provided information about exercising in both hot and cold weather. Many people have preferences for warm or cool weather for a variety of reasons. Team up with a partner to explore these reasons.

1. With your partner, decide who will take the warm weather topic and who will take the cool weather topic. If both of you prefer the same season, flip a coin to make the decision.

2. Using Word, create lists of advantages and disadvantages of your chosen climate. If you live in a climate that is more or less warm all year round, use your imagination to list the advantages and disadvantages of cold weather.

3. Exchange documents and review your partner's list. Track changes and edit the document to include your opinions. Add comments where appropriate.

4. Review the changes and comments your partner added to your document. Accept or reject each revision, and delete the comments. Make any other edits to make your argument stronger.

5. After finalizing your documents, share them with each other again and discuss with your partner whose arguments are more persuasive.

CRITICAL THINKING

ACTIVITY 14–1

If the colors fade or are inconsistent when you print a page, it's possible that the printer is low on ink or toner. The cartridges are expensive, however, so you don't want to replace them until they are empty. So, how do you know the amount of ink or toner available in the cartridge(s)? Printers vary, and there is no universal answer for this question. Explore the properties (or preferences) for the printer connected to your computer to locate the estimated levels of ink or toner your printer. When you find the information, create a list of steps that describe how you can check the level of ink or toner for your printer.

ACTIVITY 14–2

Further explore the properties for a printer connected to your computer. Identify one of the special features that interests you the most, such as printing posters, adjusting the volume of ink for faster drying time, or printing in grayscale. Examine the feature and options and use the Help screens to aid you in learning the purpose of the feature. Then write a short description about the feature and explain when you would use this feature.

ONLINE DISCOVERY

In this lesson you worked with several documents that referenced ergonomic elements. Search the Internet for *ergonomic computer* *accessories* and make a list of items that are designed to create an ergonomic computer workstation.

LESSON 15

Working with Tables

■ OBJECTIVES

Upon completion of this lesson, you should be able to:

- Create a table and insert text.
- Insert and delete rows and columns.
- Adjust column width and row height.
- Use the Draw Table and Eraser tools to create and edit a table grid.
- Format text alignment and direction within a table cell.
- Format borders and shading and apply table styles.
- Sort data in a table.
- Convert text to a table and vice versa.

■ VOCABULARY

ascending order

cell

descending order

gridlines

merging cells

Quick Tables

splitting cells

■ DATA FILES

To complete this lesson, you will need these data files:

Step15–13.docx

Project15–1.docx

Project15–2.docx

Suppose you have a document in Word that includes information you want to arrange in several lines across two or three columns. How can you create the columns you need in Word? If your answer is "Set tab stops," you're correct. However, there's also an easier and faster way. The table features in Word make the task of arranging text and numbers in columns both quick and easy. Borders and shading also help to organize information in a meaningful way.

2-2.1.13

▶ **VOCABULARY**
cell

Creating a Table

A table consists of cells to which you add content, such as text, numbers, or graphics. A *cell* represents one intersection of a row and a column in a table. In a table, rows go across and columns go down. It is common to add headings at the top of columns to label the content in the columns.

To create a table, you must first decide how many columns and rows you want in the table. You then create a table grid and enter the data.

To move the insertion point from one cell to another, you can press the arrow keys or Tab. When you reach the end of a row and press Tab, the insertion point moves to the first cell in the next row.

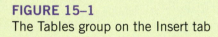

Step-by-Step 15.1

1. Open a new blank document. Click the **Insert** tab and then click the **Table** button in the Tables group shown in **Figure 15–1**. A grid of table cells appears.

FIGURE 15–1
The Tables group on the Insert tab

Table button

2. Drag the mouse pointer down the grid until seven rows of cells are highlighted, then continue to drag the mouse pointer across until the top of the grid shows 3×7 Table, as shown in **Figure 15–2**. Click, and the table is inserted in the document.

FIGURE 15–2
The Insert Table grid with the number of columns and rows selected

Three columns by seven rows

Live preview of the table

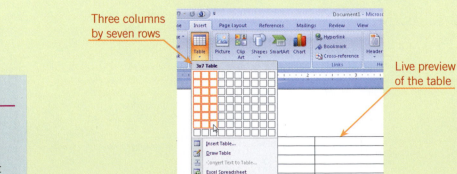

▌ **EXTRA FOR EXPERTS**

You can also create a table by opening the Insert Table dialog box and entering the number of rows and columns. On the Insert tab, click the **Table** button and then click **Insert Table** to open the dialog box.

3. Because the insertion point is now positioned in a table in the document, the Ribbon adapts and shows Table Tools, which are features you can use to format and edit tables. Compare your screen with **Figure 15–3**. There are two Table Tools tabs: the Design tab and the Layout tab.

There are two Table Tools tabs

FIGURE 15–3
The Table Tools
Design tab

4. The insertion point should be positioned in the first cell of the table. Press **Tab** to move the insertion point to the next cell to the right in the same row. Enter **20 Minutes**. Press **Tab** and then enter **40 Minutes**.

5. Press **Tab** to move the insertion point to the first cell in the next row.

6. Press the **down arrow** to move the insertion point down to the third row.

7. Enter the remaining data shown in **Figure 15–4**. Use Tab or the arrow keys to move from one cell to another.

> **HEADS UP**
>
> If nonprinting characters appear in your document, small squares will show in the left corner of each table cell. These squares are called end-of-cell markers. They will move to the right as you enter text in the cell. End-of-cell markers do not print.

FIGURE 15–4
Table content for Step-by-Step 15.1

	20 Minutes	40 Minutes
Cross-country skiing	192	384
Downhill skiing	144	288
Golf: carrying clubs	132	264
Mountain biking	204	408
Weight lifting	72	144

8. Save the document as **Calories1** and leave the document open.

Modifying the Table Structure

After you create a table, you may decide to change it. For example, you may need to add more rows or delete a column. Word has many features that make these changes easy.

2-2.1.14

Inserting Rows and Columns

To insert a new row at the end of the table, you can position the insertion point in the last table cell and press Tab. To insert a new row anywhere else in the table, or to insert new columns, you can use the insert commands on the Table Tools Layout tab.

Step-by-Step 15.2

1. If necessary, open **Calories1** from your solution files. Save the document Calories1 as **Calories2**. If necessary, click any cell in the table to show the Table Tools Design tab.

2. Position the insertion point in the last cell in the table at the lower right (*144*). Press **Tab** to create a new row. Enter the following information in the new row:

   ```
   Golf: using a cart       84       168
   ```

3. Move the insertion point to any cell in the third row (*Cross-country skiing*). Click the **Table Tools Layout** tab for more table tools, as shown in **Figure 15–5**.

FIGURE 15–5
The Table Tools
Layout tab

Delete Table button   Insert Rows Above button

Rows &
Columns
group

4. In the Rows & Columns group, click the **Insert Rows Above** button in the Rows & Columns group. A new row is entered above the row where the insertion point is positioned, and the table now has nine rows.

5. Drag across all the cells in the fourth and fifth rows (*Cross-country* and *Downhill*) to select the cells. Click the **Insert Rows Below** button **Insert Below**. Because you selected two rows, two new rows are inserted below the selection. Click anywhere in the document window to deselect the cells.

6. Enter the following information in the sixth and seventh rows:
   ```
   Walking: 15 minutes/mile      108      216
   Running: 9 minutes/mile       264      528
   ```

7. Move the insertion point to any cell in the third column (*40 Minutes*). Click the **Insert Columns to the Left** button **Insert Left**. A new column is added to the left side of the column where the insertion point is positioned.

8. Position the mouse pointer above the first row in the first column. When the mouse pointer changes to a down-pointing arrow ⬇, click to select the column. Click and drag the mouse pointer across to select both the first and the second column.

9. With the first two columns selected, click the **Insert Columns to the Right** button **Insert Right**. Two new columns are added to the right side of the second column and the width of the columns is automatically adjusted. Notice the text automatically wraps to a new line within the cells of the first column.

10. Click in the top cell of the new third column and enter **30 Minutes**. Press the **down arrow** to move down to the fourth row and enter the following numbers to complete the column:

📧 EXTRA FOR EXPERTS

You can use the number pad on your keyboard to enter numbers. Make sure that NUMLOCK is turned on.

288

216

162

396

198

306

108

126

11. Save the changes and leave the document open.

Deleting Rows and Columns

To remove rows or columns, you must choose the Delete commands on the Table Tools Layout tab. When you delete a row or column, the text in the cells is also deleted.

Step-by-Step 15.3

1. If necessary, open **Calories2** from your solution files. Save the document Calories2 as **Calories3**. If necessary, show the Table Tools Layout tab.

2. Position the mouse pointer to the left side of the ninth row (*Mountain biking*). The pointer will change to a right-pointing arrow ⇗. With the arrow pointed at the first cell of the ninth row, click the mouse button to select the entire row.

3. With all the cells selected in the ninth row, press **Delete**. When you delete the text in a cell, the cell boundaries remain.

4. With the insertion point in the ninth row, click the **Delete Table** button in the Rows & Columns group, and then click **Delete Rows**. The row where the insertion point is positioned is deleted.

5. Select the ninth row (*Weight lifting*), click the **Delete Table** button, and click **Delete Rows**.

6. Select the two blank rows, click the **Delete Table** button, and then click **Delete Rows**.

7. Position the insertion point in the first cell in the first column (a blank cell). Click the **Delete Table** button and then click **Delete Cells**. The Delete Cells dialog box will open.

8. Click the second option **Shift cells up** and then click **OK**. The cell is deleted, and the contents of the cells below the deleted cell are shifted up.

9. Click the **Undo** button to restore the table cell and the data that was in it.

> **HEADS UP**
>
> You can also select table cells by clicking the **Select Table** button in the Table group on the Table Tools Layout tab.

> **EXTRA FOR EXPERTS**
>
> You can also quickly access commands to insert and delete cells, rows, and columns by right-clicking the selected cell or cells and then choosing a command from the shortcut menu.

10. Select the two blank columns, click the **Delete Table** button, and then click **Delete Columns**.

11. Save the changes and leave the document open.

Adjusting Column Width and Row Height

When you create a table grid, Word makes all the columns the same width, and the entire width of the table is based on the settings for the margins and paper size when the table is inserted. You can adjust the width of each column automatically using the AutoFit feature. You can choose to automatically adjust the column width as needed, to accommodate the contents within the cells, or you can choose to automatically resize the table to fit in the document window. This is useful because the table width automatically adjusts when the window size changes.

The height of each row is the same when the table is first inserted, but when the text wraps to a second line within a cell, the height of all the cells in that row is automatically increased to accommodate the extra line of text.

Step-by-Step 15.4

1. If necessary, open **Calories3** from your solution files. Save the document Calories3 as **Calories4**. If necessary, switch to Print Layout view.

2. Click the **View** tab and click the **Page Width** button in the Zoom group.

3. Position the insertion point in the first cell in the table (a blank cell) and click the **Table Tools Layout** tab. In the Cell Size group, shown in **Figure 15–6**, note the height of the row that appears in the Table Row Height box.

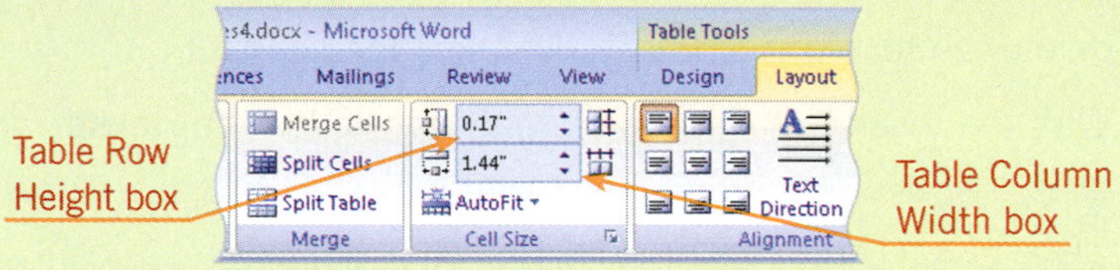

FIGURE 15–6
The Cell Size group on the Table Tools Layout tab

4. Move the insertion point to the fourth row *(Walking)*. Notice that the numbers in the Table Row Height box change to reflect the difference in the height of the row.

5. With the insertion point positioned in the first column, look at the width of the column that appears in the Table Column Width box. Click anywhere in the second and third columns. The numbers in the Table Column Width box may vary for each column.

6. With the insertion point positioned anywhere within the table, click the **AutoFit** button in the Cell Size group and then click **AutoFit Contents**. The text in the first column no longer wraps within the cells, and the extra white space in the other three columns is eliminated.

HEADS UP

When a table cell is formatted for AutoFit Contents, Word will automatically adjust the cell width each time the cell contents change.

7. With the insertion point positioned anywhere within the table, click the **AutoFit** button again and then click **AutoFit Window**. Extra space is added to the columns so that the table fills the width of the page.

8. Click the **Page Layout** tab, click the **Page Orientation** button, and then click **Landscape**. The width of each column adjusts so the table fills all the space between the left and right margins.

9. Click the **Page Orientation** button and then click **Portrait** to return to the original page orientation.

10. Click the **Undo** button arrow and then click **AutoFit Window**. This will restore the setting so that the columns are adjusted to fit the contents.

11. Click the **Table Tools Layout** tab and in the Table group, click the **Select Table** button ↳ Select ▾ and then click **Select Table.**

12. Click the up arrow in the Table Row Height box to increase the row height to 0.3".

13. Deselect the table rows. Save the changes and leave the document open.

Merging and Splitting Table Cells

When you remove the boundary between two cells, it is called *merging cells*. You can merge cells horizontally or vertically. You can merge cells when you want to create a heading to span across two or more columns.

When you convert a cell into multiple cells, it is called *splitting cells*. You can split a cell into two or more rows and/or two or more columns. You can also split a table into two separate tables.

▶ **VOCABULARY**
merging cells
splitting cells

Step-by-Step 15.5

1. If necessary, open **Calories4** from your solution files. Save the document Calories4 as **Calories5**. Also, if necessary, click in the table and then click the **Table Tools Layout** tab.

2. With the insertion point positioned anywhere within the table, click the **AutoFit** button in the Cell Size group and then click **AutoFit Window**.

3. Position the insertion point in the first row in the table and then click the **Insert Rows Above** button. A new row is added and the four cells in the new row are selected.

4. With all the cells in the new row still selected, click the **Merge Cells** button ▥ **Merge Cells** in the Merge group, shown in **Figure 15–7**. Click in the table to deselect the row. The four cells have merged into a single, wide cell.

FIGURE 15–7
The Merge group on the Table Tools Layout tab

Merge group

5. Position the insertion point in the new blank row and then click the **Split Cells** button ▦ **Split Cells** . The Split Cells dialog box will appear.

6. Change the number in the Number of columns box to **1**. Change the number in the Number of rows box to **2**. Click **OK**. Click anywhere in the table to deselect the row. You will see that the row is split into two rows.

7. Position the insertion point in the top blank row and enter **NUMBER OF CALORIES BURNED**. Press **Enter** and then enter **Body weight: 150 lbs**. The height of the cells is automatically adjusted to accommodate the two lines of text.

8. Click in the second row of the table and click the **Split Cells** button. Click **OK** to accept the proposed settings of two columns and one row. The row will be split evenly into two cells.

9. Position the mouse pointer over the border that splits the row into two cells. When the pointer changes to a double-headed arrow, drag the border to the left so that it aligns with the first column border, as shown in **Figure 15–8**.

FIGURE 15–8
Drag a cell border to resize the cell

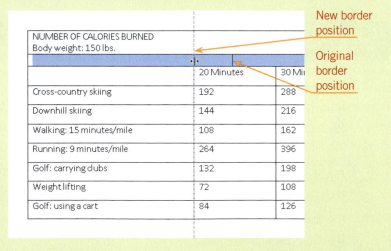

10. Click in the cell directly below *Body weight* and enter **Activity.** Click in the cell directly above the *20 Minutes* column and enter **Length of Time.**

11. Position the insertion point anywhere in the seventh row (*Running*), and then click the **Split Table** button ▦ **Split Table** . The rows now appear in two separate tables.

12. Click the **Undo** button to return the two tables to one table.

13. Save the changes and close the document.

Drawing a Table

There may be occasions when you need to create and customize a more complex table. For example, the table may require cells of different heights or a varying number of columns per row. The Draw Table tool is very useful for creating complex tables. When you use the Draw Table tool, you use the mouse to draw the table grid on the screen the same way you would use a pen to draw the grid on a sheet of paper. The document must be displayed in Print Layout view.

The Eraser tool enables you to remove cell boundaries. Click the Eraser button, and the pointer changes to an eraser. When you point and click a cell boundary, the line will be selected. When you release, the boundary is deleted.

2-2.1.3
2-2.1.13

📼 **EXTRA FOR EXPERTS**

You can also use the Draw Table tool and the Eraser tool to add, delete, split, and merge cells in an existing table.

Step-by-Step 15.6

1. Open a new blank document. Click the **View** tab, make sure the Ruler is checked, and then click the **Page Width** button.

2. Click the **Insert** tab. Click the **Table** button and then, in the menu below the grid, click **Draw Table**. The mouse pointer changes to a pencil.

3. Position the mouse pointer in the upper-left corner of the document near the flashing insertion point. Notice that as you move the mouse pointer, the position of the pointer is indicated on both the horizontal and vertical rulers.

4. To draw the outside boundary of the table grid, position the pointer in the upper-left margin. Then click and drag the pencil down and to the right. As you drag the mouse, markers on the vertical and horizontal rulers will show the table size, as shown in **Figure 15–9**. Release when the table (box) is approximately 6 ½ inches wide by 2 ½ inches high.

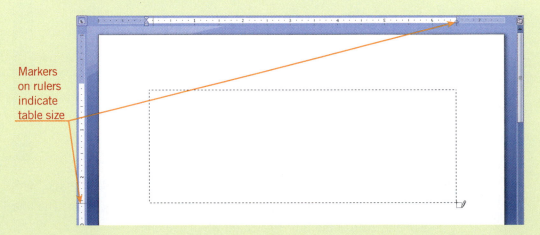

Markers on rulers indicate table size

FIGURE 15–9
Creating the outside boundary of a table grid

5. To create the cell lines inside the table, position the point of the pencil where you want the line to begin and then click and drag to the point where you want the line to end. A broken line will display as you drag the mouse. Draw all of the lines illustrated in **Figure 15–10**. Note that the four horizontal lines are ½ inch apart and the three vertical lines are positioned at 1 inch, 4 ½ inches, and 5 ½ inches on the horizontal ruler.

FIGURE 15–10
Table grid for
Step-by-Step 15.6

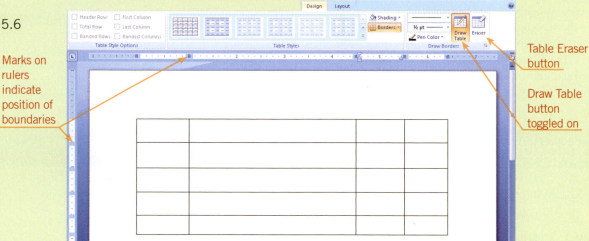

Marks on rulers indicate position of boundaries

Table Eraser button

Draw Table button toggled on

> **HEADS UP**
>
> You can also press **Escape** to toggle off the Draw Table option.

6. On the Table Tools Design tab in the Draw Borders group, click the **Draw Table** button to toggle off the Draw Table option.

7. Click the **Table Eraser** button. The pointer changes to an eraser.

8. Position the eraser in the first row on the vertical line between the first and second cells. When the lower corner of the eraser is positioned over the line and you hold down the mouse button, the line appears selected as it does in **Figure 15–11**.

FIGURE 15–11
Eraser tool with selected line

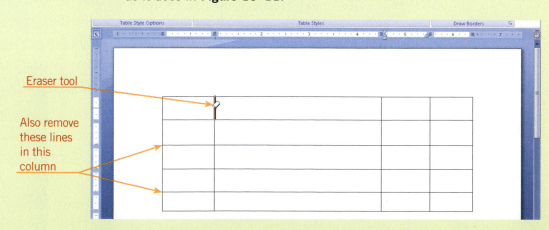

Eraser tool

Also remove these lines in this column

9. Release the mouse button to delete the selected boundary. If you click and the line is not deleted, reposition the eraser and try again. The line will only be deleted if it is selected when you click.

10. Erase two more lines in the first column as indicated in **Figure 15–11**.

11. Click the **Table Eraser** button to toggle the feature off.

12. Enter the table text shown in **Figure 15–12**.

Recycling Rate		2000	2010
PET	Soft drink bottles	48%	
	Vegetable oil bottles	12%	
HDPE	Milk jugs	29%	
	Bleach and laundry detergent bottles	14%	

FIGURE 15–12
Table content for Step-by-Step 15.6

13. Save the document as **Recycling Rate1** and leave the document open.

Formatting Tables

2-2.1.13
2-2.1.14
2-2.1.15

You can make a table easier to read by enhancing its appearance. For example, aligning numbers within a cell can make the data easier to read. Changing the border colors and adding shading to some of the cells can help the reader quickly identify different types of data.

Aligning Data within Table Cells

The Alignment group in the Table Tools Layout tab includes several buttons you can use to align text within the cells. You can align text at the top, center, or bottom of a cell, as well as to the left or right. You can also change the direction of text in a table cell. The direction of the text toggles between three text positions: top to bottom, bottom to top, and horizontal (the default position).

Step-by-Step 15.7

1. If necessary, open **Recycling Rate1** from your solutions files. Save the document Recycling Rate1 as **Recycling Rate2**. Click the **Table Tools Layout** tab.

2. Drag the mouse pointer down the left side of the table to select all the rows in the table.

3. Click the **Table Row Height** box and enter **0.5**. All the rows are now exactly the same height.

4. In the Alignment group, click the **Align Top Right** button ▤ shown in **Figure 15–13**. The text in each cell is aligned at the right side of the cell beginning at the top boundary of the cell.

FIGURE 15–13
The Alignment group on the Table
Tools Layout tab

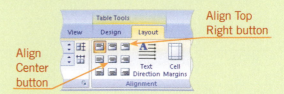

5. Click the **Align Center Left** button ▤. The text begins at the left side of the cells and is centered between the top and bottom boundaries of the cell.

6. Deselect the rows. Point to the cell with *PET* and drag down to select that cell and the cell with *HDPE*.

7. With both cells selected, click the **Text Direction** ᴬ≣ button in the Alignment group. The text rotates to the right and is shown from top to bottom.

8. Click the **Text Direction** button again. The text rotates to the right and now reads from bottom to top.

9. Notice that the buttons in the Alignment group are altered to reflect the new text direction. Click the **Align Center** button ▤ in the location shown in **Figure 15–13**. The text is centered between the left and right and top and bottom boundaries of the cell.

10. Click in the first cell (*Recycling Rate*) and then click the **Align Center** button.

11. Select the last two columns (*2000* and *2010*) and then click the **Align Center Right** button ▤. The text in each cell is aligned at the right side of the cell and centered between the top and bottom boundaries.

12. Deselect the cells. With the insertion point positioned anywhere within the table, click the **AutoFit** button, and then click **AutoFit Contents**. Your table should look like the table shown in **Figure 15–14**.

FIGURE 15–14
Table with text rotated and aligned

		Recycling Rate	2000	2010
PET		Soft drink bottles	48%	
		Vegetable oil bottles	12%	
HDPE		Milk jugs	29%	
		Bleach and laundry detergent bottles	14%	

13. Save the changes and leave the document open.

Formatting Borders and Shading

As you worked with the Calories and Recycle Rate tables you created in this lesson, the lines you saw on the screen were actually borders. By default, Word formats a ½ point single-line border around all cells in a table. Generally, the default border will be appropriate for the tables you create. However, there may be occasions when you want to customize the border and add shading or color to some of the table cells. You may even want to remove the border completely. When you remove the borders from table cells, the boundary lines for the cells still remain. These boundary lines in a table are called *gridlines*. Gridlines are used for layout purposes; they show on the screen, but they do not print.

▶ **VOCABULARY**
gridlines

Step-by-Step 15.8

1. If necessary, open **Recycling Rate2** from your solution files. Save the document Recycling Rate2 as **Recycling Rate3**.

2. Select all the cells in the table.

3. Click the **Table Tools Design** tab. In the Table Styles group, click the **Bottom Border** button arrow [Borders ▼] and then click **No Border**.

4. Click in the table to deselect it. Your document should now show lines that indicate the cell boundaries, as shown in **Figure 15–15**. If you don't see any broken blue lines in your table, click the **Table Tools Layout** tab and click the **View Table Gridlines** button [View Gridlines].

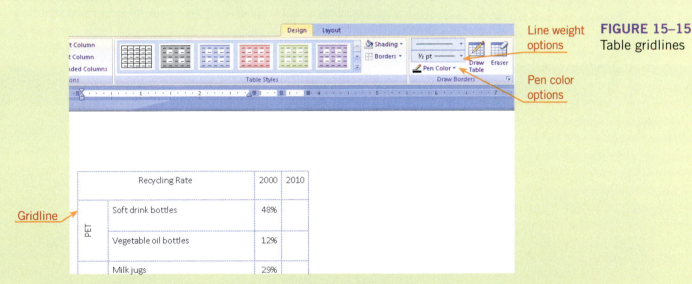

Line weight options

Pen color options

Gridline

FIGURE 15–15
Table gridlines

5. Select the first row in the table. On the Table Tools Design tab in the Table Styles group, click the **Shading** button arrow [Shading ▼]. Select a light green color. The shading is applied to the selected cells.

6. Select the cells containing *PET* and *HDPE*. Repeat the shading color format. (Hint: Press **F4**.)

7. Select all the cells in the table. In the Draw Borders group, click the **Line Weight** list arrow, and then click **¾ pt**. You must change the line weight setting before applying the border.

8. Click the **Pen Color** button arrow ✏ Pen Color ▾ and select a dark green color. You must also choose the border color before applying the border.

9. Click the **Borders** button arrow and then click **All Borders**. The ¾ pt dark green border line is applied to all selected cells.

10. Click in the table to deselect the cells. Select all the cells in the first row.

11. Click the **Line Weight** list arrow and then click **1 ½ pt**.

12. Position the mouse pointer over the **Borders** button. The ScreenTip should show *All Borders* because that was the last border format applied. The pen color is also still set for dark green. Click the **Borders** button. The 1 ½ pt dark green border is applied to all borders of the selected cells.

13. Select the cells containing *PET* and *HDPE*. Repeat the border format.

14. Click in the table to deselect the table cells. Save the changes and close the document.

Applying Table Styles

As you can see, formatting borders and shading can take time. That's why Word provides several table designs that you can apply with a single click. These styles are referred to as built-in styles.

Step-by-Step 15.9

1. Open **Calories5** from your solution files and save the document Calories5 as **Calories6**.

2. Select the first two rows, and in the Paragraph group, click the **Center** button.

3. With the insertion point positioned anywhere in the table, click the **Table Tools Layout** tab, click the **AutoFit** button, and then click **AutoFit Contents**.

4. Select all the cells that contain numbers (excluding the column headings), beginning with the calories data *192* through the calories data *168*, and then click the **Align Top Right** button in the Alignment group.

5. Click the **Table Tools Design** tab. In the Table Styles group, position the mouse pointer over the second style, **Light Shading**. A live preview of the new style will appear in the document window and the ScreenTip will show the name *Light Shading*, as shown in **Figure 15–16**.

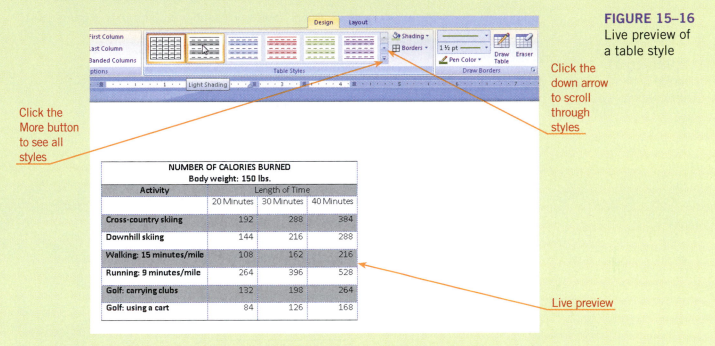

Click the More button to see all styles

Click the down arrow to scroll through styles

Live preview

FIGURE 15–16
Live preview of a table style

6. Move the mouse pointer over each of the other styles that appear in the Table Styles group to see a live preview of each style. Click the down arrow to see the next set of styles.

7. Click the **More** button to show all the built-in styles.

8. Click the **Light List – Accent 2** table style. The borders and shading are automatically applied to the table.

9. Select the column headings *Length of Time*, *20 Minutes*, *30 Minutes*, and *40 Minutes*, and apply the bold format. (Hint: Click the **Bold** button on the Mini toolbar, or press and hold **Ctrl** and then press **B**.)

10. Save the changes and close the document.

Using Quick Tables

Word also provides built-in tables, called **Quick Tables**, which include sample data and table formats. You can insert a Quick Table in a document and then replace the sample data with your own data, and you can modify the table structure and styles. Editing text in the cells of a table is a similar process to entering text in a document. You can enter and delete text, or select and replace the text. The Cut, Copy, and Paste commands are available, and you can also use drag-and-drop editing.

▶ **VOCABULARY**
Quick Tables

Step-by-Step 15.10

1. Open a new blank document.

2. Click the **Insert** tab. Click the **Table** button and then, in the menu below the grid, point to **Quick Tables**. The submenu shown in **Figure 15–17** appears.

FIGURE 15–17
The Built-In menu for
Quick Tables

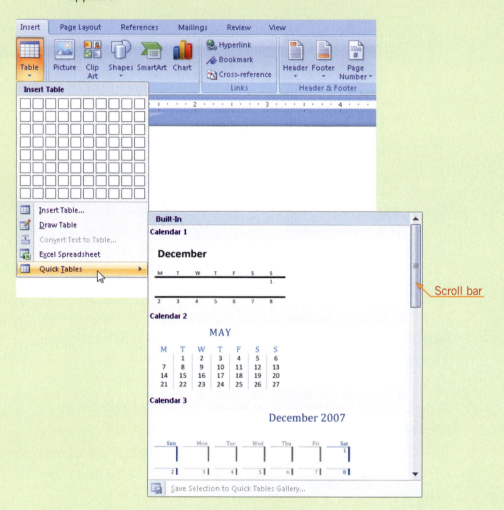

3. Scroll down and click the **Matrix** Quick Table. A table with sample data is inserted in the document.

4. Select all the rows in the table. Press **Delete** to remove all the text from the cells.

5. Click the **Table Tools Layout** tab and select the two columns at the right side of the table. In the Rows & Columns group, click the **Delete Table** button and then click **Delete Columns**.

6. Enter the data shown in **Figure 15–18** to complete the table. You will need to add two new rows at the bottom of the table grid.

Member Name	# Members in Family	Member #	# Years of Membership
Collica	5	103238	13
Sanchez	2	103241	13
O'Connell	4	103339	13
Wright	6	105166	11
Anderson	7	104655	12
Klopf	4	103210	13
Mendoza	2	104112	12

FIGURE 15–18
Table content for Step-by-Step 15.10

7. Select all the rows in the table, click the **Home** tab, and then change the font to **Arial**.

8. Click the **Table Tools Layout** tab. Select the first column and then click the **Align Bottom Left** button ▤ in the Alignment group. Select the second, third, and fourth columns and click the **Align Bottom Center** ▤ button.

9. Save the document as **Members1** and leave the document open.

Aligning and Resizing Tables on the Document Page

In this lesson, you have been selecting all the cells in a table, but you may not have actually selected the entire table. When you show nonprinting characters, you can see that every row ends with a marker. These end-of-row symbols must be included in the selection for the entire table to be selected.

To align a table on the page horizontally, you must first select the entire table. Once the entire table is selected, you can format the alignment in the same way you align text paragraphs.

You may have noticed a marker that sometimes appears at the upper-left corner of a table. This symbol is the table move handle, and you can drag the marker to reposition the table on the page. You can also use the table move handle to select the entire table.

The resize handle is another marker that sometimes appears in the lower-right corner of a table, and when you drag this symbol, you can resize the table.

Step-by-Step 15.11

1. If necessary, open **Members1** from your solution files. Save the document Members1 document as **Members2**.

2. If necessary, click the **Home** tab and then click the **Show/Hide ¶** button in the Paragraph group to show nonprinting characters.

3. Position the insertion point anywhere within the table, and click the **Table Tools Layout** tab.

4. Click and drag the **table move handle**, shown in **Figure 15–19**, to reposition the table on the page. If you do not see the table move handle, move the mouse pointer around the upper-left corner of the table until it appears.

FIGURE 15–19
Nonprinting characters in a table

Member·Name¤	#·Members·in· Family¤	Member·#¤	#·Years·of· Membership¤	¤
Collica¤	5¤	103238¤	13¤	¤
Sanchez¤	2¤	103241¤	13¤	¤
O'Connell¤	4¤	103339¤	13¤	¤
Wright¤	6¤	105166¤	11¤	¤
Anderson¤	7¤	104655¤	12¤	¤
Klopf¤	4¤	103210¤	13¤	¤
Mendoza¤	2¤	104112¤	12¤	¤

Table move handle
End of row marker
End of cell marker
Resize handle

5. Click the **table move handle** to select the entire table. Notice that the end-of-row markers are also selected.

6. Click the **Home** tab. Click the **Center** button in the Paragraph group. The table is centered horizontally.

7. Point to the lower-right corner of the table. When the resize handle appears, position the mouse pointer over the handle. The pointer will change to a double-headed arrow. Drag the handle about one inch to the right to increase the width of the table.

8. Save the changes and leave the document open.

Sorting Data in a Table

IC³

2-2.1.15

Tables organize material to make it easier to read, and you have discovered how formatting the table and the characters in the table can add clarity to the information. You can also sort the information in a table on different search criteria to organize the table contents to emphasize data in different ways.

Sorting data in *ascending order* rearranges it into alphabetical order from A to Z, or numerical order from lowest number to highest number. Sorting data in *descending order* rearranges the data in alphabetical order from Z to A, or numerical order from highest number to lowest number.

▶ **VOCABULARY**
ascending order
descending order

Step-by-Step 15.12

1. If necessary, open **Members2** from your solution files. Save the document Members2 as **Members3**.

2. Position the insertion point anywhere in the table, and click the **Table Tools Layout** tab.

3. Click the **Sort** button in the Data group, shown in **Figure 15–20**, to open the Sort dialog box.

Sort button

Data group

FIGURE 15–20
The Data group on the Table Tools Layout tab

4. Confirm that the Sort dialog box looks like the Sort dialog box in **Figure 15–21**, to sort by Member Name. The type of content to be sorted is Text.

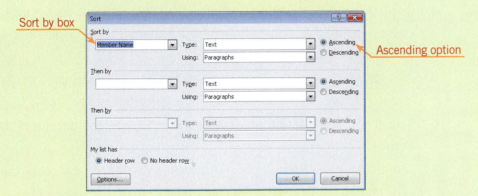

Sort by box

Ascending option

FIGURE 15–21
The Sort dialog box

5. To sort the data in descending alphabetical order according to the entries in the *Member Name* column, click the **Descending** option.

6. Click **OK**. The entries in first column of the table now appear sorted in reverse alphabetical order. Notice that the other columns in the rows were rearranged so that the correct entries for each row are in the second, third, and fourth columns also.

7. Click the **Sort** button again. In the Sort by text box, click the list arrow and then click **Member #**. Notice that the Type text box changes to Number.

8. Click the **Ascending** option, and then click **OK**. The table is now arranged so that the numbers in the third column are in order from lowest to highest, and the other columns in the rows were rearranged also to keep the entries in rows together.

9. Save the changes and close the document.

Converting Text to a Table and a Table to Text

2-2.1.13

Assume that you've already created a multicolumn list using tab settings. You decide that you want to organize the data in a table because it will be easier to format. In Word, it isn't necessary to enter all the data again. Word can quickly convert text separated by paragraph markers, commas, tabs, or other characters into a table with cells.

When converting text to a table, Word determines the number of columns needed based on paragraph markers, tabs, or commas in the text. When converting a table to text, Word inserts paragraph markers, tabs, or commas to show where the column breaks are.

Step-by-Step 15.13

1. Open **Step15–13** from your data files. Save the document as **Scores1**.

2. Select all the lines of text.

3. Click the **Insert** tab. Click the **Table** button and then click **Convert Text to Table**. The Convert Text to Table dialog box opens.

4. Under Table size, the number of columns should already be set to 3. Under AutoFit behavior, select **AutoFit to contents**. Under Separate text at, make sure Tabs is selected.

5. Click **OK**. Click anywhere in the window to deselect so you can see the revised content. The selected data is now formatted in table cells.

6. Save the changes to the document, and then save the document as **Scores2**.

7. With the insertion point positioned anywhere within the table, click the **table move handle** to select the entire table.

8. Click the **Table Tools Layout** tab. In the Data group, click the **Convert to Text** button ⊟≣ Convert to Text . The Convert Table to Text dialog box opens.

9. Replace the hyphen in the Other box with an asterisk **(*)** and click **OK**. The columns of text are now separated with an asterisk instead of a tab character.

10. Deselect the text. Save the changes and then close the document.

NET BUSINESS

Internet Fraud

Internet fraud refers to any type of scam or hoax that uses one or more components of the Internet, such as e-mail, blogs, or Web sites. The most common types of Internet fraud are auction and retail schemes, business opportunities and work-at-home schemes, identity theft, investment schemes, and credit/debit card fraud. Internet fraud is a federal crime. If you think you've been the victim of Internet fraud, you can file a complaint online at the FBI Web site, *www.fbi.gov*.

White collar crime refers to a full range of frauds committed by business and government professionals, and Internet fraud is one of the white-collar crimes that the FBI investigates. The Internet Crime Complaint Center (or IC3) is a partnership of the FBI and the National White Collar Crime Center.

SUMMARY

In this lesson, you learned:

- The table feature in Word enables you to organize and arrange text and numbers easily.

- To change the layout of information after you create a table, you can insert and delete rows and columns.

- The AutoFit feature automatically adjusts the width of a column based on the contents of the cells in a column.

- The Draw Table tool and the Eraser tool are especially useful when you need to create a complex table.

- You can format text alignment in table cells the same way you apply those formats in other Word documents.

- Borders and shading greatly enhance the appearance of a table and often make the table easier to read.

- Word provides several built-in styles to make it fast and easy to apply borders and shading to a table.

- Word provides Quick Tables that are already formatted and contain sample data, so you can quickly create a table.

- You can use the Sort feature to reorganize the table contents to emphasize data in different ways.

- Word can convert text to a table or vice versa.

 ## VOCABULARY REVIEW

Define the following terms:

ascending order
cell
descending order

gridlines
merging cells

Quick Tables
splitting cells

REVIEW QUESTIONS

TRUE / FALSE

Circle T if the statement is true or F if the statement is false.

T F **1.** Table rows go down a page, and columns go across a page.

T F **2.** You cannot hide the gridlines in a table.

T F **3.** When you remove the boundary between two cells, you are splitting the cells.

T F **4.** When you delete a row or column, the text in the cells is also deleted.

T F **5.** Word can create a table from text in which data is separated by paragraph markers, tabs, or commas.

MULTIPLE CHOICE

Select the best response for the following statements.

1. If you have already entered the data in a table, you can quickly add pre-designed borders and shading by _____.

   A. using the AutoFormat feature   C. applying a table style

   B. using Quick Table formats   D. using the Table Design command

2. The _____ option adds extra space to table columns so that the table fills the width of the page.

   A. AutoFit Contents   C. AutoSize Window

   B. AutoFit Window   D. AutoWidth Column

3. When using the mouse to draw the table grid on the screen, the document must be _____.

   A.   in Print Layout view   C.   at the zoom setting of 100%

   B.   in Draft view   D.   in Print Preview

4. Use the _____ tool to remove cell boundaries.

   A.   Remove Border   C.   Eraser

   B.   Table   D.   Cell Margins

5. Converting one cell into multiple cells is called _____ cells.

   A.   merging   C.   grouping

   B.   combining   D.   splitting

FILL IN THE BLANK

Complete the following sentences by writing the correct word or words in the blanks provided.

1. To insert a new table, you click the _____ tab on the Ribbon.

2. Built-in tables called _____ include sample data and table formats.

3. To create a complex table, use the _____ tool to position cell boundaries just where you want them.

4. Sorting text in _____ order arranges it in alphabetical order from A to Z.

5. _____ are nonprinting cell boundaries.

◼ PROJECTS

PROJECT 15–1

1. Open **Project15–1** from the data files. Save the document as **Population**.

2. Position the insertion point at the end of the document and create a grid for a 3×6 table (3 columns and 6 rows).

3. Complete the table by entering the data shown in **Figure 15–22**.

	2000	2010
18-24	30,388	28,513
25-34	52,697	44,248
45-54	27,157	40,347
55-64	42,802	50,938
65+	33,640	39,048

FIGURE 15–22   Table content for Project 15–1

4. You realize you left out the data for the 35–44 age group. Insert a row in the proper location and enter the following data:
   35–44   23,864   25,890

5. It would be helpful to see the percent change in population. Add a column to the right of the 2010 column and enter the column heading **% Change** in the first row. Insert the following information in the cells of the new column:
   -6.2
   -16.0
   +8.5
   +48.6
   +19.0
   +16.0

6. Insert a new row above the first row of the table and merge all cells in it. Enter the table title **Population by Age**. Center and bold the contents in the first two rows of the table.

7. Automatically adjust the column widths to the content.

8. Center the table horizontally on the page.

9. The data in the *% Change* column would look better if the decimal points were aligned. Right-align the numbers (but not the column heading) in this column.

10. Shade alternate rows of the data beginning with the *18–24* row.

11. Save the changes and close the document.

PROJECT 15–2

1. Open **Project15–2** from the data files. Save the document as **Hurricane History**.
2. Select only the tabbed data (not the blank line or the source line) and convert the text to a table. Accept the suggested number of columns, select AutoFit to contents, and separate the text at tabs.
3. Insert a new row at the top of the table and merge all cells in it. Enter the title **Costliest U.S. Hurricanes**, press **Enter**, and then enter **($ in Billions)**.
4. Center the text in the new heading you just entered in the first row.
5. Center the data in the *Category* column, and right-align the data in the *Damage* column.
6. The data for Hurricane Andrew is wrong. Change the year for Andrew to **1992**.
7. The data in the table is currently arranged in ascending order according to the *Year* column. Select all the cells with numbers in the *Damage* column and sort the data for Column 4 so that the storms are listed in order, with the most expensive storm first.
8. You decide the first ten entries in the table give enough information about the destructive power of hurricanes. Delete the last five rows in the table.
9. Apply a table style that will enhance the table and make it easier to read. If necessary, modify the table style to emphasize all the column headings.
10. Save the changes and close the document.

PROJECT 15–3

1. Open a new blank document and save the document as **Order Form**.
2. Use the Draw Table tool (and the Eraser tool, if necessary) to create the table shown in **Figure 15–23**.

<table>
<tr><td rowspan="4">Customer</td><td>Name</td><td colspan="5"></td></tr>
<tr><td>Address</td><td colspan="5"></td></tr>
<tr><td>City, State, ZIP</td><td colspan="5"></td></tr>
<tr><td>Phone</td><td colspan="5"></td></tr>
<tr><td rowspan="4">Clothing</td><td>Item #</td><td>Color</td><td>Size</td><td>Qty.</td><td>Price</td><td>Total</td></tr>
<tr><td></td><td></td><td></td><td></td><td></td><td></td></tr>
<tr><td></td><td></td><td></td><td></td><td></td><td></td></tr>
<tr><td></td><td></td><td></td><td></td><td></td><td></td></tr>
<tr><td rowspan="3">Accessories</td><td></td><td></td><td></td><td></td><td></td><td></td></tr>
<tr><td></td><td></td><td></td><td></td><td></td><td></td></tr>
<tr><td></td><td></td><td></td><td></td><td></td><td></td></tr>
<tr><td colspan="5">Thank you for shopping with us!</td><td>TOTAL</td><td></td></tr>
</table>

FIGURE 15–23 Table grid and content for Project 15–3

3. After completing the grid and entering the text, automatically format the table to fit the window.
4. Select all the cells in the first column, set the text direction as shown, and center all the text vertically and horizontally using the Align Center option. Select all remaining cells and center all text vertically in the table cells using the Align Center Left option.
5. Select the entire table and set the row height at **0.6 inches**.
6. Enhance the appearance of the table by adding or removing borders, adding shading, and formatting text, using bold and/or italic.
7. Save the changes and close the document.

PROJECT 15–4

1. Open a new blank document and save the document as **Agenda**.

2. Insert the **Matrix** Quick Table.

3. Edit the columns and rows and replace the sample data to create a table that matches the table shown in **Figure 15–24**.

4. Align the text in all cells, except the headings, using the **Align Center Left** format.

5. Select all the cells and change the font to **Arial**. Select the column headings and apply the bold format.

6. Save the changes and close the document.

Session	Time	Topic	Speaker	Room
1	8:30 a.m. – 9:45 a.m.	Regulatory Framework	John Preston	Indian
2	10:00 a.m. – 11:45 a.m.	Fact or Fiction?	Jo Ricci	Atlantic
3	1:30 p.m. – 2:45 p.m.	Techniques for Data Collection	Pat Swanson	Pacific
4	3:00 p.m. – 4:45 p.m.	Moving Forward	Ellis Arnold	Arctic

FIGURE 15–24   Table grid and content for Project 15–4

TEAMWORK PROJECT

If you completed Project 15–2, you learned how costly hurricanes can be in terms of property damage. The data shown in the Hurricane History table was compiled by the National Oceanic and Atmospheric Administration and is current only through 2006. You have probably heard about several powerful and costly Atlantic hurricanes in the United States. With a partner, see if you can update the table with more recent data.

1. Write down the years from 2006 to the last complete hurricane season (hurricane season begins in June and ends in November, so if you are working on this project before the end of November, do not include the current year in your list).

2. Split the years with your partner so that you each have half of them to research.

3. Using Web search tools or other research tools, try to locate a summary of hurricane damage for each year.

4. If any of the years you research total more dollar damage than the hurricanes shown in the Hurricanes table, insert new rows to add the data you have found.

5. When you have compiled the data, experiment with sorting the rows using different criteria and applying different formats to the column heads, borders, cells, and text.

6. With your partner, decide which format presents the data the way you prefer, and then add your names and the current date to the bottom of the document page.

CRITICAL THINKING

ACTIVITY 15–1

The owner of the stable where you ride horses has been complaining about the comings and goings of her part-time staff and unpaid helpers (of whom you are one). She'd like a way to keep track of names, phone numbers, what days and hours each helper is scheduled, and hourly pay (if any). Use what you have learned in this lesson to create a table that will help the stable owner organize the information about her staff. Enter several fictitious entries in the table (including yourself) to test your solution.

ONLINE DISCOVERY

In this lesson, you learned to use tables to organize data in Word. Did you realize that tables are also used to organize Web page content? Open several different Web pages and identify the table grid used for organizing the content on each page. Be sure to include all Web page elements, such as the Web page title at the top and the menu of links which often appear at the left. You will see that sometimes table border lines are used to enhance the appearance of the page, but in many cases, the table structure is not obvious in the Web page design. (Hint: Sometimes selecting all the content on the Web page will help identify the table structure.)

LESSON 16

Enhancing Documents

■ OBJECTIVES

Upon completion of this lesson, you should be able to:

- Format text in columns.
- Add borders and shading to enhance the appearance of your documents.
- Use building blocks to quickly format page numbers, headers and footers, and enter frequently used text.
- Insert data elements, such as the current date, symbols, hyperlinks, and footnotes and endnotes.
- Insert, resize, and position graphics.
- Use drawing tools to create your own graphics.
- Create a new document based on a template.
- Apply, create, and modify styles to create effective documents efficiently.

■ DATA FILES

To complete this lesson, you will need these data files:

Step16-1.docx   Project16-1.docx

Step16-3.docx   Project16-3.docx

Step16-4a.docx   Biking.tif

Step16-4b.docx   Flower.bmp

Step16-8.docx

■ VOCABULARY

AutoShape

banner

blog

boilerplate text

building blocks

clip art

crop

desktop publishing

drawing objects

fields

footer

graphics

header

manual column break

section break

sizing handles

style

text box

thumbnails

When developing a document, you must keep in mind its purpose and the needs of the reader. By using appropriate design elements, you can publish a professional-looking and effective document. *Desktop publishing* is the process of creating a document using a computer to lay out text and graphics. Word provides a number of features, including pictures, drawing tools, data elements, templates, and styles, which will all help you create an attractive document.

Formatting Columns, Borders, and Shading

One common example of desktop publishing is newsletters. Newsletter text is often formatted in multiple columns with headings, borders, and shading, and pictures and graphics are often included. All of these enhancements make the articles more appealing and easier to read. Usually, the title of the newsletter is formatted as a single-column *banner*, which is a headline that spreads the full width of the page.

Formatting Text in Columns

Word provides several multi-column formats, and you can modify these formats to meet your needs. When you format text in columns, the columns are usually balanced so that the column heights are approximately equal. There may be occasions, however, when you want to control where text breaks from one column to the next. To adjust where a column ends, you can insert a *manual column break*.

When you open a new blank document in Word, the document has just one section. All the document's formatting, including margins, page orientation, and column formats, apply to the entire section, which is the entire document. If you want to format one portion of the document in one column and another portion of the document in two columns, you must divide the document into multiple sections by creating a *section break*. After dividing the document into multiple sections, you can apply different formats in each section.

Step-by-Step 16.1

1. Open **Step16-1** from the data files and save the document as **Newsletter1**. If necessary, click the Show/Hide ¶ button on the Home tab to show the nonprinting characters.

2. Triple-click in the paragraph of text under the heading *PROTECTION FROM THE SUN* to select the entire paragraph.

3. Click the **Page Layout** tab, click the **Columns** button ▥ Columns ▾ in the Page Setup group shown in **Figure 16–1**, and then select **Two**. The selected text is formatted in two columns of approximate equal width.

FIGURE 16–1
The Page Setup group on the Page Layout tab

4. Compare your document to **Figure 16–2**. The document now has three sections. Section breaks appear with dotted lines above and below the selected paragraph. The first section contains the heading *PROTECTION FROM THE SUN* and is formatted for one column, the text in the second section is formatted for two columns, and the third section is formatted for one column.

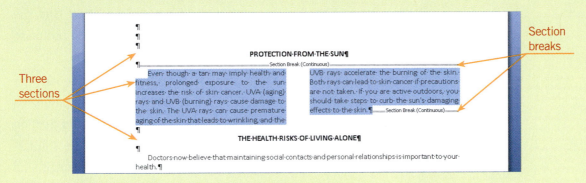

Three sections

Section breaks

FIGURE 16–2
The document divided into three sections

5. Select the three paragraphs of text under the heading *THE HEALTH RISKS OF LIVING ALONE*. Click the **Columns** button, and then click **Three**. A new section is created, and the selected text is formatted in three columns of approximate equal width.

6. In this new section, position the insertion point at the end of the first sentence which ends *important to your health*. Press the **Spacebar** and enter the following text: **They speculate that mind-body responses to human contact may be a factor.** As you enter the new text, the existing text will automatically wrap to the next column.

7. Triple-click in the paragraph of text below the heading *HIKING AND BIKING ADVENTURES* to select the entire paragraph. Click the **Columns** button, and then click **More Columns**. The Columns dialog box shown in **Figure 16–3** opens.

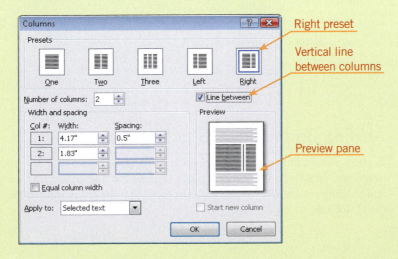

Right preset

Vertical line between columns

Preview pane

FIGURE 16–3
The Columns dialog box

8. Click the **Right** option under Presets, and then click to select the **Line between** option. The Preview pane in the dialog box is updated to show the new settings.

9. Click **OK**. The text is formatted in two columns, with the narrower column on the right. Also, a vertical line appears between the two columns.

10. Click the section break at the bottom of the document and then press **Delete**. The last section becomes part of the section above and the paragraph format changes to a single column. Click the **Undo** button to restore the right column format with a vertical line.

11. Position the insertion point in front of the third paragraph under the heading *THE HEALTH RISKS OF LIVING ALONE*. The paragraph begins *Ironically,*. In the Page Setup group, click the **Insert Page and Section Breaks** button 🗏 Breaks ▾ , and then click **Column**. The text is still formatted for three columns, but the first column break is at the beginning of the third paragraph in that section, so none of the text wraps to the third column.

12. Position the insertion point in front of the second paragraph in the same article that begins *Studies show that*. Click the **Insert Page and Section Breaks** button and then click **Column** to spread the text across the three columns again. The nonprinting characters identify the manual column break after the second paragraph, but the location of the manual column break between the first and second paragraphs does not appear. Press **Enter** two times. The second column gets longer, and the manual column break appears. Click **Undo** to remove the two blank lines.

13. Notice that the text in the first article is aligned at both the left and right sides of the columns. Select the text under the heading *THE HEALTH RISKS OF LIVING ALONE*, then click the **Home** tab and, in the Paragraph group, click the **Justify** button to change the alignment of the text. Repeat the alignment format for the text under the heading *HIKING AND BIKING ADVENTURES*.

14. Save the changes and leave the document open.

EXTRA FOR EXPERTS

Use the keyboard shortcut **Ctrl+Shift+Enter** to quickly insert a manual column break.

Adding Borders and Shading

Borders and shading also can help enhance the appearance of a document such as a newsletter or a flyer. Word offers many options for line styles, line weights, colors, and shading effects. The tools to access these options are in the Paragraph group on the Home tab, shown in **Figure 16–4**.

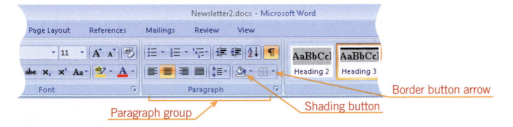

FIGURE 16–4   The Paragraph group on the Home tab

Step-by-Step 16.2

1. If necessary, open **Newsletter1** from your solution files. Save the document Newsletter1 as **Newsletter2**.

2. Position the insertion point anywhere in the heading *PROTECTION FROM THE SUN*. In the Paragraph group, click the **Border** button arrow , and then click **Top Border**. A border line is inserted across the entire top of the paragraph, which extends from the left margin to the right margin.

3. With the insertion point still positioned in the heading *PROTECTION FROM THE SUN*, click the **Border** button arrow, and then click **No Border**. The border line is removed.

4. Position the insertion point in front of the paragraph marker directly above the heading *PROTECTION FROM THE SUN*, click the **Border** button arrow, and then click **Borders and Shading** at the bottom of the menu. The Borders and Shading dialog box shown in **Figure 16–5** opens.

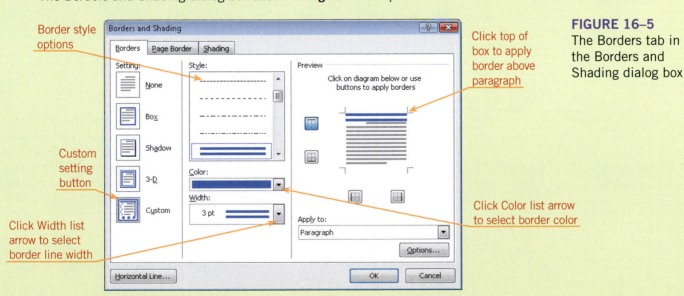

FIGURE 16–5
The Borders tab in the Borders and Shading dialog box

5. Scroll down through the Style options and click the first border style with two lines. Under Setting, click the **None** option.

6. Click the **Color** list arrow and then click **Blue, Accent 1** in the first row of Theme Colors. (The color name will appear in a ScreenTip.)

7. Click the **Width** list arrow and then click **3 pt**.

8. Under Setting at the left, click the **Custom** button. In the Preview pane at the right, click at the top of the image to add a line, as shown in **Figure 16–5**. The Preview box shows the style, color, and line width for the border at the top of the paragraph.

9. When your dialog box looks like the one shown in **Figure 16–5**, click **OK**. The border is inserted at the top of the paragraph where the insertion point is positioned.

10. Position the insertion point in front of the paragraph marker at the end of the document. Click the **Border** button arrow and click **Bottom Border**. The same double-line, blue, 3-point border is inserted at the bottom of the paragraph.

11. Position the insertion point in the first heading *PROTECTION FROM THE SUN* and then, in the Paragraph group, click the **Shading** button arrow . Click the **Blue, Accent 1**, **Lighter 80%** color in the second row. Shading is a paragraph format, so a blue shade is applied to the entire paragraph containing the heading.

12. Position the insertion point in the second heading *THE HEALTH RISKS OF LIVING ALONE*. Note that the blue color is already selected and is showing on the **Shading** button. Click the **Shading** button to apply the blue shading. Repeat the formatting for the third heading *HIKING AND BIKING ADVENTURES*.

13. Save the changes and close the document.

EXTRA FOR EXPERTS

To format shading for multiple paragraphs, select the paragraphs before clicking the Shading button.

2-2.1.9
2-2.1.10
2-2.1.16

▶ **VOCABULARY**
building blocks
fields
header

Using Building Blocks

Building blocks are built-in document parts that are already designed and formatted, enabling you to create a professional-looking document quickly. The building blocks often include *fields*, which indicate where you can insert variable text or data. Placeholder text in the fields prompts you for the information. When you click in a field, the entire field placeholder text is selected, and as you enter data, the placeholder text is replaced with the new data. The fields include codes which automatically format the data you enter.

Inserting Page Numbers and Creating Headers and Footers

Page numbers are always helpful when your document has multiple pages. When you insert page numbers in a document, the page number will appear in a header or a footer. A *header* is information and/or graphics that print in the top margin of the page; a *footer* is information and/or graphics that print in the bottom margin of the page. Your document can have a header, a footer, both, or neither. The advantage of formatting a header or footer rather than just inserting page numbers is that you can include text with the page number. The header, footer, and page number options can be accessed in the Header & Footer group on the Insert tab shown in **Figure 16–6**.

▶ **VOCABULARY**

footer

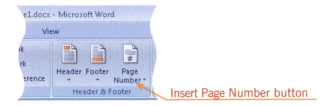

Insert Page Number button

FIGURE 16–6 The Header & Footer group on the Insert tab

Step-by-Step 16.3

1. Open **Step16-3** from the data files and save the document as **Debate1**. If necessary, change to Print Layout view and show nonprinting characters.

2. Click the **Insert** tab, click the **Insert Page Number** button, and then click **Format Page Numbers**. The Page Number Format dialog box will open. Under Page numbering, change the Start at setting to **1**. Click **OK** to accept the change and close the dialog box.

3. Click the **Insert Page Number** button again, and then point to **Bottom of Page**. Scroll down through the list to view the available styles. Under Page X of Y, click **Bold Numbers 3**. The document window is updated and shows a footer pane at the bottom of the page with *Page 1 of 4* aligned at the right margin.

4. Because the insertion point is positioned in the footer, the document text is dimmed, and the Header & Footer Tools Design tab shown in **Figure 16–7** appears on the Ribbon. Scroll through the pages of the document. Notice that a header pane appears at the top of each page, and the page number appears in a footer pane at the bottom of each page.

Header button

Different First Page check box

FIGURE 16–7
The Header & Footer Tools Design tab

5. On page 3 of 4, click at the left side of the footer pane to position the insertion point in front of the paragraph marker. Enter your first and last names. Scroll through the pages of the document. You will see that the footer has been updated on all pages.

6. Scroll to the top of one of the pages and position the insertion point in the header pane. In the Header & Footer group, on the left side of the Ribbon, click the **Header** button. Scroll down, and then click the **Conservative** option. A header with a field and a bottom line border is inserted in the header pane.

7. Click anywhere in the field placeholder text *Type the document title*, which will select the entire field. An XML tag labeled *Title* will appear at the upper-left corner of the selected field. Enter **Super Mart vs. Local Store**. The field placeholder text is replaced with the text you enter. Then click in the field placeholder text *Pick the date*, click the down arrow, and click tomorrow's date on the calendar.

8. In the Options group, click the **Different First Page** check box. Double-click anywhere in the document text. Scroll through the pages. The header and footer panes are now dimmed, and you will see that the headers and footers you just created appear on all pages except the first page.

9. Position the insertion point at the beginning of the document. Click the **Insert** tab, and in the Pages group, click the **Cover Page** button 📄 Cover Page ▾ , and then click **Conservative**. A cover page is inserted at the beginning of the document. A cover page consists of a table with fields for information such as the company name, the document title and subtitle, the date, and an abstract. The document title and date have been filled in using the information you inserted into the header.

10. Complete the information on the cover page:

    a. The Company XML tag at the top of the page should already appear. Double-click the **Company** XML tag to select the tag and the placeholder text, and then press **Delete** to remove the field placeholder text so it won't print.

    b. Click the field labeled *Type the document subtitle* and enter **The Big Debate**.

    c. Click the field labeled *Your Name* and enter your first and last name.

    d. Click anywhere in the paragraph of text at the bottom of the cover page. The Abstract tag will appear. Double-click the **Abstract** XML tag and press **Delete**.

11. Scroll down to view the first full page of text. Notice that both the header and footer now show on this page, and the page number is 2. That's because the cover page is now page 1.

12. Ideally, your first page of text should not have the header or a page number. The page numbering should begin on the second full page of text. Position the insertion point at the beginning of the heading *The Big Debate* on the first page of text. Click the **Page Layout** tab, click the

---

🖬 EXTRA FOR EXPERTS

The XML tag indicates that the information is formatted in XML (Extensible Markup Language), a universal format that allows for data transfer for use in other applications that support the XML format.

🖬 EXTRA FOR EXPERTS

You can quickly change the cover page design. With the insertion point positioned in the current cover page, click the **Cover Page** button in the Pages group on the Insert tab, and choose a new page design. The text you already entered in the fields is preserved and converted to the new cover page design.

Insert Page and Section Breaks button, and then click **Next Page**. The section break appears below the cover page table. The cover page is now in a different section.

13. The page numbering and header begin on the third page, and the cover page is included in the total page count. Double-click in the footer pane to activate the pane. Double-click the number **5** for the total page count to select it, and then enter **4**.

14. Save the changes and close the document.

Creating Your Own Building Blocks

You can create your own text entries or other document parts such as headers and footers and add them to Word's gallery of building blocks. *Boilerplate text* is a common document part that you frequently use in documents. For example, if you usually add a paragraph about your organization at the end of a document, you could save time developing future documents by creating your own building block for this boilerplate text.

Step-by-Step 16.4

1. Open **Step16-4a** from the data files and save the document as **History1**.

2. Triple-click the paragraph at the end of the document to select the entire paragraph. Click the **Insert** tab and in the Text group shown in **Figure 16-8**, click the **Quick Parts** button ▣ Quick Parts ▾, and then click **Save Selection to Quick Part Gallery**. The Create New Building Block dialog box will open.

FIGURE 16–8
The Text group on the Insert tab

3. In the Name box, enter **About Us**.

4. Click the **Gallery** box list arrow and then click **AutoText**. Then click **OK** to accept the changes and close the dialog box. You just created a building block.

5. Open **Step16-4b** from the data files and save the document as **History2**. Position the insertion point at the end of the document.

6. Click the **Insert** tab, click the **Quick Parts** button, and then click **Building Blocks Organizer** to open a dialog box similar to the one shown in **Figure 16–9**. The Building Blocks Organizer shows all the building blocks available.

FIGURE 16–9

The Building Blocks Organizer dialog box

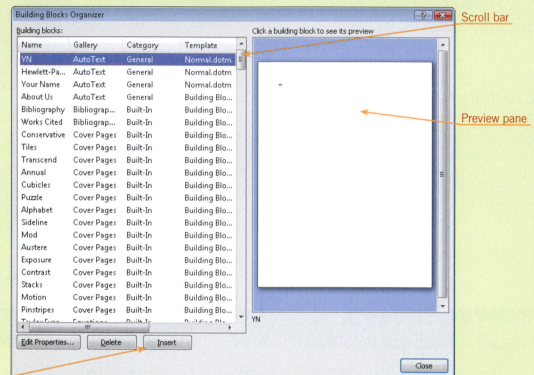

7. Scroll down through the list and you will see the document parts you used to create a cover page, insert page numbers, and add a header.

8. Scroll back to the top of the list and click **About Us** which is stored in the AutoText Gallery. The boilerplate text will appear in the preview pane on the right side of the dialog box.

9. Click **Insert**. The text is inserted in the document at the location of the insertion point.

10. Click the **Quick Parts** button, click **Building Blocks Organizer**, and then click **About Us** in the AutoText Gallery.

11. With the building block selected in the list, click **Delete** at the bottom of the dialog box to remove the boilerplate text from the gallery. When prompted to delete the selected building block, click **Yes**.

12. Close the dialog box, save the changes, and leave both documents open.

⚠ WARNING

When you exit a session of Word 2007 after creating or deleting a building block, or making changes to a built-in building block, you will be prompted to save the changes to Building Blocks.dotx. When working at a classroom computer, do not save any changes without permission.

Inserting Data Elements

Developing a document often requires inserting special data elements such as dates and times, footnotes, copyright and trademark notations, hyperlinks, and footnotes. The Insert tab provides quick access to tools that simplify the task.

2-2.1.8
2-2.2.2

Inserting the Date and Time

You can insert a field to show the current date and/or time. When you insert this field, you have the option of updating the date and/or the time whenever the document is reopened or sent to the printer queue.

AutoComplete can also make entering the current date easy (and accurate!). When you start to enter calendar terms, such as the month, the day of the week, or the current date, Word will show the complete term in a ScreenTip.

Step-by-Step 16.5

1. If necessary, open the **History1** document from your solution files. Save the document History1 as **History3**. If necessary, click the Insert tab.

2. Scroll to the bottom of the document and position the insertion point to the right of *Date posted*. In the Text group, click the **Insert Date and Time** button ⬚ Date & Time . The Date and Time dialog box opens, showing the current date and time in a variety of formats.

3. Under Available formats, click the date format MM/DD/YYYY followed by the time, showing the hours, minutes, seconds, and AM or PM (for example, 2/17/2012 8:37:39 AM).

4. At the lower-right corner of the dialog box, if necessary, enable the **Update automatically** option. When this option is checked, the date and/or time is inserted in a field, and the information will automatically be updated each time the document is opened.

5. Click **OK**. The current date and time is entered as text in your document.

6. Note the time that currently appears in the document. Save the changes and close the document. Then reopen the document. The time that appears in the document should be updated.

7. Click anywhere within the date and time to show the XML field tag. Then double-click the three dots on the left edge of the Update tag to select the tag name and the entire field. Press **Delete**.

8. Enter **Wedn**. After you enter the letter n, the complete spelling of Wednesday will appear in a ScreenTip. Press **Enter** to accept the AutoComplete entry and the full spelling of the word is inserted in the document.

9. Delete the word *Wednesday*.

HEADS UP

The full date will not appear in a ScreenTip unless the day of the week is the current day according to your computer's date and time settings.

10. Begin to enter the current day of the week. (For example, *Frid.*) When the ScreenTip appears suggesting the complete word, ignore the ScreenTip and keep entering all the letters to manually complete the word.

11. Enter a comma after the current day, and another ScreenTip will show the full date, such as *Friday, February 17, 2012*.

12. Press **Enter** again to accept the AutoComplete entry for the full date.

13. Save the changes and leave the document open.

Inserting Symbols and Creating Hyperlinks

Sometimes you need to enter characters in your document, but the characters are not on the keyboard. For example, if you are entering text in a foreign language, you will likely need to include some special characters. Or, if you're creating a math equation, you will need to use symbols. It's very likely you'll be able to find the character or symbol you need using the Insert Symbol button in the Symbols group on the Insert tab.

Another helpful tool on the Insert tab is the Insert Hyperlink button. Usually when you think of a hyperlink, you think about links on Web pages, but you can also create links in Word documents to connect users to other Word documents, other application documents, e-mails, and Web pages.

Step-by-Step 16.6

1. If necessary, open **History3** from your solution files. Save the document History3 as **History4**. If necessary, click the Insert tab.

2. Position the insertion point anywhere in one of the blank paragraphs just above the date posted line. Enter **Upcoming Events**.

3. Select the two new words and then in the Links group, click the **Insert Hyperlink** button [Hyperlink]. A dialog box similar to the one shown in **Figure 16–10** opens.

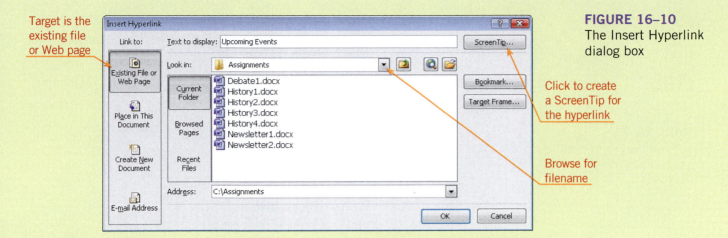

FIGURE 16–10
The Insert Hyperlink
dialog box

Click to create
a ScreenTip for
the hyperlink

Browse for
filename

4. Under Link to, make sure that the **Existing File or Web Page** button is enabled. The link will connect the user to another existing file. If necessary, in the Look in box navigate to the folder where you save your solution files. Click the solution file **History3**.

5. Click the **ScreenTip** button in the upper-right corner of the dialog box. In the Set Hyperlink ScreenTip box, enter **Click here for dates and times**.

6. Click **OK** to close the Set Hyperlink ScreenTip box, and then click **OK** to close the Insert Hyperlink dialog box. The selected text in the document is now formatted as a hyperlink.

7. Position the mouse pointer over the hyperlink text. A ScreenTip will appear, showing the text you entered. Press and hold **Ctrl** and click the hyperlink to connect to the target. The History3 document will open, and now you realize you linked to the wrong document. Close the History3 document.

8. Right-click the hyperlink and click **Edit Hyperlink** in the shortcut menu. This time click the solution file **History2**, and then click **OK**.

9. Press and hold **Ctrl** and click the hyperlink to make sure the target is the document with the upcoming events. Then close the History2 document.

10. Position the insertion point at the end of the last line of text in the document, ending *environment*. Press **Spacebar**, enter **www.westmorelandhistory.org**, and then press **Spacebar** again. When you press Spacebar (or Enter), Word recognizes that a URL has been entered and automatically formats a hyperlink to connect to the Web address.

11. Position the insertion point next to the paragraph marker at the end of the document. In the Symbols group, click the **Insert Symbol** button **Ω Symbol ▾**, and then click **More Symbols** to open the Symbol dialog box shown in **Figure 16–11**. The symbols that appear on your screen may differ from those in the figure.

FIGURE 16–11

The Symbols tab in the Symbol dialog box

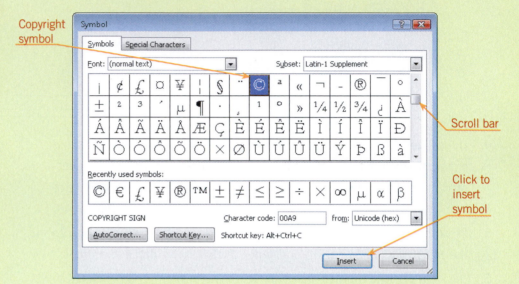

12. Scroll up and down until you see the copyright symbol shown in **Figure 16–11**. Click the symbol to select it, click **Insert**, and then close the dialog box. If you do not see the copyright symbol © on the Symbols tab, click the Special Characters tab and select the Copyright option.

13. The selected symbol is inserted in the text at the location of the insertion point. With the insertion point positioned to the right of the copyright symbol, enter the current year, press **Spacebar**, and enter **Westmoreland Historical Society**.

14. Save the changes and close the document.

Inserting Footnotes and Endnotes

Notes are most commonly seen as references in reports. However, you can also add footnotes to documents to provide additional information or comments for the reader. Footnotes are inserted at the bottom of the page on which the note is referenced in the document, and endnotes are placed together at the end of the document. Both kinds of notes are linked to an in-text reference symbol—usually a letter or numeral in superscript.

Step-by-Step 16.7

1. Open the **Debate1** document from your solution files. Save the document Debate1 as **Debate2**.

2. Press **Ctrl+F** to open the Find and Replace dialog box. Enter **The local store was founded in 1995** and press **Enter**. The first occurrence of the search text is selected. Close the Find and Replace dialog box.

3. With the search text selected, click the **References** tab and then, in the Footnotes group, click the **Insert Footnote** button. Compare your screen to **Figure 16–12**. A superscript numeral 1 is inserted at the end of the selected text, a divider line is created at the bottom of the current page, and the insertion point is positioned next to numeral 1 below the divider line.

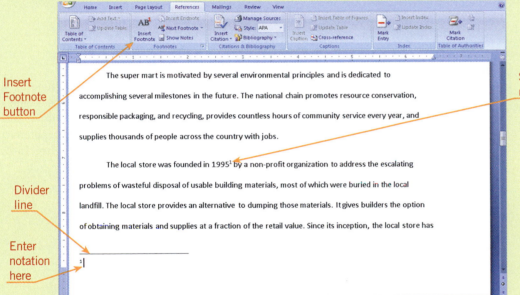

FIGURE 16–12
A footnote inserted in a document

Insert Footnote button

Superscript numeral

Divider line

Enter notation here

4. Enter the following note: **The local store I am referencing is a non-profit retail business in my home town**.

5. Position the insertion point at the end of the paragraph directly above the paragraph with the footnote reference. The paragraph ends *country with jobs*.

6. Click the **Insert Footnote** button. A new footnote reference is inserted at the location of the insertion point. Notice that the new reference is numeral 1. Because the new footnote was inserted ahead of the existing footnote, the existing footnote was renumbered and is now referenced with numeral 2.

7. With the insertion point positioned next to the numeral 1 at the bottom of the page, enter **The national chain I am referencing is one of the top three home improvement retailers**.

8. Double-click the reference symbol numeral to the left of the text you just entered. The insertion point moves to the number 1 reference above.

9. To convert the footnotes to endnotes, click the **Dialog Box Launcher** in the Footnotes group to open the Footnote and Endnote dialog box. Click **Convert** in the Location section. When prompted to convert all footnotes to endnotes, click **OK**, and then click **Close**. The notes are moved to the end of the document.

10. Scroll to the end of the document and double-click the reference number for the second endnote. The insertion point moves to the footnote reference following *founded in 1995*.

11. Position the mouse pointer over the superscript numeral ii. A ScreenTip will show the text that appears in the endnote.

12. Save the changes and close the document.

2-1.3.7

Inserting and Formatting Graphics

To illustrate an idea presented in a document, or to make a document more functional, you can include *graphics*, which are non-text items such as digital photos, scanned images, and pictures. You can also insert images created in other applications, such as a chart from a spreadsheet application or a drawing created in a computerized drafting program. The Illustrations group on the Insert tab shown in **Figure 16–13** provides buttons to easily add images to a document.

> **VOCABULARY**
>
> **graphics**
>
> **clip art**
>
> **thumbnails**

FIGURE 16–13   The Illustrations group on the Insert tab

Inserting Clip Art and Images

Clip art is a drawing that is ready to insert in a document. Word has numerous clip art images and photos that are stored in the Office Collections folder. You can also access clip art that you have saved (in the My Collections folder). If you have an Internet connection open, you can search for clip art at the Microsoft Web site. Search results appear in the task pane as *thumbnails*, which are miniature representations of the pictures. You can also insert graphics that are stored in other folders. This is called inserting a picture from a file.

> **EXTRA FOR EXPERTS**
>
> If you click the down arrow on the right side of a clip art thumbnail, a shortcut menu will show options for copying and pasting, deleting the clip from the Clip Organizer, copying the clip to a Collection folder, and so on.

Step-by-Step 16.8

1. Open **Step16-8** from the data files and save the document as **Tours1**.

2. Position the insertion point in front of the paragraph that begins *So, you can't decide.*

3. Click the **Insert** tab and then click the **Clip Art** button. The Clip Art task pane opens on the right side of the document window.

4. Position the insertion point in the Search for box. If there is text in the box, select all of the text. Enter **bicycle**.

5. Specify where Word should search for clip art. The Search in box should show *All collections*. If you see *All collections*, move on to Step 6. If you see another setting in the Search in box, click the list arrow and then click the **Everywhere** option to enable it. The option is enabled when the box to the left of the option has a check mark. Then, click anywhere in the Search in box to hide the list of options.

6. In the Results should be box, click the list arrow to show the list of options shown in **Figure 16–14**. If necessary, click the + symbol to the left of All media types so that your list matches the figure.

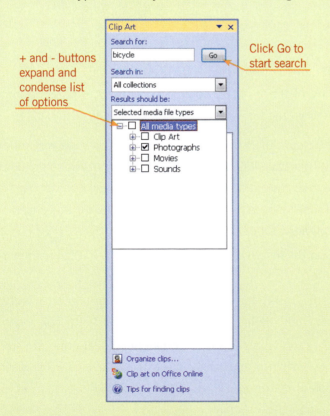

+ and - buttons expand and condense list of options

Click Go to start search

FIGURE 16–14
The Clip Art task pane with search criteria

7. Disable all options except Photographs. There should be a check mark in the box to the left of Photographs.

8. Click **Go** to start the search. The results should show several photo images as thumbnails, as shown in **Figure 16–15**.

FIGURE 16–15
The Clip Art task pane with search results

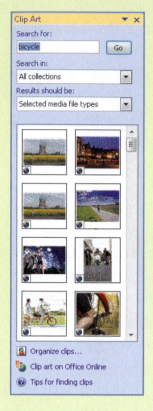

9. Click a photo of your choice to insert the image in the document at the location of the insertion point. (You can also drag and drop a clip art image from the task pane to anywhere in your document.)

10. You can leave the Insert Clip Art task pane open as you work so you can quickly access additional Clip Art images. But, we're done with Clip Art for now, so close the task pane. The image you choose may be very large when first inserted in the document, but do not be concerned because you will adjust the size later.

11. Position the insertion point at the beginning of the document in front of the title.

12. Click the **Insert** tab, and in the Illustrations group, click the **Insert Picture from File** button. The Insert Picture dialog box opens.

13. Navigate to the folder where the Lesson 16 data files are stored. Select the file **Biking.tif** and then click **Insert**. The picture is inserted at the location of the insertion point.

14. Save the changes and leave the document open.

Resizing, Cropping, and Aligning a Graphic

Once you have inserted a graphic or picture in a document, there are many ways to manipulate the picture. To work with a graphic, you must select it. You will know it is selected when you see *sizing handles*, eight small circles and squares on the border of the graphic. When a graphic is selected, you can resize, cut, copy, paste, delete, and move it just as you would text.

You can scale a graphic just vertically or just horizontally by using one of the square sizing handles on the side of the graphic, but this will distort the image. To change the size of a graphic without distorting the image, you must scale the graphic proportionally. Use one of the circle corner sizing handles to reduce or enlarge a graphic proportionally, changing both dimensions of the graphic (height and width) approximately equally.

When you *crop* a graphic, you cut off portions of the graphic that you do not want to show. You might want to crop extra white space around an image or actually remove part of the image altogether.

By default, Word inserts graphics in the line of text. This means that the graphic is positioned directly in the text at the insertion point. Instead of being in the line of text, however, you can format the text in the document to wrap around the graphic. A text-wrapping format must be applied to the graphic before you can reposition the graphic in your document. You can then drag and drop the graphic anywhere within the printable area of the page.

▶ **VOCABULARY**
sizing handles

crop

HEADS UP

You may find it easier to work with graphics in a document by reducing the view of the document. For example, you can change the zoom of the document view to 75 percent.

Step-by-Step 16.9

1. If necessary, open the **Tours1** document from your solution files. Save the document Tours1 as **Tours2**.

2. If necessary, click the View tab and enable the Ruler option.

3. Click the biking graphic at the beginning of the document. When the picture is selected, the Picture Tools Format tab shown in **Figure 16–16** will appear and eight sizing handles appear on the outside border of the image. The nonprinting border around the picture shows as well as the sizing handles. Notice that there is excess white space on the right side and bottom of the picture.

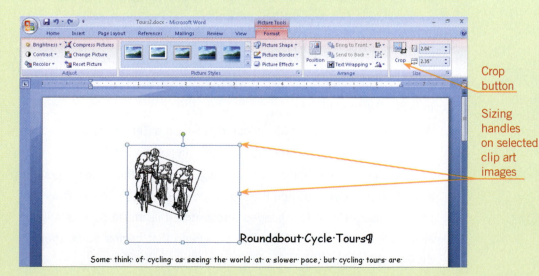

Crop button

Sizing handles on selected clip art images

FIGURE 16–16
The Picture Tools Format tab

4. Point to the lower-right corner of the image. When the pointer changes to a two-headed arrow, drag the corner sizing handle toward the center of the picture. As you drag the sizing handle, you can see the effects of the change on your screen. When the picture is approximately 1½ inches high and 1½ inches wide, release the mouse. Use the rulers at the top and left edges of the document window to judge the picture size.

5. Click the **Picture Tools Format** tab, and in the Size group, click the **Crop** button. The sizing handles change in appearance, as shown in **Figure 16–17**.

FIGURE 16–17
Cropping a graphic

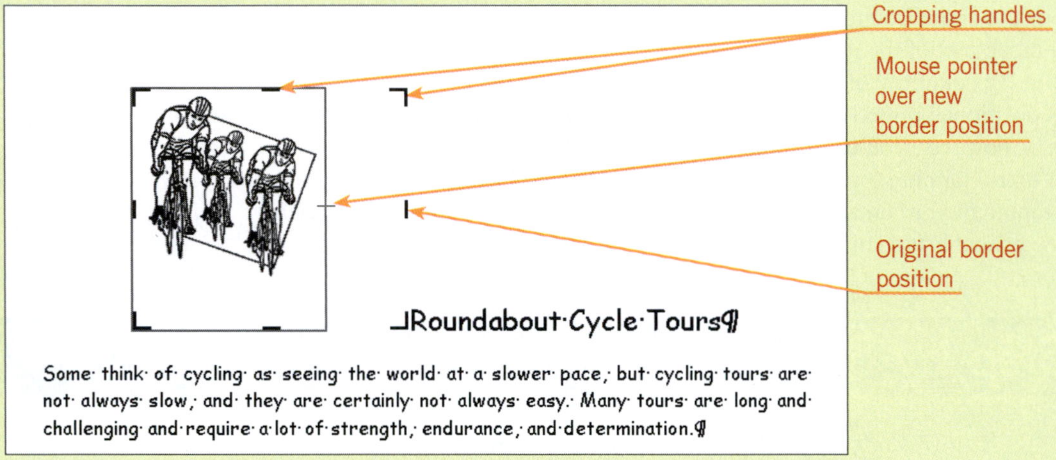

Cropping handles

Mouse pointer over new border position

Original border position

⌐Roundabout·Cycle·Tours¶

Some·think·of·cycling·as·seeing·the·world·at·a·slower·pace,·but·cycling·tours·are·not·always·slow,·and·they·are·certainly·not·always·easy.·Many·tours·are·long·and·challenging·and·require·a·lot·of·strength,·endurance,·and·determination.¶

6. Position the pointer on the sizing handle on the middle right of the picture. Then click and drag the sizing handle to the left to trim the white space. **Figure 16–17** shows how the cropping line appears as you move the image border. When you release the mouse button, the portion of the picture you cropped is gone.

7. Point to the cropping handle on the middle bottom of the image border, and crop the white space at the bottom of the picture. Click the **Crop** button to turn off the cropping feature. The image is still selected because the sizing handles are visible.

8. Drag the lower-right corner sizing handle down and to the right to increase the size of the graphic to approximately 2 inches high by 2 inches wide. Use the rulers at the top and left edges of the document to judge the picture size.

9. With the biking image still selected, click the **Text Wrapping** button ⟦Text Wrapping ▾⟧ in the Arrange group, and then click **Tight**.

10. After applying a text wrapping format to a graphic, you can move the graphic around on the page. Position the mouse pointer over the image. When the pointer changes to a four-headed arrow, drag the image so it is aligned at the upper-left corner of the first paragraph that begins *Some think of cycling*. Notice that the text wraps around the border of the image.

EXTRA FOR EXPERTS

If you want to change the size of an image to exact measurements, change the settings in the Shape Height and Shape Width boxes in the Size group on the Picture Tools Format tab.

11. Click the photo after the second paragraph. Point to one of the corner sizing handles. When the double-headed arrow appears, drag the corner to the center of the picture to reduce the size of the picture. When the picture is approximately 3 inches wide and/or 2 inches high, release the mouse.

12. With the photo selected, click the **Text Wrapping** button and then click **Square**. Then drag the picture to align with the lower-right corner of the document.

13. If time permits, select one of the pictures and roll the mouse pointer over the styles in the Picture Styles group. A live preview of the style will appear in the document. Click the **More** button to open the Picture Styles gallery.

14. Save the changes and close document.

Inserting Lines, AutoShapes, and Text Boxes

Sometimes you may need to create your own graphics. For example, you may want to illustrate a map with directions. You can use *drawing objects*, which are shapes, curves, and lines, to create your own graphic. An *AutoShape* is a predesigned drawing object, such as a star, an arrow, or a rectangle. You can resize and reposition drawing objects the same way you change the size and position of pictures and clip art, and the drawing objects can be changed and enhanced with color, patterns, and borders. A *text box* is a drawing object that enables you to add text to artwork. Because the text box is a graphic, you can resize and position it like other graphics. Within the text box, you can change the font and the alignment of the text, just as you change text in a document.

You can copy and paste lines, shapes, objects, and text boxes just like you copy and paste text and graphics. So when you are creating a drawing that requires multiple horizontal lines, create and format the first line. Then copy and paste multiple copies of the line in the document window and start building. Not only will you save time, but the objects will be more consistent. If you don't want all the objects to be exactly the same size, you can resize them after you paste them in the document.

A drawing canvas provides a frame-like boundary between your drawing and the rest of the document. Using the drawing canvas is especially helpful if your drawing contains several shapes, because it keeps your shapes together as one object. To use the drawing canvas, click the Insert tab, and in the Illustrations group, click Shapes and then click New Drawing Canvas.

▶ **VOCABULARY**
drawing objects
AutoShape
text box

HEADS UP

If you have difficulty creating or positioning the shapes as described in the activity, click the **Undo** button, then click the tool and try again.

Step-by-Step 16.10

1. Open a new blank document and if necessary, show nonprinting characters and the ruler.

2. Click the **Insert** tab, and in the Illustrations group, click the **Shapes** button and then click the **Line** tool, shown in **Figure 16–18**. The pointer changes to a crosshair when positioned in the document window.

FIGURE 16–18
The Shape options

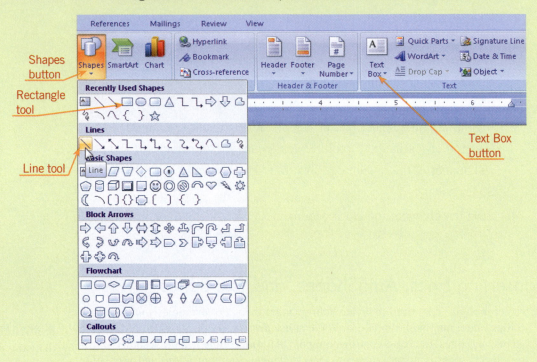

3. Point to the paragraph marker and drag the crosshair across the entire width of the document, from the left margin to the right margin. Do not release the mouse button until the line is straight, even, and the length you want. When you release the mouse button, the Drawing Tools Format tab shown in **Figure 16–19** appears on the Ribbon.

FIGURE 16–19
The Drawing Tools Format tab

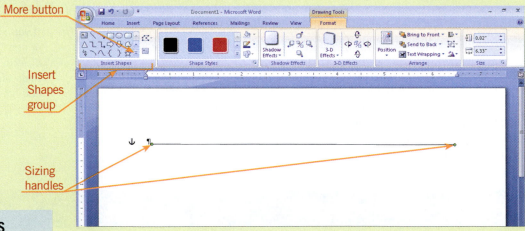

EXTRA FOR EXPERTS

To create a perfect square, hold down **Shift** as you drag the crosshair, or just click once in the document without dragging after selecting the Rectangle tool.

4. With the line still selected (the sizing handles on each end of the line indicate that the line is selected), click the **Shape Outline** button arrow in the Shape Styles group. Point to **Weight**. A live preview shows the new format. Click **3 pt**. The weight of the selected line is now heavier.

5. Notice that the shapes are available in the Insert Shapes group. Click the **More** button, and then click the **Line** tool again. Draw a second line, this time drawing the line diagonally across the document window from the paragraph marker to the lower-right corner of the screen.

6. With the line still selected, click the **Shape Outline** button arrow, and click a red color. The color of the line changes.

7. In the Insert Shapes group, click the **More** button and then click the **Rectangle** tool. Position the crosshair just above the horizontal line at the top of the document at about the 2-inch mark on the ruler. Drag the crosshair down and to the right to create a box approximately 2 inches high and 2 inches wide. This box should overlap both the horizontal and diagonal lines.

8. With the rectangle tool still selected, click the **Shape Fill** button arrow 🎨 ▾ in the Shape Styles group, and click a green color. The rectangle is filled with the green color.

9. In the Insert Shapes group, click the **More** button and in the Block Arrows section, click the **Right Arrow** tool. Begin drawing the arrow in the middle of the green rectangle and make the arrow wide enough that it extends beyond the right edge of the rectangle.

10. Click the **Insert** tab and in the Text group, click the **Text Box** button. Several built-in text box options appear. Click **Draw Text Box** below the options. Draw a box about 1 inch high by 1 inch wide in the middle of the rectangle. When you release the mouse button, the insertion point is positioned inside the box. Enter your name in the box.

11. As you create the objects, they are layered with the most recent objects placed on top. The text box is on top of the arrow, which is on top of the rectangle, which is on top of the diagonal and horizontal lines. The new text box should still be selected. In the Arrange group, click the **Send to Back** button arrow 🔲 Send to Back ▾ and then click **Send Backward**. The text box has moved backward one layer and is now positioned behind the arrow.

12. With the textbox still selected, click the **Send to Back** button. The text box is no longer visible because it is at the bottom of the stack. Click the **Undo** button.

13. Click the diagonal line to select it and then click the **Drawing Tools Format** tab. In the Arrange group, click the **Bring to Front** button arrow 🔲 Bring to Front ▾ . Click **Bring Forward**. The diagonal line moves forward one layer, in front of the rectangle but behind the text box. Click the **Bring to Front** button, and the diagonal line is on the top of the stack.

14. Save the document as **Shapes** and then close the document.

HEADS UP

When you choose one of the Callout tools from the AutoShapes menu on the Drawing Tools Format tab, the AutoShape is automatically formatted as a text box so you can add text inside the object.

15. If time permits, open a new blank document and create more objects. Select the objects and explore the shape styles, shadow effects, and 3-D effects. Save the document as **Shapes2** and then close the document.

Using SmartArt Graphics

Now that you know how to create text boxes and use the drawing tools, consider how you would create an organizational chart. You would need to create multiple text boxes, arrange and align the boxes to show a hierarchy, connect the boxes with horizontal and vertical lines, and then add text to the boxes. To create an effective chart would be a tedious task and you would likely spend a significant amount of time designing and creating the objects. But you can save yourself a lot of time and effort by using SmartArt graphics. SmartArt graphics are built-in, predesigned, and formatted graphics which you can use to illustrate concepts and ideas. The graphics are organized in a gallery under eight different categories, and each category includes several layouts. You can see live previews of the layouts which will help you choose the graphic that best suits your needs. Once you choose a design, you can focus on the content and quickly produce a professional illustration.

Like the building blocks for headers, the objects in the SmartArt graphics include fields with XML tags, and you can replace the field placeholder text. The field placeholder text does not print in SmartArt graphics, so if you don't enter data in a field, you do not need to delete the placeholder text. The designs are based on contemporary layouts and the styles and formats used in the designs are easy to modify.

Step-by-Step 16.11

1. Open a new blank document.

2. Click the Insert tab and, in the Illustrations group, click the **Insert SmartArt Graphic** button. The Choose a SmartArt Graphic dialog box opens.

3. From the Category list, click **Cycle**. Several new diagrams appear in the center of the dialog box.

4. Click the first diagram **Basic Cycle**. A color preview of the selected layout appears in the preview pane, and a description of the layout is included in the preview pane, as shown in **Figure 16–20**. Click **OK**. The graphic is inserted in the document.

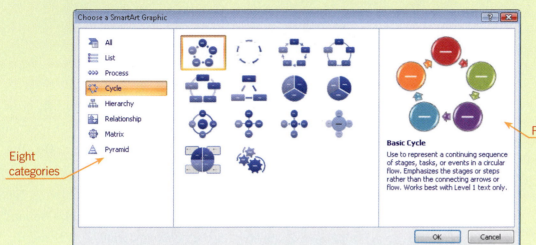

FIGURE 16–20
The Choose a SmartArt Graphic dialog box

Eight categories

Preview pane

5. When the SmartArt graphic is selected, the SmartArt Tools Design tab shown in **Figure 16–21** is active. All the objects in the diagram are contained in a canvas. Each shape in the graphic includes placeholder text. Click the tab on the left side of the canvas to show/hide the text pane.

HEADS UP

You can resize the canvas for a SmartArt graphic just as you resize other objects.

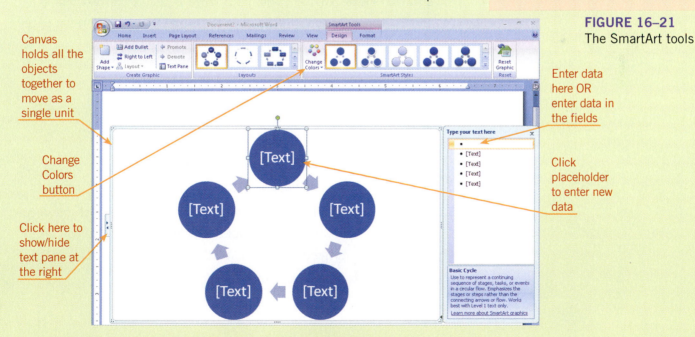

FIGURE 16–21
The SmartArt tools

Canvas holds all the objects together to move as a single unit

Change Colors button

Click here to show/hide text pane at the right

Enter data here OR enter data in the fields

Click placeholder to enter new data

6. Click the field placeholder text in the oval at the top of the diagram and enter **Ask a question**. As you enter the text, the font size adjusts so the text will fit within the oval object. Also, as you enter text in a field, the text pane updates. You can choose to enter and edit data in the graphic or the pane.

7. Enter the remaining four steps:

   `Form a hypothesis`

   `Design and conduct an experiment`

   `Analyze the results`

   `Draw a conclusion`

8. Save the document as **Process**.

9. You realize that the content you entered describes a process, not a cycle. Point anywhere within the SmartArt canvas and right-click. In the shortcut menu, click **Change Layout**. From the Category list, click **Process**. Scroll to the top of the diagram list and click the first option in the second row, labeled **Continuous Block Process**. Then click **OK**. The diagram design changes, but the content remains intact.

10. With the diagram still selected, click the **Change Colors** button in the SmartArt Styles group. Roll the mouse pointer over the color options to see a live preview of the style in the document window. A ScreenTip will show the name of each style. Click the first style in the second row, **Colorful – Accent Colors**. The colors of the rectangle objects and the arrow change in the document window.

11. With the diagram still selected, click the **SmartArt Tools Format** tab, as shown in **Figure 16–22**. Click the **Arrange** button, click **Text Wrapping**, and then click **Square**. Now you can reposition the graphic on the page.

FIGURE 16–22
The SmartArt Tools Format tab

Arrange button

12. Close the text pane and drag the image down on the page so you can insert a heading above the graphic.

13. Position the insertion point outside the graphic at the top of the document and enter **SCIENTIFIC PROCESS**. Select the heading, and on the Mini toolbar, change the font size to 18 and center the paragraph.

14. Save the changes and close the document.

Creating WordArt Objects

WordArt is a feature that enables you to transform text into a graphic. You can create your own styles or you can choose from several predefined styles in the WordArt Gallery.

Step-by-Step 16.12

1. Open the **Newsletter2** document from your solution files. Save the document Newsletter2 as **Newsletter3**.

2. Position the insertion point at the beginning of the document.

3. Click the **Insert** tab and in the Text group, click the **WordArt** button ![WordArt]. The WordArt gallery appears.

4. Click the **WordArt style 10** style. The Edit WordArt Text dialog box opens.

5. Enter **Health News** in place of the text in the text box and then click **OK**. Word formats the text as a WordArt object and positions the object in the document. The Ribbon changes to show the WordArt Tools Format tab, shown in **Figure 16–23**.

Shadow Effects button

FIGURE 16–23
The WordArt Tools Format tab

6. The WordArt object should already be selected. Point to the sizing handle in the lower-right corner, and when the mouse pointer changes to a double-headed arrow, drag the corner handle to the right margin. The WordArt object will expand to the width of the document.

7. With the object still selected, click the **Shape Fill** button arrow in the WordArt Styles group. Click the **Blue, Accent 1** color.

8. With the WordArt object still selected, click the **Shadow Effects** button in the Shadow Effects group.

9. Move the mouse pointer over some of the shadow options to see the live previews. Then, click the first Perspective Shadow option, **Shadow Style 6**.

10. With the WordArt object selected, click the **Change WordArt Shape** button in the WordArt Styles group. Choose a different shape. Notice that the shape changes but the text, fill color, line colors, and shadow effect remain unchanged.

11. Resize the WordArt object as needed so it does not extend into the right margin.

12. Save the changes and close the document.

2-1.2.1
2-2.1.11
2-2.1.16

Using Templates and Styles

It can be a time-consuming task to create documents such as fax cover sheets, resumes, and invoices. Fortunately, Word has predesigned document templates for almost any purpose you can imagine. In addition, there are preset style choices available that make creating the perfect document easy for anyone.

Depending on your Word installation, many types of document templates may be available to you. Some of the templates are already installed on your computer, and hundreds more are available at the Microsoft Web site. These templates provide default settings like the Normal.dotm template, but they include more than default settings. These templates are formatted for a specific purpose and many of them already contain a lot of boilerplate text. For example, if you want to create a fax cover sheet, you can select a fax template and create a document based on the template. When the new document opens, the fax form is already created and all you need to enter is the variable information, such as the name of the individual receiving the fax, the number of pages being sent, and the date. You can also save a document as a template so you can make the formats and styles available in other documents.

A *blog* (an abbreviated version of the term "Web log") is a journal maintained by an individual or a group and posted on a Web site for public viewing and comment. Blogs are often referred to as online diaries, and they may include graphics, photos, music, video, and links to Web sites. A typical blog Web site provides links and enables instant feedback, and many blog hosts offer free blog posting services. The Word New Blog Post template provides the necessary file formats so the blog entry content can be published on the Web. Creating a blog post is beyond the scope of this lesson because to post a blog from Word you must have an established and registered blog account with a Microsoft-enabled blog service provider.

Creating a New Document Based on a Template

Fields in the document help to ensure that you enter the variable data in the correct places, so if you leave a field blank, the field placeholder text will not appear in the printed copy of the document. The boilerplate text is protected so that you cannot accidentally change or delete it.

> ▶ **VOCABULARY**
> **blog**

Step-by-Step 16.13

1. Click the **Office Button**, and then click **New**.

2. In the Templates list at the left, click **Installed Templates**.

3. The installed templates will appear in the list at the right. Click the thumbnail for **Oriel Fax**. The template appears in the preview pane.

4. Under the preview of the fax cover sheet, make sure the **Document** option is selected. Click **Create** to create a new document based on the template.

5. The fax document opens. The boilerplate text is already entered in a table format. Save the document as **Fax1**.

6. On the right side of the document, click the fields for the company name, address, and phone numbers, and enter the following data:

    `Newstrom Getaways`

    `559 Fifth Street, Marysville, OH 43040`

    `937-555-3391`

7. Click the date field, then click the down arrow, and click **Today** below the calendar.

8. Enter the remaining data in the fields:

Recipient:	`John Croix`
Recipient Fax:	`937-555-9208`
Recipient Phone:	`937-555-6442`
From:	*Your Name*
Sender Fax:	`937-555-3392`
Sender Phone:	`937-555-3391`
Pages:	`5`
RE:	`Revised Itinerary`
CC:	`J. Moore`
COMMENTS:	`This is the revised itinerary. Let me know if you have any questions.`
	`Best,`
	Your Name

9. At the bottom of the document, position the insertion point in the box to the left of *PLEASE REVIEW*, press and hold **Shift**, and then press **X**.

10. Save the changes.

11. Each time you prepare a fax cover sheet, you enter your name, phone number, fax number, and company name. You can save time preparing future fax cover sheets by entering this information and then saving the document as a template. Delete all the variable data in the following fields:

    Date

    Recipient

    Recipient Fax

    Recipient Phone

    Pages

    RE

    CC

    Comments

VOCABULARY

style

12. Click the **Office Button** and then click **Save As** to open the Save As dialog box.

13. In the File name box, change the filename to **Fax2**. Click the Save as type box list arrow and then click **Word Macro-Enabled Template (*.dotm)**. By saving the revised file as a template, you protect the boilerplate text from getting replaced or edited.

14. Click the **Save** button in the dialog box and then close the document.

Working with Styles

Another way in which you can quickly and easily change the appearance of parts in a document is to apply a style. A *style* is a set of formatting characteristics that you can apply to characters, paragraphs, tables, and numbered and bulleted lists in your document. When you apply a style, you apply a whole group of formats in one simple step. For example, instead of taking multiple steps to format your title as 14 point, Arial, bold, and center-aligned, you can achieve the same result in one step by applying a title style.

Styles are also included in templates. The blank document template contains a set of styles already created for you. You can also create your own styles and include them in a template. As you work in the document based upon that template, all of the styles associated with that template will then be available to you. This again can ensure consistency across multiple documents.

Another advantage to formatting your document using styles is that text formatted with heading styles is easy to view, organize, and edit in Outline view.

Step-by-Step 16.14

1. Open **Debate2** from your solution files. Save the document Debate2 as **Debate3**. Position the insertion point in the first subheading on page 2, *The Big Debate*.

2. Move the mouse pointer over the thumbnails in the Styles group on the Home tab to see a live preview of the style formats.

3. Click the **Heading 1** style to format a Level 1 heading. The style is applied to all the text in the paragraph where the insertion point is positioned. The font style, font size, and font color are modified, and the Cambria font is consistent with the design elements in the cover page.

4. Scroll down and position the insertion point in the next heading *Background Information*. In the Styles group, click the **More** button to open the Quick Styles Gallery and then click the **Heading 2** style to format a Level 2 heading.

5. You don't like the second blue font for the Level 2 heading. The insertion point should still be positioned in the Level 2 heading. In the Styles

group, click the **Change Styles** button. Point to **Colors**, and then click the **Urban** built-in color theme.

6. The color for the Heading 2 style changes, and so does the Heading 1 style. Although it is a subtle change, the sample *AaBbCc* text in the thumbnails for the Heading 1 and Heading 2 styles in the Styles gallery also reflect the new font color. However, this style change will only apply to the current document.

7. To save the modified style for future use, select the heading *Background Information*. In the Styles group, click the **More** button and then click **Save Selection as a New Quick Style**. The Create New Style from Formatting dialog box opens. In the Name box enter **New H2** and click **OK**. The new style is added to the Quick Styles gallery and appears in the Styles group.

8. Apply the New H2 style to the headings *Similarities* and *Differences*. Format the last heading in the document, *Conclusion*, with the Heading 1 style.

9. Save the changes to the document. Move the insertion point to the Level 1 heading, *The Big Debate*. Click the **View** tab and then click the **Outline View** button in the Document Views group.

10. On the Outlining tab, in the Outline Tools group, click the **Show Level** list arrow and then click **Level 2**. The body text is hidden and all you see are the Level 1 and 2 headings.

11. It is easier to reorganize the content in a document when the body text is hidden. Double-click the Level 2 heading *Differences* to select the entire heading, and then drag and drop the heading so it is positioned before the Level 2 heading *Similarities*. When the headings are rearranged, the body text moves with the heading.

12. Double-click the plus sign to the left of the heading *Similarities*. All the body text under that heading is expanded and is now visible. Double-click the plus sign again to hide the body text.

13. Click anywhere in the Level 2 heading *Background Information*. Click the **Promote** button ⬕ in the Outline Tools group to promote the heading to a higher level. The heading is now formatted as a Level 1 heading. Click the **Demote** button ⬔ twice to change the format to a Level 3 heading.

14. Click the **Close Outline View** button. Right-click the **New H2** thumbnail in the Quick Styles gallery and click **Remove from Quick Style Gallery**. Then close the document. When prompted to save the changes, click **No**.

TECHNOLOGY TIMELINE

The Evolution of Text Messaging

Just like e-mail, the use of text messaging as a form of communication has grown rapidly. Short Messaging Service (SMS) is the instant communication technology that enables sending and receiving messages between mobile phones and wireless carrier networks. SMS was created in the early 1980s to send automatic alerts to notify users about e-mail or voice messages. The message was limited to 160 characters and usually provided information such as the date and time of the e-mail, and the name of the sender. Text messaging took off in the early 1990s when wireless carriers agreed to allow messages to go from one network to another. Cell phones or PDAs can be used to send short instant messages between cell phones or from a PC to a cell phone. Enter a few words or a sentence or two, and the person on the other end sees the message within seconds. The advantage of SMS over e-mail is that SMS can go with you anywhere, making communication convenient and more efficient.

Text messaging has become an integral part of our lives, not only among the young generation, but also among adults and businesses. So much is available, and right at our fingertips. Via text messages, we can get weather updates and news headlines, make donations to charities, get bank account alerts, buy concert tickets, receive coupons from retailers, see flight updates from airlines, and get emergency alerts for schools or colleges. The addition of the QWERTY keyboard on some cell phones and PDAs makes it even quicker and easier to create a text message. Many cell phones include a dictionary feature, which, like the AutoComplete feature in Word, simplifies the task of entering whole words. And, of course, many still prefer to use the shorthand often found in chat rooms, e-mail messages, and instant messages. So, if you receive a text message with shorthand and you dhac w@ d msg sez, you can translate the text message lingo to plain English at *www.lingo2word.com*.

SUMMARY

In this lesson, you learned:

- Text can be arranged in a variety of multicolumn formats, all within the same document.

- Borders and shading are effective tools for enhancing the appearance and effectiveness of a document. You can choose from a variety of options for line styles, colors, and shading effects.

- Word provides a gallery of building blocks for quickly adding page numbers and headers and footers to a document. You can also create your own building blocks and add them to the gallery.

- Word also provides several tools to insert data elements such as footnotes and endnotes, the date and time, symbols, and hyperlinks.

- Clip art and other pictures also help to enhance the appearance and effectiveness of a document. You can resize and crop the graphic, and choose from several options to align the graphic in the document.

- You can create your own artwork using the drawing tools, AutoShapes, and the WordArt feature.

- Word templates and styles provide a uniform appearance for your documents and can increase the speed and quality of your work by providing predesigned documents and preset formats.

VOCABULARY REVIEW

Define the following terms:

AutoShape	desktop publishing	section breaks
banner	drawing objects	sizing handles
blog	fields	style
boilerplate text	footer	text box
building blocks	graphics	thumbnails
clip art	header	
crop	manual column break	

 REVIEW QUESTIONS

TRUE / FALSE

Circle T if the statement is true or F if the statement is false.

T F **1.** When you insert page numbers in a document, the page number will appear in a header or a footer.

T F **2.** An AutoShape is a predesigned drawing object which cannot be changed.

T F **3.** When you size a graphic proportionally, you change both dimensions approximately equally so that no distortion occurs.

T F **4.** Building blocks are built-in document parts that are already designed and formatted, enabling you to create a professional-looking document quickly.

T F **5.** Endnotes always appear on the page on which they are referenced.

MULTIPLE CHOICE

Select the best response for the following statements.

1. _____ are built-in, pre-designed, and formatted document parts.

    A. Headers and footers   C. AutoText entries

    B. Cover pages   D. all of the above

2. _____ are small squares and circles on the border of a graphic that let you know it is selected.

    A. Banners   C. Sizing handles

    B. Footers   D. Selection marks

3. When you _____ a graphic, you remove a part of the graphic that you don't want to show.

    A. layer   C. clip

    B. crop   D. scale

4. The AutoComplete feature can help you _____.

    A. enter the current date   C. insert predesigned graphics

    B. format borders and shading   D. create a cover page

5. To adjust where a column ends, you can insert a _____.

    A. section break   C. manual column break

    B. column break   D. end-of-line break

FILL IN THE BLANK

Complete the following sentences by writing the correct word or words in the blanks provided.

1. The process of creating documents which combine text and graphics is called _____.

2. A(n) _____ graphic is a built-in, pre-designed, and formatted graphic which you can use to illustrate concepts and ideas, such as an organizational chart.

3. In a template or a building block, you can click _____ to insert variable text or data.

4. A(n) _____ is a predesigned drawing object.

5. _____ is a feature that enables you to transform text into a graphic.

◼ PROJECTS

PROJECT 16–1

1. Open **Project16-1** from the data files. Save the document as **Garden News**.

2. Justify the alignment of all the text in the document.

3. Select the first two lines of text in the document and apply a dark green shading. With the text still selected, change the font color to white.

4. Position the insertion point in the *Fall Gardening* heading. Insert a dark green 2¼ point, single line border below the heading. Click the **Repeat** button (or press **F4**) to insert borders below the other two headings.

5. Position the insertion point at the beginning of the second paragraph below the *Fall Gardening* heading. Insert a clip art image that relates to autumn, fall flowers, or gardening. Resize the picture proportionately so it is about 1½ inches tall. Choose an appropriate text-wrapping option. Adjust the position of the picture so that the top of the picture lines up with the first line of the second paragraph.

6. Apply a yellow shading to the paragraph that describes the *Annual Tree Sale*, but do not apply the shading to the blank line above the text.

7. Position the insertion point at the beginning of the second paragraph under the *Gardening Today Spotlight* heading and insert the picture file **Flower.bmp** from your data files. Crop the white space on the right side of the picture. Resize the picture to approximately 1½ inches high and 1 inch wide.

8. Apply a square text-wrapping format to the new picture. Move the picture to the right side of the page and position it so the top of the picture lines up with the first line of the second paragraph under the *Gardening Today Spotlight* heading.

9. Format a double-line border below the last line of text in the document, and use the same color green you used for shading the two headings at the top of the document.

10. Add a footer to the document that includes your name at the left margin, and then aligned at the right margin, insert a date field that shows the current month and year. Make sure the date field automatically updates.

11. Create a hyperlink for the URL provided in the last line of text by entering a blank space between "www.warrengarden.com" and the period at the end of the sentence. Add a ScreenTip that reads **Visit us online!**

12. Delete the blank paragraphs in the document so all the content fits on one page. If necessary, adjust the settings for the left and right margins.

13. Save the changes and close the document.

PROJECT 16–2

1. Open a new blank document and save it as **Map**. Change the page orientation to landscape.

2. Use the Line, Rectangle, and Fill Color drawing tools to create the map shown in **Figure 16–24**. The Rulers on the edges of the screen are included in the figure to help you judge the size and position of the objects. The line weight for the lines representing the four streets is 3 pt.

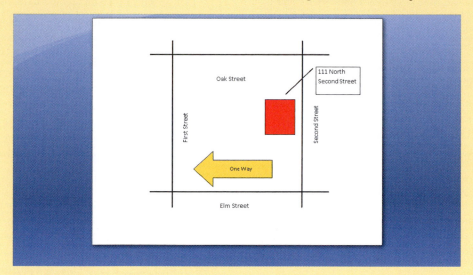

FIGURE 16–24   Map for Project 16-2

3. Fill the rectangle with a bright red color.

4. Create four text boxes for the street names:
   a. To create the First Street and Second Street text boxes, draw tall, narrow boxes. Then change the text direction in the text boxes.
   b. Increase the font size to 18 points for the text inside the text boxes. (Tip: You can use the Mini toolbar.)
   c. Remove the outline from the text boxes.

5. Use an AutoShape to create the arrow in the map and then fill the AutoShape with a bright yellow color.

6. Insert a text box on top of the arrow and enter the text **One Way**. Format the text box with the Shape Fill setting No Fill, which will allow the arrow color to show in the text box. Also, format the text box with Shape Outline setting No Outline to remove the text box border.

7. To create the callout that points out the exact address of the red rectangle, click the **Shapes** button and click the **Line Callout 2** style at the bottom of the menu. Position the mouse pointer above the red rectangle and drag to the right to create the callout object. When you release the mouse button, the insertion point will be inside a text box, and you can enter the street address.

8. Save the changes and close the document.

PROJECT 16–3

1. Open **Project 16-3** from the data files and save the document as **Creamery**.

2. Position the insertion point at the beginning of the document. Use the scroll bar to scroll down to locate the *4.00* price below the description of the Mocha Delight coffee. Press and hold **Shift** and click to the right of the price to select everything in the document except the last paragraph and the blank line above it.

3. Format the selected text in two columns of equal width and format a vertical bar between the two columns.

4. If the *THICK LIQUIDS* heading is at the bottom of the first column of text, insert a manual column break to wrap it and any other text below it to the next column.

5. Create a WordArt title for the page using the words *The Creamery*.

6. Apply the Top and Bottom text wrap option to the WordArt object, which will force the column text to move below the graphic. Position the WordArt graphic at the top of the page and center it horizontally. Modify the WordArt graphic as desired to change colors, outlines, fills, shadow effects, and 3-D effects.

7. Position the insertion point at the end of *Strawberry Fields* in the middle of the second column. Click the **References** tab and then click the **Dialog Box Launcher** for the Footnotes group to open the Footnote and Endnote dialog box.

8. Under Location, click **Endnotes**. Click the **Symbol** button and click an appropriate symbol or character for a superscript notation for a footnote and then click **OK**.

9. Click **Insert** in the Footnote and Endnote dialog box. Enter the note **Seasonal** at the bottom of the page.

10. Select the last paragraph in the document, format the text italic, and justify the alignment.

11. Position the insertion point at the end of the word *Creamery* (and before the comma) in the last paragraph, and then insert a trademark symbol.

12. Save the changes and close the document.

PROJECT 16–4

1. Click the **Office Button** and then click **New**.

2. Browse through the installed templates for a resume template. If you don't see a format that you like, search the Microsoft Web site and download one that meets your preferences. Remember, you can modify the styles that are in the template.

3. Save the document using your last name and followed by the word **Resume**—for example, *SmithResume*.

4. It is important to keep your resume up to date and to have a professional-looking final copy on hand. Enter your personal data in the fields, and approach this project seriously, knowing that you will someday use this resume.

5. Ask a classmate, friend, spouse, or other family member to review your completed resume. Ask them to look for errors and also to provide constructive feedback for improving the resume.

6. Make the necessary or recommended changes, and when the document is finalized, save the document so your instructor can review it. Save the document in XPS or PDF format and create a second digital copy that you can keep for yourself.

TEAMWORK PROJECT

In this lesson, you have learned some ways to modify the appearance of a document. Put your knowledge into practice by designing a newsletter for your class, school, or workplace. Follow these steps:

1. Divide the class members into three or four groups.

2. After determining the targeted audience for their newsletter, each group will design the layout of their newsletter, using the Word features introduced in this lesson, such as borders, shading, columns, headers and footers, and graphics.

3. Each group should then create a sample newsletter using the planned design. You do not need to write a number of real articles to fill up the pages. Instead, follow these directions to create fake text to fill the pages.

   a. Position the insertion point where you want to enter the text.
   b. Enter the following formula: **=rand(4,5)** and press **Enter**. The number 4 in the equation refers to the number of paragraphs you want to create; the number 5 refers to the number of sentences in each paragraph. To alter the number of paragraphs and sentences, change the numbers in the parentheses.

4. As a class, share and compare the newsletter designs and discuss the strengths and weaknesses of each.

CRITICAL THINKING

ACTIVITY 16–1

You have created a drawing that contains a number of drawing objects. Although you have worked as carefully as you can, you cannot place some of the objects as precisely as you would like. Is there any way to move the objects in small increments without dragging them using the mouse? Is there any way to specify that your drawing object be positioned in a specific location? Use the Help system in Word to find answers to these questions. Write a brief summary of what you learn.

ACTIVITY 16–2

In this lesson you learned about Word's New Blog Post template. Search the Microsoft Web site using the key words "blogging with Word" to learn more about creating a blog post in Word. When you find a Web page that you feel adequately explains Word's blogging features, select the URL in the Address box and copy the selected text to the Clipboard. Open a new Word document and paste the URL into the document to cite the source of your information. Write a brief summary of this feature and describe the advantages of using the New Blog Post template. Also, state whether you feel this feature will be useful to you now or in the future.

 # ONLINE DISCOVERY

As you know, Web pages change frequently. Some Web sites, such as *www.msn.com*, are updated several times a day to post current news and events. There may be times when you want to capture what you see on the Web page. You can do this by using your keyboard.

1. Open one of your favorite Web pages.

2. Press the **Print Screen** key on your keyboard. It doesn't appear that anything at all happened, but the entire image on your screen was just stored on the Clipboard.

3. Open a new blank Word document. Open the Clipboard task pane and click the thumbnail for the Web page image. The image is inserted in the document.

4. Most likely, you don't need to see the entire Web page. Select the image in the document. Click the **Picture Tools Format** tab, click the **Crop** button, and remove any unwanted parts. You can also resize and position the image as desired.

LESSON 17

Getting Started with Excel Essentials

■ OBJECTIVES

Upon completion of this lesson, you should be able to:

- Identify the parts of the Excel screen.
- Navigate through a worksheet and a workbook.
- Change views and magnification in the worksheet window.
- Enter data.
- Insert and delete rows and change column width and row height.
- Copy, clear, move, and delete data.
- Use the Undo and Redo features.
- Use the AutoFill feature to copy and enter data into a range of cells.

■ DATA FILES

To complete this lesson, you will need these data files:

Step17-2.xlsx

Project17-2.xlsx

■ VOCABULARY

active cell

AutoFill

cell

cell reference

column heading

range

row heading

spreadsheet

value

workbook

worksheet

▶ VOCABULARY

spreadsheet

worksheet

workbook

cell

cell reference

For hundreds of years, accountants have used spreadsheets to gather, organize, and summarize text and numeric data. A *spreadsheet* is a grid of rows and columns into which you enter text data (e.g., surnames, cities, states) and numerical data (e.g., dates, currency, percentages). Each time one piece of data was changed, paper spreadsheets had to be manually recalculated, which was painstaking and time consuming. Excel is an electronic application designed to replace the paper spreadsheet. When using an electronic spreadsheet, changes are relatively easy and require far less time.

2-1.1.1
2-1.1.2
2-3.1.1

Identifying the Parts of the Excel Screen

Excel refers to a spreadsheet as a *worksheet*. The worksheet is always stored in a *workbook* that contains one or more worksheets. You can have multiple Excel workbooks open at the same time.

As with Word 2007, Excel 2007 also uses the Microsoft Office Fluent user interface. The Ribbon, shown in **Figure 17–1**, provides several tabs and commands. Notice there are two sets of sizing buttons in the upper-right corner of the window. The top set of sizing buttons controls the application window. The lower set of sizing buttons controls the worksheet window. You can also see the Quick Access Toolbar and other similar features such as the Office button. The Excel document window shows the worksheet, which is divided into columns and rows. Columns of the worksheet appear vertically and are identified by letters at the top of the worksheet window. Rows appear horizontally and are identified by numbers on the left side of the worksheet window. The intersection of a single row and a single column is called a *cell*. The *cell reference* is the column letter followed by the row number (for example, A1 or B4). Usually, the top row of a worksheet is used for explanatory text or column headings that identify the type of data in each column.

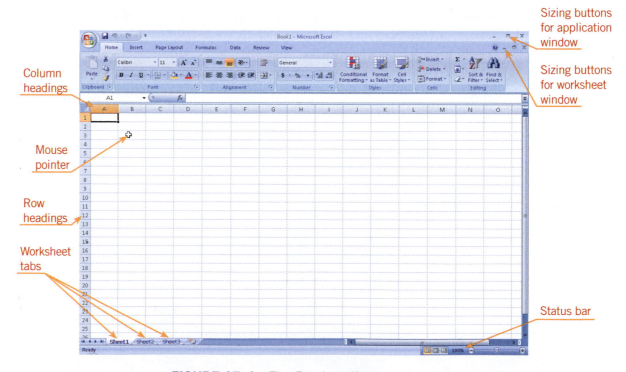

FIGURE 17–1　The Excel application window

Step-by-Step 17.1

1. Launch Excel. A new workbook titled *Book1* is opened. Sheet1 appears in the document window. There are two other worksheets in the workbook, Sheet2 and Sheet3, and the tabs for those worksheets appear at the bottom of the application window, as shown in **Figure 17–1**.

2. Compare your screen with **Figure 17–1**. Note the various components of the Excel screen and their names. The Ribbon is similar to the Ribbon that appears in Word. Some of the buttons are the same, but there are also many new buttons.

3. Move the mouse pointer around the document window. When the mouse pointer is within the worksheet cells, it changes to a large outlined plus sign. When you position the mouse pointer over the Ribbon, the pointer changes to the arrow. When you position the mouse pointer over the formula bar, the pointer changes to an I-beam.

4. Click the **Minimize** button in the upper row of sizing buttons. The application window is minimized. Click the Excel spreadsheet button in the task bar to restore the application window.

5. Click the **Minimize** button in the lower row of sizing buttons. The worksheet window is minimized, but the Ribbon still appears in the application window. A minimized title bar appears at the lower-left corner of the application window.

6. Click the **Maximize** button on the minimized title bar, and the worksheet window appears again.

7. Click the **Restore Window** button in the lower set of sizing buttons. The worksheet window is reduced in size, and when you drag the title bar for the worksheet, you can move the worksheet window around on the screen.

8. Click the **Maximize** button in the worksheet window to restore the worksheet window to full screen.

9. Leave the workbook open.

Navigating a Worksheet

To create a worksheet, you enter information into the cells. Before you can enter data into a cell, you must first select the cell. When the cell is selected, a dark border appears around the cell, and the column and row headings for the selected cell are highlighted. You can select a cell using either the mouse or the keyboard. When a cell is selected, it is called the *active cell*. The active cell is identified in the Name box at the top of the worksheet screen. You can change the active cell by using the mouse or the keyboard.

2-1.1.2
2-1.1.3
2-1.1.4
2-1.2.4

▶ **VOCABULARY**
active cell

Moving through a Workbook

To move around in a worksheet, you can use the scroll bar features or you can use keyboard shortcuts. Many of the keyboard shortcuts you learned to use in Word move the insertion point in Excel in similar ways. For example, the arrow keys move the insertion point one cell in any direction, and Page Up or Page Down moves the insertion point one screen up or down. **Table 17–1** includes other keyboard shortcuts you can use to move the insertion point in an Excel worksheet.

TABLE 17–1   Keyboard shortcuts for moving the insertion point in Excel

TO MOVE THE INSERTION POINT	PRESS
Right one cell	Right arrow or Tab
Left one cell	Left arrow or Shift+Tab
To the next row	Down arrow
To the previous row	Up arrow
To the first cell in a row	Home or Ctrl+left arrow
To the last cell with data in the row (If there is no data in the row, the insertion point will move to last cell in the row)	Ctrl+right arrow
To the last column and row with data in the document	Ctrl+End
To the next screen	Page Down
To the previous screen	Page Up
To the beginning of the document	Ctrl+Home
To a specific cell	F5 (and then enter the cell reference in the Go To dialog box)

Step-by-Step 17.2

1. Click the **Office Button**, click **Open**, and then navigate to where the data files are stored and open **Step17-2**.

2. Click the **Office Button**, click **Save As**, enter the new filename **Earnings** in the File name box, and click **Save**.

3. Cell A1 should be the active cell, as shown in **Figure 17-2**. Notice also that the cell reference *A1* appears in the Name box, and the contents of the cell appear in the formula bar. Click cell **C5** to select it. The Name box now shows the cell reference *C5*, and the formula bar shows the contents for cell C5.

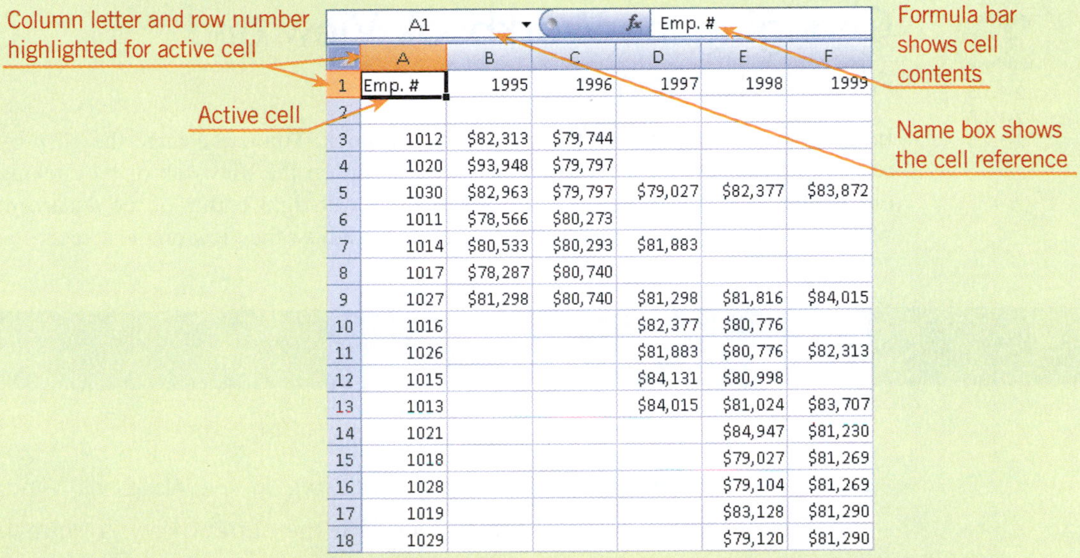

Column letter and row number
highlighted for active cell

Active cell

Formula bar
shows cell
contents

Name box shows
the cell reference

FIGURE 17-2
An active cell in
a worksheet

	A	B	C	D	E	F
1	Emp. #	1995	1996	1997	1998	1999
2						
3	1012	$82,313	$79,744			
4	1020	$93,948	$79,797			
5	1030	$82,963	$79,797	$79,027	$82,377	$83,872
6	1011	$78,566	$80,273			
7	1014	$80,533	$80,293	$81,883		
8	1017	$78,287	$80,740			
9	1027	$81,298	$80,740	$81,298	$81,816	$84,015
10	1016			$82,377	$80,776	
11	1026			$81,883	$80,776	$82,313
12	1015			$84,131	$80,998	
13	1013			$84,015	$81,024	$83,707
14	1021				$84,947	$81,230
15	1018				$79,027	$81,269
16	1028				$79,104	$81,269
17	1019				$83,128	$81,290
18	1029				$79,120	$81,290

4. Press **Tab** three times to move to cell F5. Then, press the **Home** key to move to the beginning of the row. Cell A5 is the active cell.

5. Press the **up arrow** to move to cell A4. When you use Tab or an arrow key, the active cell moves to the new location.

6. Press **F5** to open the Go To dialog box. Under Reference, enter **P76**, and click **OK** to move the insertion point to cell P76.

7. Drag the horizontal scroll bar to the right so you can see the last cell with data, cell T76. Then click the scroll up arrow on the vertical scroll bar to move up one row. The scroll bar changes the view on the screen, but it does not change the active cell.

8. Click above the scroll box on the vertical scroll bar to move up one window, and then click below the scroll box to move down one window. Click on the left side of the scroll box on the horizontal scroll bar to move one window to the left, and then click to the right of the scroll box to move one window to the right.

9. To navigate back to the beginning of the document, press and hold **Ctrl** and then press **Home**. The active cell is now cell A1.

10. Press and hold **Ctrl** and then press **End** to move to the last cell with data in the worksheet. The active cell is now cell T76.

11. Click the **Sheet2** tab at the bottom of the screen to open the second worksheet in the workbook. The cells in the worksheet are empty. Click the **Sheet1** tab to go back to the first worksheet in the workbook.

12. Press and hold **Ctrl** and then press **Home** to return to cell A1.

13. Leave the workbook open.

2-1.1.5
2-1.1.6
2-1.2.5

Changing the Workbook View and Magnification

Excel offers several options for viewing a workbook. You can change the view by selecting options from the Workbook Views group on the View tab or by clicking one of the view buttons in the status bar at the lower-right corner of the document window. You can also change the zoom settings to adjust the view on the screen.

Step-by-Step 17.3

1. If necessary, open **Earnings** from your solution files.

2. Click the **View** tab. The view commands are in the Workbook Views group, shown in **Figure 17–3**. Notice that the current view is Normal, which is the default view.

FIGURE 17–3
The Workbook Views group on the View tab

Normal View button

Page Layout View button

3. Click the **Page Layout View** button. The view changes and the column and row labels are separated from the worksheet cells because these labels will not appear in a printed worksheet. You can see the white margins that will appear when the worksheet is printed.

4. Click the **Page Break Preview** button ![Page Break Preview]. If prompted about adjusting the page breaks, click **OK**. Scroll down and you see that the worksheet will print on four pages. You will learn more about working with the Page Break Preview in Lesson 18.

5. Click the **Toggle Full Screen View** button ![Full Screen]. The full screen view hides the Ribbon, the formula bar, and the status bar.

6. To return to the previous view, press **Escape** (or right-click in the work-sheet document window and click Close Full Screen).

7. To return to the default view, click the **Normal View** button, or you can click the Normal view button on the status bar, shown in **Figure 17–4**.

Page Layout view button Page Break Preview view button

Normal view button Zoom controls

FIGURE 17–4
The view buttons and zoom settings on the status bar

8. In the Zoom group, click the **Zoom** button. The Zoom dialog box opens. Click **50%** and then click **OK**. You can see the page breaks.

9. In the Zoom group, click the **100%** button. Note that you can also find zoom controls in the status bar at the lower-right corner of the screen, as shown in **Figure 17–4**.

10. Click the **Close** button in the lower set of sizing buttons to close the workbook window. If prompted to save changes, click **No**.

EXTRA FOR EXPERTS

If you have a mouse with a wheel, you can also change the zoom settings by using the wheel. Hold **Ctrl** and roll the wheel away from you to increase the magnification; hold **Ctrl** and roll the wheel towards you to decrease the magnification.

Entering Data

You add data to the cells by entering text or numbers in the active cell. The text and numbers are often referred to as a *value*.

Inserting Data

To enter data in a cell, the cell must be active. As you begin entering text, you see the insertion point indicating where the next character of text will appear. By default, Excel shows approximately eight characters in each cell. When text is too long for the width of a cell, it spills over into the next cell if the next cell is empty. If the next cell is not empty, the text that does not fit into the cell does not appear, but it is still contained within the cell. When you enter more numbers than can fit in the cell, a series of number signs (####) appear in the cell.

2-1.3.1
2-1.3.2
2-3.1.3

▶ **VOCABULARY**
value

Step-by-Step 17.4

1. Click the **Office Button**, click **New**, click **Blank Workbook**, and then click **Create**.

2. Save the new workbook as **Cruise1**.

3. The active cell should be A1. Enter **Days**. Notice that the text you enter appears both in the cell and also in the formula bar. As new content is entered, the formula bar adapts and shows the three buttons shown in **Figure 17–5**. You will use these buttons later to edit the cell contents.

FIGURE 17–5
The formula bar with data entered in the cell

Cancel, Enter, and Insert Function buttons

As data is entered in the cell, the formula bar shows the content

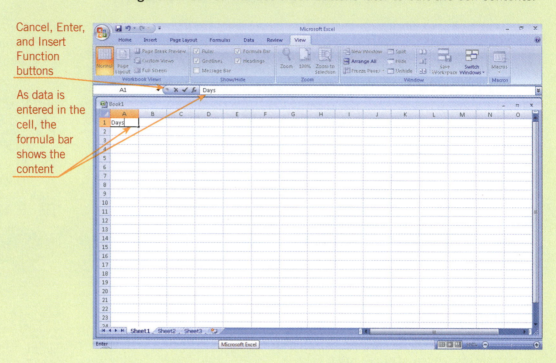

If you choose not to keep the data you have entered, you can press **Escape** or click the **Cancel** button in the formula bar. The Enter and Cancel buttons do not appear in the formula bar unless you enter data in a cell or position the insertion point in the formula bar.

4. Press **Tab**. The insertion point moves to the next cell to the right in the first row, B1.

5. Enter **Depart** and then press **Enter**. The insertion point moves down a row to the first cell in the second row, A2. The default setting aligns text at the left border of the cell.

6. Click cell **C1**, enter **Arrive**, and then press **Tab**.

7. Enter **Cruise** and then press **Enter**. The active cell is now C2.

8. Click cell **A1** to select it. *Days* shows in the cell and in the formula bar.

9. To change the text in the formula bar, position the insertion point in front of the word *Days* in the formula bar. Enter # and then press **Spacebar**. Click the **Enter** button ✓ on the formula bar. The change is made in the formula bar and in cell A1. (The Enter button in the formula bar only enters the data. It does not allow for the automatic movement to A2.)

10. Press the **right arrow** key three times to move to cell D1. The cell currently shows *Cruise*. Enter **Destination** and press **Enter**. The contents of the cell are replaced with the new text you entered, and the cell below, D2, becomes active. Also notice that the new content expands beyond the border of the D column. You'll fix that later.

11. Click cell **C1**. It currently shows *Arrive*. Press **F2**. Notice that the insertion point is now positioned at the end of the text in the cell.

12. Press **Backspace** to delete the existing text and then enter **Return**. Press **Enter**. All the contents in the cell are replaced with the new text you entered, and the cell below, C2, becomes active.

13. Click cell **A2**. Enter the following numbers, pressing **Enter** after each number. When you are done, your worksheet should look like the one shown in **Figure 17–6**. The default setting aligns numbers at the right border of the cell.

4

5

7

10

7

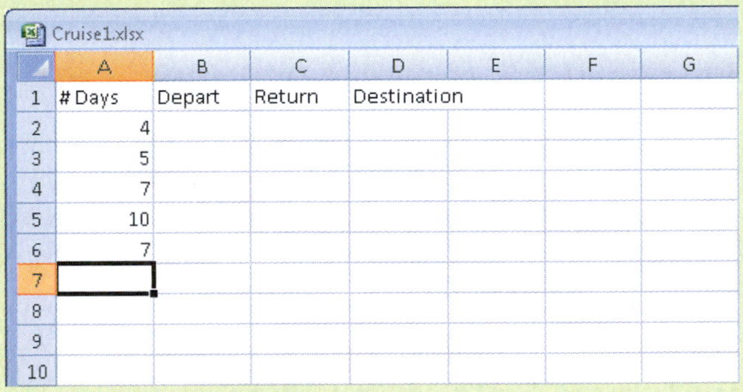

FIGURE 17–6
Worksheet with data entered

14. Click the **Save** button on the Quick Access Toolbar to save the changes and leave the workbook open.

Using the AutoCorrect and AutoComplete Features

The AutoCorrect feature in Excel corrects common mistakes as you enter data. For example, if you enter *hte*, Excel will automatically change the text to *the*. With the AutoComplete feature, Excel compares the first few characters you enter in a cell with existing entries in the same column. If the characters match an existing cell entry, Excel proposes the existing entry. You can press Enter to accept the proposed entry, or you can continue entering new text.

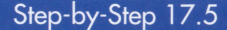

Step-by-Step 17.5

1. If necessary, open **Cruise1** from your solution files. Save the workbook Cruise1 as **Cruise2**.

2. Click cell **D2**. Enter **Caribbean** and press **Enter**.

3. Enter **Bahamas and Florida** in cell D3 and press **Enter**. The contents overlap the right border of the column. The active cell is D4.

4. Enter **C**. Notice that Excel suggests *Caribbean* because you entered it earlier in the column. Press **Enter** to accept the proposed text.

5. Enter **Alaska** and press **Enter**.

6. Enter **Belize adn**. Then look at the active cell as you press **Spacebar**. Excel automatically corrects the spelling of *and*. Enter **Cozumel** and press **Enter**.

7. Save the changes and leave the workbook open.

2-3.1.4

Modifying the Worksheet Structure

Just as you can change a Word table structure, you can change the structure of a worksheet by adding or deleting rows and columns and merging cells. You can also add and delete the worksheets stored within a workbook.

Selecting Multiple Cells in the Worksheet

▶ **VOCABULARY**
row heading
column heading
range

To select an entire row in a worksheet, click the *row heading*, which is the number at the left of the row. To select an entire column, click the *column heading*, which is the letter at the top of the column. You can also select a row, column, or section of a worksheet by clicking and dragging the mouse to highlight the area you want to select. When you select a group of cells, the group is called a *range*. All cells in a range touch each other and form a rectangle. The range is identified by the cell in the upper-left corner and the cell in the lower-right corner, separated by a colon (for example, A1:D4).

Step-by-Step 17.6

1. If necessary, open **Cruise2** from your solution files. Save the workbook Cruise2 as **Cruise3**.

2. Click the **column B** heading to select the second column. The column has a dark border and all the cells in the column are shaded except for the first cell. The lack of shading indicates the first cell is the active cell.

3. Click the **row 4** heading to select the fourth row. The entire row has a dark border, and the row number and all the cells in the row are shaded, except for the first cell, A4, which is the active cell.

4. Enter **8** and press **Enter**. Notice that this new data replaces the data in the active cell, A4. When you enter data in a selected row or column, the data is entered in the first cell.

5. Click cell **A1** and drag to the right and down to select the range **A1:D6**. Even though some of the content in column D extends beyond the cell borders, all of the content is selected.

6. Click elsewhere in the worksheet to deselect the range. Click cell **A1**. Hold down **Shift** and click cell **D6**. All cells between A1 and D6 are selected. Click elsewhere in the worksheet to deselect the range.

7. Click cell **A1**. Press and hold down **Shift** and use the right and down arrow keys to select the range **AI:D6**. Click elsewhere in the worksheet to deselect the range.

8. Save the changes and leave the workbook open.

> **EXTRA FOR EXPERTS**
>
> Instead of holding down the Shift key to select a range of cells, you can press **F8** and then press the arrow keys to select the cells. The F8 key enables the Select mode. To turn off the Select mode, press **F8** again, or press **Escape**.

Inserting and Deleting Rows and Columns

When you insert or delete a row or a column in Excel, it affects the entire worksheet. All existing data is shifted in some direction. For example, when you add a new column, the existing data shifts to the right. When you add a new row, the data shifts down a row. To add or delete rows and columns, use the buttons in the Cells group on the Home tab, shown in **Figure 17-7**. To insert or delete multiple columns and rows in a single step, select the desired number of columns or rows before executing the command.

> **EXTRA FOR EXPERTS**
>
> If the data in one cell is dependent on the data in another cell, when these cells are adjusted, Excel will keep straight what information is required where. You will learn more about this in Lesson 19.

FIGURE 17-7   The Cells group on the Home tab

Step-by-Step 17.7

1. If necessary, open **Cruise3** from your solution files. Save the workbook Cruise3 as **Cruise4**.

2. Click any cell in column D. If necessary, click the **Home** tab. In the Cells group, click the **Insert Cells** button arrow ⬛ Insert ⌄ and then click **Insert Sheet Columns**. A new column is inserted to the left of column D, and the data that was labeled Column D is now labeled Column E.

3. Click cell **D1** and enter the column heading **Agent**. Press **Enter**, and then enter the following list of travel agent initials in cells D2 through D6. Use Excel's AutoComplete feature to complete repeated entries, and remember to press **Enter** after each entry to move to the next cell in the column.

   JRK

   AMF

   JRK

   AMF

   AMF

4. Click cell **C4**. In the Cells group, click the **Delete Cells** button arrow ⬛ Delete ⌄. Four delete options appear.

5. Click the **Delete Sheet Columns** option. The column with the label *Return* is deleted from the worksheet. The content that was in column D and column E is now in column C and column D. Note that if you had selected multiple columns before clicking the Delete Sheet Columns option, all the selected columns would have been deleted.

6. Click any cell in row 6. Click the **Insert Cells** button arrow and then click **Insert Sheet Rows**. A new row is inserted above the row with the active cell and row 6 becomes row 7. The existing data shifts down, and the row labels are updated to reflect the change.

7. Enter **10** in cell A6, enter **JRK** in cell C6, and then enter **Panama Canal** in cell D6.

8. Click the **row 6** heading and drag down to include row 7 in the selection.

9. Rows 6 and 7 should both be selected. Click the **Insert Cells** button. Because whole rows were already selected, you did not need to click the button arrow to select the option to insert sheet rows. Because two rows are selected, two new rows are inserted above the selected rows.

10. Enter the following information in columns A, C, and D of the new rows:

        14   AMF   Mediterranean

        10   JRK   Caribbean

11. Click the **row 9** heading. The entire row should be selected. Click the **Delete Cells** button. Because you selected the entire row, you did not need to click the button arrow to delete the entire row.

12. Save the changes and leave the workbook open.

Changing Column Width and Row Height

Sometimes the data you enter in a cell doesn't fit in the column. When the data is too wide for the cell, the data will run outside the column if the cell to the right is empty. To accommodate the data, you can widen the column and change the height of a row. There are several options available for changing the cell width and height.

EXTRA FOR EXPERTS

The default column width is 8.43 characters with the default text font. The default row height is 12.75 points (approximately 1/6 inch).

Step-by-Step 17.8

1. If necessary, open **Cruise4** from your solution files. Save the workbook Cruise4 as **Cruise5**.

2. Point to the boundary on the right side of the column B heading. When the pointer changes to a double-headed arrow, click and drag the boundary to the right. As you drag the border, the exact column width appears in a ScreenTip. Release the mouse button when the column width is exactly 11.00 (82 pixels). **Figure 17–8** shows how you can drag a column boundary to change the column width.

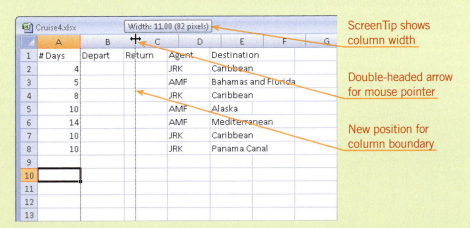

FIGURE 17–8
Dragging a column boundary to change the column width

3. Click the **column D** heading to select the entire column.

4. In the Cells group, click the **Format** button [Format], and then click **AutoFit Column Width**. The column width is automatically adjusted to fit the cell with the most content—in this case, cell D3 with the content *Bahamas and Florida*.

5. Click the **column A** heading and drag across the headings to include columns B and C in the selection.

6. With the three columns selected, position the mouse pointer over the right boundary on the column C heading. When the pointer changes to a double-headed arrow, double-click. The width of each of the three columns is automatically adjusted to fit the contents in that column.

7. Click the **row 1** heading to select the entire row.

8. Click the **Format** button and then click **Row Height**. A Row Height dialog box opens.

9. Change Row height to **25** and click **OK**.

10. Click anywhere in the worksheet to deselect the row. Note the change in row 1. The row is now about twice as high as the other rows.

11. Save the changes and leave the workbook open.

2-1.3.2
2-1.3.3
2-3.1.3

Editing the Worksheet Data

Sometimes after entering data in a worksheet, you need to reorganize it. You may even want to remove some of the data and not replace it. Or, you may want to move or copy existing data from one location to another.

Clearing, Replacing, and Copying Existing Data

You learned in Step-by-Step 17.4 that you can edit the data directly in the cell, or you can make the necessary changes to the cell contents in the formula bar. To replace cell contents, you can select the cell and enter the new data. The process for deleting data can be as simple as pressing the Delete or Backspace keys. Using these keys, you can clear the cell contents.

Copying data saves you from having to enter the same data into another location. The process, as in all Office applications, is easy. Moving data is similar to copying data, except that you cut the data from one location and paste it in the destination location. You can copy or move multiple cells of data at the same time. However, unlike copying or moving data in a Word table, when you paste data to a spreadsheet cell that already contains data, that existing data doesn't move to make room for the new data. Instead, the existing data in the destination cell is replaced. If you don't want to lose content, you need to copy or move data into empty cells.

The Undo and Redo commands are available on the Quick Access Toolbar. However, the default settings in Excel do not include the Repeat command.

Step-by-Step 17.9

1. If necessary, open **Cruise5** from your solution files. Save the workbook Cruise5 as **Cruise6**.

2. Click cell **A6**. The cell currently shows *14*. Press **Delete** to remove the contents.

3. With cell A6 still selected, enter **10** and press **Enter**.

4. If necessary, click the **Home** tab. Click cell **A6**. Click the **Delete Cells** button arrow. Click **Delete Cells**. A dialog box with four options opens. If necessary, click the **Shift cells up** option and then click **OK**. The contents in cells A7 and A8 are shifted one cell up, and cell A8 is now empty. Cell A6 is the active cell.

5. With cell A6 still the active cell, click the **Insert Cells** button arrow, and then click **Insert Cells**. *Shift cells down* should already be selected. Click **OK**. The contents in cells A6 through A8 are each shifted down one cell, and now cell A6 is empty. Enter **14** and press **Enter**.

6. Click cell **D4**. In the Clipboard group, click the **Copy** button. The contents of the cell (*Caribbean*) are copied to the Clipboard. Also, an animated border (a dotted-line marquee) appears around the selected cell, as shown in **Figure 17–9**.

> **⚠ WARNING**
>
> Use caution when using the Shift cells feature. The results may misalign data in your rows and columns.

FIGURE 17–9
Marquee around a selected cell

	A	B	C	D	E
1	# Days	Depart	Agent	Destination	
2	4		JRK	Caribbean	
3	5		AMF	Bahamas and Florida	
4	8		JRK	Caribbean	
5	10		AMF	Alaska	
6	14		AMF	Mediterranean	
7	10		JRK	Caribbean	
8	10		JRK	Panama Canal	
9					
10					

Marquee surrounding the active cell

7. Click cell **D9**. In the Clipboard group, click the **Paste** button. The copied data is pasted in the destination cell.

8. Click the **Undo** button to undo the Paste action.

9. The marquee still appears around cell D4 because you can still paste the copied data in other locations. Press **Escape** to remove the marquee around the copied cell.

10. Click cell **B1**. The cell currently shows *Depart*. In the Clipboard group, click the **Cut** button. The contents of the cell are stored on the Clipboard and a marquee appears around the cell border.

11. Click cell **E1**, and then click the **Paste** button. The contents that were cut from cell B1 are moved to cell E1.

12. Click the **column D** heading to select the entire column. Click the **Cut** button, select cell **B1**, and then click the **Paste** button. The entire column is moved, and the AutoFit Column Width format still applies. The contents are moved to column B, and although all the cells are empty, column D still exists.

13. Select rows **4** and **5**, click the **Insert Cells** button arrow, and then click **Insert Sheet Rows**. Then select rows 9 and 10, click the **Cut** button, click cell **A4**, and click the **Paste** button.

14. Save the changes and leave the workbook open.

Using AutoFill to Copy Data

Filling data is another method for copying data in a worksheet. The *AutoFill* feature enables you to repeat the same data in a column or row. Using the AutoFill feature is faster than copying and pasting because filling requires only one step. However, the Fill command can only be used when the destination cells are adjacent to the original cell. You can use the mouse to fill data up or down in the same column, or right or left in the same row.

Step-by-Step 17.10

EXTRA FOR EXPERTS

To quickly fill to the cell on the right, click the destination cell and press the keyboard shortcut **Ctrl+R**. This copies the contents of the cell at left to the destination cell on the right. To quickly fill down, click the destination cell and press the keyboard shortcut **Ctrl+D**. The contents of the cell above are copied. To fill multiple cells, select the cell containing the contents, and then drag to create a range of cells before pressing the keyboard shortcuts.

1. If necessary, open **Cruise6** from your solution files. Save the workbook Cruise6 as **Cruise7**.

2. Click cell **D1**, enter **Vacancy**, and press **Enter**.

3. Cell D2 is the active cell. Enter **Yes**, and press **Enter**.

4. Select the range **D2:D6**.

5. In the Editing group, click the **Fill** button 🔽, and then click **Down**. The content in cell D2 is copied and pasted into the cells in the D3:D6 range.

6. Click cell **D8**, enter **No**, and then press **Enter**.

7. Click cell **D7**. Click the **Fill** button and then click **Up**. The text is copied from cell D8 and pasted into cell D7.

8. Click cell **C2**. Point to the fill handle, shown in **Figure 17–10**. The pointer changes to a plus sign. Click and drag downward to select the range **C2:C6**. A ScreenTip shows the cell contents (*JRK*) that will be copied to the range of cells. Release the mouse button, and the contents of C2 are pasted and replace the contents in cells C3 through C6.

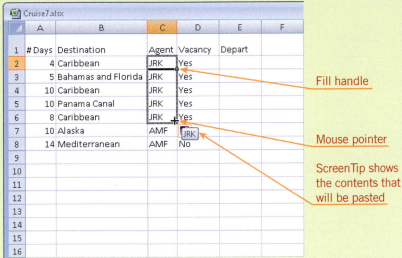

FIGURE 17–10
Filling down a range of cells

9. Save the changes and leave the workbook open.

Using AutoFill to Fill in a Series

You can also use the AutoFill feature to quickly fill in a series of numbers and dates. To fill in a series, a pattern must be established in the initial selection of cells. Then when you drag the fill handle, the pattern is continued. When you drag the fill handle down or to the right, the series will continue in ascending order. However, when you drag the fill handle up or to the left, the series will continue in descending order.

Step-by-Step 17.11

1. If necessary, open **Cruise7** from your solution files. Save the workbook Cruise7 as **Cruise8**.

2. Click cell **E2**. Enter **2/7** and press **Enter**. The default setting automatically formats the numbers for the date to appear as *7-Feb*.

3. Enter **2/14** and press **Enter**.

4. You have now established a pattern (every seven days) for the dates. Select the range **E2:E3** and click and drag the fill handle downward to cell E8. When you release the mouse button, the series of dates for the next five weeks are entered into the cells.

5. With the range **E2:E8** still selected, click the **Fill** button and then click **Series**. The Series dialog box opens, as shown in **Figure 17–11**. The settings you see are the settings that you applied when you used the fill handle. When you want to modify the settings, you can click the Fill button and access this dialog box.

FIGURE 17–11
The Series dialog box

6. Click **Cancel** to close the dialog box without making any changes.

7. Notice the AutoFill Options button, shown in **Figure 17–12**, appears to the right of the fill handle in cell E8.

FIGURE 17–12
After the range of cells is filled

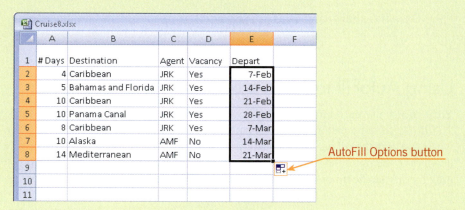

8. With the range E2:E8 still selected, point to the **AutoFill Options** button, and the button expands to show a down arrow. Click the **down arrow** to open a shortcut menu with several options. The selected option Fill Series is the option you want. Click outside the shortcut menu to deselect the cells.

9. Save the changes and close the workbook.

TECHNOLOGY CAREERS

Computer Software Engineers

More people are connecting to the Internet, and online banking is growing in popularity. Online banking enables you to check account balances, view account history, pay bills, manage accounts, and more. The service is convenient, efficient, and effective, and it is computer software engineers who make online banking possible.

Computer software engineers evaluate situations, analyze needs, develop software to perform functions (such as paying bills online), and then verify and test the software to ensure that the requirements are met. They develop many types of software, including business applications, computer games, operating systems, and technical applications used in a variety of industries. They also solve technical problems as they arise. The tasks evolve quickly, so computer software engineers must continually strive to acquire new skills to keep up with changing technology. They must pay attention to detail and have strong problem-solving and analytical skills. Much of the work is part of a team effort, so computer software engineers must be able to communicate effectively with team members and other staff. They also need skills related to the industry in which they work. For example, if they are creating or troubleshooting software for online banking, they must be familiar with and understand the banking industry.

Job prospects for computer software engineers are excellent. It is one of the fastest growing occupations.

SUMMARY

In this lesson, you learned:

- Excel uses the Microsoft Office Fluent user interface, and the Excel application window shows the Quick Access Toolbar, status bar, task bar, and other similar features. The Excel document window shows the worksheet.

- To navigate the workbook, you can use keyboard shortcuts and the scroll bars.

- You can choose from several options to view the worksheet, and you can change the zoom settings to specify the level of magnification.

- To enter data in a cell, the cell must be active.

- As you enter data, the AutoCorrect feature automatically corrects some of your keyboarding errors. If the data you are entering matches characters of existing entries in the column, the AutoComplete feature proposes the existing entry to save you time.

- When you insert or delete cells, rows, and columns, all existing data is shifted up, down, left, or right.

- To reorganize a worksheet, you can add and delete columns and rows; and you can delete, clear, copy, or move the data.

- There are several options for changing the column width. You can drag a column boundary, use the AutoFit feature, or specify an exact measurement.

- Copying and pasting data in Excel is similar to copying and pasting text in Word.

- The AutoFill feature enables you to copy data from one cell to another, and it can save you time by quickly filling in a series of data.

VOCABULARY REVIEW

Define the following terms:

active cell	column heading	value
AutoFill	range	workbook
cell	row heading	worksheet
cell reference	spreadsheet	

REVIEW QUESTIONS

TRUE / FALSE

Circle T if the statement is true or F if the statement is false.

T   F   **1.**   A worksheet is the same as a spreadsheet.

T   F   **2.**   When you position the mouse pointer over cells in the worksheet, the mouse pointer shows as a hand with a pointing finger.

T   F   **3.**   When data is too wide for a cell, the part of the data that does not fit is automatically deleted.

T   F   **4.**   By default, text aligns at the left of a cell.

T   F   **5.**   When you paste data to a spreadsheet cell that already contains data, the existing data is replaced with the new data.

MULTIPLE CHOICE

Select the best response for the following statements.

1. The _____ identifies the column letter and row number.

   A.   active reference   C.   cell reference

   B.   cell position   D.   cell name

2. When a cell is selected, it is called a(n) _____.

   A.   targeted cell   C.   cell reference

   B.   selection   D.   active cell

3. The _____ view separates the column and row labels from the worksheet cells, and you can see the white margins that will appear when the worksheet is printed.

   A.   Full Screen   C.   Page Break Preview

   B.   Page Layout   D.   Normal

4. By default, Excel shows approximately _____ characters in each cell.

   A.   10   C.   12

   B.   8   D.   18

5. The _____ automatically adjusts the column width to fit the cell with the most content.

   A.   AutoCell Width command   C.   AutoFit Column Width command

   B.   Column Width command   D.   Default Width command

FILL IN THE BLANK

Complete the following sentences by writing the correct word or words in the blanks provided.

1. A selected group of cells that touch each other and form a rectangle is called a(n) _____.

2. A(n) _____ is a grid of rows and columns into which you enter text data.

3. The _____ feature in Excel corrects common mistakes as you enter data.

4. The _____ feature is a quick and easy way to copy data to adjacent cells in a worksheet in a single step.

5. The worksheet is always stored in a(n) _____ that contains one or more worksheets.

 # PROJECTS

PROJECT 17–1

1. Open a new workbook in Excel.

2. Beginning in cell A1, enter the following data in the cells. Use the AutoComplete feature to save time entering some of the repetitive data.

female	adult	Chocolate Labrador Retriever
male	young	Beagle
male	baby	Brittany Spaniel
female	baby	Saint Bernard
male	young	Terrier
male	young	Yellow Labrador Retriever
female	adult	Brittany Spaniel
female	adult	German Shepherd
male	young	Yellow Labrador Retriever
male	young	Siberian Husky

3. Save the workbook as **Pets**.

4. Insert a new column to the left of the current column A, and add the names below.

Sasha

Sebastian

Shaggy

Lucy

Blaney

Chesterfield

Rosie

Roxy

Charlie

Max

5. AutoFit all the column widths.

6. Add three new rows at the top of the worksheet.

7. In cell A1, enter **Adoptable Pets**.

8. Enter the following column headings in the third row:

Name   Gender   Age   Breed

9. In cell C8, change *young* to **adult**.

10. Delete row 6.

11. Save the changes and close the workbook.

PROJECT 17–2

1. Open **Project17-2** from the data files. Save the workbook as **Shoes**.

2. Use the AutoFill feature to complete the series of shoe sizes. Fill the series in the range A6:A18 (sizes 7 through 13).

3. AutoFit all the column widths.

4. Edit each of the headings in row 1 so the first letter is initial caps. For example, change *court* to *Court*.

5. Add the following data to the order form:

Court:	**1** size 9
Cross-training:	**1** size 6 and **1** size 8.5
Soccer:	**2** size 10.5
Basketball:	**1** size 10
Running:	**1** size 9.5 and **1** size 12
Walking:	**2** size 9

6. Move the column F data for Basketball shoes so it is in column B before the Court shoes data. AutoFit the column width for column B.

7. Delete the empty column G, and also column E.

8. Save your changes and close the workbook.

PROJECT 17–3

1. Open a new workbook and save the workbook as **Schedule**.

2. In cell B1 enter **Monday**.

3. In cell C1 enter **Tuesday**. Use the AutoFill feature to copy the series of weekdays to the range D1:F1 (Monday through Friday).

4. In cell A2 enter **8:30 am**. The default setting will change the format to 8:30 AM.

5. In cell A3 enter **9:00 am**. Use the AutoFill feature to copy the series of times to the range A4:A17.

6. In cell B2 enter **MATH 111** and press **Enter**. Select the cell contents and copy the cell contents to the Clipboard and paste the contents in cell D2. Open the Clipboard task pane.

7. In cell C4 enter **ART 114**. Copy the cell contents to the Clipboard and paste the contents in cell E4.

8. In cell C6 enter **COMP 201**. Copy the cell contents to the Clipboard and paste the contents in cell E6.

9. In cell B8 enter **BIOL 105**. Copy the cell contents and paste the contents in cells D8 and F8.

10. In cell B11 enter **ENGL 110**. Copy the cell contents to the Clipboard and paste the contents in cells D11 and F11.

11. In cell F14, enter **BIOL LAB**.

12. You realize that your math class also meets on Friday. Click cell **F2**. On the Clipboard task pane, click the **MATH 111** content to paste it in the active cell.

13. AutoFit all of the column widths.

14. Save the changes and close the workbook.

🐾 TEAMWORK PROJECT

With a partner, explore voting statistics for your state in U.S. presidential elections from 1980 through the most recent presidential election. Follow these steps:

1. Using an almanac or Web search tools, find information on the popular vote for Republican, Democrat, and independent candidates for your state in each election. If there is more than one independent candidate, add together all the votes for all independent candidates. Collect data from 1980 through the most current presidential election. Divide the research assignment evenly so that both you and your partner gather the data.

2. Create a worksheet to hold your data. In column A, enter **1980** in one cell and then enter **1984** in the cell below it. Use AutoFill to add the remaining presidential election years up to and including the most recent presidential election.

3. Create columns for Republican, Democrat, and Independent candidates. Input the data you have gathered.

4. Add a column to your worksheet and title it **Winning Party**. Insert the political party of the candidate who won each election nationally. Use the AutoComplete feature and/or the AutoFill feature to insert parties if the same party won two or more consecutive presidential elections. Which party won most often in the years you tracked?

CRITICAL THINKING

ACTIVITY 17–1

Open **Earnings** from your solution files and scroll down past row 76. Keep scrolling. The number of rows appears to be endless. Scroll across the worksheet past column T. Keep scrolling. Again, the number of columns appears to be endless. Is there a limit, or can you create an infinite number of columns and rows? Do some exploring and find out how many columns and rows are available in a worksheet.

 # ONLINE DISCOVERY

Search online for banks in your area that offer online banking services. Create a list of the services that are provided among the banks. Then, contemplate the pros and cons of online banking from the customer perspective.

LESSON 18

Organizing and Enhancing Worksheets

■ OBJECTIVES

Upon completion of this lesson, you should be able to:

- Hide and unhide columns and rows.
- Freeze and unfreeze columns and rows.
- Create, rename, and delete worksheets.
- Merge cells and format cell contents.
- Add borders and shading to worksheet cells and apply built-in cell styles and table Quick Styles.
- Sort and filter data in a worksheet.
- Change the page setup of a worksheet and add headers and footers.
- Customize the print options.

■ VOCABULARY

cell style

filter

freeze

header row

sheet tab

split

table style

■ DATA FILES

To complete this lesson, you will need these data files:

Step18-1.xlsx

Step18-3.xlsx

Project18-1.xlsx

Project18-2.xlsx

Project18-3.xlsx

A key feature of Microsoft Excel is the ease with which you can organize the data in a worksheet. You can change the appearance of the spreadsheet to emphasize specific data using formatting, and you can sort the information to highlight significant data. You will also find it useful to print completed worksheets, and there are many options you can use to make your printed spreadsheets intelligible and professional looking.

2-3.1.1
2-3.1.2
2-3.1.4
2-3.1.10

Managing Worksheets

One of the advantages of working with electronic spreadsheets is that you can keep expanding the rows and columns, and then you can keep adding data. Eventually, though, as the spreadsheet grows in size, locating the data becomes more tedious. In this lesson you will learn how to manage worksheets so you can access data more efficiently.

Hiding and Unhiding Worksheet Data

▶ **VOCABULARY**

header row

A *header row* contains column headings or field names in a data source, such as a table or spreadsheet. In Excel, the header row provides labels which identify the content in the worksheet columns. Effective column headings make it easy to identify information in a worksheet. When navigating through a large worksheet, though, the header row sometimes scrolls out of view, which makes it difficult to continue to identify the data in the cells or locate the correct cell so you can input data accurately. One option to overcome this problem is to change the zoom setting. However, if you need to reduce the magnification significantly, you won't be able to read the data. Another option is to hide some of the rows and columns so you can focus on a particular range of data. When you hide rows and columns, the data remains intact; it's just not visible on the screen. You can access these settings in the Zoom group and the Window group on the View tab shown in **Figure 18–1**.

FIGURE 18–1   The Zoom and Window groups on the View tab

Step-by-Step 18.1

1. Open **Step18-1** and save the workbook as **Payroll1**.

2. Notice that the headings in the header row identify the years from 1995 to 2014. The labels in the first column provide employee numbers.

3. Press **F5** to open the Go To dialog box. Enter **K50** and click **OK** to move to that cell. Notice that you can no longer see the column headings at the top of the screen, so you cannot identify what year the money was earned.

4. Select the cell range **K50:N58**. Click the **View** tab and then, in the Zoom group shown in **Figure 18–1**, click the **Zoom** button.

5. Note that the default Zoom setting is 100%. Click to change the magnification setting to **50%** and click **OK**. If necessary, scroll up to show the top row in the spreadsheet. The content in the cells is much smaller now, but you can see the labels for columns K, L, M, and N, as well as the employee numbers in column A. The row numbers and column letters are highlighted, which makes it easier to identify the employee numbers and years.

6. With the cell range selected, click the **Zoom to Selection** button. The selected cells are magnified and fill the entire document window. Click the **100%** button to reduce the magnification and return to the default settings.

7. Depending on the size of your screen, you may not see the first column which shows the employee numbers, in which case you cannot identify the employee. Press and hold **Ctrl** and press **Home** to move back to cell A1.

8. You want to see the earnings for the years 2009 through 2014, so you can hide the columns for 1995–2008. Select columns **B** through **O**. Click the **Home** tab and then, in the Cells group, click the **Format** button.

9. Under Visibility, point to **Hide & Unhide** and then click **Hide Columns**. Column P showing 2009 data is now the second column on the screen, but when you scroll down, you see no cell contents appear in that column until row 51. You can also hide the rows above row 51.

10. Select rows **2** through **50**. Click the **Format** button, point to **Hide & Unhide**, and then click **Hide Rows**. Now you can quickly access the data for the years 2009 through 2014.

11. Save the changes to the workbook. Then, save the workbook as **Payroll2**.

12. Select columns **A** through **U**. Click the **Format** button, point to **Hide & Unhide**, and then click **Unhide Rows**. All 76 rows are now visible again.

13. With the columns still selected, click the **Format** button, point to **Hide & Unhide**, and then click **Unhide Columns**. Deselect the columns. All the cells in the worksheet are now visible.

14. Go to cell **A1**. Save the changes and leave the workbook open.

Freezing Rows and Columns

▶ **VOCABULARY**

freeze

split

Another way to keep rows and columns visible as you navigate a worksheet is to freeze them. When you *freeze* columns and/or rows, you lock them so you can keep an area visible as you scroll through the worksheet. By freezing rows and columns, you don't have to hide any data. An alternative way to freeze rows and columns is to split a worksheet, which divides the worksheet into two panes. You can *split* the worksheet horizontally so the panes appear on the screen one above the other, or you can split the worksheet vertically so the two panes appear side by side on the screen. This way you can show different data in each pane.

Step-by-Step 18.2

1. If necessary, open **Payroll2** from your solution files. Click anywhere in row 2. Click the **View** tab and then, in the Window group, click the **Freeze Panes** button.

2. Click **Freeze Top Row**. The top row is now locked, and a thin black border appears at the bottom of the row. Scroll down to row 76. Notice as you scroll down through the rows in the worksheet the column headings in the header row do not disappear.

3. Click anywhere in column B. Click the **Freeze Panes** button and then click **Freeze First Column**. The first column is now locked and a thick black border appears on the right side of the column. Also notice that the border line no longer appears below the header row. The first row in the worksheet is unlocked because the command was to lock only the first column.

4. Scroll across the screen to column U. Notice as you scroll across the columns in the worksheet that the first column with the employee numbers does not disappear.

5. Click the **Freeze Panes** button and then click **Unfreeze Panes**. The column is unlocked.

6. Click cell **B14**. To lock both rows and columns, click the **Freeze Panes** button and then click **Freeze Panes**. A thick black border appears at the bottom of the row above the active cell and on the right side of the column to the left of the active cell. Scroll down and across the worksheet. Column A and rows 1 through 13 are locked.

7. Save the changes to the workbook, and then save the workbook as **Payroll3**.

8. Click the **Freeze Panes** button and then click **Unfreeze Panes**. Go to cell **A1**.

9. To split the worksheet into two panes, point to the split box at the top of the vertical scroll bar shown in **Figure 18–2**.

Mouse pointer positioned over split box on vertical scroll bar

Split box on horizontal scroll bar

FIGURE 18–2
The split boxes on the vertical and horizontal scroll bars

10. When the pointer changes to a double-headed arrow as shown in **Figure 18–2**, click and drag the split box to the bottom of row 10. Release the mouse button.

FIGURE 18–3
A worksheet split into two panes

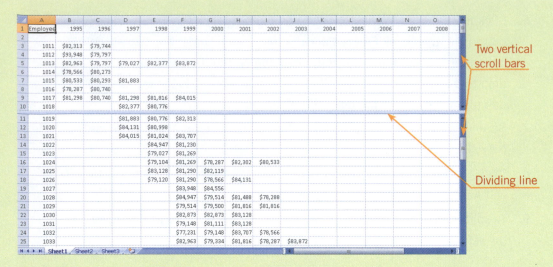

11. Your screen should look like **Figure 18–3**. Notice there are two vertical scroll bars: one for the top pane and one for the bottom pane. Use the scroll bars, the arrow buttons, or the mouse wheel to navigate in the top pane. Click in the bottom pane and scroll. The same content appears in both panes.

12. Double-click the dividing line to remove it.

13. Point to the split box at the right side of the horizontal scroll bar and drag it to the border line between columns B and C to divide the worksheet into two panes, side by side. Double-click the dividing line to remove it.

14. Leave the workbook open.

HEADS UP

You can also insert a new worksheet by clicking the **Insert** button arrow in the Cells group on the Home tab and then clicking **Insert Sheet**. When you use this button, the tab for the new worksheet will appear to the left of the active worksheet.

Working with Multiple Worksheets

Excel is useful for organizing data into categories, such as time frames, sales regions, or account names. When a spreadsheet grows to a large size, you can organize related information in multiple worksheets. A well-organized worksheet presents the data logically, and the rows, columns, and worksheets are labeled effectively.

Compare the workbook to a three-ring binder with tabs. When you need to add a new topic to the binder, you add a new tab to the binder. When you need to add a new category to an Excel workbook, you click the Insert Worksheet button at the bottom of the screen, and a *sheet tab* appears at the bottom of the screen for quick and easy access to the worksheet. At any time, you can rename the tabs in the binder, and at any time you can rename the sheet tab. When you no longer need the category, you can remove the information and the tab from the binder. Likewise, when you no longer need a worksheet, you can delete it from the workbook.

Step-by-Step 18.3

1. If necessary, open **Payroll3** from your solution files.

2. Click the **Sheet2** tab at the bottom of the screen. The blank worksheet Sheet2 opens.

3. Click the **Insert Worksheet** tab  at the bottom of the screen, as shown in **Figure 18–4**. A sheet tab for the new worksheet appears to the right of the last sheet tab. Excel automatically assigns the name *Sheet* and a sequential number to each new worksheet.

Insert
Worksheet
button

Sheet tabs

Sheet1   Sheet2   Sheet3

FIGURE 18–4
Tabs for managing worksheets

4. Sheet4 is now the active worksheet. Click the **Home** tab and in the Cells group, click the **Delete** button arrow, and then click **Delete Sheet**. The Sheet4 tab disappears. Right-click the **Sheet3** tab and click **Delete** in the shortcut menu. The Sheet3 tab disappears.

5. Click the **Sheet2** tab and hold the mouse button. The pointer changes to a sheet, and a down-pointing arrow appears at the upper-left corner of the sheet tab. Drag the sheet tab to the upper-left corner of the Sheet1 tab and then release. The order of the sheet tabs is rearranged.

6. Double-click the **Sheet2** tab. The tab name is selected. Enter **Employees** and press **Enter**. The tab name is replaced with the new name.

7. Double-click the **Sheet1** tab, enter **Earnings**, and press **Enter**.

8. Open **Step 18-3** from the data files. Select the range **A1:D51**. In the Clipboard group, click the **Copy** button. A marquee surrounds the copied cells.

9. Click the **Payroll3** spreadsheet button on the task bar. Then click the **Employees** sheet tab. Click cell **A1**, and then, in the Clipboard group, click the **Paste** button. The copied data from the Step18-3 worksheet is pasted into the Employees worksheet.

10. At the lower-right corner of the pasted cells, you will see the Paste Options symbol 📋. Point to the symbol and a ScreenTip and a list arrow will appear. Click the list arrow and you will see several options for formatting pasted contents.

11. Click the **Keep Source Column Widths** option. The width of the columns is adjusted for the cell contents. Deselect the cells.

HEADS UP

If you delete a tab for a worksheet that contains data, a prompt will appear indicating that the worksheet may contain data and asking if you want to permanently delete the data.

12. Click the **Step18-3** spreadsheet button in the task bar. Press **Escape** to remove the marquee from the selected cells. Deselect the cells and close the workbook.

13. Save the changes to the Payroll3 workbook and then close the workbook.

2-3.1.3
2-3.1.4
2-3.1.5
2-3.1.6
2-3.1.7
2-3.1.8
2-3.1.10

Formatting Cell Contents

Common uses of spreadsheets include reporting finances, managing expenses and budgets, and tracking student grades. An effective spreadsheet is well-organized and well-formatted, with consistent formatting of similar elements. Formatting the contents of a cell, like formatting in other Office applications, changes the way it appears. You can control the font styles, font sizes and colors, and you can apply attributes such as bold and italic.

When you delete the contents of a cell using the Delete key or the Backspace key, the formats for the cell remain in the cell. Therefore, if you enter new data in the cell, the existing formats will apply to the new contents. To remove the contents and the formats, you need to clear the cell. You can clear the contents and the formats from the cell, clear only the contents, or clear only the formats.

Merging Cells

There will be times when you want text to span across several columns. To do this, you can merge cells and combine several cells into a single cell. You can use merged cells to create a title or other informational text for your worksheet. The Merge & Center button in the Alignment group on the Home tab automatically centers the text in merged cells.

Changing Font Styles and Sizes

You learned in the lessons about Word that a font is the design of the typeface in your document. Fonts are available in a variety of styles and sizes, and you can use multiple fonts in one document. The font size is a measurement in points that determines the height of the font. Bold, italic, underline, and color formats can also add emphasis to the contents of a cell. When you move or copy all the data in a cell, the formats are also moved or copied.

Step-by-Step 18.4

1. Open a new blank workbook. Save the workbook as **Billing1**.

2. In cell A1, enter **Utilities Billing History for 2012** and then press **Enter**.

3. Cell A2 is the active cell. Enter **End of Billing Period**. Press **Tab** and enter **Charges**.

4. Select all the columns and double-click the right border of the last column heading to AutoFit the column widths for the cell contents.

5. Select the range **A1:C1**. Click the **Home** tab, and then, in the Alignment group shown in **Figure 18–5**, click the **Merge & Center** button. The three cells are combined into a single cell, and the existing text in cell A1 is centered in this modified cell A1.

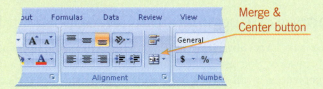

FIGURE 18–5
Alignment options for cell values

6. The semitransparent Mini toolbar does not appear above an active cell, but you can right-click the active cell to open the toolbar. Use the Mini toolbar or the buttons in the Font group on the Home tab to change the font to Cambria, 14 point. Also, apply the bold format.

7. Select the range **A2:B2**. Change the font to Cambria, 12 point and apply a red font color. The contents in cell B2 now extend beyond column B. Excel does not automatically adjust the column when you change the contents of the column. AutoFit the width for column B.

8. Click cell **B2** and press **Delete** to remove the contents. With the cell still active, enter **Amount Paid**. Deselect the cell. The new text is formatted Cambria 12 point font in red. When you clear the contents of a cell, the formats applied to the contents of that cell are not removed. AutoFit the width for column B again.

9. Select the range **A2:B2**. In the Editing group shown in **Figure 18–6**, click the **Clear** button. Click **Clear Formats**, and then deselect the cells. The font is restored to the default setting, Calibri 11 point font.

10. Select the range **A2:B2**. Change the font to Cambria 12 point and apply the italic format. Deselect the cells.

11. Save the changes and leave the workbook open.

Changing Alignment and Wrapping Text in Cells

By default, Excel aligns text at the left of the cell and numbers at the right side of the cell. However, you can also center the cell contents. You can adjust the alignment of the content of a cell vertically as well. Your choices for vertical alignment are top, middle, and bottom. You will find buttons for all of these settings in the Alignment group on the Home tab. You will also find some other interesting options, such as orientating text at an angle within the cell, and decreasing the margin between the edge of the cell and the cell contents. Also, if the text doesn't fit on one line, you can allow the text to wrap to new lines within a cell.

Step-by-Step 18.5

1. If necessary, open **Billing1** from your solution files. Save the workbook Billing1 as **Billing2**.

2. Select the range **A2:B2**. On the Home tab, in the Cells group, click the **Format** button and then click **Row Height**. Enter **100** in the Row height box and click **OK**.

3. With the cells still selected, click the **Center** button in the Alignment group. Then click the **Middle Align** button. White space now appears above and below the heading in the cell.

4. With the cells still selected, click the **Orientation** button in the Alignment group, and then click **Angle Counterclockwise**. The heading is positioned at an angle within the cell.

5. Explore the other orientation settings by clicking the **Orientation** button and then selecting a new option until you have seen all the orientations in the cell. Note also that you can change the cell alignment in the list.

6. Click the **Orientation** button and then click the current highlighted option to toggle the orientation feature off. The cell contents are centered both vertically and horizontally within the cells.

7. Click cell **C2**. Click the **Wrap Text** button 📑 in the Alignment group to apply the format. Then, enter **Percent Increase/Decrease** and press **Enter**. As you enter the text, the contents will wrap to a second and third line inside the cell.

8. Select the range **A2:C2**. In the Cells group, click the **Format** button, click **Row Height**, change the row height to **50**, and then click **OK**. Click cell **C2** and apply the italic format.

9. Click cell **B3** and enter the following data in column B:

384.83

290.44

228.51

219.44

135.59

128.56

209.31

246.16

140.61

195.11

224.59

10. Save the changes and leave the workbook open.

Formatting Numbers and Dates

Generally, numbers are displayed with no formatting and are aligned at the right side of a cell. However, dates are automatically formatted in the default styles (such as *20-Jan-12*). You can easily change the format of number data by selecting the cells and then selecting options from the Number group on the Home tab shown in **Figure 18–7**.

FIGURE 18–7   The Number group on the Home tab

Step-by-Step 18.6

1. If necessary, open **Billing2** from your solution files. Save the workbook Billing2 as **Billing3**.

2. Click cell **A3**, enter **January 20, 2012** and press **Enter**. In spite of how you entered the date, the default setting shows the date as *20-Jan-12*.

3. Enter **February 20, 2012** and press **Enter**. *20-Feb-12* appears in cell A4.

4. Select the range **A3:A4** and then click the **Dialog Box Launcher** in the Number group on the Home tab. The Format Cells dialog box opens showing the Number tab.

5. In the Category list, click **Date** to show the options. In the Type list, click ***Wednesday, March 14, 2001** and then click **OK**. The content in cells A3 and A4 changes to the new format for the two dates you entered.

6. With the two cells still selected, click the fill handle and drag down to cell A14. When you see *Thursday, December 20, 2012* in the ScreenTip on the side of the fill handle, release the mouse button.

7. Select the range **B3:B14**. (Yes, the last cell in the range is blank.) In the Number group, click the **Accounting Number Format** button arrow **$ ▾**. Click **$ English (United States)**. Notice that there is extra white space between the dollar sign and the numbers.

8. With the range of cells still selected, click the **Dialog Box Launcher** in the Number group. In the Category list, click **Currency**. The decimal places should be set at 2, and the sample should show $384.83. Click **OK**.

9. Even though there is no content in cell B14, you applied the format. Click cell **B14** and enter **297.35**. Press **Enter** (or Tab), and the currency format with two decimals is applied to the contents in the cell.

10. Select the range **C3:C14**. Click the **Dialog Box Launcher** in the Number group and under Category, click **Percentage**. If necessary, change the Decimal places number to 2. Click **OK**.

▣ EXTRA FOR EXPERTS

The keyboard shortcut **Ctrl+1** will open the Format Cells dialog box. You can also access the Format Cells dialog box by right-clicking an active cell or range and then selecting **Format Cells** in the shortcut menu.

11. Click cell **C3** and enter **10.66**. As you enter the numbers, the percent symbol appears in the cell. Press **Enter** and continue entering the following data in column C:

9.55

10.25

11.06

−4.51

6.92

8.35

9.12

−6.85

8.35

−1.19

−1.25

12. Click cell **C3** and then, in the Number group, click the **Decrease Decimal** button .00→.0. The number changes to *10.7*. The digit was rounded up to the nearest tenth. Click the **Decrease Decimal** button again. The number is rounded up to *11*.

13. With cell C3 still selected, click the **Increase Decimal** button ←.0.00 twice to restore the number to two decimal places. Deselect the cell.

14. Save the changes, and leave the workbook open.

Adding Shading and Borders

You can emphasize important information in a cell, a row of cells, or a column by applying color, shading, or border formats. You can use the Format Painter to copy the format of a worksheet cell without copying the contents of the cell. For example, after applying a date format in one cell, you may format other cells for dates by painting the format.

Applying Styles

A *cell style* is a set of predefined formats you can apply to some of the worksheet data, such as a header row, a cell showing a total, or cells showing the date and time. To apply a cell style, you must first select a cell or a range of cells to be formatted. Excel offers more than 40 styles in the Cell Styles gallery which enable you to apply quickly multiple formats and ensure that formatting is consistent.

A *table style* is a set of predefined formats that you can apply to all the worksheet data with a single click. When you apply a table style, the selected cells are converted to an Excel table. When you format a range of cells to an Excel table, you can manage, calculate, and format the table data independently of any data outside of the table. You can choose from more than 60 table styles in the Quick Styles gallery. If you don't want to work with the data in a table format, you can convert the table to a regular range and the table style format will remain intact.

▶ **VOCABULARY**

cell style

table style

The cell styles and table styles will override some or all existing formats that you have applied. If desired, you can modify the formats after they are applied, and you can save your own customized styles.

Step-by-Step 18.7

1. If necessary, open **Billing3** from your solution files. Save the workbook Billing3 as **Billing4**.

2. Click cell **C7**. In the Font group on the Home tab, click the **Fill Color** button arrow. Click a red color.

3. With cell C7 still selected, double-click the **Format Painter** button in the Clipboard group. Then click cells **C11**, **C13**, and **C14**. The red shading is copied to all three cells. Click the **Format Painter** button (or press Escape) to turn off Format Painter.

4. Go to cell **A1**. In the Font group, click the **Border** button arrow and then click **Bottom Border**. Deselect the cell. A black line is added to the bottom of cell A1.

5. Click cell **A1**, and then, in the Styles group, click the **Cell Styles** button. The Cell Styles gallery of predefined styles, shown in **Figure 18–8**, opens. If you do not see the Cell Styles button, click the More button in the Styles group.

FIGURE 18–8
The Cell Styles gallery

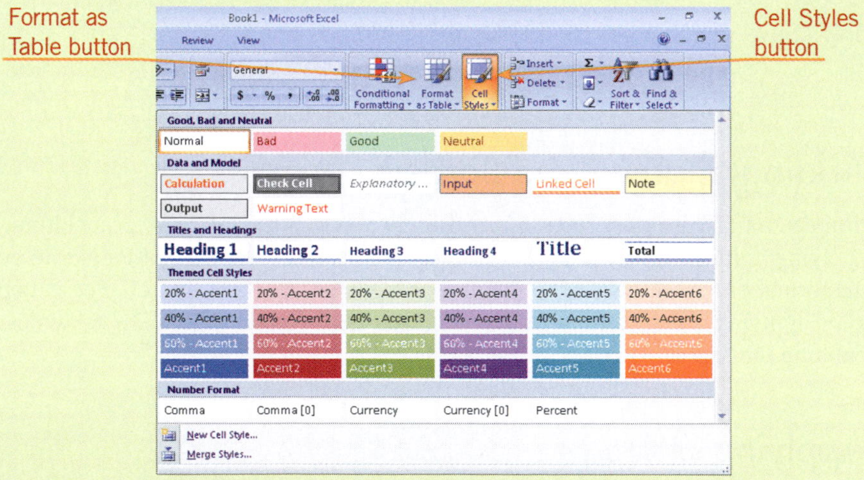

6. Click the **Heading 2** cell style. Deselect the cell. The border line you just applied is replaced with the Heading 2 cell style format.

7. Select row 2, click the **Cell Styles** button, and then click the **Heading 4** cell style. Deselect the row. The style is applied to row 2.

8. Select the range **A2:C14**. In the Styles group, click the **Format as Table** button. The Quick Styles gallery opens. In the Medium group, click **Table Style Medium 2**, the second option in the first row. The Format As Table dialog box opens.

9. The dialog box shows the range of the selection. Make sure the check box for My table has headers is enabled so the header rows will show different formats. Click **OK**.

10. Notice that the Table Tools Design tab now appears on the Ribbon when the table is selected. You can access the Quick Styles gallery by clicking the More button in the Table Styles group.

11. Deselect the cells. The worksheet is formatted as a table similar to **Figure 18–9**. Some shading is added to the cells, but the red fill color in the four cells in column C remains.

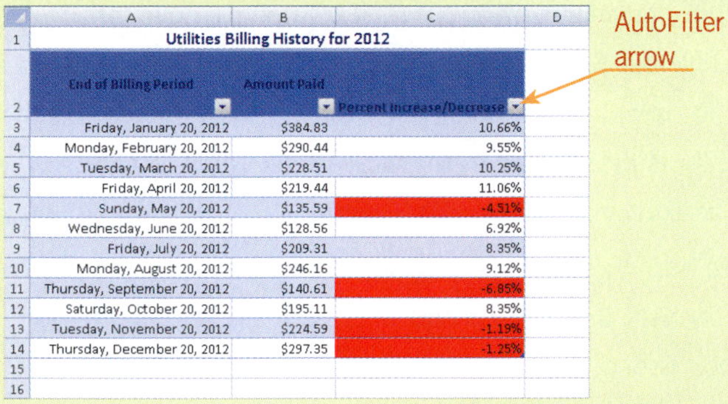

AutoFilter arrow

FIGURE 18–9
Worksheet data formatted as a table

12. You will see there are arrows in the header row, as shown in **Figure 18–9**. You will learn more about using these AutoFilter arrows in the next section. Click cell **C2**, and on the Home tab, in the Alignment group, click the **Middle Align** button.

13. To convert the table back to a range, click the **Table Tools Design** tab, and in the Tools group, shown in **Figure 18–10**, click the **Convert to Range** button. Click **Yes** to confirm that you want to convert the table to a normal range.

Convert to Range button

14. Save the changes and leave the workbook open.

HEADS UP

An alternate way to convert table cells back to a normal range is to right-click the table and in the shortcut menu, point to **Table**, and then click **Convert to Range**. Click **Yes** to confirm.

FIGURE 18–10
The Tools group on the Table Tools Design tab

2-3.2.1
2-3.2.2

▶ **VOCABULARY**
filter

Sorting and Filtering Data

Spreadsheets can function as basic databases. You can sort the data and numbers in the columns. To sort worksheet data, you must indicate the column on which you want to base the sort. If the worksheet has multiple columns of data, you can base the sort on data in as many as three different columns. For example, you can sort the worksheet contents first by the column C data, then by column A data, and then by column B data.

In addition to sorting data, you can filter worksheet data. When you *filter* data, you screen data that matches specified criteria. The data that does not meet the criteria is hidden, and only the data that meets the criteria will show.

Step-by-Step 18.8

1. Open **Billing4** from your solution files. Save the workbook Billing4 as **Billing5**.

2. Click anywhere in column B. On the Home tab, in the Editing group, click the **Sort & Filter** button. Click **Sort Smallest to Largest** to arrange the data so the lowest amounts paid are at the top of the column. The data is rearranged in the worksheet. Rows 1 and 2 were not included in the sort.

3. To sort by multiple criteria, you must open the Sort dialog box. Click the **Sort & Filter** button and then click **Custom Sort**. The Sort dialog box opens.

4. Under Column, in the Sort by box, click the list arrow and then click **Percent Increase/Decrease**. In the Sort On box, the box should already show the option **Values**. In the Order box, click the list arrow and then click **Largest to Smallest** to sort the data with the highest value at the top of the column.

5. Click **Add Level** in the dialog box. A Then by box appears under Column as shown in **Figure 18–11**. Click the list arrow and click **Amount Paid**. The Sort On option should be set to **Values**. Under Order, click the list arrow and click **Largest to Smallest**. With these settings, if two percentages are the same, the order will be determined by the Amount Paid in column B.

FIGURE 18-11
Sort options for multiple columns

6. Click **OK** to accept the settings. Look at rows 8 and 9. Both rows show *8.35%* in Column C, so the order is based on the data in Column B. The row with the amount *$209.31* was placed above the row with the amount *$195.11* because the data is arranged from largest to smallest.

7. Save the changes to the workbook. Then, save the workbook as **Billing6**.

8. Click anywhere in the data, click the **Sort & Filter** button, and then click **Filter**. The AutoFilter function is toggled on and the AutoFilter arrows appear again.

9. Click the **AutoFilter** arrow in column A and a submenu opens. Under Date Filters, click (**Select All**) to deselect all the options. Click **March** to filter out all entries which were not in March, and then click **OK**. Only one entry matches the criteria. Notice the row numbers at the left. Rows 3 and 4 and 6-14 do not contain data that meets the criteria so they are hidden.

10. Click the **Sort & Filter** button and then click **Filter** to toggle the AutoFilter feature off. All the rows appear again.

11. Click the **Sort & Filter** button and click **Filter**. Click the **AutoFilter** arrow in column C and then point to **Number Filters**. A submenu opens. Click **Greater Than Or Equal To** in the submenu. The Custom AutoFilter dialog box appears.

12. The insertion point is positioned in the first blank box. Click the list arrow in the box, scroll down the list, and click **10.25%**. Your dialog box should look like the one shown in **Figure 18–12**.

FIGURE 18–12
The Custom AutoFilter dialog box

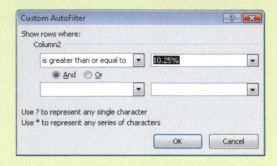

13. Click **OK**. Only those rows with a percentage increase equal to or higher than 10.25% should appear in the worksheet.

14. Save the changes and close the workbook.

2-3.1.9

Formatting the Page Layout

Before you print the worksheet, you will want to look at it in Print Preview to see what it will look like when printed. This can save you time and paper. If the worksheet does not appear correctly on the page, you have several options.

Changing the Page Setup

The Page Break Preview view will show exactly how the worksheet will print. When the worksheet is more than one page in length, Excel determines where to break the page and begin a new one. If you don't like where Excel has split the data between pages, you can create your own page break by dragging the page break to a new location. You can also insert a manual page break in a location of your choice.

Sometimes changing the page orientation will fit all the worksheet data on one page. You will recall that in Lesson 13 you learned that portrait orientation formats the content of the document with the short edge of the page at the top. This is the default setting in Excel. You can change to landscape orientation, which formats the document sideways with the long edge of the page at the top. Another option for fitting the worksheet on one page is to use the Fit to command. The default setting is 100%, and the Fit to command scales the worksheet up or down as necessary so it fits on the number of pages you designate.

> **HEADS UP**
>
> The page setup settings apply only to the current worksheet; they do not apply to all the worksheets in the workbook.

Step-by-Step 18.9

1. Open **Payroll3** from your solution files. Save the workbook Payroll3 as **Payroll4**. If necessary, click the **Employees** sheet tab to make it the active worksheet.

2. Click the **View** tab and then, in the Workbook Views group, click the **Page Break Preview** button ▣ Page Break Preview . If the Welcome to Page Break Preview dialog box appears, click OK. If your worksheet appears on one page, it may be because landscape orientation has been selected, or it may be because scaling has been adjusted to fit the worksheet on one page.

3. Click the **Page Layout** tab, and then, in the Page Setup group shown in **Figure 18–13**, click the **Page Orientation** button and make sure Portrait is selected. Then click the **Dialog Box Launcher** in the Page Setup group to open the Page Setup dialog box, which provides options similar to those in Word. Under Scaling, make sure the Adjust to option is selected and the scaling is 100%. Click **OK** to accept the settings.

FIGURE 18–13
The Page Setup group on the Page Layout tab

4. Two pages appear on the screen. The page border is indicated with a broken blue line. Drag the page border up to row 44 to divide the pages between the 44th and 45th rows.

5. Click the **View** tab. In the Workbook Views group, click the **Normal View** button. Scroll down through the worksheet data and you will see black broken lines below row 44 and to the left of column J indicating the page breaks.

6. Click the **Page Layout** tab. In the Page Setup group, click the **Page Orientation** button, and then click **Landscape**. Scroll down to the bottom of the worksheet data. Because you changed the page orientation there are now two page breaks. The first page break is after row 34 and the second page break is after row 44.

7. Click the **Page Orientation** button and click **Portrait** to return to the default setting. Now there is one page break after row 44.

8. Click anywhere in row 45. In the Page Setup group, click the **Breaks** button, and then click **Remove Page Break**. The page break between rows 44 and 45 is removed, but the worksheet data still does not fit on one page, so there is a new break between rows 47 and 48.

9. Click the **Dialog Box Launcher** in the Page Setup group to open the Page Setup dialog box. Under Scaling, click **Fit to** and keep the default settings of 1 page wide by 1 page tall.

10. Click **OK**. Notice that the dotted line no longer appears after row 47.

11. Click the **Earnings** sheet tab. Click the **View** tab and then click the **Page Break Preview** button and click OK if necessary. Scroll down to see that there are six pages of data in this worksheet.

12. Click the **Normal View** button to return to Normal view. Scroll down, and you will see a page break between rows 47 and 48.

13. Click cell **A31**. Click the **Page Layout** tab. In the Page Setup group, click the **Breaks** button and then click **Insert Page Break**. The dotted lines appear on the spreadsheet to show where the page will break.

14. Save the changes, and leave the workbook open.

Adding a Header and a Footer

Headers and footers are a means of providing useful information on a printed worksheet. A header is printed in the top margin of every worksheet page, and a footer is printed in the bottom margin of every page.

You can manually create a header or footer by entering information in the header or footer pane. Fields can be used to insert dates, times, filenames, the file path, and page numbers automatically. By using the fields instead of manually entering the information, the information is always updated automatically. For example, if you use the date field, whenever you print the worksheet, the date will reflect the current date. You can choose from several built-in headers or footers which are constructed using these fields, or you can create your own customized headers and footers by inserting the fields yourself.

EXTRA FOR EXPERTS

The information provided in the header and footer fields is obtained from the workbook properties and the application and system settings.

Step-by-Step 18.10

1. If necessary, open **Payroll4** from your solution files. Save the workbook Payroll4 as **Payroll5**.

2. Click the **Employees** sheet tab. Click the **View** tab and then, in the Workbook Views group, click the **Page Layout View** button.

3. Click the **Insert** tab. In the Text group shown in **Figure 18–14,** click the **Header & Footer** button.

FIGURE 18–14
The Text group on the Insert tab

Header & Footer button

4. The header pane, which is a row with three cells, appears at the top of the worksheet, and the Ribbon changes to show the Header & Footer Tools Design tab shown in **Figure 18–15**. The middle cell in the header pane is active.

FIGURE 18–15
The Header & Footer Tools Design tab

Footer button

Current Date button

Sheet Name button

5. In the Header & Footer group, click the **Footer** button, and then click **Page 1 of ?**. The predefined field is inserted in the middle cell of the footer pane.

6. At the bottom of the first worksheet page you'll see *Page 1 of 1* in the footer. Press the **Page Down** key. The footer for the second page shows *Page # of 1*, because at this time the page is blank.

7. Scroll to the top of the worksheet and click in the header pane where it says *Click to add header*.

8. Click the cell on the left side of the header row. In the Header & Footer Elements group, click the **Sheet Name** button. The *&[Tab]* field appears in the cell. &[Tab] is a code that refers to the worksheet name.

9. Click the cell on the right side of the header row. Click the **Current Date** button. The *&[Date]* field appears in the cell.

10. Click anywhere in the worksheet. Click the **Office Button**, point to **Print**, and then click **Print Preview** to see the document as it would print.

11. Close Print Preview. Switch to Normal view by clicking the **Normal** view button on the status bar.

12. Save the changes and leave the workbook open.

Customizing Print Options

2-3.1.9

Before you send a worksheet to the printer, take the time to see what the printed copy will look like. This will give you one more opportunity to review the page setup and confirm that the information you want to print will be included in the printed copy. For example, you might expect the printed worksheet to look like what you see on the screen. You are accustomed to seeing the worksheet gridlines, row numbers, and column letters. However, when using the default print settings, these elements will not print.

When you use the Print command, Excel prints the active worksheet with the default print settings. If you don't want to print the entire worksheet, you can identify the range you want to print before you choose the print command. When you create a print area, the print setting is saved with the workbook.

If the worksheet prints on multiple pages, you may want to print the row and/or column headings on every page so the user doesn't need to keep referring back to the first page of the worksheet to identify the cell contents.

You can easily change the print settings using commands on the Page Layout tab.

EXTRA FOR EXPERTS

By default, comments added to worksheets do not print. To print comments, click the **Dialog Box Launcher** in the Sheet Options group on the Page Layout Tab. Then, select one of the options in the Comments box.

Step-by-Step 18.11

1. If necessary, open **Payroll5** from your solution files. Save the workbook Payroll5 as **Payroll6**.

2. If necessary, click the **Employees** sheet tab to make it the active worksheet. Click the **Page Layout** tab.

3. Click the **Dialog Box Launcher** in the Page Setup group to open the Page Setup dialog box. Under Scaling, click **Adjust to**, and change the setting to **100%** normal size. Click **OK** to close the dialog box. The print area is identified with a broken line border on the left side of column J and below row 47.

4. Select the range **A1:B16**. Click the **Print Area** button and then click **Set Print Area**. The print area is modified and identified with a broken line border around the selected range of cells.

5. Deselect the cells. Select the range **A17:B31**. Click the **Print Area** button and then click **Add to Print Area**. The print area is extended.

6. Click the **Office Button**, point to **Print**, and then click **Print Preview**. Only the content in the print area appears in Print Preview. Also notice that the gridlines, row numbers, and column letters do not appear in Print Preview. Close Print Preview.

7. In the Sheet Options group on the Page Layout tab, shown in **Figure 18–16**, the check marks indicate that the settings to view the gridlines and headings are enabled. Click the **Print Gridlines** check box and the **Print Headings** check box so the gridlines and headings will also appear when the worksheet is printed.

FIGURE 18–16
Options for printing gridlines and headings

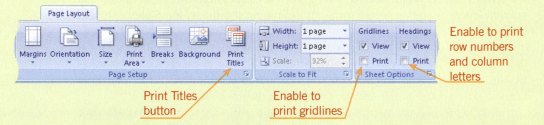

Print Titles button

Enable to print gridlines

Enable to print row numbers and column letters

8. Click the **Office Button**, point to **Print**, and then click **Print Preview**. Now the gridlines and the row and column headings also appear in the print preview. Close Print Preview.

9. You decide it would be best to print the entire worksheet. Click the **Print Area** button and then click **Clear Print Area**. The print area border is removed from the cells.

10. Because all the pages in the worksheet will be printed, you want the column headings to print on each page. Select row 1. In the Page Setup group, click the **Print Titles** button. The Page Setup dialog box shown in **Figure 18–17** opens, showing the options for printing the worksheet.

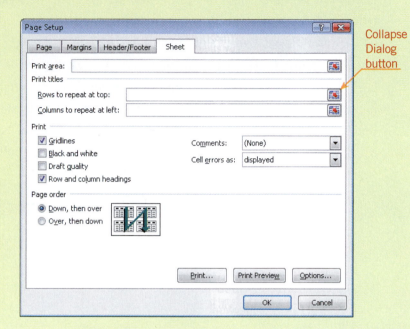

Collapse Dialog button

FIGURE 18–17
Printing options to repeat rows and columns

Stage Technician

Have you ever seen a community theater musical, attended a concert, or enjoyed a touring company's production of a popular Broadway show? The performers on stage couldn't entertain you without the help of a talented group of stage technicians who depend on computer technology to do their jobs in twenty-first century theaters. The lighting, sound, and stage sets of a theatrical production all use specialized computer programs to create the special effects we've become accustomed to seeing. The lighting designer may use a proprietary software application to program the light board, and the production's sound is enhanced with a MIDI (musical instrument digital interface) mixing board that uses sophisticated computer technology to produce digital sound effects, amplified voices, or perhaps even a "virtual" orchestra. The set designer uses a computer-aided drafting program to design the set, and he or she may also employ computer-assisted robotics to move the set pieces during the production.

But stage technicians also use more common types of computer software to do their jobs. For example, the property manager, who tracks the props used in a show, can keep track of hundreds of small items using a database or spreadsheet program such as Access or Excel that identifies which actor uses a prop in which scene, as well as where the prop is stored. The stage manager depends on a note-taking program to keep track of the director's staging instructions. Long-distance collaboration is common, and a designer may work with technicians across the country online to view designs, get input from the design team, and e-mail and send instant messages to quickly contact coworkers as work on a production proceeds.

HEADS UP

You can also quickly access the options to format row and column headings to print on each page while you are working in Print Preview. In the Print group, click the **Page Setup** button to open the Page Setup dialog box. Then, click the **Sheet** tab. Under the Print section, enable the **Row and column headings** check box, and click **OK**.

FIGURE 18–18
The Print dialog box

11. In the Rows to repeat at top box, click the **Collapse Dialog** button ![icon]. Then select row **1**. *$1:$1* appears in the Rows to repeat at top box. Click the **Expand Dialog** button ![icon] to restore the Page Setup dialog box.

12. Click **Print Preview**. Then, in the Preview group, click the **Next Page** button ![Next Page] to see that the headings are at the top of the columns on the second page. Close Print Preview.

13. Click the **Office Button**, point to **Print**, and then click **Print**. A dialog box similar to the one shown in **Figure 18–18** opens. Under Print what, notice the options which allow you to print just a selection or the entire workbook. If you enable the Selection option, only selected cells in the active worksheet will print. If you enable the Entire workbook option, all pages of all worksheets in the workbook will print.

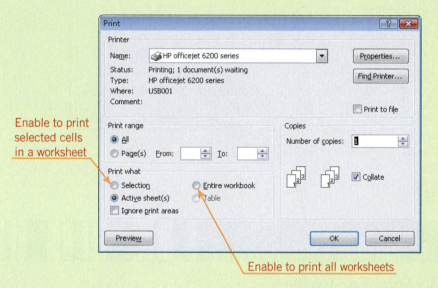

Enable to print selected cells in a worksheet

Enable to print all worksheets

14. Click **Cancel** to close the Print dialog box. Save the changes and close the workbook.

SUMMARY

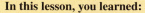

In this lesson, you learned:

- To keep the header row in view when navigating through a large worksheet, you can change the zoom setting. If that doesn't work because the worksheet is too large, you can hide some of the rows and columns so you can focus on a particular range of data, or you can freeze some rows and columns.

- You can delete or add one or several worksheets to a workbook, and you can rename each worksheet.

- There are many options available for formatting cell contents, including merging cells, changing font styles and sizes, changing the alignment within the cells, and applying number and date formats.

- To enhance the appearance and highlight data within the worksheet, you can add borders and shading to cells. There are also many predefined styles available that you can quickly apply to give the worksheet a professional look and make reading the data easier.

- To organize worksheet data numerically or alphabetically, you can sort the data based on a single column, or you can sort the data based on multiple criteria. To screen data that meets certain criteria, you can filter the data.

- You can change the page orientation or use the Fit to feature to fit all the data on one page.

- Headers and footers can be added to worksheets to provide information such as the source and date of the data.

- You can control the print output by inserting page breaks manually or creating a print area for the worksheet. With the default settings, the gridlines and row and column headings appear on screen in worksheets but they do not appear when the worksheets are printed. You can change the settings to hide these elements on the screen and/or include them in printed worksheets.

- Before you print, you can preview the worksheet to see what it will look like when it is printed. You can choose to print the active worksheet only, or you can choose to print all worksheets in the workbook.

VOCABULARY REVIEW

Define the following terms:

cell style	header row	table style
filter	sheet tab	
freeze	split	

REVIEW QUESTIONS

TRUE / FALSE

Circle T if the statement is true or F if the statement is false.

T   F   **1.**   When you create a print area, the print setting is saved with the workbook.

T   F   **2.**   With default settings, numbers are generally aligned at the left side of a cell and text is aligned at the right side of the cell.

T   F   **3.**   When worksheet rows and columns are hidden, the data remains intact.

T   F   **4.**   A workbook can contain a maximum of three worksheets.

T   F   **5.**   When you delete the contents of a cell using the Delete key or the Backspace key, the formats are also deleted.

MULTIPLE CHOICE

Select the best response for the following statements.

1. To span text across several columns, _____.

   A. split several cells   C. merge several cells

   B. insert a header row   D. create a header

2. Using default settings, _____ will print.

   A. gridlines   C. row numbers

   B. column letters   D. cell styles

3. When use the split box on the horizontal scroll bar, _____.

   A. some of the worksheet data is hidden

   B. none of the worksheet data is hidden

   C. the worksheet data appears in two panes, side by side on the screen

   D. the data in the row or column can temporarily scroll out of view

4. The header and footer fields can provide automatic updates for _____.

   A. the date   C. the file path

   B. the filename   D. all of the above

5. To sort worksheet data, you must indicate the _____ on which you want to base the sort.

   A. criteria   C. column

   B. row   D. heading

FILL IN THE BLANK

Complete the following sentences by writing the correct word or words in the blanks provided.

1. The _____ command scales the worksheet up or down as necessary to fit the worksheet data on the designated number of pages.

2. To keep a row and/or column visible as you navigate a worksheet, you can _____ the row and/or column.

3. To format cell content on multiple lines, you need to apply the _____ format.

4. To switch to a different worksheet in a workbook, click the _____ at the bottom of the screen.

5. When you _____ data, only the data that meets the criteria will show.

◼ PROJECTS

PROJECT 18–1

1. Open **Project18-1** from the data files. Save the workbook as **Classes**.

2. Someone has mistakenly formatted the class numbers with 1000s separators. Use the Clear command to clear only the formats from cells B2:B7. Then center all the numbers in the column.

3. Insert a new column to the left of column B. The new column will be very wide since it defaults to the width of the column before it. Do not be concerned. You will adjust the width later. In cell B1, enter the column heading **Fee**.

4. In cell B2, enter **120**. Format this number for Currency with no decimal places and center the number in the cell.

5. Fill down to cell B7 with the number and format in cell B2. AutoFit the column width.

6. Select the range **D2:G7** and format the cells so the contents align at the right.

7. Insert a new row above the header row. Merge and center cells A1:H1 and enter the heading **Language Classes**.

8. Change the new heading text to Arial 16 point font. Apply a light green shading to the new heading cell.

9. Select the range **A2:H2**. Apply the italic format and increase the font size to 14 point. AutoFit all column widths.

10. Apply the All Borders format to the range A1:H8.

11. Change the page orientation to landscape.

12. Change the settings so the worksheet row numbers and column letters will print.

13. Look at the worksheet in Print Preview to make sure it will print correctly on the page.

14. Close Print Preview, save the changes, and close the workbook.

PROJECT 18–2

1. Open **Project18-2** from the data files. Save the workbook as **Tutoring**.

2. Click cell **A3** and copy the cell contents to the Clipboard. Select the cell range **A4:A8** and paste the copied cell. Then click cell **A9** and copy and paste the cell contents in the range A10:A11. Continue to copy the dates to complete the data in column A.

3. Change the format for the range A3:A47 to the 3/14 date format.

4. To make it easier to find information about the students, sort the data in the worksheet. Create a custom sort and specify a sort by last name, from A to Z, and then by date, from oldest to newest.

5. Add a custom header to the worksheet that includes the current date at left, the filename in the middle, and the page number at the right. Return to Normal view.

6. Select the cell range **A3:H47**. Apply Table Style Medium 11 from the Quick Styles gallery. Because you did not select the header row cells, there are no headers in the table.

7. Convert the table to a normal range.

8. Use Format Painter to copy the format in cell A3 to cell A2. Then copy the format in cell B3 to the range B2:H2. Then hide row 3.

9. Click cell **A1** and apply the Outside Borders border format.

10. Preview the worksheet. Notice that it does not fit on one page. Close Print Preview.

11. Click the **Page Layout** tab and change the margin setting to Wide and change the page orientation to landscape.

12. In Page Break Preview, change the page break so the second page begins with row 29 (*Harris Patrick*). Switch to Page Layout view.

13. Save the changes and close the workbook.

PROJECT 18–3

1. Open **Project18-3** from the data files. Save the workbook as **Structures**.

2. Rename Sheet1 in the workbook as **Towers**. Rename Sheet2 in the workbook as **Buildings**.

3. Click the **Towers** sheet tab and sort the worksheet data based on the structure name from A to Z.

4. Select all the data in the Buildings worksheet data. Create a custom sort, first based on the number of stories from largest to smallest and then based on the year completed from largest to smallest.

5. Insert a new worksheet and rename the worksheet **Structures**.

6. Switch to the Buildings worksheet and copy all the worksheet data to the Clipboard. Switch to the Structures worksheet, and with the cell A1 selected, paste the copied data. Keep the source column widths. Deselect the pasted text and press **Escape** to cancel the marquee around the copied text on the Buildings worksheet.

7. Switch to the Towers worksheet and copy all the data in the range A2:E21 to the Clipboard. Switch to the Structures worksheet, click cell **A13** and paste the copied data. Deselect the pasted text and press **Escape** to cancel the marquee around the copied text on the Towers worksheet.

8. Sort the data in the Structures worksheet based on the height in feet, from largest to smallest.

9. Drag the column boundary to set the width for column D to **7.00** and then set the width for column E to **12.00**. Select cells **D1** and **E1** and apply the format to wrap the text in the cells.

10. Hide column F. Then set the print area for the range A1:E26.

11. Switch to the Towers worksheet. Deselect the range of cells and filter the text in column C (country) by showing all the text equal to China. Toggle off the filter feature.

12. Switch to the Structures worksheet. Freeze the top row and the first column in the worksheet.

13. Rearrange the sheet tabs so they appear in this order: Buildings, Towers, Structures.

14. Save the changes and close the workbook.

TEAMWORK PROJECT

Worksheets are excellent tools to organize information so you can make easy comparisons between sets of data. For this project, assume you need to set up a home office with new communications equipment. Because you're not yet sure of your budget, you need several price options for each piece of equipment. With a teammate, gather and organize information as follows:

1. Identify a list of at least 10 pieces of equipment that a state-of-the-art home office needs. Some of these may be a desktop or laptop computer, an all-in-one printer that includes scanning, copying, printing, and faxing functions, a wireless phone, and so on.

2. Create a worksheet to organize the list of equipment you identify. Create a header row with the column headings *Item, Low End, Moderate*, and *High End* so that you can enter descriptions for each equipment item.

3. Using computer catalogs or Web resources, find low-end, moderate, and high-end options for each equipment item. For example, low-end options for a copier would include 10 pages per minute, black-and-white copies, and automatic-document feeder. Moderate options for a copier would include 20 pages per minute, color printing, scanning, and faxing. High-end options would include 30+ pages per minute, sorting, collating, and stapling. Divide the research work so that you find information on half of the items and your teammate finds information on the other half. Enter your results in one worksheet.

4. Format the worksheet so that you can clearly see all data you have entered. Highlight cells, rows, or columns with color fill, shading, or borders to indicate the items you think are most important. Compare your worksheet with those of other teams to see what equipment items are considered most important for a home office.

CRITICAL THINKING

ACTIVITY 18–1

While previewing a worksheet before printing, you notice that the worksheet data doesn't always fill the page. The worksheet is positioned in the upper-left corner of the page, and there's a lot of white space on the right side and bottom of the worksheet. Is there a way you can format the worksheet to print in the middle of the page? Use the Excel Help screens to find an answer.

ONLINE DISCOVERY

There are many Web sites that provide unit converters so you can convert measurements, weights, currency, temperatures, speed, and much more. Search the Internet for *online unit converters* to find a site where you can convert feet to meters. Open your solution file **Structures** and save the workbook as **Tall Structures**. Add a new column to the Buildings worksheet and label the column with the heading *Height in Meters*. Use the online unit converter to convert the data in the Height in Feet column from feet to meters. Enter the conversion results in the meter column, and then save the changes. Cite your Web source by copying and pasting the URL in cell E14 and the current date in cell E15.

LESSON 19

Creating Formulas and Charting Data

■ OBJECTIVES

Upon completion of this lesson, you should be able to:

- Understand and create formulas in a worksheet.
- Understand and use relative and absolute cell references.
- Understand and use function formulas.
- Connect worksheets by using formulas with cell references to multiple worksheets.
- Identify and correct formula errors.
- Create a chart from worksheet data.
- Edit chart data and change chart formats and options.
- Interpret data from worksheets and charts.

■ DATA FILES

To complete this lesson, you will need these data files:

Step19–1.xlsx

Step19–4.xlsx

Step19–5.xlsx

Step19–6.xlsx

Step19–7.xlsx

Step19–8.xlsx

Step19–9.docx

Project19–1.xlsx

Project19–2.xlsx

Project19–3.xlsx

Project19–4.xlsx

■ VOCABULARY

absolute cell reference

argument

chart

complex formulas

embedded chart

formula

function formula

mathematical functions

mixed cell reference

operand

operator

order of evaluation

relative cell references

statistical functions

One of the primary uses of a spreadsheet is to solve problems that involve numbers. The worksheet is often used to complete complex and repetitious calculations accurately, quickly, and easily. Instead of using a calculator to perform mathematical calculations, Excel will perform the calculations for you. And you can create a chart to present the data in a way that is easily understood.

Working with Formulas

The equation used to calculate values in a cell is known as a *formula*. A formula uses numbers and cell references to perform calculations such as addition, subtraction, multiplication, and division. A formula consists of two components: an operand and an operator. The *operand* is a number or cell reference. The *operator* is a symbol that indicates the mathematical operation to perform with the operands. For example, in the formula =B5+6, the operands are B5 and 6; the operator is the plus sign. **Table 19–1** lists some of the mathematical operators used in Excel.

IC³

2-3.1.2
2-3.2.4
2-3.2.7
2-3.2.8

▶ **VOCABULARY**

formula

operand

operator

complex formulas

order of evaluation

TABLE 19–1   Operators used in Excel

OPERATOR	SYMBOL
Addition	+ (plus sign)
Subtraction	– (minus sign)
Multiplication	* (asterisk)
Division	/ (forward slash)
Percent	% (percent sign)

▶ **HEADS UP**

In Excel, use the hyphen key in the number row on the keyboard or on the number keypad to create the minus sign in a formula. You can find all the mathematical operator symbols except % on the number keypad.

All Excel formulas begin with the equal sign. This tells Excel that you are entering a formula instead of a numeric value. A formula can be as simple as a single cell reference. For example, if you enter the formula =B3 in cell C4, the cell will show the same contents as cell B3. If you then change the value in cell B3, cell C4 will automatically be updated to reflect the change.

Formulas containing more than one operator are called ***complex formulas***. For example, the formula =A4*B5+10 will perform both multiplication and addition. The sequence used to calculate the value of a formula is called the ***order of evaluation***. Multiplication and division are performed before addition or subtraction, and then calculations are performed from the left side of the formula to the right side. You can change the order of evaluation by using parentheses; calculations enclosed in parentheses are performed first. Be sure you position the parentheses correctly when you structure a formula. For example, =8/(4-2) equals 4, while =(8/4)-2 equals 0.

Table 19–2 provides examples to demonstrate the order of evaluation.

▶ **HEADS UP**

When creating formulas, there must be a closing parenthesis for every opening parenthesis. Otherwise, an error message will appear when you enter the formula.

TABLE 19–2   Examples of order of evaluation

FORMULA	RESULT
=8+4*4	8 + 16 = 24
=8*4+4	32 + 4 = 36
=(8+4)*4	12 * 4 = 48
=8-4/4	8 – 1 = 7
=8/4-4	2 – 4 = -2
=(8*4)-(4/4)	32 – 1 = 31

Computer users often make the mistake of assuming that the formula will always deliver correct results. However, computers do not evaluate or assess the worksheet values. The information is simply processed, and the worksheet results are only as good as the data and formulas that are entered. If you input an incorrect formula, or if you input invalid data, the formula produces a false result—often referred to as "Garbage In, Garbage Out" (GIGO).

Creating and Editing a Formula

Generally, cell references are used in formulas rather than the actual value in the cell. That way, if the value in the cell changes, the formula does not need to be updated. There are two ways to enter a cell reference into a formula: you can enter the cell reference, or you can click the cell. When entering the cell reference, the column letter can be entered in either uppercase or lowercase. In the Step-by-Steps in this text, the column letters you will enter are shown in lowercase, while those you click are shown in uppercase.

You can edit a formula the same way you edit text and data in cells.

Step-by-Step 19.1

1. Launch Excel and open **Step19–1** from the data files. Save the workbook as **Order1**.

2. Click cell **D2**. Enter **74.95**, which is the value of the quantity (5) multiplied by the unit price (14.99).

3. Click cell **A2** and enter **6** and press **Enter**. Because the quantity changed, you need to update the line total. Click cell **D2** and enter **89.94**.

4. The original quantity was correct. Click cell **A2**, enter **5**, and then press **Enter**. Instead of updating the line total manually, you can insert a formula that will calculate the results and automatically adjust to changes in the data.

5. Click cell **D2**. Enter **=a2*c2**. Compare your screen to **Figure 19–1**. Notice that cell A2 has a blue border and cell C2 has a green border. The color of the cell matches the color of the cell reference in the formula. Also, notice that the formula appears in both the cell and the formula bar.

FIGURE 19–1
Entering a formula in a cell

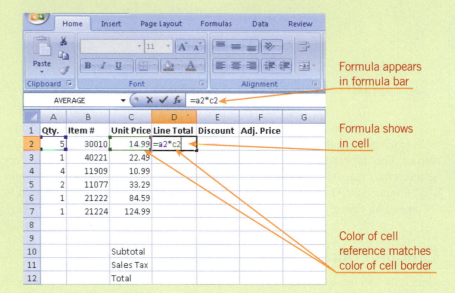

6. Press **Enter** (or click the Enter button on the formula bar). Cell D3 is the active cell and the formula bar is empty. The result of the formula *74.95* appears in cell D2.

7. Click cell **D2**. To see the formula, the cell must be active, and then you can view the formula in the formula bar.

8. Click cell **D3**. Enter **=**. Then click cell **A3**. Notice that the cell reference A3 now appears following the equal sign in both the formula bar and in cell D3.

9. Enter * and then click cell **C3**. Both the cell and the formula bar now show the formula *=A3*C3*.

10. Press **Enter**. The result *22.49* appears in cell D3.

11. Click cell **A3** and change the number to **10**. Then press **Enter**. Notice that the result in cell D4 changes to *224.90* to reflect the increase in quantity.

12. Click cell **D4**. Enter the formula **=a3*c3** and then press **Enter**. The result *224.90* appears in cell D4. Notice that this is the same number that appears in cell D3 because even though the formula is in row 4, the cell references are for cells in row 3.

13. Click cell **D4** and press **F2**. Change the 3s to 4s in the formula, and press **Enter**. The result *43.96* appears in cell D4.

14. Save the changes and leave the workbook open.

Using Relative and Absolute Cell References

By default, when you create formulas, the cell references are formatted as *relative cell references*, which means when the formula is copied to another cell, the cell references will be adjusted relative to the formula's new location. This automatic adjustment is helpful when you need to repeat the same formula for several columns or rows.

There are times, though, when you don't want the cell reference to change when the formula is moved or copied to a new cell. For example, you may be calculating a discount rate on a purchase order. The prices should always be multiplied by a fixed amount to calculate the discount. To create this formula, you format an *absolute cell reference* which does not change when the formula is copied or moved to a new location.

To create an absolute cell reference, you insert a dollar sign ($) before the column letter and/or the row number of the cell reference you want to stay the same. For example, =A1 is a formula with an absolute reference to cell A1.

A cell reference that contains both relative and absolute references is called a *mixed cell reference*. For example, you can have an absolute column reference and a relative row reference. Or, you can have a relative column reference and an absolute row reference. For example, =$A1 is a formula with a mixed cell reference. The column reference is absolute and the row reference is relative. When formulas with mixed cell references are copied or moved, the row or column references that are preceded by a dollar sign will not change. However, the row or column references that are not preceded by a dollar sign will adjust relative to the cell to which they are moved.

2-1.3.2
2-3.2.3
2-3.2.4

HEADS UP

You can use the AutoFill command to copy a formula to a range of cells.

▶ **VOCABULARY**

relative cell references

absolute cell reference

mixed cell reference

EXTRA FOR EXPERTS

You can toggle a cell reference from relative to absolute to mixed. Position the insertion point in or next to the desired cell reference in the formula bar. Each time you press **F4**, the cell reference will change. For example, the cell reference A1 toggles to A1, then to A$1, then to $A1, and then back to A1.

Step-by-Step 19.2

1. If necessary, open **Order1** from your solution files. Save the workbook Order1 as **Order2**.

2. Click cell **D4**. Drag the fill handle down to cell **D7**. AutoFill copies the formula in cell D4 to cells D5, D6, and D7, and the results appear in each of the selected cells.

3. Click cell **D4**. Notice the formula bar shows =A4*C4. A4 and C4 are relative cell references.

4. Click cell **D5**. Notice the formula bar shows =A5*C5. When you filled the formula down, Excel automatically changed the cell references from A4 and C4 to A5 and C5.

5. Click cell **E2**. Enter **=d2*c14** and press **Enter**. The cell reference C14 is an absolute cell reference.

6. Click cell **E2** and fill down the formula through cell **E7**. Click cell **E3**. Notice that the formula bar shows *=D3*C14*. The relative cell reference changed to show the new row number, but the absolute cell reference did not change.

7. Double-click cell C14 and change the value to **0.10**. Press **Enter** and watch the values in column E. The values will change as the new discount rate is entered.

8. Select the range **D2:D14**. Drag the fill handle to the right to fill across columns E and F. The # symbols appear in columns E and F.

9. Point to the **AutoFill Options** button. Click the down arrow and then click **Fill Formatting Only**. The format is applied, and the values in the Discount column remain unchanged, except that the format now shows only two decimal places.

10. Click cell **F2** and enter the formula **=d2-e2**, and then press **Enter**. Fill the formula down through cell **F7**.

11. Click the **row 4** heading to select the entire row, and then, in the Cells group, click the **Delete Cells** button. Click cell **D6**. Notice that the formula has been updated and the cell references which were for row 7 are now for row 6. Click cell **E6** and notice that the absolute reference to cell C14 has been updated to cell C13.

12. Select **row 6** and then, in the Cells group, click the **Insert Cells** button to insert a new row above row 6.

13. Click cell **D7**. Notice that the formula has been updated and the cell references are now for row 7. Click the **Undo** button to remove the blank row.

14. Deselect the cells. Save the changes and leave the workbook open.

2-3.2.5
2-3.2.6
2-3.2.7

▶ VOCABULARY

mathematical functions

statistical functions

Using Function Formulas

Excel has more than 300 built-in functions for performing calculations. *Mathematical functions* perform calculations that you could perform using a scientific calculator. *Statistical functions* are functions that describe large quantities of data. For example, a statistical function can determine the average of a range of data. Excel provides other types of functions, including trigonometric and logical functions, which are beyond the scope of this course. **Table 19–3** describes some of the most common mathematical and statistical functions available in Excel. There are several methods for entering functions in the worksheet. You can enter an equal sign, the function name, and the argument. Or, if you want help entering the formula, you can use the buttons on the Ribbon.

TABLE 19–3   Common Excel functions

MATHEMATICAL FUNCTIONS	
=PRODUCT	Multiplies values in the specified cells
=ROUND	Rounds the value to the nearest value in one of two ways: with the specified number of decimal places or to the nearest whole number
=ROUNDUP	Rounds the value up to the next higher positive value (or the next negative value away from zero) with the number of specified decimal places
=ROUNDDOWN	Rounds the value down to the next lower positive value (or to the next negative value toward zero) with the number of specified decimal places
=SUM	Adds the values in the specified range of cells
STATISTICAL FUNCTIONS	
=AVERAGE	Totals the range of cells and then divides the total by the number of entries in the specified range
=COUNT	Counts the number of cells with values in the specified range
=MAX	Shows the maximum value within the specified range of cells
=MEDIAN	Shows the middle value in the specified range of cells
=MIN	Shows the minimum value within the specified range of cells

Using the SUM Function

Although it is easy to enter a formula, if the formula consists of several cells, it could take you a long time to enter all the cell references. A shortcut for entering cell references is to name a range of cells. The AutoSum feature enables you to quickly identify a range and enter a formula. When you use the AutoSum feature, Excel scans the worksheet and identifies the most logical column or row of adjacent cells containing numbers to sum.

After identifying the range of cells, the AutoSum feature creates a function formula to calculate the sum of the range. A *function formula* is a special formula that names a function instead of using operators to calculate a result. In this case, the function is SUM. The SUM function formula is the most frequently used type of function formula. There are three components of a function formula: the equal sign, the function name, and the arguments. The equal sign tells Excel that a formula follows. The function name tells Excel what to do with the data. The *argument* is a value, a cell reference, a range, or text that acts as an operand in a function formula, and it is enclosed in parentheses after the function name. You will learn about other function formulas in the next section of this lesson. **Figure 19–2** illustrates an example of a formula containing the SUM function. The equal sign indicates that a formula follows. The function name SUM designates that the values of the five cells included in the argument (B4:B8) will be added.

▶ **VOCABULARY**
function formula

argument

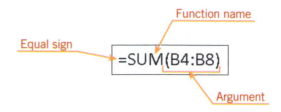

FIGURE 19–2   Parts of a function formula

Step-by-Step 19.3

1. If necessary, open **Order2** from your solution files. Save the workbook Order2 as **Order3**.

2. Click the **Formulas** tab. Click cell **F9**.

3. In the Function Library group, click the **AutoSum** button shown in **Figure 19–3**.

FIGURE 19–3
Options for function formulas

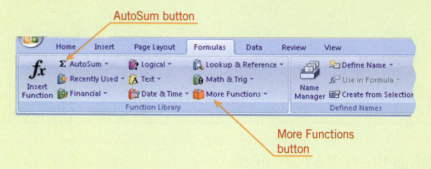

4. A marquee appears around the cell range F2:F8 and proposes the formula =SUM(F2:F8). A ScreenTip also appears showing that the formula involves adding numbers, as shown in **Figure 19–4**. Press **Enter** to accept the formula.

FIGURE 19–4
A proposed SUM function formula

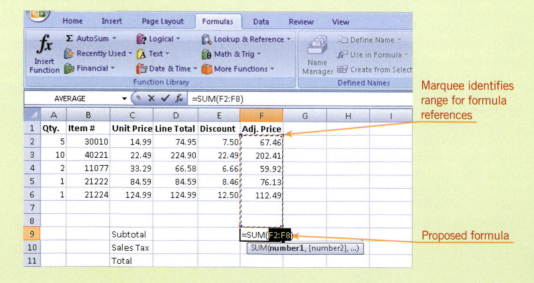

5. The result *518.41* appears in cell F9. Click cell **F9** to show the formula in the formula bar.

6. Click cell **F10**, enter **=f9*(.06)**, and press **Enter**.

7. Click the **AutoSum** button to add the subtotal and the sales tax. Notice that the marquee only surrounds cell F10. Point to the sizing handle on either the upper-left or upper-right corner of the marquee and drag the top border of the marquee up to include cell F9 in the selection.

8. Compare your screen to **Figure 19–5**. Press **Enter** to enter the formula in cell F11. The result *549.51* will show in cell F11.

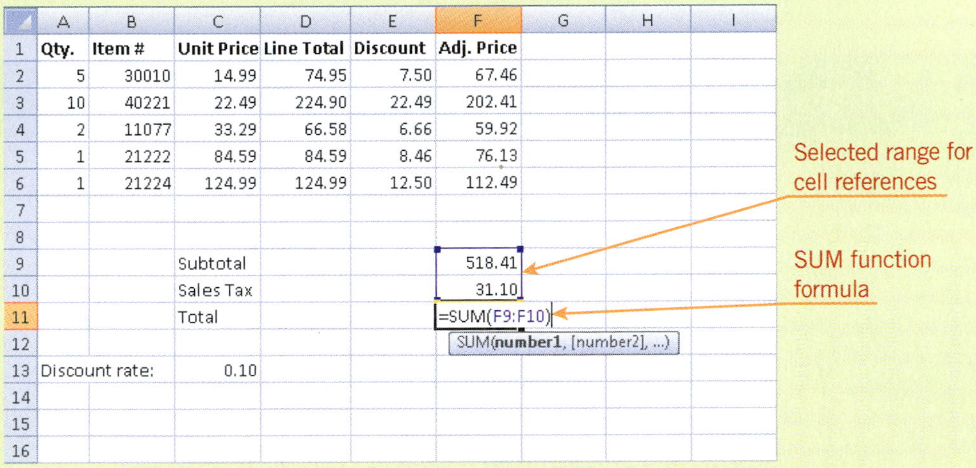

	A	B	C	D	E	F	G	H	I
1	Qty.	Item #	Unit Price	Line Total	Discount	Adj. Price			
2	5	30010	14.99	74.95	7.50	67.46			
3	10	40221	22.49	224.90	22.49	202.41			
4	2	11077	33.29	66.58	6.66	59.92			
5	1	21222	84.59	84.59	8.46	76.13			
6	1	21224	124.99	124.99	12.50	112.49			
7									
8									
9			Subtotal			518.41			
10			Sales Tax			31.10			
11			Total			=SUM(F9:F10)			
12						SUM(**number1**, [number2], ...)			
13	Discount rate:		0.10						
14									
15									
16									

Selected range for cell references

SUM function formula

FIGURE 19–5
SUM function formula

9. Click cell **F10**. Then position the insertion point after the number 6 in the formula in the formula bar and enter **5**. The formula bar should now show *=F9*(0.065)*. Press **Enter**. The result in cell F10 changes.

10. Cell F11 is the active cell. Click the **Home** tab and open the Clipboard pane. If necessary, clear the contents of the Clipboard.

11. Click the **Copy** button. Click cell **A17**, and then click the **Paste** button in the Clipboard group. The result *0.00* appears in cell A17, and the formula *=SUM(A15:A16)* appears in the formula bar. This is because you pasted the formula, and the cells referenced in the formula are empty.

12. Click cell **A18**. Click the **Paste** button arrow and then click **Paste Values**. The result *552* appears in cell A18.

13. With cell A18 still active, click the **Increase Decimal** button in the Number group two times so the entire result will show in the cell.

14. Close the Clipboard pane. Save the changes and close the workbook.

Using the COUNT Function

The COUNT function is a statistical function that shows the number of cells in the argument range that contain numerical values. It is important to distinguish the difference between the COUNT function and the SUM function. The COUNT function tallies the number of occurrences of numerical data, and the SUM function totals all the numerical data.

Like the SUM function, and several other commonly used functions, you can enter the COUNT function by clicking a button on the Ribbon. Another alternative is to open the Function Arguments dialog box, which is very useful when you use functions that are not as common. The Function Arguments dialog box is useful in the process of building a formula that contains a function. Step-by-Step 19.4 will show you how to access this dialog box and the hundreds of built-in functions that Microsoft offers.

EXTRA FOR EXPERTS

When the function formula contains more than one argument, commas are used to separate the arguments.

Step-by-Step 19.4

1. Open **Step19–4** from the data files and save the workbook as **Banquet**.

2. To calculate the number of Chicken orders, click cell **B39**, and then click the **Formulas** tab.

3. Click the **AutoSum** button arrow, and then click **Count Numbers**. The marquee indicates the B36:B38 range.

4. Click cell **B38** and then drag up to cell B5 to select the range B5:B38. Press **Enter**, and the result *10* appears in cell B39.

5. Click cell **C39**. In the Function Library group, click the **More Functions** button 📦 More Functions ▾ . Point to **Statistical**, and a complete list of statistical functions appears. Click **COUNT**. The Function Arguments dialog box shown in **Figure 19–6** opens. Notice that a brief explanation of the COUNT function is provided in the dialog box.

FIGURE 19–6
The Function
Arguments dialog box

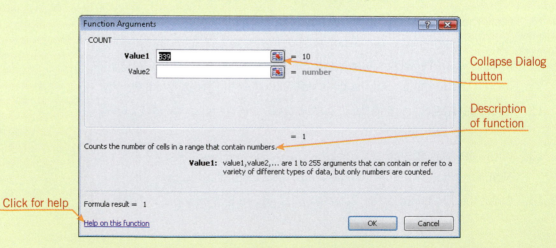

6. A proposed range *B39* appears in the Value 1 text box, which is obviously not correct.

7. Click the **Collapse Dialog** button 📧 at the right side of the Value1 text box. The dialog box minimizes so that you only see its title bar and the range of cells for Value1. The proposed formula also appears in the formula bar.

8. If necessary, drag the minimized dialog box out of the way. Scroll to the top of the worksheet and then select the range **C5:C38**. The formula in the dialog box is updated and now shows the new range you selected. Notice, too, that the formula in the formula bar is also updated.

9. Click the **Expand Dialog** 📧 button next to the Value1 text box (or press Enter). The dialog box is maximized. Click **OK**. The dialog box closes and the result *18* appears in cell C39.

10. With cell C39 still active, drag the fill handle into column D to fill the function formula across the column. The result *4* appears.

11. Deselect the cells. Save the changes and close the workbook.

> **HEADS UP**
>
> Although the intent of the Function Arguments dialog box is to guide you in creating formulas, the dialog box can get in the way when you are creating the formula. That is why the collapse and expand features are available in the Function Arguments dialog box. They allow you to minimize and maximize the dialog box as you work with it.

Using the AVERAGE, MIN, and MAX Functions

The AVERAGE function is also a statistical function. It calculates the average of the range identified in the argument. For example, the function =AVERAGE(B2,G2) calculates the average of the values contained in cells B2 and G2. Notice that in this example, the cell references are separated by a comma instead of a colon. That's because these cells are not adjacent, and only two cells are identified in the range. The comma is used to distinguish the two cell references.

The MIN (minimum) and MAX (maximum) functions are two more statistical functions. The MIN function shows the smallest number contained in the range identified in the argument. The MAX function shows the largest number contained in the range identified in the argument.

> **HEADS UP**
>
> To quickly preview the SUM, AVERAGE, or COUNT function results for a range of cells, select the range of cells. The results for all three functions appear in the status bar at the lower-right corner of the screen.

Step-by-Step 19.5

1. Open **Step19–5** from the data files. Save the workbook as **Weather**.

2. To calculate the average low temperature for the week, click cell **B11** and then click the **Formulas** tab.

3. Click the **AutoSum** button arrow and then click **Average**. The formula *=AVERAGE(B10)* is proposed. Click the formula bar and edit the formula so the argument shows the range **B2:B8**. The revised formula should appear as *=AVERAGE(B2:B8)*.

4. Press **Enter** (or click the Enter button on the formula bar). The result *9* appears in cell B11.

5. To calculate the average high temperature for the week, click cell **B11**. Drag the fill handle to the right to select cell **C11**. The formula is copied to cell C11 and the result *24* appears.

6. Click cell **B12**. Click the **AutoSum** button arrow and then click **Min**. Select the range **B2:B8** and press **Enter**. The result *-2* appears in cell B12.

7. Click cell **C12**. Click the **AutoSum** button arrow and then click **Max**. Select the range **C2:C8** and press **Enter**. The result *31* appears in cell C12.

8. You realize you entered the formula in the wrong cell. Click the **Home** tab. Click cell **C12**, click the **Cut** button, click cell **C13**, and click the **Paste** button. The formula is moved to cell C13.

9. Click cell **D14**. In the Editing group on the Home tab, click the **AutoSum** button arrow Σ ▾, and click **Max**. Press **Enter** to accept the proposed range *D2:D13*. The result *4.8* appears in cell D14.

10. Click cell **B16**. On the Home tab, click the **AutoSum** button arrow and then click **Count Numbers**. Select the range **B2:B8** and press **Enter**. The result *7* appears in cell B16.

11. Save the changes and close the workbook.

2-1.3.2
2-3.1.1

Creating Formulas that Reference Cells in Multiple Worksheets

Excel features enable you to work with multiple worksheets (pages) in three dimensions (3-D). The 3-D reference enables you to access data from three different dimensions in the workbook: length, width, and depth. Length and width refer to the worksheet rows and columns. Depth refers to the ability to connect the worksheets by creating formulas that reference the same cell or range in multiple worksheets. These 3-D references are often used in summary worksheets to condense and total data from other worksheets.

Step-by-Step 19.6

1. Open **Step19–6** from the data files. Save the workbook as **Sales**.

2. Click each worksheet tab to view all five worksheets. You will see that the Western worksheet is not complete. The cell contents for the numbers have not been formatted, and the values in the Difference column have not been calculated. Also, the Summary worksheet needs to be updated with the Western region data.

3. Click the **Central** sheet tab and then click anywhere in the cell range B3:D14, where the content is formatted for currency. With the cells selected, double-click the **Format Painter** button.

4. Click the **Western** sheet tab to switch to that worksheet. Drag the mouse pointer to select the cell range **B3:C14** and copy the number format. Deselect the cells.

5. Click the **Central** sheet tab, and press **Escape** to toggle off the Format Painter.

6. Click cell **D3** and then click the **Copy** button. Click the **Western** worksheet tab and select the cell range **D3:D14**. Click the **Paste** button arrow and click **Paste Special** to open the Paste Special dialog box shown in **Figure 19–7**.

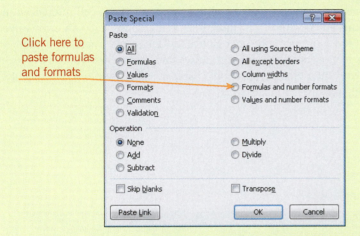

Click here to paste formulas and formats

FIGURE 19–7
The Paste Special dialog box

7. Under Paste, click **Formulas and number formats** and click **OK**. The formula is pasted with the formats.

8. Click cell **B16**. In the Editing group on the Home tab, click the **AutoSum** button. The range B3:B15 should be selected. Press **Enter** to calculate the total goal for the year. Then click cell **B16** and drag the fill handle across cells C16 and D16 to copy the formula.

9. Click the **Summary** sheet tab. Click cell **B7**. Notice the formula bar shows the formula =*Southern!B16*. The cell reference *Southern!B16* refers to cell B16 on the Southern worksheet.

10. Click cell **C8**. Enter **=**. Click the **Western** sheet tab and then click cell **C16**. A marquee surrounds the active cell. Press **Enter**. The value *$402,871* appears in cell C8 in the Summary worksheet.

11. Click cell **D8**. Enter **=**. Click the **Western** sheet tab and then click cell **D16**. Press **Enter**. The value *$871* appears in cell D8 in the Summary worksheet.

12. Take note that the value in cell C8 is $402,871 and the value in cell D8 is $871. Click the **Western** sheet tab and then click cell **C8**. Enter **33,119** and press **Enter**. The cell value is replaced and cells C16 and D16 are updated.

13. Click the **Summary** sheet tab. Notice that the values in cells C8 and D8 have automatically been updated to reflect the edits made on the Western worksheet.

14. Save the changes and close the workbook.

2-3.2.8

Troubleshooting Common Formula Errors

When Excel cannot properly perform a calculation, an error value will appear in the cell where you entered the formula. The error may exist because the cell contains text instead of a numeric value. An error value will appear if the cell referenced in the formula contains an error or if a formula tries to divide by zero. An error value will also appear if the cell is not wide enough to show the result. There are a number of common errors that occur—and common causes for those errors. **Table 19–4** lists these common errors, their typical causes, and some possible solutions. Fortunately, Excel provides help to solve formula errors.

HEADS UP

Excel has an AutoCorrect feature that automatically checks a formula for common keyboarding mistakes. Sometimes Excel is able to identify the error. If so, a suggested correction appears in an alert box.

TABLE 19–4   Common errors, their causes, and solutions

ERROR	TYPICAL CAUSE/SOLUTION
#####	**CAUSE:** Occurs when the column is not wide enough or if a negative date is entered **SOLUTION:** If the column is not wide enough, AutoFit the column or change the number format so that the number will fit within the column; negative dates usually occur when there is an incorrect formula calculating a date, so check and correct your date formula
#VALUE!	**CAUSE:** Occurs when the wrong type of argument or operand is used, which could result from a formula referencing cells with text and the formula requires a number **SOLUTION:** Trace the error to determine which of these is the cause and correct it **CAUSE:** Occurs when a cell reference in the formula refers back to its own cell, either directly or indirectly, creating a circular reference **SOLUTION:** Remove the circular reference or enable repeated recalculations
#DIV/0!	**CAUSE:** Occurs when a number is divided by zero, which is most often caused by using a cell reference to a blank cell or to a cell that contains zero **SOLUTION:** Trace the error and correct the reference
#N/A	**CAUSE:** Occurs when a value is not available to a function or formula, often caused by missing data or by referencing a cell that contains #N/A instead of data (which you can use as a placeholder for data that is not yet available) **SOLUTION:** Trace the error and replace the missing data with a real value **CAUSE:** Can be caused by giving an inappropriate value for a lookup **SOLUTION:** To resolve, make sure the lookup value argument is the correct type of value—for example, a value or a cell reference, but not a range reference

#REF!	**CAUSE:** Occurs when a cell reference is not valid, often caused by deleting cells referred to by other formulas or pasting moved cells over cells referred to by other formulas **SOLUTION:** To correct this error, trace the error and then change the formulas; if you notice the error right after deleting or pasting cells, restore the cells on the worksheet by clicking Undo immediately after you delete or paste the cells which caused the error **CAUSE:** This can also be caused by a link to a program that is not running **SOLUTION:** To resolve the error in this case, start the program to which the worksheet is trying to link
#NUM!	**CAUSE:** Occurs with invalid numeric values in a formula or function, often caused by using an unacceptable argument in a function that requires a numeric argument **SOLUTION:** To correct this, make sure the arguments used in the function are numbers—for example, even if the value you want to enter is $1,000, enter 1000 in the formula **CAUSE:** This error can also be caused by using a worksheet function that iterates, such as IRR or RATE, and the function cannot find a result **SOLUTION:** To resolve the error in this case, use a different starting value for the worksheet function or change the number of times Microsoft Excel iterates formulas
#NULL!	**CAUSE:** Occurs when using a space where it isn't appropriate **SOLUTION:** Check for inappropriate spaces in the formula; for example, when referencing two ranges, make sure a comma separates the ranges: =SUM(C1:C5, D4:D5)

Step-by-Step 19.7

1. Open **Step19–7** from the data files and save the workbook as **Quality Control**.

2. Click **D3**. Enter **=a3/b3** and press **Enter**. *#VALUE!* appears in the cell and there is a small green triangle in the upper-left corner of the cell.

3. Click cell **D3**. An exclamation point within a diamond shape, as shown in **Figure 19–8**, appears next to the cell. This is the Error Checking button, which appears when a cell may contain a formula error.

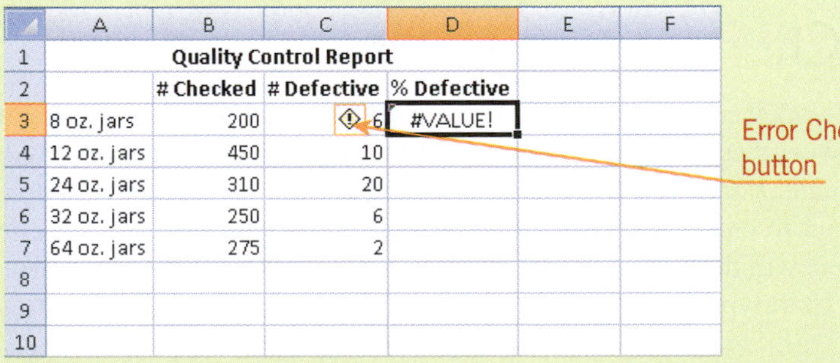

▲	A	B	C	D	E	F
1		Quality Control Report				
2		# Checked	# Defective	% Defective		
3	8 oz. jars	200	⊕ 6	#VALUE!		
4	12 oz. jars	450	10			
5	24 oz. jars	310	20			
6	32 oz. jars	250	6			
7	64 oz. jars	275	2			
8						
9						
10						

Error Checking button

FIGURE 19–8
A formula error notification

4. Point to the **Error Checking** button ⊕ to the left of the active cell, and a ScreenTip will appear describing the error.

5. Click the **Error Checking** button to show the options, and then click **Show Calculation Steps**. The Evaluate Formula dialog box shown in **Figure 19–9** opens. Under Evaluation, the formula appears with the cell values. Now you can clearly see that the problem. You are trying to divide text (*oz. jars*) with numbers.

FIGURE 19–9
The Evaluate Formula dialog box

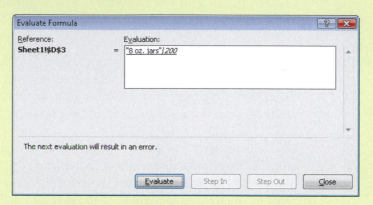

6. Close the dialog box. In the formula bar, change A3 to **D3** so the revised formula is *=D3/B3*.

7. Press **Enter**. A Circular Reference Warning opens. The cell reference *D3* in the formula refers to the cell's own value.

8. Click **OK**. An Excel Help screen opens with information about how to remove or allow a circular reference. Close the Help screen.

9. Click cell **D3**, enter **=c3/b3**, and press **Enter**.

10. Select cell **D3** and click the **Percent Style** button in the Number group. With cell D3 still selected, click the **Increase Decimal** button two times.

11. Drag the fill handle down to cell **D7** to copy the formula and the format. Deselect the cells.

12. Save the changes and close the workbook.

2-1.3.7
2-3.2.9

▶ **VOCABULARY**
chart

Using Charts to Show Data

To translate worksheet data, you can create a ***chart***, which is a graphic representation of your worksheet data. Charts help to make the data more interesting and easier to read and understand. The first step in creating a chart is to decide what type of chart you want to create. Excel provides several options for chart types. The chart type you select will depend on the data you want to represent. **Table 19–5** lists some of the Excel chart types and a description of the types of data you can illustrate with each chart.

TABLE 19–5 Chart types

CHART TYPE	DESCRIPTION
Column chart	Useful in showing changes over a period of time, or for making comparisons among individual items
Line chart	Illustrates trends in data at equal intervals
Pie chart	Compares the sizes of portions as they relate to a whole unit and illustrates that the parts total 100 percent; effective for one data series, such as one column or row of data with one column or row of column and row headings
Bar chart	Helpful when you want to make comparisons among individual items
Area chart	Effective for emphasizing trends because it illustrates the magnitude of change over time
Scatter chart	Illustrates scientific data, and it specifically shows uneven intervals—or clusters—of data
Other Charts	Stock, Surface, Doughnut, Bubble, and Radar

After you decide which chart type to create, the next step is to decide which chart options you want to use. To do this, you must first understand the elements in a chart. **Figure 19–10** identifies the chart elements. Take time to review and become familiar with the various parts.

EXTRA FOR EXPERTS

With the exception of the pie and doughnut type charts, all chart types have a horizontal and a vertical axis.

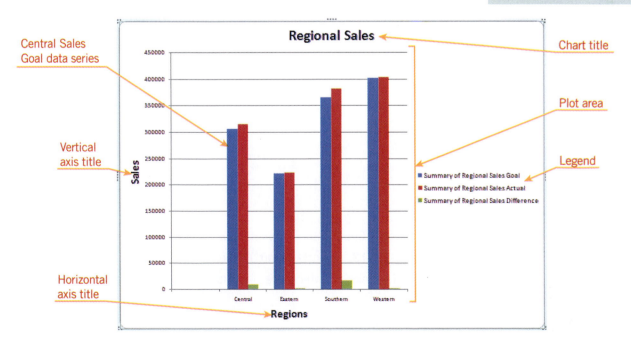

FIGURE 19–10 Chart elements

Creating and Editing a Chart

Excel provides many predesigned chart layouts and styles that make it easy for you to create professional-looking charts. The Labels group on the Chart Tools Layout tab provides several buttons for customizing the table elements such as changing the position of the chart title and the legend.

When creating a chart, you define specific data to be included in the analysis. As a result, you frequently need to select nonadjacent cells. To select nonadjacent cells, click the first cell, press and hold Ctrl, and then click the next cell.

There may be occasions when the data used to create the chart changes after the chart has been created. Fortunately, you do not need to create a new chart. When you edit the data in the worksheet, the chart is automatically updated to reflect the changes. And, if you decide the chart type isn't effective, you can choose a new chart type without starting over.

EXTRA FOR EXPERTS

You can create an instant chart by selecting the data you want to chart and then pressing **F11**. A two-dimensional column chart is created. However, there are no data labels or chart title in this chart.

Step-by-Step 19.8

1. Open **Step19–8** from the data files and save the workbook as **News1**.

2. Select the range **A5:A9** and then press and hold **Ctrl** as you select the range **C5:C9**. Two ranges of data are selected.

3. Click the **Insert** tab. In the Charts group shown in **Figure 19–11**, click the **Column** button.

FIGURE 19–11
Options to change type of chart

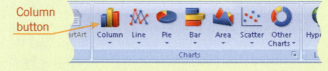

4. Under 3-D Column, click the first option **3-D Clustered Column**. The chart is inserted in a canvas on the active worksheet, similar to how a SmartArt object is inserted in a Word document. Also, the Ribbon adapts to show the Chart Tools Design tab.

HEADS UP

The Chart Tools tabs only appear on the Ribbon when the canvas for the chart is selected.

5. In the Chart Layouts group shown in **Figure 19–12**, click the third option, **Layout 3**. The chart changes to the new layout.

FIGURE 19–12
Options to change chart layout

6. Click the **Chart Tools Layout** tab. In the Labels group shown in **Figure 19–13**, click the **Chart Title** button. Then click **Centered Overlay Title**. The text box which is a placeholder for the chart title is selected.

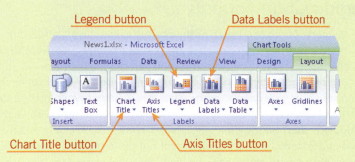

FIGURE 19-13
Options for chart elements

7. Click inside the text box and then select all of the text in the text box. Then, enter **Where People Get the News**. Click outside the text box.

8. Click the **Axis Titles** button and then point to **Primary Horizontal Axis Title**. Then click **Title Below Axis**. A new text box is positioned at the bottom of the chart. Select the text in the text box and enter **Media**. Click outside the text box.

9. You decide a pie chart will communicate the data more effectively. Click the **Chart Tools Design** tab and in the Type group, click the **Change Chart Type** button. The Change Chart Type dialog box shown in **Figure 19-14** opens.

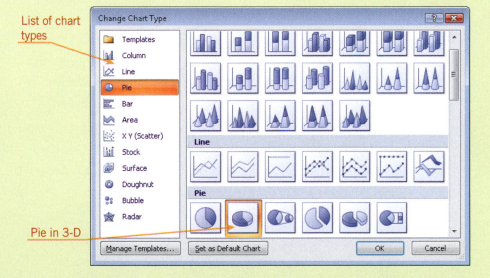

FIGURE 19-14
The Change Chart Type dialog box

10. From the list of chart types, click **Pie**. If necessary, scroll down to view the Pie chart designs. Under Pie, click the **Pie in 3-D** type, and click **OK**.

11. Click the **Chart Tools Layout** tab. In the Labels group, click the **Legend** button and then click **Show Legend at Left**.

12. Click the **Data Labels** button and then click **Best Fit**.

13. You learn that your data for Television and Internet/online are reversed. Click cell **B5**, enter **814**, and press **Enter**. Click cell **B8**, enter **864**, and press **Enter**. As you enter the new data, the values in cells C5 and C8 are updated and the chart is also updated.

14. Save the changes and leave the workbook open.

Changing Chart Formats

Many of the parts of the chart such as the chart title and the axis titles are positioned on the chart in a text box. You can click the part of the chart you want to change, the text box boundaries will appear, and then you can change the formats.

You can choose whether to keep the chart in the same worksheet as the data the chart is based on, or you can move the chart to a different worksheet. An *embedded chart* is a chart created on the same sheet as the data used in the chart. One advantage of embedding a chart on the same page as the data is that the data and the chart can be viewed at the same time. If the chart will not fit on the same sheet with the data, or if you want to create more than one chart from the same data, you will probably want to move the chart to a separate sheet.

▶ **VOCABULARY**
embedded chart

Step-by-Step 19.9

1. If necessary, open **News1** from your solution files. Save the workbook News1 as **News2**.

2. Click anywhere in the chart to select it. Position the mouse pointer over the upper-right corner of the canvas. When the pointer changes to a two-headed arrow, drag the corner of the canvas upward and to the right to increase the size of the canvas. Stop when the canvas is approximately the width of nine columns.

3. Point to any white area above the legend area, and the mouse pointer changes to a four-headed arrow. Click and drag the chart to reposition it on the worksheet. Align the upper-left corner of the canvas with the upper-left corner of cell E7.

4. Click the **Chart Tools Format** tab. With the canvas selected, click the **More** button in the Shape Styles group shown in **Figure 19–15**. Use the live preview to explore the various styles. Click the **Subtle Effect – Accent 1** style (light blue background in the second column).

HEADS UP

The chart is an object, just like a clip art image or a graphic. You can resize the chart by dragging a sizing handle. Be sure to drag a corner handle if you want to resize the chart proportionally.

FIGURE 19–15
Various styles to apply to charts

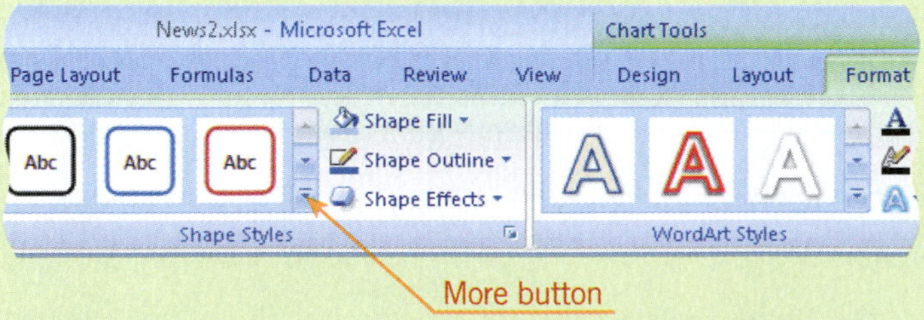

More button

5. Click to select the legend and then right-click to open the Mini toolbar. Change the font size to 12 point.

6. Click the **40%** label on the pie chart. All the labels on the chart are selected. Right-click one of the selected text boxes and change the font size to 18 point.

7. Click **40%** again, and only the 40% text box is selected. Change the font color to white. Format the 8%, 13%, and 38% labels white. Leave the 1% label formatted in the dark font color.

8. Click the **Chart Tools Design** tab and in the Location group, click the **Move Chart** button. The Move Chart dialog box opens. The current setting shows the chart is placed as an object in Sheet1.

9. Click **New sheet** and then click **OK**. A new worksheet is created with the tab name *Chart1*. The chart is moved to the new worksheet, and the chart fills the document window.

10. Save the changes.

11. Launch Word and open **Step19–9.docx** from the data files. Save the document as **Survey**.

12. Click the **News2** workbook button in the taskbar and, if necessary, make Chart1 the active worksheet. Select the canvas, and then press **Ctrl+C** to copy the chart to the Clipboard.

13. Click the **Survey** document button on the taskbar. Position the insertion point at the end of the document and press **Ctrl+V** to paste the chart into the Word document.

14. Save the changes to the Word document. Close the Word application and the Excel workbook.

Interpreting Worksheet and Chart Data

2-3.2.10

Worksheets and charts are excellent means of conveying information. But they can also be confusing or misleading if they are not set up correctly. The more you work with worksheets, the more comfortable and adept you will be at interpreting the data and analyzing charts created from the data.

Drawing Logical Conclusions from Worksheets

The results of a worksheet are only accurate if correct data and formulas have been entered. If you are certain of the accuracy of the content of the worksheet, then the next questions are: What does this worksheet tell me? What logical conclusions can I draw from it?

Obviously a worksheet can contain a great deal of information. The easiest way to summarize that information is to use the tools within Excel to obtain the information required. For example, if you want to know the average of a set of values, you would use the AVERAGE function. When using tools such as this, you can be certain of the results. And there are other ways in which you can draw conclusions from the worksheet. For example, you may notice in a column that the values are continually increasing. If this column is a chronological listing of your company's sales, you could conclude that there is a trend—that your company's sales are increasing each year. On the other hand, if this same column is not a chronological listing of sales, but rather a listing of sales by region, it is not logical to interpret a trend, but you can compare the data for each region.

Interpreting Graphical Data

An attractive chart will grab attention, but it should also convey meaning. Charts are extremely useful for summarizing, clarifying, or highlighting data. In a business, management at all levels must understand the data generated on a daily basis, but upper-level management relies on charts to look for trends and oddities. The charts are only useful, however, when the data used to create the chart is accurate and the values represented in the charts are correctly labeled. When the values and their representation are correct, the chart can help you gain an understanding that would perhaps not be clear when looking at the worksheet.

TECHNOLOGY TIMELINE

Did you know that early electronic spreadsheet programs were the "killer apps" for personal computers? Killer applications are computer programs that are so necessary or desirable that they prove the core value of some larger technology, and as a result, they substantially increase the sales of the platform that they run on.

VisiCalc is considered to be one of the earliest examples of a "killer app." VisiCalc, originally developed in 1978 for the Apple II computer, was one of the early electronic spreadsheet applications, and it spurred the sale of thousands of Apple II platform computers. In 1983, the Lotus Development Corporation released Lotus 1-2-3, a spreadsheet program, which also offered charts and basic database operations. Shortly after Lotus 1-2-3 was released, the IBM PC became the number-one selling computer. Then in 1985, Microsoft released the first version of Excel for the Mac. Two years later, Microsoft released a new version of Excel to run in the Windows environments. This new version of Excel was one of the first applications that Microsoft introduced to run on the Windows operating system, and therefore, it was also one of the first applications developed for a graphical user interface.

SUMMARY

In this lesson, you learned:

- One of the primary uses for Excel spreadsheets is to perform calculations. All formulas begin with =.

- If you do not want the cell reference to change when the formula is moved or copied to a new location, the cell reference must be formatted as an absolute cell reference.

- Functions are special formulas that do not require operators. Excel provides more than 300 built-in functions to help you perform mathematical, statistical, and other functions.

- The AutoSum feature enables you to quickly identify a range of cells and enter a formula. For a range of cells specified in the argument, the AVERAGE function finds the average, the SUM function totals the values, and the COUNT function shows the number of cells with numerical values.

- You can use the MIN and MAX functions to find the smallest or largest number in a range.

- If Excel cannot perform a calculation, an error value and an Error Checking button will appear to alert you to and help you fix the error. Then, you can edit the formula directly in the cell or in the formula bar.

- A chart shows the worksheet data visually and often helps the audience understand and interpret the information more clearly.

- When the worksheet data is changed, the chart is automatically updated to reflect those changes.

- Chart types, formats, and options can be changed at any time, even after the chart has been created.

- Excel worksheets and charts convey information and allow you to draw logical conclusions from the data; but to make a correct assessment, you must ensure that the data is accurate and that you know what the values represent.

VOCABULARY REVIEW

Define the following terms:

absolute cell reference

argument

chart

complex formulas

embedded chart

formula

function formula

mathematical functions

mixed cell reference

operand

operator

order of evaluation

relative cell references

statistical functions

■ REVIEW QUESTIONS

TRUE / FALSE

Circle T if the statement is true or F if the statement is false.

T   F   **1.**   A formula must consist of more than one cell reference.

T   F   **2.**   The Average function is a mathematical function.

T   F   **3.**   Generally, cell references are used in formulas rather than the actual value in the cell.

T   F   **4.**   In the order of evaluation, addition is performed before multiplication.

T   F   **5.**   You can reposition a chart easily by dragging the selected chart to another section of the worksheet.

MULTIPLE CHOICE

Select the best response for the following statements.

1. A(n) _____ cell reference does not change when the formula is copied or moved to a new location.

   A.   absolute   C.   relative

   B.   fixed   D.   embedded

2. The result for the formula =24-(3+3)/2 is _____.

   A.   21   C.   6

   B.   9   D.   12

3. _____ functions describe large quantities of data.

   A.   Mathematical   C.   Logical

   B.   Statistical   D.   Mass

4. A function formula has _____ components.

   A.   two   C.   four

   B.   three   D.   any of the above

5. A _____ chart is effective for emphasizing trends at equal intervals.

   A.   line   C.   scatter

   B.   pie   D.   bar

FILL IN THE BLANK

Complete the following sentences by writing the correct word or words in the blanks provided.

1. A(n) _____ cell reference contains both relative and absolute references.

2. A(n) _____ is a graphic representation of worksheet data.

3. A(n) _____ is a number or cell reference in a formula.

4. A(n) _____ is a symbol that identifies the mathematical operation to perform.

5. A(n) _____ is used to calculate values in a cell.

■ PROJECTS

PROJECT 19–1

1. Open **Project19–1** from the data files and save the workbook as **MPG**.

2. Enter a formula in cell C2 that will subtract the Odometer Start value from the Odometer End value.

3. Copy the formula to the range C3:C11.

4. Enter a formula in cell E2 to calculate the miles per gallon by dividing Total Miles by # Gallons.

5. Copy the formula to the range E3:E11.

6. Enter a formula in cell E13 to calculate the average miles per gallon for the range E2:E11.

7. Save the changes and close the workbook.

PROJECT 19–2

1. Open **Project19–2** from the data files and save the workbook as **Mileage**.

2. Open the July worksheet. Enter a formula in cell D3 to calculate the number of miles driven by subtracting the Odometer Start values from the Odometer End values. Fill the formula down to cover all the days of travel.

3. In the July worksheet, enter a formula in cell E3 to calculate the cost by multiplying the daily miles by the cost per mile. Be sure to create an absolute reference for the cost per mile cell reference. Fill the formula down to cover all the days of travel in the worksheet.

4. Copy the formulas and the format in cells D3 and E3 and paste them to the same cells in the August and September worksheets. (After pasting the cell contents, click the **Paste Options** button arrow and click **Keep Source Formatting**.)

5. Fill the formulas down to cover all the days of travel in the August and September worksheets.

6. In the July worksheet, click cell **D19** and enter a function formula to total all the daily miles in the column. If necessary, create another function formula in cell E19 to total all the expenses in that column. Enter formulas to calculate total daily miles and expenses in the August and September worksheets.

7. In the July worksheet, click cell **C23** and enter a function formula to count the number of days of travel. In cell C24, enter a function formula to calculate the minimum daily miles driven during the month. In cell C25, enter a function formula to calculate the maximum daily miles driven during the month. And in cell C26, enter a function formula to calculate the average daily miles driven during the month.

8. Copy these function formulas to the same cells in the August and September worksheets to perform the same calculations. You will need to adjust the formula in the August sheet to fit the data.

9. You just learned that the cost per mile increased to $0.58 in September. Make this change in the September worksheet only.

10. Open the 3rd Qtr. worksheet and enter cell references for the total miles and expenses from the July, August, and September worksheets. The cell references for July are cells D19 and E19, for August, cells D17 and E17, and for September, cells D19 and E19.

11. In the 3rd Qtr. worksheet, calculate the total miles and the total expenses for the three months.

12. Save the changes and close the workbook.

PROJECT 19–3

1. Open **Project19–3** from the data files and save the workbook as **Trees**.

2. Click the **Eastland Store** sheet tab. Select the range **A5:E12** and create a chart that you think would be most effective for this data.

3. Add a chart title, **Fall Tree Sale.**

4. Add the axis titles **Sales** and **Species** to the appropriate axes.

5. Move the chart so it is positioned below the data on the worksheet.

6. On the Westland Store sheet, create a chart as described in Steps 2 through 5 using the Westland Store data.

7. Click the **Eastland Store** sheet tab, and select the range **F6:F12**. Click the **Copy** button, switch to the Summary sheet, click cell **B5** and then click the **Paste** button. Click the **Paste Options** button and then click **Values and Source Formatting**.

8. Click the **Westland Store** sheet, copy the values in the range F6:F12, switch to the Summary sheet, click cell **C5** and paste the cell values. Change the paste options so the values and source formatting are pasted.

9. In all three worksheets, add a formula to total the revenues for both stores. In the Summary sheet, use the Format Painter to apply the same font format to the new values.

10. In the Summary sheet, select the range **A4:C11** and create an appropriate chart. Add a chart title **Fall Tree Sale** and add a vertical axis for **Total Sales** and a horizontal axis for **Species**.

11. Move the chart so it is positioned on a new worksheet called **Fall Tree Sale**. Increase the font size for the axis labels to 16 point.

12. Save the changes and close the workbook.

PROJECT 19–4

1. Open **Project19–4** from the data files and save the workbook as **Demographics**.

2. Select the range **A2:B7** and create a Stacked Horizontal Cylinder bar chart.

3. Change the chart title to **Centerville Population**.

4. Reposition the chart below the data on Sheet1.

5. Change the 1990 population value to **71,433**. Change the 2000 population value to **72,113**.

6. Change the chart type to a Clustered Bar chart and change the chart title to **Population Growth**. Apply the Style 35 chart style to add some color to the chart.

7. Click cell **F2** and enter the column heading **Population Density**. Format the heading text to wrap in the cell, and adjust the width of the column so the word *Population* appears on one line.

8. Click cell **F3** and enter a formula to calculate the population divided by the area. Decrease the number of decimal places to zero. Fill the formula down for the range F4:F7.

9. Select the cell range **A2:A7** and the range **F2:F7** and create a Clustered Bar chart. Add the horizontal axis title **Population per Square Mile** and apply the Style 35 chart style. Position the new chart below the Population Growth chart.

10. Select the ranges **A2:A7** and **D2:E7** and create a Stacked Horizontal Cylinder chart. Click the **Move Chart** button, and place the chart as an object in Sheet2.

11. On Sheet1, select the ranges **A2:B7** and create a Line with Markers chart. Position the new chart to the right of the Population Growth chart.

12. Select the ranges **A2:A7** and **F2:F7** and create a Line with Markers chart. Position the new chart next to the Population Density bar chart.

13. Create two new line charts based on the Housing Units and Vehicle Registration data:

    a. Select the ranges **A2:A7** and **D2:D7** and create a Line with Markers chart. Position the new chart as an object on Sheet2. Position it below the cylinder chart.

    b. Select the ranges **A2:A7** and **E2:E7** and create a Line with Markers chart. Position the new chart as an object on Sheet2. Position it next to the line chart.

14. Save the changes and close the workbook.

TEAMWORK PROJECT

As you have learned in this lesson, functions can help you analyze data in a number of ways. Excel includes hundreds of functions to help you with financial, statistical, mathematical, and other problems. In this project, explore two functions of your choice with a partner to learn how they can be applied to specific data analysis situations. Make sure your functions are not covered in this lesson. Follow these steps:

1. In a blank Excel worksheet, open the Insert Function dialog box. Review the functions in each category to find two you are interested in exploring with your teammate. (Your functions should come from two different categories.)

2. Read the Microsoft Excel Help files for the functions you have chosen to learn what kind of data the function can analyze and what kinds of information you must supply as arguments for the functions. Consider where this type of data might occur, such as the type of job where you would encounter it.

3. Construct worksheets containing data appropriate for each function and then use the functions to analyze the data.

4. After you are sure you are using the function correctly, make a team presentation to share what you have learned about your functions.

CRITICAL THINKING

Open **Demographics** from your solution files and analyze the charts to answer the following questions:

1. How does the Population Growth chart differ from the Population Density chart?

2. What, if anything, can we learn from the charts comparing houses and vehicles?

3. Compare the charts on Sheet2 that show the data for Housing Units and Vehicle Registration. Why does the comparison of the combined data look different from the data in the line charts?

4. What other questions can be answered with this data?

ONLINE DISCOVERY

There are many online Web sites available to help you find current gasoline prices. Choose four locations around the country (the East coast, the West coast, the Gulf coast, and the Midwest). Track the gas prices daily for at least seven to ten days. Also, track the price of a barrel of oil for each of those days. Enter your data in a spreadsheet, and create a chart to illustrate the data.

LESSON 20

Getting Started with PowerPoint Essentials

■ OBJECTIVES

Upon completion of this lesson, you should be able to:

- Identify the parts of the PowerPoint screen and navigate through a presentation.
- Change the slide view and magnification.
- Manage slides by adding, deleting, duplicating, and reordering them.
- Create a new presentation with effective planning.
- Apply a theme for consistent formatting and styles.
- Edit slide content by moving text and modifying placeholders.
- Work with a slide master to add universal elements for all slides in the presentation.
- Preview a presentation using Slide Show view.

■ VOCABULARY

presentation

slide layout

slide master

slide pane

theme

■ DATA FILES

To complete this lesson, you will need these data files:

Step20–1.pptx

Project20–1.pptx

Project20–2.pptx

PowerPoint helps you create, edit, and manipulate professional-looking slides that you can use to facilitate meetings, supplement classroom learning, and share information using a wide variety of media including graphics, pictures, and audio and video clips. Creating a slide show may seem like an overwhelming task, but PowerPoint provides many features that make that task easy and fun.

2-1.1.2
2-1.2.2
2-1.2.4
2-4.1.12

▶ **VOCABULARY**

presentation

slide pane

Identifying the Parts of the PowerPoint Screen

In PowerPoint, the document file is called a ***presentation***. When you first launch PowerPoint, a new blank presentation file opens. As in other Office applications, you can quickly access the most recently opened presentations by clicking the Office Button. You can search for additional files by using the Open command. In PowerPoint, the Open, Save, and Save As commands you have used in Word and Excel are again available by clicking the Office Button.

The presentation window in **Figure 20–1** shows many familiar parts, including the Ribbon, Quick Access Toolbar, title bar, sizing buttons, Close button, and status bar. Scroll bars appear when the presentation includes more than one slide. The Slides tab shows a thumbnail for each slide in the presentation file. When active, the Outline tab shows the text on each slide and it enables you to organize the content of the presentation. The ***slide pane*** is the area in the presentation window that contains the slide content, and the dotted borders in the slide pane identify placeholders where you can insert text and graphics on the slide. The Notes pane provides space for adding notes to which you can refer while preparing for and giving your presentation.

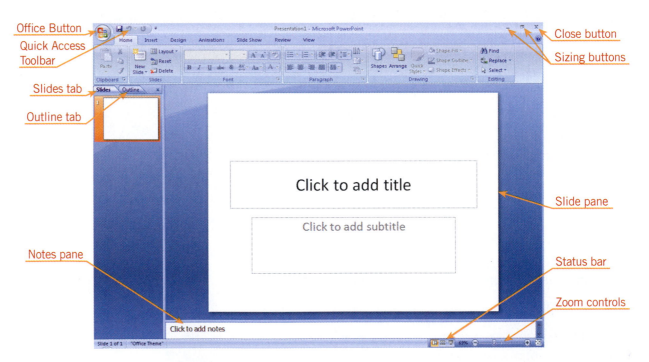

FIGURE 20–1   The PowerPoint application window

Step-by-Step 20.1

1. Launch PowerPoint. A new presentation titled *Presentation1* opens.

2. Compare your screen with **Figure 20–1** to identify the various components of the PowerPoint presentation window and their names.

3. Move the mouse pointer around the application window. When you position the mouse pointer over the Slides tab and the Ribbon, it appears as an arrow. When you position the pointer within the slide pane, it still appears as an arrow, but when you position the pointer over a placeholder, the pointer changes to an I-beam, which indicates you can add text inside the placeholder.

4. If necessary, click the **Maximize** button ☐ to change the size of the window to fill the screen. If the Maximize button does not show in the upper-right corner of the screen, the application window is already maximized.

5. Click the **Minimize** button ▬ in the row of sizing buttons. The application window is minimized. Click the Microsoft PowerPoint presentation button in the task bar to restore the application window.

6. Click the **Restore Down** button ☐ and the application window size is reduced. The Ribbon and the Slides tab adapt to the smaller size. You can drag the title bar to move the application window around on the screen, but you cannot move the slide pane like you can move a worksheet in Excel. You can also point to the window border, and when the pointer changes to a double-headed arrow, you can drag the border to resize the window.

7. Click the **Maximize** button to restore the window to its full size.

8. Click the **Office Button**, click **Open**, and then navigate to where the data files are stored and open **Step20–1.pptx**.

9. Click the **Office Button**, click **Save As**, enter the new filename **3Rs1**, and click **Save**.

10. Leave the presentation open.

Navigating Through a Presentation

2-1.1.3

You can move to a different slide in a presentation by clicking the thumbnail on the Slides tab or by clicking the slide content on the Outline tab. You can also use the vertical scroll bar or the keyboard to navigate through a presentation.

Step-by-Step 20.2

1. If necessary, open **3Rs1** from your solution files. Compare your screen to **Figure 20–2**. Note that slide thumbnails appear on the Slides tab, and the status bar shows *Slide 1 of 8*. A vertical scroll bar appears next to the thumbnails, and there is also a vertical scroll bar on the right side of the window.

FIGURE 20–2
The 3Rs1 presentation window

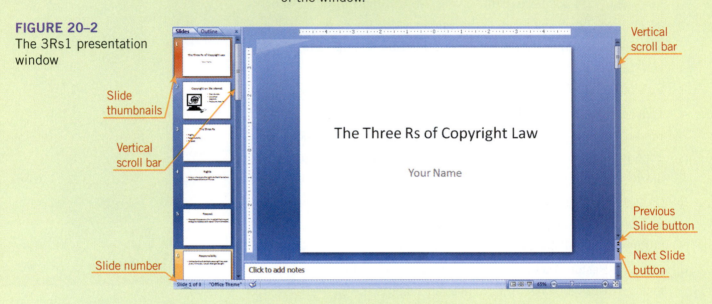

2. Press the **down arrow** key. The slide pane changes to show the second slide in the presentation. Notice that the second slide is now highlighted on the Slides tab.

3. Press **PageUp** to move to the previous slide, and then press **PageDown** to move to the next slide. The second slide is the active slide.

4. On the Slides tab, click the **slide 3** thumbnail. Again, the slide pane adapts and the highlight shows the active slide.

5. Use the scroll bar on the Slides tab to scroll down and show the thumbnail for the last slide in the presentation. Then click the **slide 8** thumbnail.

6. Drag the scroll box up the vertical scroll bar on the right side of the presentation window. As you drag the box, a ScreenTip to the left of the scroll bar shows the title and number of the slide. When you see *Slide: 2 of 8 Copyright on the Internet*, as shown in **Figure 20–3**, release the mouse button. The second slide of the presentation appears in the slide pane, and the slide 2 thumbnail is highlighted on the Slides tab.

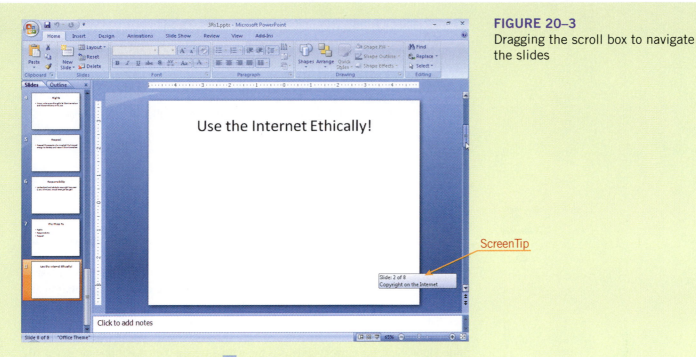

FIGURE 20–3
Dragging the scroll box to navigate the slides

7. Click the **Next Slide** button ⬇ at the bottom of the vertical scroll bar on the right side of the presentation window three times. Each time you click the Next Slide button, you move to the next slide in the presentation. The fifth slide should be active.

8. Click the **Previous Slide** button ⬆ at the bottom of the vertical scroll bar. Each time you click the Previous Slide button, you move to the previous slide in the presentation. The fourth slide should be active.

9. Click the **Outline** tab. All of the text contained on each of the eight slides in the presentation appears in outline form as shown in **Figure 20–4**.

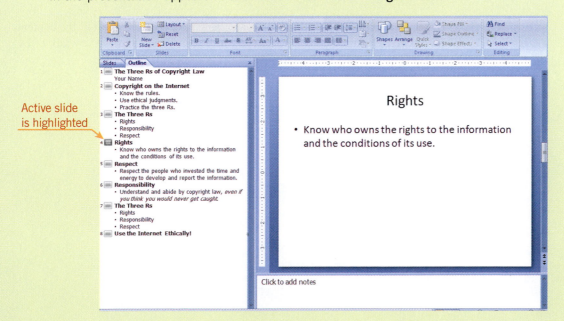

FIGURE 20–4
Outline tab for 3Rs1 presentation

10. On the Outline tab, click the slide 3 title, **The Three Rs**. The slide pane changes to show the content for the third slide.

11. Press **Ctrl+Home**. The first slide becomes the active slide. Press **Ctrl+End** to move to the last slide.

12. Click the **Slides** tab to show the thumbnails again.

13. Leave the presentation open.

2-1.1.5
2-4.1.3

Changing the Slide View

PowerPoint offers four different ways to view your presentation. Normal view is the default view and the one you've seen in PowerPoint so far. You can change the view by clicking the buttons in the Presentation Views group on the View tab shown in **Figure 20–5**. Slide Sorter view gives you an overall picture of your presentation and enables you to rearrange the order of the slides easily. Slide Sorter view also makes it easy to add and delete multiple slides and copy and move slides. In Notes Page view, you can edit your notes and see how the notes will appear when printed. In Slide Show view, the current slide fills the whole screen. You use this view when you present the show to your audience. You will learn more about using Notes Page view and Slide Show view later in this lesson.

FIGURE 20–5   Buttons for changing views

Like other Office applications, you can change the magnification of the content on the screen by using the Zoom button in the Zoom group on the View tab, or by using the zoom controls in the status bar at the bottom of the window.

Step-by-Step 20.3

1. If necessary, open **3Rs1** from your solution files. Press **PageUp** (or PageDown) until slide 3 is the active slide.

2. Click the **View** tab, and in the Zoom group, click the **Zoom** button to show the magnification options. Click **100%** and then click **OK**. The magnification of the slide pane changes.

3. Click the **Fit to Window** button to change back to the default magnification.

4. Click the **slide 2** thumbnail on the Slides tab. Click the **Zoom** button, and if necessary, click 100%. Click **OK**.

5. Click the **Zoom** button, click **66%**, and then click **OK**.

6. Click the **Slide Sorter** view button 🔲 on the status bar in the lower-right corner of the screen. The window changes to show small images (but bigger than thumbnails) of the slides in the presentation. All the slides appear in the window, as shown in **Figure 20–6**. (The layout on your screen may differ somewhat.)

Active slide is highlighted with an orange border

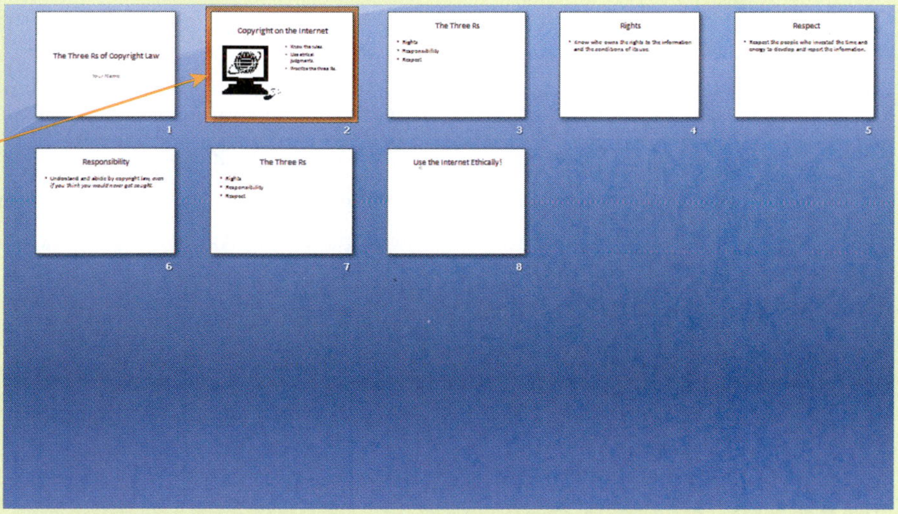

FIGURE 20–6
Slides shown in Slide Sorter View

7. Click the **Zoom** button, click **50%**, and then click **OK**. The size of the slides is decreased, so more slides will fit in the window. When the presentation contains more slides than can fit in the window, a vertical scroll bar appears so you can scroll through all the slides.

8. Click the **Fit to Window** button.

9. Click the **Normal** view button 🔲 on the status bar to return to Normal view.

10. Save the changes and leave the presentation open.

2-1.2.5
2-1.3.2
2-4.1.1
2-4.1.3
2-4.1.7

Managing Slides

As you prepare a presentation, it is common to add new slides, copy slides, and delete slides. It is also common to rearrange the sequence of the slides. You can easily manage the slides in Normal view and in Slide Sorter view.

You can use the Cut, Copy, and Paste commands to copy or move slides. The slide content and designs are stored on the Clipboard. Remember that the Clipboard is a temporary storage place in the computer's memory. You send selected slides to the Clipboard by using the Cut or Copy commands, and then you can retrieve those contents by using the Paste command. You can paste Clipboard items as many times as you want.

You can change the order of the slides by using drag-and-drop editing as well as by using the cut and paste method you used in the last lesson. It may be a little easier to use drag-and-drop editing in Slide Sorter view, where all the slides are arranged in rows in one screen, but you can also rearrange slides in the Slides tab and the Outline tab in Normal view.

Step-by-Step 20.4

1. If necessary, open **3Rs1** from your solution files. Save the presentation 3Rs1 as **3Rs2**. Move to slide 4.

2. Click the **Home** tab. In the Slides group, click the upper portion of the **New Slide** button as shown in **Figure 20–7**. (Do not click the arrow on the button.) A new blank slide is created and placed after slide 4. The slide layout for the new slide is the same as slide 4. Notice that the Slides tab is updated and shows the new blank slide, slide 5.

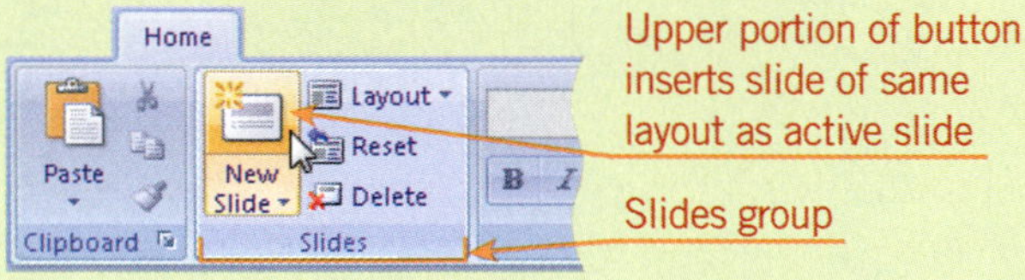

FIGURE 20–7
The Slides group on the Home tab

Upper portion of button inserts slide of same layout as active slide

Slides group

3. Click the upper portion of the **New Slide** button. A new blank slide appears after slide 5. The new slide 6 is the active slide.

4. In the Clipboard group, click the **Copy** button. The blank slide is copied to the Clipboard.

5. Scroll down on the Slides tab, and click between the slide 7 and 8 thumbnails. A flashing red horizontal line will indicate the location of the insertion point. Click the **Paste** button in the Clipboard group. The blank slide is copied to the designated location.

6. Click the **slide 6** thumbnail. Press **Delete**. The slide is removed from the presentation.

7. On the status bar, click the **Slide Sorter** view button. Notice there are two blank slides.

8. Click between slides 4 and 5 to position the insertion point between the two slides. The insertion point will appear as a flashing red vertical line between the two slides.

9. In the Slides group, click the upper part of the **New Slide** button. A new blank slide is inserted between slides 4 and 5. There are now a total of 11 slides in the presentation, and slide 5 is active.

10. Press and hold **Ctrl** and click **slide 6** and **slide 8**. Three slides are highlighted. Press **Delete**. All three slides are removed, and now there are eight slides in the presentation.

11. Click **slide 6**. In the Clipboard group, click the **Cut** button to copy the slide to the Clipboard. Then, click to the left of slide 4 to position the insertion point between slides 3 and 4. The flashing red vertical line should appear to the left of slide 4. Click the **Paste** button and the slide is moved to a new position.

12. The slides are still not in the correct order. Click **slide 4** and drag it to position it between slides 5 and 6. When you see the red vertical line between slides 5 and 6, release the mouse button, and the slides are once again rearranged.

13. Save the changes. Click the **Office Button** and then click **Close** to close the presentation. (If you click the Close button in the application window, the presentation and the application will both close.)

Creating a New Presentation

2-1.2.1
2-1.3.5
2-4.1.2
2-4.1.3
2-4.1.9
2-4.1.12

PowerPoint provides several options for creating a new presentation. You can create a new blank presentation and apply preformatted colors, styles, and layouts. PowerPoint provides several presentation templates which already contain formatted content, which you can modify to customize the presentation for your needs. You can also open an existing presentation, save it with a new filename, and then add and delete slides and edit the existing slides.

When you create a presentation, it is important to keep in mind a few basic principles for effective design. PowerPoint offers so many templates and designs that it is tempting to use many different layouts and formats in your presentation. But if your presentation is too busy, the formatting can detract from your content. You want the design features you choose to emphasize your content, not overwhelm it. Following are a few design guidelines to keep in mind when you are creating a presentation.

- Don't overload a slide with too much content—include only essential information to keep your message clear and concise.

- Select only one or two fonts that are easy to read to use in each slide, and use the same fonts for the same features in all the slides in a presentation to create a consistent appearance.

- Use bullets to present lists of information when the data does not need to be in any particular order.

- Use numbered lists to show the steps in a process or data that should be examined in order.

- Limit the number of special features, such as bullets, graphics, or numbered items, on a single slide.

- Tables and charts can illustrate numerical data or trends, but keep the charts simple and easy to read.

- Use graphics or charts only to highlight relevant information. Don't use graphics just to decorate a slide.

- Add elements such as a company name for consistency from slide to slide.

When you create a new blank presentation, the file opens with one blank slide with a proposed *slide layout*, which refers to the arrangement of the placeholders on a slide. Slide layouts contain text and object placeholders which provide placement guides for adding text, pictures, tables, or charts. You can choose from several different slide layouts. To modify the slide layout, you can resize the placeholders and move them to another position in the slide pane. If you do not use a placeholder, you can leave it blank, or you can delete it. The placeholder will not print or appear in Slide Show view.

To add text to a slide or to manipulate the text on a slide, you must display the slide in Normal view. PowerPoint automatically adjusts the layout if you insert items that don't fit the original layout. For example, if you fill a placeholder with several lines of text and keep entering text, PowerPoint will reduce the font size as needed so all the text will fit inside the text box. If there are not enough placeholders in the slide layout, you can add text boxes.

As you enter text in a placeholder, PowerPoint automatically checks for misspelled words. However, you must also proofread all of your work, because the spellingchecker will not identify all spelling errors. The AutoCorrect feature is also available, and PowerPoint will automatically correct common spelling errors. For example, when you enter "teh" it will automatically be corrected to "the."

The Notes pane provides a place for you to write speaker notes, which you can use to provide reminders about information you want to emphasize. The notes do not appear on the slide when the presentation is shown in Slide Show view. There is plenty of space available for notes, so you can even include the dialogue you want to use when you present the slide show to an audience.

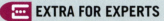
▶ VOCABULARY
slide layout

🖙 EXTRA FOR EXPERTS

You can add words to the AutoCorrect list in the AutoCorrect: English (United States) dialog box. To open the dialog box, click the **Office Button**, click **PowerPoint Options**, click the **Proofing** option, and then click **AutoCorrect Options**.

🖙 EXTRA FOR EXPERTS

In Normal view, you can only add text in the Notes pane. To add graphics or other elements to the speaker notes, click the **View** tab, and then click the **Notes Page View** button. This view also allows you to change the notes layout and background.

Step-by-Step 20.5

1. If necessary, launch PowerPoint. Click the **Office Button** and then click **New**. Then double-click **Blank Presentation** (or click Create).

2. The slide pane shows a layout for a Title Slide. Click the text **Click to add title** in the title placeholder and enter **A New Country,**. Press **Enter**, and then enter **A New Experience**.

3. Click the text **Click to add subtitle** in the subtitle placeholder and enter your first and last names. Notice the font size and color are different. These are the default settings for the presentation title slide.

4. Click the **New Slide** button arrow. The slide layout options shown in **Figure 20–8** appear.

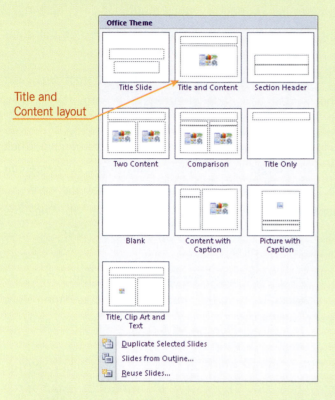

Title and Content layout

FIGURE 20–8
Slide layout options

5. Click the **Title and Content** layout. A new slide is created with two place-holders, as shown in **Figure 20–9**.

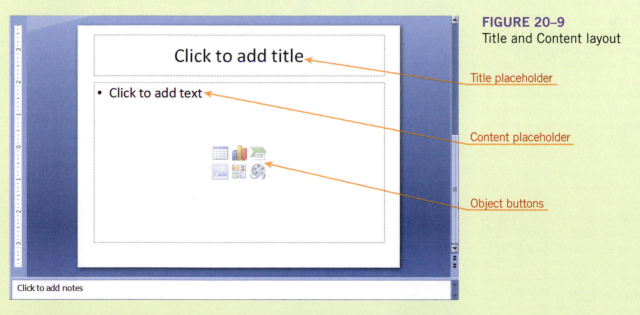

FIGURE 20–9
Title and Content layout

Title placeholder

Content placeholder

Object buttons

6. Click the title placeholder text **Click to add title** and enter **Open your door to the future...**.

7. Move the mouse point over the Object buttons in the content place-holder to see the options. You use these buttons to enter tables, charts, graphics, and video clips, which you will learn about in Lesson 21.

8. Click the content placeholder text **Click to add text** and enter **An international education is important.** and press **Enter**. The line of text is formatted with a bullet. A dimmed bullet appears for the new blank paragraph, but it will not show in Slide Show view if you do not enter text on this line.

9. Enter **Fluency in another language is more important than ever.** and press **Enter**. The second paragraph of text is also formatted with a bullet.

10. In the Notes pane at the bottom of the presentation window, click **Click to add notes** and enter **Begin by asking how many in the audience can speak a foreign language.** and press **Enter**. Notice that the note you entered does not appear in the thumbnail on the Slides tab. Click the **Outline** tab, and you will see that the notes do not appear in the slide outlines either.

11. Click the **View** tab and then click the **Notes Page View** button. The slide pane changes to show an image of the slide with the Notes pane below. This view is better for entering and viewing a long note or editing text in an existing note.

12. Click the **Normal View** button and then click the **Home** tab. Click the **New Slide** button. A new slide 3 opens with the same slide layout as the previous slide. You only need to click the New Slide button arrow when you want to change the slide layout for the new slide.

13. In the title placeholder, enter **Get Involved**. Then enter the following three lines of text in the content placeholder:

    Become a volunteer.

    Become an exchange student.

    Become a host family.

14. Save the presentation as **Global1** and leave the presentation open.

2-4.1.2
2-4.1.5
2-4.1.12

▶ **VOCABULARY**
theme

Applying a Theme

You can easily give your presentation a professional look by applying a *theme*, which specifies a color scheme, fonts, and effects. Each theme has a specific look and feel. The theme you choose for your presentation should reflect the tone of the presentation topic. Moreover, the theme should not detract from the message you want to deliver.

To apply a theme, the presentation must be shown in Normal view. The theme is applied to all the slides, but the content of the slides does not change. You can apply a different theme at any time to change the look of your presentation. If you like a theme, but you don't like the colors used in the design, you can easily change the color scheme of the theme. PowerPoint offers several standard color schemes for each theme. You can apply a new color scheme to all the slides or apply it only to selected slides.

> **HEADS UP**
>
> PowerPoint provides numerous design templates from which you can choose. If you do not find a design in the Themes gallery that meets your needs, you can look for more designs at Microsoft Office Online.

Step-by-Step 20.6

1. If necessary, open **Global1** from your solution files. Save the presentation Global1 as **Global2**. Move to the first slide and show the Slides tab.

2. Click the **Design** tab. In the Themes group shown in **Figure 20–10**, move the mouse pointer over several of the options to see live previews of the themes. The theme name appears in the ScreenTip.

Flow theme

FIGURE 20–10
The Themes group on the Design tab

3. Click the **Flow** theme. The theme is applied to all slides in the presentation, and the slide pane changes to show the updated font styles and colors. A graphic also appears at the top of the slide. You will also notice by looking at the thumbnails on the Slides tab that the first slide in the presentation has a background color, but the other two slides do not. That's because the first slide is formatted as the title slide.

4. In the Themes group, click the **Theme Colors** button to show the built-in color options. Move the mouse pointer over the options to see the live previews. Click outside the color options to leave the color scheme as is.

5. In the Themes group, click the **Theme Fonts** button to show the built-in font options. Use the scroll bar to move down through the list of fonts. Move the mouse pointer over some of the options to see the live previews. Click outside the font options without making any changes.

6. In the Themes group, click the **Theme Effects** button to show the built-in effects. When you move the mouse pointer over the options to see the live previews, you will not see any changes. That's because the theme effects are sets of lines and fill effects, which apply to graphics such as AutoShapes, WordArt, and SmartArt. Click outside the list of options without making any changes.

7. You decide you would like the background color on all slides. In the Background group on the Design tab (shown in **Figure 20–11**), click the **Background Styles** button.

FIGURE 20–11
The Background group on the Design tab

8. The background options shown in **Figure 20–12** appear. The current background style for slide 1 is the highlighted option. Position the mouse pointer over the highlighted style and a ScreenTip will appear showing *Style 7*.

FIGURE 20–12
Background styles

9. Double-click the **slide 2** thumbnail. Click the **Background Styles** button and then click **Style 7**. The background is now applied to slides 2 and 3 and will be applied to all additional slides you add to the presentation.

10. In the Background group, click the **Hide Background Graphics** check box to enable the option. The graphic is removed from the top of the current active slide, but when you look at the thumbnails on the Slides tab, you can see the graphic is still on slides 1 and 3.

11. Click the **Dialog Box Launcher** in the Background group to open the Format Background dialog box. Click **Apply to All** at the bottom of the dialog box. Look at the thumbnails on the Slides tab. The graphic is removed from all slides in the presentation. Close the dialog box.

12. Click **Undo** twice to restore the graphic on all slides.

13. Move to slide 3. Click the **Home** tab and then click the **New Slide** button to add a new slide with the same slide layout. The theme is applied to the new slide.

14. Save the changes and leave the presentation open.

Editing Slides

As you work with a presentation, you will likely want to change the content on one or more of the slides. As you change the content on a slide, you may find you need to change the slide layout and the text formats. You also may want to add some universal elements to all the slides, such as a company name or logo. PowerPoint makes it easy for you to edit and manipulate the text and objects on a slide. If you accidentally delete contents, or if you change your mind, you can undo your edits. You can also redo an undo edit, and you can repeat previous actions.

When you add and edit text, the contents that appear on the Outline tab are automatically updated. You can also change the slide layout to accommodate the text you want to add. The content and formatting will remain intact; only the layout of the slide will change. You may find that if you select a layout that does not have placeholders for all the text and content in the original slide, elements of the slide may overlap. If so, you can move any placeholder and rearrange the elements of a slide.

When you use a theme, the format of the text on each of the slides is predetermined. There may be occasions, however, when you want to alter the text format. You may want to change the font style or point size. Changing the color of the text or changing the font style can add emphasis to the slide content, but be sure you choose the font styles carefully, because sometimes the font style can make it difficult to read text. Use live preview to see the formatting effects before you apply them.

2-1.3.3
2-4.1.2
2-4.1.4
2-4.1.12

Step-by-Step 20.7

1. If necessary, open **Global2** from your solution files. Save the presentation Global2 as **Global3**.

2. Move to slide 3. Select all the text for the first bulleted item **Become a volunteer**. Notice that the boundaries of the placeholder, as indicated by the dashed line and the sizing handles, are selected. The placeholder is a text box.

3. Drag the selected text down and position the insertion point in front of the third bulleted item, then release the mouse button. The text *Become a volunteer* is now the second bulleted item.

4. Click the **Outline** tab. Notice that the text was updated on the Outline tab.

5. On the Outline tab, select all the text for the third bulleted item *Become a host family*. Drag the selected text up so it is the second item in the list. The sequence should now be *Become an exchange student*, *Become a host family*, and *Become a volunteer*.

6. On the Outline tab, select the text **exchange student** and use the Mini toolbar to apply the bold format. Although the new format does not appear on the Outline tab, it does appear in the slide pane. You are overriding the theme format.

7. Select the text **host family** and click the **Repeat** button on the Quick Access Toolbar. Select the text **volunteer** and press **F4** to repeat the bold format edit.

8. On the slide, select the title **Get Involved**. In the Drawing group on the Home tab (shown in **Figure 20–13**), click the **Shape Quick Styles** button. Several styles that fit the theme color scheme appear. Move the mouse pointer over several styles to see the live previews. Then, click **Colored Fill – Accent 3**, the fourth style in the second row.

FIGURE 20–13
The Drawing group on the Home tab

9. In the slide pane, click anywhere in the bulleted list to show the placeholder boundaries. Point to the lower-right corner of the placeholder. When the pointer changes to a double-headed arrow, drag the corner up and to the left until the width of the placeholder does not extend beyond the word *Involved* in the placeholder, as shown in **Figure 20–14**. The placeholder is significantly reduced in size and the lines of text wrap to fit inside the placeholder.

FIGURE 20–14
A modified placeholder

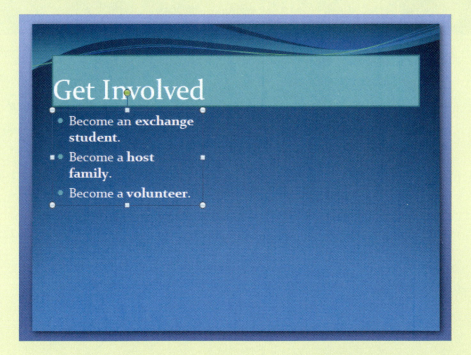

10. The placeholder should still be selected. Point to one of the borders. When the mouse pointer changes to a four-headed arrow, drag the placeholder to the center of the slide.

11. Select all the text for the three bulleted items. In the Paragraph group, click the **Bullets** button arrow 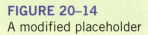 and then click the **Star Bullets** option. The round bullets are changed to star bullets.

12. In the Slides group on the Home tab, click the **Layout** button. Then click the **Two Content** layout style. Now you can add text or an object, such as a picture, on the right side of the slide.

13. In the slide pane, select **Get Involved** and use the Mini toolbar to apply center alignment.

14. Save the changes and leave the presentation open.

TECHNOLOGY CAREERS

Career Communication Skills

Chances are that you have given some thought to the kind of career or job you want when you finish school. Are you interested in entering the corporate world, perhaps as an account manager in a marketing or advertising firm? Or maybe you've always wanted to teach, in a classroom or training workers on the job. If you like science, you may be considering a career as a researcher for a large company or a university. In any of these careers, the individuals most likely to be promoted and succeed have something in common—they have good oral and written communication skills. The ability to make formal presentations is an increasingly important skill for many different occupations. In fact, communication skills can greatly enhance one's success in the classroom or on the job.

Many jobs require that an employee be able to organize, analyze, and communicate information. Moreover, employees are often called on to formally present information. For example, an account manager may use a presentation to "pitch" a new idea to a client. An instructor plans and presents material to other people every day. And a research scientist may be called on to report findings to colleagues, create a presentation on future projects for a grant application process, or even conduct a press conference to introduce a scientific breakthrough! The audience may be as small as one or two coworkers, or it may be a much larger group of people, and the presentation may be in person or on camera. In most cases, you will use some type of technology. To deliver an effective presentation, you must possess the technology skills and confidence to deliver an effective presentation.

Working with Slide Masters

A *slide master* is the main slide that stores information about the theme and layouts of the presentation. The information can include fonts, backgrounds, effects, placeholder sizes, and even text (such as a company name) or graphics (such as a company logo). The slide master ensures consistency on each slide. When you update one or more of the elements, such as the company logo, you can make a universal change and the edits will be reflected on all the slides in the presentation.

It is recommended that you create the slide master before you create a new presentation so that all new slides that you create are based on the slide master and contain all the elements and formats specified on the slide master.

2-4.1.3
2-4.1.12

▶ **VOCABULARY**
slide master

Step-by-Step 20.8

1. If necessary, open **Global3** from your solution files. Save the presentation Global3 as **Global4**.

2. Click the **View** tab. In the Presentation Views group, click the **Slide Master View** button. The slide master, similar to **Figure 20–15**, opens in the Slide pane. Notice that the Ribbon adapts to show options for the slide master.

FIGURE 20–15

Slide master for Global4 presentation

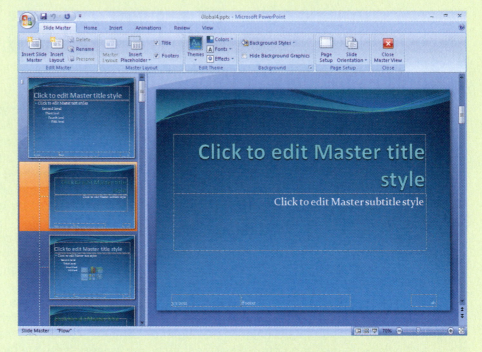

3. Notice that the Slides tab and the Outline tab are no longer visible. Also, there are several new thumbnails at the left. The first thumbnail is the slide master for the presentation, and the thumbnails below the slide master are the supporting default slide layouts that are associated with the slide master.

4. Click the **Insert** tab. In the Text group, click the **Header & Footer** button. The Header and Footer dialog box shown in **Figure 20–16** opens.

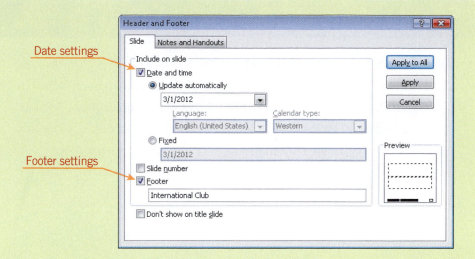

Date settings

Footer settings

FIGURE 20–16
The Header and Footer dialog box

5. Under Include on slide, click the **Date and time** check box, and if necessary enable Update automatically. Then click the list arrow and select the MM/DD/YYYY format.

6. Click the **Footer** check box and then in the text box, enter **International Club** in the text box. The settings should match those shown in **Figure 20–16**.

7. Click **Apply to All**. Click the **Slide Master** tab, and then, in the Close group, click the **Close Master View** button. As you can see in the slide pane and in the thumbnails on the Slides tab, the footer with the date and club name have been added to all three slides.

8. Save the changes and leave the presentation open.

Previewing a Presentation

Now that you have had some practice creating and editing presentation slides, you probably want to see what the slides look like in Slide Show view. As you view the presentation, you can click the left mouse button or press Spacebar to advance to the next slide. You can also use the arrow keys or the Page Up and Page Down keys to navigate forward or backward.

You can click the Slide Show View button on the View tab, or you can show the Slide Show tab for more options. In Slide Show view, when you move the mouse pointer around the lower-left corner of the screen, four buttons appear that help you navigate and add annotations to the slides while in Slide Show view.

If your computer is capable of supporting more than one monitor, and if you have access to two monitors, you can show the presentation in Presenter view. In Presenter view, the presentation appears on two monitors. One of the monitors can show the speaker notes in large clear type, and with thumbnails of slides to preview text. The second monitor shows the presentation in Slide Show view for the audience.

If your presentation time is cut, you may need to cut some slides from your presentation. Instead of deleting the slides, you can create a custom slide show by selecting only those slides you want to include.

2-4.1.10
2-4.1.11

EXTRA FOR EXPERTS

To hide a slide so it doesn't appear in Slide Show view, right-click the slide in Normal view or Slide Sorter view, and then click **Hide Slide** in the shortcut menu. To restore the slide so it does appear when you run the presentation, right-click to select the slide, open the shortcut menu, and click **Hide Slide** again to toggle the feature off.

Step-by-Step 20.9

1. If necessary, open **Global4** from your solution files.

2. Click the **Slide Show** tab. In the Start Slide Show group shown in **Figure 20–17**, click the **Slide Show From Beginning** button. The first slide shows full screen. Click the mouse button to advance to the next slide. Slide 2 shows full screen.

FIGURE 20–17
The Start Slide Show group on the Slide Show tab

3. Press **PageUp** to move to the previous slide. Then, click the down arrow to move to the next slide. Move the mouse pointer across the screen. You can use the arrow to point out parts of the slide during your presentation.

4. Position the mouse pointer in the lower-left corner of the screen. As you drag the pointer over the bottom edge of the screen (which happens to be over the date in the footer), four different semitransparent buttons will appear. Click the **Back in Slide Show** button ← to move to the previous slide. Then move the mouse pointer, and when it shows, click the **Forward in Slide Show** button → to move to the next slide.

5. Continue to move the mouse pointer around the date in the footer and click the **Pen** button ✎. In the shortcut menu, point to **Ink Color** and then select a bright yellow color. Click the **Pen** button again and then click **Highlighter** and then drag the mouse across the first line of text in the bulleted list, just as you would highlight text on paper.

6. You can also use the pen tool to add annotations to the slides during a presentation. Click the **Pen** button. Click **Felt Tip Pen** in the shortcut menu, and use the pen tool to underline the text *more important than ever* on the screen. The pen marks overlay the text and objects that appear on the slide.

7. Move the mouse pointer down to the lower-left corner and click the **Shortcut Menu** button ▤. In the shortcut menu, point to **Screen** and then click **Show/Hide Ink Markup** to hide the highlighted text and the underlines. Press **Escape** to toggle off the felt tip pen.

8. Right-click anywhere on the screen. The shortcut menu opens. Point to **Go to Slide**. The slide numbers with the slide titles appear in a submenu, and the active slide is checked. Click **Get Involved** to show that slide.

9. Press **B**, and the entire screen goes black. This option is helpful when you stop for a discussion or a break because you can stop the projection of the slide without exiting Slide Show view. Press **B** again to toggle the black screen off.

10. Press **Escape** to return to Normal view. When prompted to keep your ink annotations, click **Discard**.

11. In the Start Slide Show group, click the **Custom Slide Show** button. Click **Custom Shows**, and then click **New**. A list of the slides appears in the Define Custom Show dialog box.

12. In the Slide show name text box, accept the proposed slide show name, such as *Custom Show 1*. Under Slides in presentation, click **1. A New Country, A New Experience**. Press and hold **Ctrl** and then click **3. Get Involved**.

13. Click **Add** and the selected slides are copied to the box on the right. Click **OK** and then click **Show** in the Custom Shows dialog box. The custom slide show opens with just two slides. Press **PageDown** twice to view the two slides, and then press **PageDown** one more time to end the slide show.

14. Close the document without saving any changes.

HEADS UP

You can also toggle a white screen on and off by pressing **W**.

SUMMARY

In this lesson, you learned:

- In addition to using the Slides and Outline tabs to move to a different slide, you can use the scroll bar, mouse, or keyboard to navigate through a presentation in Normal view.

- You work in either Normal view or Slide Sorter view as you create and edit your presentation. You use Slide Show view when you present the show to an audience.

- You can use the Cut, Copy, and Paste commands to delete, move, or copy slides in a presentation. You can also easily rearrange the order of slides using drag-and-drop editing.

- The slide theme automatically formats slides with color schemes, font styles, and effects. A theme ensures that all slides in a presentation have a consistent look. You can apply a theme at any time without affecting the contents of the slides.

- You can change the slide layout even when the slide contains content, and you can modify the slide layout by resizing and repositioning the placeholders.

- You can add elements such as a company logo to the slide master. Then when you want to update the elements, you can make a global change and the edits will be reflected on all the slides in your presentation.

- In Slide Show view, the slides appear full screen, and you can move through the presentation using the mouse or keyboard.

- You can add annotations to slides and highlight text when showing slides in Slide Show view.

- You can create a custom slide show so that only designated slides appear in Slide Show view.

VOCABULARY REVIEW

Define the following terms:

presentation   slide master   theme

slide layout   slide pane

 # REVIEW QUESTIONS

TRUE / FALSE

Circle T if the statement is true or F if the statement is false.

T   F   **1.**   You can use the Outline tab to quickly navigate through a presentation.

T   F   **2.**   The background color and graphics must be the same for all the slides in a presentation.

T   F   **3.**   If you want to skip some slides in a presentation, you can hide them.

T   F   **4.**   PowerPoint checks spelling and automatically corrects commonly misspelled words.

T   F   **5.**   You can edit text on the Outline tab or in the slide pane.

MULTIPLE CHOICE

Select the best response for the following statements.

1. When planning slide content, use _____ to illustrate numerical data or trends.

   A.   bulleted lists   C.   font styles and colors

   B.   annotations   D.   tables and charts

2. The _____ view gives you an overall picture of the presentation.

   A.   Slide Show   C.   Normal

   B.   Slide Sorter   D.   Main

3. To provide consistent format for universal elements, add the text or graphics to the _____.

   A.   theme template   C.   slide master

   B.   slide layout   D.   design template

4. _____ provide guides for adding text, tables, charts, pictures, SmartArt, and media to a slide.

   A.   Quick Styles   C.   Slide guides

   B.   Slide organizers   D.   Placeholders

5. The _____ enables you to add annotations to a slide during a presentation.

   A.   annotation feature   C.   slide writer

   B.   pen tool   D.   slide editor

FILL IN THE BLANK

Complete the following sentences by writing the correct word or words in the blanks provided.

1. The document file in PowerPoint is called a(n) _____.

2. _____ refers to the arrangement of text and graphics on a slide.

3. A(n) _____ specifies a color scheme, fonts, and effects for the slide designs.

4. In _____ view, you can see how speaker's notes will appear when printed.

5. _____ view is available for computers that are set up to show a presentation on two monitors.

■ PROJECTS

PROJECT 20–1

1. Open **Project20–1** from the data files. Save the presentation as **International**.

2. Change to Slide Sorter view.

3. Delete slide 5.

4. Move slide 2 to the end of the presentation. Move slide 6 so that it is positioned before slide 4. Then move slide 5 so it is positioned after slide 6. Then move slide 2 so that it is positioned before slide 7.

5. On the View tab, change the zoom setting to fit to the window.

6. Change to Normal view and navigate to the first slide in the presentation.

7. Click the **title** placeholder and enter the title **International Students**. Click the **subtitle** placeholder and enter the subtitle **An international education opportunity**.

8. Drag a corner of the subtitle placeholder to decrease the size so that it is about 2 ½ inches wide and the text wraps to four lines. Then position the mouse pointer on a border. When the pointer changes to a four-headed arrow, drag the subtitle placeholder to center it under the title on the slide.

9. Copy slide 8 and paste it after slide 1.

10. Apply a theme of your choice. Change the color scheme. Change the background style. Make any desired modifications, such as text alignment or font colors.

11. Save the changes and then preview the presentation.

12. In Slide Show view, toggle on the Highlighter option. Change the ink color to yellow and then use the highlighter to highlight *Benefits* on slide 4. Press **Escape** to toggle off the highlighter.

13. Exit Slide Show view. When prompted to keep the annotations, click **Keep**.

14. Save the changes and close the presentation.

PROJECT 20–2

1. Open **Project20–2** from the data files. Save the presentation as **Searching**.

2. Delete slide number 2.

3. Insert a new slide after slide 2 with the Title Only layout.

4. Click the title placeholder in the new slide number 3 and enter **Then, choose a tool.**.

5. Add a slide at the end of the presentation with the Title Slide layout. In the title placeholder, enter the title **Other Resources**.

6. Change the slide layout for the new slide to Title and Content layout.

7. Enter the following items as bullets in the content placeholder:

    ```
    Resource lists
    Guides
    Clearinghouses
    Virtual libraries
    ```

8. Delete slide number 6.

9. Apply a design of your choice. Change the color scheme and theme fonts if desired.

10. Show the slide master and add the footer **Internet Search Tips**. Apply the footer to all slides.

11. Save your changes and preview the presentation.

12. Create a custom slide show, and include only slides 1, 2, 5, 6, 7, and 8. View the slide show.

13. Close the presentation and then close PowerPoint. When prompted to save changes, click **No**.

TEAMWORK PROJECT

One of the best uses of a PowerPoint presentation is to persuade an audience to adopt a particular point of view. With a partner, explore both sides of a specific issue. Follow these steps:

1. As a class, brainstorm some topic issues of interest to the entire class (such as a proposal for a new community park or bike path). Or, your instructor may have a list of issues already prepared.

2. Form groups of two learners who have different opinions on one topic. Each learner will create a slide show that presents their position.

3. Gather information on the issue from surveys or research and then create a presentation to support your own particular point of view.

4. Organize the slide content to emphasize your points clearly. Select a theme and slide layouts that present your information effectively.

5. Each team member will then present their argument, and classmates will critique each presentation for design, content, and persuasiveness.

 # CRITICAL THINKING

ACTIVITY 20–1

One of the files you worked with in this lesson, 3Rs, addressed the importance of knowing the rules and using ethical judgments. If a classmate copies pictures from Web pages and uses the pictures in a report for a class assignment, is the classmate violating copyright laws? Search the Internet for information about copyright laws, and then explain why you think the classmate has or has not broken any copyright rules. Use the information gathered from your Internet search to support your argument. Be sure to respect those who provided the information at the Web site and give them credit by citing your sources!

 # ONLINE DISCOVERY

Microsoft provides several PowerPoint templates to help you create professional-looking presentations. Explore the categories of templates. With an online connection, you can see thumbnails and previews as well as some customer ratings, which will help you decide if you want to download the template. Focus on two or three categories and write a brief paragraph about why you think PowerPoint is a good application for these categories.

Explore the photo album templates available at Microsoft Office Online, and if permitted, download one or more of the templates. Review the features provided in the template. Create a simple presentation, briefly describing each feature. In a summary slide at the end of the presentation, list reasons why PowerPoint is better than Word for creating a photo album.

The list below will help you get started.

- Backgrounds
- Themes
- Overall order and album layout
- Specific page layouts
- Captions
- Frames
- Picture handling

LESSON 21

Enhancing Presentations with Multimedia Effects

■ OBJECTIVES

Upon completion of this lesson, you should be able to:

- Add clip art, shapes and drawn objects, SmartArt graphics, and pictures from files to a slide.

- Change the size and position of a graphic object, and add borders and shading to graphic objects on a slide.

- Create charts and tables using Excel and Word features.

- Create hyperlinks on slides to link to Web pages, e-mails, and other documents.

- Add slide transitions to control how the slides are introduced in a slide show.

- Animate objects on a slide to draw attention and add emphasis.

- Insert sound and video clips to add an extra dimension to a slide show.

- Prepare hard copies for handouts and speaker's notes and distribute presentations via soft copies.

■ DATA FILES

To complete this lesson, you will need these data files:

Step21-1.pptx

Step21-3.pptx

Photo1.jpg

Photo2.jpg

Video1.wmv

Project21-1.pptx

Project21-3.pptx

Photo3.jpg

Video2.wmv

■ VOCABULARY

animation

emphasis effects

entrance effects

exit effects

motion paths

slide transitions

trigger

A good presentation holds your audience's attention without distracting them from understanding the information you are presenting. PowerPoint allows you to use color, design, graphics, sound, and video to illustrate your points effectively. These options can all be used to emphasize your points and clarify your information.

2-1.3.7
2-4.1.2
2-4.1.12

Inserting and Editing Graphics

Graphics can help your audience remember your message. Graphics include shapes, clip art, photographs, text art, SmartArt graphics, tables, and charts. PowerPoint provides special content placeholders in slide layouts to make the task of adding graphics easy. But don't let your message get lost by overloading your slide show with the abundant special effects available. Use graphics only when they illustrate relevant points in a presentation.

Adding Clip Art to a Slide

When you insert a graphic in a placeholder, the graphic replaces the placeholder. You can insert clip art and photographs from the Clip Art task pane, and you can also insert a picture from a file, such as a digital photograph or a scanned image of a drawing.

When a graphic is selected, eight small squares and circles called sizing handles appear on the border of the graphic. When the graphic is selected, you can cut, copy, paste, delete, move, or resize it. To resize the graphic, drag a sizing handle, and you will see the effects on the screen as you drag. To resize the graphic proportionally, drag a corner sizing handle.

Step-by-Step 21.1

1. Launch PowerPoint and open **Step21-1** from the data files. Save the presentation as **Time1**.

2. Go to slide 2. It is a blank slide. Notice that the slide layout includes title and content placeholders. The content placeholder shows six different graphics buttons, as shown in **Figure 21–1**.

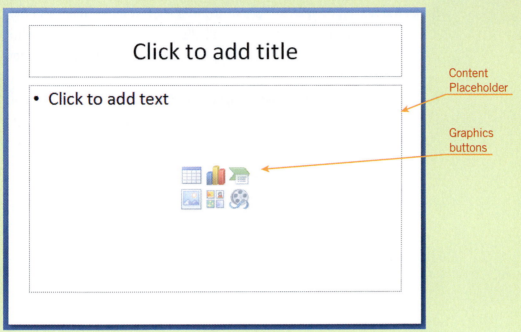

FIGURE 21–1
Placeholder for text or
graphics content

3. Point to each of the graphics buttons to show the ScreenTips. Notice that you can insert tables, charts, SmartArt graphics, pictures from files, clip art, and media clips.

4. In the content placeholder, click the **Clip Art** button . The Clip Art task pane, as shown in **Figure 21–2**, appears. Do not be concerned if there is text in the Search for text box in your task pane. Make sure the options in the Search in and Results should be boxes match those shown in the figure.

FIGURE 21–2
The Clip Art task pane

5. In the Search for text box, select any existing text, enter **time**, and then click **Go**. PowerPoint searches for all clip art related to this word. Scroll through the thumbnails, which may include clip art, photographs, movies, and sounds.

6. Click the clip art identified in **Figure 21–3**. (If that clip art is not available, click something similar. You may need to scroll down through the thumbnails to find a suitable clip art.) The clip art replaces the content placeholder on the slide. Close the Clip Art task pane.

FIGURE 21–3
Clip art related to the search text "time"

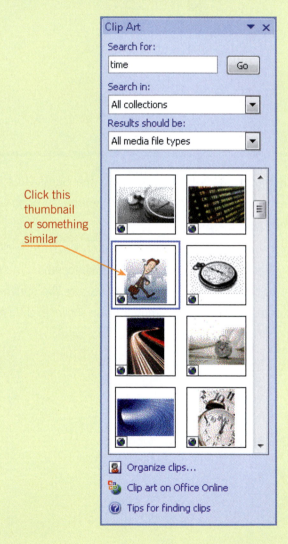

7. Eight sizing handles should appear around the clip art, similar to **Figure 21–4**. Point to the sizing handle in the upper-left corner. When the pointer changes to a two-headed arrow, drag the sizing handle up and to the left to make the clip art bigger. The clip art will overlap the title placeholder.

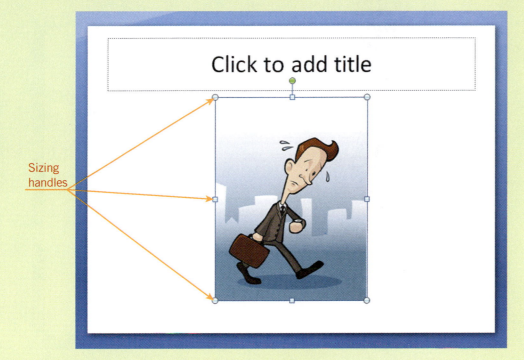

FIGURE 21–4
Selected clip art with sizing handles

8. Point to the center of the clip art. The pointer will change to a four-headed arrow. Drag the clip art to center it on the slide.

9. Go to slide 3. In the content placeholder on the left, click the **Clip Art** button. In the Clip Art task pane, change the Search for text to **search**, and then click **Go**. Search for clip art similar to the photograph shown in **Figure 21–5** and click the thumbnail to insert it in the content placeholder. Close the Clip Art task pane.

FIGURE 21–5
Slide with graphic and text

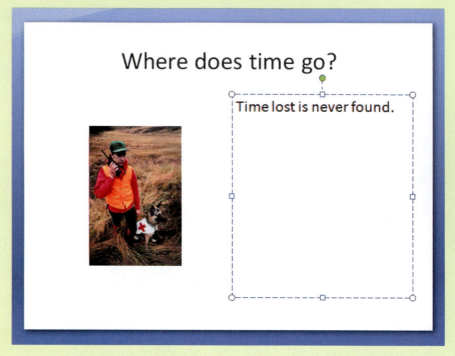

10. In the content placeholder on the right, click above the graphics buttons and enter **Time lost is never found.**. The text is contained in a text box. Click anywhere within the line of text. In the Paragraph group on the Home tab, click the **Bullets** button to remove the bullet format. Your presentation window should look like **Figure 21–5**.

11. You can resize and reposition this text box just as you would change a graphic. Drag the bottom middle handle of the text box border up towards the text, as shown in **Figure 21–6**, to reduce the size of the text box.

FIGURE 21–6
Adjusting the size of the text box

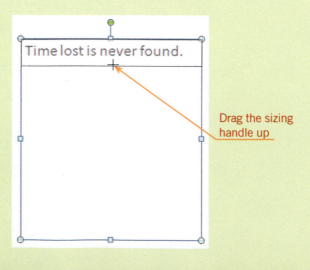

Drag the sizing handle up

12. The text box should still be selected. Click the **Drawing Tools Format** tab, and in the Shape Styles group, click the **More** button to open the Shape Styles gallery. Click the last style in the bottom row, **Intense Effect – Accent 6**, and then click outside the text box to see the results of the new style.

13. Go to slide 4. Click anywhere within the bulleted list to select the text box. Then, select all of the text in the text box. In the Paragraph group on the Home tab, click the **Numbering** button. The bullets are converted to numbers.

14. Deselect the text. Save the changes and leave the presentation open.

Adding WordArt, Drawn Objects, and SmartArt Graphics to a Slide

You can also create WordArt objects and draw objects on a slide using the same shapes tools that you learned to use in Word. SmartArt graphics enable you to convert text to a professional-looking visual. As you already know, SmartArt graphics are easy to create, and you can even create them from existing text.

Step-by-Step 21.2

1. If necessary, open **Time1** from your solution files. Save the presentation Time1 as **Time2**.

2. On slide 1, click anywhere within the title text box. The sizing handles on the border of the text box are white, and the border appears with broken lines. Point to the text box border, and when the pointer changes to a four-headed arrow, click to select the text box. When the text box is selected, the borders are solid lines and the sizing handles are blue.

3. Press **Delete** to remove the text box contents. Select the text box again, and then press **Delete** to remove the text box.

4. Click the **Insert** tab, and then in the Text group, click the **WordArt** button. Click the first option, **Fill – Text 2**, **Outline – Background 2**. A new text box is inserted on the slide. Enter **Time Management**.

5. Point to one of the text box borders, and when the pointer changes to a four-headed arrow, drag the text box to the left to center it horizontally on the slide.

6. Go to slide 3 and insert a new slide with the Title and Content layout.

7. In the Drawing group, click the **Shapes** button, and under Basic Shapes, click the **Smiley Face** shape tool. (If you do not see the Shapes button, click the More button.) The mouse pointer changes to a cross hair. Starting above and to the left of the graphics buttons, click and drag the mouse pointer diagonally down and to the right to create a smiley face object that covers all the graphics buttons.

8. The smiley face object should still be selected. In the Drawing group, click the **Shape Fill** button arrow, and under Standard Colors, click the **Yellow** option.

9. To change the smile to a frown, point to the diamond shape on the smile and click and drag the line upward, as shown in **Figure 21–7**.

FIGURE 21–7
Changing the smile on the smiley face

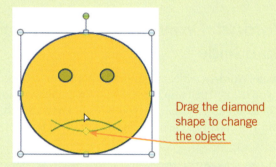

Drag the diamond shape to change the object

10. Go to slide 5. Click anywhere within the numbered list to select the text box. In the Paragraph group on the Home tab, click the **Convert to SmartArt Graphic** button. Then click the first option, **Vertical Bullet List**. The contents in the text box are converted to a graphic.

11. There are two blank rows in the SmartArt graphic. Right-click the first empty row, and click **Cut** in the shortcut menu to remove the row. Repeat the process to remove the other empty row.

12. Save the changes and close the presentation.

Adding Tables, Charts, and Pictures to Slides

You can add tables and simple charts to illustrate numerical data or trends. The placeholders make it easy to create a table or chart on a slide using features with which you are already familiar in Word and Excel. You can also copy and paste tables and charts from Word and Excel documents. To further enhance a slide and add another type of visual element, you can insert from a file a photo, a drawing, or a scanned image.

Step-by-Step 21.3

1. Open **Step21-3** from the data files and save the presentation as **Dogs1**.

2. On slide 1, in the subtitle placeholder, enter your first and last name.

3. Go to slide 3. In the content placeholder, click the **Insert Table** button ⊞. The Insert Table dialog box opens. Change the settings to **4** columns and **6** rows.

4. Click **OK**. A table is inserted on the slide. Enter the table data shown in **Figure 21-8**.

Name	Gender	Age	Breed
Sebastian	Male	Young	Beagle
Lucy	Female	Baby	Saint Bernard
Rosie	Female	Adult	Brittany Spaniel
Blaney	Male	Young	Terrier
Max	Male	Young	Siberian Husky

FIGURE 21-8
Table data for slide 3

5. Go to slide 4. If necessary, maximize the presentation window. In the content placeholder, click the **Insert Chart** button 📊. The Insert Chart dialog box opens.

6. The first option, Clustered Column, should already be selected. Click **OK**. An Excel workbook opens and the screen is split to show both your PowerPoint presentation and an Excel worksheet. The worksheet contains sample data, and a sample chart is inserted on the PowerPoint slide, as shown in **Figure 21-9**.

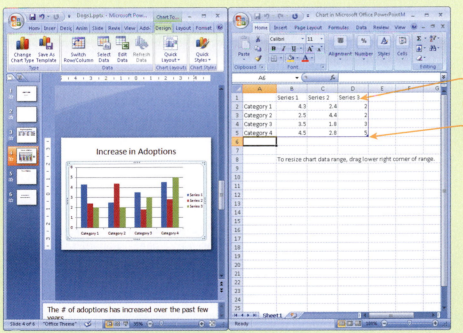

FIGURE 21-9
A presentation and worksheet shown side by side

Replace this data

Click and drag to resize the data range

7. Point to the lower-right corner of the selected data range. When the pointer changes to a double-headed arrow, drag the border down to cell D6 to add one more row to the data range. The data range should now be A1:D6.

8. In the worksheet, replace the sample data with the data shown in **Figure 21–10**. As you enter the data, the chart in the slide is updated.

	A	B	C	D	E	F	G
1		Baby	Young	Adult			
2	2007	45	38	37			
3	2008	52	44	39			
4	2009	61	58	47			
5	2010	79	66	64			
6	2011	86	71	72			
7							
8		To resize chart data range, drag lower right corner of range.					
9							
10							

9. Save the worksheet as **DogData** and then close the Excel application. The PowerPoint application is still open, and the updated chart is shown on slide 4.

10. Go to slide 5. In the content placeholder on the left, click the **Insert Picture from File** button . The Insert Picture dialog box opens. Navigate to the data files, click **Photo1.jpg**, and then click **Insert** at the bottom of the dialog box. The photograph is inserted in the placeholder on the slide.

11. In the text placeholder above the picture, enter **Taffy**.

12. In the content placeholder on the right, click the **Insert Picture from File** button. If necessary, navigate to the data files folder. Click **Photo2.jpg**, and then click **Insert**. The photographs are positioned side by side on the slide.

13. In the text placeholder above the picture, enter **Blue**.

14. Save the changes and leave the presentation open.

Creating Hyperlinks

IC³

2-4.1.2
2-4.1.11

In PowerPoint, you can create hyperlinks to slides in the same presentation, to slides in another presentation, or to an e-mail address, a Web page, or another file. You can create the hyperlink from text on a slide, and you can also create the hyperlink from a graphic object.

Step-by-Step 21.4

1. If necessary, open **Dogs1** from your solution files. Save the presentation Dogs1 as **Dogs2**.

2. Go to slide 6. Select *www.clintonadoptadog.org*.

3. Click the **Insert** tab, and in the Links group, click the **Insert Hyperlink** button. The Insert Hyperlink dialog box, similar to the one shown in **Figure 21–11**, opens.

Copy this URL

Target is existing Web page

Paste URL here

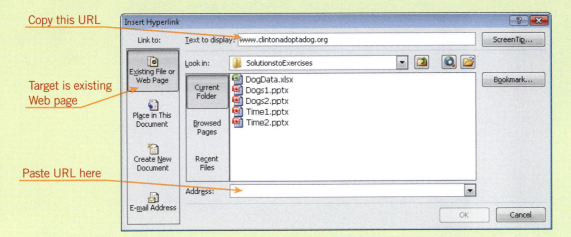

FIGURE 21–11
The Insert Hyperlink dialog box

4. The option to link to an existing Web page is already selected, and the text to display in a ScreenTip when you position the mouse pointer over the hyperlink appears at the top of the dialog box. Select the text to display and press **Ctrl+C** to copy the URL to the Clipboard.

5. Click to place the insertion point in the Address box. Press **Ctrl+V** to paste the URL in the box, and then click **OK**. Deselect the text, and the hyperlink format becomes visible.

6. Go to slide 4. Click anywhere in the chart to select it.

7. Click the **Insert Hyperlink** button to open the Insert Hyperlink dialog box. If necessary, click the list arrow in the Look in box to navigate to the folder where you saved the DogData file. Click **DogData.xlsx** and then click **OK**. The link will help you quickly access the worksheet if you need to update the data.

8. Go to slide 5. Click the photograph on the left to select it, and then click the **Insert Hyperlink** button.

9. In the Insert Hyperlink dialog box, under Link to, click **Place in This Document**. A list of the slides with the slide titles appears, as shown in **Figure 21–12**. Click **3. Dogs Looking for Homes**. The slide shows in the preview pane. Click **OK**. This creates a link to slide 3.

FIGURE 21–12
Options for hyperlinks to places in this document

Click slide 3 as hyperlink target

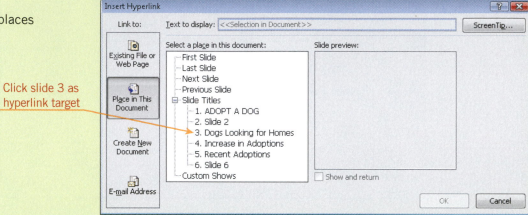

10. Go to slide 4. Click the **Slide Show** view button in the status bar to change to Slide Show view. Slide 3 appears full screen. Position the mouse pointer over the chart, and the pointer changes to a hand indicating a hyperlink. A ScreenTip with the hyperlink information also appears.

11. Click anywhere in the chart and the Excel worksheet opens. Close Excel.

12. Press **Page Down** to move to the next slide. Position the mouse pointer over the graphic on the left. When the pointer changes to a hand, click. Slide 3 appears.

13. Press **Escape** to return to Normal view in PowerPoint.

14. Save the changes and leave the presentation open.

2-4.1.6

▶ **VOCABULARY**
slide transitions

Formatting Slide Transitions

Slide transitions are settings that determine how a slide is introduced as you move from one slide to another in Slide Show view. For example, you can format the transition so the current slide fades to black before the next slide appears. Or you can choose to have the next slide automatically appear after a designated number of seconds. You can even choose a sound effect that plays as the transition occurs. When used effectively, the transitions you add between the slides add interest and help keep the attention of your audience focused on the presentation. You can apply the transition settings to a single slide or to all the slides in the presentation.

Step-by-Step 21.5

1. If necessary, open **Dogs2** from your solution files. Save the presentation Dogs2 as **Dogs3**.

2. Go to slide 1. Click the **Animations** tab to show the transition options, shown in **Figure 21–13**.

FIGURE 21–13
Transition options

More button   Click to select
                                                     transition sound

3. Move the mouse pointer over the transition options to see a live preview of each transition. Click the **More** button to show more transition options, and use the Live Preview feature to explore more of the options.

4. Scroll down through the options, and under Push and Cover, click the **Push Up** option. As you apply the option, a quick preview of the transition occurs.

5. In the Transition to This Slide group, click the **Transition Speed** list arrow [Transition Speed: Fast] and change the speed setting. A preview of the transition shows again. Click the **Transition Speed** list arrow again and change the setting to **Slow**.

6. In the Transition to This Slide group, click the **Apply To All** button [Apply To All]. The transition settings are applied to all slides in the presentation.

7. Go to slide 5. In the Transition to This Slide group, click the **Transition Sound** list arrow [Transition Sound: [No Sound]] and point to an option. A preview of the sound occurs. Click the **Push** option. Because you did not click the Apply to All button, the transition sound occurs only with this slide.

8. In the Transition to This Slide group, under Advance Slide, click to enable the **Automatically After** check box [Automatically After: 00:00]. Then, in the box to the right, click the up arrow five times to set the timer for 5 seconds. The box should show *00:05*. When in Slide Show view, the slide show automatically advances to the next slide after five seconds.

9. Go to slide 1. Click the **Slide Show** view button in the status bar and click the mouse to move through the slides to see the effects of the transitions. You do not need to click the mouse when the slide with the two photos appears. The slide show automatically advances after five seconds.

10. Press **Escape** to return to Normal view.

11. Go to slide 3. Click the **Home** tab, and in the Drawing group, click the **Shapes** button. Under Basic Shapes, click the **Text Box** tool. Drag the mouse pointer to create a text box approximately four inches wide. Position the text box so it is just below the table and aligned with the left side of the table.

12. Enter **This list changes daily.**, and apply the italics format to the new text. Click outside the text box to deselect it.

13. Save the changes and close the presentation.

14. If time permits, reopen **Dogs3** from your solution files and explore other transitions and speed and sound options, then close the presentation without saving the changes.

Formatting Animations

2-4.1.2

When you add *animation*, you add special visual or sound effects to text or an object. Without animation, text and objects automatically appear all at once when a slide is opened in Slide Show view. However, when you format animations for the text boxes and graphics, you can determine how and when the text or graphics appear on each slide.

Customizing Animations

PowerPoint provides some built-in animations, but you'll more likely want to customize the animations. You can customize the animations by modifying the effects and controlling the timing of the effects. For example, you can make text disappear very subtly by fading away, or you can make an object disappear with a much more dramatic exit by making it disappear quickly.

PowerPoint also provides several animation effects. *Entrance effects* control how the object enters onto the slide. *Emphasis effects* draw attention to an object that is already visible on the slide, and *exit effects* control how an object leaves the slide. *Motion paths* enable you to create a path for the object to follow on the slide. The animation options are organized in four categories: Basic, Subtle, Moderate, and Exciting. You can also add sound to a slide show, and even specify a *trigger* that starts a sound effect or animation segment.

▶ **VOCABULARY**
animation
entrance effects
emphasis effects
exit effects
motion paths
trigger

Step-by-Step 21.6

1. Open **Time2** from your solution files, and save the presentation Time2 as **Time3**. Go to slide 2.

2. Click the clip art object, and click the **Animations** tab. In the Animations group shown in **Figure 21–14**, click the **Animate** list arrow `⟦Animate: No Animation ▾⟧` and then click **Fade**. A preview of the animation occurs. To see the animation again, at the far left side of the Animations tab in the Preview group, click the **Preview Animations** button.

FIGURE 21–14
Animation options

3. Go to slide 3. Click the *Time lost is never found* text placeholder to select it. In the Animations group, click the **Custom Animation** button . The Custom Animation task pane shown in **Figure 21–15** opens at the right side of the slide pane.

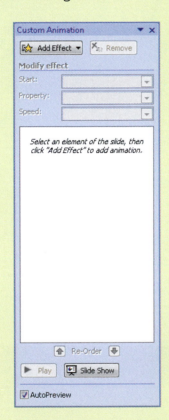

FIGURE 21–15
The Custom Animation task pane

4. In the task pane, click **Add Effect** and then point to **Entrance**. In the submenu, click **More Effects**. Point to the title bar of the Add Entrance Effect dialog box and drag the box to the left to reposition it so you can see the clip art and the text box on the slide. In the dialog box, under Basic, click **Wipe**. A live preview of the animation occurs.

5. Click **OK** to apply the animation. Notice in the task pane that the On Click option shows in the Start box. On Click is the trigger, and the animation does not occur until you click the mouse button when in Slide Show view. Notice that there are two numbers on the slide pane to the left of the text box. These numbers indicate that there are two animations applied.

6. In the task pane, click the double arrows shown in **Figure 21–16** to expand the contents. Both animations now appear in the task pane.

FIGURE 21–16
The Custom Animation task pane with animation selected

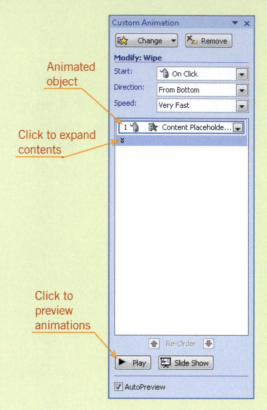

Animated object

Click to expand contents

Click to preview animations

ETHICS IN TECHNOLOGY

Respecting Intellectual Property

The term "intellectual property" is used to refer to information, material, or processes that were created by and belong to a person or corporation. The types of things included in the definition of intellectual property include books, poems, plays, and other works of literature; music and artwork; inventions and ideas; product names and logos; and scientific or business procedures. Computers make it very easy to copy and disseminate art, documents, inventions, and music, and this has created many legal concerns about the rights of a creator. Intellectual property law ensures that the original output of a human mind is considered valuable and entitled to protection.

Often people think that any information available on the Internet is in the public domain and free for the taking. This is not always the case. There are protections for intellectual property, including copyright for literary works, art, and music; patents for inventions and procedures; trademarks for company and product logos; and trade secrets, which include recipes, codes, and manufacturing processes.

Be careful not to use protected material in your own work without permission from the person who owns the material. And when referencing this information in classroom assignments, give credit to those who own the material by citing sources in the slide show and in your presentation handouts.

7. Click the **2 Time lost is never found** animation, and then click the list arrow to show the options shown in **Figure 21–17**. This submenu provides options for the animation. Click **Start With Previous**. Notice now that the numbers to the left of the text box on the slide are both the numeral 1, indicating that both animations occur at the same time.

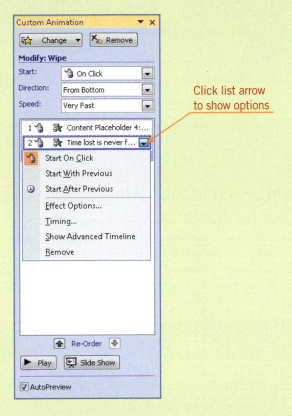

FIGURE 21–17
Options for expanded animation contents

8. In the task pane, click the **Direction** box list arrow and then click **From Left**. Click the **Speed** box list arrow and then click **Medium**.

9. Click the picture object to select it. In the task pane, click **Add Effect** and then point to **Entrance**. In the submenu click **More Effects**, and then, in the dialog box under Basic, click **Dissolve In**. Then click **OK**. The numeral 2 to the left of the picture indicates that this object is formatted with the second animation on this slide.

10. With the picture object still selected, click **Add Effect**, and then point to **Exit**. In the submenu, click **Diamond**. This setting controls how the object exits the slide. In the task pane, click the **Start** box list arrow and then click **With Previous**. This setting causes the picture to exit as the text box appears.

11. You need to change the order of the animations so that the picture appears first, and then the text box appears. In the task pane, click the **2 Picture 2** animation to select it, and then drag it to the top of the list of animations. When you see a black horizontal line above the 1 Picture 2 animation, release the mouse button. The sequence of animations should now be *1 Picture 2*, *2 Content Placeholder 4* and *Time lost is never found*, and then *Picture 2*.

12. On the Animations tab, in the Preview group, click the **Preview Animations** button to preview the effect. The picture dissolves in, and then as the text box starts to appear, the picture begins to exit.

13. Save the changes and leave the presentation open.

HEADS UP

You can also preview the animations by clicking **Play** at the bottom of the task pane.

Changing and Removing Custom Animations

If you change your mind after applying animations, you can change the animation, or you can remove the animation from the object completely. To modify an animation effect, you need to use the Change command. If you format a new effect without using the Change command, the existing effect is not removed, and the new effect is added to the object. In other words, the object would have two animations, not one.

Step-by-Step 21.7

1. If necessary, open **Time3** from your solution files. Save the presentation Time3 as **Time4**. If necessary, click the Animations tab and click the Custom Animation button to open the Custom Animation task pane.

2. Go to slide 4. Click the smiley face object and press **Ctrl+C** to copy it to the Clipboard. Deselect the object and then click outside the placeholder and press **Ctrl+V** to paste the object on the slide. Drag the diamond on the mouth down to create a smile.

3. With the copied smiley face object still selected, click **Add Effect** on the Custom Animation task pane, point to **Entrance**, and then click **More Effects**. In the dialog box, under Basic, click **Dissolve In**, and then click **OK**.

4. Reposition the copied smiley face object so it is positioned exactly over the original smiley face object. (*Hint*: Use the arrow keys to move the object.) Preview the animation to see the frown turn into a smile.

5. You decide you don't like the entrance effect. In the Custom Animation task pane, click the **1 Smiley Face 4** animation. Then, click **Change** at the top of the task pane. Point to **Entrance**, click **More Effects**, and in the dialog box under Subtle, click **Fade**. Click **OK**.

6. Preview the animation, and if necessary, change the Speed setting to **Fast**.

7. In the task pane, click the **1 Smiley Face 4** animation list arrow. Click **Timing** to open the Fade dialog box to the Timing tab. In the Delay box, change the setting to **1.5**. When you click to trigger the animation, there is a pause of 1.5 seconds before the animation begins. Click **OK**.

8. Go to slide 2. Click the clip art to select it. In the task pane, click **Add Effect**, point to **Emphasis**, and then click **More Effects**. In the dialog box under Moderate, click **Teeter** and then click **OK**.

9. In the task pane, change the Start setting to **After Previous** and change the Speed setting to **Medium**.

10. Preview the animations and make any necessary changes. Close the Custom Animation task pane.

11. Save the changes and close the presentation.

Inserting Audio and Video Clips

Sound and video add an extra dimension to a presentation. You can use sound and video at any point in a presentation to add emphasis or set the mood for the audience. Animated clip art graphics and sound clips are available in the Clip Art task pane. You can also use clips from other sources. To play a sound during a presentation, the sound clip must be in one of the following formats: .aiff, .au, .mid or .midi, .mp3, .wav, or .wma. To play a video during a presentation, the video must be in one of the following formats: .asf, .avi, .mpg, .mpeg, or .wmv.

Adding audio and video clips is similar to adding graphics. When you insert the video and sound files into the slide presentation, the files are either embedded and stored with the presentation, or the files are linked to the presentation. By default, .wav sound files under 100 kilobytes (KB) are embedded. All other media file types and .wav sound files that are 100 KB and over are linked and stored outside the presentation file. Movie files are always linked and stored outside the presentation file.

2-1.3.7
2-4.1.2

EXTRA FOR EXPERTS

Video and audio files can be quite large, so to avoid making the presentation file so large, a link is created. When you show the slide show, the link locates and opens the video file. Therefore, it is important that the link for the target file is maintained and the computer you are using for the slide show is able to access the target file.

Step-by-Step 21.8

1. Open **Dogs3** from your solution files, and save the presentation as **Dogs4**.

2. Go to slide 2. In the content placeholder, click the **Insert Media Clip** button ![icon]. The Insert Movie dialog box opens. Navigate to the data files folder and click **Video1.wmv**. Then click **OK** to link the video file to the presentation file.

3. A prompt appears. Click **Automatically**. The video starts as soon as the slide becomes active in Slide Show view. The trigger When Clicked enables you to control when the video starts.

4. Compare your screen to **Figure 21–18**. A graphic representing the video appears on the slide. When you advance to this slide in Slide Show view, the video will start to play.

FIGURE 21–18
Video object positioned on a slide

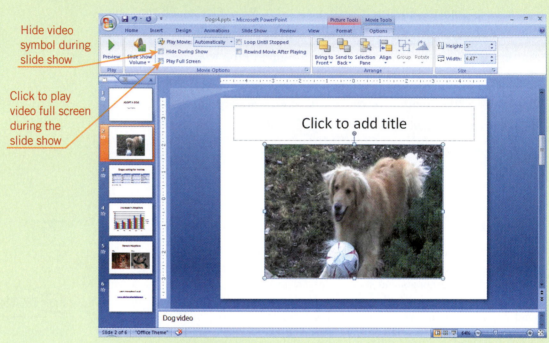

5. In the Movie Options group, enable the options **Hide During Show** and **Play Full Screen**.

6. Click the **Slide Show** view button in the status bar to preview the video in full screen. Then press **Escape** to return to Normal view.

7. Go to slide 6. Click the **Insert** tab. In the Media Clips group shown in **Figure 21–19**, click the **Sound from File** button arrow. Click **Sound from Clip Organizer**. The Clip Art task pane opens.

FIGURE 21–19
Buttons to insert video or sound files

8. In the Clip Art task pane, in the Search for box, enter **dog**. Click the **Results should be** box list arrow. Notice that Sounds is the only media selected. Click **Go**. A list of audio clips appears.

9. Click a sound clip of a dog barking. When prompted, click **Automatically**. An audio symbol is inserted in the center of the slide. (You can drag the symbol to the side so that it does not appear on top of the hyperlink.) When the slide is active in Slide Show view, the audio clip plays automatically. Close the Clip Art task pane.

10. Click the **Sound Tools Options** tab. In the Sound Options group shown in **Figure 21–20**, enable the options **Hide During Show** and **Loop Until Stopped**.

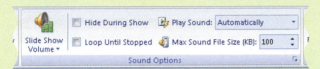

FIGURE 21–20
The Sound Options group on the Sound Tools Options tab

11. Go to slide 1. Click the **Slide Show** view button in the status bar to preview the presentation. Click to advance to slide 2. When the video stops playing, you need to click to advance to slides 3 and 4.

12. To advance to slide 5, press **Page Down**. (If you accidentally click the chart, the Excel spreadsheet opens.) When slide 5 (*Recent Adoptions*) appears, you do not need to click the mouse button to advance to the next slide. After five seconds, the slide show advances to the last slide, and the barking audio automatically plays.

13. The audio clip continues to play until you exit the slide show. Exit the slide show.

14. Save the changes and leave the presentation open.

Distributing Presentations

2-4.1.8
2-4.1.9

PowerPoint offers several options for distributing your presentation. Obviously, the primary way to distribute the presentation is to project the slide show before an audience. In addition, you can provide hard copies of slides, handouts, and notes, and you can also distribute electronic copies (soft copies) of the presentation. If you are unable to make your presentation in person, you can instead share the presentation via e-mail, Web pages, or over networks.

Printing Handouts and Speaker Notes

You can print individual slides, handouts, the presentation outline, and speaker notes. You can also prepare handouts by formatting the slides in the various page layouts available in Word documents.

Step-by-Step 21.9

1. If necessary, open **Dogs4** from your solution files.

2. Click the **Office Button**, point to **Print**, and then click **Print** to open the Print dialog box shown in **Figure 21–21**.

FIGURE 21–21
The Print dialog box

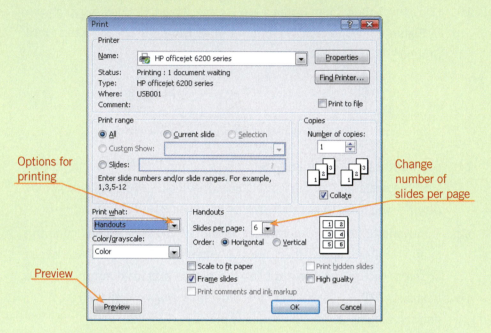

Options for printing

Change number of slides per page

Preview

3. In the Print what box, the Slides option is already selected. Click **Preview** in the lower-left corner of the dialog box. Notice in the preview that each slide is on a separate page. If you were to print the slides, each slide would fill the page and would print in full color in landscape orientation. In the Preview group, click the **Close Print Preview** button.

4. Open the Print dialog box again. (*Hint*: Press **Ctrl+P**.) Click the **Print what** box list arrow and then click **Handouts**. Under Handouts, click the **Slides per page** list arrow and then click **3**. Notice that the preview changes to show three slides instead of six.

5. Click **Preview**. Scroll down and you see that the images of three slides appear on one page. Click the **Close Print Preview** button.

6. Open the Print dialog box again. Click the **Print what** box list arrow and then click **Notes Pages**. Click **Preview**. Scroll down and you see that an image of each slide appears on a page by itself, and the notes from the Notes pane appear below the image. You can use the extra white space on the page to add written notes. Click the **Close Print Preview** button.

7. Open the Print dialog box again. Click the **Print what** box list arrow and then click **Outline View**. Click **Preview**. A list of all six slides appears. Click the **Zoom** button, click **100%** to magnify the preview, and then click **OK**. If the slide contains text in placeholders, that text appears in the outline. However, when you add a text box to a slide, that text does not appear in the outline. Click the **Close Print Preview** button.

8. Click the **Office Button** and then point to **Publish**. Click **Create Handouts in Microsoft Office Word**. The Send to Microsoft Office Word dialog box opens, and provides several options for page layouts.

9. Click **Blank lines next to slides** to enable the option, and then click **OK**. A new Word document is created.

10. Click the Word document button in the task bar. Images of the slides are positioned three on a page with blank lines on the right side of each slide. Save the document as **DogsHandouts**, and then close the Word document and the Word application.

11. Leave the presentation open.

Preparing Presentations for Distribution

When distributing electronic copies of the presentation, you can attach the file as an attachment to an e-mail message. Before sharing the presentation, you may want to control what others can see in the file. For example, you may not want them see the author of the presentation or the date the presentation was created. Information like this can easily be removed from the file.

In Word, you learned how to save documents in PDF and XPS formats. You can also save presentations in these formats. Readers can see the slides, but they cannot edit them or use them in a slide show.

It is also common for presentations to be published on Web pages. Instructors of online courses often make course information available in this format.

Another way to distribute a presentation is to publish the presentation to a document management server or to a document workspace. Of course, you must be connected to a network or the Internet, and you must have sufficient bandwidth for transferring the electronic files. You must have authorization to publish to or access files from a document workspace or document management server. Accessing files in a document management server or creating a new document workspace is beyond the scope of this lesson.

> **HEADS UP**
>
> A computer must be properly configured to output or receive and open PDF and XPS documents. Microsoft provides a free add-in that you can download so you can use the PDF and XPS formats.

Step-by-Step 21.10

1. If necessary, open **Dogs4** from your solution files. Save the presentation Dogs4 as **Dogs5**.

2. Click the **Office Button**, point to **Prepare**, and then click **Inspect Document**. The Document Inspector dialog box opens.

3. Make sure all options are enabled, and then click **Inspect** at the bottom of the dialog box.

4. The results appear in the Document Inspector dialog box. An exclamation point appears next to Document Properties and Personal Information and also next to Presentation Notes. Click both **Remove All** buttons in the dialog box to remove this information from the file.

5. The dialog box adapts to update the status. Click **Reinspect**, and then click **Inspect** to check one more time. Close the dialog box. Save the changes to the document.

6. Click the **Office Button**, point to **Save As**, and then click **PDF or XPS**. The Publish as PDF or XPS dialog box opens. Navigate to the folder where you save your solution files. If necessary, change the Save as type box to PDF (*.pdf). Click **Publish**. The presentation opens in Adobe Reader.

7. Scroll through and preview the slides in PDF format, and then close Adobe Reader.

8. Click the **Office Button**, point to **Save As**, and then click **Other Formats**. The Save As dialog box opens. Click the **Save as type** box list arrow and then click **Single File Web Page (*.mht; *.mhtml)**. Click **Publish** near the bottom of the dialog box, and the Publish as Web Page dialog box shown in **Figure 21–22** opens.

FIGURE 21–22
Options for publishing a presentation as a Web page

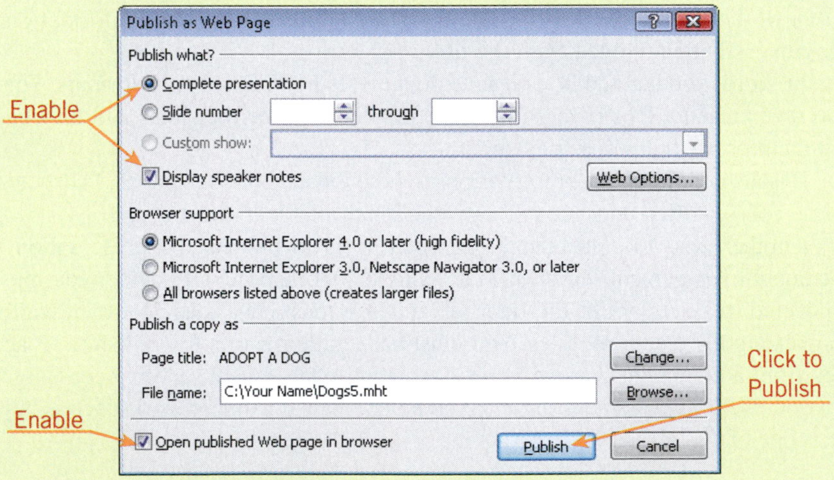

9. Compare your screen to **Figure 21–22**, and, if necessary, enable or disable some options.

10. Under Publish a copy as, a page title may or may not appear. Click the **Change** button. In the Page title box, enter **ADOPT A DOG** and then click **OK**.

11. Click **Publish**. The presentation should open in your Internet browser. If you see a message bar containing a warning about ActiveX controls, click the message bar and then click to allow the blocked content. The presentation opens, and you can click the links at the left side of the slides to navigate through the presentation.

12. Close the browser window.

13. Click the **Office Button** and then point to **Send**. Notice that you can attach the file to an e-mail or format the file in PDF or XPS format and then attach it to an e-mail. Click outside the submenu to close it.

14. Save the changes and close the presentation.

SUMMARY

In this lesson, you learned:

■ Graphics help to clarify the message of your presentation. Graphics can make your audience remember your message, and PowerPoint makes it easy for you to add graphics to a slide.

■ You can create WordArt, drawn objects, and SmartArt graphics to add visual effects to slides.

■ You can easily reposition and resize graphic objects on slides, and you can also format the objects with borders and shading.

■ You can add hyperlinks to text and graphics so you can link slides to other slides, other documents, or Web pages.

■ The slide transition affects how each new slide appears. You can apply transition settings to a single slide or to all the slides in the presentation.

■ PowerPoint provides special effects that can add emphasis, animation, or sound to the text and graphics, or that can enhance how a slide opens or closes.

■ You can easily insert sound and video clips on slides and format the clips to play automatically.

■ PowerPoint provides several options for printing a presentation, including slides, handouts, notes pages, and an outline of the slide show content.

 # VOCABULARY REVIEW

Define the following terms:

animation	exit effects	trigger
emphasis effects	motion paths	
entrance effects	slide transitions	

■ REVIEW QUESTIONS

TRUE / FALSE

Circle T if the statement is true or F if the statement is false.

T   F   **1.**   You cannot create a hyperlink to a slide in the same presentation.

T   F   **2.**   You can copy and paste tables and charts from Word and Excel documents.

T   F   **3.**   When you format a slide transition, it must be applied to all slides in the presentation.

T   F   **4.**   You can only create hyperlinks from text.

T   F   **5.**   Without animation, text and objects automatically appear all at once when a slide is opened in Slide Show view.

MULTIPLE CHOICE

Select the best response for each of the following statements.

1. Sound effects can be applied to _____.

   A.   objects   C.   text

   B.   slide transitions   D.   any of the above

2. Before sharing a presentation, you can control the personal information users can see by _____ the file.

   A.   encrypting   C.   inspecting

   B.   protecting   D.   publishing

3. Animation effects are organized in four categories: Basic, Subtle, Moderate, and _____.

   A.   Extreme   C.   Intense

   B.   Exciting   D.   Excessive

4. The _____ effect is used to draw attention to an object that is already visible on the slide.

   A.   emphasis   C.   exit

   B.   entrance   D.   none of the above

5. The print options for a presentation include _____.

   A.   slides, handouts, and notes pages

   B.   slides, handouts, notes pages, and an outline

   C.   handouts and notes pages

   D.   slides and notes pages

FILL IN THE BLANK

Complete the following sentences by writing the correct word or words in the blanks provided.

1. The entrance effects and exit effects are accessed in the _____ task pane.

2. A(n) _____ starts a sound effect or animation segment on a slide.

3. When a graphic is selected, eight small circles and squares called _____ appear on the border of the graphic.

4. When you add special visual or sound effects to the text or graphics on a slide, you add _____.

5. You can quickly access clip art graphics and photos in the _____.

PROJECTS

PROJECT 21–1

1. Open **Project21-1** from the data files and save the presentation as **Refuge**.

2. Go to slide 2. Select the bulleted list and convert the text to a SmartArt graphic.

3. Go to slide 3. Insert clip art or a photograph that helps describe hiking or biking. Resize the graphic as necessary. Leave the Clip Art task pane open.

4. Go to slide 4. Because the Clip Art task pane is open, you do not need to click the graphic button in the placeholder. Insert clip art or a photograph that helps describe the wildlife viewing. Resize and reposition the graphic as necessary, and delete the empty content placeholder.

5. Format a border for the graphics on slides 3 and 4.

6. On slide 5, insert a table and add the data below.

Activity	Regulation
Fishing/crabbing	Permitted in designated areas
Hiking/biking	Trails open year round
Boats	Permitted from Sept. 1 to March 14
Camping	Not permitted
Open fires	Prohibited except by special permit

7. Resize and reposition the table as needed so that it fits in the center of the slide, and format the table contents as you like.

8. Go to slide 6. Remove the bullet format from the last line of text. Insert a blank line before the URL, center the text for the URL, and then create a hyperlink to the URL.

9. Apply an appropriate theme and add a sound clip to one or more slides. Modify the color and/or font styles if desired.

10. Apply appropriate slide transitions to all the slides.

11. Preview the slide show and make any necessary changes.

12. Save the changes.

13. Save the presentation in PDF format.

14. Close Adobe Reader and then close the presentation.

PROJECT 21–2

1. In this project, you will complete a presentation that you worked on the lesson Step-by-Steps. Open **Time4** from your solution files and save the presentation Time4 as **Time5**.

2. Go to slide 2. Insert a new slide with the Title and Content layout. Enter the title **Racing the Clock**.

3. Search the Clip Art task pane and insert a movie clip that helps describe "racing the clock." Resize and position the object so that it is an appropriate size and is positioned in the center of the slide.

4. Go to slide 5 and insert a new slide with the Two Content layout. Enter the title **Organize**.

5. Insert clip art or a photograph in the content placeholder on the left to illustrate a messy or cluttered desk. Then insert clip art or a photograph in the content placeholder on the right to illustrate organized documents, such as a file cabinet. If you use clip art on the left, then use clip art on the right.

6. Add custom animation effects so that the cluttered desk image appears first triggered by a click, and then the filing cabinet appears on the right triggered by a click. The cluttered desk should go away as the file cabinet appears. Resize the images as needed so they are approximately the same size, and position the objects side by side on the slide.

7. Insert a new slide after slide 6, using the Comparison layout. Enter the title **Plan Ahead**. In the subheading placeholder on the left, enter **Daily/Weekly Planner**. In the subheading placeholder on the right, enter **Monthly Planner**.

8. Insert an appropriate clip art or a photograph below each subheading to illustrate using planners and calendars. If you use a photograph on the left, then use a photograph on the right. Resize and reposition the graphics as needed.

9. Go to slide 8 and insert a new slide with the Title and Content layout. Enter the title **The clock is ticking…**.

10. Insert a movie clip of a clock. Resize and position the clip as needed. If necessary, format the clip to play automatically. Insert a sound clip of a clock ticking. Hide the audio symbol during the show and loop the audio clip until stopped.

11. Apply slide transitions with sound effects, if desired. Preview the presentation in Slide Show view.

12. Inspect the document and remove the document properties, personal information, and the presentation notes.

13. Save the changes. Then, save the presentation as a single file Web page.

14. Close the Web browser and the presentation. When prompted to save the changes, click **No**.

PROJECT 21-3

1. Open **Project21-3** from the data files and save the presentation as **Community**.

2. On slide 1, enter your name in the subtitle placeholder.

3. Go to slide 2. In the placeholder, create a Pie in 3-D chart by adding the data below in the Excel spreadsheet.

	% of Waste
Residential	45.9
Commercial	39.7
Construction	8.9
Yard	5.5

4. Save the workbook as **Waste** and then close Excel.

5. Go to slide 3. In the placeholder on the right, insert the picture file **Photo3.jpg** from the data files folder.

6. Go to slide 6. In the placeholder, create a 5 x 5 table, and enter the data below in the Word table.

	1995	2000	2005	2010
Aluminum	18%	23%	28%	36%
Glass	12%	15%	18%	23%
Paper	21%	39%	43%	50%
Plastics	3%	5%	6%	7%

7. Go to slide 7. Insert a new slide with the Title and Content layout. In the content placeholder, on the new slide 8, insert the media clip **Video 2.wmv** from the data files folder. Format the movie to play automatically. Hide the image during the show, and enable the settings so the movie fills the screen when playing.

8. On slide 7, format a transition so that slide 8 appears automatically after 2 seconds.

9. Apply an appropriate slide theme or slide background, and modify the color and font style if desired.

10. Go to slide 3. Create a custom animation for the bulleted list with the following settings:

    Entrance: **Wipe**

    Start: **On Click**

    Direction: **From Left**

    Speed: **Fast**

11. On slide 3, create a custom animation for the picture with the following settings:

    Entrance: **Fade**

    Start: **On Click**

    Speed: **Medium**

12. Go to slides 4 and 5. Apply the same settings specified for the bulleted list in Step 10.

13. Go to slide 1 and preview the slide show. After the *Make a Difference* slide appears, you should not have to click. The next slide appears automatically and the video starts. Press **Escape** to return to Normal view.

14. Save the changes and close the presentation.

TEAMWORK PROJECT

PowerPoint provides many features that empower you to be creative and show your preferences of styles. In this lesson and in Lesson 20, the point was made that the theme, graphics, and colors you use should fit the purpose of the presentation and its content. Choose a partner and sit down with that partner to review your solution files for Projects 1, 2, and 3 in this lesson. Explain to your partner why you chose the themes, colors, graphics, slide transitions, and sound effects for each presentation. Ask your partner to provide constructive feedback regarding whether or not he or she thinks your choices were effective.

CRITICAL THINKING

ACTIVITY 21-1

Several weeks ago, you prepared a presentation with 32 slides. Most of the slides include a title and a picture or a graphic, and only a few of the slides included bulleted lists with text. You added comments in the Notes pane as reminders for the key points related to each slide. You will be presenting the slide show again in a few days. Consider all the printing options, and then choose which option would be most useful to you when showing the slide show in front of an audience. Write a few sentences explaining which print option you would use and why.

ONLINE DISCOVERY

Microsoft provides thousands of free clip art images, photographs, and movie and sound clips at Microsoft Office Online. Choose a topic that interests you, such as basketball or mountain climbing. Explore the free clip art and media at *www.microsoft.com* to see what is available for that topic. Then search the Internet for other Web sites that offer *free* clip art, *free* photographs, and *free* sound and video clips. Explore and evaluate five to seven Web sites. Write a sentence or two about each site explaining whether you believe that the site is credible and if the media is truly free and in the public domain. Comment on whether the site offers quality images and media.

LESSON 22

Getting Started with Access Essentials

■ OBJECTIVES

Upon completion of this lesson, you should be able to:

- Identify the parts of the Access screen.
- Identify and navigate objects in a database.
- Create a database, then create a new table and enter records in Datasheet view.
- Change the column width in a table in Datasheet view.
- Add and delete fields in Design view.
- Change field data types and field properties.
- Add and edit records in a table in Datasheet view.
- Delete and copy records and fields in Datasheet view.

■ DATA FILES

To complete this lesson, you will need these data files.

Step22-1.accdb

Step22-6.accdb

Project22-1.accdb

■ VOCABULARY

data type

database

datasheet

entry

field

field name

field properties

primary key

record

relational database

table

A *database* is a collection of related information. Databases can contain all types of data—from an address list to schedules for a soccer tournament. Access is the Microsoft Office database program that enables you to organize, retrieve, and analyze data in many ways.

You might wonder what the difference is between a spreadsheet and a database. Actually, they are very similar. Like spreadsheets, databases are composed of rows and columns. While both applications enable you to organize, sort, and calculate the data, Access offers much more comprehensive functions for manipulating data. Access is a relational database management system. In a *relational database*, information is organized into separate subject-based tables, and the relationship of the data in one or more tables is used to bring the data together. For example, a relational database can be used to track the customers, orders, and the inventory for a retail business. One table stores information about the customers, one table stores information about the customers' orders, and yet another table stores product information. In Access, the information in the tables can be used to generate invoices based on customer orders. The invoices contain contact information from the customer table, as well as product details from the products table. If the business is planning to send out notices of a sale on a certain product brand, Access can quickly use the information in the orders table and the customers table to generate mailing labels for all those customers who have purchased products of that brand in the past.

Furthermore, in Access you can import or link data from other Access databases, Excel, Outlook, and many other data sources. And, Access data can be exported to many other data formats for use in other applications. Access is a powerful program that offers many features, most of which are beyond the scope of this course. The Access lessons in this module will introduce you to some of the basic features for viewing, entering, editing, querying, and reporting data.

Identifying the Parts of the Access Screen

The Access screen is similar to other Office 2007 applications, with the title bar, Ribbon, Quick Access Toolbar, application window sizing buttons, Close button, and status bar. You can open only one database at a time in an Access window. To open a new database from the Office Button menu, you will need to close the current database. If you would like to work with multiple databases at the same time, you must launch Access multiple times and then open a different database in each application window.

Unlike Word and Excel, Access does not have a standard document view. An Access database is composed of several objects, and each object contains several elements. The Access document window changes based on the object with which you are working. **Table 22–1** describes four basic objects that you will work with in this lesson and in Lesson 23. These objects help you organize and report the information that is stored in the database. You will learn to create tables in this lesson, and you will learn to create forms, reports, and queries in Lesson 23.

TABLE 22–1   Basic database objects

OBJECT	PURPOSE
Table	Stores data in columns and rows; all data is stored in a table
Form	Makes it easy for you to view, enter, and edit data in a table
Report	Organizes data in a specific layout
Query	Finds and shows data that meet a specified criteria

The objects are organized into categories in the Navigation Pane so you can quickly find and access the objects. The Navigation Pane can be collapsed to allow more space for the object elements.

Step-by-Step 22.1

1. Launch Access. The Getting Started with Microsoft Office Access window shown in **Figure 22–1** opens. Do not be concerned that the files listed in the Open Recent Database section are different. Notice that the most recently accessed documents appear in the list. Up to nine most recently accessed documents appear in this list.

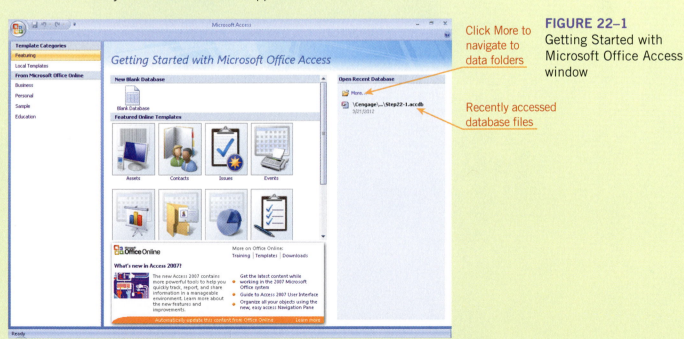

Click More to navigate to data folders

Recently accessed database files

FIGURE 22–1
Getting Started with Microsoft Office Access window

2. In the Open Recent Database section, click **More**. The Open dialog box opens.

3. Locate and open the file **Step22-1** from the data files. The Step22-1: Database (Access 2007) window, similar to that shown in **Figure 22–2**, appears. Compare your screen with the figure and identify the parts of the Access screen to familiarize yourself with the application. If you see a Security Warning message pane, close it.

FIGURE 22–2
Step 22-1: Database
(Access 2007) window

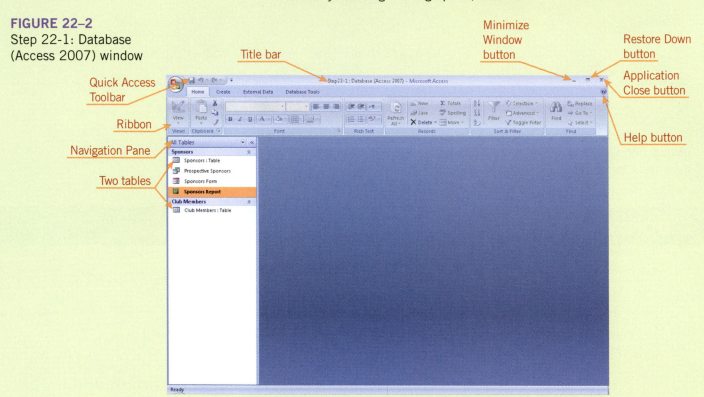

4. Note that there are two tables in this database: *Sponsors* and *Club Members*. In the Navigation Pane, under Sponsors, double-click **Sponsors : Table**. The table shown in **Figure 22–3** opens in the object window.

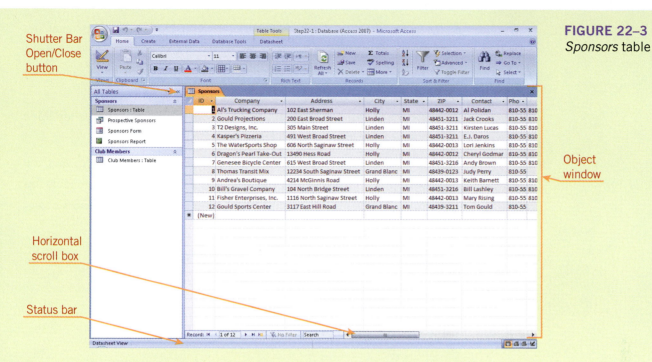

FIGURE 22–3
Sponsors table

5. To allow more space to show the table contents, click the **Shutter Bar Open/Close** button « in the Navigation Pane. The pane collapses, as shown in **Figure 22–4**, and you can see more of the table columns.

FIGURE 22–4
Collapsed
Navigation Pane

6. Drag the scroll box on the horizontal scroll bar (at the bottom of the screen) to view the columns to the right. This table provides data about companies that currently provide sponsorship for a club as well as companies that could potentially become sponsors.

7. Click the **Shutter Bar Open/Close** button to expand the Navigation Pane and show the objects in the database.

8. In the Navigation Pane, double-click **Club Members : Table**, and the table opens on top of the *Sponsors* table and is the active table, as shown in **Figure 22–5**. In the Object window, click the **Sponsors** object tab to show that table.

FIGURE 22–5
Club Members table

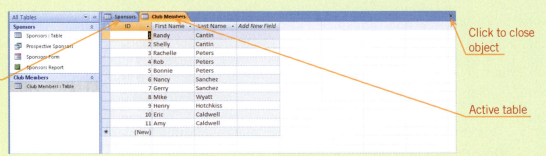

Click object tab to make *Sponsors* table active

Click to close object

Active table

9. Click the **Close** button for the table at the upper-right corner of the object window. The *Sponsors* table is closed, but the *Club Members* table is still open.

10. In the Navigation Pane, under Sponsors, double-click **Sponsors Form**. A form object appears in Form view, which makes it easy for you to enter data. All data entered in the form is saved in the *Sponsors* table.

11. Under Sponsors, double-click **Prospective Sponsors**, and a query object opens on top of the *Sponsors Form* object. This query object finds and shows only the companies that are considered to be prospective sponsors. The information comes from the *Sponsors* table.

12. Under Sponsors, double-click **Sponsors Report**. A report object opens on top of the query object and shows the data contained in the *Sponsors* table in a report design.

13. In the object window, click the **Sponsors Form** object tab. Then click the **Prospective Sponsors** object tab. Four objects are open, but you can only work with one object at a time.

14. Click the **Office Button** and then click **Close Database**. The objects and the database are closed and the Getting Started with Microsoft Office Access window appears. Leave Access open.

Creating a New Database

You can create a new database file using a blank database template or by using templates that are predefined with tables, reports, forms, and queries already created. In this lesson and in Lesson 23 you will learn to create each of these objects. Then when you open a predesigned database template, you will be familiar with all the object elements and you will be able to modify and customize the objects as needed.

Saving a Database File

When you create a new database, the first step is to name the database file. Before you enter any data, you need to assign a filename.

In all other lessons in this module, you have saved data files using a new filename. However, in Access, you can only use the Save As command to name and save objects in the database, or to save the database or object in a different format. You cannot use the Save As command to save the entire database under a new name. To rename an Access file, you can open My Computer (or Windows Explorer) from the desktop or the Start menu. Then locate and select the filename, right-click to open the File menu, and click Rename. You can copy or save the file in a new location before you rename it.

Creating a Table in Datasheet View

The second step is to create a table. A *table*, often referred to as a *datasheet*, is the primary object in the database. Each of the objects and everything you do in a database relies on the data stored in the tables. Therefore, at least one table must be created before any additional objects can be created. You can create as many tables as you need to store the information.

A database table contains fields and records. A *field* is a single piece of database information, such as a first name, a last name, or a telephone number. Fields appear as columns, and each column has a *field name*, which is a label that helps identify the field. A *record* is a group of related fields in a database, such as all the contact information for an individual, including first and last name, address, postal code, telephone number, and so forth. When you create a table in Access, the default setting creates a *primary key* for each record, which uniquely identifies each record in the table. The primary key is useful in sorting records, and it prevents duplicate entries. For example, you may have a student ID number, and no other student has exactly the same number as you.

By default, a table opens in Datasheet view, and the table data is shown in a row-and-column format. In this view, the table looks much like a spreadsheet. The intersection of a row and a column is called a cell, just as in an Excel worksheet. Field names are used for column headings, and each row in the table contains one single record of the entire database.

EXTRA FOR EXPERTS

A file in the Access 2000 or the Access 2002–2003 file format (.mdb) can be opened in Access 2007. When you create a new database file, the default setting is to save the file in the Access 2007 file format. You can change this setting so new files you create are saved in the Access 2000 or the Access 2002–2003 file format. Click the **Office Button** and then click **Access Options**. Under Creating databases, change the format setting in the Default file format box, and then click **OK**.

▶ VOCABULARY

table

datasheet

field

field name

record

primary key

Step-by-Step 22.2

1. If necessary, launch Access. The Getting Started with Microsoft Office Access window should be open.

2. Under the first heading, New Blank Database, click the **Blank Database** icon. A Blank Database section similar to the one shown in **Figure 22–6** appears on the right side of the screen.

FIGURE 22–6
Creating a new blank database

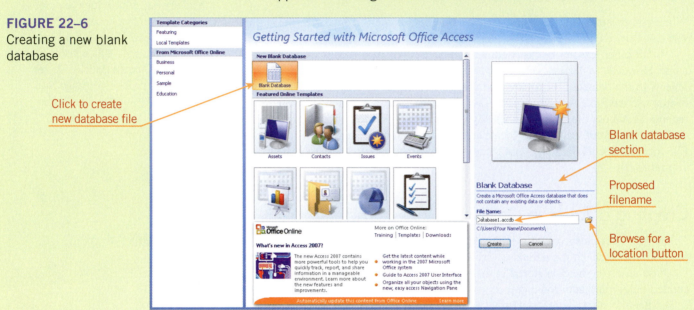

3. A proposed filename, such as *Database1.accdb*, appears in the File Name box. Click the **Browse for a location** button 📂. The File New Database dialog box opens. Locate the folder where you save your solution files.

4. In the File New Database dialog box, replace the proposed filename in the File name box with **Customers**. Click **OK**. The new filename now appears in the File Name box on the Blank Database section. Click **Create**. A new database window like the one shown in **Figure 22–7** opens.

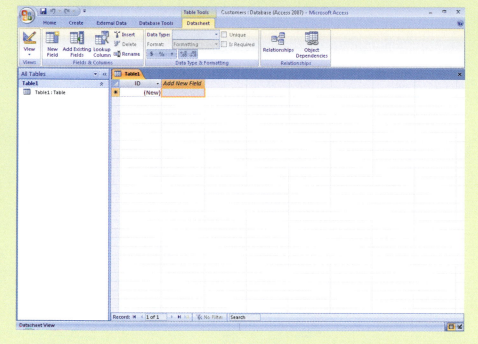

FIGURE 22–7
New database window

5. In the second column of the table, double-click the **Add New Field** column heading. When the column heading is gone, enter **Last Name** and press **Enter**. The new field name is entered as the column heading, and the insertion point is positioned in the column heading for the third column.

6. Enter **Address** and press **Enter**. Continue using the same procedure to enter the following additional field names:

   `City`

   `State/Province`

   `Postal Code`

   `Country/Region`

7. Click the **Save** button on the Quick Access Toolbar to open the Save As dialog box. In the Table Name box, enter **Contact Information** and then click **OK**.

8. To create a second table in the database, on the Ribbon, click the **Create** tab. In the Tables group shown in **Figure 22–8**, click the **Table** button. A new table appears in the object window on top of the *Contact Information* table, and the Navigation Pane also shows the new table.

FIGURE 22–8
The Tables group on the
Create tab

9. The Ribbon changed to show the Table Tools Datasheet tab. In the Fields & Columns group shown in **Figure 22–9**, click the **New Field** button. A Field Templates pane opens on the right to show fields to insert in the table.

FIGURE 22–9
The Fields & Columns group on the
Table Tools Datasheet tab

10. If necessary, click the plus signs to the left of *Assets* and *Contacts* to expand the list, as shown in **Figure 22–10**.

FIGURE 22–10
Expanded list of field templates

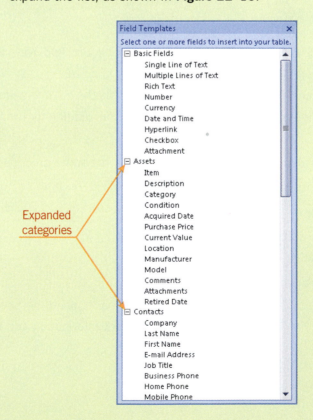

11. Under Contacts, double-click **First Name**. The field name is inserted at the top of the second column. Under Contacts, double-click **Last Name**. The field name is inserted at the top of the third column.

12. Under Assets, double-click to add the field names **Item**, **Description**, and **Purchase Price**. Then, close the Field Templates pane.

13. Click the **Save** button. In the Table Name box, enter **Orders**, and then click **OK**.

14. Leave the tables and database open.

Entering Records in Datasheet View

When you enter data into a cell, it is called an *entry*. To move from one cell to another, you can use the mouse to click in a cell. You can also use the keyboard to navigate in a table. **Table 22–2** describes the keys you can use to move around in a table in Datasheet view.

▶ **VOCABULARY**
entry

TABLE 22–2   Keys for navigating in Datasheet view

KEY	DESCRIPTION
Enter, Tab, or right arrow	Moves the insertion point to the next field
Left arrow or Shift+Tab	Moves the insertion point to the previous field
Home	Moves the insertion point to the first field in the current record
End	Moves the insertion point to the last field in the current record
Up arrow	Moves the insertion point up one record and stays in the same field
Down arrow	Moves the insertion point down one record and stays in the same field
Page Up	Moves the insertion point up one screen
Page Down	Moves the insertion point down one screen

Step-by-Step 22.3

1. If necessary, open the **Customers** database from your solution files.

2. In the Navigation Pane, double-click Contact Information : Table, if necessary, to open the table.

3. To enter the first record, press **Tab** to move to the cell under the field name *Last Name* and enter **McGuirk**. Notice that as you create the entry in the *Last Name* field, Access automatically assigns the primary key *1* in the *ID* field.

4. Press **Tab** to move to the next field, and complete the record by entering the following information in the respective fields:

    Address: 610 Brae Burn

    City: Mansfield

    State/Province: OH

    Postal Code: 44907-1112

    Country/Region: USA

5. Press **Tab** twice to move to the *Last Name* field in the next row. Enter the following data for two more records:

    Last Name: Bain

    Address: 117 Yorkshire Road

    City: Lexington

    State/Province: OH

    Postal Code: 44904-3455

    Country/Region: USA

    Last Name: Smith

    Address: 4645 Rule Road

    City: Bellville

    State/Province: OH

    Postal Code: 44813-3231

    Country/Region: USA

6. Click the **Save** button on the Quick Access Toolbar to save the changes. Leave the table and the database open.

Modifying a Database Table in Design View

The default column widths are often too wide or too narrow for the data in the table. This is the case with your database. The *Address* field is not wide enough to show all the text in the street address, and the *ID* field has extra white space. You can adjust the column widths in a database table just as you adjust the column widths in an Excel spreadsheet.

Adding and Deleting Fields

Often, after you create a table and enter data, you decide you want to add or delete fields. You can add fields in either Datasheet view or Design view. However, Design view provides features that make the task easier. Design view shows details about the structure of the object, including the data type and the field properties. The *data type* determines what type of data the field can store, such as text or numbers. *Field properties* define the characteristics and behavior of a field, such as the number of characters allowed.

▶ **VOCABULARY**

data type

field properties

You can change views using the View button. When you click the View button arrow, you can select the desired view. The upper portion of the button always shows the icon for an alternative view, which you can click to switch to that view. For example, when you are in Design view, the upper portion of the View button shows the icon for the Datasheet view. Clicking the upper portion toggles your view to the Datasheet view.

Step-by-Step 22.4

1. If necessary, open the **Customers** database from your solution files and then open the *Contact Information* table.

2. Point to the right border of the cell containing the field name (column heading) *Address*. When the pointer changes to a two-headed arrow, drag the column border to the right until the column is wide enough to show the complete entry for all records.

3. Point to the field name *ID*. When a down arrow appears, click and drag to the right until all the columns in the table through *Country/Region* are selected.

4. Position the mouse pointer over the right cell border for the field name *Country/Region*. When the pointer changes to a two-headed arrow, double-click. All the column widths are automatically adjusted for the contents in each column.

5. Click the first cell in the table. Click the **Home** tab. In the Views group shown in **Figure 22–11**, click the **View** button arrow and then click **Design View**.

Click View button arrow to select from the list of available views

Click top portion of button to toggle to view shown

FIGURE 22–11
The Views group on the Home tab

6. The table appears in Design view, as shown in **Figure 22–12**. The Ribbon changes. The field names appear in the first column, and the second column shows the data type for each field. Notice that a data type appears for each field name, and field properties for the active field appear in a pane at the bottom of the window.

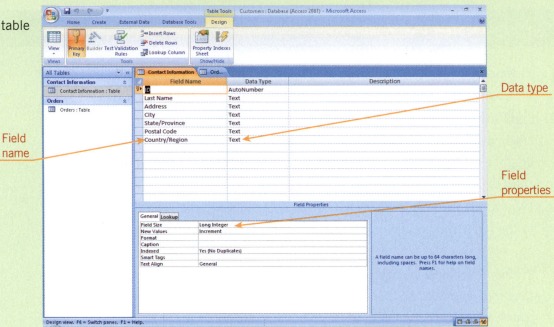

Field name

Data type

Field properties

7. Position the mouse pointer to the left of the *Country/Region* field name. When a right-pointing arrow appears, as shown in **Figure 22–13**, click to select the entire row.

Right-pointing arrow for selecting a row

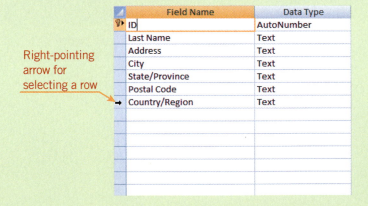

8. In the Tools group on the Table Tools Design tab, click the **Insert Rows** button **Insert Rows** .

9. Click the blank cell directly below the field name *Postal Code*. Enter **E-mail** and press **Enter**.

10. Click the blank cell directly below the field name *Country/Region*. Enter **Birth Date** and press **Enter**. The new field is entered and the Data Type cell to the right is active and shows the default data type, *Text*.

11. Select the row for the field name *Last Name*, and click the **Insert Rows** button. In the blank cell above *Last Name*, enter **First Name** and then press **Enter**.

12. Select the row containing the *Country/Region* field. In the Tools group on the Table Tools Design tab, click the **Delete Rows** button .

13. When prompted to delete the field and all the data in the field, click **Yes**. The field and all the data entered in the field are removed from the table.

14. Save the changes to the table. Leave the table and the database open.

> **WARNING**
>
> Use caution when deleting rows in Design view. Once you confirm the deletion, you cannot undo the deletion.

Changing Field Data Type and Field Properties

As you saw in the previous Step-by-Step, the default data type for a field is Text. In Design view, you can specify the data type for each field. For example, you can specify Text, Number, Currency, and even Yes/No. Text is appropriate for most of the fields in the *Contact Information* table. However, for some fields, such as the Birth Date field, you may want to specify a Date/Time data type instead of Text.

When you choose a data type, you can also change the field properties. The field properties available depend on the data type selected. For example, the default Field Size property for the Text data type is 255 characters, but you can specify that the field allow up to only 50 characters. Most data types include a Format property. The Format property specifies how you want Access to show numbers, dates, times, and text.

Step-by-Step 22.5

1. If necessary, open the **Customers** database from your solution files and then open the *Contact Information* table. Show the table in Design view.

2. Click the **Text** data type cell for the *Birth Date* field. A list arrow appears at the right side of the cell. Click the list arrow, and then click **Date/Time** to change the data type. Notice that the Field Properties pane changes to show the values for the Date/Time data type.

3. In the Field Properties pane, click the **Format** property box, and when the list arrow appears, click it to open the list of Format property options shown in **Figure 22–14**. Click **Short Date**.

FIGURE 22–14
Date/Time
format options

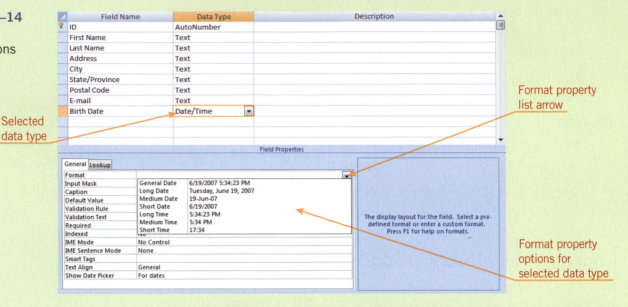

4. Click the **Text** data type cell for the *State/Province* field. In the Field Properties pane below, click the **Field Size** property box. The field size is currently set at *255*. Change the field size to **2**. This requires that the user use two-letter state abbreviations when entering the state name in the table.

5. Click the **View** button to toggle to Datasheet view. When prompted to save the table, click **Yes**. When prompted that some data may be lost, click **Yes** to continue.

6. Click the **Shutter Bar Open/Close** button to collapse the Navigation Pane.

7. Enter the following data in the *First Name*, *Birth Date*, and *E-mail* fields. Notice that as you enter the birth date data, Access automatically formats the date using the short date format you specified in the field properties.

ID	First Name	Birth Date	E-mail
1	Jaimey	Jmcguirk@nets.com	March 13, 1978
2	Jesse	Jbain@LFSC.com	June 18, 1980
3	Matt	Msmith@qry.com	April 11, 1979

8. Enter the following new record. Remember that as you enter the state name, Access will not permit you to enter more than two characters. You must enter the two-letter state abbreviation for Ohio.

First Name:	Kelsey
Last Name:	Erwin
Address:	2038 Leiter Road
City:	Lucas
State/Province:	Ohio
Postal Code:	44843-3197
E-mail:	Kerwin@csfa.com
Birth Date:	October 6, 1979

9. Select the *E-mail* and *Birth Date* columns and automatically adjust the column widths. Click one of the entries in the table to deselect the columns.

10. Click the **Shutter Bar Open/Close** button to expand the Navigation Pane.

11. Save the changes to the table.

12. Click the **Office Button** and then click **Close Database**.

Adding and Editing Database Records

It is common for data to change after you have entered it into your database. For example, people move, so you have to change their addresses and probably their phone numbers. Access provides several navigation features that make it easy for you to move around in a table to make necessary edits. These features are especially useful when you are working in large databases.

   If you make a mistake adding or editing data in a record, you can choose the Undo command to reverse your last action. As soon as you begin editing another record, however, the Undo command is no longer available. That is because Access constantly saves the changes. As you experienced in the previous Step-by-Step, when you make changes in Design view and then switch to Datasheet view without first saving the object, Access prompts you to save the changes. However, when you work in Datasheet view, the changes are saved as they are made. When you switch from Datasheet view to a different view, or when you close the database, you are not prompted to save the changes because they were already saved.

Step-by-Step 22.6

1. Click the **Start** button, click **Computer**, and navigate to the folder where the data files are saved. Locate the file **Step22-6**. Do not open the file. Instead, right-click the filename and click **Copy** in the shortcut menu to copy the file to the Clipboard.

2. Navigate to the location where you save your files. Open the appropriate folder, right-click in a blank area inside the folder and click **Paste** in the shortcut menu to paste the Step22-6 file in that folder. Then, double-click **Step22-6**, and then click **Rename**. Enter **Books** and press **Enter**.

3. Double-click the **Books** filename to open the database. In the Navigation Pane, double-click **Classics : Table** to show the table.

4. An orange highlight indicates that the first cell in the table (ID number 1) is the active cell. In the Navigation bar, shown at the bottom of the table in **Figure 22–15**, click the **Next record** navigation button. The highlight moves to the ID number 2 in the second row in the table.

FIGURE 22–15
Navigation bar

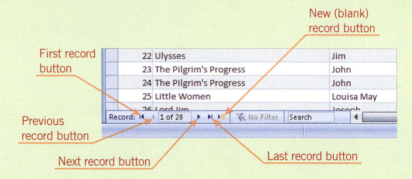

5. In the Navigation bar, click the **Previous record** navigation button to move back to ID number 1. Notice that the highlight moves to a new row, and the active cell is still in the *ID* field.

6. Select the number **1** in the Current Record number box in the middle of the navigation buttons and enter **22**. Press **Enter**. The highlight moves to the cell in the ID field with the ID number 22.

7. Click the *ID* field entry **22**. Press **Tab** twice to move the insertion point to the *Author First* field in the same row. The entry in that cell is selected. Enter **James** to change the entry. Notice that a pencil appears at the left edge of the row, indicating that the record is being edited.

8. Click the **Next record** navigation button. The highlight moves to the next row in the *Author First* field, and the entry in that cell is selected. The pencil no longer appears to the left of row 22 because when you clicked the Next record navigation button, the edit was completed. When you navigate out of the row, the entry is updated.

9. Click the **First record** navigation button. The insertion point moves to the *Author First* field in the first row in the table.

10. Click the **Last record** navigation button. The insertion point moves to the *Author First* field in the last row in the table.

11. Press **Tab** two times to move to the *Cover* field in the same row. Enter **Paperback** to replace the current entry.

12. Click the **Previous record** navigation button to move to the row above. Enter **Paperback** to replace the entry. Press **Tab**.

13. The last change was not necessary. Click the **Undo** button on the Quick Access Toolbar. The action is reversed and the cell shows *Hardcover*.

14. Save the changes. Leave the table and the database open.

Deleting and Copying Records and Fields in Datasheet View

Deleting records is similar to deleting rows in an Excel spreadsheet. To delete a record, you must first select the record. You can delete multiple records at the same time by selecting more than one row. After a record(s) is selected, you can press the Delete key to remove the data. Take care, though. Once you have deleted a record, you cannot use the Undo command to restore it.

Selected data can also be copied or moved from one location in an Access table to a new location within the same table or to a different table. The Cut, Copy, and Paste commands you have used in other Office applications are also available in Access. Access stores cut or copied text in the Clipboard.

To remove a table field and all the data for the field, you delete the column, similar to how you delete a column in Excel. To change the sequence of the fields in the table, you can rearrange the sequence of the columns.

> ### ▣ EXTRA FOR EXPERTS
>
> To select multiple rows, select a row and then drag the mouse pointer down (or up) to include adjacent rows. You can also select multiple rows by selecting the first row, pressing and holding **Shift**, then positioning the mouse pointer to the left of the last row to include in the selection. When the right-pointing arrow appears, click once and the rows between the two clicks are selected.

Step-by-Step 22.7

1. If necessary, open the **Books** database from your solution files and then open the *Classics* table. Collapse the Navigation Pane.

2. In the group of navigation buttons at the bottom of the table, click the **New (blank) record** button ▸▦ . The first empty cell in the *ID* field is highlighted.

3. Press **Tab** to move to the *Title* field. Access automatically inserts an ID number for the primary key when you begin to enter data. Enter the following data for the new record. Press **Enter** after you enter the price.

Title:	Crime and Punishment
Author First:	Fyodor
Author Last:	Dostoyevsky
Cover:	Hardcover
# Pages:	499
Publisher:	HarperCollins Publishers, Inc.
Price:	$16.99

4. Point to the left of the record with ID 26. (The record is fourth from the bottom in the table.) When the pointer changes to a right-pointing arrow, click to select the entire row.

5. Press **Delete**. When prompted to confirm the deletion of the record, click **Yes**. The record is deleted from the table. Notice that the ID numbers for the records below the deleted row do not change.

6. Point to the left of the *ID* field 27 (*Emma*). When the pointer changes to a right-pointing arrow, click to select the entire row.

7. Click the **Copy** button in the Clipboard group, point to the left of the *ID* field in the empty row (*New*) at the bottom of the table. When the pointer changes to a right-pointing arrow, click to select the entire row.

8. Click the upper portion of the **Paste** button to paste a copy of record 27 in the new row. Change the title to **Northanger Abbey**, the number of pages to **220**, and the publisher to **Modern Classics Library**. Press **Enter**.

9. If necessary, drag the horizontal scroll box to the left to show the *ID* column. In record 28 (*The Red Badge of Courage*), double-click the *Cover* field entry **Paperback**, and then press **Ctrl+C** to copy the entry.

10. In the new *Northanger Abbey* record, double-click the *Cover* field entry **Hardback**, and then press **Ctrl+V** to replace the entry with the data on the Clipboard (*Paperback*).

11. Position the mouse pointer over the field name *# Pages*. When the pointer changes to a down-pointing arrow, click to select the entire column.

12. Click the **Table Tools Datasheet** tab. In the Fields & Columns group, click the **Delete** button ![Delete icon]. When prompted to permanently delete the fields and data, click **Yes**.

13. The *Publisher* column should already be selected. Click the column heading and drag to the left. When the black vertical border shown in **Figure 22–16** appears to the left of the *Cover* column, release the mouse button. The *Publisher* column is now repositioned and is before the *Cover* column.

FIGURE 22–16
Repositioning a table column

Drag pointer to position vertical line for new location

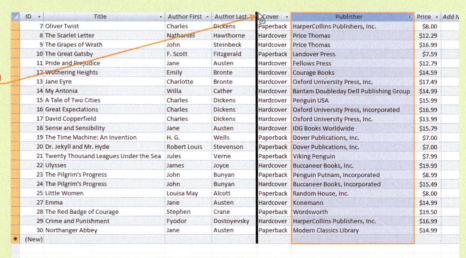

14. Save the changes. Click the **Office Button** and click **Close Database**. Close the Access application.

ETHICS IN TECHNOLOGY

Software Piracy

One of the biggest problems facing the computer industry today is software piracy, the illegal copying or use of programs. Some low-level software costs less than $25, but more specialized software can cost hundreds or even thousands of dollars. Billions of dollars are lost every year as a result of pirated software.

Software is pirated in many ways. You may be surprised to know that not only individual users copy software illegally—so do businesses. Of course, the easiest way is to copy from the original disks. But software can also be copied from the server of a network or via e-mail. Shareware, software that can be accessed for free, is also abused. It is based on an honor system, and if you use the software on a regular basis, you are asked to pay a registration fee. Many people use shareware with no intention of ever paying for it.

You, too, may ask, "What is the big deal about copying software?" Developing software programs is an expensive process, and highly trained programmers spend hundreds of hours creating programs. Software is a form of intellectual property, and the creators of software programs own the rights to their work, just as an author owns the rights to what he or she writes. The Copyright Act of 1976 was passed to update the previous Copyright Act of 1909 to address intellectual property issues raised by technology. In 1983, a Software Piracy and Counterfeiting Amendment was added. It is no longer a misdemeanor to copy software illegally—it is a felony.

SUMMARY

In this lesson, you learned:

- Many parts of the Access screen are similar to other Office 2007 applications. However, Access also has different views to perform tasks unique to Access.

- The first step in creating a new database is to assign a filename to the database. The second step is to create a table. Tables are the primary objects in a database. A database can have multiple tables. All other objects are based on data stored in tables.

- You can automatically adjust table column widths in Datasheet view similar to how you adjust column widths in Excel.

- A table can be modified after it is created, and you can add or delete fields even after records have been entered. You can modify a table in Datasheet view or in Design view.

- You can change views using the View button. Clicking the upper portion of the View button toggles you to an alternative view, such as switching from Design view to Datasheet view.

- In Design view, you can specify the data type and properties for each field. Text is the default field data type. The field properties control the characteristics and behavior of a database field, such as the maximum number of characters.

- If you make a mistake adding or editing data in a record, you can choose the Undo command to reverse your last action, but once you begin entering another record, the Undo command is no longer available.

- Deleting records is similar to deleting rows in Excel. Once you have deleted a record, you cannot use the Undo command to restore it.

- Selected data can be copied or moved from one location to another in an Access table, or to another table, using the Cut, Copy, and Paste commands.

- To change the sequence of fields in a table, you rearrange the sequence of columns.

■ VOCABULARY REVIEW

Define the following terms:

data type   field   record
database   field name   relational database
datasheet   field properties   table
entry   primary key

■ REVIEW QUESTIONS

TRUE / FALSE

Circle T if the statement is true or F if the statement is false.

T   F   **1.** Database information is stored in tables, forms, and reports.

T   F   **2.** You can open multiple database files in the same Access application window.

T   F   **3.** You can work with only one object at a time.

T   F   **4.** You can add and delete fields in Datasheet view or Design view.

T   F   **5.** If you change your mind after deleting a row, you can undo the deletion.

MULTIPLE CHOICE

Select the best response for each of the following statements.

1. A _____ is a single piece of information in a database, such as a first name, a last name, or a telephone number.

   A. row   C. record

   B. field   D. column

2. _____ view shows the table data in a row-and-column format.

   A. Table   C. Normal

   B. Design   D. Datasheet

3. The _____ uniquely identifies each record in a table.

   A. primary key   C. entry number

   B. field name   D. entry

4. _____ are specifications that allow you to customize a field beyond choosing a data type.

   A. Record settings   C. Primary keys

   B. Field properties   D. Record entries

5. You can only use the Save As command in Access to _____.

   A. save the database with a new filename or to a new location

   B. name and save an object in the database

   C. save the database or object in a new format

   D. B and C

FILL IN THE BLANK

Complete the following sentences by writing the correct word or words in the blanks provided.

1. A(n) _____ is a group of related fields, such as all the personal information about an employee.

2. A(n) _____ is a label that helps to identify the field.

3. When you enter data into a cell, it is called a(n) _____.

4. The _____ object organizes data in a specific layout.

5. The _____ object finds and shows data that meet a specified criteria.

■ PROJECTS

PROJECT 22–1

1. Click the **Start** button, click **Computer**, and locate and open the data files folder. Copy the file **Project22-1** to the Clipboard. Then locate and open the folder where you save your files. Paste the file in the folder, and then rename the file **Films**.

2. Open the **Films** database. This database stores membership information and the current video collection of the Oak Creek Film Society (OCFS), a club for lovers of classic films. Notice that this database contains two tables: *Collection* and *Members*.

3. Open the **Collection** table to see the films the OCFS has collected so far.

4. Close the table and double-click **Members Form** to see the form used to insert member data.

5. Close the form and double-click **Suspense Query** to see the films in the collection that belong to the *Suspense* category. Close the query.

6. Create a new table for the database to store information on special events that the OCFS sponsors. Use the Field Templates pane to add new fields. Under *Events*, add the following fields to the new table in this order: **Title**, **Location**, **Start Time**, **End Time**, and **Description**.

7. Close the Field Templates pane and save the table with the name **Events**.

8. Enter the following data in Datasheet view:

Title	Location	Start Time	End Time	Event Description
Holiday Classics	Odeon Theatre	12/15/2012	12/16/2012	Christmas theme
Horror Classics	Odeon Theatre	1/17/2013	1/19/2013	Horror theme
Hitchcock Classics	Odeon Theatre	2/22/2013	2/24/2013	Suspense theme

9. Automatically adjust the column widths so that complete entries are shown in all columns.

10. Save the changes. Leave the table and database open.

PROJECT 22–2

1. If necessary, open the **Films** database from your solution files and then open the **Events** table.

2. You decide your table needs some modifications. With the *Events* table open, switch to Design view.

3. Change the Field Name *Title* to **Event**.

4. The *Description* field does not add much to the table because the subject of each event is clear from the event name. Delete the *Description* field and all contents.

5. It would be helpful to see the time for each event. First edit the two fields *Start Time* and *End Time* to read as **Start Date** and **End Date**.

6. Insert a new field following the *End Date* field named **Start Time**. Change the data type to **Date/Time**. Set the Format property for the new field to **Medium Time**.

7. Each event includes clips from classic films. Insert a new field named **Films** following the *Start Time* field. Change the Field Size property for the new field to **200**.

8. Save the changes to the design and return to Datasheet view. Insert the following data in the new fields:

Event	Start Time	Films
Holiday Classics	7:00 PM	A Christmas Story, A Christmas Carol
Horror Classics	7:00 PM	Dracula, Frankenstein
Hitchcock Classics	6:30 PM	The Birds, Vertigo

9. Insert the following new record.

Event:	Spoofing the Classics
Location:	Odeon Theatre
Start Date:	3/15/2013
End Date:	3/17/2013
Start Time:	4:00 PM
Films:	The Pink Panther, Young Frankenstein, Dr. Strangelove

10. Adjust the column widths to show all entries in the fields.

11. Save the changes. Close the table and leave the database open.

PROJECT 22–3

1. If necessary, open the **Films** database from your solution files. Open the **Collection** table.

2. Adjust the width of the columns to show the complete entry for all records.

3. Collapse the Navigation Pane.

4. Go to record 24 (*The Haunting*). You think the film title is incorrect. In the *Title* field, change the title to **The Haunting of Hill House**. Press **Enter**.

5. Whoops, you were wrong. That was the title of the book, not the film. Your original title was correct after all. Click **Undo** to restore the original title *The Haunting*.

6. You need to add two new films that were acquired for recent events. Enter the data below.

Title:	Vertigo
Year:	1958
Length:	128 m
MPAA:	NR
Color/BW:	Color
Director:	Hitchcock
Category:	Suspense
Actor:	James Stewart
Actress:	Kim Novak

Title:	Dr. Strangelove
Year:	1964
Length:	93 m
MPAA:	NR
Color/BW:	BW
Director:	Kubrick
Category:	Comedy
Actor:	Peter Sellers, George C. Scott

7. You have another new film to add. Copy record 29 (*Star Wars*) and paste it in a new record. Change the title to **The Empire Strikes Back**, the year to **1980**, the length to **124 m**, and the director to **Kershner**. Replace *Alec Guinness* in the *Actor* field with **Billy Dee Williams**. Replace the existing entry in the *Award* field with **Sound**.

8. You have discovered that the 1969 version of Hamlet (record 14) is damaged. Delete this record from the table.

9. Expand the Navigation Pane.

10. Save your changes and then close the table and the database.

TEAMWORK PROJECT

Databases are ideal for storing statistics such as those of sports teams. With a partner, create a database to record statistics for a sports team. Follow these steps:

1. With your teammate, choose a sports team for further study.

2. Determine the categories of statistics you need to gather for your database. For example, players' names, number of games completed in the current season, scores, and individual or team statistics for each game. Divide up the categories so you share the responsibility for gathering the data.

3. Create a database table with appropriate file names and data types to store the data you collect.

 # CRITICAL THINKING

ACTIVITY 22–1

If possible, look at two computer screens, side by side. On one computer, open an Access table in Datasheet view. On the other computer, open an Excel worksheet. Compare the two screens, and create two lists—one to describe at least three similarities and one to describe at least three differences.

 # ONLINE DISCOVERY

Contact information generally includes postal codes. If you mail a letter or a package without a postal code, the item must be manually sorted at the post office, and the delivery of the item can be delayed by several days. Furthermore, if the data for the postal code is incorrect, mailed documents and packages may be returned as undeliverable. So, how can you find a postal code or verify that the postal code you have in your record is correct? The United States Postal Service provides an online Zip Code Lookup feature. You can search for zip codes by address, city, or company. You can also search for a list of all the cities within a specified zip code. The search results can verify a correct address and zip code, and the proper standard postal format for the address is also provided.

1. Go to *www.usps.com*.

2. Navigate to the Find a Zip Code feature, and find the zip code for the following address:

   892 Hickory Drive

   Marysville, OH

3. Verify the zip code for the following company address. Make any necessary changes for the standardized format.

   Cengage Learning

   20 Channel Center Street

   Boston, MA 02200-3401

LESSON 23

Managing and Reporting Database Information

■ OBJECTIVES

Upon completion of this lesson, you should be able to:

- Create a form.
- Enter and edit data in a form.
- Sort data in Datasheet view.
- Find and replace data in Datasheet view.
- Create a query.
- Create and print a report.
- Create mailing labels.

■ DATA FILES

To complete this lesson, you will need these data files:

Step23-1.accdb

Step23-2.accdb

Project23-1.accdb

■ VOCABULARY

form

query

report

As the amount of data in a database increases, it becomes more difficult to manage records and find information. Access has several useful features that help you work with larger databases. These features help you enter the data, order the data, find the data, and summarize and report the data.

Creating a Form

▶ VOCABULARY
form

Access offers another way to enter data in a table. You can create a *form*, a database object which provides a convenient way to enter, edit, and view data from a table. A professional-looking form can also make the process of entering data more efficient and more accurate. When you create a form, you add a new object to the database. Although you can design and create a form manually, Access offers two features that make the process quick and easy: the Form tool and the Form Wizard.

When you work with a form, you have three options for viewing the object. Form view is used for adding, editing, and viewing data. Layout view enables you to make changes to the form design, such as font styles and colors and pre-designed styles. In this view, data appears, so you can see how the changes you make will look when you open the form in Form view. Design view provides a detailed view of the structure of the form, and you can use this view to change the properties and add new fields.

Creating a Form Using the Form Tool

You can create a form with a single click using the Form tool. All the fields from the table or query are included on the form, and the form is pre-designed. If desired, you can modify the form layout and design using either Layout view or Design view.

Step-by-Step 23.1

1. Click the **Start** button, click **Computer**, and locate and open the data files folder. Copy the file **Step23-1** to the Clipboard. Then, locate and open the folder where you save your files. Paste the file in the folder, and then rename the file **Books2**.

2. Double-click the **Books2** filename to open the database.

3. In the Navigation Pane, open both tables (*Book List* and *Officers*) to look at the data stored in the tables. Close both tables.

4. In the Navigation Pane, click **Book List : Table** to select it. Click the **Create** tab. In the Forms group shown in **Figure 23–1**, click the **Form** button.

FIGURE 23–1
The Forms group on the Create tab

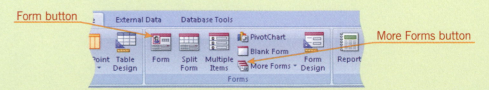

5. The form shown in **Figure 23–2** appears. The form appears in Layout view, and the Ribbon shows the Form Layout Tools Format tab. Labels identify the fields included on the form, and text boxes show the field data for the first record in the *Book List* table.

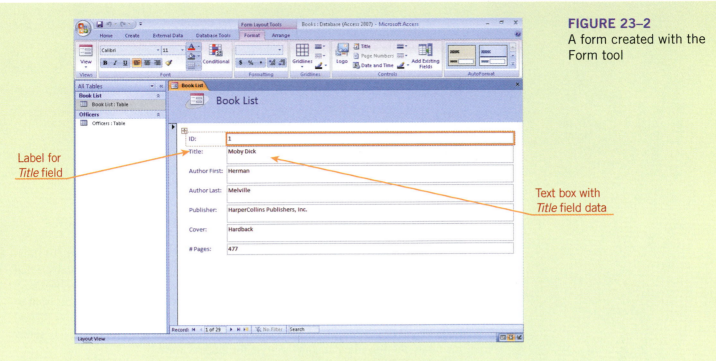

FIGURE 23-2
A form created with the Form tool

6. In the AutoFormat group shown in **Figure 23–3**, click the **More** button.

More button

FIGURE 23-3
The AutoFormat group on the Form Layout Tools Format tab

7. A gallery of several pre-designed formats appears. Click the **Equity** style (the fourth option in the second row). This style applies only to the form; the table style remains unchanged.

8. Click the text box for the *Title* field to select the text box. In the Font group, click the **Font Color** button arrow. Under Access Theme Colors, click the **Highlight** color in the first row of colors. As you enter the title for each record, the text will appear in the orange color, but only on the form. The formats applied to the font have no effect on the data stored in the *Book List* table.

9. Click the text box for the *Author First* field. Click the **Font Color** button arrow. Click the **Dark Red** color, the first color in the bottom row.

10. With the text box still selected, click the **Font** list arrow. Scroll up in the list of font styles and click **Arial**. Click the **Font Size** list arrow and then click **12**.

11. With the *Author First* text box still selected, double-click the **Format Painter** button. Then, click the text boxes for the *Title, Author Last, Publisher, Cover,* and *# Pages* fields to apply the new font formats to those text boxes.

12. Click the **Format Painter** button (or press Escape) to toggle off the Format Painter mode.

13. Click the **Save** button on the Quick Access Toolbar. The Save As dialog box appears. In the Form Name text box, enter **Book Form** and then click **OK**. The new form appears in the Navigation Pane under the *Book List* table.

14. Close the database.

Creating a Form Using the Form Wizard

You may not always want to include all the database fields on the form. To illustrate, consider the following scenario. You are working with a vendor database that includes contact information as well as data about past purchases, billings, and payments. You want to create a form to add new vendors to the database. You want to include only the fields related to contact information on the form. The Form Wizard makes it easy to create a form with your preferences because it prompts you to select the fields, the form layout, and the style for the new form.

Step-by-Step 23.2

1. Click the **Start** button, click **Computer**, and locate and open the data files folder. Copy the file **Step23-2** to the Clipboard. Then, locate and open the folder where you save your files. Paste the file in the folder, and then rename the file **VGInc**.

2. Double-click the **VGInc** filename to open the database. Open the *Vendors* table. Scroll through the table to view the data stored in the table. Leave the table open.

3. Click the **Create** tab. In the Forms group, click the **More Forms** button 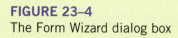 and then click **Form Wizard**. The Form Wizard dialog box shown in **Figure 23–4** opens.

FIGURE 23–4
The Form Wizard dialog box

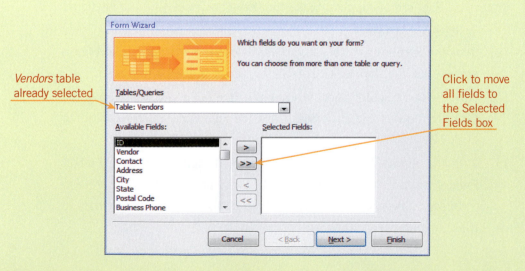

4. Notice that under Table/Queries, *Table: Vendors* is already selected. This indicates that the form will be based on the *Vendors* table. Also notice that under Available Fields all the fields that are available in the *Vendors* table are listed.

5. You need to identify the fields you want to appear on the form. Click the right-pointing double arrows button (**>>**). All of the field names are moved to the Selected Fields list. This tells Access to include all the fields in the form.

6. You decide you don't want the *Account Balance* and the *Last Purchase* fields to appear on the form. In the Selected Fields list, click **Account Balance** to select the field name. Then click the left-pointing single arrow button (**<**) to remove the field from the list.

7. In the Selected Fields list, the field name *Last Purchase* is already selected. Click the left-pointing single arrow button (**<**) to remove that field from the list.

8. Click **Next** to advance to the next step in the wizard. The new Form Wizard dialog box prompts you to select a layout for the form. Select each of the four layout options to see a preview of each layout.

9. Select the **Columnar** layout option, and then click **Next**. The dialog box changes and prompts you to select an AutoFormat style for the form. Select the **Concourse** style. The preview box shows you what this AutoFormat style looks like.

10. Scroll down through the list and select some of the other styles to see what they look like. Then scroll to the bottom of the list and click **Windows Vista**.

11. Click **Next** to advance to the next step in the wizard. The final Form Wizard dialog box prompts you to create a name for the form. A proposed title appears in the text box. Edit the proposed form name so it is **Vendor Form**.

12. If necessary, click the check box to enable the **Open the form to view or enter information** option. Click **Finish**. Access creates and shows the new form in Form view. (When you enable the *Modify the form's design* option, the new form opens in Design view.)

13. Compare your screen to **Figure 23–5**. Notice that data from the first record in the *Vendors* table appears in the form text boxes. Notice, too, that the new form object appears in the Navigation Pane under the *Vendors* table.

FIGURE 23–5
Vendor Form object

New form added to list of objects

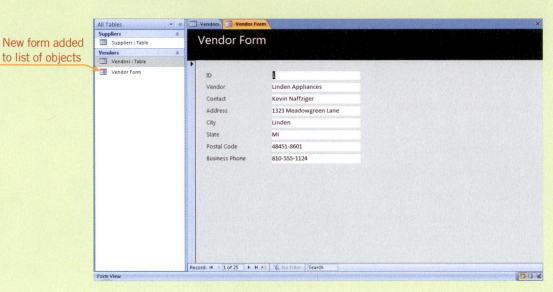

14. Leave the form, the table, and the database open.

Entering and Editing Data in a Form

Entering data in a form is similar to entering data in a table in Datasheet view. You can use the Tab key and the arrow keys to move the insertion point among the fields. Furthermore, the same navigation buttons are available at the bottom of the form. When you enter or edit a record in Form view, Access automatically updates the records in the table.

Step-by-Step 23.3

1. If necessary, open the **VGInc** database from your solution files. If necessary, open the *Vendor Form* object.

2. In the Navigation bar at the bottom of the form, click the **New (blank) record** navigation button. A new record appears with labels, but there is no data entered.

3. Press **Tab** to position the insertion point in the text box for the *Vendor* field. Access will assign an ID number when you begin to enter data. Enter **Ray's Refrigerator Repair**. Notice that the pencil icon appears at the upper-left corner of the form, indicating that you are editing the record.

4. Press **Tab** and enter **Ray Fowler**.

5. Press **Tab** and enter the following information into the form:

   Address: 2531 Owen Road
   City: Fenton
   State/Province: MI
   Postal Code: 48430-2082
   Business Phone: 810-555-6609

6. Press **Tab** (or Enter). A new blank form appears.

7. Select the number **27** (or triple-click) in the Record Number box at the bottom of the form, enter **8**, and press **Enter**. A form containing the data for the eighth record appears.

8. The business phone number has changed. Click the text box for the *Business Phone* field and edit the phone number so it is **810-555-9937**. Press **Enter**. The revised data is saved.

9. Click the **Vendors** object tab to view the *Vendors* table. Scroll to the bottom of the table. You'll notice that the table has not yet been updated, and the new record does not appear. In the Records group on the Home tab, click the upper portion of the **Refresh All** button that is shown in **Figure 23–6**. The table is updated, and the new record now appears.

Click to update table   Refresh All button arrow

FIGURE 23–6
The Records group on the Home tab

10. If necessary, close the Field List pane. Navigate to record 8. If necessary, scroll to the right to view the *Business Phone* field. Notice that the phone number has been updated and now shows *810-555-9937*.

11. Leave the table, the form, and the database open.

Sorting Data in Datasheet View

Databases typically contain numerous records. Organizing records in a specific order can help you access the data more quickly. You can sort text and numbers in either ascending or descending order. As you may recall, ascending order sorts alphabetically from A to Z and numerically from the lowest to the highest number. Descending order sorts alphabetically from Z to A and numerically from the highest to the lowest number.

If you change your mind after sorting the data, you can use the Undo command to undo the action. You can also easily restore the table to its original arrangement.

Step-by-Step 23.4

1. If necessary, open the **VGInc** database from your solution files. If necessary, open the *Vendors* table.

2. Click any record in the *City* column. In the Sort & Filter group on the Home tab, shown in **Figure 23–7**, click the **Ascending** button. The records in the table are rearranged and placed in alphabetical order from A to Z by city, and a vertical arrow appears at the top of the column indicating that the data is sorted.

FIGURE 23–7
The Sort & Filter group on the Home tab

3. Click any record in the *Account Balance* column. In the Sort & Filter group, click the **Descending** button. The records are rearranged and placed in numerical order with the largest account balance listed first.

4. Scroll to the right and click any record in the *Last Purchase* column. Click the **Descending** button. The records are rearranged in numerical order with the most recent purchase listed first.

5. You change your mind about the sort order. Click the **Undo** button on the Quick Access Toolbar. The records are restored to the arrangement prior to the last sort.

6. Click any record in the *Vendor* column. Click the **Ascending** button. The records are rearranged and placed in alphabetical order from A to Z.

7. In the Sort & Filter group, click the **Clear All Sorts** button. The records are restored to the original order.

8. Save the changes and close the *Vendors* table.

9. Close the *Vendor Form* object and the database.

Finding and Replacing Data

In a small database, you can locate data by scrolling through the records. However, if the database is quite large, finding a particular record or value can be tedious and time-consuming. Sometimes, records contain common data, and that data needs to be updated. Whether the database has a few records, hundreds of records, or even thousands of records, using the Find and Replace commands simplifies this task.

Finding Data

Let's assume that you want to see if there are any books about Huckleberry Finn included in the *Books2* database. You could sort the records in the *Book List* table in alphabetical order by title and then scroll down through the list to look for the title. However, if the database had hundreds or thousands of records, scrolling through the records to find the title could take a lot of time. The Find command provides a quick and easy way for you to locate specific records or find certain values within fields. You can search for data within a specific field, or you can search the entire table.

Step-by-Step 23.5

1. Open the **Books2** database from your solution files. Open the *Book List* table.

2. Position the insertion point in the first row in the *Title* column. Be careful, though, not to select any text in the cell.

3. In the Find group on the Home tab, shown in **Figure 23–8**, click the **Find** button.

4. The Find and Replace dialog box opens. With the insertion point already positioned in the Find What text box, enter **Huckleberry Finn**. If there is already text in the box, it will be replaced when you enter the new search text.

5. Notice that *Title* appears in the Look In box. This option is correct as is. It tells Access to look for all occurrences in the *Title* field. (To search the entire table, you would click the list arrow and select the table name.)

6. Change the options, if necessary, to match the following:

   a. Click the Match box list arrow and select **Any Part of Field**. Access will locate any book title that has the words *Huckleberry* and *Finn* in it.

   b. Select **All** in the Search box.

   c. The Match Case and the Search Fields As Formatted options should not be selected. If they are selected, click the option once to uncheck the box and turn the option off. When these options are turned off, Access ignores capitalization and data formats when searching for matching text.

7. Compare your screen to **Figure 23–9**. When the settings in your dialog box match those in the figure, click **Find Next**.

8. Access scrolls to the first record that matches the search criteria. The search text in the *Title* column for record 6 is selected.

9.   Click **Find Next** again. A message appears indicating that there are no more occurrences of the search text. Click **OK** in the message box to close the message. Leave the Find and Replace dialog box open.

10. In the *Book List* table, position the insertion point in the first record in the *Author Last* column. Be careful not to select the contents in the cell.

11. In the Find and Replace dialog box, select the text in the Find What box and enter **Dickens**. Notice that the option in the Look In box changes to *Author Last*. Click **Find Next**. The first occurrence of the search text is selected in record 7. Click **Cancel** to close the dialog box.

12. Press **Shift+F4** to find the next occurrence for *Dickens* without opening the Find and Replace dialog box. Access searched for the values entered for the last search and the search text in the *Author Last* column for record 15 is selected.

13. Press **Ctrl+F** to open the Find and Replace dialog box. In the Find What box, enter **Bronte**. Click the **Search** box list arrow and then click **Up**. Click **Find Next**. The first occurrence of *Bronte* moving upward in the table is selected (record 13).

14. Click **Cancel** to close the dialog box. Leave the *Book List* table open.

Using the Replace Command

The Replace command locates the search text and replaces it with new text that you specify. For example, in the *Classics* field there is no consistency in the spelling of the word "Incorporated." Sometimes it is spelled out completely, and sometimes it is abbreviated ("Inc."). You can search for all the occurrences when the word is abbreviated and then automatically replace those abbreviations with the complete spelling.

When you use the Replace command, you can choose to view and confirm each replacement individually or you can choose to replace all occurrences of the search text with a single click. You should use the Replace All command only when you are confident about making all the replacements without reviewing them first.

Step-by-Step 23.6

1.   If necessary, open the **Books2** database from your solution files, and open the *Book List* table.

2.   Position the insertion point at the beginning of the text in the first record in the *Publisher* column. Be careful not to select the contents in the cell.

3.   In the Find group, click the **Replace** button to open the dialog box.

4. Notice that the Find What box still contains the text from your last search. Enter **Inc.** to replace the old search text.

5. In the Replace With text box, enter **Incorporated**.

6. Compare your screen to **Figure 23–10** and make any necessary changes to the settings. The Search box should show *All*, and the Search Fields As Formatted check box should be enabled.

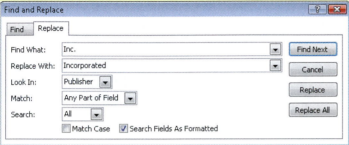

FIGURE 23–10
The Find and Replace dialog box with replace settings

7. Click **Find Next**. Access selects the first occurrence of *Inc.*, which is in the first record.

8. Click **Replace** in the dialog box. The next occurrence of *Inc.* (record 3) is selected. Leave the dialog box open, and scroll up to view record 1. In the record entry, *Inc.* was replaced with *Incorporated*, and the other selected text in the publisher name was not changed.

9. You change your mind. Click the **Undo** button on the Quick Access Toolbar. You can use the Undo command to reverse the action; however, you must choose the Undo command before editing another record.

10. Position the insertion point in any one of the records in the *Publisher* column. Be careful not to select the contents.

11. Click the **Replace All** button. When prompted to continue, click **Yes**. Access replaces all occurrences of *Inc.* with *Incorporated* throughout the column.

12. Scroll up and down to view all the entries in the column. Notice that there are no more abbreviations *Inc.*

13. Click the **Cancel** button to close the dialog box.

14. Save the changes and close the table. Leave the database open.

> **HEADS UP**
>
> There may be times when you do not want to replace the selected text. On those occasions, simply click **Find Next** to go to the next occurrence. No changes are made until you click the Replace button.

Creating a Query

Although the Find command provides an easy way to find data, you may need to locate multiple records, all containing the same values. If you have a large database, and several records contain the value you are searching for, this is another task that can be tedious. In this case, you can use a *query*, a database object which enables you to locate multiple records matching specified criteria. Remember, you learned in Lesson 22 that a query is one of the types of database objects that appears in the

▶ **VOCABULARY**
query

Navigation Pane. The query provides a way for you to ask a question about the information stored in one or more database tables. Access searches for and retrieves data from the table or tables to answer your question.

To illustrate, consider the following example. Suppose you just read a book by Charles Dickens. You really enjoyed the book and you would like to read another book authored by him. You could locate the books by Charles Dickens one at a time in the Classics database by using the Find command. But a query makes your search easier, and it also creates a list of the titles for you.

When you create a query, you must identify all the fields for which you want to retrieve and show information. For example, you might want to retrieve records and show only the title and the author name. The order in which you select the fields will be the order in which the information appears in the query results.

Step-by-Step 23.7

1. If necessary, open the **Books2** database from your solution files. Note that there are currently no query objects for this database.

2. Click the **Create** tab. In the Other group shown in **Figure 23–11**, click the **New Object: Query** button.

FIGURE 23–11
The Other group on the Create tab

New Object:
Query button

3. The Show Table dialog box opens on top of a query grid. If necessary, select Book List to base the query on the *Book List* table records. Click **Add**. A new dialog box opens, showing the fields in the *Book List* table.

4. Close the Show Table dialog box. You can now see the entire object window, as shown in **Figure 23–12**. The query object is currently open in Design view.

FIGURE 23–12
Query window

Run button

Query Tools
Design tab

Click list
arrow to show
field list

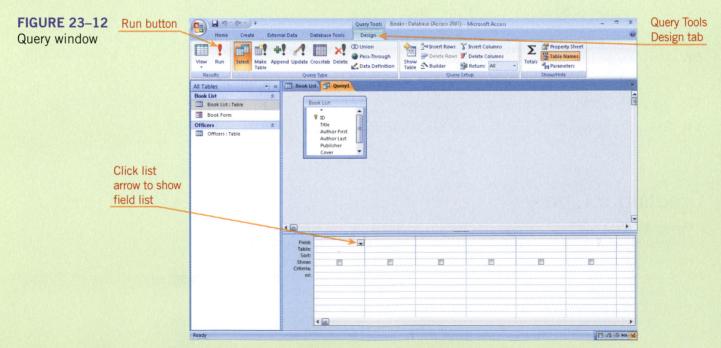

5. In the query grid, click the list arrow in the first column next to the label *Field* and then click **Author Last**.

6. Click the cell in the second column to the right of the label *Field*, click the list arrow, and then click **Title**.

7. Click the cell in the third column to the right of the label *Field*, click the list arrow, and then click **Cover**. The query will retrieve data from three fields.

8. Click the cell in the first column next to *Criteria*. Enter **Dickens** and then press **Enter**. This tells Access to retrieve any records written by authors with the last name *Dickens*. Access places quotations around the text.

9. In the *Author Last* column, click to uncheck the check box in the Show row. The data in this field will be used to retrieve records with Dickens as the author, but the data from this column will not show in the query results.

10. Compare your screen with **Figure 23–13** and make any necessary corrections so that your screen matches the figure.

Click to
uncheck
Show option

Enter
criteria here

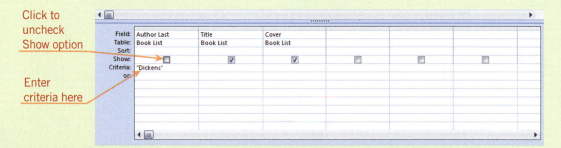

FIGURE 23–13
Completed query grid

11. Click the **Save** button on the Quick Access Toolbar. Because the query has not yet been saved, the Save As dialog box opens. Enter **Dickens Query** to replace the text in the Query Name text box and then click **OK**.

12. In the Results group, click the **Run** button. The results of the query appear in a datasheet. Although data was retrieved from three fields, only the data from two fields appears in the database.

13. Close the query. Notice that the *Dickens Query* object appears in the Navigation Pane, under the *Book List* table.

14. Leave the database open.

Creating and Printing a Report

You can print a database in Datasheet view, but when you do, all of the data contained in the database is printed. This can be very cumbersome if the database is large or if you only need certain information from the database. A ***report*** is a database object which allows you to organize, summarize, and print all or a portion of the data in a database. You can create a report based on a table or a query.

▶ **VOCABULARY**
report

Although you can prepare a report manually, the Report Wizard provides an easy and fast way to design and create a report. The wizard will ask you questions about which data you want to include in the report and how you want to format that data. One of the format options you will apply in the report is page orientation. Remember, you learned in earlier lessons that the orientation determines how the report will print on the page. Landscape orientation formats the report with the long edge of the page at the top. Portrait orientation formats the report with the short edge of the page at the top.

Step-by-Step 23.8

1. If necessary, open the **Books2** database from your solution files. Note that there are currently no report objects for this database.

2. Click the **Create** tab. In the Reports group, click the **Report Wizard** button . The Report Wizard dialog box shown in **Figure 23–14** opens. If necessary, click the list arrow in the text box under Tables/Queries and click **Table: Book List**.

FIGURE 23–14
The Report Wizard dialog box

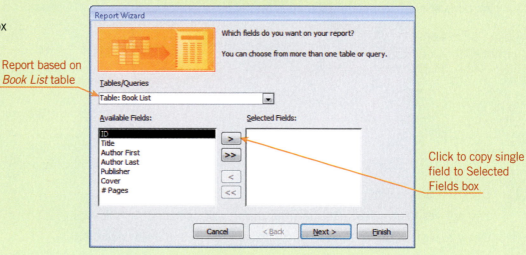

Report based on *Book List* table

Click to copy single field to Selected Fields box

3. Choose the field names from the Available Fields list and arrange them in the order you want them to appear in the report:

    a. Click **Author First**, then click **>** to move the field name to the Selected Fields list.

    b. Author Last is already selected. Click **>**.

    c. Click **Title** and then click **>**.

    d. Publisher is already selected. Click **>**.

4. Click **Next** to advance to the next step in the wizard. The options for grouping the fields are not necessary for this report. Click **Next** to move on to the next step.

5. Options for the sort order of the records appear. In the first box, click the list arrow, and then click **Author Last**.

6. Next to the first box, click **Ascending**. The option toggles to *Descending*. Click **Descending** to toggle back to the default Ascending setting.

7. Click the list arrow in the second box and then click **Title**. If there are two or more books by the same author, the titles will be ordered first by the author last name, then by the book title.

8. Click **Next** to move to the next step. Options for layout and orientation appear. If it is not already enabled, click the Tabular option. Then click the **Landscape** option to enable it. The option to adjust the field width to fit all fields on a page should be selected.

9. Click **Next**. Options for styles appear. Click the **Concourse** style. A preview of the new style appears.

10. Click **Next** to move to the last step. The new dialog box prompts you to add enter a title for the report. The current title is *Book List*, because that is the name of the table. Change the title to **Classic Books**.

11. If necessary, enable the Preview the report option. Then, click **Finish**. A preview of the report opens in Print Preview, and the Print Preview tab appears on the Ribbon.

12. In the Zoom group, click the **Print Preview Zoom** button arrow and then click **50%**. The preview of the report is reduced so you can see the entire page. Compare your screen to **Figure 23–15**.

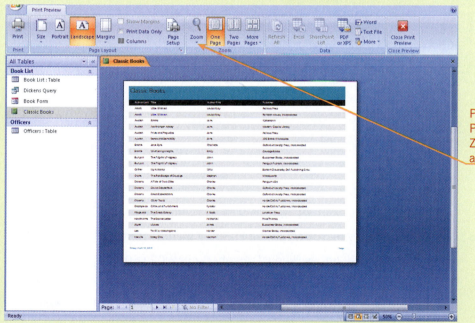

FIGURE 23–15
Report shown in Print Preview

Print
Preview
Zoom button
arrow

13. Notice that the *Classic Books* report object appears in the Navigation Pane. Close the report.

14. If necessary, close the *Dickens Query* object and then close the database, but leave Access open.

Creating Mailing Labels

Because databases often contain data regarding names and addresses, it is common to create mailing labels based on the database information. For example, you can quickly create labels for the vendors or suppliers in the *VGInc* database. Access provides a wizard to use a report format to create the labels.

The wizard includes a step to sort the database records. For bulk mail rates, the mail must be sorted by postal code, so sorting the labels before printing them saves a lot of time.

Step-by-Step 23.9

1. Open the **VGInc** database from your solution files.

2. In the Navigation Pane, make sure the *Vendors* table is selected. (The wizard will not prompt you to choose a table, so you must make sure the correct table is selected.)

3. Click the **Create** tab. In the Reports group, click the **Labels** button ⊞ **Labels**. The Label Wizard dialog box shown in **Figure 23–16** opens.

FIGURE 23–16
The Label Wizard
dialog box

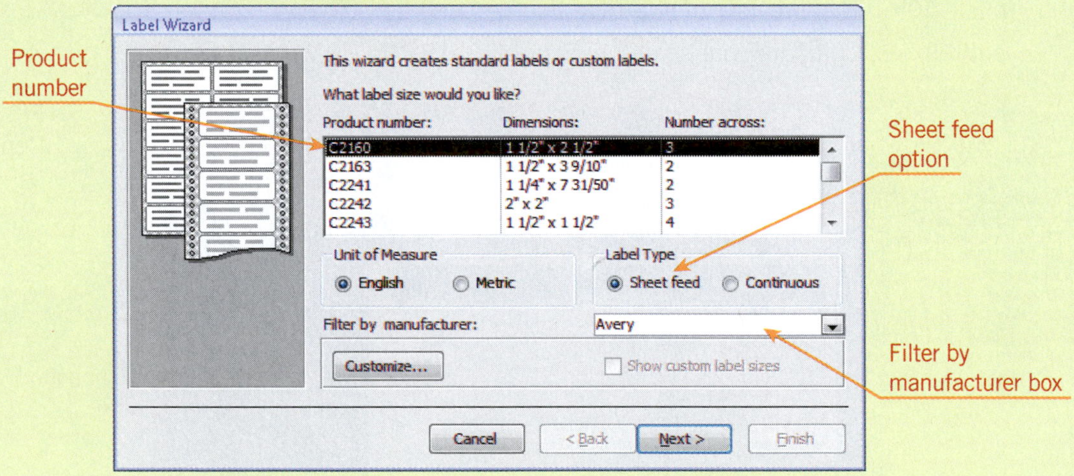

4. If necessary, under Label Type, enable the **Sheet feed** option. Also, if necessary, select **Avery** in the Filter by manufacturer list box.

5. If necessary, under Product number, click **C2160** to specify the label size. Product numbers appear on the label packaging.

6. Click **Next**. The next step in the wizard describes the text appearance on the mailing label. If necessary, change the font name to **Arial**, the font weight to **Light**, and the font size to **10**. Notice that the preview in the dialog box reflects the font changes as you apply them. Compare your screen to **Figure 23–17**, and if necessary, make changes so your dialog box looks like the one shown in the figure.

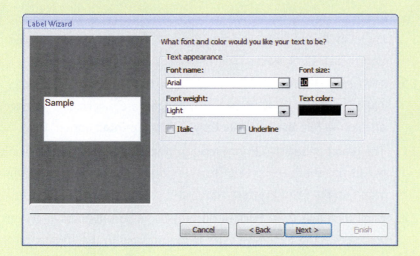

FIGURE 23–17
The Label Wizard dialog box
showing selected font options

7. Click **Next** to move to the next step. In this step you choose the fields and arrange them on a prototype label. Select and arrange the fields as follows:

   a. Under Available fields, click **Vendor**. Click **>**, and then press **Enter**. Brackets are inserted before and after the field name.

   b. With the insertion point still positioned in the Prototype label box, enter **ATTN** and then press **Spacebar**.

   c. Under Available fields, double-click **Contact**. The *Contact* field is inserted at the location of the insertion point. Press **Enter**.

   d. Under Available fields, double-click **Address** and then press **Enter**.

   e. Under Available fields, double-click **City**. Press **Spacebar** and then double-click **State**. Press **Spacebar** and then double-click **Postal Code**.

8. When your prototype label looks like the one shown in **Figure 23–18**, click **Next**.

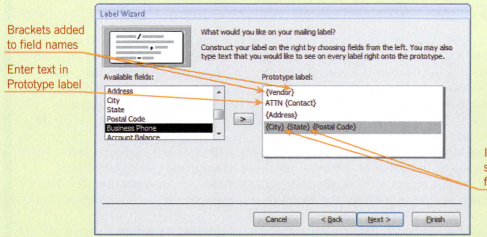

Brackets added to field names

Enter text in Prototype label

Insert a blank space between field names

FIGURE 23–18
The Label Wizard dialog box showing a prototype label

9. The next step in the wizard is to sort the labels. In the Available fields list, click **Postal Code**, and then click **>**. The field name is moved to the Sort by list. Click **Next**.

10. The last step in the wizard is to name the report. The proposed name *Labels Vendors* is good, so no changes are necessary. If necessary, enable the **See the labels as they will look printed** option. Click **Finish**.

11. The report appears in Print Preview. If you were printing the labels, you would put the label sheets in your printer and choose the Print command on the Print Preview tab.

12. Click the **Close Print Preview** button. The report appears in Design view. Notice that the *Labels Vendors* report appears in the Navigation Pane.

13. On the Home tab, click the **View** button arrow and then click **Report View**. The labels appear in a single column. Click the **View** button arrow again and then click **Layout View**. The information appears as it will print only in Print Preview.

14. Close the *Labels Vendors* report object, and then close the database.

TECHNOLOGY CAREERS

Data Entry Keyers

The amount of information that businesses maintain continues to grow, and this information needs to be entered into a database. If you're a fast and accurate keyboarder, have a good eye for detail, and enjoy working at the computer all day, a data entry job might be the right career choice for you. Generally, data entry keyers use computers to enter numbers and information in a form on the computer screen. In addition to entering data, keyers verify the accuracy of the data they enter. They proofread entries, perform accuracy tests, correct errors, and compile and sort data. Accuracy is emphasized; inaccurate data means inaccurate records and errors can cost the business a lot of money.

Keyers are employed in every sector of the economy. Primary employers include data processing firms; accounting, auditing, and bookkeeping firms; banks and credit unions; and state and local governments. Typical job titles include billing clerk, accounting clerk, production clerk, data entry operator, and key data operator. A data entry job can help you get your foot in the door with an employer, and then you can work your way up to a better paying job with more responsibilities.

Many keyers are able to work flexible hours, both part- and full-time. Also, they can often work out of their homes on personal computers and upload the data to the main office. Data entry keyers sit for long periods of time, and they must take preventive measures to avoid repetitive strain injuries such as carpal tunnel syndrome.

SUMMARY

In this lesson, you learned:

- The Form Wizard helps you create a professional-looking, customized form for entering data.

- Entering and editing data in a form is similar to entering and editing data in a table in Datasheet view. You use the same navigation buttons to move from one record to another.

- You can sort records in Datasheet view in either ascending or descending order.

- The Find command can save you time looking for records and specific values in a table. The Replace command can save you time finding and replacing specific text.

- You can create a query to find records that match specified criteria. Access searches for and retrieves data from the table that matches the criteria you specify.

- A report allows you to organize, summarize, and print all or a portion of the data in a database. You can choose the Report Wizard to guide you through the process in creating and formatting a report.

- When you want to create mailing labels, you create a report object using the Label Wizard.

■ VOCABULARY REVIEW

Define the following terms:

form
query
report

■ REVIEW QUESTIONS

TRUE / FALSE

Circle T if the statement is true or F if the statement is false.

T F 1. When you work with a form, you have only two options for viewing the object.

T F 2. The navigation buttons at the bottom of a form are the same as the navigation buttons at the bottom of a table in Datasheet view.

T F 3. If you change your mind immediately after you sort data, you can choose the Undo command to return the data to its original order.

T F 4. When you create a report, you can choose the order in which the information appears.

T F 5. When you use the Label Wizard to create mailing labels, you must use a predesigned layout of the fields that controls how the data appears on the label.

MULTIPLE CHOICE

Select the best response for each of the following statements.

1. A _____ can make the process of entering data more efficient and more accurate.

    A. query   C. report

    B. table   D. form

2. When you create mailing labels, you create a new _____.

    A. report   C. form

    B. query   D. table

3. _____ view enables you to make changes to the form design.

    A. Form   C. Layout

    B. Design   D. B or C

4. A _____ enables you to locate all records that match certain criteria.

    A. report   C. form

    B. query   D. sort

5. When searching for a record, you can search for data contained in _____.

    A. a specific field   C. all the tables in the database

    B. the entire table   D. A and B

FILL IN THE BLANK

Complete the following sentences by writing the correct word or words in the blanks provided.

1. In _____ view, you can see how the changes you make will look when you enter data in the form.

2. In _____ view, you can change the properties and add new fields to a form.

3. To enter data in a form, the form must be opened in _____ view.

4. To locate specific records or find certain values within fields, use the _____ command.

5. To arrange data with the most recent date at the top of the list, sort the data in _____ order.

■ PROJECTS

PROJECT 23–1

In this project and the next two, you will work with a database containing information about the River Cleanup Crew, a volunteer program that coordinates annual events to clean up and remove trash from the local rivers, creeks, and streams.

1. Click the **Start** button, click **Computer**, and locate and open the data files folder. Copy the **Project23-1** file to the Clipboard. Then, locate and open the folder where you save your files. Paste the file in the folder, and then rename the file **RiverCC**.

2. Open the **RiverCC** database.

3. Use the Form Wizard to create a form for the *Volunteers* table:

    a. Include all the fields except *# Hours*.

    b. Apply the Columnar format.

    c. Choose a style.

    d. Name the form **Volunteer Form**. Preview the form in Print Preview.

4. Use the new form to add the following two new records to the *Volunteers* table:

First Name:	Justin
Last Name:	Kane
Address:	4513 Cove Trail
City:	Anderson
State:	SC
Postal Code:	29621-2133
Phone:	864-555-4911
Birth Date:	6/11/1997
River:	Savannah
Join Date:	5/1/2012
First Name:	Jessica
Last Name:	Taylor
Address:	506 Heritage Drive
City:	Anderson
State:	SC
Postal Code:	29621-1666
Phone:	864-555-1984
Birth Date:	4/18/1987
River:	Savannah
Join Date:	5/1/2012

5. Close the form. Open the *Volunteers* table, find Marcia Pruitt (search for the last name), and change her phone number to **864-555-5005**.

6. Gary Phillips has moved. Find his record and change his street address to **2114 Woodside Avenue, Anderson, SC 29625-2810**. His new phone number is **864-555-9651**.

7. Several of the area codes in the *Phone* field are incorrect. The numbers have been transposed. Search the *Phone* field for all occurrences of *846* and replace all occurrences with **864**.

8. Sort the data in ascending order based on the *Last Name* field.

9. Save the changes to the table. Leave the table and the database open.

PROJECT 23–2

1. If necessary, open the **RiverCC** database.

2. You would like to contact the volunteers who clean up the Saluda River. Create a query for the *Volunteers* table:

   a. Include the *Last Name*, *First Name*, *Phone*, and *River* fields, in this order.

   b. The criteria for the query is for those who clean the Saluda River.

   c. The *River* field does not need to show in the query.

3. Save the query as **Saluda Volunteers**.

4. Run the query, and then close the query. If necessary, close the *Volunteers* table.

5. You would like to print a list of the names and phone numbers of all sponsors. Use the Report Wizard to create the report from the *Sponsors* table:

   a. Include the *Name* and *Phone* fields, in that order.

   b. Do not group the report.

   c. Sort the report by name in ascending order.

   d. Choose the Columnar layout and Portrait orientation.

   e. Choose a style.

   f. Name the report **Sponsors Phone List** and preview the report.

6. Close Print Preview, and then close the report.

7. For an upcoming recognition event, you want to prepare a list of all the volunteers and the number of hours they have devoted to the organization. Use the Report Wizard to create the report:

   a. Include the *# Hours, First Name*, and *Last Name* fields from the *Volunteers* table, in that order.

   b. Do not add any grouping levels.

   c. Sort the report by the *# Hours* field, in descending order.

   d. Choose the Columnar layout and Portrait orientation.

   e. Apply a style.

   f. Name the report **Volunteers Hours** and preview the report.

8. Close Print Preview and the report. Leave the database open.

PROJECT 23–3

1. If necessary, open the **RiverCC** database.

2. To mail the quarterly newsletter to the volunteers, create mailing labels. Launch the Label Wizard and accept the default label and font settings.

3. In the prototype label:

   a. Enter the *First Name* and *Last Name* fields on the first line, separated by a space.

   b. Insert the *Address* field on the second line.

   c. Insert the *City*, *State*, and *Postal Code* fields on the third line. Enter a blank space after the *City* and *State* fields, and do not use any punctuation between the city and state fields.

4. Sort the labels by the *Postal Code* field.

5. Name the report **Volunteers Mailing Labels** and preview the report.

6. Close the report and then close the database.

TEAMWORK PROJECT

Create a roster for your computer class or workgroup to record the names, addresses, phone numbers, e-mail addresses, and other information about your classmates or coworkers. Follow these steps:

1. With a teammate, determine what information you want to gather and organize.

2. Divide the names of your classmates or coworkers so that each of you will gather information for half the group.

3. After you have gathered the information, create a new database and a table with the fields you identified in Step 1. Then create a form to make data entry easier. Select the options you think will present the information you've collected in the best way, and give your form a relevant title.

4. Enter the information into the form.

CRITICAL THINKING

ACTIVITY 23–1

In Projects 23-1, 23-2, and 23-3, you worked with a database for a community volunteer program. The program manager wants to recognize the youth volunteers. How can the *Volunteers* table data be arranged so the program manager can easily identify those volunteers who are under 18 years old? Write two or three sentences explaining how you would manipulate the table data to help the manager.

ONLINE DISCOVERY

When mailing a letter to another country, how can you be sure you have addressed the envelope or package correctly? Go to *www.usps.com*, and then search for information regarding addressing international mail. Also search online for this information on the destination country's postal services. Using the information you find online, edit the following information to show the address data in the correct format required for delivery in the destination country. Cite the Web page URLs where you find the supporting information.

First and Last Name

36 Silvergrove Court N.W.

Calgary, Alberta

Canada

T3B5A3

First and Last Name

P.O. Box 30009

Wonderbooj Poort

0033 South Africa

First and Last Name

38 Upland Drive

Brookmans Park

Hatfield, Hertfordshire

AL9 6PT

England

First and Last Name

Blk 35 Mandalay Road

15 Mandalay Towers

Singapore 308215

Singapore

MODULE 2 REVIEW

 Estimated Time:
2.5 hours

Key Applications

■ REVIEW QUESTIONS

TRUE / FALSE

Circle T if the statement is true or F if the statement is false.

T   F   **1.**   Portrait orientation is the default setting for Word, Excel, and Access.

T   F   **2.**   The Undo command is always available in all Office applications.

T   F   **3.**   By default, Excel automatically wraps text in a cell.

T   F   **4.**   When a number value is too wide to fit in a cell, Excel shows a series of asterisks (*****).

T   F   **5.**   As you enter data in a datasheet, Access automatically corrects commonly misspelled words.

T   F   **6.**   In PowerPoint, you can edit slide contents in Normal view and in Slide Sorter view.

T   F   **7.**   When you apply a style, you apply a whole group of formats in one simple step.

T   F   **8.**   In Excel, the COUNT function shows the number of cells with numerical values in the argument range.

T   F   **9.**   In PowerPoint, text boxes enable you to position text anywhere on a slide, even outside a placeholder.

T   F   **10.**   You can automatically adjust column widths in Word tables, Excel worksheets, and Access datasheets.

MULTIPLE CHOICE

Select the best response for each of the following statements.

1. The _____ serves as the primary interface between the user and the application.

   A.   application window   C.   status bar

   B.   document window   D.   task bar

2. In _____ mode in Word, the existing text shifts to the right to make room for the new text.

   A.   Insert   C.   Edit

   B.   Overtype   D.   Replace

3. _____ are settings that determine how a slide is introduced as you move from one PowerPoint slide to another in Slide Show view.

   A.   Triggers   C.   Entrance effects

   B.   Slide transitions   D.   Motion paths

4. In an Excel worksheet, you can edit a cell by _____.

   A. double-clicking the cell and then editing the formula in the cell

   B. pressing F2 and then editing the formula in the cell

   C. selecting the cell and then editing the formula in the formula bar

   D. all of the above

5. When a Word paragraph is formatted with a _____, the first line of text begins at the left margin, and all other lines of the paragraph are indented to the right of the first line.

   A. first-line indent   C. right indent

   B. hanging indent   D. none of the above

6. To protect the content from change as well as preserve the visual appearance and layout of each page and enable fast viewing and printing, save a Word document in a(n) _____ format.

   A. compatible   C. read-only

   B. encrypted   D. PDF or XPS

7. A(n) _____ is a number or cell reference in an Excel formula.

   A. operand   C. argument

   B. operator   D. function

8. To prevent users from seeing personal data related to a file, _____.

   A. protect the document with a password

   B. inspect the document and remove hidden text

   C. inspect the document and remove metadata

   D. restrict access

9. A _____ is a database object that enables you to organize, summarize, and print all or a portion of the data in an Access database.

   A. form   C. query

   B. report   D. table

10. The _____ define(s) the characteristics and behavior of an Access database field.

   A. field name   C. field data type

   B. field properties   D. primary key

FILL IN THE BLANK

Complete the following sentences by writing the correct word or words in the blanks provided.

1. _____ is a standard method for encoding data.

2. A(n) _____ is a small window with descriptive text that appears when you position the mouse pointer on a command or control in the application window.

3. _____ are the boundary lines in a table or a worksheet.

4. When you remove the boundary between two cells in a table or worksheet, you are _____ the cells.

5. _____ formulas contain more than one operator.

6. The _____ is a small arrow in the lower-right corner of a group on the Ribbon. When clicked, it provides access to additional options related to the group.

7. The _____ is a temporary storage place in your computer's memory that is shared among all the Office applications.

8. The _____ identifies the disk and any folders relative to the location of a document.

9. The _____ is the main slide that stores information about the theme and layouts of a PowerPoint presentation.

10. A(n) _____ is a group of related fields in an Access database, such as all the contact information for an individual.

■ DATA FILES

To complete these projects, you will need these data files:

ProjectUR-1.docx	ProjectUR-2.xlsx	JobUR-1.xlsx
Bird.jpg	ProjectUR-2.docx	JobUR-2.docx
Elephant.jpg	ProjectUR-3.pptx	JobUR-3.pptx
Giraffe.jpg	ProjectUR-4.accdb	JobUR-4.accdb

■ PROJECTS

PROJECT 2–1

1. Launch Word and open **ProjectUR-1.docx** from the data files and save the document as **Safari**. The document is a promotional flyer for visitors at the Madikwe Game Reserve, and the document will be printed using a duplex printing setting.

2. Change the margin settings so that all margins are 1".

3. Several words are misspelled, and there are a few grammatical errors. Locate these errors and make the necessary corrections. All occurrences of *Madikwe* are spelled correctly.

4. Find the first occurrence of *Big Five*. Change *Five* to **5**, and then add the following sentence immediately after that sentence. **The Big 5 are the lion, elephant, rhino, buffalo, and leopard, which are all considered to be the most dangerous animals to hunt.**

5. Search from the beginning of the document and find the phrase *constantly train*. This text appears twice in this article, so change this first occurrence so that it is not used repetitively. Use the Thesaurus feature to find and replace the word *constantly* with a synonym.

6. Under the subheading *Wildlife and Ecosystem*, select all the italicized text and apply a bullet format. Then, indent all paragraphs in the document, excluding the subheadings and the bulleted list, with a .25" first-line indent.

7. Position the insertion point in front of the paragraph marker under the subheading *Safari Options*, and then create a 2x5 table and enter the following data. AutoFit the column widths for the content and apply a table style.

```
Safari Name             Description
Bush Walk               A guided walking tour; approximately 3 miles; 1 day
The Expedition          Combines hiking and camping for those who want to get close to
                        nature; 3 days, 2 nights
Photo Workshop          Photography instruction in prime wildlife locations; overnight stay
                        in thatch roof guesthouses; 4 days, 3 nights
Classic Experience      Morning, afternoon and evening game drives in safari vehicle; lodge
                        suites are ideal for families with children; 3 days, 2 nights
```

8. In the article with the subheading *History*, format the two paragraphs in two columns, using the right preset with a line between the columns. In the article with the subheading *Excellent Bird Watching and Wildlife Viewing*, format the three paragraphs of text in two columns of equal width. Apply justified alignment to all paragraphs under both subheadings.

9. In the article *Excellent Bird Watching and Wildlife Viewing*, insert the **Bird.jpg** picture file from the data files folder. Resize the picture so it is approximately 1.5" wide by 1.5" high. Position the picture at the left side of the first paragraph. Apply square text wrapping.

10. In the same article, insert the **Elephant.jpg** picture file. Resize the picture so it is approximately 3" wide by 2" high. Position the picture in the second column below the last paragraph in the article. If necessary, reduce the size of the pictures so that the two articles fit on the first page of the document.

11. Position the insertion point at the end of the document and insert the **Giraffe.jpg** picture file. Resize the picture so it is approximately 3.5" wide by 3" high. Center the picture below the last paragraph in the document. Add a black, 1½ point border to each of the three pictures.

12. Select the first subheading *History*. Change the font to Cambria, 16 point. Add a double-line border above and below the paragraph, using a color that complements the colors in the pictures. Then add appropriate shading for the paragraph. Center the text. Use the Format Painter to copy the paragraph formats to the three other subheadings.

13. View the document in Print Preview. Make adjustments to the margins and the picture sizes as needed so that the entire document fits on two pages, with two articles on each page.

14. Save the changes. Then save the document in PDF format as **Safari.pdf**. Close the document.

PROJECT 2–2

1. Launch Excel and open **ProjectUR-2.xlsx** from the data files and save the workbook as **Expenses**.

2. Rename the *Sheet1* tab **Expenses**. Rename the *Sheet2* tab **Hours**.

3. In the Expenses worksheet, insert a new column to the left of the *Fuel* column. Add the heading **Enter.** at the top of the new column. *Enter.* is an abbreviation for Entertainment, which refers to expenses incurred for entertaining clients, such as taking them to dinner.

4. Click cell **F1** and enter the heading **Total**. Insert a new row at the top of the worksheet. Select the range **A1:F1** and merge and center the cells. Enter the heading **Monthly Expense Report**. Select the first two rows and apply the bold format.

5. Click cell **A14** and fill down the cell contents through cell A32 so that all the dates in the month of June appear. Then open **ProjectUR-2.docx** from the data files. This document simulates handwritten notes for incurred expenses. Enter this new data in the Expenses worksheet. Close the document.

6. Select the range **A3:A32**, and then apply the Date: 3/14 format. Select the range **B3:F34**. Apply the Currency number format.

7. Click cell **F3** and enter a formula to calculate the sum of the values in the range B3:E3. Then, fill the formula down to cell F34. Many adjacent cells are empty, so do not be concerned when the error flag appears with the results.

8. Click cell **A34**. Enter **Total** and format the text bold. Click cell **B34** and enter a formula to calculate the sum of the values in the range B3:B32. Then, fill the formula to the right for the range C34:E34.

9. AutoFit the column widths for the cell contents.

10. Switch to the *Hours* worksheet. Delete column B. Then, select the range **B2:B36** and increase the number of decimal places to 2.

11. Click cell **A32** and enter **Total days worked**. Click cell **B32** and enter a formula to count the number of cells in the column that contain numbers. Click cell **A33** and enter **Total hours worked**. Click cell **B33** and enter a formula to calculate the total number of hours worked.

12. Enter some formulas to calculate the data recorded for the month.
    a. Click cell **A34** and enter **Fewest hours worked**. Click cell **B34** and enter a formula to calculate the fewest hours worked in one day.
    b. Click cell **A35** and enter **Most hours worked**. Click cell **B35** and enter a formula to calculate the most hours worked in one day.
    c. Click cell **A36** and enter **Average daily hours worked for 21 days**. Format the text to wrap in the cell. Click cell **B36** and enter a formula to calculate the average daily hours worked for 21 days. (*Hint*: You cannot use the AVERAGE function to perform this calculation; you must create your own formula.)

13. AutoFit the column widths for the content.

14. Save the changes and close the workbook.

PROJECT 2–3

1. Launch PowerPoint and open **ProjectUR-3.pptx** from the data files and save the presentation as **Everest**.

2. Show the slides in Slide Sorter view. Delete the fourth slide. Then move slide 6 to follow slide 3.

3. Switch to Normal view. Add a new slide with the Title and Content layout after slide 3. Enter the title **Risky Business**. In the lower place-holder text box, enter **1 out of 10**. Increase the font size to 96. Remove the bullet format and center the text.

4. Go to slide 5. Change the title *Risky Business* to **What happens?**

5. Go to slide 2. Insert clip art or a photograph of mountains. Resize the picture to fill the slide. Send the picture to the back so the title *29,035 feet high* appears at the top of the photograph. If necessary, change the font color to white or a light color so you can easily read the title.

6. Go to slide 3. Change the slide layout to Two Content. Position the bulleted list on either the left or right side of the slide. On the other side of the slide, insert clip art or a photograph that helps illustrate the words in the bulleted list. For example, insert an image of a calendar or the number 6.

7. Go to slides 5 and 6. Insert clip art or a photograph that helps to illustrate the text in the bulleted list, such as blowing snow, a thermometer, or a mountain climber on the side of the mountain. Remember, you can format pictures with styles and special effects.

8. Go to slide 7. Convert the bulleted items to a SmartArt graphic. Edit the 2001 record so that it reads **Youngest climber: Age 15, Tsheri**.

9. Apply a theme or custom background to all the slides. If you choose to apply a theme, make any necessary adjustments if the slide titles are not positioned correctly relative to inserted pictures.

10. Format custom animations for the objects and text boxes on each slide. Be sure to set the trigger and speed for each animation.

11. Format a slide transition for one or more slides. Be sure to set the transition speed.

12. Preview the slide show and make any necessary changes so that the content flows smoothly. Make sure the animations and transitions are effective.

13. Go to slide 6. In the Notes pane, enter **There is a short window of time in the spring to climb the mountain.**

14. Save the changes and close the presentation.

PROJECT 2–4

1. Click the **Start** button, click **Computer,** and locate and open the data files folder. Copy the file **ProjectUR-4.accdb** to the Clipboard. Then, locate and open the folder where you save your files. Paste the file in the folder, and then rename the file **Wildlife.**

2. Open the **Wildlife** database, and then double-click **Species : Table.**

3. Rearrange the order of the fields so that the *Common Name* field appears in the table before the *Group* field.

4. Adjust the widths of all the columns so you can see the complete entry in every field column.

5. Show the *Species* table in Design view and rearrange the field names so the *Common Name* field appears in the list before the *Group* field name. Close the *Species* table.

6. Create a form for all the fields in the *Species* table, in the same order that they appear in the table. Name the form **Species Form.**

7. Use the form to enter the following two new records, and then close the form.

    | Common Name: | Mandarin duck | Grant's zebra |
    | Group: | Birds | Mammals |
    | Species Name: | Aix galericulata | Equus burchelli |
    | Order: | Angeriformes | Perissofactyla |
    | Family: | Anatidae | Equidae |
    | Habitat: | Eastern Asia | Southeastern Africa |

8. Open the *Species* table and go to record 22, *Arctic wolf*. In the *Species Name* field, change the entry to **Canis lupus tundranum.**

9. In the *Order* field, search for all occurrences of *Arteodactyly* and replace all occurrences with **Artiodactyla.**

10. You would like to see a list of only the mammals. Create a query for the *Species* table:
    a. Include the *Common Name, Group, Species Name,* and *Habitat fields*, in that order.
    b. Add the criteria **Mammals** in the *Group* field.
    c. All fields should show in the query.
    d. Name the query **Mammals.**

11. Preview the query in Datasheet view and then close the query.

12. Use the Report Wizard to create a report:
    a. Include the *Common Name, Group, Habitat, Family, Species Name,* and *Order* fields, in that order.
    b. Do not group the report.
    c. Sort the report by the *Common Name* field in ascending order.
    d. Choose the Tabular layout and Landscape orientation.
    e. Choose a style.
    f. Name the report **Species Report** and preview the report.

13. Close the Print Preview of the report, and then close the report, the table, and the database.

■ INTEGRATED PROJECT

You volunteer at the local Rails-to-Trails organization, which converts old, unused railroad beds into trails for public use. These trails can be used for a variety of activities including walking, jogging or running, biking, and in-line skating. The organization has asked you to help communicate information about rail trails in your area. You want to prepare an announcement to distribute throughout the community, and create a slide show to present at the community meeting next week.

JOB 2–1

You decide to begin by organizing some data in an Excel spreadsheet.

1. If necessary, launch Excel. Open **JobUR-1.xlsx** from the data files and save the new workbook as **Survey.**

2. Click cell **C4.** Enter a formula to calculate the percentage of positive responses. (*Hint:* Divide the number of positive responses by the total surveyed. In the equation, the value for the total surveyed needs to be an absolute reference.)

3. Apply the Percent Style to cell C4. Then, fill the formula down through cell C8.

4. Copy the formula in cell C4 to the Clipboard and then paste the formula in cells E4 and G4. Then, fill the formula down in both of those columns.

5. Hide columns B, D, and F. Then select rows 3 and 4. Create a 3-D pie chart. If necessary, add a legend and data labels. Format data labels for Best Fit. If necessary, change the color and increase the font size for the legend and the labels to 14 point so the text can be read easily. Apply the bold format to the labels. In the chart title, change *crime rate* to **Crime Rate**.

6. Position the chart below the data.

7. Select rows 3 and 5 and create a second pie chart, using the same settings described in Step 5. In the chart title, change *home value* to **Home Value**. Move the chart to Sheet2.

8. Save the changes to the workbook and leave the workbook open.

JOB 2–2

A new section of a popular rail trail is about to open, so the timing is perfect to provide general information to community residents about rail trails. You already created a draft of an announcement, and you asked another member of the organization to review it and provide feedback.

1. If necessary, launch Word. Open **JobUR-2.docx** from the data files folder, and save the document as **Announcement**.

2. Navigate through the revisions and comments and review the markup.

3. Accept all the revisions and delete the comments. Toggle off Track Changes.

4. Select the title at the top of the document. Apply the bold format and change the font size to 14 point.

5. Select the third paragraph beginning *Rail trails such as* and move the paragraph so it follows the introductory paragraph.

6. Find every occurrence of *rail-trail* and replace the hyphen with a blank space.

7. Find the occurrence of *14,000* and change it to **15,000**.

8. If necessary, open the **Survey.xlsx** workbook from your solution files. Select the chart on Sheet2 (*Impact on Home Value*) and copy it to the Clipboard. Switch back to the Announcement document. Position the insertion point at the beginning of the last paragraph of text beginning *Rail trails are not only*. Paste the chart in the Word document.

9. Format the chart for square text wrapping. Change the zoom setting so you can see the entire page. Position the chart in the lower-right corner of the page. Make sure the entire document fits on one page. Resize the chart if necessary.

10. Save the changes to the document. Then, save the document as a single file Web page. Save the document as **Announcement.mht**. Do not be concerned if the chart is repositioned in the Web page file.

11. Close the Web page file and leave the workbook open.

JOB 2–3

The next step is to prepare the slide show for next week's community meeting.

1. Open **JobUR-3.pptx** from the data files, and save the presentation as **RailTrail**.

2. Instead of adding words to the presentation, add visuals to deliver the message. Tips in the Notes pane for each slide will help you choose appropriate clip art and photographs.

3. After you insert the images on the slides, change to Notes Page view and replace the tips with points you want to emphasize during the presentation. Open the **Announcement.docx** document from your solution files and use it as a guide.

4. Switch to Normal view and insert a new slide after slide 5 with the blank layout. Into the new slide, copy and paste the *Impact on Home Value* chart from the Survey workbook. If necessary, enlarge the chart title, legend text, and label text.

5. Select the image on slide 7 and create a hyperlink to slide 3 in the same presentation. In Slide Show view, when you point to the image on this slide, the pointer will change to a hand. When you click the image, slide 3 will open and you can use this slide for the closing comments in the presentation. Then to exit the presentation instead of advancing to slide 4, you can press Escape.

6. Add a background or theme to all the slides, and add custom animations and/or sounds for the clip art and photographs to appear on the slide. If desired, also format one or more slide transitions.

7. Preview the slide show and make any necessary edits to the triggers and timing for the animations and transitions.

8. Save the changes to the presentation and close the presentation, the Announcement document, and the Excel workbook.

JOB 2–4

The final step is to prepare mailing labels so you can mail copies of the announcement to other volunteers in the organization who will then assist in distributing the copies of the announcement throughout the community.

1. Click the **Start** button, click **Computer**, and locate and open the data files folder. Copy the file **JobUR-4.accdb** to the Clipboard. Then, locate and open the folder where you save your files. Paste the file in the folder, and then rename the file **Volunteers**.

2. Open the **Volunteers** database, and then open the *Volunteers* table.

3. Use the Label Wizard to create mailing labels:
   a. Create labels for the Avery C2160 label type.
   b. Change the font to Comic Sans MS, 12 point, Normal weight.
   c. Add the fields to the prototype label for the appropriate mailing format.
   d. There is no need to sort the records.
   e. Accept the proposed report name *Labels Volunteers*.

4. Review the labels in Print Preview to make sure they look correct, and make any necessary changes.

5. Close Print Preview and switch to Report view. Close the report and the table, and then close Access.

MODULE 3

LIVING ONLINE

LIVING ONLINE

LESSON 24
Network Fundamentals

3-1.1.1	3-1.1.4	3-1.1.7
3-1.1.2	3-1.1.5	
3-1.1.3	3-1.1.6	

LESSON 25
Communication Services

3-2.1.1	3-2.2.2	3-2.2.6
3-2.1.2	3-2.2.3	3-2.2.7
3-2.1.3	3-2.2.4	3-2.2.8
3-2.2.1	3-2.2.5	3-2.2.9

LESSON 26
Communications and Collaboration

3-2.3.1	3-2.3.4	3-2.3.7
3-2.3.2	3-2.3.5	
3-2.3.3	3-2.3.6	

LESSON 27
Using the Internet and the World Wide Web

3-3.1.1	3-3.1.6	3-3.1.11
3-3.1.2	3-3.1.7	3-3.1.12
3-3.1.3	3-3.1.8	3-3.1.13
3-3.1.4	3-3.1.9	3-3.1.14
3-3.1.5	3-3.1.10	

LESSON 28
Web Content

3-3.2.1	3-3.2.3	3-3.2.5
3-3.2.2	3-3.2.4	3-3.2.6

LESSON 29
Technology and Society

3-4.1.1	3-4.1.2	3-4.1.3
		3-4.1.4

LESSON 30
Computer Safety and Ethics

3-4.2.1	3-4.2.5	3-4.2.9
3-4.2.2	3-4.2.6	3-4.2.10
3-4.2.3	3-4.2.7	3-4.2.11
3-4.2.4	3-4.2.8	

LESSON 24

Network Fundamentals

■ OBJECTIVES

Upon completion of this lesson, you should be able to:

- Describe a network.
- Explain the benefits of a network.
- Identify the risks of network computing.
- Describe the roles of clients and servers on a network.
- List and describe the types of networks.
- List and describe communications media and hardware.
- Describe network security.

■ DATA FILES

You do not need data files to complete this lesson.

■ VOCABULARY

biometric security measures

cable modem

client

client/server network

communication channels

digital subscriber line (DSL)

extranet

firewall

hacker

hub

Internet

intranet

local area network (LAN)

modem

node

peer-to-peer network

proxy server

Public Switched Telephone Network (PSTN)

router

server

server operating system

T-1 line

wide area network (WAN)

WiMAX

wireless Internet service provider (WISP)

wireless LAN (WLAN)

As companies grow and purchase more computers, they often find it advantageous to connect those computers through a network, a group of two or more computers linked together. This allows users to share software applications and to share hardware devices such as printers, scanners, and other hardware add-ons. In addition to using a local network, companies and organizations also use networks to connect employees and subsidiaries nationally and even internationally. The locations can be in the same city or in different locations all over the world.

3-1.1.1

Introducing Networks

When most people think of networks, they envision something fairly complicated. At the lowest level, networks are not that complex. In fact, a network is simply a group of two or more computers linked together. As the size of a network increases and more devices are added, installation of devices and management of the network becomes more technical. Even so, networking concepts and terminology basically remain the same regardless of size or type.

Different types of networks transfer different types of data. For instance, over a computer network, you can transfer a variety of data, including text, images, video, and audio files. A telephone network is similar in makeup to a computer network. The *Public Switched Telephone Network (PSTN)* supports telephone service and is the world's collection of interconnected commercial and government-owned voice-oriented systems. Digital, mobile, and standard telephones are supported through this network (**Figure 24–1**).

▶ **VOCABULARY**

Public Switched Telephone Network (PSTN)

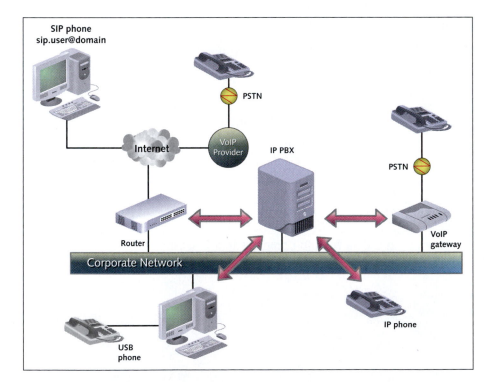

FIGURE 24–1   Telephone network

Network Benefits

3-1.1.2

To consider the topic of network benefits, you first might think about the biggest network of all—the Internet. Consider some of the many changes that have occurred in our society because of the Internet. Perhaps the most profound of all of these changes is electronic mail. A network provides almost instant communication, and e-mail messages are delivered almost immediately. Other network benefits include the following:

■ *Information sharing*: Authorized users can access computers on the network to share information, data, and other resources. This could include special group projects, news groups, databases, blogs, FTP, Internet telephony, instant messaging, chat rooms, and so on.

■ *Collaborative environment*: A shared environment enables users to work together on group projects by combining the power and capabilities of diverse equipment and software, thus increasing personal productivity.

■ *Hardware sharing*: It is not necessary to purchase a printer or a scanner or other frequently used peripherals for each computer. Instead, one device connected to a network can serve the needs of many users.

■ *Software sharing*: Instead of purchasing and installing a software program on every single computer, it can be installed on the server. All of the users can then access the program from this one central location. This also saves money because companies can purchase a site license for the number of users. This is less expensive than purchasing individual software packages, and updating software on the server is much easier and more efficient than updating on individual computers.

■ *Enhanced communications*: Electronic mail has changed the way the world communicates. Some of the advantages are almost instantaneous delivery of e-mail. The cost for e-mail does not depend on the size of the message or the distance the message has to travel (**Figure 24–2**).

FIGURE 24–2 Information sharing

3-1.1.3

Risks of Networked Computing

As with any technology, disadvantages also exist. For instance, data security and the vulnerability to unauthorized access is a primary weakness with many networks. The security of a computer network is challenged every day by equipment malfunctions, system failures, computer hackers, and virus attacks.

Equipment malfunctions and system failures are caused by a number of factors, including natural disasters such as floods or storms, fires, or electrical disturbances, such as a brownout or blackout. Server malfunctions or failures mean users temporarily lose access to network resources, such as printers, drives, and information.

Computer hackers and viruses present a great risk to networked environments. *Hackers* are people who break into computer systems to steal services and information, such as credit card numbers, passwords, test data, and even national security information. Hackers can also delete data. Other people threaten networks and data by creating viruses and other malicious software, which are particularly dangerous to networked computers as they usually are designed to sabotage shared files (**Figure 24–3**).

▶ **VOCABULARY**
hacker

FIGURE 24–3   Computer criminal

The following are some of the other disadvantages of networks:

- *Individual loss of autonomy*: Networks can also play a part in taking away an individual's autonomy through the controlling of which software programs are accessible, keeping a record of how the computer is used, what sites are accessed, and so on.

- *Malicious code*: Networks are more vulnerable than stand-alone computers to viruses, worms, Trojan horses, E-mail bombs, and spyware.

- *Network faults*: Network equipment problems can result in loss of data or resources.

- *Setup and management costs*: Setting up a network requires an investment in hardware and software; ongoing maintenance and management of the network requires the care and attention of at least one IT professional.

- *E-mail is not necessarily private*: Messages travel through a number of systems and networks and provide opportunities for others to intercept or read the messages (see **Figure 24–4**). Junk e-mail can also become a problem.

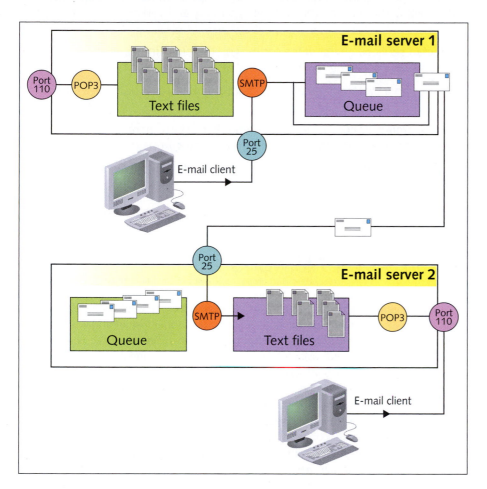

FIGURE 24–4   E-mail system

On the other hand, a standalone system is not vulnerable to many of these risks since it does not share interconnection with other computers.

ETHICS IN TECHNOLOGY

Hackers

Computer security violations are one of the biggest problems experienced on computer networks. People who break into computer systems are called hackers. The reasons they do this are many and varied. Some of the more common reasons are as follows:

- *Theft of services*: Many password-protected services charge a fee for usage. A hacker finds a way to bypass the password and uses the service without paying for it.

- *Theft of information*: A hacker may break into a system to steal credit card numbers, test data, or even national security data.

- *Hatred and vengeance*: Many people have groups or companies they do not like. These people may hack into a company's system to destroy files or to steal information to sell to opposing groups.

- *For thrill of it*: Some hackers break into sites just to see if they can do it. The thrill for them is in breaking the code.

3-1.1.4

▶ **VOCABULARY**

client/server network

client

server

server operating system

local area network (LAN)

wide area network (WAN)

Client/Server Networks

The term *client/server network* describes a software architectural model relationship. Most common network functions such as database access, e-mail exchange, Internet access, and so on, are based on this model. Likewise, most of today's software applications are also based on this model. In most instances, the *client* is a software program such as Internet Explorer. The *server* is hardware and can be one of many types of servers, such as a mail server, a database server, an FTP server, an application server, a Web server, and so on. When you access the Internet using a browser, the browser is the client and is used to access any accessible server (computer) in the world. This access enables the server and client to share files and other resources such as printers, external storage devices, and so on.

Selecting a server can be a simple or complicated task, depending on the network size, the amount of storage needed, the number of users, and so on. Similar to a desktop computer, a network server also requires an operating system.

Server operating systems are high-end programs designed to provide network control and include special functions for connecting computers and other devices into a network. Three of the more popular operating systems are Microsoft Windows, Apple's Macintosh, and UNIX/Linux. The selection of an operating system is determined by the way in which the server will be accessed, security issues, if the server will host a database, if forms will be processed, if programs such as Microsoft FrontPage or Adobe Dreamweaver will be used, and other individual factors. Client access to the server can be through various devices, including desktop or notebook computers, handheld devices, game systems, and other similar electronic devices.

3-1.1.5

Network Types

Networks are divided into two main types: *local area networks (LANs)* and *wide area networks (WANs)*.

Local Area Networks

Most LANs connect personal computers, workstations, and other devices such as printers and scanners in a limited geographical area, such as an office building, a school, or a home. Each device on the network is called a *node*, and each node generally shares resources such as a printer, programs, and other hardware. A *wireless LAN (WLAN)* is a variation of the LAN that uses no physical wires. To communicate on a WLAN, the computer and other devices that access the WLAN must contain some type of wireless device such as a network card, flash card, PC card, a USB network adapter, or other type of built-in wireless capability or a wireless network card (see **Figure 24–5**).

▶ **VOCABULARY**
node
wireless LAN (WLAN)
router
communication channels

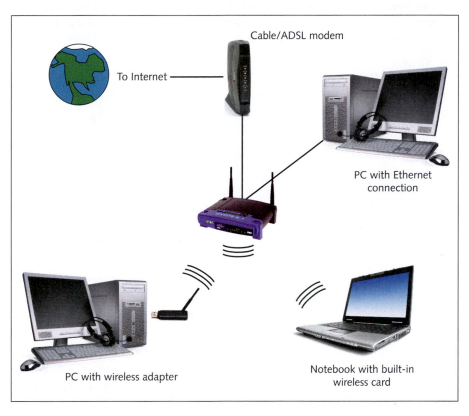

Cable/ADSL modem

To Internet

PC with Ethernet connection

PC with wireless adapter

Notebook with built-in wireless card

FIGURE 24–5   Wireless LAN

Wide Area Networks

A WAN covers a large geographical area and can contain communication links across metropolitan, regional, or national boundaries. The communications area might be as large as a state or a country or even the world. The largest WAN is the Internet. Most WANs consist of two or more LANs and are connected by *routers*. *Communication channels* can include telephone systems, fiber optics, satellites, microwaves, or any combination of these.

▶ **VOCABULARY**

hub

peer-to-peer network

Several different types of networks are available:

■ *Client/server network*: In this type of architecture, one or more computers on the network act as a server. The server manages network resources. Depending on the size of the network, several different servers might be connected. For example, a print server manages the printing, and a database server manages a large database. In most instances, a server is a high-speed computer with considerable storage space. The network operating system software and network versions of software applications are stored on the server. All of the other computers on the network are called clients. They share the server resources and other peripherals such as hubs, firewalls, and routers. A *hub* is a small, simple, inexpensive device that joins multiple computers together. Users access the server through a user name and password. See **Figure 24–6**. Some legacy networks use a switch, which performs the same tasks as a hub and is about 100 times faster.

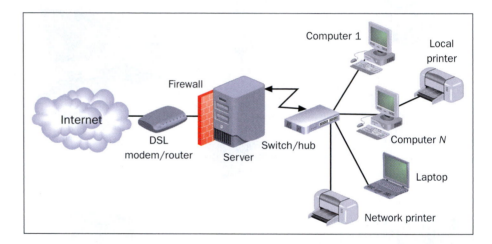

FIGURE 24–6   Client/server local area network

■ *Peer-to-peer network*: In a **peer-to-peer network**, all the computers are equal. No computer is designated as the server. People on the network each determine what files on their computer they share with others on the network. This type of network is much easier to set up and manage. Many small offices use peer-to-peer networks. See **Figure 24–7**.

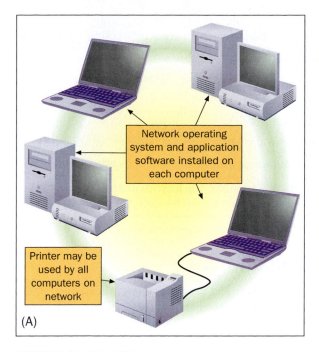

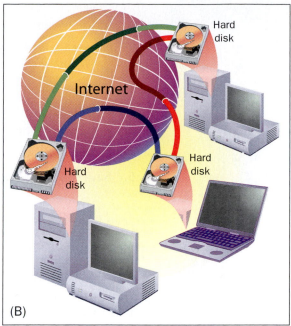

FIGURE 24–7   (A) Peer-to-peer network using a printer resource
(B) Internet peer-to-peer network

- *Intranet*: An ***intranet*** is designed for the exclusive use of people within an organization. Many businesses have implemented intranets within their own organizations. Documents such as handbooks and employee manuals, newsletters, employment forms, and other relevant company documents are the types of files that are stored on an intranet server.

- *Extranet*: An ***extranet*** is similar to an intranet, but it allows specific users outside of the organization to access internal information systems. Like the Internet, intranets and extranets use and support Web technologies, such as hyperlinks and Web pages coded in hypertext markup language (HTML).

- *Internet*: The ***Internet*** is a worldwide system composed of thousands of smaller networks. This global network allows computers worldwide to connect and exchange information. The World Wide Web and electronic mail are two of the more popular components of the Internet.

    In Step-by-Step 24.1, you research home networks.

▶ **VOCABULARY**
intranet

extranet

Internet

Step-by-Step 24.1

1. Click the **Start** button 🪟 on the taskbar, and then click **Help and Support**.

2. Search for Help topics on networking.

3. Select the **How is a network at home different from one at work?** link.

4. Read the information and then use your word processing program to answer the following questions:

   ■ How are computers on a home network different from the ones at a workplace?

   ■ What is the main difference?

   ■ What are the most common types of home network technologies?

   ■ What process would you use to diagnose your home network problems?

5. Save your file as **networking** and submit it to your instructor.

3-1.1.6

Network Communications

Most networks consist of a network server and computer clients. In addition to the server and the client, there are two other categories of network hardware: communication devices and devices that connect the network cabling and amplify the signal.

Communication Hardware

Communication hardware devices facilitate the transmitting and receiving of data. When we think about communication hardware, the first thing that generally comes to mind is the desktop computer and router. However, there are other types of computers and devices that send and receive data. Some examples are large computers such as supercomputers, mainframe computers, and minicomputers; handheld and laptop computers; and even fax machines and digital cameras. All of these devices require some type of transmitting hardware device. Examples are as follows:

▶ **VOCABULARY**

modem

cable modem

■ *Modem*: The word **modem** is an acronym for *mo*dulate-*dem*odulate, which means to convert analog signals to digital and vice versa. This device enables a computer to transmit voice data over telephone lines. Computer information is stored digitally (in binary code of 0s and 1s), whereas information sent over telephone lines is transmitted in the form of analog waves. Both the sending and receiving users must have a modem. The speed at which modems can transmit data has increased dramatically in the past few decades. The first modems introduced in the 1960s could send data at a rate of about 300 bits per second (bps). By the early 1990s, the speed of data transmission via modem had increased to 9600 bps, and today the standard modem has a speed of 56 Kbps (kilobits per second). There are special modems capable of transmitting data as fast as 8 Mbps (megabits per second) over telephone lines.

■ *Cable modem*: A **cable modem** uses coaxial cable to send and receive data. This is the same type of cable used for cable TV. The bandwidth, which determines the amount of data that can be sent at one time, is much greater with a cable modem than with a traditional dial-up modem connection. Cable modems allow as many as 1,000 users to transmit data on one 6-MHz (megahertz) channel and is capable of transmitting data at speeds of 30 to 40 Mbps. A cable modem can be connected directly to your computer, enabling you to connect to the Internet, or it can be connected to a set-top box used with your television. With a set-top box, you can access and surf the Web from your TV. **Figure 24–8** shows a dial-up modem and a cable modem.

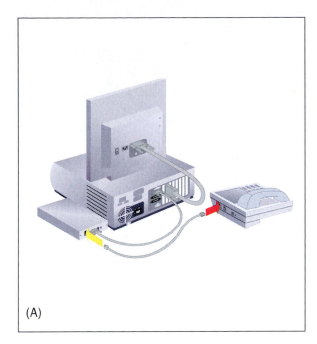

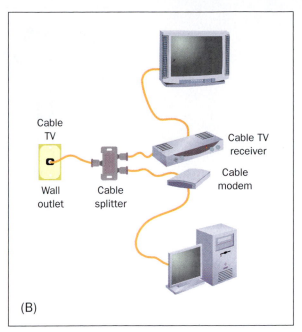

FIGURE 24–8   (A) Computer with dial-up modem attached (B) Computer with cable modem attached

- *Digital subscriber line (DSL)*: **Digital subscriber line (DSL)** is an Internet connection technology that provides for the transfer of information to a computer at a high-speed bandwidth over ordinary copper telephone lines. A DSL can carry both data and voice. The data part of the line is a dedicated connection to the Internet. High bit-rate DSL (HDSL) was the first DSL technology to use twisted pair cables. Very-high DSL (VDSL) is capable of supporting HDTV, telephone services, and Internet access over a single connection. Cable modems and DSL are widely used to provide broadband Internet access. Both are routers, which businesses use for security and stability on their Internet-connected networks.

- *T-1*: A **T-1 line** is a type of fiber-optic telephone line that can transmit up to 1.544 megabits per second or can be used to transmit 24 digitized voice channels. It can be used for data transfer on a network or to provide phone service for a commercial building (see **Figure 24–9**).

▶ **VOCABULARY**
digital subscriber line (DSL)
T-1 line

▦ **EXTRA FOR EXPERTS**

Broadband is high-speed Internet access; most Internet users in the United States have broadband access.

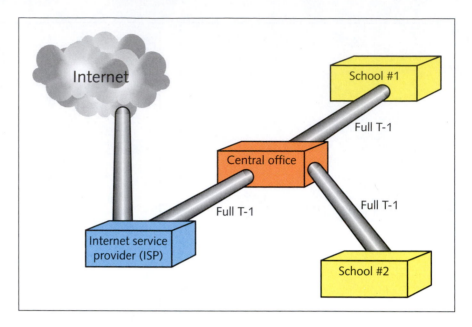

FIGURE 24–9   T-1 lines

▶ **VOCABULARY**

wireless Internet service provider
   (WISP)

WiMAX

- *Wireless*: **Wireless Internet service providers (WISPs)** provide connection speeds more than 30 times faster than dial-up connections—from 384 Kbps to 2.0 Mbps. **WiMAX** (Worldwide Interoperability for Microwave Access) is a recent wireless technology that can deliver maximum speeds of up to 7 Mbps to your cell phone, home computer, or car.

As indicated earlier, connecting to the Internet requires special devices—a dial-up device, cable, or DSL access. To connect wirelessly, however, requires different equipment than that used for a wired connection. To connect any devices (personal computers, cell phones, game systems, and so on) wirelessly to the Internet, the following components are needed:

- A notebook computer or some other type of device such as a computer game system, an iPhone or cell phone, minicomputer, or similar device
- An internal wireless adapter or a USB port for connecting an external adapter. The adapter must be compatible with the wireless provider's protocols.
- A high-speed, wireless Internet access plan from a provider
- "Sniffer" software, used to locate hot spots

Communication standards enable all of these different devices to communicate with each other.

3-1.1.7

Network Security Issues

Establishing and maintaining computer security is necessary to keep hardware, software, and data safe from harm or destruction. Some risks to computers are natural causes, some are accidents, and others are intentional. It is not always evident that some type of computer crime or intrusion has occurred. Therefore, it is necessary that safeguards for each type of risk be put into place. It is the responsibility of company or an individual to protect their data.

The best way to protect data is to effectively control access to it. Generally, this protection is the responsibility of the network administrators and security personnel. If unauthorized persons gain access to data, they may obtain valuable information or trade secrets. Perhaps worse, they might change data outright so that no one can use it.

The most common form of restricting access to data is the use of passwords, as shown in **Figure 24–10**. Users may need a password to log on to a computer system or to specific parts of it. Companies often establish password-protected locations on hard drives and networks so that certain people have access to certain areas but not to others.

FIGURE 24–10   Password-protected computer

To maintain secure passwords, they should be changed frequently so that people who no longer need access are locked out. Tips for creating secure passwords include using a mixture of upper- and lowercase letters, using numbers as well as letters, and adding punctuation keys such as & or % to the password. The challenge is to create passwords that are easy for you to remember but difficult for anyone else to decipher, because you should never write down a password or share it with anyone else (see **Figure 24–11**). More password protection is broken by people who gain access through a shared password or lost "cheat sheet" than by anyone guessing your "secret code."

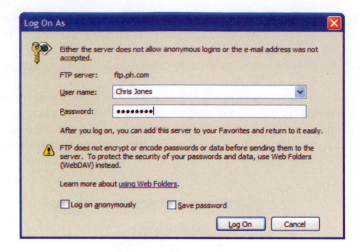

FIGURE 24–11   Passwords are used to protect data against unauthorized use

It is important for all users to maintain password security in order to keep out unauthorized users, hackers, and other computer criminals. Never reveal a password to anyone without authorization. Inform the appropriate people if you discover that someone knows passwords he or she shouldn't know. Avoid using the same or similar passwords for other applications or Internet accounts.

Other security measures include the following:

VOCABULARY

firewall

proxy server

biometric securiy measures

- Electronic identification cards are used to gain access to certain areas within a building or department.

- *Firewalls*, which consist of special hardware and software, protect individual companies' networks from external networks. A firewall gives users inside the organization the ability to access computers outside of their organization but keeps outside users from accessing the organization's computers.

- Antivirus software is used to protect data on your computer. It should always be running on a computer to protect data and programs from corruption or destruction.

- A *proxy server* acts like a switchboard through a firewall. The server acts as an intermediary between a user and the Internet. This process ensures security, administrative control, and caching service. A cache (pronounced *cash*) is a place to store something temporarily.

Planning for Security

Companies must plan for security before it is needed rather than handling breaches in security as they occur. For example, any company that handles sensitive information or needs to protect its data should consider the following guidelines:

- Institute a selective hiring process that includes careful screening of potential employees. Do not keep employees on staff who refuse to follow security rules. This measure can prevent internal theft or sabotage.

- Regularly back up data and store it off site.

- Employ *biometric security measures*, which examine a fingerprint, a voice pattern, or the iris or retina of the eye. These must match the entry that originally was stored in the system for an employee to gain access to a secure area. This method of security usually is applied when high-level security is required.

Wireless Security

Predictions are that in the near future, wireless networking (Wi-Fi) will be so common that you can access the Internet just about anywhere at any time. Most laptop computers have wireless cards preinstalled. Wireless networking, however, has many security issues, and hackers have found it very easy to access wireless networks. For example, one way to access a wireless network is through accidental association, when the user turns on the computer and the computer automatically connects to a wireless access point (see **Figure 24–12**). In Step-by-Step 24.2, you research wireless network security.

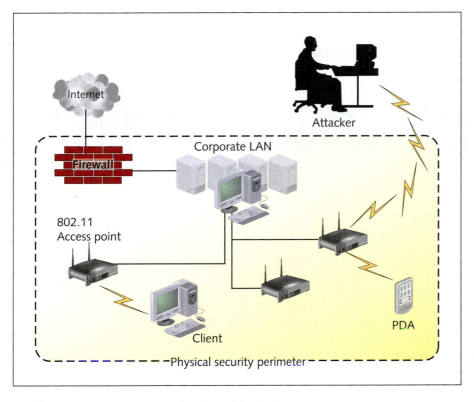

FIGURE 24–12   Securing wireless networks

Step-by-Step 24.2

1. Click the **Start** button on the taskbar, and then click **Help and Support**.

2. Search for Help topics on wireless networks, and then click the **How do I know if a wireless network is secure?** link.

3. Read the information and then use your word processing program to summarize what you learned.

4. Define the terms network security key, certificate, and Internet service provider (ISP).

5. Submit your word processing document to your instructor.

TECHNOLOGY CAREERS

Building Communities with Computers

Computer modeling is a term that describes the use of computers to create a mathematical model of a real-life system or process and then test it under different conditions. If you have ever played the computer game SimCity, you already have some experience with computer modeling. When you play the game, create a city, and then change certain data, such as the population or the layout of a utility system, you can see what changes occur in different situations. The future is still bright for computer gaming and simulation. If you are looking for a career that follows the future development technology and stays on top of the latest innovations, consider one in computer simulation.

SUMMARY

In this lesson, you learned:

- A network is a group of two or more computers linked together.

- A telephone network is similar in makeup to a computer network. The Public Switched Telephone Network (PSTN) supports telephone service, and it is the world's largest collection of interconnected commercial and government-owned voice-oriented systems.

- You can use a network for information sharing, hardware sharing, software sharing, and as a collaborative environment.

- Networks are divided into two main types: local area networks and wide area networks.

- Local area networks (LANs) connect personal computers, workstations, and other devices such as printers and scanners in a limited geographical area, such as an office building, a school, or a home.

- A wide area network (WAN) is made up of several connected local area networks.

- In a client/server network, one or more computers on the network act as a server. The server manages network resources. In a peer-to-peer network, all of the computers are equal. No computer is designated as the server. People on the network each determine what files on their computer they share with others on the network.

- Data security is a risk with many networks. Some risks to computers are natural causes, some are accidents, and others are intentional.

- The best way to protect data is to effectively control the access to it. Generally, this protection is the responsibility of the network administrators and security personnel. If unauthorized persons gain access to data, they may obtain valuable information or trade secrets. Hackers are people who break into computer systems to steal services and information.

- Transmission media can be either physical or wireless.

- A modem is a type of communication device. A hub is a device that controls the incoming and forwarding of data. A router directs traffic on the Internet or on multiple connected networks.

VOCABULARY REVIEW

Define the following terms:

biometric security measures
cable modem
client
client/server network
communication channels
digital subscriber line (DSL)
extranet
firewall
hacker

hub
Internet
intranet
local area network (LAN)
modem
node
peer-to-peer network
proxy server
Public Switched Telephone Network
   (PSTN)

router
server
server operating system
T-1 line
wide area network (WAN)
WiMAX
wireless Internet service provider (WISP)
wireless LAN (WLAN)

■ REVIEW QUESTIONS

TRUE / FALSE

Circle T if the statement is true or F if the statement is false.

T   F   **1.** A modem converts analog signals to digital signals.

T   F   **2.** The best way to protect data is to effectively control the access to it.

T   F   **3.** All users should maintain password security.

T   F   **4.** Hackers invade other people's computers only for fun.

T   F   **5.** Software sharing is one of the benefits of networking.

MULTIPLE CHOICE

Select the best response for the following statements.

1. A _____ is confined to a limited geographical area.

   A.   wide area network   C.   tiny area network

   B.   local area network   D.   metropolitan area network

2. _____ software should always be running on a computer to protect data and programs from corruption or destruction.

   A.   Word processing   C.   Connection

   B.   Antivirus   D.   Preview

3. A proxy server acts like a switchboard through a _____.

   A.   firewall   C.   bridge

   B.   NIC   D.   modem

4. A _____ is made up of several connected local area networks.

   A.   hub   C.   wide area network

   B.   bridge   D.   router

5. A _____ directs traffic on the Internet or on multiple connected networks.

   A.   server   C.   router

   B.   hub   D.   client

FILL IN THE BLANK

Complete the following sentences by writing the correct word or words in the blanks provided.

1. A(n) _____ is a small, simple, inexpensive device that joins multiple computers together.

2. A(n) _____ is a type of fiber-optic telephone line.

3. A(n) _____ is a place to store something temporarily.

4. _____ are people who break into computer systems to steal services and information.

5. A(n) _____ is a type of network that covers a large geographical area.

PROJECTS

PROJECT 24–1

Many colleges and universities have formal statements regarding the ethical use of their computer systems, often called an *acceptable use policy*. Complete the following:

1. Use the Internet or contact a local college or university to obtain a copy of a school's ethical computing statement.

2. After reading it carefully, rewrite it to include any additional rules you believe should be included.

3. Submit the revision to your instructor as requested.

PROJECT 24–3

You want to set up a network in your home with the following elements:

- DSL, cable, or satellite Internet connection
- Switch, PC, wireless router, and a wireless laptop that all share the same Internet connection
- No additional charges to your Internet service provider

1. Use the Internet to research how to set up the home network according to this description.

2. Describe the network in a one- or two-page document.

3. Submit the document to your instructor as requested.

PROJECT 24–2

You use passwords to protect data and equipment. Complete the following:

1. Research the importance of a good password.

2. Find out what is considered a strong password and why it is better than a weak one.

3. Write a paragraph explaining why this is important and what could happen if your password was stolen.

4. Submit the paragraph to your instructor as requested.

TEAMWORK PROJECT

You work at a local restaurant. Your supervisor at work is interested in learning about the various networking options and which would be best for your particular environment. Assume that your restaurant has 10 employees and is not part of a national chain. Develop a plan that you think would best serve the needs of your restaurant.

CRITICAL THINKING

Use the Internet and other resources to identify early security measures that were used to protect computers and computer data. Describe how these measures counteracted the intrusions made. Then, visit the Web sites of some companies that make computer security devices such as *www.pcguardian.com*. Compare these early security measures to today's current needs and practices. Write a report of your findings.

ONLINE DISCOVERY

You now have three computers, a scanner, a DVD player, a printer, and a copier spread throughout several rooms in your home. You and your family have decided it is time to network the equipment. Your goal is to determine whether to go wireless or wired. Use the Internet to help you decide on the technology you will use, and then write a one-page report explaining why you selected this technology. Include a diagram of your network plan.

LESSON 25

Communication Services

■ OBJECTIVES

Upon completion of this lesson, you should be able to:

- Identify types of electronic communication.
- Describe users of electronic communication.
- Identify the major components of electronic communication.
- Manage e-mail with Microsoft Office Outlook.
- Send and receive e-mail.

■ DATA FILES

You do not need data files to complete this lesson.

■ VOCABULARY

Address Book

archiving

attachment

distribution list

electronic mail (e-mail)

e-mail address

instant messaging

mailing list

packets

signature

spam

text messaging

user agent

Windows Mail

The Internet, electronic mail (e-mail), and other forms of electronic communications provide new ways to communicate. Using e-mail, you can combine numerous media—text, graphics, sound, video—into a single message, and then quickly exchange information in dynamic, two-way communications. Using the Internet, you quickly can transmit information to and receive information from individuals and workgroups around the world.

3-2.1.1

Electronic Communication Categories

As a worldwide electronic communications system, the Internet provides many communication services, which can be organized into the following categories:

▶ **VOCABULARY**

electronic mail

e-mail

instant messaging

text messaging

- *Electronic mail*: **Electronic mail**, or **e-mail**, is similar to regular mail. You have a message, an address, and a carrier that figures out how to transfer the message from one location to another. You can send e-mail to other people on a network at an organization, or you can use an Internet service provider to send e-mail to any computer in the world.

- *Instant messaging (IM)*: You use **instant messaging** services to send messages in real time. In other words, you can send and receive messages while you and someone else are both connected to the Internet.

- *Text messaging*: Instead of using a computer, with **text messaging** you use a cell phone or other mobile device to send and receive written messages.

- *Voice over IP (VoIP)*: Sometimes called audio over IP, you use this service to make phone calls with an Internet connection instead of a regular telephone line. Your voice is converted into a digital signal that travels over the Internet. With VoIP, you can make a call directly from a computer, a special VoIP phone, or a traditional phone connected to a special adapter.

- *Online conferencing*: Also referred to as video conferencing, you can conduct a conference with yourself and one or more other participants at different sites by using computer networks to transmit audio and video data.

- *Chat rooms*: Chat rooms are Web sites that allow real-time communication so you can exchange messages with others through the computer. You use the keyboard to type text, which is displayed on the other person's monitor.

- *Social networking sites*: These Web sites provide a way to build online communities of people who share common interests or activities.

- *Blog postings/comments*: A blog (short for Web log) is a type of personal journal created by one person or by a group; entries are published in reverse chronological order.

- *Message boards and newsgroups*: Both of these services provide bulletin board systems that serve as discussion sites; users can post messages asking for assistance.

3-2.1.2

Identifying Users of Electronic Communication

Millions of people use the Internet, and each is required to have unique identification in the form of an e-mail address, sign-in or log on credentials, and password in the same way that each person has a unique phone number. Your e-mail address is not only used to send and receive e-mails, but it is also used for a variety of other options. For example, you use it to fill out a form to subscribe to a Web site, to set up your checking account, to order a book from Amazon, to use instant messaging, and so on. Other services that require a unique logon are blogs, social networks, and video conferencing services.

Components of Electronic Communications

3-2.1.3

Electronic communication is the technology that enables computers to communicate with each other and other devices. It is the transmission of text, numbers, voice, and video from one computer or device to another. Electronic communication has changed the way the world does business and the way we live our lives.

When computers were developed in the 1950s, they did not communicate with each other. This all changed in 1969. ARPANET was established and served as a testing ground for new networking technologies. ARPANET was a large wide-area network created by the United States Defense Advanced Research Project Agency (ARPA).

Today's electronic communication requires the following components:

- *Software*: Software applications (**user agents**) installed on the local PC, network, or Web, such as e-mail, text message, and instant messaging programs
- *Sender*: The computer sending the message (server)
- *Receiver*: The computer receiving the message (server)
- *Channel*: The media that carries or transports the message: telephone wire, coaxial cable, radio signal, microwave signal, or fiber-optic cable
- *Communication*: The information that is transferred between user agents
- *Protocols*: The rules that govern the transfer of data and ensures that information created by one system can be interpreted and read by another

This technology has made it possible to communicate around the globe using tools such as the Internet, electronic mail (e-mail), faxes, e-commerce, and electronic banking. See **Figure 25–1**.

EXTRA FOR EXPERTS

On Labor Day in 1969, the first message was sent via telephone lines from a computer at UCLA to another computer at Stanford Research Institute. This was the beginning of the Internet and electronic communication as we know it today.

▶ **VOCABULARY**

user agent

e-mail address

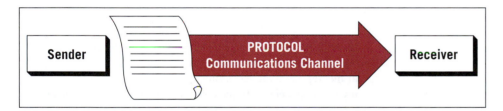

FIGURE 25–1   Transmitting a message from sender to receiver

Interpreting E-Mail Addresses

3-2.2.1

When you send postal mail to someone, you must know the address of that person. The same thing is true for e-mail. For instance, David Edward's e-mail address could be *dedwards@msn.com*. Each user on the Internet must have a unique e-mail address.

An *e-mail address* consists of three parts:

- The user name of the individual
- The @ symbol
- The user's domain name

David Edward's e-mail address *dedwards@msn.com* ends with the domain code .com. The first set of domain codes were defined in October 1984 and are used on the Internet's Domain Name System. This set of codes included the following:

- .com (commercial)
- .edu (education)
- .gov (government)
- .mil (military)
- .org (organizations)

Currently, a limited range of 21 top-level domains are available. A number of other less popular specialty domain codes are .cat, .jobs, .mobi, .post, .tel, .info, and .travel.

Parts of an E-mail Message

When you compose an e-mail message, it should contain four main components. First, enter the address of one or more people to whom you are sending the message. Be sure to include a subject line, which should grab the recipient's attention or fully but briefly describe the purpose of the message. Many people scan the subject lines of their messages before opening them, so your subject lines should be meaningful and accurate. Next, include the body of the message, which should be clear, concise, and free of spelling errors. Any attachments should be noted in the body of the message.

E-Mail Options

E-mail programs include a variety of options when responding to a message, including the following:

- *Reply to Sender*: One way to reply to an e-mail message is to click the Reply button, type your reply message, and then send the message. With this type of reply, the original message is included along with your reply message, so it is appropriate when you are answering a question or responding to specifics in the original message. When you reply to an e-mail message, the recipient normally sees the letters *Re* preceding the text in the subject line to indicate that it is a reply message.
- *Reply All*: If more than one person is listed on the To or From line of the e-mail message, you can click the Reply All button instead of Reply. You then follow the same steps as when replying, except your message is sent to everyone who received the original message.
- *Forward*: This option is similar to replying to a message; however, when you forward a message, you send it to people other than those who sent the original message. Forwarding a message helps cut down on the time you spend creating messages from scratch. It is also a quick way to share information with a number of people. When you forward a message, a recipient normally sees the letters *FW* preceding the text in the subject line to identify it as a message that is being forwarded.
- *Copy (cc) and blind copy (bcc)*: To send a copy of an e-mail to another person, type his or her e-mail address into the Cc text box, or click the Cc button and then select the person's name. To send a blind copy to someone, type the e-mail address in the Bcc text box, or click the Bcc button and then select the person's name. The recipient of the Bcc is not visible to the other people receiving the message.

Unless a technical problem occurs, e-mail travels much faster than regular mail (sometimes referred to as "snail mail"). When you send someone an e-mail message, it is broken down into small chunks called *packets*. These packets travel independently from server to server. You might think of each packet as a separate page within a letter. When the packets reach their final destination, they are recombined into their original format. This process enables the message to travel much faster. In fact, some messages can travel thousands of miles in less than a minute.

Accessing E-Mail

Since e-mail has become a widespread way of communicating in our business and personal lives, the methods used to access e-mail have multiplied. Many Web sites and Internet service providers offer e-mail as part of a monthly fee or even at no charge. Google's Gmail, Hotmail, and AltaVista are examples of Web-based e-mail services. After you set up an e-mail account with a service, you access your account using the company's Web site and entering your account name (usually your e-mail address) and a password. The Web site often directs you to a built-in e-mail program where you can read and send messages and manage your electronic communication.

Wireless communication also has expanded the ways e-mail can be transmitted and retrieved. Many people have cell phones or handheld computers that can send and receive e-mail almost anywhere.

Managing E-Mail with Microsoft Office Outlook

3-2.2.7

Microsoft Outlook is an Office application you can use to manage e-mail. The e-mail features of Outlook are very similar to the features of *Windows Mail* (a scaled-down version of Outlook provided with Windows Vista), so after you practice using Outlook in the exercises in this lesson, you will find that you can also use Windows Mail. Outlook is a versatile application that you can use to organize appointments, tasks and to-do lists, addresses, and e-mail.

When you start Outlook, a window similar to the one shown in **Figure 25–2** is displayed. The default opening window is the Outlook Today window, which gives you an overview of the calendar, tasks, and mail features of the program. **Figure 25–2** shows the Outlook Inbox, which displays the messages you receive.

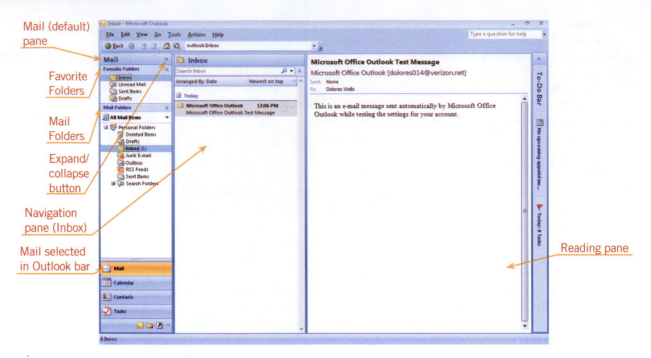

FIGURE 25–2   The Outlook window

Mail management is primarily handled through the Inbox. The Inbox contains a number of elements. Using the Inbox, you can organize your mail by creating mail folders for various topics, special projects, and individuals. The folders can be divided into favorites and general mail folders. The Inbox contains a list of your messages. The messages can be arranged by date with the newest on top or the oldest on top. When a message first arrives in the Inbox, it is displayed in bold type. Once the message is read, it is no longer bolded.

The current task selected in the Outlook bar at the left of the window is Mail. The name of the selected task appears in the task banner at the top of the Outlook bar. When Mail is selected, the left pane lists a number of standard folders, including Inbox, Deleted Items, Drafts, Junk E-mail, and Outbox. When you select a folder in the left pane, such as Inbox, its contents appear in the middle pane, or Navigation pane, as shown in **Figure 25–2**. Click an item in the folder to see the full text in the Reading pane, the large window at the right of the Outlook screen.

You can manage the folders in the Mail pane in the following ways:

- To create a new folder in the Mail pane, click File on the menu bar, point to New, and then click Folder.

- To delete a folder, right-click the folder name and then click Delete "folder name".

- To select, move, and copy mail to and from one folder to another, click the folder name containing the item you want to copy. This selects the folder and displays folder contents in the Inbox. Drag the file you want to move to the new folder. To copy and paste a file, select the file name, click Edit on the menu bar, and then click Copy. Click the name of the folder you want to copy the file to, click Edit on the menu, and then click Paste.

- To save a mail message, click the item that you want to save as a file, click the File menu and then select Save As, select the location where you want to save the file, type a name for the file, select the File type, and then click Save.

- To delete mail, select the message to be deleted, select Edit on the menu bar, and then click Delete. Deleted items are stored in the Deleted Items Mail folder. To undelete an item, click the Deleted Items folder and select the file name to be undeleted. Click Edit on the menu, select Move to Folder, select the folder, and click OK to move the item. To permanently delete a message or to delete the contents of the Deleted Items folder, select the item or items in the Deleted Items Mail folder, right-click and then select Delete.

- To search for a message, click Tools on the menu bar, point to Instant Search and then select Search All Mail Items.

- To sort mail, click the Newest on top or Oldest on top column heading to organize the messages by date. You can also click View on the menu bar, point to Arrange, and then click Date.

Archiving is the process of backing up your e-mail messages. When you first run Outlook, AutoArchive automatically runs every 14 days and saves the backup file with a .pst extension. You can change how often Archive runs by clicking Tools on the menu bar, clicking Options, clicking the Other tab, and then clicking the AutoArchive button. When you make your regular backups, be sure to back up the archive file with the .pst extension. If your hard disk fails (and they all eventually do), you will lose your messages and attachments such as pictures and videos unless you have a backup copy of the .pst file.

Outlook can synchronize with other devices such as a desktop computer, a cell phone, or other handheld devices. To use this service generally requires that you download and install updates for the particular device that you want to use.

Although you do not apply all of Outlook's options in this lesson, you can take a short tour of Outlook in the following Step-by-Step exercise by opening several Outlook folders. You can customize most Outlook folders to display information in a number of ways. When you open a folder, you will see the view that was used the last time that folder was opened.

▶ **VOCABULARY**
archiving

Step-by-Step 25.1

1. Click the **Start** button 🟦 on the taskbar, point to **All Programs**, click **Microsoft Office**, and then click **Microsoft Office Outlook 2007**.

   If your computer is on a network, you might be prompted to enter your profile name and a password when launching Outlook. If a dialog box appears asking you to make Outlook your default program for e-mail, calendar, and contacts, click **No**.

2. Click **Calendar** in the Outlook bar. You use this feature to set up appointments and meetings. If no one has entered any meetings in Outlook yet, this folder will be empty.

3. Click **Contacts** in the Outlook bar. This feature stores information about personal and business contacts. If no one has entered any contacts in Outlook yet, this folder will be empty. (Additional information on using the Address book is provided later in this lesson.)

4. Click **Tasks** in the Outlook bar. A grid used to organize information about tasks you want to accomplish is displayed in the Reading pane. If no one has yet entered any tasks in Outlook, this folder will be empty.

5. Click **Mail** in the Outlook bar and then click the **Deleted Items** folder in the All Mail Items list in the Outlook bar. The Deleted Items folder opens in the Navigation pane. When you delete items from other mail folders, the items are stored here until you delete them permanently. If no one has deleted any items in Outlook, this folder will be empty.

6. Click the **Inbox** folder. Any messages waiting for you are displayed in the Navigation pane, with a closed envelope icon next to items in the inbox that have not been read yet. The first time you start Outlook, you receive a message in the inbox folder from Microsoft, similar to the one shown in **Figure 25–2**. **Figure 25–3** shows the Inbox with many more messages.

FIGURE 25–3
Navigation pane and Reading pane in the Mail window

Name of selected folder in Navigation pane

The (6) indicates six unread messages

Plus sign

Open envelope icon

Closed envelope icon

Reading pane

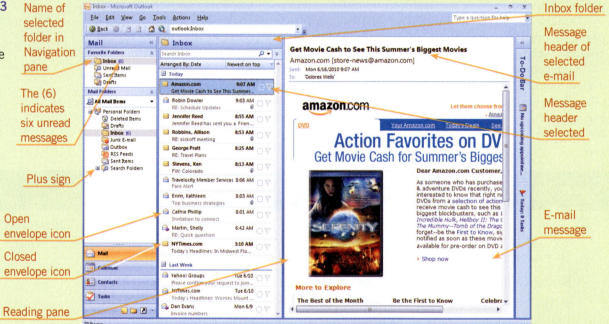

Inbox folder

Message header of selected e-mail

Message header selected

E-mail message

WARNING

You might not have any messages in your Inbox when you open the Inbox folder in this exercise. You can still perform the steps without any problems.

7. Click the **Outbox** folder. This folder is used to hold completed messages that have not yet been sent. If this folder contains messages, notice the icon, which looks like a small addressed and stamped envelope, that indicates the message is ready to send.

8. Leave this folder open for the next Step-by-Step exercise.

Sending and Receiving E-Mail

3-2.2.4
3-2.2.5
3-2.2.6

As you have seen, if your computer is set up to handle e-mail, you can use the Inbox folder in Outlook to send and receive e-mail messages. An advantage to using Outlook as your e-mail application is that as you create messages you have easy access to the other Outlook folders. You can quickly address the message to someone on your contacts list, check your calendar to make sure you are available for a meeting, or add a task to your task list when a message requests further action. In addition to sending a message, you can include attachments such as pictures or documents.

Receiving E-Mail

When you open Outlook, it sends a request to your mail server to check if you have any messages waiting. If you do, Outlook receives them and displays them in the Inbox folder. The Navigation pane displays message headers for any new messages. The message header tells you who sent the message, the subject of the message, and the date and time your server received it. The Reading pane of the Inbox window displays the actual text of the message. If you have a number of messages, you can read each one by clicking its message header to display the message text in the Reading pane.

If you already are working in Outlook, you can check your e-mail at any time. Open the Inbox folder and click the Send/Receive button on the Standard toolbar. After you have finished reading your messages, if you do not need to keep the messages, you can delete them by selecting each message header and clicking the Delete button on the Standard toolbar.

E-Mail Features

3-2.2.8

▶ **VOCABULARY**

Address Book

distribution list

mailing list

Sending e-mail is as easy as clicking a few buttons and typing your message. The Outlook *Address Book* stores names, e-mail addresses, phone numbers, and other contact information so you can access it easily while you are sending and receiving e-mail messages. Some of the tasks you can perform in Address Book include the following:

- To add new data to the Address Book, click Tools on the menu bar and then click Address Book to display the Address Book: Contacts screen, or copy and paste an address from an e-mail message that you received.

- To modify an e-mail address, display the Address Book: Contacts screen, double-click the address, and then make the modifications.

- To delete an e-mail address, display the Address Book: Contacts screen, click File, and then click Delete.

You can use a *distribution list* to send the same message to a group. To create a distribution list (also called a *mailing list*), click File on the menu bar, point to New, and then click Distribution List. In the Name box, type the name of your distribution list. On the Distribution List tab, click Select Members. In the Address Book list box, click the address book that contains the e-mail addresses you want to include in your distribution list.

3-2.2.4

Sending E-Mail

You enter an e-mail address in the To text box either by typing the address or by inserting an address stored in your address book. The Address Book generally contains a list of e-mail addresses of those individuals with whom you frequently correspond. You also enter e-mail addresses in the Cc text box if you are sending copies of the message to other recipients. See **Figure 25–4**.

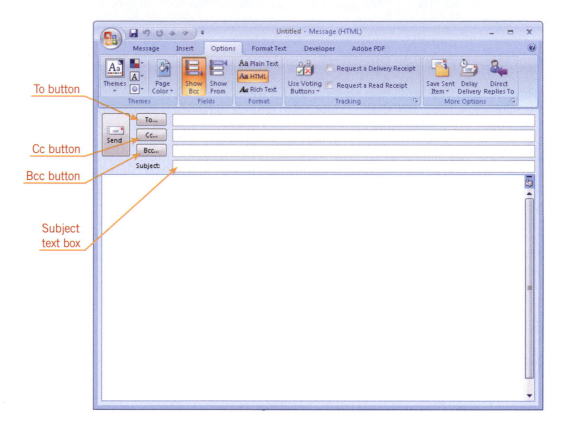

FIGURE 25–4   Message window

You can add another field labeled *Bcc* to enter e-mail addresses for recipients who are to be "blind" copied, meaning the primary addressee does not see that others are copied on the message. You can also add a From field to add your own name. To add these fields, click the Options tab and select the field you want to add to the message form.

It is good e-mail etiquette to include a subject for your mail message. As mentioned earlier, the subject should be brief, yet it should be descriptive enough to tell the recipient what the message is about. Then enter the text of your message.

After you have entered the addresses, subject, and text of your message, click the Send button to send the e-mail message.

In the following Step-by-Step exercise, you practice creating an e-mail message that you will send to yourself or to someone else in your class. If necessary, check with your instructor regarding the e-mail address (or addresses) to be used for the exercises in this lesson.

EXTRA FOR EXPERTS

The Cc in the e-mail window is the abbreviation for *carbon copy*. This originated with the old-fashioned typewriter. To send someone a copy of a letter or to create a file copy required that the typist use a sheet of carbon paper between each sheet of paper.

Step-by-Step 25.2

1. In Microsoft Office Outlook, click **File** on the menu bar, point to **New**, and then click **Mail Message**. The Untitled - Message window appears.

2. If necessary, click the **To** box. Type your e-mail address (or the e-mail address of the person to whom you are sending the message). If you do not know what e-mail address you should use, check with your instructor.

3. Click the **Subject** box and type **Caribbean cruise**.

4. Click in the message area. The title of the window changes to *Caribbean cruise*.

5. Type the following message:

   I am looking forward to going on the cruise next month. Our ports of call are Grand Cayman, Belize, and Cozumel. You can find additional information at www.cruise.com.

   Press **Enter** two times and type your name. Your screen should look similar to **Figure 25–5**.

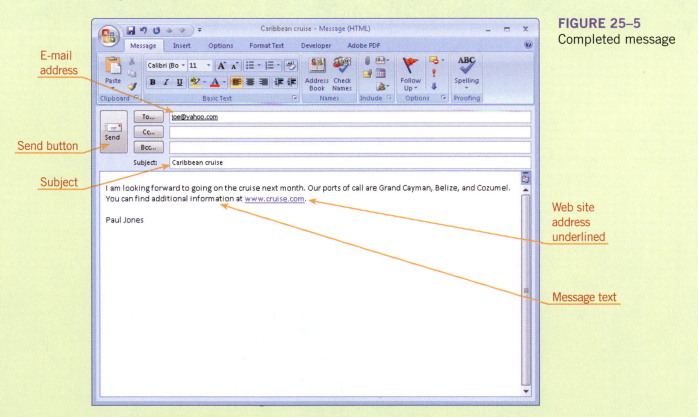

FIGURE 25–5
Completed message

E-mail address

Send button

Subject

Web site address underlined

Message text

EXTRA FOR EXPERTS

After you send a message, Outlook closes the Message window and temporarily stores the message in the Outbox folder. After the message is sent, Outlook moves the message to the Sent Items folder.

Notice that when you type the Web site address, it is underlined. It also might appear in a different color. Some e-mail programs require you to click, double-click, or hold down the CTRL key and click to activate the link and open the associated Web page.

6. Click the **Send** button to send the message. Leave Outlook open for the next Step-by-Step exercise.

Receiving and Opening E-Mail Messages

Now that you have sent a message to yourself (or someone in your class has sent you a message), you should receive it in the Inbox. You can click the Send/Receive button on the Standard toolbar to check for messages. In the following Step-by-Step exercise, you check for messages and then open the message you sent to yourself or the message you received from another student. In some instances, your instructor might have sent you a message.

Step-by-Step 25.3

1. Click **Tools** on the Standard toolbar, point to **Send/Receive** and then click **Send/Receive All**. The Inbox receives the message, and the message header is displayed, like that shown in **Figure 25–6**.

FIGURE 25–6
Receiving a message

Message header displayed in Inbox

Send/Receive button

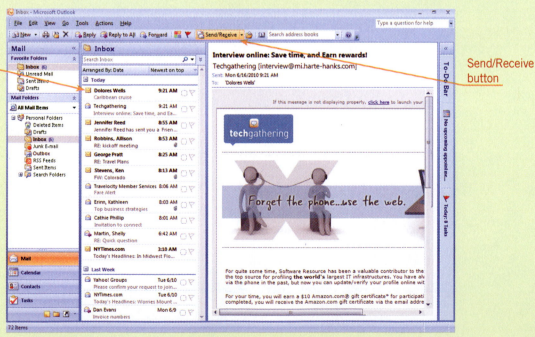

2. Click the message header in the Inbox pane. The message is displayed in the Reading pane, as shown in **Figure 25–7**. Leave Outlook open for the next Step-by-Step exercise.

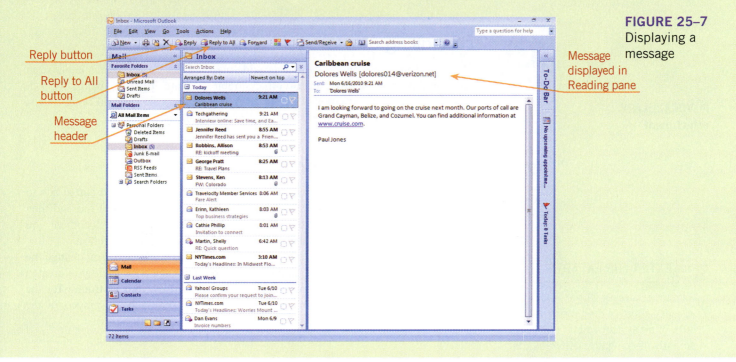

FIGURE 25–7
Displaying a message

Message displayed in Reading pane

Saving a Message

3-2.2.7

When you receive a message, Outlook automatically saves the message in the Inbox or another designated folder until you delete the message. You can save a message, however, as a text file, an HTML document, or a template. To save a message in one of these formats, click File on the menu bar and then select the Save As command. When the Save As dialog box is displayed, type a name in the File name text box, and then select the format by clicking the Save as type text box arrow. Click the Save button to save the file.

E-mail messages require file management skills similar to any other references (electronic or hard copy) you want to keep and manage. Most of the time, you will want to reply to messages you receive, and save important messages for future reference. On the other hand, you probably will want to delete unneeded messages and spam. *Spam* is unsolicited e-mail, essentially electronic junk mail. In many instances, spam is used to advertise products and services. Other spam messages might contain phony offers.

VOCABULARY
spam

Replying to a Message

3-2.2.4

When replying to a message, first select the message. Then click the Reply or Reply to All button on the Standard toolbar, type your message, and click the Send button. With this format, the original message is included along with your reply message. Suppose, for example, you received an e-mail from a friend and the friend sent a cc of the message to several other people. To reply to the friend, click the Reply button. To reply to the friend and send a copy of the message to the others who were sent a cc, use the Reply to All button. Using the Reply or Reply to All option is appropriate when you are answering a question or responding to specifics in the original message.

When you reply to a message, a Message window is displayed. This window is similar to the window that was displayed when you created a new message. Recall that when you use this format to reply to an e-mail message, the recipient(s) normally sees the letters Re preceding the text in the subject line to indicate that it is a reply message.

3-2.2.4

▶ **VOCABULARY**
attachment

3-2.2.5
3-2.2.6

Formatting a Message

The formatting tools on the Ribbon provide many of the same features as those in your word-processing program and other similar software. You can change the font type, font size, and text color of an e-mail message. You can also add bold, italics, and an underline to text as well as center it and add bullets.

Attaching a File to an E-Mail Message

Attachments are documents, images, figures, and other files that you can attach to your e-mail messages. To attach a file to a message, click the Insert tab and then click the Attach File button in the Include group, locate the file or document you want to attach in the Insert File dialog box, and then click the Insert button.

In the following Step-by-Step exercise, you reply to a message. You change the font and text color, attach a file, and then send the message. Use a file you created in one of the other lessons in this course or as directed by your instructor for the attachment. Outlook should be open and a message should be displayed in the Reading pane.

EXTRA FOR EXPERTS

Some messages might contain viruses—most of the time in the form of an attachment. If you have an antivirus program, generally the program identifies the message as having a virus. Many Internet service providers use firewalls to protect their customers from viruses. Do not open an attachment if you suspect that it has a virus, and immediately delete the message to which it is attached.

Step-by-Step 25.4

1. Click the **Inbox** and then double-click the message once, or right-click the message and then click **Open**. Click the **Reply** (or **Reply to All**) button on the Message tab. The message window is displayed, similar to that shown in **Figure 25–8**. The e-mail address is displayed automatically in the To box, and the insertion point is blinking in the message area.

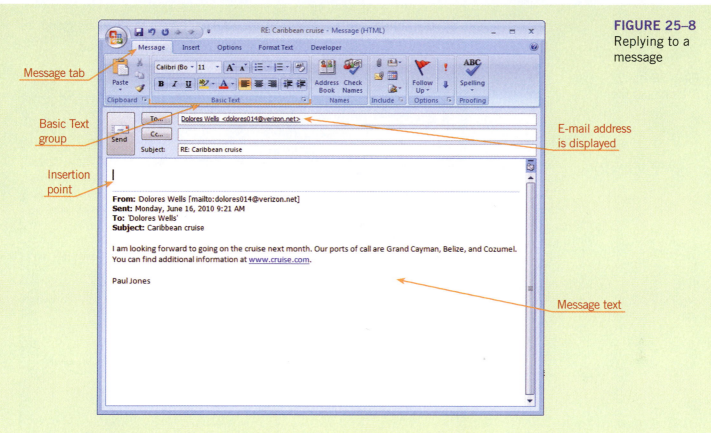

FIGURE 25–8
Replying to a message

2. Type the following:

   Dolores, (substitute the name of your recipient, and then press **Enter** two times).

   Good to hear from you. I also am preparing for the cruise and look forward to seeing you. I have attached some information for you.

   Press **Enter** two times and type your name.

3. Select the text of your message. Use the buttons on the Message tab to change the font to a style of your choice and the font size to **12**. Change the color to one of your choice. Format all of the text in bold.

4. Click the **Insert** tab and then click **Attach File** in the Include group, as shown in **Figure 25–9**. The Insert File dialog box is displayed.

FIGURE 25–9
Attaching a file

Attach File button

Formatted message

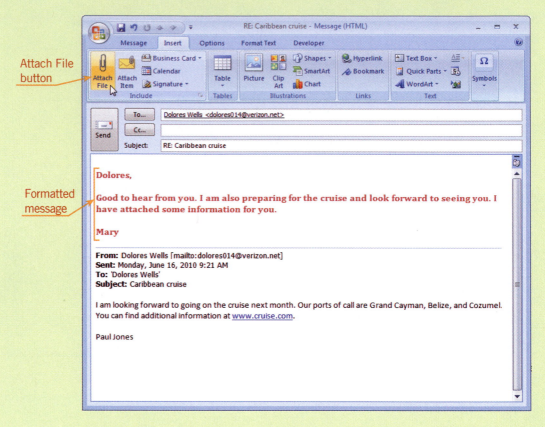

5. Locate and select a file that you want to attach, and then click the **Insert** button. The file is attached, as shown in **Figure 25–10**.

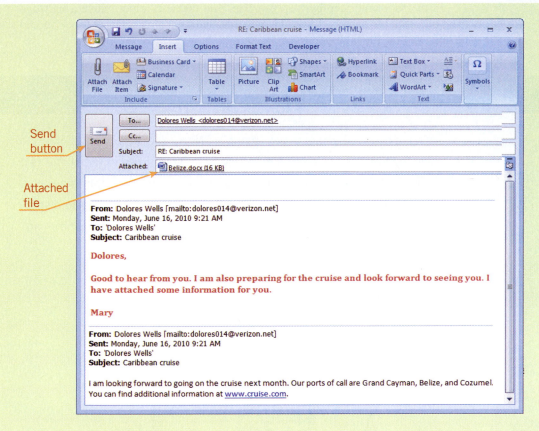

FIGURE 25–10
Message with attached file

6. Click the **Send** button. The message is sent. Close the message, but leave Outlook open for the next Step-by-Step exercise.

Managing Attachments

3-2.2.6

When you receive an attachment you can read the attachment in a few ways. You can preview it without opening it by clicking Outlook's Reading Pane. You can also open the message that contains the attachment, and then click the attachment, or you can open the attachment by double-clicking the attachment in the Reading Pane or the Message List. To save an attachment, you can right-click the attachment that you want to save in the open or previewed message, click Save As on the shortcut menu, select a location, and then click Save. To remove an attachment, right-click the attachment, and then click Remove on the shortcut menu.

Message Icons

Icons in the message headers listed in the Navigation pane offer clues about each message. For example, an icon that looks like the back of a sealed envelope indicates a message that has been received but not read; an exclamation point icon means the sender considers it an urgent or high-priority message; a paper clip icon indicates that the message has an attached file. You can also manually mark a message as read or unread, or add a flag icon as a reminder to follow up on the message.

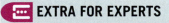 **EXTRA FOR EXPERTS**

When Outlook is open, you can check your e-mail at any time. Just click the Send/Receive button on the Standard toolbar.

In the following Step-by-Step exercise, you create a folder, move a message from one folder to another, forward a message, and print a message. Outlook should be open and the Inbox displayed.

Step-by-Step 25.5

1. Click **File** on the menu bar, point to **New**, and then click **Folder** to display the Create New Folder dialog box. Type **Cruise** in the Name text box. Click **Personal Folders** in the Select where to place the folder box. If necessary, click the plus sign to the left of Personal Folders to display the subfolders. The dialog box should look similar to that shown in **Figure 25–11**.

FIGURE 25–11
Create New Folder dialog box

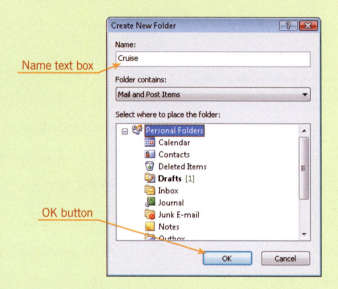

2. Click the **OK** button. The folder is displayed as a subfolder in the Personal Folders folder, as shown in **Figure 25–12**.

FIGURE 25–12
New folder created

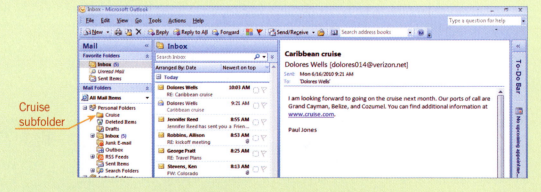

3. You should have two messages in your Inbox regarding the cruise. Click the first Cruise message; hold down the **Ctrl** key and click the second Cruise message. Both messages are selected. (If you are creating other messages and/or do not have two cruise messages, select any other two messages.)

4. Right-click the selected messages to display the shortcut menu. Point to **Move to Folder**, as shown in **Figure 25–13**.

Shortcut menu

Move to Folder command

5. Click **Move to Folder** to display the Move Items dialog box. If necessary, select the **Cruise** folder, as shown in **Figure 25–14**.

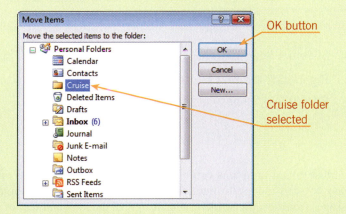

OK button

Cruise folder selected

6. Click the **OK** button. Click the **Cruise** folder to display the two messages.

7. Right-click the first message to display the shortcut menu. Click **Forward**. The message is displayed with *FW:* indicated in the Subject box.

8. Type your e-mail address or one of your classmates' in the To box. Type your instructor's e-mail address (or an e-mail address to another classmate) in the Cc box. (See **Figure 25–15**.)

FIGURE 25–15
Message to be forwarded

FW: is displayed

E-mail addresses

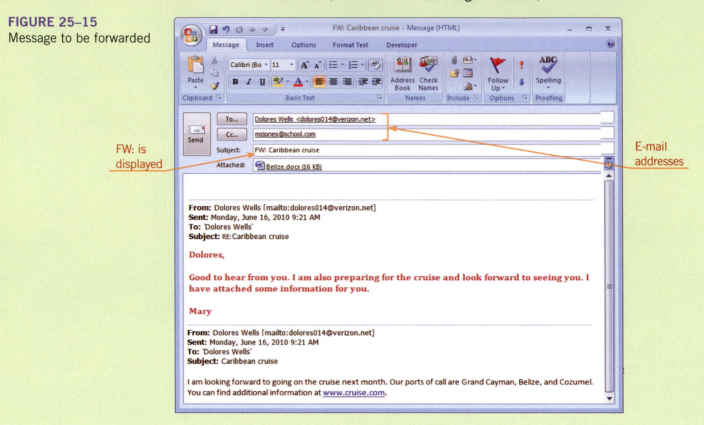

9. Click the **Send** button.

10. Right-click the first cruise message to display the shortcut menu. Click **Print** to print a copy of the message.

11. Close Outlook.

Most e-mail programs come with a variety of features and options that make it easy to send a copy to multiple recipients, generate an automatic reply, block messages from specific senders, and customize the look and feel of your messages.

Copying to Multiple Recipients

As previously indicated, you can insert more than one address in the To, Cc, and Bcc boxes. The message goes to all the addressees at the same time. If you are sending or copying an e-mail to more than one person, each e-mail address should be separated by a semicolon.

Mail Configuration Options

You can configure e-mail programs such as Outlook to deal automatically with e-mail messages you receive. The automatic controls you can set in Outlook include the following:

3-2.2.9

- *Automatic "out of the office" response*: Automatically replies to all received e-mail messages when you are unable to reply to messages yourself. This feature requires special e-mail servers and might not be available on your system.

- *Forwarding command*: Automatically redirects your mail to another e-mail address; this feature is accessed through the Actions command on the menu.

- *Redirect messages to your mobile phone*: Automatically redirects your mail to your mobile telephone; this feature is accessed through the Options command on the Tools menu. Click Preferences to display the option.

- *Block Senders List*: Prevents messages from designated addresses from being placed in your Inbox; this is particularly useful to block unwanted advertisements that often are sent repeatedly to the same e-mail address.

- *Safe Senders/Safe Recipients List*: Similar to the Block Senders list, selecting this option indicates to Outlook to accept all e-mails from the sender names contained in the list. A similar feature is the Safe Senders Domain List, which contains a list of all safe domains (*@msn.com*, for example) that you want to accept.

The Block Senders and Safe Senders lists are accessed through the Actions menu Junk E-mail command. Click the Junk E-mail options and click Safe Senders, Safe Recipients, or Blocked Senders. Type the e-mail address and then click the Add button.

A *signature* consists of text and/or pictures that you create and that automatically is added to the end of any outgoing messages. You can create unique signatures for different addresses (see **Figure 25–16**). For instance, you might want a signature for friends and family and another signature for business purposes.

▶ **VOCABULARY**
signature

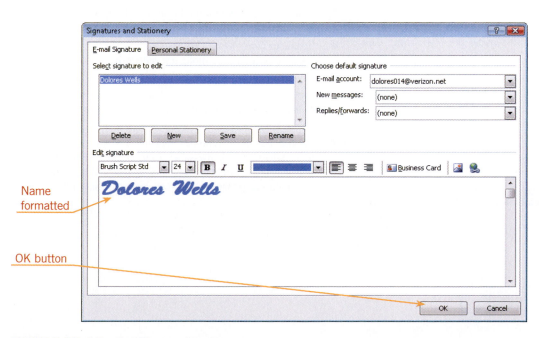

Name formatted

OK button

FIGURE 25–16   Creating a signature

ETHICS IN TECHNOLOGY

E-Mail/E-Aches

Although e-mail is one of the more popular services of the Internet, its widespread use has created several problems. One of the more time-consuming problems it causes is the overflow of e-mail messages many users find in their Inboxes. Similar to your telephone number, marketers and news groups can locate your e-mail address, enabling them to send you many unwanted e-mails.

E-mail communications can also lead to confusion and misinterpretation. Receivers are often guilty of not thoroughly reading an e-mail message before they reply, or they might not use the Reply All option correctly. It is important to pay close attention to whom you are sending your messages and replies. You do not want to reply automatically to all addressees if the content of the message is not relevant to everyone.

SUMMARY

In this lesson, you learned:

- Electronic communication includes e-mail, instant messages, text messages, VoIP phone calls, online conferences, chat rooms, blogs, and social networks.

- The components of electronic communication include software, a sender, a receiver, channel, communication content, and protocols.

- Wireless communication makes it possible to send and receive e-mail using a handheld computer or cell phone with e-mail capabilities.

- E-mail addresses consist of three parts: the user name, the @ symbol, and the domain name.

- Microsoft Office Outlook includes features to manage appointments, tasks, and e-mail. The Outlook bar displays shortcuts that give you quick access to each of the Outlook folders.

- Electronic mail is similar to regular mail because it requires an address, a message, and a carrier to get it from the sender to the receiver.

- You can access e-mail on a computer using a program such as Microsoft Outlook, or you can send and receive e-mail messages using a Web site with a built-in e-mail program, such as Gmail or Hotmail.

- An e-mail message header includes the address of the recipient, the subject of the message, and information about to whom the message is sent as a copy.

- You can use the Inbox folder in Outlook to send and receive e-mail messages.

- An attachment is a file that is sent with an e-mail message and that can be opened by the recipient.

- You can reply to an e-mail message, forward a message to a new recipient, delete a message, or save a message.

- Spam, or junk e-mail, consists of unsolicited messages that take up space in your Inbox unnecessarily.

- E-mail messages are organized in folders of incoming messages, sent messages, deleted messages, and junk e-mail. You can also create additional folders to organize your own e-mail.

- Special e-mail features let you add an automatic signature to messages, block messages from certain addresses, create personalized stationery for your messages, and set up an automatic response or forward your messages to another address.

◼ VOCABULARY REVIEW

Define the following terms:

Address Book

archiving

attachment

distribution list

electronic mail (e-mail)

e-mail address

instant messaging

mailing list

packets

signature

spam

text messaging

user agent

Windows Mail

◼ REVIEW QUESTIONS

TRUE / FALSE

Circle T if the statement is true or F if the statement is false.

T   F   **1.**   Electronic communication is the technology that enables computers to communicate with each other and other devices.

T   F   **2.**   A distribution list is used to send the same message to a group.

T   F   **3.**   Reply to All is the same process as reply, except your reply goes to all those individuals to whom the original message was sent.

T   F   **4.**   You can type only one e-mail address in the Cc text box.

T   F   **5.**   Mail management primarily is handled through the Inbox.

MULTIPLE CHOICE

Select the best response for the following statements.

1. An e-mail address consists of _____ parts.

    A.   two

    B.   three

    C.   four

    D.   five

2. An e-mail message is broken into small chunks called _____ as it is sent to the recipient.

    A.   attachments

    B.   packets

    C.   user names

    D.   domain names

3. A file sent with an e-mail message is called a(n) _____.

    A.   attachment

    B.   program

    C.   packet

    D.   interface

4. In Outlook, the _____ pane displays message headers for any new messages.

    A.   Incoming

    B.   Outgoing

    C.   Navigation

    D.   Exit

5. You enter an e-mail address in the _____ text box.

    A.   To

    B.   From

    C.   Access

    D.   Send

FILL IN THE BLANK

Complete the following sentences by writing the correct word or words in the blanks provided.

1. You use _____ to make phone calls with an Internet connection instead of a regular telephone line.

2. The media that carries or transports the message is called the _____.

3. _____ are documents, images, figures, and other files that you can attach to your e-mail messages.

4. If you are sending or copying an e-mail to more than one person, each e-mail address should be separated by a(n) _____.

5. _____ is the process of backing up your e-mail messages.

■ PROJECTS

PROJECT 25–1

You can use Outlook to send messages to your cell phone. Complete the following:

1. Access the Web site at *http://blogs.techrepublic.com.com/msoffice/?p=584* and read the information.

2. Write a paragraph describing how to use this option and include your opinion. Do you think it is useful? Assume you have a cell phone. Would you personally use this? If so, how would you use it? If not, why not?

PROJECT 25–2

Microsoft has several free audio courses that are accessible through your browser. A list of these courses is available at *http://office.microsoft.com/en-us/FX010857931033.aspx*. Complete the following:

1. Access the Web site at *http://office.microsoft.com/en-us/FX010857931033.aspx*.

2. Scroll down to the Learn the basics link, and then complete the tutorial.

3. Write a report listing at least three things you learned from the tutorial.

PROJECT 25–3

To learn about the Web and communication, complete the following:

1. Access the Web site at *http://websearch.about.com/od/whatistheinternet/a/usewww_2.htm* to read the article, "The World Wide Web and Effective Communication."

2. After you read the article, write a report expressing your opinion about the article. Do you agree or disagree with the author's statements? Explain why you agree or disagree.

TEAMWORK PROJECT

People who use e-mail for frequent communication are often annoyed by unsolicited e-mail called spam. Spam can be obnoxious, offensive, and a waste of your time. Some countries have laws against spam. Your Internet service provider might try to block spam before it reaches your mailbox. However, you still might be inconvenienced by junk e-mail. Working with a partner, research spam to learn more about what it is used for, how marketers get addresses, how effective spam is, and ways that you can stop spam. Prepare a report on your findings. Include information on both good and bad instances of spam, if it is a nuisance or problem, and how you can stop it before it reaches your e-mail Inbox. At the end of your report, answer the following questions: Is spam ever useful? Should there be laws to restrict spam? Do you think you can block all spam from reaching your Inbox?

■ CRITICAL THINKING

A number of Web sites provide free access to e-mail. What kind of features would you like to have for a personal e-mail account? You might want to investigate some Web sites, such as *www.hotmail.com*, *www.gmail.com*, or *www.yahoo.com*, to find out about the options available and then list the ones you think are most important. Why do you believe you would need these features for your e-mail account?

■ ONLINE DISCOVERY

Instant messaging is another type of electronic communications. Access and read the information at *http://en.wikipedia.org/wiki/Instant_messaging*. After you read the information, write a paragraph describing at least five new things you learned about instant messaging.

**Estimated Time:
2 hours**

LESSON 26

Communications and Collaboration

■ OBJECTIVES

Upon completion of this lesson, you should be able to:

- Identify appropriate uses for different communication methods.
- Identify the advantages of electronic communications.
- Identify common problems associated with electronic communications.
- Identify the elements of professional and effective electronic communications.
- Identify appropriate use of e-mail attachments and other supplementary information.
- Identify issues regarding unsolicited e-mail.
- Describe how to minimize or control unsolicited e-mail.
- Identify effective procedures for ensuring the safe and effective use of electronic communications.

■ DATA FILES

You do not need data files to complete this lesson.

■ VOCABULARY

biometric security measures

filtering

fraud

hoax

logic bomb

netiquette

phishing

pyramid schemes

RDF Summary

spam

tagging

teleconferencing

time bomb

Trojan horse

urban legend

virus

worm

In Lesson 25, you learned about e-mail. In this lesson, you expand your knowledge of e-mail and learn about other electronic communication methods, the appropriate use of each of these methods, and the advantages and disadvantages associated with each one.

3-2.3.1

Communication Methods

A variety of electronic communication methods is available. In most instances, the person or persons with whom you are corresponding and the topic of the correspondence will determine which communication method is the more appropriate. Electronic mail (e-mail), which was discussed in detail in Lesson 25, is best used in the following situations:

- When the correspondence might require a paper trail
- When the correspondence covers multiple points
- When the correspondence needs to be accessed frequently

Instant messaging, also introduced in Lesson 25, is best used when correspondence needs to be accessed in real time. Each person can send and receive messages while everyone is logged on to the Internet at the same time. The message can be sent from a computer, from a cell phone, or from other mobile devices (see **Figure 26–1**).

FIGURE 26–1   Instant messaging

Teleconferencing uses a telecommunications system to serve groups, permitting the live exchange and sharing of information between two or more people. Generally the communications media is a telephone line.

Syndication (Really Simple Syndication or RSS), also known as Rich Site Summary and *RDF Summary*, are formats originally developed to facilitate the syndication of news articles. This communication method now is widely used to share the contents of blogs.

In some instances, a combination of the above communication methods may be used. For example, a group of individuals who live in various areas of the country may be enrolled in an online class. This group can use electronic mail, instant messaging, and teleconferencing to communicate on various aspects of the project. Or, in some instances, they could use a blog to post project updates. In another example, electronic communications helps some students to overcome the fear of asking questions or contributing to a class discussion.

Advantages of Electronic Communications

3-2.3.2

Electronic communications offers many advantages. The communication is not restricted to a specific place and time. Secondly, in most instances, it uses text and graphics rather than voice. These tools also provide for different types of correspondence such as one to one, one to many, or many to many. For instance, in a many-to-many example, a discussion board is used where all parties can post and read all of the postings. Other advantages are as follows:

- Speed is almost instantaneous, which means increased accessibility and enhanced interaction.

- Cost is minimal or even free in some instances. E-mail, for example, is a service that is part of most networked computers. Price remains the same regardless of sending and receiving a hundred messages or a thousand messages. Based on the device that is being used, instant messaging is a free service or has a minimal fee. Teleconferencing, on the other hand, generally involves a fee for the host. In many instances, however, using this service can eliminate travel expenses for those individuals who would otherwise need to meet in person.

- Access is available from various devices such as computers and cellular telephones.

- Forwarding and routing of messages can be accomplished in an instant. Simply click the message, select the address of the individual to whom it is to be forwarded, and then click the Forward button.

Routing is the process of selecting paths in a network along which to send network traffic. It can be an automatic or an individual process. For example, the network administrator receives a message that a server is going to be offline for a specific time. The administrator then can route this message to all personnel who would be affected.

One-to-one/one-to-many communications is the act of an individual or computer communicating with another individual/individuals or computer. In Internet terms, this can be done by e-mail, FTP, and Telnet. The most widely used one-to-one communication on the Internet is e-mail. Many-to-many communications such as file sharing, blogs, wikis, and tagging enable people to both contribute and receive information. *Tagging* is used in blogs and other informational sites to simplify the search process.

▶ **VOCABULARY**
tagging

Collaborative communications is a type of software program that allows people to use live voice, full-motion video, and interactive desktop sharing from between two individuals to an unlimited number (see **Figure 26–2**).

FIGURE 26–2   Collaborative communications

Community building connects members of a group with the same general interest. The community could be connected by a blog, a mailing list, a message board, or other type of electronic communication. Text, audio, and video communications require specialized intercommunication systems within the community. The network and the network interface card must be optimized to accommodate audio and video traffic. You might find this type of communications in a school, a hospital, a large office building, and so on.

Another advantage is online document sharing, which allows users to create and edit documents online while collaborating in real-time with other users. Google Docs is an example of this type of program.

History tracking and recording helps you keep track of visited Web sites. When a Web site is accessed, certain information is saved and stored on your computer hard drive. This information, also called Temporary Internet Files (TIF) or cache, decreases the amount of time it takes for a browser to load and display the site. Information such as Web site addresses, total times the site was accessed, images, file types, file size, specific dates and times of last access are stored on the hard drive.

In the following Step-by-Step exercise, you use the History button to search the Favorites list.

Step-by-Step 26.1

1. Click the **Start** button 🪟 on the taskbar, and then click **Internet Explorer** (or start Internet Explorer the way you usually do).

2. Click the **Favorites Center** button to display the Favorites Center. If necessary, click the **History** button arrow and then select **By Site** (see **Figure 26–3**).

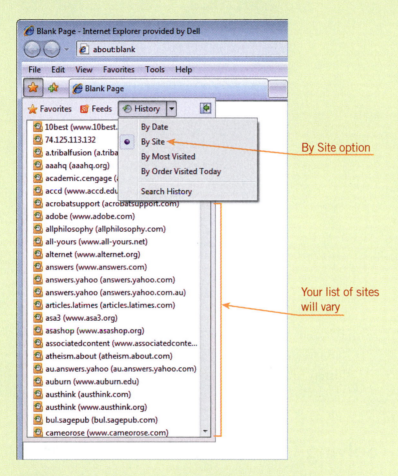

FIGURE 26–3
Displaying the History list sorted by site

By Site option

Your list of sites will vary

3. Click the **History** button arrow and then select **By Date** (see **Figure 26–4**).

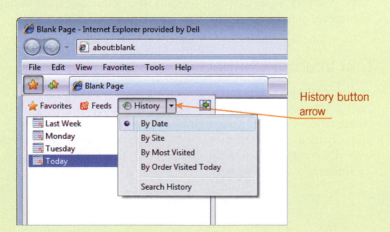

FIGURE 26–4
Displaying the History list sorted by date

History button arrow

4. Click and view the other options—**By Most Visited** and **By Order Visited Today**.

5. Click the **Search History** button, type **Microsoft** (or another word or phrase) into the search text box, and then click the **Search Now** button (see **Figure 26–5**). Most likely, your screen will display different Web site addresses.

FIGURE 26–5
Searching the History list

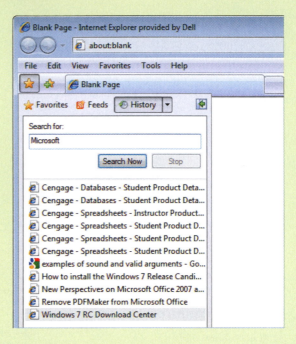

6. Use your word-processing program and write a summary of each of the options available through the History button. Save your document as **history_tracking** and submit it to your instructor.

3-2.3.3

Solving Communication Problems

Similar to other electronic devices, electronic communications is not without problems. Windows Vista, however, contains troubleshooting tools to help you identify and resolve communication problems.

Lost Internet Connection

Accessing the Internet is one of the primary reasons many people use their computers. Losing your connection can be frustrating, especially if you are in the middle of an online or video conference or uploading important data. Depending on the problem, you may need to call your provider. However, you may be able to repair the problem with the Network Connection Repair tool. The following Step-by-Step exercise illustrates how to use this tool.

Step-by-Step 26.2

1. Click the **Start** button 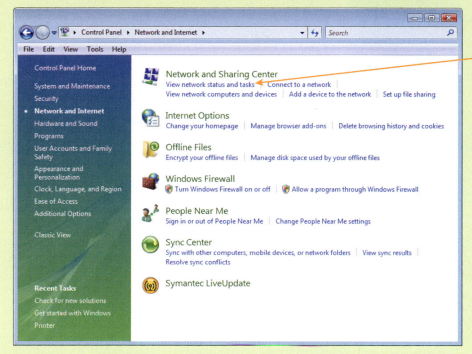 on the taskbar, and then click **Control Panel** to display the Control Panel Home window.

2. Click **Network and Internet** to display the Network and Internet window (see **Figure 26–6**).

Click to open the Network and Sharing Center window

FIGURE 26–6
Network and Internet window

3. Click **View network status and tasks** to display the Network and Sharing Center window (see **Figure 26–7**).

FIGURE 26–7
Network and Sharing Center window

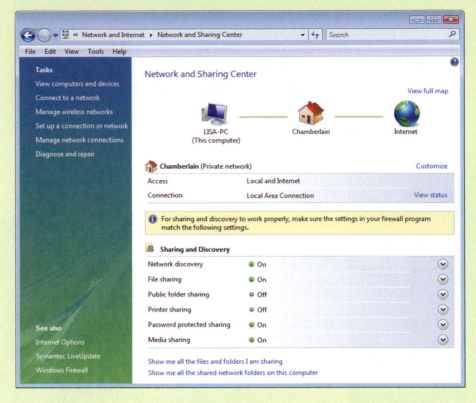

4. In the Tasks column, click **Diagnose and repair** to run the Windows Network Diagnostics program. If there are no problems, then Windows will return a message similar to that in **Figure 26–8**. If there are problems, Windows will attempt to fix the problem or suggest other solutions.

FIGURE 26–8
Windows Network Diagnostics dialog box

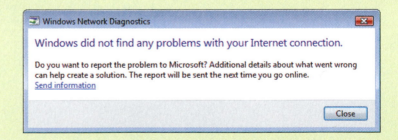

5. Click the **Close** button to close the dialog box.

6. Use your word-processing program and write a summary of why you think the Diagnose and repair tool is important. Provide an example of when and how you would use this tool. Submit your assignment to your instructor.

E-Mail Software Problems

E-mail failure to send and/or receive messages can result from various problems. Your server provider's connection could be down. If your connection to the Internet is still available, then checking your server provider's Web site could provide answers to your problem. Windows Help and Support also provides possible answers to the problem. In Step-by-Step 26.3, you have an opportunity to review this Help file.

Step-by-Step 26.3

1. Click the **Start** button 🪟 on the taskbar, and then click **Help and Support** to display the Windows Help and Support window (see **Figure 26–9**).

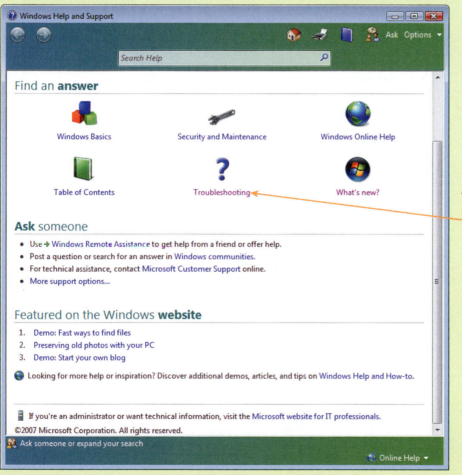

FIGURE 26–9
Windows Help and Support window

Troubleshooting link

2. In the Windows Help and Support window, click **Troubleshooting** to display the Troubleshooting in Windows window (see **Figure 26–10**).

FIGURE 26–10
Troubleshooting in
Windows window

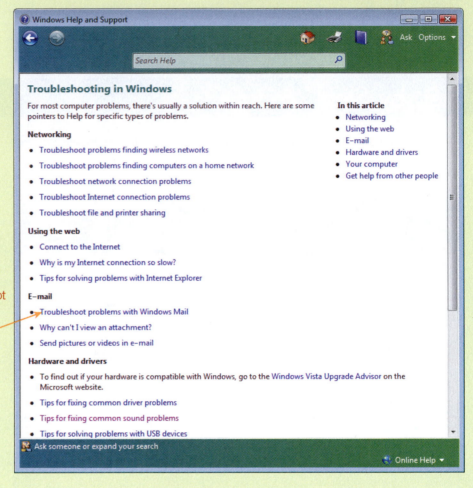

Click Troubleshoot
problems with
Windows Mail

3. In the Troubleshooting in Windows window, click **Troubleshoot problems with Windows Mail** to display the Troubleshoot problems with Windows Mail window (see **Figure 26–11**).

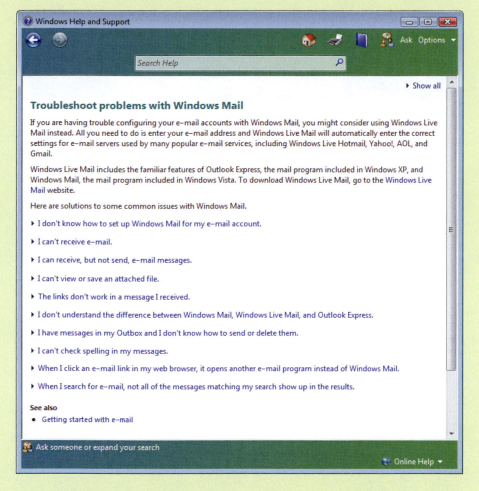

FIGURE 26–11
Troubleshoot problems with Windows Mail window

4. Click the links and then read the information. Leave the Windows Help and Support window open for the next Step-by-Step exercise.

5. Use your word-processing program to describe the different options and summarize what you learned about each. Submit your word-processing document to your instructor.

EXTRA FOR EXPERTS

You can send an open Microsoft Office document without closing the file. Click the Office button, point to Send, and then click E-mail to send the document. This process can be used, for example, during a conference call when more than one person is working on a document.

Downloading and Viewing E-Mail Attachment Problems

If you are unable to download or view an e-mail attachment, this could be due to the size of the attachment. Some e-mail programs limit attachment size and the number of attached files. If the message contains a virus, this also could be another problem. A third issue could relate to the sender and the type of e-mail—advertising, pornographic materials, or other unrecognizable documents, which may be blocked by your e-mail program.

Windows Help also provides suggestions on why you cannot view an attachment. In Step-by-Step 26.4, you access and review this Help information.

Step-by-Step 26.4

1. In the Windows Help and Support window you opened in the last exercise, click **I can't view or save an attached file** (see **Figure 26–12**).

FIGURE 26–12
Troubleshooting attachment problems

Click to display a possible solution

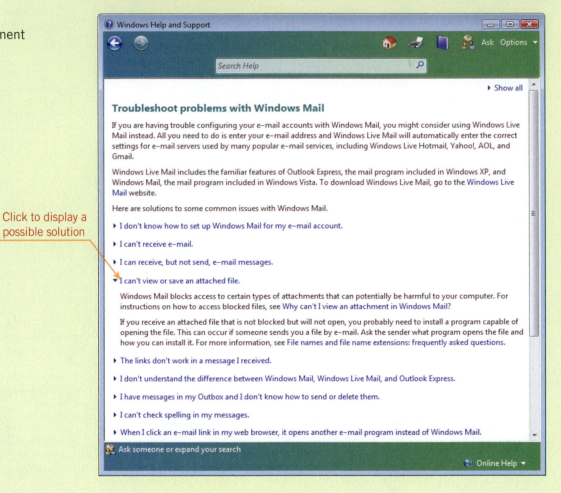

2. Read the information and then use your word-processing program to summarize what you learned. Close the Windows Help and Support window.

3. Submit your word-processing document to your instructor.

Delivery Failure

E-mail delivery failure refers to a returned or "bounced" e-mail. This can happen for a number of reasons, including the following:

■ The e-mail address was mistyped.

■ The e-mail may have a virus or worm attached. The receiving program detects the problem and will not accept the message.

- The receiver has a spam-filtering program. Based on the e-mail content or subject, the program may identify the message as spam.

- The sender is known and the person to whom the message is sent has blocked the sender.

- The recipient's mailbox is full.

Some e-mail programs return delivery failure (bounce) notices for e-mail that cannot be delivered. Others do not provide this service.

Garbled Messages/No Guaranteed Delivery

Occasionally, e-mail and other transmissions over the Internet are lost or spliced together. This occurs most often when Internet traffic is heavy. E-mail messages sent in rich text format (RTF) are garbled frequently (see **Figure 26–13**). The person sending the message should change the format to HTML. In some instances, the sender does not receive a notification of delivery failure and is unaware that the message was not delivered properly.

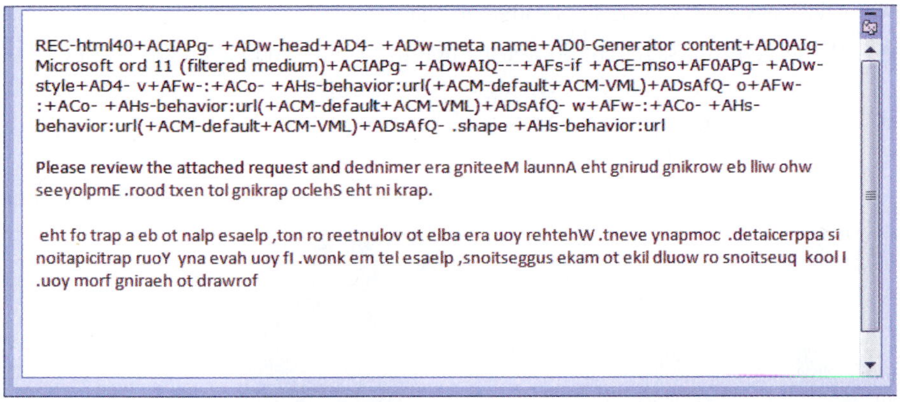

REC-html40+ACIAPg- +ADw-head+AD4- +ADw-meta name+AD0-Generator content+AD0AIg-Microsoft ord 11 (filtered medium)+ACIAPg- +ADwAIQ---+AFs-if +ACE-mso+AF0APg- +ADw-style+AD4- v+AFw-:+ACo- +AHs-behavior:url(+ACM-default+ACM-VML)+ADsAfQ- o+AFw-:+ACo- +AHs-behavior:url(+ACM-default+ACM-VML)+ADsAfQ- w+AFw-:+ACo- +AHs-behavior:url(+ACM-default+ACM-VML)+ADsAfQ- .shape +AHs-behavior:url

Please review the attached request and dednimer era gniteeM launnA eht gnirud gnikrow eb lliw ohw seeyolpmE .rood txen lot gnikrap oclehS eht ni krap.

eht fo trap a eb ot nalp esaelp ,ton ro reetnulov ot elba era uoy rehtehW .tneve ynapmoc .detaicerppa si noitapicitrap ruoY yna evah uoy fI .wonk em lel esaelp ,snoitseggus ekam ot ekil dluow ro snoitseuq kool I .uoy morf gniraeh ot drawrof

FIGURE 26–13   Garbled message

Lost Formatting

Windows Mail and other mail programs provide two formatting options: HTML (Hypertext Markup Language) and Plain Text. HTML provides formatting options such as multiple fonts, bold text, colored headings, graphics, and links to Web sites. To use HTML when creating a message, click Format on the New Message menu bar and select Rich Text (HTML). To format as plain text, click Format on the New Message menu bar and select Plain Text. When sending an HTML formatted message, keep in mind that not all e-mail programs support HTML-formatted messages. If the recipient's e-mail program does not support HTML, the message will display as plain text with an HTML file attached.

Lack of a Paper Trail

A paper trail is a written record, history, or collection of evidence created by a person or organization in the course of activities. Paper trails have been used in legal cases for evidence proof and in other situations. E-mail and other electronically stored information, for example, provide a paper or electronic trail similar to that of traditional mail and other written documents. Other types of electronic communications such as instant messaging, teleconferencing, online conferences, and collaborations do not provide a paper trail. Depending on the circumstances, electronic communication that does not produce a paper or electronic trail could create problems.

Hasty Responses

At one time or another, everyone has said something, sent an e-mail, or a letter that they wish they could take back. For instance, if you receive an e-mail message that makes you angry, your immediate response may be to send a quick reply. This could create a more intense situation. To avoid sending a message you later may regret, consider the following options:

- Discuss your response with someone else.
- Write your message, but do not include the e-mail address in the To line. This will prevent an accidental sending of the message.
- Save your message overnight as a draft and then later reevaluate your response (see **Figure 26–14**).

FIGURE 26–14   Avoid hasty responses to e-mail messages

Professional Versus Informal Communication

With the advent of quick and easy online communication formats, the boundary between professional and informal communication has blurred. Computer technology has provided the tools to make the composing process easier and faster. The fast-paced media used for electronic communications demands a writing style that is clear and concise without sacrificing speed. Professional communications, however, should be of a more formal nature.

Volume of E-Mail Replies

Communications *netiquette*, a combination of the words net and etiquette, refers to good manners and proper behaviors when communicating through electronic media. Because most e-mail users report that their biggest problem is not spam but too much e-mail, keep the following netiquette guidelines in mind when replying to an e-mail message:

- You have received an e-mail message and now you want to send a reply to the user. Click the Reply button, type your message, and then click the Send button. Verify, however, that your reply is necessary, and do not send responses that are not applicable.

- Reply All is another e-mail option. If you receive a message that also was sent to and/or copied to other recipients, for example, clicking the Reply All button sends your reply message to the sender and the other recipients. If the reply message is not applicable to the other recipients, then Reply should be used rather than Reply All to reduce the volume of e-mail replies.

- Two other options are cc and bcc. The cc abbreviation is derived from carbon copy. This refers to the technique of using carbon paper to produce one or more copies of a document during the creation of paper documents with a typewriter. A sheet of carbon paper is inserted between two sheets (or more) of paper. Typing or writing on the top sheet transfers the text or image to the copy. The initials bcc represents blind carbon copy. A bcc is a copy sent to recipients and is not visible to the primary and cc addressees. This practice rarely is used any longer, but the cc and bcc abbreviations were carried over into electronic communications.

Junk Mail (Spam)

Just as you might receive unsolicited advertisements, flyers, and catalogs in your regular mail, you most likely receive junk e-mail, also called *spam*, in your e-mail inbox. This type of e-mail might include advertisements, fraudulent schemes, pornography, or other illegitimate offers. This method of advertising is very inexpensive, and it is not uncommon for most people to receive numerous spam messages.

To help prevent spam/junk e-mail:

- Use caution in giving out your e-mail address. Do not publish it online, on a Web site, in newsgroups, or other public areas on the Internet.

- Check the Web site's privacy statement before you provide your e-mail address. Verify that it does not permit the sharing of your e-mail address with other companies.

- Never reply to a junk e-mail message. Once you reply, the sender will know that your e-mail address is valid. More than likely, you will receive even more junk e-mail, and the sender also may sell your e-mail address to others.

- Windows Mail includes a junk e-mail filter that is turned on by default. The protection level is set to low and identifies only the more obvious junk e-mail messages. The program analyzes the content of your messages and moves suspicious messages to a special junk e-mail folder. You then can view and/ or delete them. If a junk e-mail message is received in your inbox, you can specify that future messages from the sender be moved automatically to the junk e-mail folder.

In the following Step-by-Step exercise, you examine junk e-mail options in Windows Mail.

Step-by-Step 26.5

1. Click the **Start** button 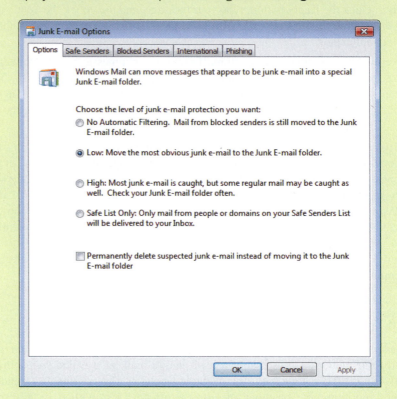 on the taskbar, and then click **Windows Mail** (or start Windows Mail the way you usually do).

2. Click **Tools** on the menu bar, and then click **Junk E-mail Options** to display the Junk E-mail Options dialog box (see **Figure 26–15**).

FIGURE 26–15
Junk E-mail Options dialog box in Windows Mail

3. Review the Options page, and then click the **Safe Senders** and **Blocked Senders** tabs and view that information.

4. Use your word-processing program and write a summary of the information contained under each of these three tabs—Options, Safe Senders, and Blocked Senders. Submit your word-processing document to your instructor.

Fraud, Hoaxes, and Other False Information

Similar to other types of fraud and false information incurred outside of the Internet, similar types of *fraud*, such as e-mail fraud, also exist within the Internet. This type of computer crime involves the manipulation of a computer or computer data in order to dishonestly obtain money, property, information, or other things of value, or to cause loss. The U.S. Secret Service indicates that hundreds of millions of dollars are lost annually due to fraudulent activities.

▶ **VOCABULARY**
fraud

E-Mail Fraud

E-mail messages are one of the more popular formats used for fraudulent activities. In many instances, the messages are well-written and appear to be legitimate. Unless you know it to be true, a response should not be made to a message that requests that you send money or personal information. Some of the more common fraudulent type of messages include *phishing*, which are personal information scams. This type of message appears to come from a legitimate source, such as your bank. The message asks that you update or verify your personal information. However, the information is used to commit identify theft. *Pyramid schemes* are an illicit business model where profits are based on the investor's ability to recruit other individuals who are enrolled to make payments to their recruiters. Generally, neither a product or service is delivered.

Hoaxes

A *hoax* is an attempt to deceive an audience into believing that something false is real. Sometimes this is perpetrated as a practical joke with a humorous intent; other times, it is an attempt to defraud and mislead. Many e-mail hoaxes appear to be warnings about potential viruses, but actually contain viruses themselves.

Perhaps one of the most well-known media hoaxes—one that many consider the single greatest of all time—occurred on Halloween eve in 1938. Orson Welles shocked the nation with his Mercury Theater radio broadcast titled "The War of the Worlds." Despite repeated announcements before and during the program, many listeners believed that invaders from Mars were attacking the world.

It is not always easy to spot an e-mail or chain letter containing a virus, but looking for some of the following will help detect possible harmful files.

- The e-mail is a warning message about a virus.
- The message might be very wordy, be in all capital letters, or include dozens of exclamation marks.
- The message urges you to share this information with everyone you know.
- The message appears credible because it describes the virus in technical terms.
- The message comes with an attachment, and you do not know who it is from.

If you identify any of the above, it is wise to delete the e-mail immediately. Also, use antivirus software and keep it updated.

In the 21st century, hoaxes, along with urban legends, myths, and chain letters, grow and flourish through the Internet. *Urban legends* are stories which at one time could have been partially true, but have grown from constant retelling into a mythical yarn. Much of this false information is harmless; however, some of these, such as chain letters, can have viruses attached to the message. One of the more popular Web sites displaying information about myths and hoaxes is the Vmyths Web site. You visit this site in Step-by-Step 26.6.

VOCABULARY

phishing

pyramid scheme

hoax

urban legend

EXTRA FOR EXPERTS

The first known computer crime, electronic embezzlement, was committed in 1958.

Step-by-Step 26.6

1. Click the **Start** button on the taskbar, and then click **Internet Explorer** (or start Internet Explorer the way you usually do).

2. Type **http://www.vmyths.com** in the Address text box. Click the **Go** button or press **Enter** to display the Vmyths.com Web site, similar to that shown in **Figure 26–16**.

FIGURE 26–16
Vmyths Web site

3. Click the **Hoaxes**, **myths**, **ULs** link in the right column. Select one of the myths and/or legends. Follow your instructor's directions to either print a copy or write a paragraph summarizing what you read.

Viruses and Security

In an information-driven world, individuals and organizations must manage and protect against risks such as viruses, which are spread through electronic communications.

Viruses

▶ **VOCABULARY**
virus

A *virus* is a program that has been written, usually by a hacker, to cause corruption of data on a computer. The virus is attached to a file such as a program file, a document, or an e-mail message, and spreads from one file to another once the program is executed.

A virus can cause major damage to a computer's data or it can do something as minor as display messages on your screen. There are different types of viruses:

- A *worm* makes many copies of itself, resulting in the consumption of system resources that slows down or actually halts tasks. Worms don't have to attach themselves to other files.

- A *time bomb* is a virus that does not cause its damage until a certain date or until the system has been booted a certain number of times.

- A *logic bomb* is a virus triggered by the appearance or disappearance of specified data.

- A *Trojan horse* is a virus that does something different from what it is expected to do. It may look like it is doing one thing while in actuality it is doing something quite opposite (usually something disastrous).

To protect your computer against virus damage:

- Use antivirus software. This software should always run on your computer and should be updated regularly.

- Be careful in opening e-mail attachments. It is a good idea to save them to disk before reading them so you can scan them.

- Do not access files copied from USB drives, other media, or downloaded from the Internet without scanning them first.

You can prevent a virus from infecting your computer and spreading to other computers by diligently scanning files that you did not create to make sure they are clean. Many programs have a built-in virus scan feature that activates when a new file is opened; in other cases, you can use an antivirus program to scan a file before opening it (see **Figure 26–17**).

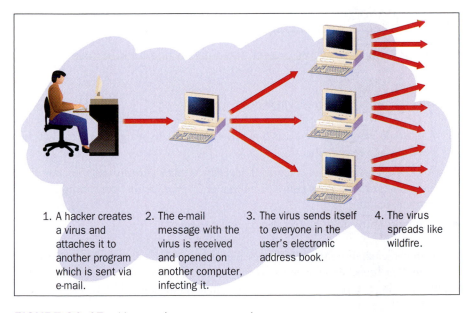

1. A hacker creates a virus and attaches it to another program which is sent via e-mail.

2. The e-mail message with the virus is received and opened on another computer, infecting it.

3. The virus sends itself to everyone in the user's electronic address book.

4. The virus spreads like wildfire.

FIGURE 26–17   How a virus can spread

General Security Risks

Computer security is necessary in order to keep hardware, software, and data safe from harm or destruction. Some risks to computers are natural causes, some are accidents, and some are intentional. It is always not evident that some type of computer crime or intrusion has occurred. Therefore, it is necessary that safeguards for each type of risk be put into place. It is the responsibility of a company or an individual to protect their data.

The best way to protect data is to effectively control access. If unauthorized persons gain access to data, they may obtain valuable information, as shown in **Figure 26–18**. Users may need a password in order to log on to a computer system or to specific parts of it. Companies often establish password-protected locations on hard drives and networks so that designated individuals have access to certain files but not to others. In order to maintain secure passwords, they should be frequently changed. This ensures that individuals who no longer need access will not be able to log in.

FIGURE 26–18   Passwords protect data against unauthorized use

Other security measures include using the following:

- Electronic identification cards that provide access to designated areas within a building or department.

- A firewall, which is an integrated security system that prevents unauthorized electronic access to a network computer system while permitting outward communication.

- Antivirus software to protect data on your computer.

Companies and organizations must plan for security before it is needed rather than handling breaches in security as they occur. For example, any company that handles sensitive information or needs to protect its data should take the following precautions:

- Institute a selective hiring process that includes careful screening of potential employees. Do not keep employees on staff who refuse to follow security rules. This measure will prevent internal theft or sabotage.

- Regularly back up data and store it offsite.

- Employ *biometric security measures*, which examine a fingerprint, a voice pattern, or the iris or retina of the eye, as shown in **Figure 26–19**. These must match the entry that was originally stored in the system for an employee to gain access to a secure area. This method of security usually is employed when high-level security is required.

FIGURE 26–19 Biometric security measures

Another common security concern on the Internet is credit card information. Effective encryption technologies help keep credit card numbers secure, but you can add additional security by following some simple precautions. For example, purchase from Web sites that you know are reputable and trustworthy. Read and understand the company's privacy and consumer-protection policy before you buy. Verify that any credit card information is transmitted in a secured, encrypted mode.

Professional and Effective Communications

Electronic communications, as previously discussed, are available in a variety of formats—e-mail, instant messaging, teleconferencing, social networks, and so on. The levels of formality and informality is based on the type of communication.

Statistics indicate that e-mail is the most popular of all Internet activities and that 85 percent or so of all Internet users use e-mail. When used in the workplace for business communications, certain rules of etiquette and formality should be applied similar to those applied to other business communications. The following list discusses elements of professionalism as applied to electronic communications.

 VOCABULARY
biometric security measures

 EXTRA FOR EXPERTS

You can create secure passwords that you can remember. String together the first letter of a line from a song or poem, for example, to create a password such as IlmhiSF!—all you have to remember is, "I left my heart in San Francisco," then add that punctuation mark. A password like this is nearly impossible for someone to guess.

WARNING

Several e-mail scams have been uncovered that appear to be from legitimate companies but ask you to provide a Social Security number to verify your account. Most companies assure customers they would never ask for sensitive information in an e-mail, so it is best to be suspicious of any solicitation for private information via e-mail.

IC³
3-2.3.4

MODULE 3   Living Online

■ Is it a business, professional, social, or personal type of communication? Writing for a business or professional audience is different from writing for a personal or social audience. When composing a business message, you should assume that your audience has limited time and most likely will skim the contents. In other words, they want to know the "bottom line." The content should be clear and the message should not contain spelling or other errors.

■ Personal and social messages can be less formal. They should, however, be checked for spelling and punctuation errors. The purpose should be clearly stated. Avoid using sarcasm or too much humor unless the message is to someone you know very well.

■ The nature of the communication also is important. What is the purpose of the communication? For example, is it to invite someone to dinner or to submit a proposal? Instant messaging should be short and to the point. An e-mail message can contain more content.

■ Timely response is another consideration. When responding to a message, the response should be timely. In many instances, the type of message dictates response time. For example, if a customer needs immediate assistance or has a complaint, then the reply should be within 30 minutes to two to three hours. Or, if a student needs assistance on how to upload an assignment for his online class, the response time should be within 5 to 10 hours. Other non-emergency responses should be made within a 24-hour time period.

■ Messages should be concise and to the point. Ideally, the recipient should not have to scroll past one page to read the message. If the message is longer than that, then most likely the message should be put into document format and added as an attachment.

■ Include one subject per e-mail message. The subject line should be short and direct and describe the message content.

■ Reply options should be considered carefully. Do you really need to send a copy (cc) to others? If so, to whom should it be sent? Is the carbon copy really necessary and if so, should it be a bcc or cc?

■ The purpose of the message and the recipients of the message will determine the level of formality. The addition of elements should as emoticons, abbreviations, jokes, and so on are appropriate in some instances and inappropriate in others. Business correspondence, for example, should be of a more formal nature than social correspondence. Even within the social correspondence is a degree of formality and informality.

■ Repeating of information and inclusions of materials from previous e-mail messages is another consideration. Verify that you are not duplicating something that was sent previously. Also check that the recipient was not previously sent a copy of any attachments that you are adding.

3-2.3.5

Other E-Mail Options

In addition to the e-mail options discussed previously, other alternatives are available. The ability to send and receive e-mail attachments and other supplemental information is of great benefit and often a timesaver.

■ An attachment is a file that is sent along with an e-mail. More than one file can be attached to the same message, and the files do not need to be of the same type. When the recipient receives the message, they can click the file name to open the file.

- Most e-mail services have a limit on the size, although the size, based on the server settings, can be anywhere from 30 MB up to 2 GB or more. Some companies, however, now support delivery of files of unlimited size.

- Some companies set security on some types of files, such as executable programs (.exe extensions) so they are rejected. In other instances, some companies set security on e-mails so that all attachments are rejected.

- When creating an e-mail, it also is possible to add a hyperlink to the message rather than attaching a file. With this format, the recipient can click the link rather than opening an attachment. There are two ways to add hyperlinks to an e-mail message. You can type the Web site address. Most e-mail programs will recognize this and convert it to a hyperlink. The second method is to attach the Web site address to a word or a phrase in the message. This makes the word or phrase the hyperlinked text. To embed hyperlinks in an e-mail message requires that the HTML setting be selected. The recipient of the message also must use a program which can display hyperlinks.

- Some mail readers cannot display embedded graphics or animation. Generally, this happens if the mail program reader is set to text only.

- Viruses and other similar threats can be delivered as e-mail attachments. To protect a system requires a number of security tools. Nearly all e-mail programs provide security settings, phishing filters, and anti-spam tools. Other protective tools and procedures include firewalls, encryption, antivirus tools, spam filters, and educating the users (see **Figure 26–20**).

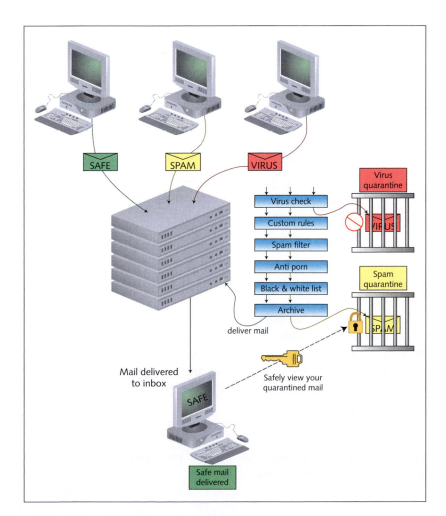

FIGURE 26–20   Controlling viruses and spam

3-2.3.6

Controlling Unsolicited E-Mail

E-mail filtering allows you to define rules to manage incoming e-mail. Filters automatically sort your incoming messages according to the rules you set up.

You can filter your incoming e-mail messages to:

- Sort incoming messages into folders
- Automatically tag messages
- Forward messages
- Discard messages

For example, you could define a filter rule to identify mail coming from your immediate supervisor and move it to a folder called "From My Boss" or to automatically move messages from a specific address to the Trash folder.

Filtering Mail by Mail Servers

E-mail spam, or junk mail, was discussed earlier in this lesson. From the beginning of the Internet, spam has existed. It is estimated that the yearly cost of spam for U.S. businesses is more than $20 plus billion.

Although some of it still will get through, a number of ways exist to reduce the amount. In the past few years, the amount of spam received by most users has decreased because of *filtering*. Software filtering is one process that can be used to cut down on or eliminate most junk mail. Windows Outlook contains a junk e-mail option to filter mail. (This option was discussed earlier in this lesson.) Another preventive measure is to avoid posting your e-mail address in a public place. Marketers use database matching to obtain e-mail addresses. For example, the marketer has a database that contains names, addresses, and telephone numbers. They pay to have their database matched against another database that contains e-mail addresses.

▶ **VOCABULARY**

filtering

3-2.3.7

Guidelines for Electronic Communications

Most companies, institutions, governmental agencies, and other businesses and groups have guidelines for the use of electronic communications. The following is a checklist of guidelines, as discussed throughout this lesson.

- All incoming e-mail messages and attachments should be checked for viruses. It is critical that a virus program is used and is updated on a regular basis.
- E-mail, instant messages, and other electronic communications should be reviewed prior to sending.
- Understand and apply the rules of netiquette, company/school policies, cultural issues, and other guidelines.
- Verify that your e-mail program includes the feature that enables the encryption of messages. To encrypt an e-mail message requires that you obtain a digital signature from a commercial digital ID group such as GlobalSign or VeriSign.
- Filtering by your Internet service provider (ISP) could, in some instances, be a determinant if messages from reputable organizations, such as the Red Cross or Salvation Army, are flagged.
- A policy should be in place that outlines the backing up and archiving of correspondence on a regular basis.

- All employees within a company or an organization should have an understanding of the sensitive nature of data and of the rules related to sending data electronically.

- Everyone should be aware that electronic communications can leave an "electronic trail". Messages left on public sites such as blogs or message boards or posts to social networking sites can be publicly and/or permanently accessible.

- Schools, other organizations, and company guidelines for state and national law for electronic communications should be followed.

ETHICS IN TECHNOLOGY

Physical Security

E-mail and attachments often contain information valuable to people and organizations, such as records of decisions, internal documents, and upcoming plans. Users should take steps to protect this information, including securing computer hardware and other equipment. It generally is fairly easy for an unauthorized person to access systems by removing them from a valid user's desk.

Computers and their devices should be kept in a secure place. Only a limited number of people should have access. A list of authorized users should be kept up to date. Some organizations have security guards to monitor computer rooms and control entry.

Remember that limited access means less opportunity for computer equipment or data to be stolen. Alternative methods for getting into a computer room should not be available. This includes hidden spare keys in an unsecured place.

Some organizations have taken computer safety a step further by securing equipment physically to desks and tables. This might seem like overkill, but you should protect your investment and your data by whatever means necessary.

SUMMARY

In this lesson, you learned:

- Teleconferencing uses a telecommunications system to serve groups, permitting the live exchange and sharing of information between two or more people.

- Syndication (Really Simple Syndication or RSS), also known as Rich Site Summary and RDF Summary, are formats originally developed to facilitate the syndication of news articles.

- Electronic communication offers many advantages. The communication is not restricted to a specific place and time. Secondly, in most instances, it uses text and graphics rather than voice. These tools also provide for different types of correspondence such as one to one, one to many, or many to many.

- Typical communication problems include failing to connect to the Internet or to your e-mail server. Being unable to download or view an e-mail attachment could be due to the size of the attachment, a virus in the message, or the sender and the type of e-mail.

- Communications netiquette, a combination of the words net and etiquette, refers to good manners and proper behaviors when communicating through electronic media.

- Fraud and false information are computer crimes that involve the manipulation of a computer or computer data in order to dishonestly obtain money, property, or other value or to cause loss.

- A virus is a program that has been written, usually by a hacker, to cause corruption of data on a computer. The virus is attached to a file and then spreads from one file to another once the program is executed.

- Computer security is necessary in order to keep hardware, software, and data safe from harm or destruction. The best way to protect data is to effectively control access.

VOCABULARY REVIEW

Define the following terms:

biometric security measures
filtering
fraud
hoax
logic bomb
netiquette

phishing
pyramid schemes
RDF Summary
spam
tagging
teleconferencing

time bomb
Trojan horse
urban legend
virus
worm

REVIEW QUESTIONS

TRUE / FALSE

Circle T if the statement is true or F if the statement is false.

T   F   **1.**   Routing is the process of selecting paths in a network along which to send network traffic.

T   F   **2.**   The network and the network interface card must be optimized to accommodate audio and video traffic.

T   F   **3.**   Once you lose an Internet connection, it is impossible to restore it.

T   F   **4.**   E-mail delivery failure refers to a returned or bounced e-mail.

T   F   **5.**   E-mail paper trails cannot be used as legal documents.

MULTIPLE CHOICE

Select the best response for the following statements.

1. _____ is a communications method primarily used to serve groups.

   A. Teleconferencing   C. Instant messaging

   B. E-mail   D. Routing

2. _____ is used in blogs to simplify the search process.

   A. Searching   C. Tagging

   B. Listing   D. Sharing

3. Junk e-mail also is called _____.

   A. baloney   C. carbons

   B. spam   D. netiquette

4. Phishing is a type of e-mail _____.

   A. listing   C. fraud

   B. controller   D. hardware

5. A(n) _____ can cause corruption of data.

   A. virus   C. instruction

   B. processor   D. USB drive

FILL IN THE BLANK

Complete the following sentences by writing the correct word or words in the blanks provided.

1. Communications _____ refers to good manners and proper behaviors when communicating through electronic media.

2. E-mail _____ allows you to define rules to manage incoming e-mail.

3. _____ _____ are one of the more popular formats used for fraudulent activities.

4. A(n) _____ is an attempt to deceive an audience into believing that something false is real.

5. A(n) _____ is a program that has been written, usually by a hacker, to corrupt data on a computer.

PROJECTS

PROJECT 26–1

Access the eHow Web site at *www.ehow.com/how_2003276_e-mail-hoaxes-scams.html*. This site contains an activity on *How to Learn About the Latest E-mail Hoaxes and Scams*. Below the heading Instructions, there are five steps. Read the instructions and follow the steps. Then use your word-processing program to describe how you answered each of the steps.

PROJECT 26–3

Using the Internet or other resources, see what you can find about the history of instant messaging. Then answer the following questions:

1. In what year did instant messaging become popular?

2. What was ICQ as related to instant messaging?

3. When did AOL adopt instant messaging?

PROJECT 26–2

Viruses have been around for quite a while. Use the Internet and other resources to research the history of early computer viruses. Prepare a report to share with your classmates on the types of viruses and the damage they caused. Also, include any information you might find on the person who programmed the virus, if possible. Use a search engine and the keywords *computer viruses or early computer viruses*.

TEAMWORK PROJECT

Individuals who use e-mail for frequent communication are often annoyed by unwanted e-mail called *spam*. Spam is unsolicited e-mail messages that can be obnoxious, offensive, and a waste of your time. Some countries have laws against spam. Your Internet service provider may try to block spam before it reaches your mailbox. However, you may still be inconvenienced by junk e-mail.

Working with a partner, research spam to learn more about what it is used for, how marketers get addresses, how effective spam is, and ways you can stop spam. Then, you and your teammate should each select one of the two positions—pro spam, how effective it is and what it is meant to do; or against spam, if it is a nuisance or problem and how you can stop it before it reaches your e-mail inbox. Write a brief summary of your findings and compare them with your partner. Then, at the end of your report, answer the following questions together: Is spam ever useful? Should there be laws to restrict spam? Do you think you can block all spam from reaching your inbox?

CRITICAL THINKING

If you do not have a personal e-mail address, how would you go about opening a free account for personal e-mail? There are a number of Web sites that provide free access to e-mail, and even if you do not have a computer, public libraries, schools, and even some "Internet cafes" offer free or inexpensive computer access to the World Wide Web that you can use to check incoming messages and send your own e-mail. If you wanted to set up a personal e-mail account, what kind of features would you like to have for your account? You might want to investigate some Web sites, such as *www.hotmail.com*, *www.usa.net*, or *www.yahoo.com*, to find out about the options available and then list the ones you think are most important. Why do you believe you would need these features for your e-mail account?

ONLINE DISCOVERY

The Web site located at *http://www.albion.com/netiquette/book/index.html* contains an online version of the book *Netiquette* by Virginia Shea. Access this Web site and then review Chapter 3 Core Rules of Netiquette. Provide a brief overview of the 10 rules contained in this chapter.

LESSON 27

Using the Internet and the World Wide Web

■ VOCABULARY

ActiveX

client

cookie

digital certificate

domain

File Transfer Protocol (FTP)

geographic imaging

hit

home page

Hypertext Markup Language (HTML)

Hypertext Transfer Protocol (HTTP)

Internet Protocol (IP) address

Internet service provider (ISP)

Mosaic

podcast

portal

Really Simple Syndication (RSS)

Secure Sockets Layer (SSL)

social networking site

Uniform Resource Locator (URL)

Web 2.0

Web cache

Web site

webapp

wiki

■ OBJECTIVES

Upon completion of this lesson, you should be able to:

- Understand the difference between the Internet and the World Wide Web.
- Identify terminology related to the Internet and the World Wide Web.
- Identify different items on a Web page.
- Identify different types and purposes of Web sites.
- Use a browser to navigate the Web.
- Refresh a Web page.
- Show a history of recently visited Web sites.
- Navigate to and delete history of recently visited Web sites.
- Manage bookmarked sites.
- Copy elements from a Web site to another program.
- Identify problems associated with using the Web.

■ DATA FILES

You do not need data files to complete this lesson.

Each day millions of people "surf," or explore, the Internet and its popular service, the World Wide Web. People use the Internet to research information, shop for goods and services, go to school, communicate with family and friends, read the daily newspaper, and make airplane and hotel reservations, for example. They use the Internet at work, at home, and while traveling. Anyone with access to the Internet can connect to and communicate with anyone else in the world who also has Internet access.

3-3.1.1

The Internet and the World Wide Web

The Internet is made up of many services. Some of the more popular of these services include blogs, chat rooms, e-mail, FTP (file transfer protocol), instant messaging, mailing lists, newsgroups and bulletin boards, online conferencing, and Voice over Internet Protocol (VoIP). Its most popular service is the World Wide Web.

Many people use the terms World Wide Web, or *Web* for short, and *Internet* interchangeably. In reality, they are two different things. The Web is part of the Internet. The Internet can exist without the Web, but the Web cannot exist without the Internet. The Web actually began in 1990, when Dr. Tim Berners-Lee, currently the director of the World Wide Web Consortium, wrote a small computer program for his own use. This program, called **Hypertext Transfer Protocol (HTTP)**, became the language computers use to transmit hypertext documents over the Internet. Dr. Berners-Lee next designed a scheme to give documents addresses on the Internet, and then developed a text-based program called **Hypertext Markup Language (HTML)** that creates hyperlinked documents. Clicking linked text or images in a hyperlinked document transfers you from one Web page to another or to another part of the same Web page. Dr. Berners-Lee's contributions laid the foundation, but they were not the catalyst that made the Web what it is today.

In 1993, the number of people using the Web increased significantly. This increase occurred when Marc Andreessen, working for the National Center for Supercomputing Applications at the University of Illinois, released Mosaic. **Mosaic** was the first graphical browser. See **Figure 27–1**.

> ▶ **VOCABULARY**
> **Hypertext Transfer Protocol (HTTP)**
>
> **Hypertext Markup Language (HTML)**
>
> **Mosaic**

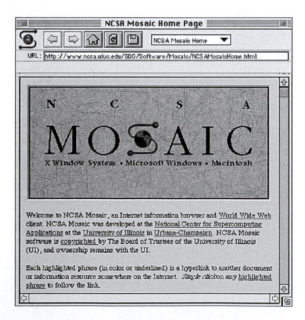

FIGURE 27–1   Mosaic Web page

In 1994, Marc Andreessen cofounded Netscape Communications. With the introduction of Mosaic and the Web browsers that followed, the Web became a communications tool for a much wider audience.

In 2004, the phrase **Web 2.0** was coined. Also called the *participatory Web*, this term has several definitions, although the most popular one refers to Web sites where users can modify the content. Web 2.0 includes a new generation of Web-based services such as blogs, social-networking sites, wikis, and application software built into the site. Because of these enhancements, the Web is one of the most widely used services on the Internet.

Internet Terminology

The Internet and the World Wide Web have their own terminology. This section introduces Internet-related vocabulary in alphabetic order and provides definitions.

ActiveX is a programming interface developed by Microsoft for Windows. This set of rules controls Windows applications that are downloaded from the Internet and then run in a browser.

As you become an experienced Internet user, you may find that you want to change how your browser handles cookies. Windows Help defines a *cookie* as "A small text file that Web sites put on your computer to store information about you and your preferences." Web sites store cookies on your computer so that when you return to a site, it displays any preferences or other customized settings you selected, such as sign-in information or items stored in a shopping cart. However, some unscrupulous Web sites use cookies to track your Web habits, which might invade your privacy. You need to balance the ease of use provided by cookies with security concerns and the amount of storage space available on your computer. For the most part, the default settings for cookies and stored pages are appropriate for most Internet users. In Step-by-Step 27.1, you use the Windows Vista online Help to find out more about cookies.

EXTRA FOR EXPERTS

Currently, the most popular Web browser is Internet Explorer. Other popular browsers include Firefox, Mozilla, Netscape, Safari, Google Chrome, and Opera.

3-3.1.2

VOCABULARY
Web 2.0
ActiveX
cookie

Step-by-Step 27.1

1. Click the **Start** button 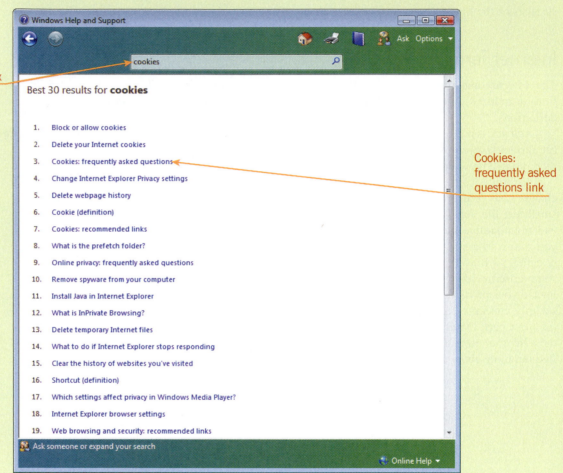 on the taskbar, click **Help and Support**, type **cookies** in the Search text box, and then click the **Search Help** button to display a list of results for cookies (see **Figure 27–2**).

FIGURE 27–2
Search results for cookies

cookies in the Search text box

Cookies: frequently asked questions link

Windows Help and Support

cookies

Best 30 results for **cookies**

1. Block or allow cookies
2. Delete your Internet cookies
3. Cookies: frequently asked questions
4. Change Internet Explorer Privacy settings
5. Delete webpage history
6. Cookie (definition)
7. Cookies: recommended links
8. What is the prefetch folder?
9. Online privacy: frequently asked questions
10. Remove spyware from your computer
11. Install Java in Internet Explorer
12. What is InPrivate Browsing?
13. Delete temporary Internet files
14. What to do if Internet Explorer stops responding
15. Clear the history of websites you've visited
16. Shortcut (definition)
17. Which settings affect privacy in Windows Media Player?
18. Internet Explorer browser settings
19. Web browsing and security: recommended links

Ask someone or expand your search

Online Help ▼

2. Click the **Cookies: frequently asked questions** link, and then click each
    question to read the answers (see **Figure 27–3**).

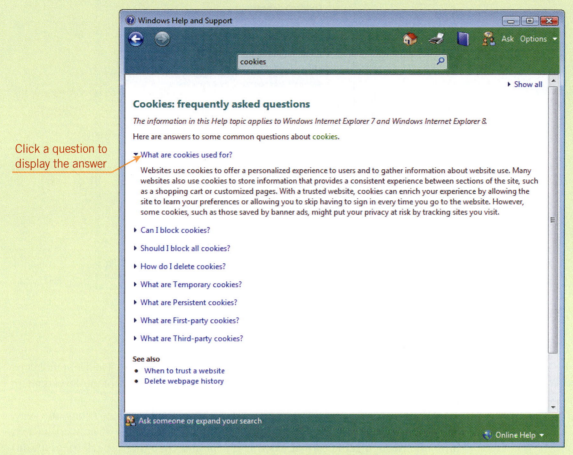

FIGURE 27–3
Cookies: frequently
asked questions
Help page

3. Use your word-processing program to write a brief explanation of what
    you learned from each of the questions. Save the document as **ic3-ch27**.
    Keep the document open for the next Step-by-Step exercise.

A *digital certificate* is an electronic document similar to an ID card. This digitally
signed statement verifies the identity of a person or company and confirms that they
own a public key. Also referred to as digital IDs, digital certificates are issued by third
parties known as certification authorities (CAs). The certificate is designed to prevent
fraud or other illegal activities and is validated by the CA. A typical digital certificate
includes a serial number, issuer, private key, public key, signature algorithm, subject,
thumbprint algorithm, thumbprint, valid from, and valid to dates (see **Figure 27–4**).

▶ **VOCABULARY**
digital certificate

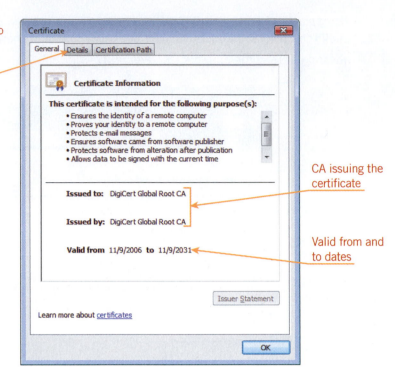

Click the Details tab
to display more
information about
the certificate

CA issuing the
certificate

Valid from and
to dates

FIGURE 27–4 Digital certificate

A *domain* identifies a computer or Web site on the Internet. The Domain Name System (DNS) converts domain names to IP addresses. Examples of top-level domain names are .com, .edu, .org, .gov, and .net.

When data is sent over the Internet, it is sent in packets. Along the way, these packets can be intercepted. *Encryption* is the process of converting text into an unrecognizable format when it is sent and changing it back (decryption) into plain text when it reaches its destination. This process is used for sensitive online transactions, such as credit card purchases.

You use *File Transfer Protocol (FTP)* to transfer files between computers. You can upload (send) files from one computer to another and retrieve (download) files from a server to a computer.

A *home page* is the first page that appears in the browser when you visit a Web site. An example of a home page for a community college is shown in **Figure 27–5**. (The home page also refers to the first page that is displayed when you start your browser.)

FIGURE 27–5 Home page for a community college

▶ **VOCABULARY**
home page
client
Internet service provider (ISP)
Internet Protocol (IP) address
podcast
Really Simple Syndication (RSS)
Secure Sockets Layer (SSL)

As mentioned earlier, *HTML* is the programming language used to create Web pages. The code is written using a text editor such as Windows Notepad or by using an application such as Adobe Dreamweaver. *HTTP/HTTPS* is the underlying protocol for the Web. This protocol defines how messages are formatted across the Internet. An HTTP client program is required at one end, and an HTTP server program is required on the other end. (A *client* is a type of computer program that makes a service request from a server.) For example, when you enter a Web site address in your browser, you send an HTTP command to the Web server to tell it to locate and transmit the requested Web page.

An *Internet service provider (ISP)* is an organization or company that provides connectivity to the Internet through a telecommunications line or wireless system.

An *Internet Protocol (IP) address* is a numerical addressing system that uniquely identifies computers and networks linked to the Internet. IP addresses consist of four sets of numbers separated by periods. Every client and server must have a unique IP address. A domain name server (DNS) translates the IP address into a domain name such as networksolutions.com.

A *podcast* is a method of publishing files (primarily audio) to the Internet that can be streamed or downloaded for playback on a computer or a personal digital audio player. In other words, podcasts are downloadable audio broadcasts.

Really Simple Syndication (RSS), also known as Rich Site Summary and RDF Summary, is a format originally developed to syndicate news articles online. This communication method now is used widely to share the contents of blogs.

Secure Sockets Layer (SSL) is a protocol for managing the security of message transmissions on the Internet.

A *Uniform Resource Locator (URL)* is the address of a Web page, FTP site, audio stream, or other Internet resource.

A *Web browser* is a software program you use to view and retrieve documents from the World Wide Web and to display the documents in a readable format. The browser is the interface between the user and the Internet. The browser sends a message to a Web server to retrieve a requested Web page. The browser then renders the HTML code to display the page.

A *Web cache* is a temporary storage area on your computer for collecting data. Once the data is stored in the cache, a Web site can quickly access the stored copy rather than downloading the data again.

A *Web site* is a collection of related HTML-formatted Web pages located on the World Wide Web. All pages within the site are accessible from the Web site address. The pages within the Web site can contain text, images, and multimedia elements such as sound, video, and animation files.

A *wiki* is a collaborative Web site that people can use to add, edit, remove, and organize Web page content. **Figure 27–6** shows the Wikipedia.com Web site, a popular online wiki.

FIGURE 27–6   Wikipedia Web site

XML is the abbreviation for *Extensible Markup Language*, which is a flexible text format for creating structured computer documents. For example, application software programs, such as Microsoft Office, save files in a particular format. Generally, the file must be opened by the same program. However, leading software makers have introduced a new method of saving files: XML. This method saves the document as a simple text file, along with information on how the application interprets the text. Programs such as Microsoft Office, OpenOffice, and WordPerfect Office create their own versions for different operating systems such as Windows, Apple Macintosh, and Linux/UNIX. Recent versions of these programs provide the option to save in XML format, thus enabling easier file exchange.

Understanding Web Page Elements

A Web page can be a simple text document or it can contain a variety of the following elements:

- Web site addresses that link to other Web sites
- Text, video, or other media
- Hyperlinked text and graphics
- Interactive objects such as buttons, text boxes, option buttons, check boxes, menus, and lists
- Images such as photos, pictures, maps, and drawings

Figure 27–7 shows a Web page that contains most of these items.

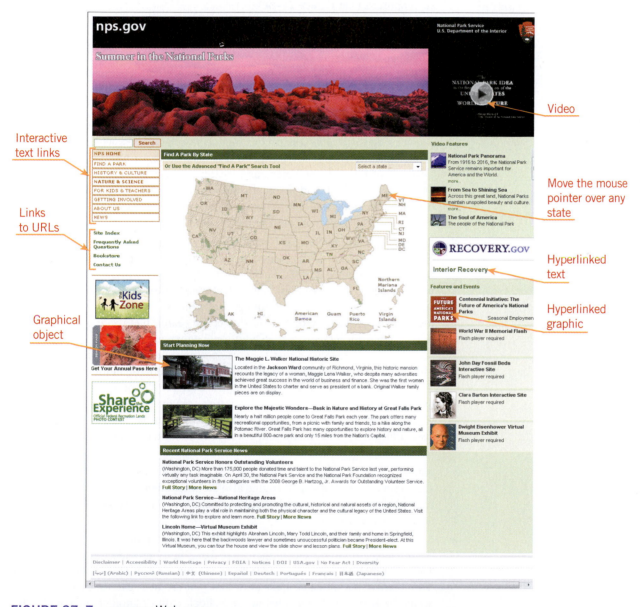

FIGURE 27–7   nps.gov Web page

3-3.1.4

Web sites can be organized into different categories, each with a different purpose. The following list provides an overview of the types of Web sites available.

- *Commercial*: Also known as an e-commerce site, a commercial site sells or promotes products or services. Almost every business today has a business/commercial Web site. Many of these companies also provide options to purchase products or services online (see **Figure 27–8a**).

- *Academic*: Most educational facilities, elementary to university and public to private, have a Web site. Most of the higher education Web sites provide online registration, online courses, and various other options. Many research facilities and private or public companies also provide online training for their employees (see **Figure 27–8b**).

- *Organizational*: Examples include nonprofit organizations such as the Red Cross and the Salvation Army, and advocacy groups such as wildlife and clean air supporters (see **Figure 27–8c**).

- *Governmental*: Most local, state, regional, and national governments have a Web site or numerous Web sites. For instance, a medium-sized city could have a number of Web sites for employment, news of the day, parks and recreation, local services, utilities, visitors guide, citizens guide, customer service, and other public announcement sites (see **Figure 27–8d**).

- *Web sites hosted in different countries*: International Internet marketing of a product or service sometimes require that Web sites be hosted in other countries because each country has unique search engines, which use different mathematical algorithms. Web page text also needs to be translated into the language of the country. Values and customs vary, so an effective Web site in one country may not work in other countries. Finally, local agencies most likely have a better understanding of the population and search engine optimization related to that population (see **Figure 27–8e**).

- *Search sites*: A search engine is a software program used for online searching. Hundreds of search engines have been developed to find information on the Internet (see **Figure 27–8f**). Each search engine may work a little differently, but most share some common search features. For example, all search engines support keyword searches. Although keyword searches may not always be the most effective way to search, this is the search method most people use. Some search engines support an additional enhancement called concept-based searching. The search engine tries to determine what you mean and returns hits on Web sites that relate to the keywords. *Hits* are the number of returns or Web sites based on your keywords. If you search for "video games," the search engine might also return hits on sites that contain Nintendo and Playstation. One of the best-known search engines using concept-based searching is Excite. Its search engine uses intelligent concept extraction (ICE) to learn about word relationships.

  Another feature supported by some search engines is stemming. When you search for a word, the search engine also includes other "stems" of the word. For example, you enter the search word *play*, and you may also get back results for *plays*, *playing*, and *player*.

- *Secure sites*: Some Web sites, such as those used for financial transactions or e-commerce, are more secure than sites that simply provide information. Most Web sites require you to log on using an account or user name and a password. You might see a message indicating that you are now entering (or leaving) a secure Web site, and you often see a padlock icon or another indicator in the status bar of a Web page to indicate the information is secure. In Internet Explorer 7 and later, the Address bar turns green when you display secure Web

▶ **VOCABULARY**
hit

sites. Occasionally, messages appear questioning the security of a site you are entering. Read the information in the message carefully before deciding whether to provide sensitive or private information on such a site (see **Figure 27–8g**).

You might also be required to provide a password for a Web site that limits access to members or subscribers. For example, if you access a university's Web site, you might be able to browse and link to many parts of the site, but need a password to access a professor's class-specific Web sites or your student account. Or, you might be able to read the current online edition of a newspaper, but if you want to search the paper's archives, you need to provide a password to show that you are a subscriber.

Recall that HTTP is a protocol for sending data back and forth between Web servers and clients. You often see this abbreviated in the browser window as http:// and https://. The letter *s* stands for *secure*. You should never enter personal information, such as your credit card number, in an http:// Web site. You should always verify that the Web address begins with https://.

■ *Online applications*: Also known as **webapps**, these sites host software applications you can access with your Web browser. When using a webapp, the browser functions as a client. Users interact with the software through their browser. Some programs allow the user to store data on their local computer while others store users' data and information on their servers. Some Web sites provide the service free of charge, and others charge a fee. For instance, TurboTax Online is a free service. However, if you choose to file online or to print a copy, a minimum fee is charged. Google Docs is another example of this type of software. Using this software program, you can share your work, edit from anywhere, share your documents in real time and so on. And it is all free (see **Figure 27–8h**).

■ *Portal*: A **portal** is a Web site that features useful content, but also contains links to other sites. You can use a portal as your home page. For example, besthistorysites.net, shown in **Figure 27–8i**, is a portal that includes links to Web sites about prehistory, ancient history, medieval history, and American history, for example.

■ *Weblog*: A Weblog, or blog, is a Web site designed as an online journal. These sites generally are maintained by one person or a small group and are similar to a diary. Postings generally are about personal experiences, hobbies, school, work, and opinion. Some companies also sponsor blogs. The blog in **Figure 27–8j** focuses on cooking.

■ *Social networking*: This type of Web site is an online community that provides interaction for groups of people who share a similar interest or activity. Users can post online profiles, pictures, video, music, and other information. There are dozens of **social networking sites**, but some of the more popular include MySpace, Facebook, LinkedIn, Twitter, and Digg (see **Figure 27–8k**).

■ *Geographic imaging*: Mapping and geographic imaging Web sites use technology to change imagery of the Earth's surface into valuable information. This information is used by geographical information systems (GIS) to capture, store, analyze, and manage images. Google Earth is one example of this type of programming. **Figure 27–8l** shows mapping and imaging of Mt. Everest.

▶ **VOCABULARY**

webapp

portal

social networking site

geographic imaging

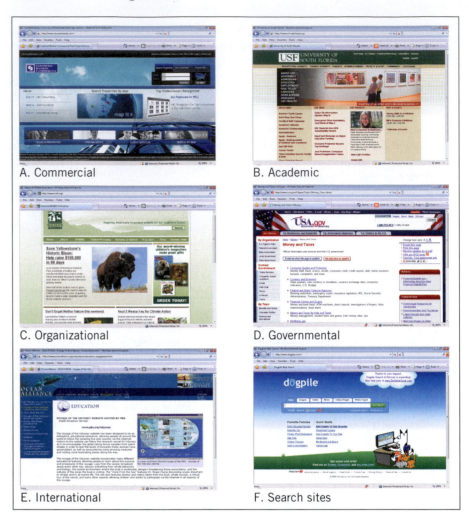

A. Commercial   B. Academic

C. Organizational   D. Governmental

E. International   F. Search sites

FIGURE 27–8   Types of Web sites

G. Secure sites

H. Online applications

I. Portal

J. Weblog

K. Social networking

L. Geographic imaging

FIGURE 27–8 CONTINUED   Types of Web sites

Connecting to the Internet

3-3.1.5

Before you can access the Internet, you have to connect to it. If you connect to the Internet from an office or academic setting, you probably are connecting through a local area network (LAN). You connect to the Internet using a network interface card (NIC). This is a special card inside your computer that allows the computer to be networked. A direct connection is made from the LAN to a high-speed connection line leased from the local telephone company.

Home users connect to the Internet using a dedicated high-speed digital telephone line ("dedicated" means it is always available for Internet access), a cable modem, or a wireless connection. Dial-up modems linked to telephone lines are becoming less common.

Connecting to the Internet is fairly simple, but there are a few steps you need to take:

1. Locate an ISP or an online service. Of the thousands of ISPs, many are small local companies. Their service is primarily to provide a connection to the Internet. Other providers are large national and international companies, such as Verizon, AT&T, Comcast, and MSN. Generally, the local ISP is less expensive, but many people use the more expensive national services if they offer additional speed.

2. After you find an ISP, you must install some type of telecommunications software. This software enables your computer to connect to another computer. Your ISP or online service company provides this software, or you might be able to use software already installed on your computer. Most newer computers are set up for a wireless connection.

3. You need a Web browser to visit Web sites. Most computers purchased today come with a browser already installed.

After you contract with an ISP and install telecommunications software and a browser, you are ready to connect to the Internet. This is the easy part. You may have to give instructions to your computer to dial a local telephone number if you are using a dial-up modem, but if you have a high-speed dedicated phone line, a cable connection, or a wireless service, you start your browser. This connects you to your ISP's computer, which in turn connects you to the Internet. You are then online with the world. **Figure 27–9** shows an application that searches for available wireless hookups, called hotspots.

FIGURE 27–9   Searching for a hotspot

Different types of Internet connections provide a range of options. Be prepared to balance the features you want, such as connection speed and reliability, with the cost and availability of the options. For example, broadband connections can transmit multiple channels of information over a single link, so they can carry video, voice, and computer data simultaneously. Cable modems, digital subscriber lines (DSL), and T-1 lines offer high bandwidth, as opposed to a dial-up telephone modem, which has only a single bandwidth that can transmit voice or data, but not at the same time. Broadband cable connections allow home computer users to enjoy the benefits of faster connection speed and multiple channels to transmit data.

Browser Basics

Recall that a browser is a software program you use to retrieve documents from the World Wide Web and to display them in a readable format. The Web is the graphical portion of the Internet. The browser functions as an interface between you and the Internet. Using a browser, you can display both text and images. Browsers also support multimedia information, including sound and video.

To connect to the Internet, the browser sends a message to the Web server to retrieve your requested Web page. The browser then renders the HTML code to display the page. (Recall that HTML is the language used to create documents for the Web.) You navigate through the Web by using your mouse to point and click hyperlinked words and images.

Parts of the Browser Window

This lesson uses Microsoft Internet Explorer 7.0 as the browser. You should understand the parts of the browser window to use a browser effectively. **Figure 27–10** identifies parts of the browser window. **Table 27–1** defines each part.

FIGURE 27–10   Parts of the browser window

TABLE 27–1   Parts of the Internet Explorer window

COMPONENT	DEFINITIONS
Address bar	Contains the URL or address of the active Web page; also, where you type the location for the Web page you want to visit
Back button	Displays the page you viewed prior to the current page displayed in the browser window
Command bar	A horizontal toolbar located on the right side of the window; provides a selection of options used to execute common commands
Document window	Displays the active Web page
Forward button	Displays the next page in the series of pages you have previously viewed; this button is not active until the Back button has been clicked at least one time
Menu bar	Lists menu commands if you select the option to display the menu bar
New Tab button	Tabbed browsing lets you open multiple Web pages within the same browser window
Quick Tabs button	Displays a thumbnail of open Web pages; the Quick Tabs button is displayed when you have more than one Web page open
Refresh button	Refreshes or reloads the current Web page
Scroll bars	Vertical and horizontal scroll bars that let you scroll vertically and horizontally if the Web page is too long or too wide to fit within one screen
Search box	Lets you search for Web pages containing information that you specify
Status bar	Located at the bottom of the browser; shows the progress of Web page transactions
Tab List button	Displays a list of all open Web pages
Title bar	The bar on top of the window that contains the name of the document

Navigating the Web

This lesson assumes that you have an Internet connection, such as a direct connection through school or a broadband connection at home. If you have a direct high-speed connection or a wireless connection, you start your Web browser to display your home page. In most instances, you can double-click the browser icon located on your computer's desktop. If the icon is not available, open the browser from the Start menu. If you have a dial-up modem, first start your browser and then dial the Internet connection.

Your browser was installed with a default home page. The Address bar located near the top of the browser window contains the URL of the current page. The URL tells the browser where to locate the page on the Internet. If you want to visit a specific Web site, you need to know the address, which you enter in the Address bar. After you type the URL, press Enter to go to the Web site. In Step-by-Step 27.2, you visit the National Parks Service Web site and navigate through various options. Then you click the New Tab button to open another site.

Step-by-Step 27.2

1. Start your Web browser the way you usually do. The first page you see is your home page.

2. In the Address bar, type **www.nps.gov** and then press **Enter** to access the National Park Service Web page (see **Figure 27-11**).

Web site address entered in the Address bar

Search box

Links panel

FIGURE 27-11
National Park Service Web page

Play button for viewing a video

Other videos

3. You can navigate through the pages of the site using a number of navigation tools:

   a. In the Links panel on the left side of the Web page, click a link of your choice and review the information on the page.

   b. Click the browser's **Back** button to return to the nps.gov home page.

   c. In the upper-right corner of the page, click the **Play** button to view a video. After the video finishes, play another video listed under the Video Features link.

   d. Point to the state in which you live to display a pop-up window (see **Figure 27-12**).

FIGURE 27–12
Pop-up window for states

New Tab

Site Index link

Point to a state
to display the
pop-up window

e. Read the information and then move the pointer away from the pop-up window.

f. Click the **Search** box in the upper-left part of the page, type **Denali**, and then click the **Search** button. Click the first link in the search results. Review the Denali Park Web page, and then click the **Back** button ◕ twice to return to the nps.gov page.

g. Below the Links panel is a list of links, including Site Index. Click the **Site Index** link and then scroll to view the entire page. Click the **Back** button ◕ to return to the home page.

h. Click **New Tab** to open a new window. Type **nature.org** in the Address bar and then press **Enter** to display the home page of the Nature Conservancy Web site (see **Figure 27–13**).

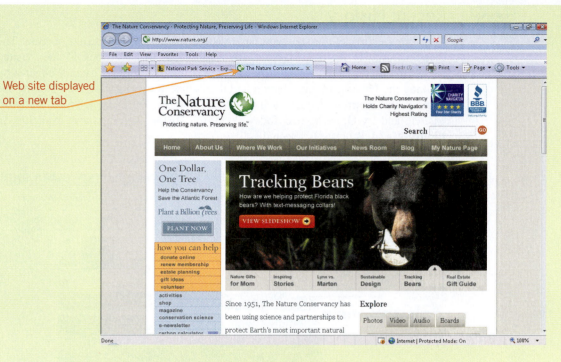

Web site displayed on a new tab

FIGURE 27–13
Nature Conservancy
Web site

i. Use your word-processing program to write a paragraph describing the activities in this Step-by-Step. Save your file using the file name **ic3-ch27**.

j. Keep the document open for Step-by-Step 27.3.

Refreshing or Reloading a Web Page

Cache memory is high-speed RAM that serves as a temporary storage area for data you access frequently. When you visit a Web page, a copy of the contents of the Web page are stored in your cache. If you access a Web page that contains updated information, such as a daily newspaper, most likely you will need to refresh or reload the information. Internet Explorer provides three options for reloading your browser:

- Click the Refresh button on the Address bar.
- Select View on the menu bar and then click Refresh.
- Press the F5 key.

3-3.1.6

EXTRA FOR EXPERTS

Clear the cache on a regular basis so you do not run out of disk space or slow down the loading, displaying, and exiting of a Web page. To do so, click Tools on the Command bar, and then click Delete Browsing History. This deletes temporary files, browsing history, cookies, saved form information, and saved passwords, but not your list of Favorites or subscribed feeds.

3-3.1.7

Recent History

Your browser tracks the sites you have visited for a specified period of time. The default setting in Internet Explorer, for example, is to keep track of sites visited for approximately three weeks. You can view a list of recently visited Web sites by clicking the Favorites Center button and then click the History button. Clicking the History button arrow displays a list of View options: By Date, By Site, By Most Visited, and By Order Visited Today. A Search History option is also available. In **Figure 27–14**, By Date is selected.

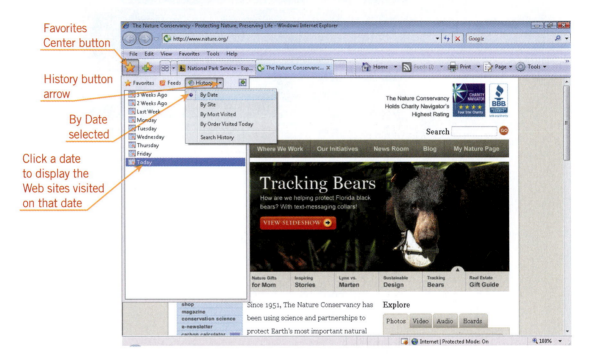

FIGURE 27–14   Viewing visited sites by date

In Step-by-Step exercise 27.3, you learn how to clear the History list, reload a Web page, and then show the history of recently visited Web sites.

Step-by-Step 27.3

1. If necessary, close the nature.org page by clicking the **Close** button on The Nature Conservancy tab, and then click the **Home** button to return to your home page.

2. Click the **Refresh** button to make sure the most recent version of the page is loaded. Do you notice any changes to the page after it has reloaded?

3. Click **Tools** on the Command bar, and then click **Delete Browsing History** to display the Delete Browsing History dialog box (see **Figure 27–15**).

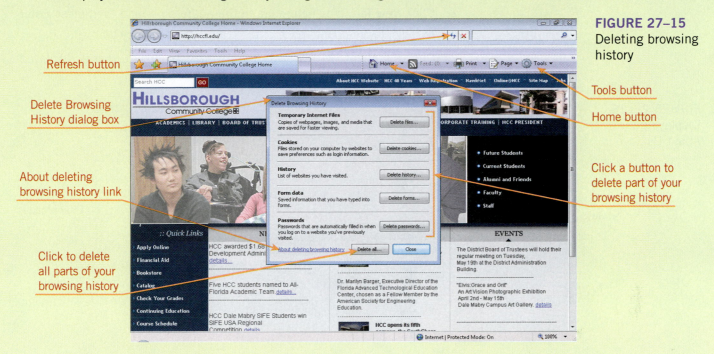

Refresh button

Delete Browsing History dialog box

About deleting browsing history link

Click to delete all parts of your browsing history

FIGURE 27–15
Deleting browsing history

Tools button

Home button

Click a button to delete part of your browsing history

4. The Delete Browsing History dialog box provides buttons to delete temporary Internet files, cookies, history, form data, and passwords. Clicking any of these buttons displays a warning dialog box asking if you are sure you want to delete the selected files. Click the **Delete cookies** button, for instance, to display the warning dialog box. Unless instructed to do so, click **No** to close the warning dialog box.

5. At the bottom of the Delete Browsing History dialog box is the About deleting browsing history link. Click this link, read the information, and then close the window.

6. Click the **Close** button in the Delete Browsing History dialog box.

7. If necessary, open your **ic3-ch27** document. Write a paragraph describing the activities in this Step-by-Step exercise. Save your document, but keep your ic3-ch27 file open.

Finding Text on a Web Page

3-3.1.8

When searching for information on the Internet, the most widely used tool is a search engine. Many large Web sites contain a large number of pages and links and provide a search tool specific to the site. In Step-by-Step 27.2, you used such a search engine when you searched for Denali in the National Park Service Web site and then accessed the Denali National Park Web page. Other Web pages contain links to other pages within the site. You can also use the Find command. Complete Step-by-Step 27.4 to use the Find command.

Step-by-Step 27.4

1. Click **New Tab**, type **nature.org** in the Address bar and then press **Enter** to redisplay the home page of the Nature Conservancy Web site.

2. Click the **About Us** link. Note the About Us submenu that is displayed below the main menu (see **Figure 27–16**).

FIGURE 27–16
Displaying the About Us page

About Us link

About Us submenu

Search nature.org text box

Main menu

3. Scroll the page and view the other links. In the Search nature.org text box, type **climate** and then click the **GO** button. Approximately how many results were displayed?

4. Press **CTRL+F** to display the Find dialog box, type **conservation**, and then click the **Next** button to find the first instance of "conservation."

5. If necessary, open your **ic3-ch27** document. Write a paragraph describing the activities in this Step-by-Step exercise. Save your document, but keep your ic3-ch27 file open for the next Step-by-Step exercise.

3-3.1.9

Organizing and Managing Favorites

Internet Explorer and other browsers provide a tool that makes it easy for you to return to a particular Web site or to easily access a Web site that you visit frequently. Internet Explorer refers to these links as favorites. Other browsers refer to these as bookmarks. The Favorites list contains the addresses (URLs) of designated sites. When you add a Web site to your Favorites list, you can access the site by clicking the site name. In Step-by-Step 27.5 you add a Web page to your Favorites list.

Step-by-Step 27.5

1. Make sure the nature.org Web site is still displayed.

2. Click **Favorites** on the menu bar to display the Favorites list. Your browser probably displays a list different from that in **Figure 27–17**.

Add to Favorites command

Favorites list on this computer

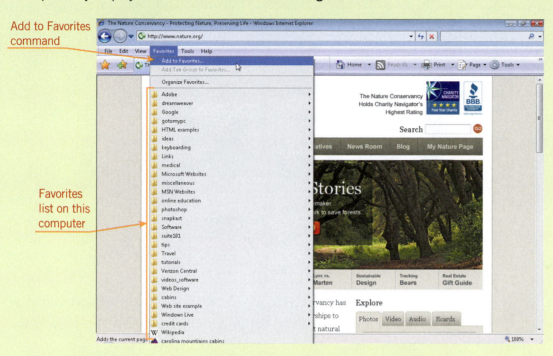

FIGURE 27–17
Favorites list

3. Click the **Add to Favorites** command to display the Add a Favorite dialog box. The Web site name is displayed in the Name text box. Type **Nature Conservancy** (see **Figure 27–18**).

Add a Favorite dialog box

New Folder button

FIGURE 27–18
Adding a favorite site

4. Click the **New Folder** button, and then type **environment** as the folder name (see **Figure 27–19**).

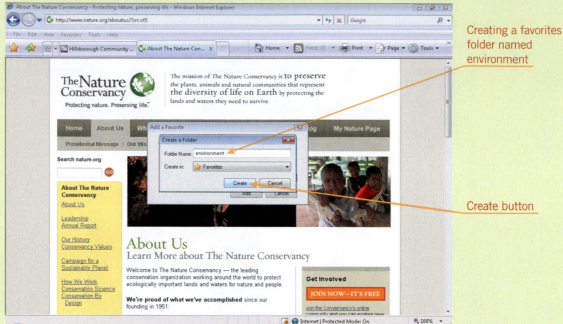

Creating a favorites
folder named
environment

Create button

5. Click the **Create** button to create the folder. Click the **Add** button in the Add a Favorite dialog box to add the folder and Web page to the Favorites list.

6. Close the Nature Conservancy Web page, and then write a paragraph describing your activities in this Step-by-Step exercise. Save your document, and keep your ic3-ch27 file open for the next Step-by-Step exercise.

Once you have a Web site added as a favorite or bookmarked site, you can access a site, move a favorite or bookmarked site between folders, and share favorite or bookmarked sites with other users. To access a favorite site:

1. Open Internet Explorer, and then click the Favorites Center button on the Favorites bar.

2. If the site is not stored in a folder, click the site name to access the site. If the site is stored in a folder, click the folder name and then click the site name.

To move favorite or bookmarked sites between folders:

1. Open Internet Explorer and then click the Add to Favorites button.

2. Click Import and Export to display the Import/Export Wizard, and then click the Next button.

3. Select Export Favorites, and then click the Next button.

4. Select the individual folder (or all folders) that you want to export, and then click the Next button.

Internet Explorer creates a file titled bookmark.htm in your Documents folder and then exports your favorites into this folder. You can rename the folder if you want to do so.

To export favorites or bookmarked sites to share with other users, first export your favorite or bookmarked sites into a separate folder as described on the previous page. Then select one of the following options:

- Option 1: Compress the folder and send it as an e-mail attachment.
- Option 2: If the Google toolbar is stored on your computer, an option is available to export the favorite or bookmarked sites.

EXTRA FOR EXPERTS

If you have a Gmail account, it includes a personalized Google Bookmarks service.

IC³

3-3.1.11

Downloading a File from a Web Site

You can download a file such as a program, graphic, or document from a Web page. Note that you should only download files from reliable sources, but there are many of these on the Web, including shareware and freeware sites. These sites offer useful computer programs and games that you can download for a small fee or at no cost. In other instances, you may need to download a patch or an update from the software manufacturer for a program installed on your computer, or you may want to download clip art, an informational file, or an audio or video clip. Most sites that have files to download provide an interface that makes the process of downloading simple. In the next Step-by-Step exercise, you download clip art.

Step-by-Step 27.6

1. In Internet Explorer, type **microsoft clip art** in the Search text box and then press **Enter**. A list of search results is displayed.

2. One of the links in the search results list (probably the first one) is the Microsoft Office Clip Art and Media Home Page. Click the link to open the page, which should be similar to the one shown in **Figure 27–20**.

Microsoft Clip Art Web page

Clip Art text box

Search button arrow

FIGURE 27–20
Microsoft Office clip art collection

Text entered in Search text box

3. Type **computer** in the Clip Art text box, click the **Search** button arrow, and then click **Clip art**.

4. Click the **Search** button.

5. When the results appear, select one of the clip art images of a computer or computer-related item by clicking the check box under the picture. You should see a check mark in the box after you select it (see **Figure 27–21**).

FIGURE 27–21
Searching for computer clip art

Check mark

Select a clip art graphic

6. Click the **Download 1 item** link at the bottom of the Selection Basket section in the left pane. Notice that the information in the Download window indicates that the clip art will be stored in the Microsoft Clip Organizer folder (see **Figure 27–22**).

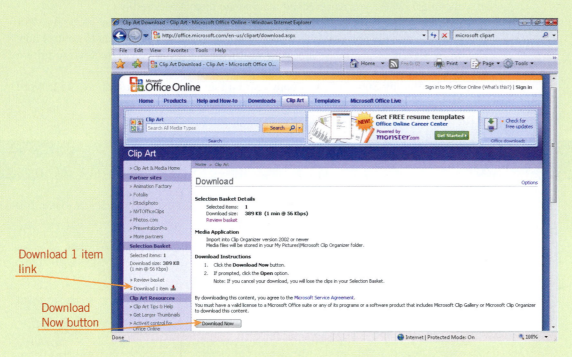

FIGURE 27–22
Downloading clip art

Download 1 item link

Download Now button

7. Follow the Download Instructions in the window: Click the **Download Now** button, and if prompted, click the **Open** option.

8. When the file has been downloaded, the graphic is displayed in the Microsoft Clip Organizer window. Click the **Close** button to close the window.

9. Open a blank document in Word.

10. Click the **Clip Art** button on the Insert tab to open the Clip Art pane.

11. Type **computer** in the Search for text box, make sure that **All collections** is the option displayed in the Search in text box, and then click **Go**.

12. Locate the computer clip art graphic you downloaded, click it, and then insert it into the Word document.

13. Save the document in your assignments folder and then close the document.

14. Write a paragraph describing your activities in this Step-by-Step exercise. Save your document, and keep your ic3-ch27 file open for the next Step-by-Step exercise.

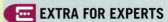 **EXTRA FOR EXPERTS**

The size and approximate time it will take to download the clip art file is indicated under the Download link in the Selection Basket section of the Microsoft Office Clip Art page.

3-3.1.10
3-3.1.12

Copying and Printing Information from a Web Page

You can copy and save specific elements of a Web page to disk and use them in a new document or file. For example, you might want to save a photographic image to disk or copy a paragraph of text you want to quote in a report. You can then open these in other applications or paste them into new files, such as a word-processing document, where you can edit and manipulate them as desired.

You can also print a copy of a Web page directly from your browser. Most browsers provide previewing and page setup options that enable you to control how the Web page prints. Make sure your instructor has given you permission to print a Web page before completing the following exercise.

In Step-by-Step 27.7, you copy text and an image from a Web site to a Word document and you print information from a Web site.

Step-by-Step 27.7

1. Return to the nature.org page you accessed earlier. (*Hint*: Use the Favorites list to return to the page.)

2. Select a paragraph of text, click **Edit** on the menu bar, and then click **Copy** to copy the text (see **Figure 27–23**).

FIGURE 27–23
Copying text on a
Web page

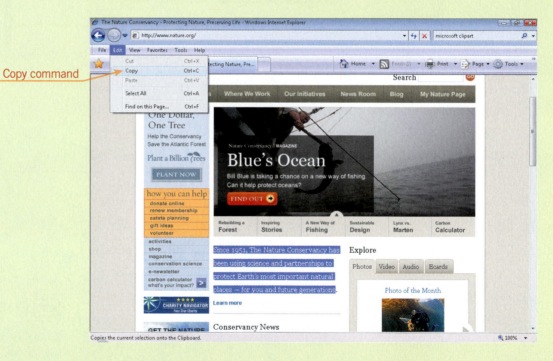

3. Open Word and paste the text into a new blank document.

4. Save the file with a name of your choice in the location where you save your assignments.

5. Return to your browser. Right-click a graphic image of your choice and then choose the **Save Picture As** command on the shortcut menu. Select a format for the image and use the **Insert Picture** command to insert it in the same document in which you saved the text in Step 3 (see **Figure 27–24**).

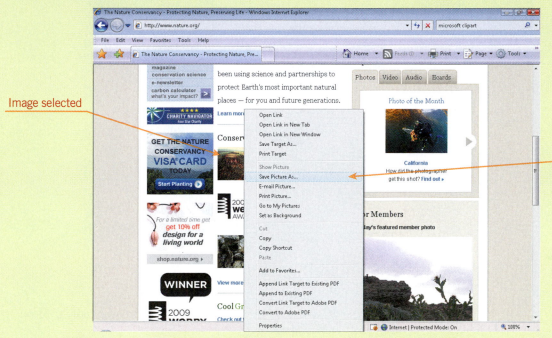

Image selected

Save Picture As selected

FIGURE 27–24
Saving a picture on a Web page

6. Return to your browser and find another graphic image. Right-click the image and then click **Copy** on the shortcut menu.

7. Return to your Word document and use the **Paste** command to paste the image you copied from the Web page.

8. Save the document to the location where you save assignments, using a file name of your choice. Then close the file and Word and return to your browser.

9. Click **File** on the menu bar, and then click **Print Preview** to preview the Web page (see **Figure 27–25**).

FIGURE 27–25
Displaying a Web page in Print Preview

Print Document button

Page Setup button

Print Preview toolbar

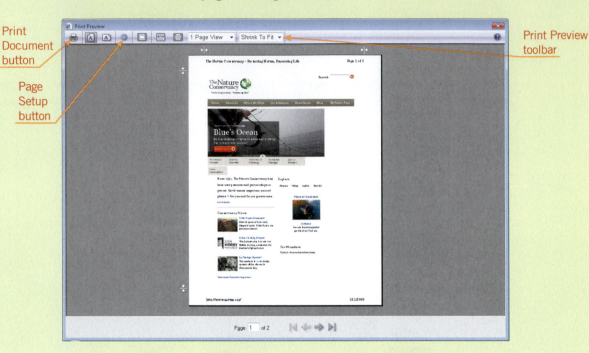

10. To print the Web page:

   a. Click the **Page Setup** button on the Print Preview toolbar to open the Page Setup dialog box.

   b. Change the top margin to **1.5** inches and then click **OK** to close the Page Setup dialog box.

   c. Click the **Print Document** button on the Print Preview toolbar to open the Print dialog box.

   d. Verify that the **All** option is selected in the Page Range section.

   e. Click the **Print** button to print your document.

11. You return to the browser window. Leave the browser open for the next Step-by-Step exercise.

3-3.1.13

Web Browser Settings

As you become an experienced Internet user, you may find that you want to change your browser's security settings. In Step-by-Step 27.8, you review Internet Explorer's Security options.

Step-by-Step 27.8

1. In Internet Explorer, click the **Tools** button on the Command bar, click **Internet Options** to open the Internet Options dialog box, and then click the **Security** tab. See **Figure 27–26**.

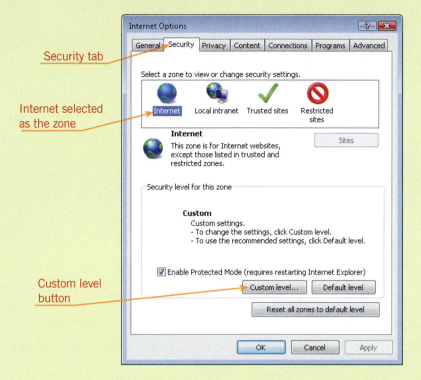

Security tab

Internet selected as the zone

Custom level button

FIGURE 27–26
Security tab in the Internet Options dialog box

2. Internet should be selected as the zone. Click **Local intranet** and review those settings. Then review the settings for Trusted sites and for Restricted sites.

3. Click the **Internet** icon and then click the **Custom level** button to display the settings. Use the scroll bar to view the various options (see **Figure 27–27**).

FIGURE 27–27
Security Settings - Internet Zone dialog box

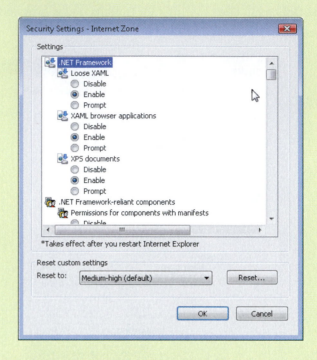

4. Click the **Cancel** button to return to the Internet Options dialog box.

5. Click the other three zones, click the **Custom level** button, and review the settings for each zone.

6. Write a paragraph describing your activities in this Step-by-Step exercise. Save your document, and then close your **ic3-ch27** file and submit it to your instructor as requested.

3-3.1.14

Browser Issues

The Internet and browsers are not without their problems. Web sites might not be displayed, a page is slow to load or the text is garbled, or pop-up ads distract you from or block the content on the page.

When you enter a Web site address and receive a "Page not found" message, the Web site might display a "404 error," which you receive because (a) the page was moved, (b) an old index is still maintained in a search engine, or (c) you made a typing error when entering the Web site address. In some instances, the Web site is temporarily unavailable because the server is offline or the site is being updated.

A Web page may load slowly because of heavy server traffic or the page may contain a large number of images. A garbled page could result from a number of issues, such as "fit-to-width" rendering used by the browser. If this option is used instead of the default rendering, it must be enabled for all pages. Earlier versions of Internet Explorer (4.0, 4.01, and 4.5) are known to have this problem. Some Web pages contain advertising in the far-left or far-right column, which results in only a portion of the page being displayed.

Pop-up ads are more recent phenomena. Advertisers place these ads on Web pages and they pop up in the middle of a page that you are reading to call attention to their content. Internet Explorer contains a pop-up blocker that limits most pop-ups. The pop-up blocker is turned on by default. To turn it off, complete the following steps:

1. Open Internet Explorer, click Tools on the menu bar, and then point to Pop-up Blocker.

2. Click Turn Off Pop-up Blocker. A confirmation window is displayed asking if you are sure you want to turn off the blocker. Click the Yes button to turn off the blocker or click the No button to cancel the request.

You can also change the settings to allow specific sites to display pop-ups. The following steps show how to select specific sites:

1. Open Internet Explorer, click Tools on the menu bar, and then point to Pop-up Blocker.

2. Click Pop-up Blocker Settings to display the Pop-up Blocker Settings dialog box.

3. Select the address of a site to allow pop-ups and the click the Add button.

4. You can also set the Filter level from High to Low. High blocks all pop-ups, Medium blocks most automatic pop-ups, and Low allows pop-ups from secure sites (see **Figure 27–28**).

FIGURE 27–28   Pop-up Blocker Settings dialog box

SUMMARY

In this lesson, you learned:

- The Internet and the World Wide Web have their own terminology. You should be familiar with terms such as ActiveX, cookies, digital certificate, and domain.

- A Web page can be solely a text document or it can be made up of elements such as Web site addresses that link to other Web sites; audio, video, graphics, or other media; hyperlinked text and hyperlinked graphics; and interactive objects such as buttons, text boxes, option buttons, check boxes, menus, and lists.

- Select an Internet connection to balance the features you want, such as connection speed and reliability, with the cost and availability of the different options. For example, broadband connections allow multiple channels of information to be transmitted over a single link so more than one channel of video, voice, and computer data can be carried simultaneously,

- Parts of the Internet Explorer browser window include the Address bar, document tabs, status bar, and command bar.

- A browser displays a home page when it starts. You use the Address bar to verify the address of the current page and enter addresses to visit other pages. A Web address is called the Uniform Resource Locator (URL), which uniquely identifies each Web page and tells the browser where to locate the page.

- Internet Explorer and other browsers provide a favorite or bookmarked sites list to make it easy for you to return to a particular Web site you visit frequently. Internet Explorer provides a Favorites Center that lists and organizes the Web pages in your Favorites list.

- Web sites used for financial transactions or e-commerce usually use encrypted communication to make them more secure than sites that simply provide information. Some Web sites also require you to log on using an account or user name and a password.

- Problems associated with using the Web include not being able to display Web sites, navigating to pages that are slow to load or contain garbled text, or finding pop-up ads distract you from or block the content on the page.

 ## VOCABULARY REVIEW

Define the following terms:

ActiveX	Hypertext Markup Language (HTML)	social networking site
client	Hypertext Transfer Protocol (HTTP)	Uniform Resource Locator (URL)
cookie	Internet Protocol (IP) address	Web 2.0
digital certificate	Internet service provider (ISP)	Web cache
domain	Mosaic	Web site
File Transfer Protocol (FTP)	podcast	webapp
geographic imaging	portal	wiki
hit	Really Simple Syndication (RSS)	
home page	Secure Sockets Layer (SSL)	

■ REVIEW QUESTIONS

TRUE / FALSE

Circle T if the statement is true or F if the statement is false.

T   F   **1.**   The number of search engines on the Internet is limited to three.

T   F   **2.**   Online Web applications are known as webapps.

T   F   **3.**   A social networking site is an online community that provides interaction for groups of people who share a similar interest or activity.

T   F   **4.**   Cable modems provide low bandwidth.

T   F   **5.**   A browser is a software program that you use to retrieve documents from the World Wide Web.

MULTIPLE CHOICE

Select the best response for the following statements.

1. A _____ is a temporary storage area for a collection of data.

    A.   Web cache   C.   Web site

    B.   Web page   D.   client page

2. _____ is also called the participatory Web.

    A.   Web 4.0   C.   Internet Web

    B.   Web 2.0   D.   Web bound

3. A(n) _____ is an electronic document similar to an ID card.

    A.   active file   C.   domain

    B.   digital certificate   D.   home page

4. _____ is a flexible text format for creating structured computer documents.

    A.   RSS   C.   XML

    B.   RPS   D.   LMX

5. Which of the following is *not* a reason you might receive a "Page not found" or "404 error?"

    A.   You made a typing error when entering the Web site address.

    B.   The browser uses "fit-to-width" rendering.

    C.   The page was moved.

    D.   The site contains pop-up ads.

FILL IN THE BLANK

Complete the following sentences by writing the correct word or words in the blanks provided.

1. To connect to the Internet, the browser sends a message to the _____ to retrieve your requested Web page.

2. _____ _____ is high-speed RAM that serves as a temporary storage area for data that is accessed frequently.

3. Another word for favorite sites is _____.

4. _____ are small text files that are created by some Web pages when you visit the site.

5. A(n) _____ _____ may load slowly because of heavy server traffic.

PROJECTS

PROJECT 27–1

This lesson discussed online applications and mentioned Turbo Tax and Google Docs. However, many other online applications are available. Complete the following:

1. Use your Web browser and search for online applications or webapps.

2. Select and research at least three that are interesting to you.

3. Use your word-processing program to write a short description of the application, including if it is free or fee based, and then explain why you would or would not use this software.

PROJECT 27–2

The Web site at *www.ibiblio.org/pioneers* contains a profile of 10 Internet pioneers. Complete the following:

1. Visit the *www.ibiblio.org/pioneers* Web site and select one of the pioneers.

2. Read the biography of the pioneer you selected.

3. Copy a photo of the pioneer to a word-processing document and write a paragraph describing his or her contributions to the Internet.

PROJECT 27–3

Several countries, including the United States, have proposed a taxing plan for the Internet. Complete the following:

1. Research the proposal for taxing Internet usage online.

2. Prepare a one-page report discussing this topic. Answer questions such as the following:
   - Do you think Internet usage will eventually be taxed? Why or why not?
   - Do you think Internet usage should be taxed? Explain your answer.
   - Discuss the pros and cons of taxing the Internet.

TEAMWORK PROJECT

This lesson describes several Internet features. Work with a partner to determine which of these features each of you would most likely use and why you would use it.

1. Make a list that includes all the features that were mentioned in this lesson, and make two columns, one for each member of your team.

2. Use a ranking scale of 1 to 5 (1 means you would probably never use this feature and 5 means that you would definitely use it) to rank how important you and your partner think each feature is.

3. Work together to prepare a report that explains your rankings and why you ranked each feature as you did.

CRITICAL THINKING

Wikis are quickly becoming a popular way to share information on the Internet. Use your favorite search engine to find out more about wikis, including the following information:
- Definition of "wiki"
- Why wikis are useful
- How businesses use wikis
- Characteristics of wikis
- Security concerns
- Examples (4–5) of wikis

ONLINE DISCOVERY

Google offers a wealth of services. Consider now how convenient it would be to access many of these services from your cell phone. Thanks to Google Mobile, you can use your cell phone to send and receive Gmail, get driving instructions, search online for text and/or images, view a calendar, display a location map or a satellite map, and read Google news. Visit the Google Mobile Help Center located at *www.google.com/support/mobile* and review the Help topics. If you have a cell phone, locate your phone model and then create a list of services applicable for your particular phone. Write a short overview of which service or services you most likely would use. If your cell phone is not listed, select one that you would purchase.

**Estimated Time:
1 hour**

LESSON 28

Web Content

■ OBJECTIVES

Upon completion of this lesson, you should be able to:

- Identify how content is created on the Internet.
- Identify methods of searching for information.
- Use a search engine.
- Identify issues regarding the quality of information.
- Identify how to evaluate the quality of information.
- Identify responsible and ethical behaviors related to online content.

■ DATA FILES

You do not need data files to complete this lesson.

■ VOCABULARY

blog

Boolean logic

copyright

directories

feed

indexes

keywords

libel

link lists

math symbols

news feed

peer-to-peer (P2P)

phrase searching

plagiarism

podcatcher

public domain

related search

search engine

shared bookmark

social networking sites

trademark

wiki

wildcard character

As the use of online technology has continued to grow, you should understand how to find and evaluate content on the Web. This lesson explores how to develop, locate, and use information available in Web sites.

3-3.2.1

Internet Content

You typically create content for the Internet by publishing it on a Web page and providing links for navigation. As the author, you control the content of the Web page and access to it. Viewers visit your site and interact with the information you provide. With the advent of Web 2.0, you can allow other types of interaction. Recall from the discussion of Web 2.0 in Lesson 27 that a new generation of Web design and development options are available, accessible, and easy to use. For example, you can now invite Web page viewers to contribute information to a site or exchange information, messages, and files with other viewers. You can create online content in the following ways:

- Web pages and Web sites are created by schools, governments, institutions, companies, nonprofit agencies, individuals, and others. Examples of Web site types include personal, entertainment, e-commerce, special causes, political, and government services. Lesson 27 contains an extensive overview of the various types of Web sites.

▶ **VOCABULARY**

blog

- A *blog* (short for Weblog) generally is managed by one person or a small group. The authors post commentary, journal entries, video, graphics, and other content and invite viewers to read and comment on the entries, which are usually displayed in reverse-chronological order. **Figure 28–1** shows an example of a blog for Adobe Dreamweaver, a program you use to create Web sites.

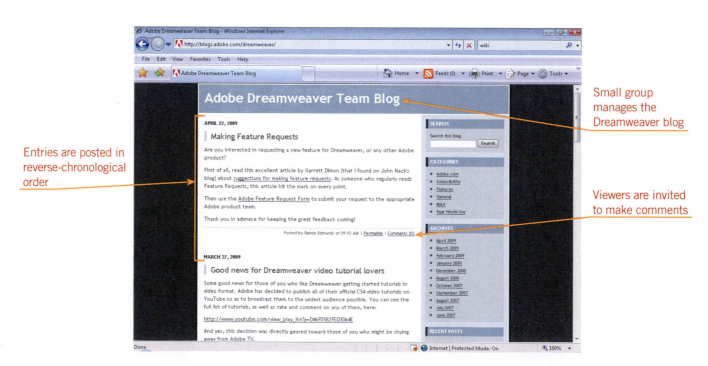

FIGURE 28–1 Adobe Dreamweaver team blog

■ A *wiki* is a collaborative Web site that can be edited by anyone with access. ("Wiki" means quick in Hawaiian.) **Figure 28–2** shows an example of a wiki that focuses on Blender, a graphics animation and video program.

▶ **VOCABULARY**
wiki

social networking sites

Use the wiki to contribute to the documentation

Sign up for editing rights to collaborate with others

FIGURE 28–2   Blender wiki

■ *Social networking sites*, such as Facebook, MySpace, Bebo, Twitter, LinkedIn, hi5, Orkut, and others attract millions of users. These sites basically are groups of people who share similar interests or activities. The sites provide ways for users to interact such as through instant messages and e-mail. **Figure 28–3** shows an example of a MySpace page.

Interact with other users

FIGURE 28–3   MySpace social networking site

▶ VOCABULARY

podcatcher

feed

peer-to-peer (P2P)

- A podcast is a collection of multimedia files, usually audio or video files, that can be downloaded from the Internet to a mobile device or personal computer. You can download the files manually one at a time or automatically through a subscription using Really Simple Syndication (RSS). To subscribe to a podcast, you use a software program called a *podcatcher*. This program checks a *feed* for new content on a regular basis. When the podcatcher finds a new podcast, it downloads the podcast to your specified device (see **Figure 28–4**). For example, you can download podcasts from the Apple iTunes Store to view video or listen to audio developed by independent creators or media outlets such as ESPN, *The Onion*, and *The New York Times*.

FIGURE 28–4   Podcast

- The Web contains several types of file-sharing sites, including those for sharing photos, music, and video. When you share files, you post them on a Web site to make them available to other users. To do so, you usually use a *peer-to-peer (P2P)* network, which connects computers directly instead of through a central server. **Figure 28–5** shows the home page of Shutterfly, a peer-to-peer site for sharing photographs.

🖳 EXTRA FOR EXPERTS

MP3 is a file format that allows audio compression at close to CD-quality. Audio file sharing is an area that is changing rapidly on the Internet; free download sites that were prevalent a few years ago have been replaced by more regulated sites where you can download high-quality audio files for a small fee.

FIGURE 28–5   Peer-to-peer media sharing site

■ A *news feed* (also known as a Web feed) is a data format used for providing users with frequently updated content. Content distributors such as media outlets syndicate news feeds so that users can subscribe to them. Similar to a podcast, news related information is usually delivered using the RSS family of formats (see **Figure 28–6**). You can receive a news feed through your browser or using a dedicated feed reader program.

▶ **VOCABULARY**
news feed

EXTRA FOR EXPERTS

In Windows Vista, you can add an RSS Feed gadget to your desktop to display current headlines or up-to-date sports and weather information.

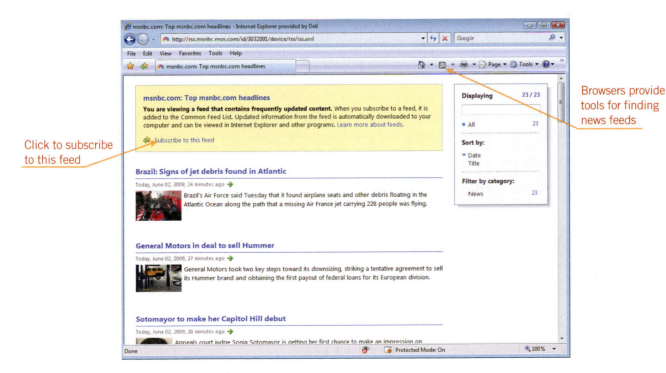

FIGURE 28–6   News feed

3-3.2.2

▶ **VOCABULARY**

search engine

keywords

indexes

directories

link lists

Searching for Information on the Web

When searching online, one of the primary tools you can use to find information is a *search engine*. You use a search engine to search for *keywords*. Search engines are automated indexes, so you might find that your search results include information that is irrelevant, but you will learn how to refine your search in this lesson. You can use general search engines and special-purpose search engines.

No single tool indexes or organizes the entire Web. When using an online search tool, you are searching and viewing data extracted from the Web. This data has been placed into the search engine's database. It is the database that is searched—not the Web itself. This is one reason you often have different results when you use different search engines.

You search the Internet to find answers to questions and information on any topic that interests you. The following are just a few examples of the types and availability of online data.

- You need to do some research for that paper due in your continuing education class next week.

- Your grandfather is losing his hearing and has asked you to help him find some information on hearing aids.

- You plan to take a trip to Mexico this summer and would like to get information on some of the best places to stay.

In addition to search engines, you can find online information using other tools, including the following:

- *Indexes*, also called *directories*, are Web sites which are organized by categories. Some examples of online directories include Libdex, which is a worldwide index of library catalogs, libraries, and books; online books, which contains a listing of over 35,000 free books on the Web; the National Geographic index; technical indexes, and dozens of others.

- *Link lists* are collections of links on a particular topic. You can find hundreds of link list sites on a variety of topics throughout the Internet. Most link lists, such as Cyndi's List of Genealogy Sites shown in **Figure 28–7**, contain a search engine, which you use to find information on the site.

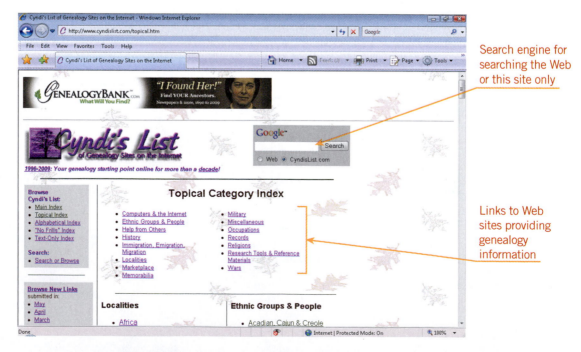

FIGURE 28–7   Genealogy link list Web site

■ A *shared bookmark* is a form of collaborative information sharing that lets users organize and share favorites, or bookmarks. Also called social bookmarking, you use this technology to store, organize, search, and manage a collection of links to Web pages. Many libraries use this process to provide lists of informative links on various topics. Delicious (*delicious.com*) was one of the pioneer Web sites in this technology (see **Figure 28–8**).

▶ VOCABULARY
shared bookmark

FIGURE 28–8 Social bookmarking site

Besides using one of these tools to search the Web, you can use the links on Web pages to discover content on other Web sites. For example, blogs often contain links. A typical blog generally combines text, images, and links to other blogs, Web pages, and other related media. Many Web sites, including social network sites, also contain links within their content. Clicking one of the links can transfer you to a new Web site page or open another Web page within the same site. Other online content, such as a traditional Web site, an informational site, or government sites, generally contains links within the content. **Figure 28–9** shows an example of the Internal Revenue Service Web site, which contains numerous links.

Links for getting help

Links for downloading forms

Links for finding information on other sites

Links for finding information on this site

FIGURE 28–9   Internal Revenue Service Web site

3-3.2.3

Using a Search Engine

As the Internet continues to expand and more pages are added, effective searching requires new approaches and strategies. When you use a search engine such as Google, the more specific your keywords, the more likely you will find what you want. To make your keywords more specific, you can use phrases, math symbols, Boolean operators, and wildcards.

Phrase Searching

▶ **VOCABULARY**

phrase searching

If you want to search for words that appear next to each other, then *phrase searching* is your best choice. When you enter a phrase within quotation marks, the search engine matches those words that appear adjacent to each other and in the order you specify. For example, if you are searching for baseball cards, enter the phrase "baseball cards" in quotation marks. The results contain Web sites with the words "baseball" and "cards" next to each other. Without the quotation marks, the search engine finds Web pages that contain the words "baseball" and "cards" anywhere within each page.

If you are searching for more than one phrase, you can separate phrases or proper names with a comma. To find Mickey Mantle baseball cards, for example, enter "baseball cards", "Mickey Mantle." It is always a good idea to capitalize proper nouns because some search engines distinguish between upper- and lowercase letters. On the other hand, if you capitalize a common noun such as "Bread," you find fewer Web pages than if you entered "bread."

Search Engine Math

Math symbols are another available option to make keywords more specific and narrow your search results. You can use *math symbols* such as plus (+) and minus (–) to enter a formula that filters out unwanted listings. For example:

- Insert a plus sign (+) before words that must appear (also called an inclusion operator).
- Insert a minus sign (–) before words that you do not want to appear (also called an exclusion operator).

Suppose you are making cookies for a party and want to try some new recipes. Your keywords are "+cookie+recipes." Only pages that contain both words would appear in your results. Now suppose that you want recipes for chocolate cookies. Your keywords are "+cookie+recipes+chocolate." This would display pages with all three words.

To take this a step further, you do not like coconut, so you do not want any recipes that contain the word "coconut." Use the minus (–) symbol to reduce the number of unrelated results. Enter the search phrase as "+cookie+recipes+chocolate-coconut." This tells the search engine to find pages that contain cookie, recipes, and chocolate and then to remove any pages that contain the word coconut. To extend this idea and to find chocolate cookie recipes without coconut and honey, your search phrase would be "+cookie+recipes+chocolate-coconut-honey." Subtract terms you do not want to find to produce better results. Nearly all of the major search engines support search engine math. You also can also use math symbols with most directories.

Boolean Searching

Recall that when you search for a topic on the Internet, you are not going from server to server and viewing documents on that server. Instead you are searching databases. *Boolean logic* is another way that you can search databases. This works on a similar principle as search engine math, but has a little more power. Boolean logic consists of three logical operators:

- AND
- NOT
- OR

Returning to the cookie example, suppose you want only cookie recipes, not Web pages about cookies in general or about recipes for other food. Search for "cookies AND recipes." The more terms you combine with AND, the fewer pages you find. If you want chocolate cookie recipes without coconut, you would search for "cookies AND recipes AND chocolate NOT coconut."

You can use OR logic to search for similar terms or concepts. If you do want to find Web pages about cookies in general or recipes for other food, you can search for "cookies OR recipes." In contrast to the AND operator, the more terms you combine in a search with OR logic, the more results you will receive from your search. You can combine OR with AND to produce sophisticated results. For example, search for "cookies AND recipes OR chocolate" to retrieve results containing one term or the other or both.

▶ **VOCABULARY**

math symbols

Boolean logic

Some search engines assist you with your logical search through the use of forms. For example, look for a hyperlink that says *Advanced Search* or *Advanced Options* on a search engine's main page to open an advanced search form. Using this form, you can add words, and phrases to include and to omit topics such as in **Figure 28–10**. Some search engines do not support Boolean logic, but most do provide a form that allows searching to be refined with filters or specific criteria. Some advanced search forms also provide options to specify a time period, a language, and other options. In Step-by-Step 28.1, you use Google's search engine to search for the cookie recipe.

Step-by-Step 28.1

1. Start your Web browser as you normally do, open **google.com**, and then click the **Advanced Search** link to display the Advanced Search page.

2. In the all these words text box, type **cookies AND recipes AND chocolate**, and then click the **Advanced Search** button.

3. Note the number of pages the search engine finds. Click the **Back** button ◀ to return to the form.

4. In the all these words text box, type **cookies AND recipes AND chocolate** again, if necessary.

5. In the any of these unwanted words text box, type **coconut** (see **Figure 28–10**).

FIGURE 28–10
Google's Advanced Search

Complete search term is shown here

Search for Web pages that contain these words

Exclude Web pages that contain this word

Advanced Search button

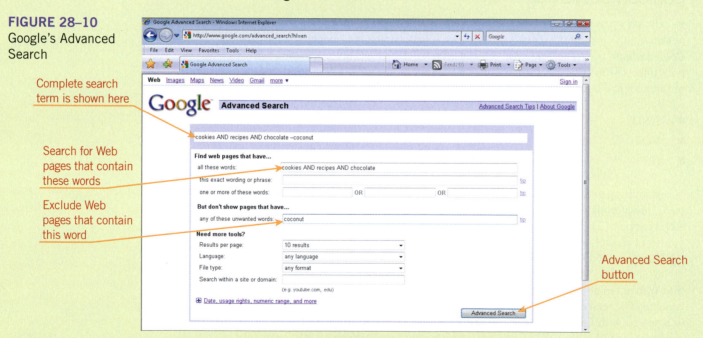

6. Click the **Advanced Search** button. Again, note the number of hits; the number should be much less than in the first search.

7. Click one or more of the links in the search results to review the information provided by some of the Web sites.

8. When you are done, leave your browser open for the next Step-by-Step exercise.

Wildcard Searching

The * symbol, or asterisk, is considered a ***wildcard character***. If you do not know the spelling of a word or you want to search plurals or variations of a word, use the wildcard character. For example, if you want to search for "baseball cards and Ichiro Suzuki," but you're not sure how to spell Ichiro, enter the search term using a wildcard—"baseball cards" and "I* Suzuki."

Some search engines only permit the * at the end of the word; with others you can insert the * at the end or beginning. Some search engines do not support wildcard searches.

▶ **VOCABULARY**
wildcard character

Title Searching

When a Web page author creates a Web page, it generally contains an HTML title. The title is contained within the Web page HTML code and entered between title tags:

<Title>Internet Tutorials</Title>

When you visit a Web site, the title appears in the title bar at the top of the Web page. In **Figure 28–11**, the title bar indicates the subject of the Web site.

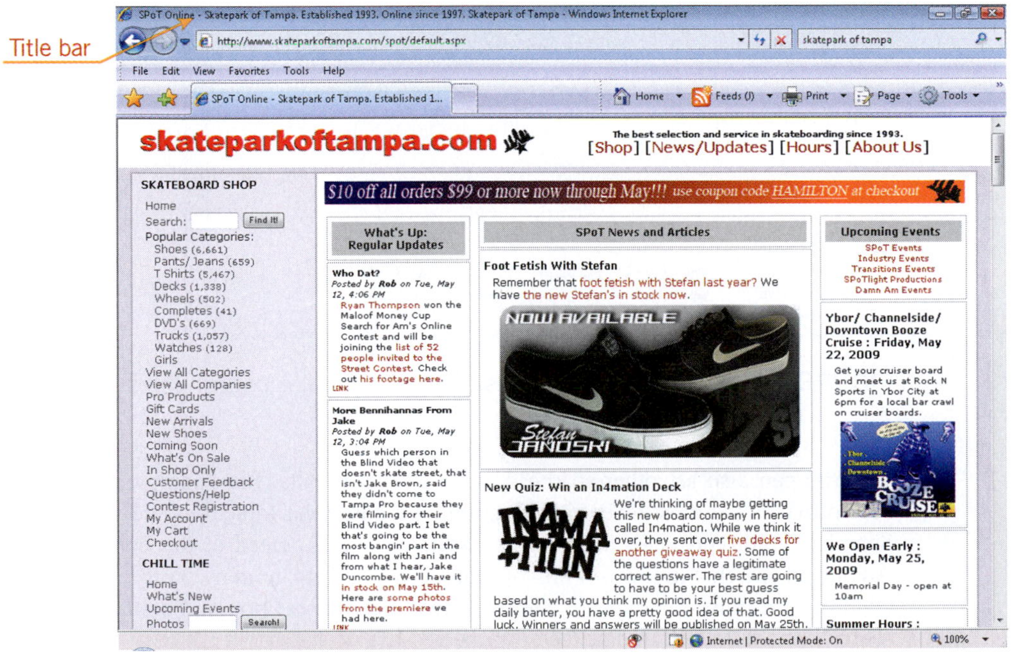

FIGURE 28–11   Web page title in the title bar

Many major search engines allow you to search within the HTML document for the title of a Web page. If you did a title search for "skateparks," then most likely one of your results would be the page shown in **Figure 28–11**. Not all search engines support title searches.

Other Search Features

▶ **VOCABULARY**

related search

Another feature provided by several search engines is a ***related search***. These are preprogrammed queries or questions suggested by the search engine that often lead to other Web pages containing similar information. A related search can improve your odds of finding the information you are seeking. Several search engines offer this feature, although they may use different terminology. Look for terms such as "similar pages," "related pages," or "more pages like this." All of these terms mean basically the same thing. Google uses the phrase *Similar pages*, as shown in **Figure 28–12**, to provide links to pages that are related to the selected search result. In addition, many search engines list search terms at the bottom of the search results that are related to the search term you entered to help you refine your search.

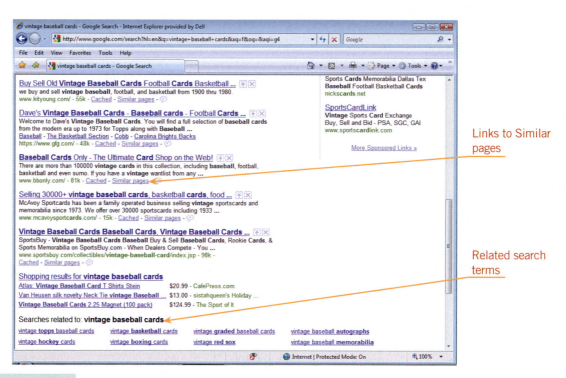

FIGURE 28–12   Google search results with "Similar pages" links

📧 **EXTRA FOR EXPERTS**

Google streamlines typical searches on its Search Features page (*www.google.com/intl/en/ help/features.html*). For example, you can search for current local weather conditions, sports scores, and stock quotes. You can also search for information available only within your zip code, such as movie show times, or travel details such as flight status and maps.

You can also set other search options to sort results. For example, sorting by date provides the most recent information on a particular topic. Google's Advanced Search window provides an option to sort by date. Located at the bottom of the Advanced search window is a link (+ Date, usage, rights, numeric range, and more). Clicking the plus sign expands the Advanced Search text box and contains several search options related to date (see **Figure 28–13**).

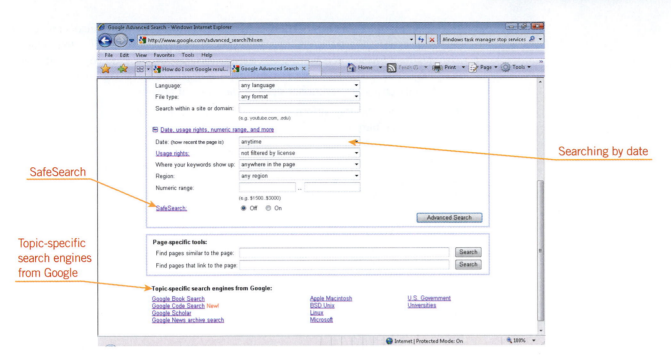

FIGURE 28–13   Searching by date

Note also that this page includes the Safe Search and the Topic-specific search engines from Google.

Evaluating the Quality of Internet Information

3-3.2.4
3-3.2.5

Anyone can publish information on the Internet of any type—factual or false, true or untrue. The Internet does not enforce rules or quality controls about content. Therefore, you should not accept everything as accurate. The following guidelines include criteria that you should consider.

- *Relevance and reliability*: When considering whether to use the content of a Web page, ask yourself the following questions to assess the relevance and reliability of the information. Does the information on the site meet the needs of your research? Is the purpose of this Web site stated? Is the information accurate? Is the information deep enough? Has the information been reviewed? Does the information come from a source that can be trusted? Is the information current? Do not accept any information presented on the Internet at face value. The source of the information should be clearly stated, whether it is original or borrowed from somewhere else.

- *Page layout*: The overall layout of the page is also important. Is the site organized and well designed? The page should be free of spelling and grammatical errors. Even if the page appears to contain valuable information, misspelled words and incorrect grammar can be warning signs that the information itself is not completely reliable.

- *Validity and bias*: Be sure you understand the agenda of the site's owner. Is the purpose of the site to sell a product or service? Is it trying to influence public opinion? As you read through the information, pay close attention to determine whether the content covers a specific time period or point of view or whether the content is more broad. To determine the validity of the information, check other resources, such as books or journals at the local library, that contain similar information.

- *Writing style*: The style of writing and the language used also can reveal information about the quality of the site. If the style is objective, the chances are the information is worthy of your attention. However, if it is opinionated and subjective, you may want to reconsider viewing it. Ideas and opinions supported by references are additional signs of the value of the site.

- *Coverage*: Is the information presented on the site sufficient for your particular purpose? Or will you also need to access other sites to complete your requirements?

Evaluating Web Sites

The Internet contains Web sites on every imaginable topic and come from sources around the world. When accessing a Web site, remember that even professional-looking Web sites can contain inaccurate or misleading information. Unlike most traditional information media (books, magazines, and newspapers, for example), no one has to approve the content on a Web site before it is published. As with any other document, you must evaluate the nature and source of the information. Some options to be considered are as follows:

- Institutional sites such as for a school, nonprofit organization, or government should clearly state their mission. You should also be able to verify that the site represents the organization by contacting a representative by phone or e-mail.

- Blogs generally represent the views and beliefs of the owner. Information might be skewed based on the owner's personal experiences and preferences, so you may or may not agree with information contained on the blog.

- A wiki can contain entries from any numbers of users. An entry could be from an expert or from a lay person. No qualifications or expertise is required for the person contributing to the wiki.

You can use the information in this lesson to construct a survey to assess the electronic resources you find. **Figure 28–14** shows a sample survey form.

CRITERIA FOR EVALUATING ELECTRONIC RESOURCES

1. Can you identify the author of the page?   Yes _____   No _____

2. Is an e-mail address listed?   Yes _____   No _____

3. Can you access the site in a reasonable time?   Yes _____   No _____

4. Is the text on the screen legible?   Yes _____   No _____

5. Are the commands and directions easy to follow?   Yes _____   No _____

6. Is the information current?   Yes _____   No _____

7. When you perform a search, do you get what you expect? Yes _____   No _____

8. Are instructions clearly visible?   Yes _____   No _____

9. Is the information updated regularly?   Yes _____   No _____

10. Make any comment here you would like concerning the site.

_____

_____

FIGURE 28–14   Criteria for evaluating electronic resources

Other evaluation processes that you can consider are as follows:

- Do you consider that the information is accurate?
- Is there an option to communicate with the Web site author?
- Review the site and determine if the site contains external links. If so, to what sites does it link? Do the linked sites contain valuable information that enhances your knowledge or do they contain information of personal opinions and beliefs?
- Use a search engine such as Google and then evaluate the ranking results.
- Compare the Web site information with other resources, such as professional journals, books, and other offline sources.

Web Sites and Intellectual Property Laws

For the most part, information displayed on a Web site is easy to copy. Often you can select the text or graphics that you want to copy, use your browser's Copy command, and then paste the content onto another document. Or you can display a page on your monitor and print the entire page. The ease with which information can be copied, however, does not mean that users have the right to do this.

Most sites have copyright protections. *Copyright* is the exclusive right, granted by law for a certain number of years, to make and use literary, musical, or artistic work, which is considered intellectual property. Even if the copyright notice isn't displayed prominently on the page, someone wrote or is responsible for the creation of the content on a Web page. This means that you cannot use the information as your own. You must give credit to the person who created the work.

If Internet content, such as music files, is copyrighted, it cannot be copied without the copyright holder's permission. To do so is a violation of copyright laws. Violating these laws can lead to criminal charges for theft as well as civil lawsuits for monetary damages.

A company's logo or other graphic information may be protected as a *trademark*, which means much the same thing as copyright but relates specifically to visual or commercial images rather than text or intellectual property. In addition, processes and business methods may be protected by patents, which guarantee the inventor exclusive rights to the process or method for a certain period of time.

Copyright and patent law do provide certain exceptions to the general prohibition against copying. If copyright or patent protection has lapsed on certain material, then it is considered to be in the *public domain* and is available for anyone to copy or use. Also, the law allows for the fair use of properly identified copyrighted material that is merely a small part of a larger research project, for instance, or cited as part of a critique or review.

Citing Internet Resources

You must cite Internet resources used in reports and other documents. In an academic setting, claiming someone else's words as your own is *plagiarism*. You must give proper credit to any information you include in a report that is not your original thought. Providing credits and citations also provides the reader of the document with information about additional research. You can find general guidelines for citing electronic sources in the *MLA Handbook for Writers of Research Papers*, published by the Modern Language Association. *The Chicago Manual of Style* is another source for this information.

3-3.2.6

EXTRA FOR EXPERTS

Many libraries and schools publish guidelines for evaluating Web content. Use your favorite search engine to search for *how to evaluate Web content* to find criteria and explanations.

▶ **VOCABULARY**
copyright
trademark
public domain
plagiarism

Following are some samples of citing Internet resources as suggested in the *MLA Handbook for Writers of Research Papers*:

- *Online journal article*: Author's last name, first initial. (date of publication or "NO DATE" if unavailable). Title of article or section used [Number of paragraphs]. Title of complete work. [Form, such as HTTP, CD-ROM, E-MAIL]. Available: complete URL [date of access].

- *Online magazine article*: Author's last name, first initial. (date of publication). Title of article. [Number of paragraphs]. Title of work. [Form] Available: complete URL [date of access].

- *Web sites*: Name of site [date]. Title of document [Form] Available: complete URL [date of access].

- *E-mail*: Author's last name, first name (author's e-mail address) (date). Subject. Receiver of e-mail (receiver's e-mail address).

Respecting Others

The Web site Wikipedia defines *libel* as follows: "In law, libel (for written words) is the communication of a statement that makes a claim, expressly stated or implied to be factual, that may give an individual, business, product, group, government or nation a negative image." The Internet does not relieve anyone of the burden of ensuring that information they publish is true. If someone publishes information about another person or organization and it is not true, they can be sued for libel and forced to pay compensation for any damages they caused. Treating others with respect is just as important online as it is in other environments. These same guidelines apply to online bullying and harassment.

Online Responsibilities

Responsibilities for your behavior online are the same as in an academic or similar environment. Information that you publish online should be as accurate and timely as possible. Some other suggestions to be considered are as follows:

- Use common sense as to what you publish online; the content and tone should be appropriate for the intended audience.

- Behave online the way you would behave in your daily life.

- Indicate if a statement is fact or your opinion. If it is your opinion, provide backup information and/or links to supportive documents. Opinions should be presented in a respectful format.

- Include contact information.

- Update your information on a regular basis.

- Do not berate or harass others.

- Verify that your content is appropriate for your designated audience.

TECHNOLOGY CAREERS

Web Content Writer or Producer

If you like to work with Web pages, consider a career as a Web content writer or producer. Writers often create press releases, articles, and journal entries for company blogs. You need to be familiar with how search engines work so that your Web pages appear in search results. You also need to be proficient with HTML, particularly with writing and formatting text and adding links and keywords to a page. Web producers often work with other media such as video or audio and coordinate those sources into a Web site. For example, a Web producer might work for a television network and integrate TV show content into a Web site.

To produce Web content, you need to have training in writing, editing, and graphic design as well as Web site design and maintenance. In some cases, you work with Web content using a content management system (CMS), which is software that helps you create, edit, manage, and publish content in a consistent format and organization. You might also need to use Web analytics, which are tools for tracking visitors to a Web site and determining whether the site meets your business objectives.

SUMMARY

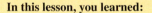

In this lesson, you learned:

- You typically create content for the Internet by publishing it on a Web page and providing links for navigation. Viewers visit your site and interact with the information you provide. Web 2.0 technology lets you invite Web page viewers to contribute information to a site or exchange information, messages, and files with other viewers.

- When searching online, one of the primary tools you can use to find information is a search engine. You use a search engine to search for keywords.

- Keywords describe the information you are trying to locate and most search engines support keyword searches. Use double quotation marks around a set of words for phrase searching.

- Use the plus and minus sign for inclusion and exclusion of words within a search. Boolean searches use the three logical operators OR, AND, and NOT.

- Many search engines offer advanced search options that let you filter search results with specific criteria. Use the * symbol for wildcard searching.

- To evaluate Web sites, consider relevance and reliability, page layout, validity and bias, writing style, and coverage.

- Cite any information that you use from the Internet. The MLA style is widely used for citing electronic resources.

VOCABULARY REVIEW

Define the following terms:

blog	link lists	related search
Boolean logic	math symbols	search engine
copyright	news feed	shared bookmark
directories	peer-to-peer (P2P)	social networking sites
feed	phrase searching	trademark
indexes	plagiarism	wiki
keywords	podcatcher	wildcard character
libel	public domain	

REVIEW QUESTIONS

TRUE / FALSE

Circle T if the statement is true or F if the statement is false.

T   F   **1.**   You can assume that all information found on the Internet is accurate.

T   F   **2.**   Keywords describe the information you are trying to locate.

T   F   **3.**   Everyone who puts information on the Internet is an authority on the particular subject.

T   F   **4.**   Spelling and grammatical errors on a Web page should not affect a user's opinion of a site.

T   F   **5.**   All sites should have an e-mail address for the author so the user can make contact.

MULTIPLE CHOICE

Select the best response for the following statements.

1. All of the following are types of Internet resources *except* _____.

   A.   online articles   C.   CD-ROMs

   B.   commercial sites   D.   e-mail

2. Some information on the Internet is classified as _____, which means it can be used without citation or permission.

   A.   patented   C.   copyrighted

   B.   public domain   D.   precited

3. An asterisk is a symbol for a _____ character in a search.

   A.   wildcard   C.   math

   B.   Boolean   D.   meta

4. A news _____ is a data format used for providing users with frequently updated content.

   A.   article   C.   search engine

   B.   bookmark   D.   feed

5. All of the following are criteria for evaluating information on a Web site *except* _____.

   A.   coverage   C.   bias

   B.   popularity   D.   page layout

FILL IN THE BLANK

Complete the following sentences by writing the correct word or words in the blanks provided.

1. A(n) _____ is used for the chronological posting of commentary, journal entries, video, and graphics.

2. To subscribe to a podcast requires that you use a software program called a(n) _____.

3. A(n) _____ is a form of collaborative information sharing that lets users organize and share favorites.

4. When using search engine math, you put a(n) _____ before words that must appear (also called an inclusion operator).

5. Responsibilities for your behavior online are _____ as in an academic or similar environment.

PROJECTS

PROJECT 28–1

You can conduct research on the Web on almost any topic. Complete the following.

1. Search the Internet for Web sites containing information on Olympic gold medalists.

2. In the results list, pick at least two sites that you think might contain useful information.

3. Using the survey form shown in **Figure 28–14**, evaluate each site.

4. Write a one-page report on your evaluation of the sites. Be sure to include the URL of the site and elaborate on what you found in response to each of the survey questions.

PROJECT 28–3

Evaluate the Web sites you use for research. Complete the following:

1. Choose a topic to research on the Internet. Using the techniques you learned in this lesson, search for Web sites related to your topic.

2. Print the home pages of the first two sites that you find.

3. Using the information you studied in this lesson, evaluate the content on each site.

4. Report your findings by comparing and contrasting the reliability and validity of the two sites in a short report.

PROJECT 28–2

Using the advanced search option provided by search engines can produce valuable results. Complete the following.

1. Use the advanced search option on your favorite search engine to search for information about your favorite band or musical group.

2. Check the size of some of the Web pages listed in your search results and save a small site (less than 50K) as a text file in your assignments folder if your instructor gives you permission to do so.

3. Link to some of the other sites in your search results list and use the information you find to create a one-page report that includes at least one example of a graphic or excerpted text that you have saved or copied from a Web page.

4. Also include within the report what search engine you used and why, how many sites you found, and how you were able to narrow the search.

TEAMWORK PROJECT

You have been assigned to work as a group on a science project. The project involves selecting a type of insect and providing information about the life and habits of the insect. Working in a group with two other students, decide what insect you would be interested in researching and then create a "Search Strategy" form that you can use to search the Internet. Within the form, list possible search tools and ways in which to search. Include the URLs for any suggested search engines or directory Web sites. Make a copy of the form for each student in your group, and then individually use the form to find information about the insect. Then, meet as a group again and compare the information you found. Did you all find similar information, exactly the same information, or very different information when you did your searches?

CRITICAL THINKING

You want to design a Web site on a topic of your choice. Sketch a design for the home page of the Web site. Review the evaluation criteria discussed in this lesson and make sure your Web site follows the criteria of a reputable site with accurate information.

ONLINE DISCOVERY

Select a topic of your choice to research on the Web. Try to be as specific as possible in the topic you choose—for example, "Apollo missions" or "national parks in the Eastern United States." Search for information using three different search engines. Be sure to use exactly the same search techniques (such as keywords, Boolean operators, or related searches) for each search. Create a table with a separate column for each search engine. Then under the column headings, list the top 10 sites that the search engine locates. Determine which engine provided you with the highest-quality results.

LESSON 29

Technology and Society

■ OBJECTIVES

Upon completion of this lesson, you should be able to:

- Identify how information technology and the Internet are used at work, home, and school.
- Identify settings in which computers and the Internet are used.
- Identify how computers and the Internet have transformed traditional processes.
- Identify technologies that support or provide options for the physically challenged.

■ DATA FILES

You do not need data files to complete this lesson.

■ VOCABULARY

business-to-business (B2B)

business-to-consumer (B2C)

business-to-government (B2G)

critical thinking

digital cash

electronic commerce (e-commerce)

keyless entry system

online learning

telecommuting

Technology has changed and continues to change every aspect of life—from home to school to the workplace. These changes are swift and dramatic. A little more than 20 years ago, IBM hired Paul Allen and Bill Gates to create an operating system for a new PC, which was the beginning of Microsoft Corporation. About 10 years ago, Google and PayPal were founded, and early versions of the Web browsers Internet Explorer and Netscape Navigator were released. MySpace was founded in 2003 with YouTube following in 2005. Clearly, the trend of electronic innovation affecting daily life is bound to continue.

3-4.1.1

Using Computers at Work, School, and Home

It is becoming increasingly difficult to find a job or employment that does not require some knowledge of computers. If you do not have a working knowledge of or exposure to technology, you will most likely feel the effects on your career options. Technology today is integrated into almost every facet of life and influences how you work, use computers at home, and learn about the world outside your doors.

This section discusses how computers facilitate and enhance your everyday activities.

Collecting Information

The Internet and the World Wide Web are the major forms of technology affecting your life today. Using the Internet is a fast and easy way to find the information you need. At home and at work, if you need to find the telephone number of a local company, or order a pizza for lunch, you can use the computer to search for and find the data, and then store this information on your hard disk using software such as Windows Mail or Microsoft Office Outlook.

Not so long ago, if a science teacher gave the class a project to find out how a television works, the students would go to the library and do the research. In most of today's classrooms, the students go to the Internet and visit a Web site such as the ScienceProject.com Web site to collect this information. See **Figure 29–1**.

FIGURE 29–1   ScienceProject.com Web site

Organizing Information

Computer software helps you organize information. You can use databases and spreadsheets to arrange and calculate data in a variety of ways. After entering data into a spreadsheet, you can format, sort, and chart the data. If you are in the working world, the company you work for uses spreadsheets for statistical data, tax information, or financial reporting, for example. At home, you might use spreadsheets to track a personal budget, list a collection of items such as baseball cards, and maintain expenses for income tax purposes. At school, spreadsheets are integrated into courses on mathematics, business, and personal finance, to name only a few.

A database program also organizes and sorts data. For example, a database might contain a table with fields for data such as names, addresses, city, state, and zip code. You can sort the data by any of these fields, whether they contain text or numbers.

Evaluating Information

In addition to using spreadsheet applications to calculate numeric data, you can use spreadsheets to ask what-if questions and evaluate information. Spreadsheets contain mathematic and trigonometry functions as well as statistical functions such as Average, Count, Maximum, Minimum, and Percentile. Arranging data in tables, charts, and lists helps you see patterns or trends in the data and evaluate it by comparing one set of calculation results to another.

Communicating Information

When computers are connected through a network or the Internet, they can exchange information instantaneously. Technology provides communication options such as e-mail, instant messaging, blogs, and social Web sites such as MySpace and Twitter.

Increasing Productivity

Access to the Internet and the Web can increase your productivity by providing online access to multiple resources, including communications with experts and specialists. Application programs, such as those discussed in this and previous lessons, can also enhance output and productivity.

Collaborating with Others and Solving Problems

You can take advantage of Web services to supplement project-based learning. With this dynamic approach, you explore real-world problems and challenges. Using online communities, you can collaborate with other people all over the world who might otherwise never meet or know of each other. The exchange and sharing of ideas on a global basis helps you see a problem from different viewpoints. One example of this is the Social Media for Social Change Web site (see **Figure 29–2**), which is dedicated to exploring how technology can promote good in the world.

FIGURE 29–2   Social Media for Social Change Web site

Creating Communities

Online communities and social networking sites such as Facebook and MySpace have been discussed in other lessons. This type of Web site provides an opportunity to socialize with others who have common interests. For example, the Wikipedia Web site shown in **Figure 29–3** contains a list of major active social networking Web sites from all over the world.

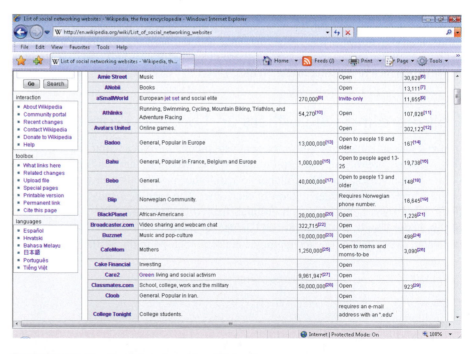

FIGURE 29–3   Social networking Web sites

Facilitating Learning

You can use the Internet as a resource for learning and discovering new facts and information. As mentioned previously, however, you should not take all online information at face value. Be sure to carefully evaluate and verify the source and the information itself.

Many textbooks published today have an associated Web site where students can access Web-based projects, find study aides to accompany the text, and do homework. Look in the front pages of a textbook that has been recently published to see if there is a Web site that accompanies it. It is even possible for students using a particular textbook to open an online version of the textbook with a password provided by their instructor. This can lighten the load in your backpack as you travel back and forth to school. Publishers might provide a Web site for a series of textbooks or for each individual book.

Promoting Creativity

Integrating technology in the classroom provides you with an opportunity to demonstrate your inventiveness, individuality, and creativity. Modern technology provides tools you can use to create a range of artistic work that can be published for a real audience anywhere in the world. Project-based collaborations can further enhance creative learning and problem solving (see **Figure 29–4**).

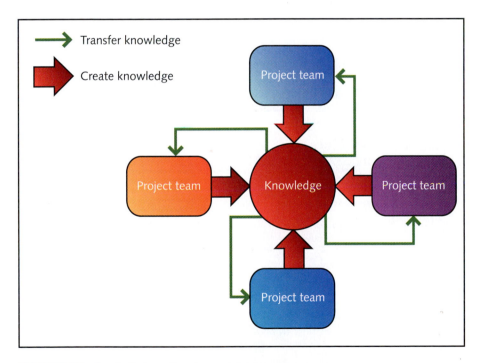

Transfer knowledge

Create knowledge

Project team

Project team

Knowledge

Project team

Project team

FIGURE 29–4   Collaborating in project teams

Supporting Critical Thinking

When searching for information on the Internet, you need to use critical thinking. Researching the phrase *critical thinking* provides a number of definitions such as "consisting of a mental process of analyzing or evaluating information," "the process of evaluating propositions or hypotheses and making judgments," and "shows

▶ **VOCABULARY**
critical thinking

or requires careful analysis before judgment." When reading information online, particularly pages that persuade you to buy or do something, evaluate the information critically, analyze the point of view and motivations, and wait to act until you have gathered and considered all the information.

Facilitating Daily Life

Electronic commerce, or *e-commerce*, means conducting business on the Internet. It primarily refers to purchasing and selling products or services on the Internet or through other computer networks. Commercial Web sites let you conduct business online. You can access electronic catalogs, select goods, store them in a digital cart or bag, and then check out by paying with a credit card or online account. Organizations provide more than goods online. For example, if you need tickets for the basketball playoffs or an upcoming concert, you can purchase the tickets online, order a program, and probably select your seats.

Online local, state, and national government Web sites provide access to many services. For example, many local government agencies provide Web sites where you can pay your water bill, renew your driver's license, and sign up for municipal services. Perhaps you need a tax form. The Internal Revenue Service site provides all types of forms and other services such as how to check on your refund and how to file forms electronically (see **Figure 29–5**).

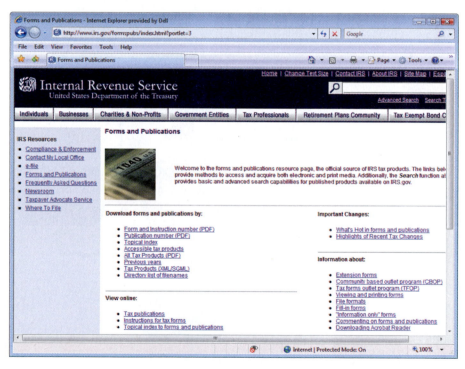

FIGURE 29–5   Forms on the Internal Revenue Service Web site

3-4.1.2

Computer Technology in Everyday Life

You probably perform day-to-day activities without thinking about computers and how they affect your life. In fact, using desktop and laptop computers represents only a fraction of your interactions with computer technology. This section discusses how computers are used in daily life.

Automated Teller Machines

Almost everyone with a bank account now takes advantage of the convenience of automated teller machines (ATMs) to deposit or withdraw money. These automated banking machines are located at most banks but are also in supermarkets, convenience stores, restaurants—even at the ballpark or museum. They allow you to do your banking almost anywhere, anytime. Banker's hours from 9:00 a.m. to 5:00 p.m. are definitely a thing of the past.

You might not even need to get cash from an ATM for your shopping. Electronic checks and debit cards are making cash more obsolete every day. If you swipe your ATM card or debit card through the machine at the cashier's station at your local store and then enter your personal identification number (PIN), information about your account is transferred to the store's computers and the amount of your purchase is deducted from your checking or savings balance (see **Figure 29–6**).

> **EXTRA FOR EXPERTS**
>
> ATMs are usually computers running the Windows XP operating system.

FIGURE 29–6   Automated teller machine

Credit Card and Other Commerce Systems

Many people no longer carry large sums of money while traveling. They prefer to use ATM or credit cards. The magnetic strip on the back of the card increases efficiency. When you travel, using a card helps you keep track of your travel expenses. If you lose a credit card, it can be canceled immediately; whereas if your money is lost or stolen, the chances of recovery are very small.

A security concern on the Internet, however, is credit card information. Because the Internet makes transactions so quick and easy, credit card numbers that fall into the wrong hands can cause lots of headaches for cardholders very quickly. Although effective encryption technologies keep credit card numbers secure, you can make yours even more secure by following simple precautions. Only purchase from Web sites that you know are reputable and trustworthy. Read and understand the privacy and consumer-protection policies of online companies before you buy. Be sure that any credit card information is transmitted in a secured, encrypted mode.

Credit card information is not the only personal information you should protect. Take the same precautions whenever you are asked to disclose anything personal, such as to market research companies. For example, avoid providing your telephone number on Web forms. It usually is not a required field even for online purchases. Disclose only what you think is legitimately necessary for the intended purpose. Do not provide personal information to unknown parties. Use code names when appropriate to protect your identity and personal security.

Automated Industrial Processes

The use of robots on assembly lines and in other industrial processes has expanded production capabilities in the manufacturing world. Some automated systems are equipped with vision technology. Performance is precise, measurements are exact, and production is increased. Most manufacturing companies report that once they install automated systems, they realize a high return on investment (see **Figure 29–7**).

FIGURE 29–7   Industrial robots

Point-of-Sale Systems

A terminal used for electronic processing of payment transactions in a retail outlet is called a point-of-sale (POS) system. When the cashier scans a product you purchase, the pricing comes from a centralized database thousands of miles away. If you use a frequent buyer card, the POS system might record information about your purchase so that you receive coupons or other promotions for similar items. Many of the POS systems include a complete accounting, inventory, and management system. The POS in **Figure 29–8** contains an onscreen menu.

FIGURE 29–8   POS system

Weather Predicting and Reporting Systems

Several weather prediction software tools are available. Numerical weather prediction programs are used by most professional meteorologists. In most programs, the user can select the map output or the model output statistics option. The output statistics model allows the user to customize the output for particular locations.

Embedded Computers in Appliances and Equipment

Though you might not see them, embedded computer systems play an important role in your daily life. An embedded computer is a special-purpose computer system that is incorporated into other devices such as automobiles, appliances, and mechanical equipment. Also defined as a single-purpose system, it is designed to perform one or a few dedicated functions. Embedded computers are preprogrammed to perform a specific task within a device or appliance.

Newer cars, for example, have embedded computers that control such systems as ignition timing and antilock brakes. This is accomplished by using input from a number of built-in sensors.

Almost every home has appliances with embedded computers. Any appliance that has a digital clock, for instance, has a small embedded microcontroller that displays the time. Other examples of appliances and mechanical devices with embedded computers are microwaves, refrigerators, cell phones, MP3 players, compressors, propellers, and water pumps (see **Figure 29–9**).

FIGURE 29–9   Refrigerator with an embedded computer

Embedded computers are also an important element in medical and scientific equipment. In the operating room, computers are integrated into virtually all medical equipment, including blood pressure monitors, pulse devices, and stethoscopes.

Global Positioning Systems

A global positioning system (GPS), combined with cell phone technology, can provide location information and directions. A GPS can also be a communications device for a driver who needs help or has been in an accident.

Security Systems

Many cars today include a remote keyless system and can include a remote keyless ignition system. Pressing a button opens or locks the doors. Pressing another button starts the car. *Keyless entry systems* are also available for entrance doors to houses, businesses, and other buildings. Most of these systems include a keypad. To open the lock, you press a button on a remote control device or enter a combination on the keypad.

Some security systems require more sophisticated user identification. Biometrics applies statistics to biology. A biometric device can match patterns stored in a database with a person's iris, retina, voice, fingerprint, or handprint to confirm or deny someone's identity (see **Figure 29–10**).

▶ **VOCABULARY**
keyless entry system

FIGURE 29–10   Biometric security

Transforming Traditional Processes

3-4.1.3

Integrating personal computers and Internet services has transformed many of the traditional procedures and methods in business, education, and government. This section discusses these transformations.

E-Commerce

You probably have read about the Industrial Revolution and how it affected our world. The Internet economy is being compared to the Industrial Revolution. As mentioned earlier, e-commerce, which means having an online business, is changing the way the world does business.

Statistics indicate that over a billion people are connected to the Internet. Internet speed will continue to increase as more people add fiber-optics, cable modems, or digital subscriber lines (DSL). All of this activity and high-speed connections indicate more online businesses. Some analysts predict that within the next 10 years, Internet-based business will account for up to 30 percent or more of the world's consumer sales. The Center for Research in Electronic Commerce at the University of Texas indicates that out of the thousands of online companies, most are not the big Fortune 500 companies—they are smaller businesses.

Using e-commerce, you can buy and sell just about any product through the Internet. Many people hesitate before making online purchases because they fear someone will steal their credit card numbers. However, *digital cash* is a technology that might ease some of those fears. The digital cash system allows you to pay by transmitting a number from one computer to another. The digital cash numbers

▶ **VOCABULARY**
digital cash

are issued by a bank and represent a specified sum of real money; each number is unique. When you use digital cash, no one can obtain information about you. As an alternative, some credit card companies have a virtual account option.

As you read about electronic commerce, you might wonder about the effects it will have on you personally. You or someone in your family probably has made a purchase online. Buying online will become much more common in the future, and you might find it becomes a way of life. You could also continue to see an increase in spam—junk mail sent to your e-mail address. Several states are looking at ways to legislate against junk mail.

Electronic commerce has also generated a number of new jobs and new categories of jobs, which could influence your future career. Some examples include Webmasters, programmers, network managers, graphic designers, and Web developers. You might also consider starting an online business for yourself. People with imagination and ambition discover that the greatest source of wealth is their ideas.

Business Connections

Business-to-business (B2B) describes e-commerce transactions between businesses, such as between a company and a supplier. This includes the online exchange of products, services, or information. *Business-to-consumer (B2C)* describes online transactions between businesses and consumers. A third category is *business-to-government (B2G)*, which includes transactions between businesses and governmental agencies.

Retail businesses often use radio-frequency identification (RFID) tags, which are small electronic devices that identify and track goods from the point of delivery or manufacturing to the point of sale, similar to a bar code. Unlike bar codes, however, scanners can read information from RFID tags from several feet away. Businesses use RFID to improve the efficiency of inventory tracking and management. Governments are using them in passports and in transportation, such as electronic toll collection on highways and in mass transit passes.

Media

In the past, the distribution of media was primarily through newspapers, magazines, television, and radio. The Internet opened a new category of communications media. Media can be distributed by anyone who has an Internet connection. Music, video, audio, pictures, text—all can be distributed online through e-mail, blogs, Web sites, and other types of Internet distribution channels.

Online Learning

For some time, people have been able to obtain their education via distance learning methods. Earlier nontraditional methods include television and correspondence courses that are completed through the mail. In the last few years, the Internet has become a way to deliver *online learning*. At the elementary and secondary school levels, the Department of Education supports an initiative called the Star Schools Program. This program provides online education learning to millions of learners annually.

Imagine being able to complete high school from home. This is possible in many states. For instance, any high school student who is a Florida resident can attend the Florida Virtual School online for free. This is a certified diploma-granting school, open any time—night or day. Students enroll, log on, and complete their work through the guidance of a certified Florida high school teacher. Several other states also provide similar programs, including Utah. See **Figure 29–11**.

▶ **VOCABULARY**

business-to-business (B2B)

business-to-consumer (B2C)

business-to-government (B2G)

online learning

🔲 **EXTRA FOR EXPERTS**

Project Gutenberg was one of the earliest educational uses of the Internet. It began as a text-based project by Michael Hart in 1971, before the World Wide Web even existed. More than 13,000 books, mostly older works of literature in the public domain in the United States, are available to download at *www.gutenberg.org*.

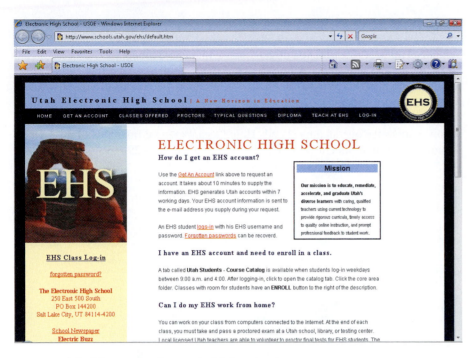

FIGURE 29–11 Utah electronic high school

Learning management system programs help teachers deliver online courses. These programs are an integrated set of Web-based teaching tools that provide guidance and testing for the student. Three of the more popular of these learning management systems are Blackboard, Moodle, and Angel. See **Figure 29–12**.

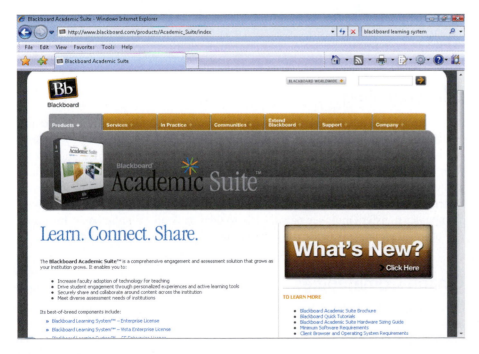

FIGURE 29–12 Blackboard online learning

Robotics

When you think of robotics, you might think of humanoid robots such as those in Star Wars. In real life, however, robotic design did not originally take this path. Robots have been used mostly in assembly plants, often doing dangerous or repetitive tasks. More recently, some specialized robots have been developed that do have a humanoid appearance, and robot devices such as NASA's Mars Rover Spirit, and Jason, the robotic submarine operated by Woods Hole Oceanographic Institute, allow exploration of hostile environments unsafe for humans. See **Figure 29–13**.

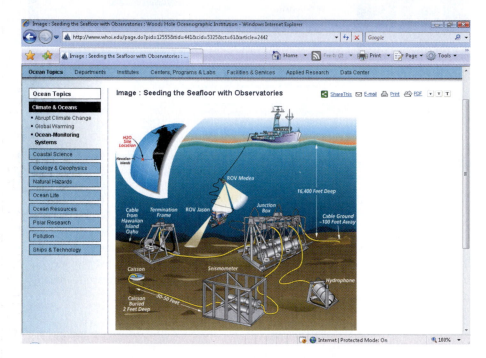

FIGURE 29–13   Woods Hole Oceanographic Institution Web site

Telecommuting

Many employers allow their employees to work from home. This arrangement is called ***telecommuting***. It involves using communications technology to keep the employee connected to the office. Telecommuting has many advantages for both the employer and the employee. It saves traveling time and expense, and it allows the employee to work at a time that is convenient. Projects and other relevant information can be shared through e-mail and other online distribution options. Companies transfer employee pay directly to their bank on a regular basis. Insurance and other employment-related activities are handled automatically online.

VOCABULARY
telecommuting

Online Communities

Online communities, also known as social networks, virtual communities, and e-communities, enable groups of people to interact online through a communication media rather than face-to-face. Social and professional groups use this type of communication to exchange ideas around various topics and to share personal information. Facebook (see **Figure 29–14**) and Flickr were two of the earlier virtual communities.

FIGURE 29–14   Facebook sign-up page

Some of the more popular social networks today include Yahoo Groups (see **Figure 29–15**) and Google Groups (see **Figure 29–16**).

FIGURE 29–15   Yahoo Groups

FIGURE 29–16   Google Groups

Disaster Recovery

Hurricanes, tornadoes, and other recent disasters have increased awareness of the need for disaster recovery planning for communities, cities, and states. The content of a disaster recovery plan and online resources will vary, based on the location and potential hazards. A segment of the plan, however, should include options for electronic communications, such as a Web site that is updated periodically, e-mail availability, and available resources and locations where help can be provided.

3-4.1.4

Supporting the Physically Challenged

Many of today's technologies can be used to support those who are physically challenged. This section describes some of these technologies.

Assistive Technologies

People around the world can communicate with each other almost instantaneously. Advances in technology affect how you are treated for illnesses and injuries, how cars are manufactured and how they work, even how the meter reader calculates your water bill.

Computers are working behind the scenes to assist in most endeavors. For example, computer programs make it possible to predict dangerous weather and warn people in time to prepare for storms. Electronic devices help disabled people communicate, become more mobile, and participate in activities. For example, telecommunications device for the deaf (TDD) technology allows hearing-impaired people to use a telephone, "smart" buses can lower steps to allow disabled people to board the bus or provide a lift for a wheelchair, and personal computers offer accessibility options that permit people with many types of disabilities to work and communicate more easily.

Several adaptive software options are also available for the blind or individuals with limited sight. These software options are as follows:

- Screen readers that provide alternative sensory guidance for computer navigation
- Scanning and reading software
- Internet browser readers that read HTML pages
- Braille translators (see **Figure 29–17**)
- Other miscellaneous applications for the blind such as talking checkbooks

FIGURE 29–17 Braille translator

Electronic Learning

Education today is no longer confined to the classroom. E-learning and online courses are offered throughout the world by public and private education institutions. Many educational institutions also offer public service and non-credit courses at reduced fees.

Public Service

The Federal government provides a number of free educational resources such as those at *http://free.ed.gov*. The Discovery Channel (*discovery.com*) and the Learning Channel (*tlc.discovery.com*) have a number of educational resources ranging from animals to global warming. In many cities and towns, local community centers and libraries also provide free and/or inexpensive educational opportunities (see **Figure 29–18**).

FIGURE 29–18   Online learning resources

Electronic Government

All states and most cities have a Web site that provides information about the city or state. In **Figure 29–19**, for instance, the City of Tampa Web site contains information resources, news and events, services, and key topics. Links at the top of the page provide a site map and FAQ link. Links for program services, utility bill payments, recycling, information resources, and a number of other Web pages are contained in the menu bar on the left side of the screen.

FIGURE 29–19   City of Tampa Web site

TECHNOLOGY CAREERS

Simulation Analyst

Simulation analysts and consultants work with all types of companies of any size. Their primary job is to investigate different options to determine which would be the best for a particular situation. For instance, health care company administrators might want to implement a new system for filing and processing insurance claims. Before spending a huge amount of money, they might hire a simulation analyst to determine which system would best meet their needs. Or a bank that is going to bring in a new system to process checks may hire an analyst to do simulation modeling of what the system might and might not do.

Some necessary skills include the ability to see detail in a system and to be a good technical writer. The person should be a logical thinker and have good analytical skills. A good memory is an additional asset. Opportunities and the need for simulation analysts are increasing. One of the reasons for the increase is that more and more companies are applying simulation to a larger variety of problems.

As a consultant, you would probably do some traveling. Consulting fees are usually quite generous, with some simulation analysts making as much as $75,000 or more per year. You might find some analysts with only a two-year degree, but generally you need at least a bachelor's degree in computer information systems or computer engineering.

SUMMARY

In this lesson, you learned:

- Computers are used in different areas of work, school, and home to collect, organize, evaluate, and communicate information; increase productivity; collaborate with others; and facilitate learning and daily life.

- Desktop and laptop computers represent only a fraction of interaction with computer technology. Embedded computers in automobiles, appliances, and mechanical equipment, for example, are more prevalent. These computers are programmed to perform a specific task within the equipment.

- Traditional processes for banking, news delivery, and education have been transformed due to e-commerce, online news content, and online learning.

- Robotics and other automated systems have increased the efficiency of manufacturing and production.

- Online communities provide communication links for people who share similar interests. They also bridge geographical boundaries between people. Online learning and other learning opportunities are available through the Internet.

- New jobs and new job categories are being developed related to the Internet and electronic commerce. People can telecommute and collaborate globally using e-mail, networks, and automated systems.

- Electronic communication is used to distribute disaster information.

- Technologies such as voice recognition software are available for the blind.

- Local, state, and national governments can provide access to related information.

VOCABULARY REVIEW

Define the following terms:

business-to-business (B2B)   critical thinking   keyless entry system
business-to-consumer (B2C)   digital cash   online learning
business-to-government (B2G)   electronic commerce (e-commerce)   telecommuting

 REVIEW QUESTIONS

TRUE/FALSE

Circle T if the statement is true or F if the statement is false.

T F **1.** With digital cash, you can pay someone by transmitting a number from one computer to another.

T F **2.** Robots are used in e-commerce transactions.

T F **3.** Keyless entry systems are available for entrance doors to houses.

T F **4.** An embedded computer is a special-purpose computer system that is incorporated into another device such as an automobile.

T F **5.** It is not possible to enroll in an online high school.

MULTIPLE CHOICE

Select the best response for the following statements.

1. _____ is an example of a social Web site.

   A. MySpace   C. E-commerce

   B. Systems   D. Each of the above

2. _____ software can be used to evaluate information.

   A. Word-processing   C. E-mail

   B. Spreadsheet   D. GPS

3. A terminal used for electronic processing of payment transactions in a retail outlet is called a(n) _____ system.

   A. internal   C. POS (point-of-sale)

   B. external   D. e-processing

4. _____ means conducting business on the Internet.

   A. Simulation   C. Virtual reality

   B. E-commerce   D. Each of the above

5. _____ combined with cell phone technology can provide location information and directions.

   A. GPS   C. MP3

   B. SPG   D. Each of the above

FILL IN THE BLANK

Complete the following sentences by writing the correct word or words in the blanks provided.

1. When someone works from home, it is called _____.

2. Google Groups is a type of _____ _____.

3. A screen reader is an example of _____ software, which is available for the blind or people with limited sight.

4. _____ commerce has generated a number of new jobs and new categories of jobs.

5. A(n) _____ device can match patterns stored in a database with a person's iris, retina, voice, fingerprint, or handprint.

 # PROJECTS

PROJECT 29–1

Many government, nonprofit, and commercial Web sites provide online learning opportunities. Complete the following:

1. Start your Web browser, and then go to the Intel Web site at the following address:

   http://educate.intel.com/en/DesignDiscovery/ ImplementationExamples/student_projects.htm

2. Review the student projects on this site, and then select three of the projects.

3. Prepare a report on what you learned. Share this information with your class.

PROJECT 29–3

As indicated in this lesson, an embedded computer is a special-purpose computer system that is incorporated into another device. Complete the following:

1. Examine the electronic devices in your classroom or in your home.

2. Use your word-processing program to list and describe the objects that you found that contain an embedded processor.

PROJECT 29–2

Online local, national, and state government Web sites were discussed in this lesson. Complete the following:

1. Use the Internet to locate a government Web site that applies to your community or city.

2. Evaluate the Web site and write a review of what is contained on the Web site.

3. Comment on what you found the most helpful and informational. Also identify what is missing from the Web sites you examined.

 ### TEAMWORK PROJECT

Your instructor has assigned to you and a team member a project relating to the global economy and electronic commerce. You and your partner are to prepare a report on what information you would need to know before setting up an e-commerce Web site. Create a PowerPoint presentation and present it to your class.

 # CRITICAL THINKING

Congratulations on your new job at Bank International. Assume that your supervisor has asked you to research and prepare a report on biometric security measures. After you thoroughly research this project, create a report listing each item you selected and explain why you selected that particular item. Submit your report to your instructor.

ONLINE DISCOVERY

Most dentists today use computers in one way or another. For instance, instead of obtaining a film of an x-ray, it can be sent to a computer screen. Some dentists use a sonic device to clean teeth. Use search engines such as google.com and altavista.com to see what you can discover about how dentists are using computers. Prepare a presentation and share it with the class.

LESSON 30

Computer Safety and Ethics

■ OBJECTIVES

Upon completion of this lesson, you should be able to:

■ Explain how to maintain a safe working environment and use computer equipment in a way that prevents personal injury.

■ Identify injuries that can result from the use of computers for long periods of time.

■ Identify software threats and risks to data.

■ Understand methods you can use to prevent data loss.

■ Identify various security measures.

■ Identify the principles regarding when information can or cannot be considered personal.

■ Identify the risks associated with electronic commerce.

■ Understand how computer use can affect your privacy and personal security.

■ Identify how to stay informed about changes and advancements in technology.

■ Understand how to be a responsible user of computers.

■ VOCABULARY

browser hijacking

brute force attacks

hacking

hardware firewall

keylogger

private key

public key

repetitive strain injury (RSI)

Secure Sockets Layer (SSL)

sniffer

spyware

strong password

Transport Layer Security (TLS)

■ DATA FILES

You do not need data files to complete this lesson.

While using computers and the Internet offers unrivaled access to commerce, entertainment, and information, it also exposes you to breaches in security, privacy, and ethics. This lesson explores the risks of computing and the measures you can take to minimize those risks. In addition, this lesson examines software threats and how to protect and restrict access to your files and data. As a computer user, you have certain responsibilities that govern your use of technology, including following guidelines and policies, exercising ethical conduct online, and maintaining a safe work environment.

3-4.2.1

Maintaining a Safe Computing Environment

Make sure you use a computer in a way that supports your comfort, health, and safety. Whether you use a desktop computer provided by your school or other organization, a notebook computer at home or in an outdoor café, or a smart phone when you are on the go, pay attention to your posture, lighting, and activity level. For example, sitting in the same position for long periods of time causes muscle fatigue and discomfort. Staring at a computer screen can cause eye strain. Be sure to change your position as you use a computer to encompass a range of motion and sight. Arrange the computer area so that you can work comfortably.

Using a notebook computer introduces risks not associated with desktop computers. Avoid setting a notebook computer directly on your lap or on a soft, flexible surface such as a cushion, which might obstruct air vents and cause the computer to overheat. Use a cooling pad to keep air flowing around the notebook and the battery or AC adapter.

Review product safety guidelines provided with your computer and any electronic devices. For example, if you need to connect your computer to a power source using a plug that has a third pin for grounding, make sure you insert it into a grounded outlet only. If you are maintaining computer equipment yourself, pay attention to icons and other symbols that warn about the hazards of electrical shock, excessive heat, or sharp edges.

The Occupational Safety and Health Administration (OSHA) provides guidelines for using and purchasing computer equipment. See *www.osha.gov* for more information.

3-4.2.2

Computer Related Injuries

When you use a computer, take precautions to avoid chronic physical maladies such as eyestrain, back problems, and *repetitive strain injury (RSI)*, which can result when a person makes too many of the same motions over a long period of time. Ergonomic design, which adapts equipment and the workplace to fit the worker, can help prevent RSIs, which can develop over time and eventually lead to long-term disability. A well-designed work area, use of ergonomic furniture, good posture, and changing positions throughout the day are effective ways to minimize these types of injuries. Avoid or minimize eyestrain by using a high-resolution monitor, providing adequate and properly positioned lighting, and taking regular breaks to allow eye muscles to relax. See **Figure 30–1**.

(Photography by Hader Goren)

FIGURE 30–1   Ergonomic workstation

Security Risks

3-4.2.3

As the use of computers has grown in volume and importance, protecting computer systems and the information they hold has become increasingly important. Wireless networking, for example, is popular because it provides many benefits to computer users. However, it also creates serious risks if it is not properly secured.

For example, your next door neighbor can easily use your broadband connection if it is not password protected. This normally does not cause harm or damage to your network, but it could slow down your Internet access. In other instances, you could be charged for actual usage, which would mean additional costs.

An unauthorized user could also tap into your connection for illegal or criminal activity. If the unauthorized user is part of the network and is working behind a gateway device, any activity coming from the intruder could appear to be coming from your computer, meaning you could be held responsible for the illegal activity.

An intruder could connect directly to your computer, bypassing any firewalls. Once connected, the intruder can scrutinize your computer for personal information such as tax records and other personal information. The intruder could use a *sniffer* to find usernames and passwords. A sniffer is a program that hackers use to capture IDs and passwords on a network. To access an unsecured wireless connection, a hacker only needs a computer with a wireless network card and eavesdropping software that can be downloaded free from the Internet.

▶ **VOCABULARY**
sniffer

Using Network Protection

Almost all routers and access points have a factory-set administrator password and generally use a word such as "password." Some devices do not have a default password at all. When setting up your wireless network, your first step should be to change the default password and then write it down so that you can refer to it if needed. Secondly, turn on some form of encryption. Several forms of encryption technologies are available. You need to select the one that works best with your wireless network devices. Turn off the network during extended periods when you are not using it.

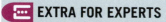
Computer Hacking

Computer *hacking* involves invading someone else's computer, usually for personal gain or the satisfaction of defeating a security system. Hackers usually are computer experts who enjoy having the power to invade someone else's privacy. They can steal, change, or damage data stored on a computer. It is estimated that hacking causes millions of dollars of damage each year, along with the theft of important and valuable data.

Most servers have built-in security features, but they need to be turned on and the server's security setting configured. Firewalls are essential. If the network is small, a software firewall is sufficient. If the network is large, however, a *hardware firewall* that controls the computers from one point should be implemented. This type of firewall is more secure and easier to monitor.

Avoiding Data Loss

One ever-present threat to a computer system is an electrical power failure. Electricity not only provides the power to operate a computer, but it is the medium by which data is stored. An unexpected power outage, for example, can wipe out any data that has not been saved properly. One easy way to avoid data loss is to save frequently. Most software programs contain a command that can be set to save data on a regular basis. For instance, suppose you are working on a 10-page report. If your computer loses power, you lose your work. However, if your software is set to save on a regular basis, such as every 10 minutes, then you can retrieve at least a portion of your report.

To safeguard computer systems against power outages, secure electric cords so that people cannot accidentally disconnect or trip over them. Recall from Lesson 3 that another option is to install an uninterruptible power supply, usually a battery that provides power if the normal current is interrupted. You should also plug surge suppressors into electric outlets to protect against power spikes, which can damage computer hardware and software.

Even saved data can be lost or corrupted by equipment failure, software viruses or hackers, fire or flood, or power irregularities. To protect your data, you should back up important files regularly. Also recall from Lesson 3 that backing up files entails saving them to removable disks or another independent storage device that can be used to restore data if your primary system becomes inaccessible. Because hard drives are mechanical devices, they all eventually fail, preventing access to the data stored on them. A hard disk crash can result in a catastrophic loss of data if it occurs on a critical system and the files have not been backed up properly. For home users, external hard drives are available, and many Web sites provide an online backup service for a minimal price. **Figure 30–2** shows Windows Vista Backup and Restore Center window, which you use to back up files on your computer.

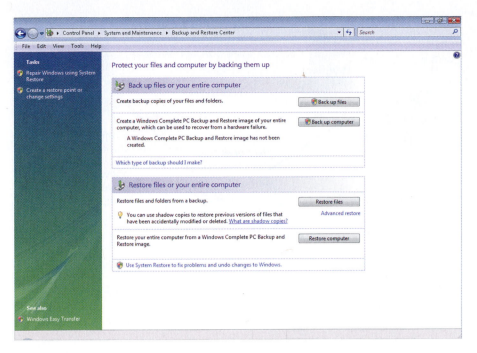

FIGURE 30–2   Using Windows Vista to back up files

Your backup procedures should place a priority on files that would be difficult or impossible to replace or reconstruct if you lost them, such as your data files. Secure backup procedures used by large organizations include a regular schedule for backing up designated files and a means of storing backup files off site so that they will survive intact if the main system is destroyed either by natural disaster or by criminal acts.

Safeguarding Against Software Threats

3-4.2.4

Recall from Lesson 26 that a virus is a program that has been written, usually by a hacker, to corrupt data on a computer. The virus is attached to a file (such as a document or program file) and spreads from one file to another once the program is executed. Often, you can inadvertantly run the virus program by opening an e-mail message or attachment. To protect against viruses, you should use strong passwords, download and install the latest security updates for your operating system, and use an up-to-date antivirus program, as shown in **Figure 30–3**.

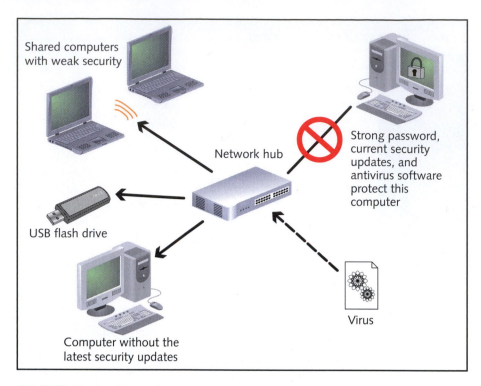

FIGURE 30–3   Protecting against viruses

A *strong password* is both complex and secure—it contains numbers, letters, and special characters that do not include personal information such as name or birth date. In addition, strong passwords contain at least eight characters, and at least one letter, number, and special character (such as @ , $, * , or ?).

Strong passwords are more resistant to *brute force attacks*, also called dictionary attacks, that use a script or program to log on to an account using hundreds of words or phrases stored in a dictionary file.

Other types of software threats include worms and keyloggers. Recall from Lesson 26 that a worm makes many copies of itself, resulting in the consumption of system resources that slows down or actually halts tasks, and don't have to attach themselves to other files to infect your computer. A *keylogger* is a malicious program that records keystrokes. For example, a keylogger might record your keystroke to keep track of the Web sites you visit, the username and password you enter, and private information such as credit card and account numbers. Because they can aid identify theft, keyloggers are a particularly dangerous type of harmful software.

Worms can spread *spyware*, also called adware and privacy-invasive software, which is software installed surreptitiously on a personal computer. The goal is to collect information about the user, the user's browsing habits, and other personal information. Spyware can significantly slow the performance of your computer, display annoying pop-up ads, and change system settings. Hackers often use spyware to control your browser, a practice called *browser hijacking*. The spyware might replace your home page with another, often to increase the number of visits to the replacement page, which can boost advertising revenue. Spyware is also discussed in the "Preserving Privacy" section later in this lesson.

To guard against these types of software threats, be sure to use an antivirus program to regularly scan your system for harmful software and scan files before you open them (see **Figure 30–4**).

FIGURE 30–4   Antivirus protection

You can also use antispyware software such as Windows Defender to protect your system against spyware (see **Figure 30–5**). Make sure you use reputable antispyware programs—some spyware disguises itself as antispyware to gain access to your system.

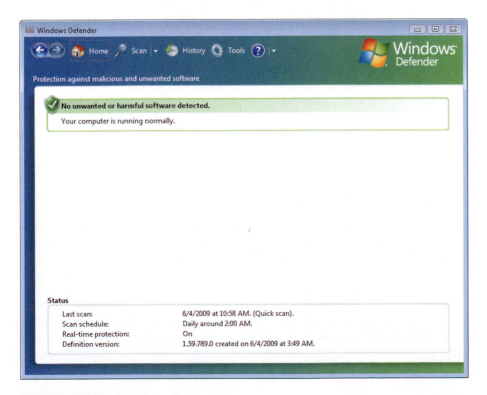

FIGURE 30–5   Windows Defender

Access Restrictions

System administrators and users often restrict access to files, storage devices, various computers, networks, the Internet, or specific Internet sites. They do so to protect data and other users.

Most organizations use firewalls and other methods to protect data. These devices, however, do not protect data from employees. For instance, competition among companies for a government contract or a bid on a new hotel can encourage some employees to share information with competitors. At universities and other educational institutions, copies of final exams and other files are copied and shared. Malicious tampering also can result in data loss. A disgruntled employee can willfully delete vital records and other important data.

Protecting children from unsuitable Web sites also is a concern for parents, teachers, libraries, and other areas where children have computer access. Software is available that lets you monitor computer usage, including Web sites, e-mail messages, social networks, instant messaging and chats, and applications. Some programs keep track of keystrokes typed and even create screenshots. When using this type of protection and this type of program, it is recommended that protecting users be balanced with preserving privacy.

Private Property—But Not Yours

If you work for a company that provides you with e-mail services, the information you send is available to the company; in fact, it is the company's property. It can be accessed from backup copies made by the system.

Generally, any information gathered from a company's computer system is company property and not an individual worker's personal property. The employee normally has no right to personal privacy regarding those issues. The company has a right to access any data on their computers and use it for its legitimate purposes. If the company monitors its Internet logs, for instance, and discovers that an employee has been spending time visiting Web sites that bear no relation to work-related duties, it can discipline the employee. Similarly, if an employee uses a company computer in a way that harms the company—contracting a computer virus through unauthorized activities, for example, or allowing hackers into the company's system—he or she can be disciplined or fired. Likewise, the same laws apply to educational institutions. Any information stored on a computer in an educational facility is school property.

Many organizations have computer or network usage policies that provide guidelines for using the organization's systems ethically, professionally, and legally. Before you access the Internet, send e-mail, exchange files, or otherwise use a computer at school or work, make sure you are familiar with the usage policies.

E-Commerce Issues

E-commerce issues and safety measures were discussed in detail in Lesson 29. The following provides a recap of how to avoid possible hazards of e-commerce and provides information on how sensitive data is encrypted.

Before providing personal information or credit card information on an e-commerce or similar site, first verify that the site is secure. Several companies such as VeriSign (*verisign.com*), GoDaddy (*godaddy.com*), Network Solutions (*networksolutions.com*), and others provide a *Transport Layer Security (TLS)* or *Secure Sockets Layer (SSL)* certificate for e-commerce sites, sites that process sensitive data, and sites that require privacy and security requirements. See **Figure 30–6**.

▶ **VOCABULARY**
Transport Layer Security (TLS)

Secure Sockets Layer (SSL)

Online merchants can purchase SSL certificates from vendors such as VeriSign

FIGURE 30–6 SSL certificates

TSL and SSL technology enables encryption of sensitive information by establishing a private communication channel. Data transmitted through this channel is encrypted during transmission. The SSL Certificate consists of a **public key** and a **private key**. The public key encrypts information and the private key deciphers the information.

The Federal Trade Commission (FTC) offers the following guidelines on its Web site (*www.ftc.gov*) to make sure your e-commerce transactions are secure and to protect your private information:

- *Use a secure browser*: Make sure you are using the most current version of your browser because contemporary browsers have the most up-to-date encryption features. When submitting your purchase information, look for the padlock icon in the browser's status bar and the "https" protocol in the Address bar. Internet Explorer versions 7 and 8 also display secure Web sites using a green Address bar.

- *Check privacy policies*: Before you provide any personal financial information to a Web site, look for and read the site's privacy policy. A link to the privacy policy is often listed at the bottom of the home page.

- *Keep personal information private*: Don't provide personal information such as a password, bank account number, or credit card number unless you know who's collecting the information and how they'll use it. Give payment information only to businesses you know and trust.

▶ **VOCABULARY**

public key

private key

EXTRA FOR EXPERTS

Safe ways to pay for online purchases include using a perishable credit card, which assigns a credit card number to an online purchase or online merchant only for a specific amount of time. You can also use third-party payment services such as PayPal. You set up and fund an online account and make payments from that account without exposing your real credit card or bank account information. E-wallets are a type of online account you can maintain for small purchases, such as magazine subscriptions.

3-4.2.8

Preserving Privacy

The amount of personal information available online for the average computer user is astonishing. The major source of revenue for some companies comes from gathering information about consumers and other computer users to create databases and sell or trade this information to others.

Any time you submit information on the Internet, it is possible for this information to be gathered by many persons and used for various situations. Information can also be gathered from online data regarding school, banking, hospitals, insurance, and any other information supplied for such everyday activities.

Much of the information gathered and sold results in your name being added to mailing lists. These lists are used by companies for marketing purposes. Junk e-mails are used for the same purpose. Information regarding one's credit history is also available to be sold.

Phishing, introduced in Lesson 26, is a type of computer fraud that attempts to steal your private data. A hacker tries to fool you into providing information such as usernames, passwords, and bank account numbers. They do so by posing as a trustworthy entity in an electronic communication such as an e-mail or text message. Typical phishing messages come from social network sites, auction sites, banks, and the IRS. The message directs you to enter details at a fake Web site that looks identical to the legitimate one. See **Figure 30–7**.

Seems to be from a reputable bank

Tricks you into providing a bank account number

Misspelled words often signal a phishing message

TrustedBank™

Dear valued customer of TrustedBank,

We have recieved notice that you have recently attempted to withdraw the following amount from your checking account while in another country: $135.25.

If this information is not correct, someone unknown may have access to your account. As a safety measure, please visit our website via the link below to verify your personal information:

http://www.trustedbank.com/general/custverifyinfo.asp

Once you have done this, our fraud department will work to resolve this discrepency. We are happy you have chosen us to do business with.

Thank you,
TrustedBank

Member FDIC © 2005 TrustedBank, Inc.

FIGURE 30–7   Phishing message

Cookies and Spyware

You might be surprised at how much information about your computer use is tracked by cookies and spyware. Cookies, as you may remember, are small files that are created when you visit a Web site and are stored on your computer, then accessed again the next time you visit the same site. They may make it easier for you to use the Web site when you return, but they may also provide the Web site owner with information about you and your computer, and they often take up disk storage space that you might want to use for other data. It's a good idea to clean up the unnecessary cookies on your computer frequently with a utility program designed for that purpose.

Spyware does not have any redeeming qualities. As mentioned earlier, spyware not only tracks your Web habits, it can even take over control of your computer and direct you to Web sites you have not chosen to visit. Spyware can be harmful as well as annoying. The FTC Web site includes a page advising consumers how to lower the risk of spyware infection (see **Figure 30–8**). Firewalls consisting of hardware and software features can protect your computer from unauthorized spyware programs.

FIGURE 30–8   Avoiding spyware infection

Securing Data

You secure data to protect it from harm or destruction from natural causes, accidents, and intentional damage. It is not always evident that some type of computer crime or intrusion has occurred. Therefore, you need to set up safeguards for each type of risk. It is the responsibility of a company or an individual to protect their data.

The best way to protect data is to effectively control the access to it. You might need a password to log on to a computer system or to specific parts of it (see **Figure 30–9**). Companies often establish password-protected locations on hard drives and networks so that certain people have access to some areas but not to others. To maintain secure passwords, you or the system administrator should change them frequently so that people who no longer need access cannot continue to use the passwords. The challenge is to create strong passwords that are easy for you to remember but difficult for anyone else to decipher. If you write down a password, keep it in a secure place and do not share it with anyone else. Unauthorized access is much more likely to be caused by people who gain access through a shared password or lost "cheat sheet" than by anyone guessing your "secret code."

Log on to access network services, such as e-mail

FIGURE 30–9   Signing in with a username and password

Some other privacy considerations are as follows:

- The security and privacy of personal information on the Internet is improving all the time. It still is necessary, however, to take precautions to protect both personal and business-related information. Use code names instead of real names. This also applies to protecting personal or family information in public places as well.

- When communicating on a forum, blog, or social network or other similar Internet-related sites, use an alias.

- Verify that you have logged off a computer used in a public place such as a public library, a school, or other similar institutions.

3-4.2.9

Using the Internet Safely and Legally

The Internet makes widespread publication of information easy. It also creates the potential for huge damages if the information turns out to be false. The ease of obtaining information from the Internet and of publishing information on the Internet can contribute to legal problems. Just because information is available on a Web site does not mean that anyone can copy it and claim it as their own, even non-copyrighted information. That is plagiarism. The Internet does not relieve an author of responsibility for acknowledging and identifying the source of borrowed material. Likewise, the Internet does not relieve anyone of the burden of ensuring that information they publish is true. If someone publishes information about another person or organization and it is not true, they can be sued for libel and forced to pay compensation for any damage they caused.

Nearly all schools, government agencies, companies, libraries, and other similar institutions have written policies and guidelines regarding Internet usage. These policies protect the organization as well as the user. If these policies are not readily available, ask a system administrator or other employee for a copy of the policy.

Additional information on safe use of computers can be found on numerous Web sites, in books and magazines, and other similar media. The FBI and other government agencies provide resources for Internet safety (see **Figure 30–10**).

FIGURE 30–10   Resources for Internet safety

Technology Changes and Individual Responsibilities

3-4.2.10
3-4.2.11

It is your responsibility to stay informed about changes and advancements in computer technology, product upgrades, and virus threats. If you have a computer, you must keep your antivirus protection up to date. You can find out how to do this at the Web site of your antivirus program provider; you also can find updates and bulletins about software and hardware at company Web sites.

As a responsible computer user, keep in mind that you can lead by example when you recycle products such as used computer paper and ink cartridges. In addition, old computer hardware such as monitors can create an environmental hazard if disposed of improperly. Consider asking your school or business to donate unneeded computer hardware to charitable organizations that refurbish it and provide it to individuals and organizations who would otherwise be unable to take advantage of computer technology. Before the computer is donated, however, the data on the hard drive should be backed up and the data then deleted from the hard drive. In addition, your knowledge and experience using computers is also a commodity you can share generously. Community centers, schools, and other organizations welcome knowledgeable volunteers to serve as tutors to help other people learn how to use computers effectively.

ETHICS IN TECHNOLOGY

The Golden Rule of Computer Ethics

You probably heard the Golden Rule when you were in elementary school—"Do unto others as you would have them do unto you." The Golden Rule applies to computer ethics, too. Do not give in to the urge to snoop around in other people's files or interfere with their work by accessing and changing data in files. And if you had spent a few months creating a great computer game, how would you feel if all your friends started passing copies of the game around to all their friends, without even giving you credit for the program, not to mention cheating you out of any potential profit for your work?

If you do write computer programs, think about the social consequences of the programs you write. Do not copy software illegally, and do not take other people's intellectual property and use it as your own. Just because something is posted on the Web does not mean it is "free" for anyone to use. Use your computer in ways that show consideration of and respect for other people, their property, and their resources. In short, think of the Golden Rule and follow it whenever you face an ethical dilemma at your computer.

SUMMARY

In this lesson, you learned:

- Make sure you use a computer in a way that supports your comfort, health, and safety. When you use a computer, take precautions to avoid chronic physical maladies such as repetitive motion injuries, eyestrain, and back problems that can arise over time. Ergonomic design, which adapts equipment and the workplace to fit the worker, can help to prevent repetitive strain injuries.

- When setting up your wireless network, your first step should be to change the default password to protect access to the network.

- Computer hacking involves invading someone else's computer, usually for personal gain or the satisfaction of defeating a security system.

- To avoid data loss, you can use techniques and devices for preventing power interruptions. You can also devise and follow a regular procedure for backing up your data.

- A virus is a program that has been written, usually by a hacker, to corrupt data on a computer. The virus is attached to a file and spreads from one file to another once the program is executed. To protect your computer against virus damage, use up-to-date antivirus software, download and install security updates for your operating system, and avoid opening files sent via e-mail from people you do not know.

- System administrators and users often restrict access to files, storage devices, various computers, networks, the Internet, or specific Internet sites.

- If you work for a company that provides you with e-mail services, the information you send is available to the company and is the company's property.

- TSL and SSL technology enables encryption of sensitive information by establishing a private communication channel. Data transmitted through this channel is encrypted during transmission.

- Nearly all schools, government agencies, companies, libraries, and other similar institutions have written policies and guidelines regarding Internet usage.

VOCABULARY REVIEW

Define the following terms:

browser hijacking
brute force attacks
hacking
hardware firewall
keylogger

private key
public key
repetitive strain injury (RSI)
Secure Sockets Layer (SSL)
sniffer

spyware
strong password
Transport Layer Security (TLS)

REVIEW QUESTIONS

TRUE / FALSE

Circle T if the statement is true or F if the statement is false.

T   F   **1.** Being able to easily copy information from an Internet site does not mean that someone can use it and claim it as their own.

T   F   **2.** Ergonomic design can help to prevent repetitive strain injuries.

T   F   **3.** Generally, any information gathered from a company's computer system is the individual worker's personal property.

T   F   **4.** Data theft is one way in which data can be lost.

T   F   **5.** A strong password contains numbers, letters, and special characters that do not include personal information such as name or birth date.

MULTIPLE CHOICE

Select the best response for the following statements.

1. _____ is a criminal act that is committed through the use of a computer.

   A. Hacking   C. Copyright

   B. Privacy   D. Biometrics

2. _____ software should always be running on a computer to protect data and programs from corruption or destruction.

   A. Biometrics   C. Copyright

   B. Fraud   D. Antivirus

3. An intruder can use a(n) _____, a program design to find usernames and passwords on a network.

   A. public key   C. sniffer

   B. antivirus program   D. detector

4. _____ control access to computer data.

   A. Passwords   C. Trojan horses

   B. Hackers   D. Worms

5. Hackers often use spyware to control your browser, a practice called _____.

   A. phishing   C. browser control

   B. browser hijacking   D. sniffing

FILL IN THE BLANK

Complete the following sentences by writing the correct word or words in the blanks provided.

1. To keep data safe, your _____ should be changed often.

2. _____ is a type of program that tracks information about the user, the user's browsing habits, and other personal information.

3. _____ is when a hacker attempts to fool you into providing private information such as usernames and passwords.

4. The SSL Certificate consists of a(n) _____ and private key.

5. A(n) _____ is a malicious program that records keystrokes.

■ PROJECTS

PROJECT 30–1

The U. S. Federal Trade Commission has a Web site dedicated to the privacy, security, and functionality issues caused by spyware. Complete the following:

1. Access the FTC Web site at *www.ftc.gov/bcp/edu/microsites/ spyware/index.html*.

2. Review the information contained on the site and on the site links.

3. Prepare a report on what you learned. Include information on how to avoid spyware and how to remove it from your computer.

PROJECT 30–3

In May, 2009, the University of California at Berkeley was found to be the target of a major data theft involving 160,000 Berkeley students. This data theft had gone on for six months. Complete the following:

1. Use your research skills to find out additional information about this theft.

2. Use a word-processing program to write a description of the incident.

3. Locate two more articles related to data theft and describe what was taken and how it was used.

PROJECT 30–2

As mentioned in this lesson, many organizations provide guidelines for using their computers and networks. Complete the following:

1. Access the Nassau Library Web site at *www.nassaulibrary.org/ gardenc/comproom.html*.

2. Read the Rules & Guidelines document.

3. Use your word-processing program to respond to the following questions:
   - Which three rules do you think are the most important and why?
   - Which three rules do you think are the least important and why?
   - Do you agree with the guidelines contained in this set of rules? Explain your answer.
   - Locate two similar Web sites. List their Web site addresses. How do their guidelines compare to the Nassau Library Web site?

■ TEAMWORK PROJECT

Repetitive strain injuries have become a serious concern for computer users and members of the medical profession. Work with a partner to learn about the types of RSIs, their causes, and their treatments. Create a PowerPoint presentation and present it to your class.

CRITICAL THINKING

Use your browser and do a search for *Internet+Safety+Week* and then answer the following questions:

1. Approximately how many hits did you receive?

2. Is there a national week set aside for Internet Safety Week? If so, when is it celebrated?

3. Access three Web sites that are relevant to Internet Safety Week. Review each site and then use your word processing program to write a paragraph describing each of the sites. Include the Web site address in your review.

ONLINE DISCOVERY

Social networking online is a recent technology that has become very popular. Research this technology and then prepare a report defining what you consider the definition of a social network site, list at least four examples of social network sites, and then discuss why you think this technology has become so popular. Select one site (other than Facebook or MySpace) and describe the differences between the network site you selected and Facebook or MySpace.

MODULE 3 REVIEW

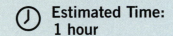

Estimated Time:
1 hour

Living Online

 ## REVIEW QUESTIONS

TRUE / FALSE

Circle T if the statement is true or F if the statement is false.

T F **1.** With text messaging, you use a cell phone or other mobile device to send and receive written messages.

T F **2.** An e-mail address consists of three parts.

T F **3.** An intranet is designed for the exclusive use of people within an organization.

T F **4.** ARPANET was the name of the first Web browser.

T F **5.** Computers on the Internet communicate with each other using the TCP/IP protocol.

T F **6.** Government agencies typically use the .irs domain name extension.

T F **7.** A newsgroup is an Internet-supported discussion forum.

T F **8.** The home page is the first Web page displayed when you launch your browser.

T F **9.** You can only save text on a Web page to disk.

T F **10.** Google is an example of a search engine.

MULTIPLE CHOICE

Select the best response for the following statements.

1. _____ is the process of backing up your e-mail messages.

   A. Archiving   C. Retrieving

   B. Podcasting   D. Encrypting

2. _____ is a method of publishing files (primarily audio) to the Internet.

   A. Archiving   C. Uploading

   B. Podcasting   D. Phishing

3. An asterisk is a symbol for a _____ character in a search.

   A. wildcard   C. math

   B. Boolean   D. meta

4. One way you can lose data is through _____.

   A. copyrights   C. encryption

   B. decryption   D. data theft

5. A(n) _____ is the address of a Web page, FTP site, audio stream, or other Internet resource.

   A. SSL   C. HTML

   B. URL   D. ISP

6. A(n) _____ is a computer program written to cause corruption of data on a computer.

   A. virus   C. algorithm

   B. sniffer   D. cookie

7. You use a(n) _____ to encrypt information.

   A. backup   C. archive

   B. public key   D. USB flash drive

8. Hackers use a program called a(n) _____ to capture user IDs and passwords.

   A. phisher   C. worm

   B. sniffer   D. user bomb

9. _____ is a method that you can use to search databases.

   A. Wildcard   C. Bookmark

   B. Really Simple Syndication   D. Boolean logic

10. Some information on the Internet is classified as _____, which means it can be used without citation or permission.

   A. patented   C. copyrighted

   B. public domain   D. encrypted

FILL IN THE BLANK

Complete the following sentences by writing the correct word or words in the blanks provided.

1. A(n) _____ is used for the chronological posting of commentary, journal entries, video, and graphics.

2. A(n) _____ is a type of network that covers a large geographical area.

3. You use _____ to make phone calls with an Internet connection instead of a regular telephone line.

4. Junk mail also is called _____.

5. A(n) _____ is an attempt to deceive an audience into believing that something false is real.

6. To subscribe to a podcast requires that you use a software program called a _____.

7. The media that carries or transports the message is called the _____.

8. File sharing generally requires a(n) _____ model where files stored on a personal computer are accessible to other users.

9. In an academic setting, copying information from an Internet resource claiming it as your own is called _____.

10. When someone works from home, it is called _____.

PROJECTS

PROJECT 3–1

1. Start your Web browser and create a Favorites folder. Give the folder a name of your choice, such as *Project 1 Sites*.

2. Use a search engine of your choice to find information on the following topics:
   - Popular Web browsers
   - Viruses
   - Protecting online privacy

3. Save the most informative Web site addresses to your Favorites folder.

4. Write a paragraph describing what you found on each of the topics.

5. Save the document with a filename of your choice, and then print the documents if instructed to do so. Close all open files.

PROJECT 3–2

Technology has changed considerably the way in which instruction is delivered in the classroom. Complete the following:

1. Use the Internet and other sources to research how technology will continue to change education and how the classroom of the future will be different.

2. Prepare a report identifying and describing at least two new educational technologies that will affect education in the future.

PROJECT 3–3

1. Go to one of the Web sites you found in Project 3–1.

2. Evaluate the Web site using the form in Figure 28–14 from Lesson 28.

3. Prepare a one-page report on the design and quality of content you found at this site. Be sure to address all the criteria listed in Figure 28–14.

SIMULATION

JOB 3–1

The human resources manager at your company has asked you to help her create a training presentation for employees about responsible computer use. The presentation should cover topics such as computer security, Internet use, and proper disposal of printouts and storage media that are no longer needed. She wants you to provide information on the following:

- Backing up data
- Using passwords to access company computers
- The company's policy on employee use of the Internet
- Appropriate ways to safely dispose of discarded paper, used CDs, and other computer waste

Search the Web for examples of employee handbooks to see how other companies address these issues. Or, interview the human resource managers of some local companies and ask them about their policies on these issues. Then create a slide presentation that explains your company's policies, how the policies can be followed effectively by employees, and any consequences that can result from failing to follow the policies.

JOB 3–2

You have noticed that many students in your computer classes are having difficulty selecting appropriate electronic resources for their term papers and citing the selected sources. They are spending hours surfing the Internet to locate legitimate information. As a result, you have asked your instructor if you could develop and give a presentation on the criteria for evaluating electronic resources. Use the information in this module and other sources to develop a five- to six-slide presentation.

APPENDIX A

A Comprehensive Guide to IC³

IC³ - MODULE 1: COMPUTING FUNDAMENTALS 2009 STANDARD

STANDARDIZED CODING NUMBER	OBJECTIVES & ABBREVIATED SKILL SETS	PAGE
OBJECTIVE 1.1	**Identify types of computers, how they process information, and the purpose and function of different hardware components**	
IC³-1 1.1.1	Identify different types of computer devices	Mod1-6, Mod1-7
IC³-1 1.1.2	Identify the role of the central processing unit (CPU) including how the speed of a microprocessor is measured	Mod1-9
IC³-1 1.1.3	Identify concepts related to computer memory (measurement of memory, RAM, ROM)	Mod1-10
IC³-1 1.1.4	Identify the features and benefits (storage capacity, shelf-life, etc.) of different storage media	Mod1-17
IC³-1 1.1.5	Identify the types and purposes of standard input and output devices on desktop or laptop computers	Mod1-28, Mod1-32
IC³-1 1.1.6	Identify the types and purposes of specialized input devices (e.g. cameras, scanners, game controllers, etc.)	Mod1-36
IC³-1 1.1.7	Identify the types and purposes of specialized output devices (e.g. printers, projectors, etc.)	Mod1-41
IC³-1 1.1.8	Identify how hardware devices are connected to and installed on a computer system	Mod1-42
IC³-1 1.1.9	Identify factors that affect computer performance	Mod1-45

STANDARDIZED CODING NUMBER	OBJECTIVES & ABBREVIATED SKILL SETS	PAGE
OBJECTIVE 1.2	**Identify how to maintain computer equipment and solve common problems relating to computer hardware**	
IC³-1 1.2.1	Identify the importance of protecting computer hardware from theft or damage	Mod1-54
IC³-1 1.2.2	Identify factors that can cause damage to computer hardware or media (e.g. environmental factors, magnetic fields, etc.)	Mod1-56
IC³-1 1.2.3	Identify how to protect computer hardware from fluctuations in the power supply, power outages, and other electrical issues (such as use of computers on different electrical systems)	Mod1-57
IC³-1 1.2.4	Identify common problems associated with computer hardware	Mod1-58
IC³-1 1.2.5	Identify problems that can occur if hardware is not maintained properly	Mod1-68
IC³-1 1.2.6	Identify maintenance that can be performed routinely by users	Mod1-69
IC³-1 1.2.7	Identify maintenance that should ONLY be performed by experienced professionals, including replacing or upgrading internal hardware (especially electrical) components (such as processors or drives) that are not designed to be user accessible	Mod1-84
IC³-1 1.2.8	Identify the steps required to solve computer-related problems	Mod1-90
IC³-1 1.2.9	Identify consumer issues related to buying, maintaining, and repairing a computer including: ■ Factors that go into an individual or organizational decision on how to purchase computer equipment ■ Factors relating to maintenance and repair responsibilities	Mod1-98
OBJECTIVE 2.1	**Identify how software and hardware work together to perform computing tasks and how software is developed and upgraded**	
IC³-1 2.1.1	Identify how hardware and software interact	Mod1-106
IC³-1 2.1.2	Identify the difference between an operating system and application software	Mod1-110
IC³-1 2.1.3	Identify issues relating to software distribution (e.g. licenses, upgrades)	Mod1-114

STANDARDIZED CODING NUMBER	OBJECTIVES & ABBREVIATED SKILL SETS	PAGE
OBJECTIVE 2.2	**Identify different types of application software and general concept relating to application software categories**	
IC³-1 2.2.1	Identify fundamental concepts relating to word processing and common uses for word-processing applications (e.g. reviewing, editing, formatting, etc.)	Mod1-124
IC³-1 2.2.2	Identify fundamental concepts relating to spreadsheets and common uses for spreadsheet applications (e.g. worksheets, data sorting, formulas, and functions, etc.)	Mod1-127
IC³-1 2.2.3	Identify fundamental concepts relating to presentation software and common uses for presentation applications (e.g. slides, speaker notes, graphics, etc.)	Mod1-130
IC³-1 2.2.4	Identify fundamental concepts relating to databases and common uses for database applications (e.g. fields, tables, queries, reports, etc.)	Mod1-134
IC³-1 2.2.5	Identify fundamental concepts relating to graphic and multi-media programs and common uses for graphic or multimedia software (e.g. drawing, painting, animation tools, etc.)	Mod1-138
IC³-1 2.2.6	Identify fundamental concepts relating to education and entertainment programs (e.g. computer based training (CBT), video, audio, etc.)	Mod1-140
IC³-1 2.2.7	Identify the types and purposes of different utility programs (e.g. virus, adware, and spyware detection programs, etc.)	Mod1-140
IC³-1 2.2.8	Identify other types of software (e.g. chat, messaging, Web conferencing, accounting software, etc.)	Mod1-140
IC³-1 2.2.9	Identify how to select the appropriate application(s) for a particular purpose, and problems that can arise if the wrong software product is used for a particular purpose	Mod1-141
IC³-1 2.2.10	Identify how applications interact and share data	Mod1-141

STANDARDIZED CODING NUMBER	OBJECTIVES & ABBREVIATED SKILL SETS	PAGE
OBJECTIVE 3.1	**Identify what an operating system is and how it works, and solve common problems related to operating systems**	
IC³-1 **3.1.1**	Identify the purpose of an operating system and the difference between operating system and application software	Mod1-146
IC³-1 **3.1.2**	Identify different operating systems (e.g. Windows, Macintosh OS, Linux, etc.)	Mod1-146
IC³-1 **3.1.3**	Identify that a computer user may interact with multiple operating systems while performing everyday tasks	Mod1-151
IC³-1 **3.1.4**	Identify the capabilities and limitations imposed by the operating system including levels of user rights (administrative rights, etc.), which determine what a user can and cannot do (install software, download files, change system settings, etc.)	Mod1-152
IC³-1 **3.1.5**	Identify and solve common problems related to operating systems	Mod1-154
OBJECTIVE 3.2	**Use an operating system to manipulate a computer's desktop, files, and disks**	
IC³-1 **3.2.1**	Shut down, restart, log on, and log off the computer	Mod1-164
IC³-1 **3.2.2**	Identify elements of the operating system desktop	Mod1-167
IC³-1 **3.2.3**	Manipulate windows (e.g. minimize, maximize, resize)	Mod1-170
IC³-1 **3.2.4**	Start and run programs	Mod1-171
IC³-1 **3.2.5**	Manipulate desktop folders and icons/shortcuts	Mod1-172
IC³-1 **3.2.6**	Manage files (e.g. identifying files, folders, directories, moving and retrieving files, display file properties, etc.)	Mod1-173
IC³-1 **3.2.7**	Identify precautions one should take when manipulating files including using standardized naming conventions	Mod1-180
IC³-1 **3.2.8**	Solve common problems associated with working with files (e.g. incompatibility of application programs, corruption of files, denied access, etc.)	Mod1-182
OBJECTIVE 3.3	**Identify how to change system settings, install and remove software**	
IC³-1 **3.3.1**	Display control panels/system preferences	Mod1-188
IC³-1 **3.3.2**	Identify different control panel/system preference settings	Mod1-196
IC³-1 **3.3.3**	Change simple settings (e.g. date and time, audio, security, etc.)	Mod1-196
IC³-1 **3.3.4**	Display and update a list of installed printers	Mod1-202
IC³-1 **3.3.5**	Identify precautions regarding changing system settings	Mod1-204
IC³-1 **3.3.6**	Install and uninstall software including installing updates from online sources	Mod1-205
IC³-1 **3.3.7**	Identify and troubleshoot common problems associated with installing and running applications	Mod1-210

IC³ - MODULE 2: KEY APPLICATIONS 2009 STANDARD

STANDARDIZED CODING NUMBER	OBJECTIVES & ABBREVIATED SKILL SETS	PAGE
OBJECTIVE 1.1	**Be able to start and exit an application, identify and modify interface elements, and use sources of online help**	
IC³-2 1.1.1	Start and exit a Windows style application	Mod2-4, Mod2-12, Mod2-172
IC³-2 1.1.2	Identify on-screen elements common to applications (e.g., toolbars, Ribbon, document windows)	Mod2-6, Mod2-8, Mod2-172, Mod2-173, Mod2-250
IC³-2 1.1.3	Navigate around open files using scroll bars, keyboard shortcuts, and Go To command	Mod2-6, Mod2-8, Mod2-39, Mod2-173, Mod2-251
IC³-2 1.1.4	Display and use onscreen command buttons	Mod2-8, Mod2-13, Mod2-173
IC³-2 1.1.5	Change views	Mod2-32, Mod2-176, Mod2-254
IC³-2 1.1.6	Change magnification level	Mod2-32, Mod2-176
IC³-2 1.1.7	Display options for changing application defaults (e.g., where files are stored, print and AutoSave options)	Mod2-13, Mod2-29, Mod2-50
IC³-2 1.1.8	Identify and prioritize help resources, including online help, printed documentation, and external help resources	Mod2-21
IC³-2 1.1.9	Use automated help, including navigating help resources and employing logical search strategies	Mod2-21

STANDARDIZED CODING NUMBER	OBJECTIVES & ABBREVIATED SKILL SETS	PAGE
OBJECTIVE 1.2	**Perform common file-management functions**	
IC^3-2　1.2.1	Create files	Mod2-28, Mod2-160, Mod2-257
IC^3-2　1.2.2	Open files within an application and from the desktop, identify extensions associated with applications	Mod2-13, Mod2-250
IC^3-2　1.2.3	Switch between open documents	Mod2-4, Mod2-13
IC^3-2　1.2.4	Save files in specified locations/formats	Mod2-13, Mod2-29, Mod2-173, Mod2-250
IC^3-2　1.2.5	Close files	Mod2-12, Mod2-176, Mod2-256
IC^3-2　1.2.6	Identify and solve common problems relating to working with files (e.g., product or version incompatibility, AutoSave recovery options)	Mod2-13
OBJECTIVE 1.3	**Perform common editing and formatting functions**	
IC^3-2　1.3.1	Insert text and numbers into a file	Mod2-30, Mod2-37, Mod2-177
IC^3-2　1.3.2	Perform simple editing (e.g., select, cut, copy, paste, and move information)	Mod2-50, Mod2-177, Mod2-184, Mod2-227, Mod2-234, Mod2-256
IC^3-2　1.3.3	Use the Undo, Redo, and Repeat commands	Mod2-50, Mod2-184, Mod2-263
IC^3-2　1.3.4	Find and/or Find and Replace information	Mod2-63
IC^3-2　1.3.5	Check spelling	Mod2-50, Mod2-257
IC^3-2　1.3.6	Perform simple text formatting, including using Format Painter	Mod2-63
IC^3-2　1.3.7	Insert pictures and other objects into a file, including clip art, drawn objects, text art, and images created in another application	Mod2-148, Mod2-238, Mod2-274, Mod2-291

STANDARDIZED CODING NUMBER	OBJECTIVES & ABBREVIATED SKILL SETS	PAGE
OBJECTIVE 1.4	**Perform common printing/outputting functions**	
IC³-2 1.4.1	Format a document for printing	Mod2-63, Mod2-96
IC³-2 1.4.2	Preview a file before printing	Mod2-63
IC³-2 1.4.3	Print files, specifying common print options	Mod2-96
IC³-2 1.4.4	Manage printing and print jobs	Mod2-96
IC³-2 1.4.5	Identify and solve common problems associated with printing (e.g., printer, connection, print setting issues)	Mod2-96
IC³-2 1.4.6	Output documents in electronic format, including PDF, fax, e-mail attachment, and Web content	Mod2-99
IC³-2 1.4.7	Identify issues related to outputting files in electronic format	Mod2-99
OBJECTIVE 2.1	**Be able to format text and documents, including the ability to use automatic formatting tools**	
IC³-2 2.1.1	Change spacing options	Mod2-63
IC³-2 2.1.2	Indent text	Mod2-63
IC³-2 2.1.3	Display the ruler	Mod2-63, Mod2-117
IC³-2 2.1.4	Use tabs	Mod2-63
IC³-2 2.1.5	Insert and delete a page break or section break	Mod2-63, Mod2-134
IC³-2 2.1.6	Display non-printing characters and identify on-screen formatting information, including breaks and paragraph, tab, and indent markers	Mod2-36, Mod2-37
IC³-2 2.1.7	Create and modify single- and multi-level bulleted and numbered lists	Mod2-63
IC³-2 2.1.8	Insert symbols/special characters	Mod2-143
IC³-2 2.1.9	Insert, modify, and format page numbers	Mod2-138
IC³-2 2.1.10	Create, modify, and format headers and footers	Mod2-138
IC³-2 2.1.11	Create, modify, and apply styles	Mod2-160
IC³-2 2.1.12	Create and modify columns	Mod2-134

STANDARDIZED CODING NUMBER	OBJECTIVES & ABBREVIATED SKILL SETS	PAGE
IC^3-2 2.1.13	Work with tables, including creating, inserting, and editing data in a table	Mod2-110, Mod2-117, Mod2-119, Mod2-127
IC^3-2 2.1.14	Modify table structure	Mod2-111, Mod2-119
IC^3-2 2.1.15	Format tables, including sorting data	Mod2-119, Mod2-126
IC^3-2 2.1.16	Identify common uses for word processing, and identify elements of a well-organized document	Mod2-63, Mod2-134, Mod2-138, Mod2-160
OBJECTIVE 2.2	Be able to use word-processing tools to automate processes such as document review, security, and collaboration	
IC^3-2 2.2.1	Use language tools	Mod2-50
IC^3-2 2.2.2	Insert and modify data elements into a document, including footnotes and endnotes	Mod2-143
IC^3-2 2.2.3	Use tools that support collaborative creation and editing of documents	Mod2-84
IC^3-2 2.2.4	Protect a document from unauthorized viewing or modification	Mod2-93
OBJECTIVE 3.1	Be able to modify worksheet data and structure and format data in a worksheet	
IC^3-2 3.1.1	Identify how a table of data is organized in a spreadsheet	Mod2-172, Mod2-196, Mod2-234
IC^3-2 3.1.2	Identify the structure of a well-organized, useful worksheet	Mod2-196, Mod2-224
IC^3-2 3.1.3	Insert and modify data	Mod2-177, Mod2-184, Mod2-202
IC^3-2 3.1.4	Modify table structure	Mod2-180, Mod2-196, Mod2-202

STANDARDIZED CODING NUMBER	OBJECTIVES & ABBREVIATED SKILL SETS	PAGE
IC³-2 3.1.5	Identify and change number formats, including Number, Currency, Date and Time, Percentage, and number of decimal places	Mod2-202
IC³-2 3.1.6	Apply borders and shading to cells	Mod2-202
IC³-2 3.1.7	Specify cell alignment	Mod2-202
IC³-2 3.1.8	Apply table AutoFormats	Mod2-202
IC³-2 3.1.9	Specify worksheet/workbook-specific print options, including page breaks, print area, repeating rows and columns, and headers and footers	Mod2-212, Mod2-215
IC³-2 3.1.10	Identify common uses of spreadsheets, as well as elements of a well-organized, well-formatted spreadsheet	Mod2-196, Mod2-202
OBJECTIVE 3.2	**Be able to sort data, manipulate data using formulas and functions, and create simple charts**	
IC³-2 3.2.1	Sort worksheet data	Mod2-210
IC³-2 3.2.2	Filter data	Mod2-210
IC³-2 3.2.3	Demonstrate an understanding of absolute vs. relative cell references	Mod2-227
IC³-2 3.2.4	Insert arithmetic formulas into worksheet cells	Mod2-224, Mod2-227
IC³-2 3.2.5	Demonstrate how to use common worksheet functions (e.g., SUM, AVERAGE, MIN, MAX, COUNT)	Mod2-228
IC³-2 3.2.6	Use AutoSum	Mod2-228
IC³-2 3.2.7	Insert and modify formulas and functions	Mod2-224, Mod2-228
IC³-2 3.2.8	Identify common errors people make when using formulas and functions	Mod2-224, Mod2-236
IC³-2 3.2.9	Insert and modify simple charts in a worksheet	Mod2-238
IC³-2 3.2.10	Draw conclusions based on tabular data or charts in a worksheet	Mod2-243

STANDARDIZED CODING NUMBER	OBJECTIVES & ABBREVIATED SKILL SETS	PAGE
OBJECTIVE 4.1	**Be able to create and format simple presentations**	
IC³-2 4.1.1	Manage slides	Mod2-256
IC³-2 4.1.2	Add information to a slide	Mod2-257, Mod2-260, Mod2-263, Mod2-274, Mod2-282, Mod2-286, Mod2-291
IC³-2 4.1.3	Change slide view	Mod2-254, Mod2-256, Mod2-257, Mod2-265
IC³-2 4.1.4	Change slide layout	Mod2-263
IC³-2 4.1.5	Modify a slide background	Mod2-260
IC³-2 4.1.6	Assign transitions to slides	Mod2-284
IC³-2 4.1.7	Change the order of slides in a presentation	Mod2-256
IC³-2 4.1.8	Identify different ways presentations are distributed (e.g., printed, projected to an audience, distributed over networks or the Internet)	Mod2-293
IC³-2 4.1.9	Create different output elements (e.g., speaker's notes, handouts, Web page)	Mod2-257, Mod2-293
IC³-2 4.1.10	Preview the slide show presentation	Mod2-267
IC³-2 4.1.11	Navigate an on-screen slide show	Mod2-267, Mod2-282
IC³-2 4.1.12	Identify common uses of presentation software as well as effective design principles for simple presentations	Mod2-250, Mod2-257, Mod2-260, Mod2-263, Mod2-265, Mod2-274

IC³ - MODULE 3: LIVING ONLINE 2009 STANDARD

STANDARDIZED CODING NUMBER	OBJECTIVES & ABBREVIATED SKILL SETS	PAGE
OBJECTIVE 1.1	**Identify network fundamentals and the benefits and risks of network computing**	
IC³-3 1.1.1	Identify that networks (including computer networks and other networks such as the telephone network) transmit different types of data	Mod3-4
IC³-3 1.1.2	Identify benefits of networked computing	Mod3-5
IC³-3 1.1.3	Identify the risks of networked computing	Mod3-6
IC³-3 1.1.4	Identify the roles of clients and servers in a network	Mod3-8
IC³-3 1.1.5	Identify networks by size and type	Mod3-8
IC³-3 1.1.6	Identify concepts related to network communication (e.g. high speed, broadband, wireless (wifi), etc.)	Mod3-12
IC³-3 1.1.7	Identify fundamental principles of security on a network including authorization, authentication, and wireless security issues	Mod3-14
OBJECTIVE 2.1	**Identify different types of electronic communication/collaboration and how they work**	
IC³-3 2.1.1	Identify the different methods of electronic communication/ collaboration and the advantages and disadvantages of each (e.g. e-mail, instant messaging, blogging, social networking, etc.)	Mod3-22
IC³-3 2.1.2	Identify how unique users are identified with communication services such as instant mail, text messaging, online conferencing, and social network sites	Mod3-22
IC³-3 2.1.3	Identify how communication tools such as electronic mail or instant messaging are accessed and used	Mod3-23
OBJECTIVE 2.2	**Identify how to use an electronic mail application**	
IC³-3 2.2.1	Identify how electronic mail identifies a unique e-mail user by e-mail address	Mod3-23
IC³-3 2.2.2	Identify the components of an electronic mail message or instant message	Mod3-24
IC³-3 2.2.3	Identify when to use different electronic mail options	Mod3-24
IC³-3 2.2.4	Read and send electronic mail messages	Mod3-29, Mod3-30, Mod3-33, Mod3-34
IC³-3 2.2.5	Identify ways to supplement a mail message with additional information	Mod3-29, Mod3-34

STANDARDIZED CODING NUMBER	OBJECTIVES & ABBREVIATED SKILL SETS	PAGE
IC³-3 2.2.6	Manage attachments	Mod3-29, Mod3-34, Mod3-37
IC³-3 2.2.7	Manage mail	Mod3-25, Mod3-33
IC³-3 2.2.8	Manage addresses	Mod3-29
IC³-3 2.2.9	Identify the purpose of frequently used mail-configuration options (e.g. automatic signatures, out-of-office assistance, blocking messages, etc.)	Mod3-41
OBJECTIVE 2.3	**Identify the appropriate use of different types of communication/collaboration tools and the "rules of the road" regarding online communication ("netiquette")**	
IC³-3 2.3.1	Identify appropriate uses for different communication methods (e.g. e-mail, instant messaging, teleconference, and syndication)	Mod3-46
IC³-3 2.3.2	Identify the advantages of electronic communication	Mod3-47
IC³-3 2.3.3	Identify common problems associated with electronic communication (e.g. delivery failure, junk mail, fraud, hoaxes, viruses, etc.)	Mod3-50
IC³-3 2.3.4	Identify the elements of professional and effective electronic communications (e.g. timely responses, correct spelling and grammar, appropriate level of formality, etc.)	Mod3-65
IC³-3 2.3.5	Identify appropriate use of e-mail attachments and other supplementary information (e.g. large attachments, embedding a URL, security issues, etc.)	Mod3-66
IC³-3 2.3.6	Identify issues regarding unsolicited e-mail ("spam") and how to minimize or control unsolicited mail	Mod3-68
IC³-3 2.3.7	Identify effective procedures for ensuring the safe and effective use of electronic communication including "netiquette", understanding school or company policies, and following guidelines	Mod3-68
OBJECTIVE 3.1	**Identify information about the Internet, the World Wide Web, and Web sites, and be able to use a Web browsing application**	
IC³-3 3.1.1	Understand the difference between the Internet (a worldwide network of computers) and the World Wide Web (a set of linked pages containing information and applications that uses the Internet to facilitate online communications)	Mod3-74
IC³-3 3.1.2	Identify terminology related to the Internet and the World Wide Web (e.g. domain, home page, HTML, URL, wiki, etc.)	Mod3-75
IC³-3 3.1.3	Identify different items on a Web page (e.g. text, graphic objects, hyperlinked text, etc.)	Mod3-81
IC³-3 3.1.4	Identify different types of Web sites and the purposes of different types of sites (e.g. government sites, secure vs. unsecure sites, search sites, etc.)	Mod3-82

STANDARDIZED CODING NUMBER	OBJECTIVES & ABBREVIATED SKILL SETS	PAGE
IC³-3 3.1.5	Navigate the Web using a browser (e.g. opening a new browser or tab, going to a Web site's home page, etc.)	Mod3-85
IC³-3 3.1.6	Reload/refresh the view of a Web page	Mod3-91
IC³-3 3.1.7	Show a history of recently visited Web sites, navigate to a previously visited site, and delete history of visited sites	Mod3-92
IC³-3 3.1.8	Find specific information on a Web site	Mod3-93
IC³-3 3.1.9	Manage Bookmarked sites/Favorite sites	Mod3-94
IC³-3 3.1.10	Copy appropriate elements from a Web site to another application (such as copying text or media to a word processing document or presentation or copying data to a spreadsheet)	Mod3-100
IC³-3 3.1.11	Download a file from a Web site to a specified location	Mod3-97
IC³-3 3.1.12	Print information from a Web site or Web page	Mod3-100
IC³-3 3.1.13	Identify settings that can be modified in a Web browser application	Mod3-102
IC³-3 3.1.14	Identify problems associated with using the Web (e.g. "Page Not Found" errors, pop-up ads, etc.)	Mod3-104
OBJECTIVE 3.2	Understand how content is created, located, and evaluated on the World Wide Web	
IC³-3 3.2.1	Identify ways content is created on the Internet (e.g. blogs, wikis, podcasts, social networking sites, etc.)	Mod3-110
IC³-3 3.2.2	Identify ways of searching for information	Mod3-114
IC³-3 3.2.3	Use a search engine to search for information (e.g. using effective key words, using advanced search tools, etc.)	Mod3-116
IC³-3 3.2.4	Identify issues regarding the quality of information found on the Internet including relevance, reliability, and validity	Mod3-121
IC³-3 3.2.5	Identify how to evaluate the quality of information found on the Web	Mod3-121
IC³-3 3.2.6	Identify responsible and ethical behaviors when creating or using online content (e.g. copyright, trademark, avoiding plagiarism, etc.)	Mod3-123

STANDARDIZED CODING NUMBER	OBJECTIVES & ABBREVIATED SKILL SETS	PAGE
OBJECTIVE 4.1	**Identify how computers are used in different areas of work, school, and home**	
IC³-3 4.1.1	Identify how information technology and the Internet are used at work, home, or school to collect, analyze, evaluate, and create communities, etc.	Mod3-130
IC³-3 4.1.2	Identify that traditional desktop and laptop computers represent only a fraction of the computer technology people interact with on a regular basis (e.g. ATMs, embedded computer devices in household appliances, GPS, etc.)	Mod3-134
IC³-3 4.1.3	Identify how computers and the Internet have transformed traditional processes (e.g. e-commerce, telecommuting, online learning, etc.)	Mod3-139
IC³-3 4.1.4	Identify technologies that support or provide opportunities to the physically challenged and disadvantaged (e.g. voice recognized software, electronic government, etc.)	Mod3-144
OBJECTIVE 4.2	**Identify the risks of using computer hardware and software, and how to use computers and the Internet safely, ethically, and legally**	
IC³-3 4.2.1	Identify how to maintain a safe working environment that complies with legal, health, and safety rules	Mod3-152
IC³-3 4.2.2	Identify injuries that can result from the use of computers for long periods of time (e.g. back strain, eye strain, etc.)	Mod3-152
IC³-3 4.2.3	Identify risks to personal and organizational data (e.g. theft, data loss, etc.)	Mod3-153
IC³-3 4.2.4	Identify software threats, including viruses and WORMS	Mod3-155
IC³-3 4.2.5	Identify reasons for restricting access to files, storage devices, computers, networks, the Internet or certain Internet sites including protection of data and restricting sites to children with adult content	Mod3-158
IC³-3 4.2.6	Identify the principles regarding when information can or cannot be considered personal, including the difference between computer systems owned by schools or businesses that may have rules and guidelines as to who owns data stored on the system, and computers owned by individuals where the owner of the computer has control over his or her own data	Mod3-158
IC³-3 4.2.7	Identify how to avoid hazards regarding electronic commerce (e.g. sharing credit card information on non-secure sites, checking the legitimacy of online offers, etc.)	Mod3-158
IC³-3 4.2.8	Identify how to protect privacy and personal security online (to avoid fraud, identity theft, and other hazards)	Mod3-160

STANDARDIZED CODING NUMBER	OBJECTIVES & ABBREVIATED SKILL SETS	PAGE
IC³-3 4.2.9	Identify how to find information about rules regarding the use of computers and the Internet	Mod3-162
IC³-3 4.2.10	Identify how to stay informed about changes and advancements in technology	Mod3-163
IC³-3 4.2.11	Identify how to be a responsible user of computers (e.g. recycling products like printer cartridges, safely disposing of hardware, etc.)	Mod3-163

GLOSSARY

A

absolute cell reference   A reference that does not change when the formula is copied or moved to a new location.

active cell   A selected cell in an Excel worksheet.

active window   The window currently in use. The title bar of the active window is always darker (or displayed in a different color) to distinguish it from other open windows that may be visible in a tiled or cascaded screen.

ActiveX   A set of rules developed by Microsoft for Windows that controls Windows applications that are downloaded from the Internet and then run in a browser.

Address bar   The space in some application windows that displays the name of the open folder or object.

Address Book   Part of most e-mail programs; used to keep a list of contacts and their e-mail addresses.

administrative rights   Permission to make changes on a computer system.

administrator account   A collection of information that determines which files you can access and which settings you use.

algorithm   A set of clearly defined, logical steps that solve a problem.

alignment   How text is positioned between the left and right margins.

American Standard Code for Information Interchange (ASCII)   Coding system that computers of all types and brands can translate.

animation   Special visuals or sound effects added to text or an object.

Appearance and Personalization category   Control Panel tools that provide options to personalize the desktop by selecting a new color scheme, changing the background, and adjusting the screen resolution.

application file   A file that is part of an application program, such as a word-processing program, a graphics program, and so on.

application file icons   Icons that start an application, such as a word processor or spreadsheet program.

application software   Also called productivity software; helps you perform a specific task such as word processing, spreadsheets, and so forth.

application window   The main window that serves as the primary interface between the user and the application.

archive   To save or transfer data to a storage device or folder for the purpose of saving space or organizing the data.

argument   A value, a cell reference, a range, or text that acts as an operand in a function formula; it is enclosed in parentheses after the function name.

arithmetic/logic unit (ALU)   The part of the central processing unit that performs arithmetic computations and logical operations.

artificial intelligence   Type of software that can process information on its own without human intervention.

ascending order   Alphabetical order from A to Z, or numerical order from lowest number to highest number.

attachment   A document, image, figure, or other file that you can attach to an e-mail message.

attributes   Style characteristics applied to text such as bold, italic, and underline.

audio input   The process of inputting sound into the computer.

AutoShape   A predesigned drawing object, such as a star, an arrow, or a rectangle.

B

background   A pattern or picture that can be used on the desktop.

backup   Procedures that place a priority on files that would be difficult or impossible to replace or reconstruct if they were lost, such as a company's financial statements, important projects, and works in progress.

banner   A full-width headline that spans multiple newsletter-style columns, such as the title for a newsletter or report.

beta testing A process that releases commercial software in development to a cross-section of typical users who evaluate the program and report any problems or "bugs" in the software before it is released to the public.

biometrics A technique or device that examines a fingerprint, voice pattern, or the iris or retina of the eye.

bit In binary, a bit represents a zero or one.

bitmapped graphics Images created with a matrix of picture elements (pixels).

blog An abbreviated version of the term "Web log"; a journal maintained by an individual or a group and posted on a Web site for public viewing and comment.

boilerplate text A common document part that you frequently use in documents.

Boolean logic Way to search databases; consists of three logical operators—AND, NOT, OR.

boot The process of starting a computer.

bot Type of robot used by search engines on the Internet.

bridge A special computer that connects one local area network to another.

browser Software program used to retrieve documents from the World Wide Web (WWW or Web) and to display them in a readable format.

browser hijacking A program or practice that takes control of your browser without your knowledge.

brute force attack An attack that uses a script or program to log on to an account using hundreds of words or phrases stored in a dictionary file. Also called a *dictionary attack*.

building blocks Document parts that are already designed and formatted, enabling you to create a professional-looking document quickly.

bundleware Software included with the purchase of a new computer.

business-to-business (B2B) E-commerce transactions between businesses, such as between a company and a supplier.

business-to-consumer (B2C) E-commerce transactions between businesses and consumers.

business-to-government (B2G) Online transactions between businesses and governmental agencies.

byte A byte is another word for character; generally represented by eight bits.

C

cable management A technique or kit that gathers cables together and stores them so they are not a hazard.

cable modem A device that uses coaxial cable to send and receive data.

cache A storage location on a computer's hard disk used to temporarily store Internet files.

CD-ROM Disk that can store up to 680 MB of data; data can only be read from it.

cell One intersection of a row and a column in a table.

cell reference Identifies the column letter and row number in a worksheet (for example, A1 or B4).

cell style A set of predefined formats you can apply to some of the worksheet data.

central processing unit (CPU) Also known as the microprocessor; the brains of the computer.

channel Media, such as telephone wire, coaxial cable, microwave signal, or fiber-optic cable, that carry or transport data communication messages.

chart A graphic representation of worksheet or table data.

circuit board A thin plate or board that contains electronic components.

clicking Pressing and releasing the left (primary) mouse button.

client A computer that uses the services of another program.

client/server network Computer configuration in which one or more computers on the network acts as a server.

clip art A drawing that is ready to insert in a document.

Clip Organizer A wide variety of pictures, photographs, sounds, and video clips that you can insert in your document.

Clipboard A temporary storage place in your computer's memory that is shared among all the Office applications.

Clock, Language, and Region category Control Panel tools to change the language your system uses or the date, time, or time zone.

command buttons Rectangular buttons in a dialog box that execute an instruction. An ellipsis following a command button name (i.e., Browse…) indicates that another dialog box will appear if this command is chosen.

commands Instructions to perform an operation or execute a program. In Windows, commands can be issued by making menu selections, clicking on a toolbar button, or clicking on a command button in a dialog box.

comment An electronic note that the author or a reviewer adds to a document; it is not part of the text but is viewable in the margin or in a separate pane.

communication channel Link from one computer to another through which data can be transmitted.

complex formulas   Excel formulas containing more than one operator.

computer   Electronic device that receives, processes, and stores data and produces a result.

computer-based learning   Using the computer for learning and instruction.

computer crime   Criminal act committed through the use of a computer, such as getting into someone else's system and changing information or creating a computer virus and causing damage to others' information.

computer fraud   Manipulation of a computer or computer data to obtain money, property, or value dishonestly or to cause loss.

computer system   Hardware, software, and data working together.

Computer window   A utility program designed to help you find, view, and manage files easily and effectively.

contacts   Persons with whom you communicate.

Control Panel   A program accessed from the Windows Start menu that provides specialized features used to change the way Windows looks and behaves.

control unit   The part of the central processing unit that controls the flow of information through the processor.

controller   Device that controls the transfer of data from the computer to a peripheral device and vice versa.

cookies   Small text files created by some Web pages when you visit the site that may include information about your preferences for the Web page; cookie files are stored on your computer.

copy   To duplicate a selection, file, folder, and so forth so that you can place it in another position or location.

copyright   The exclusive right, granted by law for a certain number of years, to make and dispose of literary, musical, or artistic work.

corona wire   Wire used to generate a field of positive charges on the surface of the drum and the paper.

critical thinking   The process of evaluating propositions or hypotheses and making judgments.

crop   To cut off portions of a graphic that you do not want to show.

currency   On a Web page, this refers to the age of the information, how long it has been posted, and how often it is updated.

D

data   Information entered into the computer to be processed that consists of text, numbers, sounds, and images.

data communications   Transmission of text, numeric, voice, or video data from one machine to another.

data file   A file you create when working with an application program.

data theft   Removing data from a computer without authorization.

data type   A field property in Access that determines the type of data a database field can store.

database   A collection of related information organized for rapid search and retrieval.

database software   Software that makes it possible to create and maintain large collections of data.

datasheet   A database table that stores subject-based data; a primary object in a database.

Datasheet view   A view in Access that displays the table data in columns and rows.

default   (1) A setting that is automatically used unless another option is chosen. (2) In any given set of choices, the choice that is preselected, the selection that is in effect when you open a program, or the settings established during the installation process.

defragmentation   A utility that reduces the amount of fragmentation by physically organizing the contents of the disk to store the pieces of each file contiguously.

descending order   Alphabetical order from Z to A, or numerical order from highest number to lowest number.

Design view   A view in Access that displays the field names and what kind of values you can enter in each field; used to define or modify the field formats.

desktop   The first screen you see when the operating system is up and fully running. It is called the desktop because the icons are intended to represent real objects on a real desktop.

desktop publishing   The process of creating a document using a computer to lay out text and graphics.

desktop shortcuts   Icons you can create and place on the desktop to represent an application, folder, or file. When you click the shortcut icon, the application, folder, or file opens immediately.

desktop theme   A set of predefined elements, such as icons, fonts, colors, and sounds, that determine the look of your desktop.

destination   When copying or moving a file, the location (disk and/or folder) where the copied or moved file will reside.

dialog box   An information-exchange window in which the user selects options, sets defaults, chooses items from lists, or otherwise provides information Windows needs before it can execute a command.

dialog box launcher   A small arrow in the lower-right corner of a group on the Ribbon; when clicked, it opens a dialog box with additional options and commands.

digital camera   A camera that takes and stores photographs as digital files.

digital cash   Allows someone to pay by transmitting a number from one computer to another.

digital certificate   An electronic document similar to an ID card.

digital subscriber line (DSL)   An Internet connection technology that provides for the transfer of information to a computer at a high-speed bandwidth over ordinary copper telephone lines.

directory   A container for files and other directories. Windows Vista generally uses the term *folder*, while operating systems such as Linux use the term *directory*.

Disk Cleanup   A program that enables you to clear your disk of unnecessary files.

Disk Defragmenter   A tool that rearranges disk files, storing each file in contiguous blocks.

distance learning   Schooling concept in which students in remote locations receive instruction via telecommunications technology.

distribution list   A list of e-mail address you can use to send the same message to a group.

document   A data file in a software application.

document file icons   Icons that share the same distinctive feature, a piece of paper with a superimposed graphic, that help create a link between a document and an application.

document management server   A central location for storing, managing, and tracking files.

Document window   The area in an application window where you enter new text and data or change existing text and data.

Document workspace   A Windows SharePoint Services Website that provides tools for sharing and updating files.

domain   A name or other attribute that identifies a computer or Web site on the Internet.

domain name   Identifies a site on the Internet.

double-clicking   Pointing to an object and then quickly press and release the primary mouse button twice.

drag-and-drop editing   Using the mouse to drag selected from the existing location and then dropping the selected text in a new location.

dragging   Placing the mouse pointer on an object and then pressing and holding down the primary mouse button while moving the object on the desktop.

Drawing canvas   An area upon which you can draw, arrange, and resize multiple shapes.

drawing objects   Shapes, curves, and lines to create your own graphic.

driver   A small program that instructs the operating system on how to operate specific hardware.

duplex printing   Printing on both sides of the paper.

DVD   Also called Digital Versatile Disk; video output, including full-length movies, can be stored on this medium.

E

Ease and Access category   Control Panel tools to adjust hardware and operating system settings for users with vision, hearing, and mobility disabilities.

edit   Modify or adapt and make revisions or corrections.

electronic commerce (e-commerce)   Business conducted over the Internet.

electronic mail (e-mail)   Transmission of electronic messages over networks.

embedded chart   A chart created on the same sheet as the data used in the chart.

embedded operating system   Similar in principle to operating systems such as Windows or Linux, embedded operating systems are smaller and generally less capable than desktop operating systems.

emoticons   Keyboard symbols used in e-mail and other electronic communication to show emotion, such as :-o to show surprise.

emphasis effects   Settings used to draw attention to an object that is already visible on a slide in a PowerPoint presentation.

emulation card   A card that provides the ability for the computer to run a program that was designed for a different operating system.

encryption   A standard method for encoding data.

endnote   A note that appears at the end of a document and provides the source of borrowed material or explanatory information about specific text.

entrance effects   Settings used to control how an object enters onto a slide in a PowerPoint presentation.

entry   Data entered in a datasheet cell.

ergonomic keyboard   A keyboard that allows for a more natural positioning of your arms and hands.

Execution cycle (E-cycle)   The amount of time it takes the central processing unit to execute an instruction and store the results in RAM.

exit effects   Settings used to control how an object leaves a slide in a PowerPoint presentation.

expansion slot   Opening on the motherboard where an expansion board, also called an *adapter card*, can be inserted.

extranet   A network configuration that allows selected outside organizations to access internal information systems.

F

field   In Access, a single piece of database information, such as a first name, a last name, or a telephone number; in Word, an indication of a location in which variable text or data can be inserted.

field name   A label that helps identify the field.

field properties   Definitions of the characteristics and behavior of a database field.

field selector   A small box or bar that you click to select a column in a table in Datasheet view.

file   A collection of information saved as a unit.

file compatibility   The ability to open and work with files without a format conflict.

file extension   Three or four characters automatically added to the filename when the document is saved; a period separates the filename and the extension, which typically identifies the type of file.

file name   A name assigned to a file for identification.

file properties   Characteristics that help you locate and organize files.

file system   Determines the way an operating system stores files on disk.

File Transfer Protocol (FTP)   Internet standard that allows users to download and upload files with other computers on the Internet.

fill handle   A small square in the lower-right corner of an active cell in a worksheet.

filling   A method for copying data in a worksheet.

filter data   To screen for data matching specified criteria.

filtering   A process that can be used to cut down on or eliminate most junk mail.

firewall   A combination of hardware and software that creates a buffer between an internal network and the Internet to prevent unauthorized access.

FireWire   Also known as IEEE 1394 and IEEE 1394b. The IEEE 1394 bus standard supports data transfer rates of up to 400 Mbps and can connect up to 63 external devices; IEEE 1394b provides speeds up to 3200 Mbps.

first line indent   Only the first line of the paragraph is indented.

flowchart   A diagram that shows different paths a program will take depending on what data is inputted.

folder   A means for organizing files into manageable groups.

font   The design of the typeface.

footer   Information and/or graphics that prints in the bottom margin of each page.

footnote   A note that appears at the bottom of a page and provides the source of borrowed material or explanatory information about specific text on that page.

form   A database object which provides a convenient way to enter, edit, and view data in a table.

Format Painter   A Microsoft Office feature used to quickly copy and apply font and paragraph formatting as well as some basic graphic formatting, such as borders, fills, and shading.

format   To change the appearance of the text or of the whole document.

formula   Equations using numbers and cell references to perform calculations such as addition, subtraction, multiplication, and division.

fragmentation   Files that are not stored in contiguous clusters, but rather are divided into subparts and stored in different disk locations. It takes longer for a disk drive to access fragmented files than unfragmented files.

fraud   Something intended to deceive; deliberate trickery intended to gain an advantage.

freeze   To lock a row or column to keep an area visible as you scroll through the worksheet.

function formula   A special formula that names a function instead of using operators to calculate a formula.

G

gadgets   Small programs such as a clock or calendar.

gateway   A combination of software and hardware that links two types of networks that use different protocols or rules to exchange messages.

geographic imaging   Technology to change imagery of the Earth's surface into valuable information.

graphics   Items other than text, such as digitized photographs, scanned images, and pictures.

graphics software   An application used to create artwork with a computer.

gridlines   Boundary lines in a table used for layout purposes; they show on the screen, but they do not print.

H

hacker   Expert computer user who invades someone else's computer either for personal gain or simply for the satisfaction of being able to do it.

hacking   Invading someone else's computer.

handheld operating system   Operating system for mobile devices.

hanging indent   The first line of text begins at the left margin, and all other lines of the paragraph hang, or are indented, to the right of the first line.

hard column break   A manual column break.

hard copy   A printed copy of a document.

hard disk   A data storage unit inside a computer that can store a large quantity of data (60GB or more), but cannot easily be removed from the computer.

hardware   The tangible, physical equipment that can be seen and touched.

Hardware and Sound category   Control Panel tools to manage hardware devices such as printers, the mouse, and the keyboard.

hardware firewall   A device that controls computers from one point.

header   Information and/or graphics that prints in the top margin of each page.

header row   Column headings or field names at the top of columns in a data source.

hidden file   A file like any other except it is not displayed in a folder window.

hit   Any time a piece of data matches search words you specify.

hoax   An attempt to deceive an audience into believing that something false is real.

home page   First page that is displayed when a browser is launched.

hub   A junction where information arrives from connected computers or peripheral devices and is then forwarded in one or more directions to other computers and devices.

humidity   Moisture in the air that can cause computers to short circuit, resulting in the loss of data and damage to hardware.

hyperlink   Text or graphic in a Web page or other document that a user clicks to jump to another location in the file, another file, or another Web page.

Hypertext markup language (HTML)   Protocol that controls how Web pages are formatted and displayed.

Hypertext transfer protocol (HTTP)   Protocol that defines how messages are formatted and transmitted over the World Wide Web.

I

I-beam   The shape the mouse pointer takes when it is positioned on text in a document.

icons   Graphic images or symbols that represent applications (programs), files, disk drives, documents, embedded objects, or linked objects.

identity theft   The crime of obtaining someone else's personal data and using it for financial gain or to defraud or deceive.

impact printers   Type of printer that uses a mechanism that actually strikes the paper to form characters.

indent   A space inserted between the margin and where the line of text appears.

index   A Web site organized by categories.

information   The output produced by a computer after it processes data.

inkjet printer   A type of printer that uses a nonimpact process. Ink is squirted from nozzles as they pass over the media.

input   Data or instructions, which must be entered into the computer and then stored temporarily or permanently on a storage media device.

input devices   Enable the user to input data and commands into the computer.

inputting   The process of using an input device to enter data.

Insert mode   In this default mode, when you enter new text in front of existing text, the existing text shifts to the right to make room for the new text.

insertion point   A vertical blinking line in the document window that indicates the location in the document where new text and data will be entered.

instant messaging   A form of electronic communication that allows you to send and receive text messages in "real time" from friends and colleagues who are currently online.

Instruction cycle (I-cycle)   The amount of time it takes the central processing unit to retrieve an instruction and complete the command.

Internet   The largest network used as a communication tool.

Internet Explorer   A Web browser used for communication on the Internet.

Internet Protocol (IP) address   A numerical addressing system that uniquely identifies computers and networks linked to the Internet.

Internet service provider (ISP) An organization or company that provides connectivity to the Internet through a telecommunications line or wireless system.

intranet A network designed for the exclusive use of computer users within an organization that cannot be accessed by users outside the organization.

K

keyboard Common input device for entering numeric and alphabetic data into a computer.

keyboard shortcut A combination of two or more keystrokes that, when pressed, carries out a specific action or function.

keyless entry system A system in which to open a lock, you press a button on a remote control device or enter a combination on the keypad.

keylogger A malicious program that records keystrokes.

keywords Words that describe the information the user is trying to locate.

L

landscape orientation Page layout in which the content of the document is formatted with the long edge of the page at the top.

language translators Systems software that converts code written in a programming language into machine language that the computer can understand.

laser printer A printer that produces images using the same technology as copier machines.

linking Feature that allows data to be transferred among programs and updated automatically.

link list A collection of links on a particular topic.

Linux A variant of the UNIX operating system.

Linux PC A standard personal computer that runs the Linux operating system.

local area network (LAN) A series of connected personal computers, workstations, and other devices, such as printers or scanners, within a confined space, such as an office building.

log off To exit the account you are using, but keep the computer on for you or another user to log on at a later time.

log on To access a computer system by identifying yourself and, if prompted, entering a password.

logic bomb Computer virus triggered by the appearance or disappearance of specified data.

M

Mac OS X The Macintosh operating system.

Mail Setup Tools you use to create e-mail accounts and directories, change settings for Outlook files, and set up multiple profiles of e-mail accounts and data files.

mailing list See *distribution list*.

main memory Also called random access memory, or RAM, it is like short-term memory. It stores data while the computer is running. When the computer is turned off or if there is a loss of power, any data in the main memory disappears. The computer can read from and write to this type of memory.

mainframe computers Large, powerful computers that are used for centralized storage, processing, and management of very large amounts of data.

maintenance Tasks you perform to keep equipment in working order.

manual column break A command inserted by the user to adjust where a column ends.

manual line break A paragraph mark created by pressing the Enter key.

manual page break A command inserted by the user to force a page break at a specific location.

margin The blank space around the edges of the page.

markup The revision marks and comments that appear in a document.

math symbols The plus and minus signs used to filter out unwanted hits when searching online.

mathematical functions Perform calculations that you could do using a scientific calculator.

maximize To enlarge a window on the computer to fill the computer screen.

memory Where data is stored on the computer's motherboard.

menu A list of commands or options grouped under specific headings or titles (e.g., File, Edit) on a window's menu bar.

merging cells In Excel, combining multiple cells by removing the boundaries between the cells, usually done to create a title or informational text for the worksheet.

metadata Data that describes other data.

microcomputer Usually called a personal computer; used at home or the office by one person; can fit on top of or under a desk.

microprocessor An integrated circuit silicon chip that contains the processing unit for a computer or a computerized appliance.

minicomputer Type of computer that is designed to serve multiple users and process significant amounts of data; larger than a microcomputer, but smaller than a mainframe.

minimize To reduce a window on the screen to a button on the taskbar.

mixed cell reference A cell reference that contains both relative and absolute references.

mobile devices Electronic devices that fit into the palm of your hand, such as personal digital assistants (PDAs), calculators, smart phones and other cell phones, electronic organizers, and handheld games.

modem Communications hardware device that facilitates the transmission of data.

monitor The display device on a computer, which includes the screen and the housing for its electrical components.

Mosaic The first graphical browser.

motherboard A circuit board that contains all of the computer system's main components.

motion paths Settings used to create a path for an object to follow on a PowerPoint slide.

mouse A pointing device that serves as a faster, more effective alternative to the keyboard in communicating instructions to the computer.

mouse buttons Special buttons placed on the mouse that, when pressed, perform various tasks, such as starting applications and moving elements around the screen.

move To cut or remove a selection, file, folder, and so forth from one position or location and place (paste) it in another position or location.

MS-DOS Microsoft's Disk Operating System; originally introduced with the IBM PC in 1981.

multimedia The use of text, graphics, audio, and video in some combination to create an effective means of communication and interaction.

multimedia software Application used to create output that integrates several different types of media such as text, images, audio, video, and animation.

multitasking Running two or more distinct computer operations simultaneously: one in the foreground, the other(s) in the background.

N

navigation Ability to move through a Web page.

netiquette A combination of the words net and etiquette, refers to good manners and proper behaviors when communicating through electronic media.

network Connects one computer to other computers and peripheral devices.

Network and Internet category Control Panel tools that help you connect to and view a network and network computers and devices, sync with other computers, and perform other networking tasks.

network drive A disk drive located on another computer or server that provides space you can use for data storage.

network interface cards (NICs) An add-on card for a computer in a network that enables and controls the sending and receiving of data in a network.

network license A type of license that gives the organization the right to install a program on a server which can be accessed by a specific number of computers.

network operating system An operating system that runs on a network server.

news feed A data format used for providing users with frequently updated content. Also known as a Web feed.

newsgroup Discussion forum or a type of bulletin board.

node A device on the network.

nonimpact printers Type of printer in which characters are formed without anything striking the paper.

Normal view A view of a PowerPoint presentation that shows the Slide and Outline tabs, the slide pane, and the Notes pane.

Normal.dotm template A file containing default styles and customizations that determine the structure and page layout of a document.

notebook computer Similar to a microcomputer; however, it is smaller and portable.

notification area The right side of the Windows taskbar.

O

object A discrete item that provides a description of virtually anything known to a computer.

object linking and embedding (OLE) A technology developed by Microsoft that lets you create a document or object in one program and then link and/or embed that data into another program.

Office Assistant An animated Help character that offers tips and messages in Microsoft Office applications.

online learning Classes and other educational opportunities provided on the Internet.

open To load a file into an application.

operand A number or cell reference.

operating system (OS) System software that provides an interface between the user or application program and the computer hardware.

operator A symbol that indicates the mathematical operation to perform with the operands.

optical storage devices Devices that enable the computer to give the user the results of the processed data.

option buttons Allow you to choose one option from a group of options; also called *radio buttons*.

order of evaluation   The sequence used to calculate the value of a formula.

orientation   Determines whether your document will be printed lengthwise or crosswise on the sheet of paper. The default page orientation in all Office applications is portrait (taller than wide), but you can change it to landscape (wider than tall).

output   Data that has been processed into a useful format.

output devices   Enable the computer to give you the results of the processed data.

Overtype mode   In this mode, new text replaces existing characters.

P

packets   Units of data sent across a network. When a large block of information is sent, it is broken up into smaller data packets that are sent separately and then reassembled in their original order at the other end.

Palm OS   An operating system that runs on Palm handhelds and other third-party devices.

parallel ports   Computer ports that can transmit data eight bits at a time; usually used by a printer.

parent folder   A folder containing one or more subfolders.

patch   Software applied over software that you already have installed.

path   The route the operating system uses to locate a document; the path identifies the disk and any folders relative to the location of the document.

peer-to-peer (P2P) network   Computer architecture in which all of the computers on a network are equal and there is no computer designated as the server.

personal information management software (PIMS)   Software designed to organize and manage personal tasks, appointments, and contacts.

phishing   Types of personal information scams.

phrase searching   Searching for words that appear next to each other.

ping   A DOS command that tests connectivity and isolates hardware problems and any mismatched configurations.

placeholders   Provide placement guides for adding text, pictures, tables, or charts.

plagiarism   Claiming someone else's words as your own.

plotter   An output device used to produce charts, engineering plans, and other large-size printed material with lines drawn by pens that move on rails.

Plug-and-play   Technology that allows a hardware component to be attached to a computer so that it is automatically configured by the operating system, without user intervention.

podcast   A method of publishing files (primarily audio) to the Internet that can be streamed or downloaded for playback on a computer or a personal digital audio player.

podcatcher   A program that checks a feed for new content on a regular basis, and then downloads the podcast to your specified device.

pointer   On-screen object (whose shape changes depending on the function) that can be moved and controlled by the mouse.

pointing device   Device, such as a mouse or trackball, that allows the user to select objects on the screen.

points   The units of measure for fonts. The larger the point number, the larger the font size. (One inch equals approximately 72 points.)

port   An interface to which a peripheral device attaches to or communicates with the system unit.

Portable Document Format (PDF)   A format developed by Adobe Systems designed to preserve the visual appearance and layout of each page and enable fast viewing and printing.

portal   A Web site that features useful content, but also contains links to other sites.

portrait orientation   Page layout in which the content of the document is formatted with the short edge of the page at the top.

power spike   A short, fast transfer of electrical voltage, current, or energy.

presentation   The document file in PowerPoint.

presentation software   Software that is used to create and edit information to present in an electronic slide show format.

primary key   Unique identifier of each record in an Access table.

Print Layout view   The display of a document that shows the document as it will look when it is printed.

print queue   Shows information about documents that are waiting to print.

printer   A device that produces a paper or hard copy of the processing results.

private key   The part of encryption process that deciphers an encoded certificate.

problem solving   A systematic approach of going from an initial situation to a desired situation.

Program Compatibility Wizard   A Windows Vista tool for changing the compatibility settings for a program.

Programs category   Control Panel options to install, change, or remove software and Windows components; see a list of installed software; control access to certain programs; and add gadgets to the Sidebar.

protocol   Standard format for transferring data between two devices. TCP/IP is the agreed-upon international standard for transmitting data.

proxy server   A server that acts as an intermediary between a user and the Internet.

public domain   Information or content to which copyright protection does not apply and that is available for anyone to copy.

public key   The part of encryption process that encodes a certificate.

Public Switched Telephone Network (PSTN)   The world's collection of interconnected commercial and government-owned voice-oriented systems.

pyramid schemes   An illicit business model where profits are based on the investor's ability to recruit other individuals who are enrolled to make payments to their recruiters. Generally, neither a product or service is delivered.

Q

query   A database object which enables you to locate multiple records matching specified criteria.

Quick Launch toolbar   A toolbar on the Windows taskbar that starts a program with one mouse click.

Quick Tables   Built-in tables with sample data and table formats.

R

radio buttons   Allow you to choose one option from a group of options; also called *option buttons*.

random access memory (RAM)   Computer location where instructions and data are stored on a temporary basis. This memory is volatile.

range   A group of adjacent cells selected in a worksheet. All cells in a range touch each other and form a rectangle.

RDF Summary   A format originally developed to facilitate the syndication of news articles.

read-only document   Users can open and view the document, but they won't be able to make any changes to the document.

read-only memory (ROM)   Permanent storage; instructions are burned onto chips by the manufacturer.

Really Simple Syndication (RSS)   A format originally developed to syndicate news articles online, this communication

method now is used widely to share the contents of blogs. Also known as *Rich Site Summary* and *RDF Summary*.

receiver   Computer that receives a data transmission.

record   A group of related fields in a database, such as all the contact information for an individual.

record selector   In Access, a small box or bar that you click to select a row in a table in Datasheet view.

Recycle Bin   A holding area for files and folders before their final deletion from a storage device.

related search   Preprogrammed queries or questions suggested by the search engine.

relational database   A database in which information is organized into separate subject-based tables, and the relationship of the data in one or more tables is used to bring the data together.

relative cell references   Cell references which will be adjusted relative to the formula's new location when a formula is copied or moved to a new location.

repetitive strain injury (RSI)   An injury that can result when a person makes too many of the same motions over a long period of time.

report   A database object which allows you to organize, summarize, and print all or a portion of the data in a database table or query.

restore   To return a maximized or minimized window to its previous size.

Ribbon   A banner in the Office Fluent user interface that organizes commands in logical groups presented on tabs.

right-click   To quickly press and release the shortcut menu button (usually the right button).

router   A device that directs traffic on a network by dividing data into smaller packets that travel by different routes and then are reassembled at their destination.

S

save   To store a document on a disk or other storage medium.

scanner   An input device that can change images into codes for input to the computer.

ScreenTip   A small window with descriptive text that appears when you position the mouse pointer on a command or control in the application window.

scroll   To move text and content vertically or horizontally on a display screen when searching for a particular section, line, option, and so on.

scroll bar   Bar on the right side or bottom of a window that you click to bring different parts of a document into view.

search To examine the contents of a computer file, folder, disk, database, or network to find particular information.

search engines Tools that allow you to enter a keyword to find sites on the Internet that contain information you need.

section break Divides the document into multiple sections.

sectors Divisions on magnetic media used for storing digital information.

Secure Sockets Layer (SSL) A protocol for managing the security of message transmissions on the Internet.

security Protecting a computer from tampering or harm.

Security category Control Panel tools for maintaining the security of a computer.

seek time The time it takes for a read/write head to move to a specific data track; one of the delays associated with reading or writing data on a computer disk drive.

select (highlight) To point to an object and then press and release the primary mouse button. Also to identify blocks of text or objects you want to edit.

sender Computer that sends a data transmission.

serial ports Computer ports that can transmit data one bit at a time; often used by a modem or a mouse.

server A computer that handles requests for data, e-mail, file transfers, and other network services from other computers (clients).

server operating system High-end programs designed to provide network control and include special functions for connecting computers and other devices into a network.

service pack A collection of updates, fixes, or enhancements to a software program delivered as a single file.

shared bookmark A form of collaborative information sharing that lets users organize and share favorites, or bookmarks. Also called *social bookmarking*.

sheet tab A tab in the horizontal scroll bar to provide quick and easy access to a worksheet.

shortcut A pointer to an application or document file; double-clicking the shortcut icon opens the actual item to which the shortcut is pointing.

shortcut menu A list of the command options most commonly performed from the current window display.

shortcut menu button The secondary mouse button, usually the right button.

Sidebar A Windows Vista panel that contains gadgets.

signature Text or graphics added to the end of outgoing e-mail messages.

simulations Models of real-world activities.

single-user license A license that gives you the right to install software on a single computer.

sizing handles Small circles and squares on the border of a graphic or object indicating that it is selected.

slide design Specifies a color scheme, text format, background, bullet style, and graphics for all the slides in a PowerPoint presentation.

slide layout The arrangement of placeholders on a slide.

slide master The main slide that stores information about the theme and layouts of a presentation.

slide pane The area in the presentation window that contains the slide content.

Slide Show view Allows you to view a PowerPoint slide in full screen.

Slide Sorter view Displays PowerPoint slides as thumbnails.

slide transitions Settings that determine how a slide is introduced as you move from one PowerPoint slide to another in Slide Show view.

sniffer A program that hackers use to capture IDs and passwords on a network.

social networking site An online community that provides interaction for groups of people who share a similar interest or activity.

soft copy A digital copy of data.

soft page break A page break that is automatically inserted when you fill a page with text or graphics.

software Intangible set of instructions that tells the computer what to do.

Software as a Service (SaaS) A software delivery method where an application is licensed for use as a service. The software is provided to customers on demand through the Internet, an intranet, or through a network.

software development The multistep process of designing, writing, and testing computer programs.

software license A license that gives you permission to use a program.

software piracy The illegal copying or use of computer programs.

sorting The process of creating a list organized on a specific criterion.

source When copying a file, the file that is being copied.

spam Unsolicited commercial e-mail that is sent to many people at the same time to promote products or services; also called *junk e-mail*.

spider   Program that searches the Web; called a spider because it crawls all over the Web.

split   To divide a worksheet into two panes.

splitting cells   Converting a cell into multiple cells by adding cell boundaries.

spreadsheet   A grid of rows and columns into which you enter text data (i.e., surnames, cities, states) and numerical data (i.e., dates, currency, and percentages).

spreadsheet software   An application used to store, manipulate, and analyze numeric data.

spyware   Software installed surreptitiously on a personal computer, with the goal of collecting information about the user, the user's browsing habits, and other personal information.

standard desktop   The screen you see immediately after logging on to Windows.

Standard toolbar   The bar, usually located near the top of a window, that contains buttons that instantly execute commands or access various functions.

Start button   A button on the taskbar that, when clicked, opens the Start menu.

startup program   A program that runs when a computer system starts.

statistical functions   Functions that describe large quantities of data.

status bar   A message or information area, usually located at the bottom of a window, that displays specific details about the currently selected object or the task being performed.

strikethrough   A type attribute that makes text appear as if it is crossed out.

strong password   A password that is complex and secure—it contains numbers, letters, and special characters that do not include personal information such as name or birth date. In addition, strong passwords contain at least eight characters, and at least one letter, number, and special character.

style   A set of formatting characteristics that you can apply to characters, paragraphs, tables, and numbered and bulleted lists.

subfolder   A folder within another folder.

submenu   A menu within another menu. A submenu is indicated when there is a right-pointing arrow next to a menu option.

supercomputers   Largest and fastest computers, capable of storing and processing tremendous volumes of data.

superscript   A letter or numeral set above the text base line in a document.

support agreement   A list of services specifically designed to provide assistance to a company or organization.

surge protectors   Devices that protect electronic equipment from variations in electric current.

surge suppressors   Devices that protect against power spikes.

system administrator   A user who has an administrator account.

System and Maintenance category   Control Panel tools that include settings for a variety of system tasks, such as backup and restore, systems options, power options, and Windows Update.

system clock   An electronic pulse that is used to synchronize processing; it controls the speed of the central processing unit.

system file   An essential file necessary for running Windows or another operating system.

system settings   A collection of settings that affect an entire computer.

system software   A group of programs that coordinate and control the resources and operations of a computer system.

T

T-1 line   A type of fiber-optic telephone line that can transmit up to 1.544 megabits per second or can be used to transmit 24 digitized voice channels.

table   A datasheet that stores subject-based data. It is a primary object an Access database.

table style   A set of predefined formats that you can apply to all the worksheet data.

tablet PC   A personal computer similar in size and thickness to a notepad on which you can take notes using a stylus or digital pen on a touch screen.

tagging   The practice of adding keywords to content to simplify searching.

taskbar   The horizontal bar at the bottom of the desktop that includes the Start button, minimized window buttons, and a row of icons usually related to input and output devices.

technology   The application of scientific discoveries to the production of goods and services that improve the human environment.

telecommunications   Electronic transfer of data.

teleconferencing   Telecommunications service in which parties in remote locations can participate via telephone in a group meeting.

template   A file that contains formatting and text that you can customize to create a new document similar to, but slightly different from, the original.

text box   A drawing object that enables you to add text to artwork.

text editor   A basic word-processing application.

text messaging   Using a cell phone or other mobile device to send and receive written messages.

Thesaurus   A feature in Word that allows you to quickly find alternative words or synonyms for a word in your document.

thumbnails   Miniature representations of pictures.

time bomb   Computer virus that does not cause its damage until a certain date or until the system has been booted a certain number of times.

title bar   The horizontal band in a window that displays the name of the program, data file, or another type of window.

toggle   To alternate between the off and on states by repeating a procedure, such as clicking a button.

toolbar   A bar near the top of a window that has groups of icons or buttons that will execute certain commands when clicked.

touchpad   A pointing device you can use instead of a mouse. These devices sense the position of your finger and then move the pointer accordingly.

trackball   A pointing device that works like a mouse turned upside down; the ball is on top of the device.

trademark   Similar to a copyright, but relates specifically to visual or commercial images rather than text or intellectual property.

transmission media   Media used to transmit data from one device to another; may be wireless or physical.

Transport Layer Security (TLS)   A protocol for managing the security of message transmissions on the Internet.

trigger   An instruction that will start a sound effect or animation segment on a PowerPoint slide.

Trojan horse   Computer virus that does something different from what it is expected to do.

troubleshooting   Analyzing problems to correct faults in the system.

U

Uniform Resource Locator (URL)   Address that tells the browser where to locate a Web page.

uninterruptible power source (UPS)   A battery power source that provides electric current during a power outage.

universal serial bus (USB)   Standard for computer ports that support data transfer rates of up to 12 million bits per second.

UNIX   Operating system developed by AT&T. It is considered portable, meaning it can run on just about any hardware platform.

update   A collection of files for updating released software that fixes bugs or provides enhancements.

upgrade   Replacing software with a newer or better version to bring the system up to date or to improve its characteristics.

urban legend   A story which at one time could have been partially true, but has grown from constant retelling into a mythical yarn.

USB flash drive   A small removable data storage device.

User Accounts category   Control Panel tools that let you change user accounts and passwords, change a user's mail profile, and change your Windows password.

user agent   A software application installed on the local PC, network, or Web, such as e-mail, text message, and instant messaging programs.

user interface   Part of the computer's operating system that users interact with.

utility software (utility program)   Systems software that performs tasks related to managing the computer's resources, file management, diagnostics, and other specialized chores.

V

vector graphics   Graphics that use points, lines, curves, and shapes based on mathematical equations to represent images.

virtual reality   An artificial environment used in education, medicine, training, research, and other fields.

virus   A computer program that is written to cause corruption of data.

voice recognition   Input devices and software that are used to issue spoken or voice commands to the computer.

W

warranty   A written guarantee that a product or service meets certain specifications.

Web application   An application without platform constraints or installation requirements that is accessed through a Web browser over a network such as an intranet or the Internet.

Web Layout view   A Word view that allows you to see text and graphics as they would appear in a Web browser.

Web server   Computer that houses and delivers Web pages.

wide area network (WAN)   Computer network that covers a large geographical area. Most WANs are made up of several connected LANs.

wiki   A collaborative Web site that can be edited by anyone with access.

wildcard characters   The asterisk (*) and question mark (?) characters used to represent unknown characters in a search for filenames, words, or phrases.

WiMAX   A recent wireless technology that can deliver maximum speeds of up to 7 Mbps to your cell phone, home computer, or car. Stands for Worldwide Interoperability for Microwave Access.

window   Rectangular area of the screen used to display a program, data, or other information.

Windows CardSpace   A Windows Vista feature that provides a system for creating relationships with Web sites and online services that use credit cards and membership cards for payment or credentials.

Windows Embedded CE   An operating system designed for devices such as digital cameras, security robots, intelligent appliances, gaming devices, GPS, and set-top boxes.

Windows Explorer   A program that lets you browse, open, and manage your computer's disk drives, folders, and files (that is, move, copy, rename, and delete files).

Windows Mail   E-mail software provided with Windows Vista.

Windows Mobile   A version of the Windows operating system that runs on smart phones and other types of handheld computers.

wireless Internet service provider (WISP)   An ISP that provides connection speeds more than 30 times faster than dial-up connections—from 384 Kbps to 2.0 Mbps.

wireless keyboard   A keyboard that uses radio or infrared frequencies to connect to a computer rather than a cable.

wireless LAN (WLAN)   A variation of a LAN that uses no physical wires.

wizard   A Windows program that simplifies a task by guiding you through a series of prompts and questions.

word wrap   A feature by which Word automatically wraps the text to the next line.

word-processing software   Software used to prepare text documents such as letters, reports, flyers, brochures, and books.

workbook   Where worksheets are stored; a workbook contains one or more worksheets.

worksheet   A spreadsheet in Excel, consisting of a grid of rows and columns containing numbers, text, and formulas.

worm   Computer virus that makes many copies of itself, resulting in the consumption of system resources that slows down or actually halts tasks.

X

XML Paper Specification (XPS)   A format developed by Microsoft designed to preserve the visual appearance and layout of each page and to enable fast viewing and printing.

INDEX

PHOTO CREDITS

Lesson 1:

Figure 1–1	© Inti St Clair /Getty Images
Figure 1–2	U.S. Army Photo
Figure 1–3	Courtesy of IBM Archives
Figure 1–4	© Thomas Lammeyer /iStockphoto
Figure 1–6b	AP Photo/Jason DeCrow
Figure 1–6c	© CostinT /iStockphoto
Figure 1–6d	Yomiuri Shimbun/MCT/Landov
Figure 1–6e	Courtesy of IBM Corporation
Figure 1–6f	Courtesy of Los Alamos National Laboratory
Figure 1–7	AP Photo/Mark Lennihan
Figure 1–8	Courtesy of Intel Corporation
	iStockphoto.com
	Courtesy of Creative Technology Ltd.
	Courtesy of Advanced Micro Devices, Inc.
	Courtesy of Zoom Technologies
	Courtesy of 3Com Corporation
	Courtesy of Hewlett-Packard Company
Figure 1–9	Courtesy of Intel Corporation
Figure 1–10	Courtesy of Advanced Micro Devices, Inc.
Figure 1–13	Courtesy of Corsair
Figure 1–18	Gennady Imeshev / Photo Researchers, Inc.
Figure 1–21	© Photodisc/Getty Images

Lesson 2:

Figure 2–1	Courtesy of Dreamware Computers
Figure 2–2	Courtesy of Microsoft Corporation
Figure 2–3	Courtesy of Matias Corporation
Figure 2–4	Courtesy of Virtual Devices, Inc
Figure 2–5	Courtesy of Microsoft Corporation
Figure 2–6	Courtesy of PCD Maltron Ltd.
Figure 2–7	Courtesy of Hewlett Packard Company
Figure 2–11	Courtesy of Hewlett Packard Company
Figure 2–12	Courtesy of Logitech

PHOTO CREDITS

Figure 2–13	Courtesy of Socket Mobile Inc
	Courtesy of Metrologic Instruments Inc
Figure 2–14	UPI Photo/Aaron Kehoe/Landov
Figure 2–15	Courtesy of iRex Technologies
Figure 2–16	PRNewsFoto/Pay By Touch
	PRNews/Foto/Kwikset
Figure 2–17	Courtesy of Virtual Devices Inc.
Figure 2–18	Courtesy of Hewlett Packard Company
Figure 2–19	Courtesy of Nokia
Figure 2–20	Courtesy of Hewlett Packard Company
Figure 2–24	Courtesy of Intel Corporation

Lesson 3:

Figure 3–1	iStockphoto
Figure 3–2	Courtesy of Microtechnologies, Inc.
Figure 3–3	Courtesy of Panamax
Figure 3–4	Courtesy of Adafruit Industries
Figure 3–5	Courtesy of CLAS Computer Support Group/University of Connecticut

Lesson 4:

Figure 4–1	Courtesy of Cable-Safe LLC
Figure 4–2	Courtesy of Cable-Safe LLC
Figure 4–3	© Lon C. Diehl/ PhotoEdit
Figure 4–4	Source: "Got Fear?," by G.D. Warner, at http://www.cheapandsleazy.net/gotfear.html, copyright G.D. Warner, 2009; used with permission
Figure 4–5	Courtesy of HK Wentworth Limited
Figure 4–6	© PhotoAlto/Corbis
Figure 4–7	iStockphoto
Figure 4–10	Courtesy of Microsoft Corporation
Figure 4–11	Courtesy of Microsoft Corporation
Figure 4–12	Courtesy of Cirque Corporation

Lesson 5:

Figure 5–1	Image copyright 2009, foment. Used under license from Shutterstock.com
Figure 5–3	Image copyright 2009, Monika Wisniewska. Used under license from Shutterstock.com
Figure 5–4	© René Mansi/iStockphoto
Figure 5–5	AP Photo/Ben Margot
Figure 5–6	© Mark Richards/PhotoEdit
Figure 5–10	AP Photo/Steve Yeater

Lesson 6:

Figure 6–1	© Yu-Feng Chen/iStockphoto
Figure 6–2	Image copyright Pelham James Mitchinson, 2009. Used under license from Shutterstock.com

Lesson 8:

Figure 8–5	© Image Source/Getty Images
Figure 8–6	Courtesy of Palm, Inc.

Lesson 24:

Figure 24–2	© Alex Slobodkin/iStockphoto
Figure 24–3	Image copyright 2009, Jozsef Szasz-Fabian. Used under license from Shutterstock.com
Figure 24–5a	Image copyright 2009, Norman Chan. Used under license from Shutterstock.com
Figure 24–5b	Image copyright 2009, ene. Used under license from Shutterstock.com
Figure 24–5c	Image copyright 2009, kzww. Used under license from Shutterstock.com
Figure 24–5d	Image copyright 2009, Alexander Kalina. Used under license from Shutterstock.com
Figure 24–5e	Image copyright 2009, Stuart Monk. Used under license from Shutterstock.com
Figure 24–10	Image copyright 2009, zimmytws. Used under license from Shutterstock.com

Lesson 26:

Figure 26–1	Courtesy of Microsoft Corporation
Figure 26–2	Stuart Ramson/Bloomberg News /Landov
Figure 26–14	© croftsphoto / Alamy
Figure 26–19	AP Photo/Ric Field

Lesson 29:

Figure 29–6	Image copyright 2009, Stephen Coburn. Used under license from Shutterstock.com
Figure 29–7	© Arno Massee/iStockphoto
Figure 29–8	Courtesy of ICG Software
Figure 29–9	PRNewsFoto/Samsung Electronics
Figure 29–10	© David Paul Morris/Getty Images
Figure 29–17	Courtesy of Seonkeun Park

Lesson 30:

Figure 30–2	Courtesy of Ergo Concepts, LLC; photograph by Hadar Goren